Effective Instructional Design Informed by AI

Scott Gregory
Fort Hays State University, USA

IGI Global
Scientific Publishing
Publishing Tomorrow's Research Today

Vice President of Editorial — Melissa Wagner
Managing Editor of Acquisitions — Mikaela Felty
Managing Editor of Book Development — Jocelynn Hessler
Production Manager — Mike Brehm
Cover Design — Phillip Shickler

Published in the United States of America by
IGI Global Scientific Publishing
701 East Chocolate Avenue
Hershey, PA, 17033, USA
Tel: 717-533-8845
Fax: 717-533-8661
Website: https://www.igi-global.com E-mail: cust@igi-global.com

Library of Congress Cataloging-in-Publication Data

Names: Gregory, Scott, 1975- editor.
Title: Effective instructional design informed by AI / Edited by Scott Gregory.
Description: Hershey, PA : IGI Global Scientific Publishing, [2025] | Includes bibliographical references and index. | Summary: "The objective of this book is to identify the latest empirical, conceptual, theoretical, and ethical "knowledges" that will assist teachers at all levels, in providing informed AI-situated classroom strategies as they relate to the domains of instruction, assessment, grading, and curriculum"-- Provided by publisher.
Identifiers: LCCN 2024054402 (print) | LCCN 2024054403 (ebook) | ISBN 9798369365274 (hardcover) | ISBN 9798369365281 (paperback) | ISBN 9798369365298 (ebook)
Subjects: LCSH: Instructional systems--Design. | Artificial intelligence--Educational applications.
Classification: LCC LB1028.38 .E383 2025 (print) | LCC LB1028.38 (ebook) | DDC 371.3--dc23/eng/20241214
LC record available at https://lccn.loc.gov/2024054402
LC ebook record available at https://lccn.loc.gov/2024054403

British Cataloguing in Publication Data
A Cataloguing in Publication record for this book is available from the British Library.

This book is dedicated to Dawn Gregory, who is the light of my inspiration and the fire of my work.

Table of Contents

Detailed Table of Contents

map (Sandoval, 2014), which includes a hypothesis, design features, embodiments (interventions), mediating processes, and outcomes. This design aims to create a learning environment where students engage in attentive and collaborative thinking with the aid of GenAI.

This research paper investigates the integration of Artificial Intelligence (AI) within instructional design (ID), highlighting its potential to enhance learning experiences while maintaining a human-centered approach. It addresses the existing knowledge gap among instructional designers regarding AI applications and aims to develop a framework that aligns AI tools with ID practices. The study employs a mixed-methods approach, combining qualitative and quantitative analyses to assess the impact of AI-assisted design on learner outcomes across various educational contexts. Key findings suggest that AI can automate content creation and personalize learning paths, thereby augmenting the expertise of instructional designers rather than replacing it. Ultimately, this research seeks to empower instructional designers to optimize their workflows and improve learner engagement and achievement through effective AI integration

AI-driven adaptive learning, intelligent systems, and ethical issues will transform education. AI adaptive learning systems adjust content, pace, and feedback based on student performance and learning preferences. These technologies provide highly tailored education, student engagement, and scalable learning solutions across multiple contexts. Virtual tutors and automated grading systems are projected to minimize administrative workloads for teachers, allowing them to focus on creative instruction. Data privacy, algorithmic discrimination, and the possible loss of human engagement in learning are ethical concerns with AI in education. As AI becomes more prevalent in education, equitable access, data security, and openness in algorithmic decision-making are needed. Using AI to overcome these challenges may lead to a more efficient, inclusive, and ethical education system.

Education has greatly changed in the last 20 years, especially in the previous five years, with AI in learning and teaching. This change has affected both instructional design and special education and opened new possibilities for personalization, accessibility, and efficiency in education. The book chapter will explore how AI can improve special education and instructional design to create inclusive and effective learning environments. The authors will review the basics and challenges of special education and instructional design and then discuss how AI can enhance them. In special education, AI-powered tools and applications such as assistive technologies, personalized learning platforms, and adaptive learning systems can help students with special needs and improve their education outcomes and experiences (Kumar, 2023). Within an instructional design framework, AI also has the capability to provide real-time feedback and create personalized learning pathways, thereby making education more efficient and effective.

Artificial Intelligence (AI) is taking over the operations of universities globally because of the multiple benefits associated with it which include transparent forms of assessment, immediate feedback to students and a reduced workload on the part of the instructors. There are also challenges that are associated with the use of AI, such as unethical practices which may undermine academic rigour and integrity. A number of theories are employed in this chapter which includes statistical modelling, Unified Theory of Acceptance and Use of Technology, (UTAUT) and Evidence Based Learning (EBL). The chapter presents a case for Africa to adopt AI in a conscientious way in order to meet the Sustainable Development Goal No 4, of providing quality and inclusive education. The opportunities for using AI in assessment in higher education are explored as well as the constrictions that Africa faces in transitioning to this form of technology.

This chapter explores the utilization of ChatGPT, an artificial intelligence (AI) language model, in deconstructing K-12 content standards or Student Learning Outcomes (SLOs) to facilitate the development of assessments and rubrics following Rick Stiggins' deconstructing standards process. Sections of the chapter explore understanding ChatGPT and its educational applications, detailing Stiggins' deconstructing standards process and providing scenarios for deconstructing learning standards. Further, the chapter delineates the flexibility in deconstructing standards and steps for application, leveraging ChatGPT for SLO deconstruction, developing assessments and rubrics, offering examples, and discussing the implications of AI integration in education. The chapter aims to equip educators with insights and practical guidance to enhance assessment practices, fostering well-rounded student development.

This chapter explores the transformative potential of Generative Artificial Intelligence (GAI) in educational assessment, examining its impact on learners, educators, and educational institutions. Through a comprehensive literature review and analysis of existing GAI-based assessment systems, we investigate how GAI is reshaping traditional assessment practices, enabling more personalized, adaptive, and continuous evaluation of student learning. The chapter discusses the major challenges and opportunities associated with GAI, including issues of data privacy, fairness, and the evolving role of educators. We also examine concrete examples of GAI applications in assessment, such as adaptive learning platforms and automated grading systems. The chapter concludes by outlining future research directions and considering the ethical implications of widespread GAI adoption in education. While GAI offers opportunities for enhancing educational assessment, its implementation requires careful consideration of ethical, pedagogical, and technical challenges

This chapter examines the integration of Artificial Intelligence (AI) in Caribbean educational assessments, focusing on its potential to enhance instructional quality and ethically streamline evaluations. This quantitative study used structured surveys, with reliability confirmed by Cronbach's Alpha (0.767 for students, 0.91 for teachers). The analysis revealed a significant positive correlation between teachers' belief in the need for strict ethical guidelines for AI-based assessments and their comfort with AI integration, r(104) = .42, p < .01. Teachers' willingness to adopt AI is shaped by ethical concerns, particularly the need for guidelines and collaborative decision-making. Among students, those using AI tools (M = 2.98) reported slightly higher comfort than non-users (M = 2.85). However, this difference was not statistically significant, t(59.65) = 0.53, p = .60. Privacy concerns are central to shaping student perceptions of AI in education. The chapter concludes with recommendations for ethical frameworks, teacher training, and inclusive decision-making.

The hype around AI today has been ubiquitous and exciting. The use of AI behind the scenes has been implemented in many different areas such as the use of GPS for driving instructions, the use of natural language assistants such as smart speakers, and the ability of social media apps to keep tabs on what you are watching and reading (Masoud & Kamran, 2024). All of these are examples of AI that has been in use for decades now. It seems like a new tool, and a rather miraculous one, at that. As generations Z and Alpha have made their way to the K-12 school system in 2000s and beyond, the use of AI in school has increased. As administrators, teachers and parents try to understand what it appears their digital natives who are in many ways, born AI literate, the middle person who can help bring everyone to the same page is the person who serves everyone in the school – the school librarian.

Preface

We live in a new epoch of instructional design. In our current educational paradigm, educators find themselves challenged to incorporate artificial intelligence effectively to advance student learning. At present, there is a lack of studies and resources for educational stakeholders on how best to incorporate artificial intelligence into the classroom (Chang, et al., 2023). This book provides promising insights into applying instructional design principles that center on artificial intelligence and utilize its notable strengths to further instructional achievement through informed lesson implementation and assessment. The first chapter provides information on instructional design and artificial intelligence. The subject-specific implementation of artificial intelligence is the focus of the second part of the chapters provided.

CHAPTER OVERVIEW

Chapter 1. A Basic Toolkit for Instructional Design by AI in Elementary-Level Teaching

Instructional design informed by AI in the elementary classroom is the focus of Chapter 1. The elementary practitioner learns to identify student learning needs, identify learning objectives, and develop teaching strategies and supports with four phases. The first constitutes analysis, implementation, and evaluation, followed by instructor decision-making regarding learning purposes and goals. The third phase is planning content, while the fourth is predicated on selecting activities for students to engage in involved participation. The authors then outline contemporary and traditional design elements before articulating the main principles of instructional design informed by AI. Explicitly identified activities and applications are provided to assist instructional designers and educators in moving toward coherent AI-informed instructional design.

Chapter 2. The Ethical and Pedagogical Challenges of AI-Powered Language Instruction: The Case of Writing Skills from a Moroccan University

Marhaoui, Chniet, El Boubekri, & Fadli address the challenge of incorporating A.I. into the writing and language arts classroom. The authors identify questions relating to AI and its role in supplementing learning in the traditional language classroom, areas of language instruction that AI may excel at, and the ethical issues that arise through using AI in the language classroom. The last question centers upon strategies that can effectively meet ethical concerns. A literature review addresses the two-prong challenge of finding a fit between AI and language learning, as well as short-term corresponding long-term challenges.

Of particular interest to the reader will be the highlighting of what aspect of language learning AI excels at, as well as the use of AI to create authentic, immersive, and highly engaged learning environments. From individualized support to streamlining common tasks, AI benefits learners in language classrooms.

In the second chapter, the reader is presented with how to create personalized, efficient, and engaging learning experiences through A.I.-informed instructional design. The authors outline how AI addresses the instructional design challenges of meeting the needs of diverse learners and the burdensome nature of curating content lessons and assessments in a timely manner. The description of creating "learning paths" is explained to address the challenge of meeting diverse learning needs, while automation of common tasks is provided to assist the instructor. As a result of incorporating AI into a quality instructional design framework, the educator will see a trifecta of positive results. These benefits are higher student achievement, the freeing of time that was formerly taken up through routine tasks, and increased engagement by the learner, respectively.

Chapter 3. AI-Driven Instructional Design: Enhancing Learning Experiences Through Personalization and Efficiency

Instructional design with AI is the central focus of Babu, Gururaja V., Bhavesh, and Venkatesh's informative chapter. AI has notable distinctions of providing greater personalization of learning, an increase of efficiency when it comes to the teacher's work, and the creation of learning experiences that are engaging and maintain students' attention. The authors point out that these strengths address key challenges relating to the need to serve students with diverse learning needs and the time it takes to create class content and assessments.

From this vantage point, the reader is taken along a pathway to learn how different learning "paths" can be set up by integrating AI into instructional design. Readers then learn how routine teaching tasks can be automated to achieve greater efficiency, resulting in more time to utilize for more productive teaching tasks. Lastly, readers are provided insight into how student data can be utilized to craft effective, personalized instruction for learners with diverse learning needs. This chapter provides a useful guide on integrating evidence-based practices effectively and ethically into instructional design. This chapter provides the teacher with a comprehensive framework for effective use in the contemporary classroom, crossing the boundaries of initial notation of potential to actualized results.

Chapter 4: Slow and Connected: Deliberate GenAI-Enhanced Instructional Design Fostering the Essence of Critical Thinking

Hsiao, Wolff, & Rajagopal address the integration of AI into the educational setting through the introduction of pedagogical frameworks designed to engage students in in-depth critical thinking. These frameworks are based on slowing down the critical thinking process to allow for greater student access. This methodical effort concentrates on increasing time for task completion, focusing on the learning process, and dividing group work and solo work. In discussing effective pedagogical frameworks, readers will appreciate their ability to center the critical thinking and decision-making of the "humans" involved in the learning process.

Social-emotional learning considerations are also addressed by outlining relational pedagogy that fosters stronger teacher and student relationships. The critical thinking aspect of these frameworks is also called upon to examine and discern bias in generated content. More importantly, the chapter is a powerful contribution in its ability to encourage the slowing down of thinking in a fast-paced technological age, which is great for on-demand and "instant" information, to the detriment of critical thinking and extended consideration of a topic or idea at hand.

Chapter 5. Demystifying AI for Instructional Designers: A Research Overview

A key challenge when it comes to instructional design and the incorporation of AI is the limited research that is available regarding the designer's knowledge of AI. From this insight, Abdullah synthesizes research through a literature review to address this key gap in understanding. To assist designers, a detailed explanation of AI tools and functionalities that are effective for designers to utilize is provided, along with an outline of how to integrate AI into instructional design with consideration of space and place and human expertise. These considerations work to "demystify" the integration of AI into instructional design, thereby creating a personalized learning environment for the learner and through which a more efficient instructional design is crafted.

Chapter 6. The Future of Education with AI: Adaptive Learning, Intelligent Systems, and Ethical Challenges

In seeking to incorporate AI into the classroom, instructional designers and educators of all levels can benefit from increased teacher productivity by automating rote tasks. They will also benefit from producing learning activities that engage learners in learning. This dual benefit is addressed in the chapter through the scope of the need to identify ethical AI practices and the need to take practical steps to integrate AI into classroom practice. Through this holistic diagnostic lens, the authors introduce the multitude of ways AI can assist in meeting the dual benefits mentioned previously.

In the automation of rote tasks, AI offers promising features such as automated assessment and grading, which saves time and delivers accurate assessment results. Personalized learning creates greater efficiency through organizing and re-arranging curricula based on students' individual needs. The creation of engaging content is addressed through a wide variety of features that the authors outline. Most notable is language processing, which improves language learning and acquisition through voice recognition. AI-based virtual labs create a simulated experience for students to understand concepts and processes. Along with addressing the dual benefits to educators, the authors provide a wealth of information on data privacy, bias, and addressing the digital divide.

Chapter 7. Integrating AI in Special Education and Instructional Design: A Synergistic Approach

Instructional design with AI and its impacts concerning special education is the focal point of examination in chapter 13. Greater learner personalization, accessibility, and efficiency are three highlighted strengths mentioned. The reader is introduced to AI tools and applications that span the range of assistive technologies, personalized platforms, and adaptive systems that enhance learning. Due to the broad range of tools available to teachers, AI in instructional design can improve educational outcomes and experiences for special education learners.

Practical considerations such as frameworks and models are presented, not to mention the outlining of case studies and examples from practice that readers can utilize in their own learning environments. Greater use of AI with instructional design will require greater training of teachers to manage data privacy, mitigate bias, and engage in training opportunities to keep their skills current with an ever-changing tool.

The special education classroom of the future is bound to have AI involved with instructional design. To address this reality, educators must be aware of policy and the implications to practice. From this chapter, readers will also glean insightful recommendations for educators and policymakers concerning instructional design and its ethical use.

Chapter 8. Assessment in Higher Education in the Age of Artificial Intelligence: Possibilities and Constrictions in Africa

The promise of AI and its use in education in Africa is the central focus of Chakabwata's chapter, which begins with an initial dive into AI and its related areas that touch upon robotics, virtual reality, 3D printing, and computers. From this vantage point, the introduction shifts to an exploration of how AI may be used for assessment in higher educational settings in Africa. Chakabwata details the need to include AI in the various frameworks and models of practice that relate to assessment and the use of technology in assessment. AI holds promise in assisting at-risk learners and tailoring individual outcomes from prior experienced assessments.

No topic on AI and instructional design is complete without a synthesis of challenges and ethical considerations that go along with the need to integrate AI into pedagogy. Educators must maintain a strong emphasis on high educational standards and honesty and ensure that relevant assessment practices that are in place now, are not discarded without considerable thought. AI models of assessment steeped in research are discussed and how to improve formative assessment practices.

Chapter 9. Using ChatGPT to Deconstruct K-12 Student Learning Outcomes for Developing Assessments and Rubrics

How to use AI to identify and deconstruct student learning objectives (SLOs) is the focus of Bolton who begins the selection by introducing the reader to AI's potential in the field of education and how ChatGPT can be utilized to facilitate the creation of SLO based assessments and rubrics. The reader is then provided with a broad understanding of ChatGPT can be utilized effectively in education and how it can be utilized in the creation of lesson planning, in focusing on student engagement, and in working towards personalized learning experiences. From this point, Bolton includes the Deconstruction Standards Process by Rick Stiggens to guide the use of ChatGPT in working through SLO goals.

In the deconstructing process, educators will be able to parse out learning and assessment goals relating to knowledge, reasoning, performance, product, and flexibility, respectively. The chapter concludes with describing how to adapt the process to fit specific standards and learning contexts. The reader will also be able to identify the most relevant components related to the deconstruction process that are most beneficial for student learners.

Chapter 10. Generative Artificial Intelligence and Assessment of Learning: Challenges and Perspectives

Chapter 10 is a prescient contribution as it relates to AI instructional design for online courses and MOOCS (massive, online, open courses). This specialized contribution highlights the complexity of assessment for online environments, especially as they deal primarily with assessments that can be time-consuming and various students who require individualized feedback. With teachers being tasked with addressing achievement gaps and closing them from identified knowledge and skills that are missing, this contribution shows the importance of creating assessments that are adaptable based on student needs to ensure equity.

Contemporary assessments without AI face notable obstacles of being a true "end point" of instruction, as opposed to being a living tool that enhances student learning and achievement. On top of this, frustrated students drop out of their programs, and this presents a challenge for institutions to address. Even most notably, traditional assessments have limited use and suitability for the online learning environment.

Through AI-infused assessment, assessment tools can be created that are faster and more efficient. For those in online and MOOC teaching situations, the benefits of automating routine tasks are a reality that teachers can have as a result of incorporating AI into assessment for online learning. Promoting equity and inclusion can be addressed through personalized feedback and responsiveness to learning styles. The chapter concludes with detailed information to ensure ethical compliance across the spectrum of ensuring inequalities are not exacerbated, to the replication of bias, as well as to ensure the teacher's proper role as a central provider of educational content in the learning process.

Chapter 11. Navigating New Frontiers: AI in Assessments From the Perspectives of Teachers and Students

Incorporating AI with assessment considerations requires a comprehensive understanding of assessment theory, conceptual models, and ethical considerations. Roberts begins her analysis of these elements with the inclusion of understanding AI from the vantage point of teachers and students. In surveying current research on AI use in testing and grading, Roberts provides the reader with a detailed description of data-informed assessment decision-making that fully addresses learning goals and standards.

The alignment of AI with traditional assessment and teaching methods is provided through a comparison of practices and exploring the role of AI within different teaching method schools of thought. Roberts provides case studies that highlight successful integration of AI and provides examples of what specific AI tools have been utilized. Roberts concludes with recommendations for broader policy and curriculum considerations and emphasizing decision-making frameworks to assess the effectiveness of AI tools being considered.

Chapter 12. Librarians Leading the Way to AI Literacy

Burress, Gross, and Weimar shared the understood roles of school librarians today before providing information on how AI can be used as a support in education. From this vantage point, the authors show how learned expertise in information literacy, technology integration, and resource curation can be utilized with AI. Practical insights include strategies to integrate lessons through working with teachers to integrate technology into classroom lessons and supporting teachers to make their initial foray into using AI in a sound, pedagogical way. From the library services spectrum, demonstrating the use of how AI can support research and introduce powerful applications such as ISTE's Stretch AI are some examples that are provided. Lastly, readers will learn how AI use and development continues to change and what contemporary news, research, and resources are available to encourage more significant student curiosity and collaboration.

Chapter 13. Architectural Education: AI Integrative Challenges and Prospects

The focus of Nag, Boricha, & Sarkar in chapter 7 is integrating artificial intelligence into architectural pedagogy. The reader is introduced to the authors' initial foray into providing artificial intelligence as a tool, into architectural education courses. The introduction contains a second prong of discussion comparing the intersection of artificial intelligence and architecture. As a content area, the authors contend that architectural education is at a critical point pedagogically and that it architecture is not alone in being a profession that faces change at an increasing pace that educators face. For those who are concerned with architectural education, the challenge of AI incorporation into architectural pedagogy contains three major hurdles. First, the inclusion of AI into pedagogical methods requires the meeting of ethical concerns related to AI's use. Second, AI presents a pathway to collaboration among related disciplinary fields.

Successful AI integration into architectural education programs will lead to programs accelerating creativity and problem-solving abilities of students as well as ensuring that students have relevant, field-ready skills at their disposal, saving employers time and money in training costs. A third benefit is the ensuring of continued relevance and alignment of architectural programs with up-to-date skills. AI inclusion into architectural education recognizes the need to adapt AI into the curriculum, pedagogical methods, and assessments. As we stand at the initial stages of AI incorporation into content-specific areas, this chapter provides an initial step forward in aligning practices for the future.

Scott Gregory
Fort Hays State University, USA

REFERENCES

Chang, D. H., Pin-Chuan Lin, M., Hajian, S., & Wang, Q. Q. (2023). Educational design principles of using AI chatbot that supports self-regulated learning in education: Goal Setting, feedback, and personalization. *Sustainability (Basel)*, 15(17), 12921. DOI: 10.3390/su151712921

Chapter 1
A Basic Toolkit for Instructional Design by AI in Elementary Level Teaching

Gamze Türkmen
https://orcid.org/0000-0002-4695-9159
Manisa Celal Bayar University, Turkey

Sinem Sözen Özdoğan
https://orcid.org/0000-0002-4692-2305
TED University, Turkey

ABSTRACT

Reporting pathways between instructional design and specific AI models for elementary education is considered highly valuable for the educational field, based on recent developments. Therefore, the aim of this study is to provide an instructional design practice guide for elementary school teachers. Drawing on the capabilities of current educational AI models and the most frequently requested areas of support in instructional design, sample practices were provided as part of in-service teacher training. Four AI tools were selected based on their availability and usability for anyone with internet access. These tools were integrated into the teachers' instructional practices. Ultimately, teachers can utilize educational AI models in every aspect of their instructional design at the elementary level.

DOI: 10.4018/979-8-3693-6527-4.ch001

INTRODUCTION

Recently, the integration of artificial intelligence, both informal and formal, has become a hot topic in the education field. Its unpredictable spread without concrete evidence on positive impact has been quite a challenging issue to discuss. On the other hand, artificial intelligence as a tool in education has been offered by the authorities and considerable investments have been made (see recent reports U.S Department of Education, Office of Educational Technology, 2023, 2024). Moreover, artificial intelligence developers need to be supported in the field of education due to the practices and theoretical background of education in terms of end users, teachers (Luckin & Cukurova, 2019). Therefore, educational experts and teachers should investigate the potential benefits of emergent artificial intelligence models with consideration of educational needs and provide several pathways to the other stakeholders, especially teachers about how to integrate them for the efficient teaching and learning process (Celik et al., 2022).

Instructional design, one of the areas that artificial intelligent (AI) models have potential benefits (Chen et al., 2020), is the systematic planning and process management to achieve educational goals. This process begins with identifying student needs, followed by setting learning objectives and developing instructional materials and strategies. The primary aim of instructional design is to ensure the effective implementation and evaluation of teaching. In this process, which includes analysis, design, development, implementation, and evaluation phases, teachers start by determining the purpose and goals of their lessons (Merrill, 2007; Sweller, 2021). They plan the content by identifying the necessary knowledge and skills to achieve the goals and develop instructional strategies and activities that ensure active student participation. Additionally, they use assessment tools such as exams, performance tasks, and projects to measure students' learning levels and continuously improve the teaching process. In relation to this, potential benefits have been revealed by a review study considering advantages of AI use for teachers in terms of planning, implementing, and assessment (Celik et al., 2022) as well. Reporting pathways between instructional design and specific AI models for elementary education is considered highly valuable for the educational field, based on recent developments. Therefore, the aim of this study is to provide an instructional design practice guide for elementary school teachers.

BACKGROUND

Artificial Intelligence Use in Instructional Design

Planning activities that encourage active student participation and integrating visual, auditory, and tactile elements that can adapt to different learning approaches are some important steps for effective instructional design. Furthermore, providing feedback to students at regular intervals according to their needs to support their development is considered one of the essential components of the instructional design process. Teachers confront challenges while developing instructional design due to its complicated process (see Conca et al., 2024). Integrating technology into instructional design can enrich the learning experience by using digital tools and resources, as well as adjusting instructional methods and materials by identifying students' needs, prioritizing a student-centered instructional approach, and personalizing their instruction.

On the other hands, instructional design through artificial intelligence aims to create more personalized, adaptable, and effective learning experiences by integrating advanced data analytics and machine learning techniques into traditional instructional design processes (Ruiz-Rojas et al., 2023). AI, which collects large amounts of data from students' interactions and performance data, helps determine the subjects that students struggle with, the learning materials they find more effective, and their individual learning speeds. It is important for teachers to process the data generated by AI systems and provide appropriate instructional materials to their students and collaborate with these systems (Weng & Chiu, 2023). Although systems have advanced in making data-driven decisions, teachers still play a crucial role in designing the instruction for their students' classroom and extracurricular activities at the elementary level. However, achieving more focused results on topics such as each student's motivation, frequently repeated mistakes, and misconceptions in the classroom can be possible through these learning analytics processes.

Moreover, it is possible to structure activities designed for students through artificial intelligence. One important element is for the teacher to determine the content, context, and student needs before designing these activities. The prepared activities can vary at the elementary level. Planning activities such as digital storytelling, lesson plans, and conversation environments where students can individually learn the ideas of different historical figures will undoubtedly be among the applications that facilitate data storage for the teacher and improve the instructional design processes through AI.

Teacher-AI Collaboration: What A Teacher Gets and What an AI Model Gives

Without a teacher as an agent, AI supported systems developed for better learning processes such as intelligent tutoring systems (see Nesbit et al., 2014), have taken the greatest attention compared to the teacher-AI collaboration for the best teaching-learning systems. Due to the limits of AI models for now and a variety of opportunities that AI provides for teachers, education requires a good collaboration between teacher and AI which is supposed to develop teaching and learning processes. Furthermore, an experience with AI models may help teachers to overcome misconceptions related to AI such as "AI is dangerous" or "AI is for tech giants only" (Antonenko & Abramovitz, 2023).

Although K-12 level teachers' requests for guidance on artificial intelligence are increasing day by day, realizing these demands can be considered one of the important challenges, considering their limited or lack of experience in computer science or artificial intelligence. However, it is not easy to access resources for artificial intelligence (Touretzky et al., 2019). At the other extreme, countries such as the United States, Finland, Singapore, and China have already integrated artificial intelligence technologies into their curriculum (Kajamaa & Kumpulainen, 2020; Kim et al., 2021; OECD, 2017; Ouyang & Jiao, 2021; Vartiainen et al., 2020; Zhang & Aslan, 2021). Since K-12 level is at the focus of many different institutions and organizations teaching materials for teachers and course resources for students are being developed (see AI4K12, 2024).

In this context, the literature provides a rather limited context about how to support teachers. Considering AI4K12, there are artificial intelligence training materials at the K-12 level prepared for educators and special training sessions to raise awareness (Touretzky et al., 2019). In the study conducted with 24 computer teachers about what kind of artificial intelligence education application teachers can make at the K-12 level, apart from the materials, teachers' opinions were asked about the four basic components of program development (content, product, application, process) (Chiu et al., 2021). Artificial intelligence knowledge, the functioning of artificial intelligence, the impact of artificial intelligence on society, student interest, teacher-student communication and flexibility issues are discussed under these four basic components. Although this proposed model has not been implemented, it offers a holistic perspective for artificial intelligence and ethics developers, researchers, and users. Similar developed applications are available for different countries (see Kim et al., 2021). In a recent literature review study conducted by Salas-Pilco et al. (2022) on artificial intelligence and learning analytics, teachers and teacher candidates stated that in 30 artificial intelligence studies conducted between 2017 and 2021, most research was conducted on behaviors of teachers. Research conducted after

2021 has shown that the focus is on teachers and teaching materials targeting the K12 level. In the research conducted by Lee et al., (2022), an artificial intelligence book club proposal was made, and design principles were presented, considering the professional development of teachers on artificial intelligence and ethical issues. Considering the theoretical framework in which it is constructed, this book club model has been reported to be effective in attracting and maintaining teachers' interest in artificial intelligence literacy and creating a community of practice (Lee et al., 2022).

Reasons for Use

Educational technology and its effective use for instruction and the development of learning is crucial for student-centered learning environments which considers diverse needs and engagement of learners. Although its effective use enhances learning environment, recent studies reported that the teachers are still reluctant to use educational technology (Hsu et al., 2022) which may give an implication for AI utility for teaching and learning process due to their lack of knowledge and skills (Alwaqdani, 2024; Ottenbreit-Leftwich et al., 2023). Consequently, providing basic understanding and utility paths of AI in education is an urgent topic.

The role of AI in the classroom is not in the way of primacy over teachers' role. The aim is to empower teachers to give more time on the quality of teaching and learning. Apart from AI embedded robots (Timss, 2016), AI embedded software is more commonly infused in all the sectors as in education to enhance teaching and learning experiences. In a recent review study explored that the education system is reported to use artificial intelligence in the areas of assessments of schools and learning, grading and evaluation of students' artifacts, personalized teaching, smart school and online education (Chen et al., 2020). Administrative issues, instructional processes, program development, learning enhancement are the target issues to enrich. Reducing the administrative tasks on the school stakeholders, tailoring the learning experiences to satisfy students' needs, increasing students' engagement with the content, utilizing data analytics to raise the quality of instruction are main concerns for AI embedded web-based tools.

Areas of Use in Instructional Design Process

AI embedded web-based learning platforms make all the learners and teachers reach materials from anywhere in the world according to their needs (Chen et al. 2020). Since teachers are the primary responsible stakeholders in education for instructional design, they consider the curriculum, the materials and the students' need and prior knowledge. Based on this, they need to collect data from the students and need to follow a curriculum or program for content-based knowledge, skills and experience development. Therefore, artificial intelligence embedded web-based platforms provide designing lesson plans, content and assessment development, and evaluation of learning to improve teaching quality (Celik et al., 2022; Owoc et al., 2021). Specifically, the AI web-based tools may identify students' learning progress; provide a variety of resources for learning and personalized feedback; flourish student-teacher interaction; interpret students' data and so on (Kim, 2024).

AI web tools play a significant role in identifying students' learning progress by continuously collecting and analyzing data on students' interactions with learning materials, assessments, and participation. These tools use algorithms to track various indicators of progress, such as completion rates, time spent on tasks, performance on quizzes, and overall engagement with the content. Through this analysis, AI platforms can identify patterns, such as which concepts students struggle with or excel at, enabling personalized feedback and adjustments to their learning paths. AI can also predict future performance based on historical data (Fok et al., 2018; Gashout et al., 2023), allowing for early interventions to address learning gaps before they widen.

Teachers can utilize these insights in several ways. First, they can access real-time dashboards that present student progress in a clear, organized manner, helping them quickly identify which students are excelling and which need additional support (Aleven et al., 2022; Gobert et al., 2024). For example, AI can flag students who consistently struggle with specific topics, enabling teachers to provide targeted remediation or recommend additional resources. Teachers can also use the data to adapt lesson plans and instructional strategies, ensuring that the pacing and content are aligned with the class's overall performance and individual learning needs (Safsouf, 2021). This personalized approach helps to create more engaging and effective learning environments, as teachers can customize their teaching strategies based on precise, data-driven insights provided by AI tools.

Case Studies: AI in Action in Elementary Classrooms

In the K-12 process, AI tools can be integrated into two distinct ways: as a tool for learning and a tool for the design of teaching. First, AI might be a goal or a tool for learning; for example, a course on how to use ChatGPT (AI as a goal) or using ChatGPT to develop a student's essay writing (AI as a tool). For this case AI is explicitly used in the classroom. It was well-known that these kinds of specific courses on AI are involved in primary, middle and secondary education. However, A few examples from the field have demonstrated that AI embedded web-based applications were used all around the world for various reasons. Limited research studies have shown us that elementary students are capable of using AI in the classroom

(Vartiainen et al., 2020) but it was also reported that children and their teachers do not have substantial knowledge and skills (Ottenbreit-Leftwich et al., 2023).

In addition, it shows that AI has a small but positive effect on students' mathematics achievement (Hwang, 2022). In conjunction with this, Ottenbreit-Leftwich et al. (2023) suggested that integrating AI education into elementary classrooms requires addressing both student misconceptions and teacher preparedness. The study highlights the importance of thoughtfully designed curricula that connect AI concepts to students' prior knowledge, while also ensuring that teachers are confident and well-equipped to teach AI. Additionally, the co-design process, involving collaboration between teachers and students, is essential for creating effective and engaging AI learning experiences.

KEY CONCEPTS OF AN AI-DRIVEN INSTRUCTIONAL TOOLKIT

In this section, four practical applications that teachers can reach and use in their instructional design processes will be discussed, and activity suggestions will be provided within these applications. The presentation of activity suggestions will also include instructional design processes. These activities will cover the analysis, design, development, implementation, and evaluation processes. Each activity will emphasize these processes and discuss the application steps for teachers. These activities are classified into four main groups: (i) student interaction, (ii) digital storytelling, and (iv) smart classroom. The selected toolkits include a basic user interface in which a user can transfer the learning experience into similar AI models. Moreover, these tools have common characteristics which are significant for teachers to construct their own toolkit.

- Allows auto-generation of contents
- Offers several tools to create content
- Has more than 20 language support
- Has user-friendly interface

Student Interaction

Student interaction can be important at every stage of the instructional design process (Sims, 2006). However, it becomes especially significant during the design of the course assessment and evaluation process. It is anticipated that teachers' inability to observe students' work processes and to understand whether they have pre-existing misconceptions before the lesson, as well as how they use an environment where they can receive support for lesson outcomes, will be facilitated.

Interaction and feedback are crucial in instructional design to enhance student success. With the advent of AI and large language models, chatbots can be developed to address students' individual feedback and interaction needs. These chatbots provide instant feedback, answer questions, and personalize learning, thereby boosting motivation and enriching learning experiences. They also help identify and address students' weaknesses, easing teachers' workloads and contributing to more efficient educational environments. Large language models enable natural communication, encouraging students to participate actively in learning. To sum up, AI-supported chatbots are valuable tools in modern instructional design, optimizing student learning experiences. Chen et al. (2023) found that chatbots can effectively help students learn basic content interactively and confidentially. In which they make students use a new experimental chatbot to teach basic AI concepts, showing that chatbots can be engaging and responsive learning tools. The study highlights the opportunities and ethical considerations of using chatbots for inclusive learning as well.

In this context, Mizou is a tool designed to facilitate student interaction with an AI assistant around specific concepts. Its flexibility allows educators to customize concept sets, information sheets, AI response strategies, and student roles to fit any class level, enabling effective planning of the interaction.

Creating an Account

Teachers can proceed with their existing account on the Mizou.com platform or create a new account using an email address. After creating an account, it is important to familiarize themselves with the platform's interface (see Figure 1).

Figure 1. Build a Chatbot button

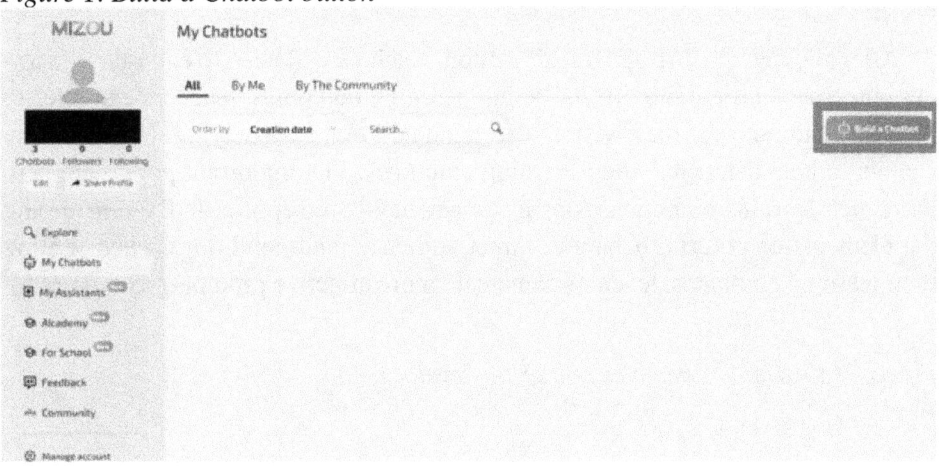

Setting Rules When Creating a Chat Room

After clicking the "build a chatbot" button, teachers can select either the "Custom" or "AI-driven" options. This way, teacher can create a chatbot with AI support according to the current learning outcomes of their lesson (see Figure 2).

Figure 2. AI-Generated chatbot button

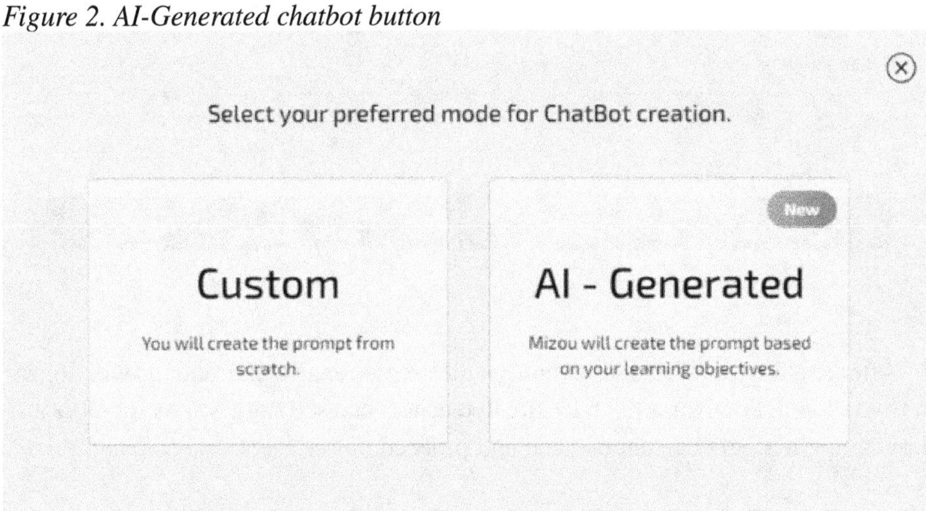

Defining Learning Outcomes

After clicking the “AI-generated” button, teachers will need to enter their learning outcomes in this field. To define the learning outcomes, teachers can refer to their curriculum or, if they wish to create an additional activity, they can use any chatbot to help determine their learning outcomes. The important point here is to write their learning outcomes using a competency-based approach. By considering the elements of criteria, behavior, target audience, and conditions when writing their learning outcomes, teachers can create more effective prompts (see Figure 3).

Figure 3. Learning objectives and grade level screen

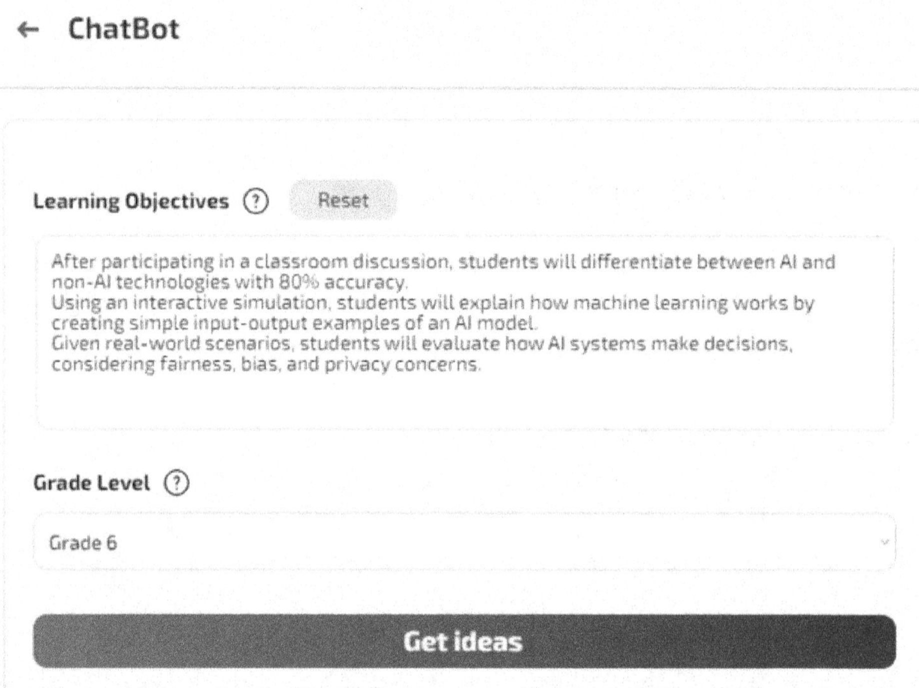

After clicking the “Get ideas” button, different scenario alternatives will appear in front of you. For example, in Figure 4, teachers can see suggestions for Quiz and Simulation. teachers can choose one and proceed.

Figure 4. Chatbot offer

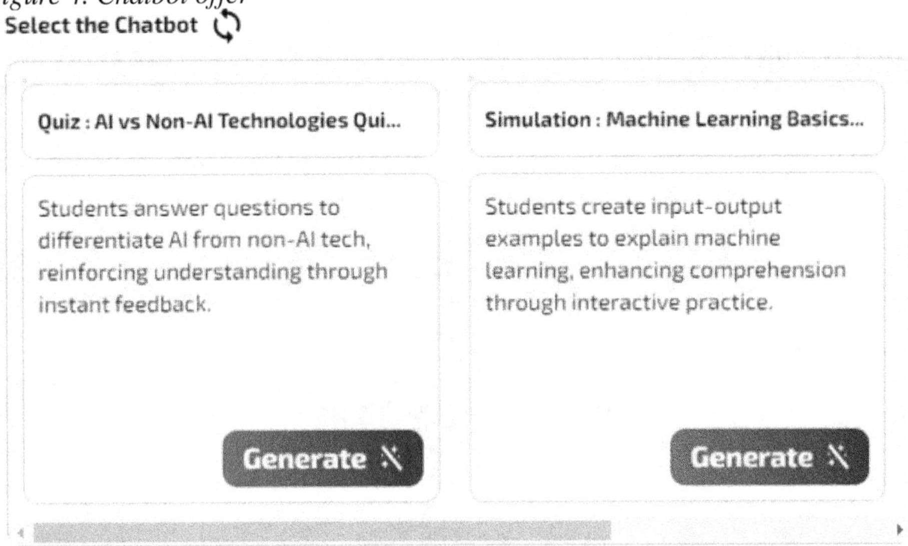

This AI-driven chatbot brings teachers different suggestions again. They can update areas such as their quiz title, statements on how to train the AI, student level, and the name of the AI if teachers wish. What is seen in Figure 5 are the recommendations made by Mizou.

Figure 5. Chatbot instructions screen

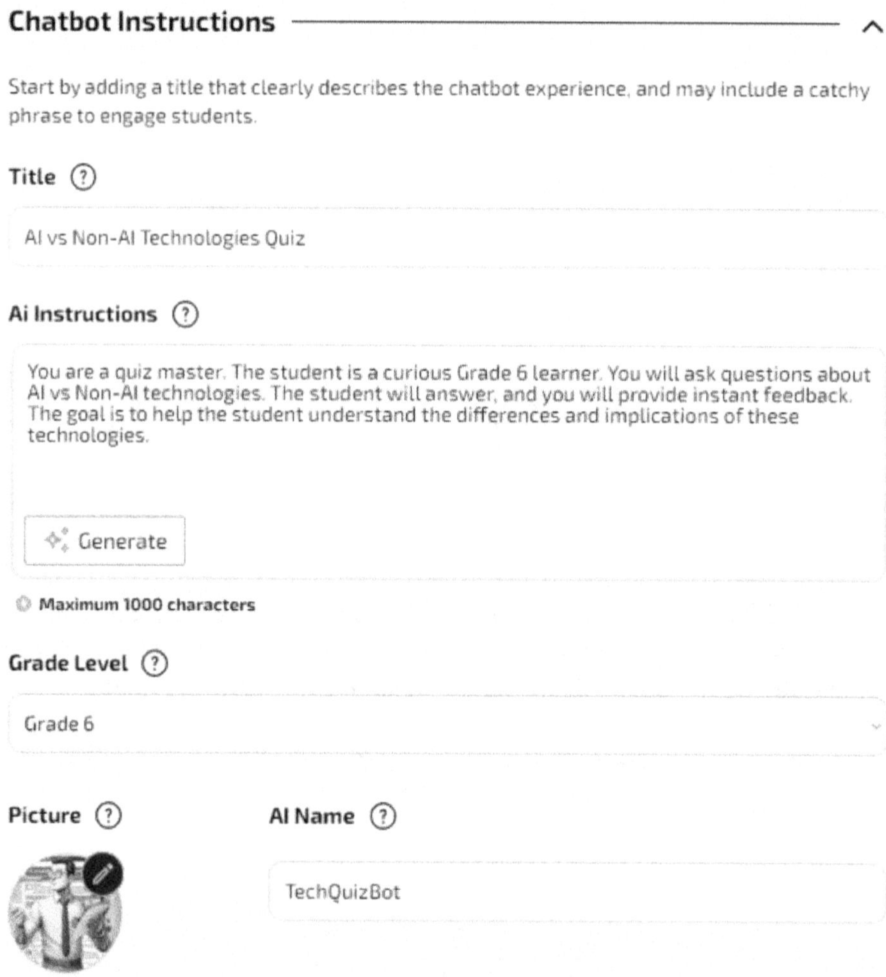

When teachers click on the “More options” button, they can provide guidelines on how the AI should approach students' questions and answers. Additionally, they can upload their lesson information file in this area. Figure 6 shows a scenario where the instructions are generated by the AI.

Figure 6. More options for generation

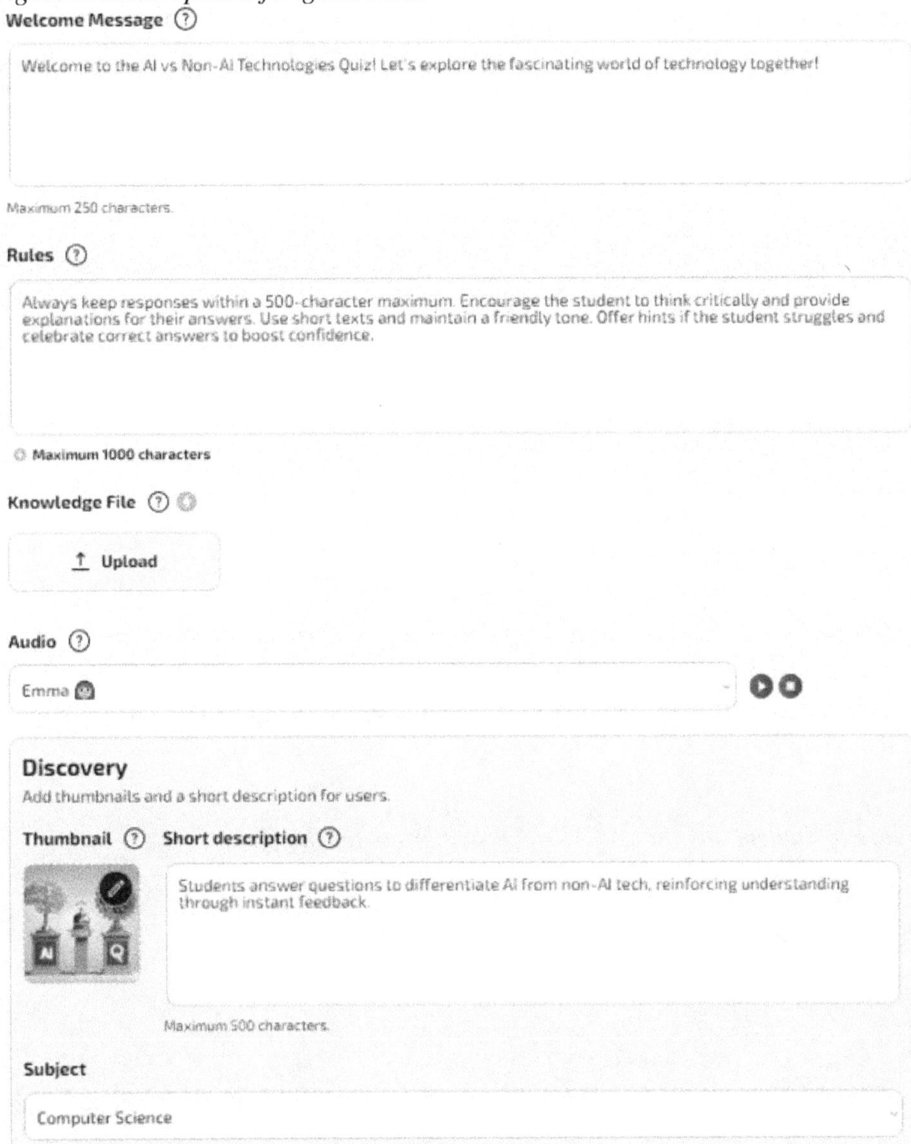

By clicking the "Publish" button in the top right corner, teachers can choose between private or public options. Right after that, with the link teachers shared, they will be able to see what their students have written and shared if they have had any chatbot experience. To share the link with their students, click the "Share" button on the screen that appears and select the student box. This will bring up the screen shown in Figure 7. On this screen, teachers can also personalize the chatbot based on the student they are sending it to and train the AI chatbot accordingly. After clicking the "Launch" button, teachers can copy the link and share it with their students. When any of their students use the chatbot, teachers can access the details of their session under this chatbot session.

Figure 7. Launch for sharing chatbot screen

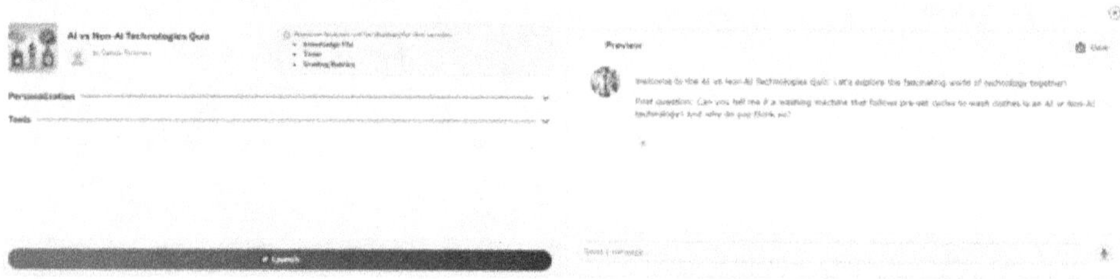

Monitoring Student Responses

In Figure 8, teachers can access the student's chat room and observe the score recommended by the AI. Based on this score, the AI suggests grade A; however, as a teacher, it is their responsibility to review the details of the grade recommended by the AI.

Figure 8. Student answer and AI suggested grade for the Quiz

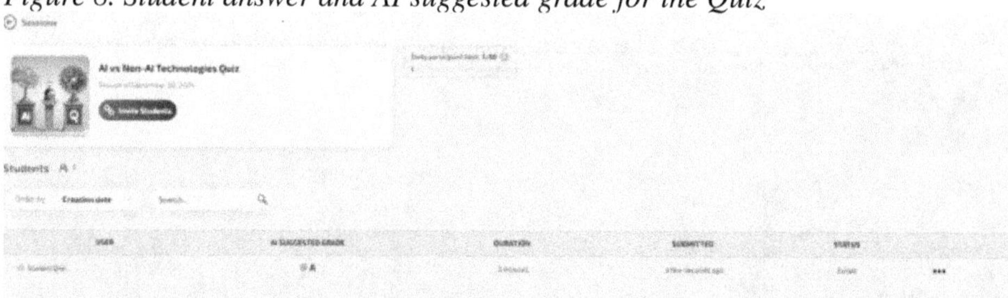

Here, the AI provides feedback for the student on the left side. On the right side, teachers can observe the student's responses and the questions the AI asked the student (see Figure 9).

Figure 9. Student chat screen and AI feedback

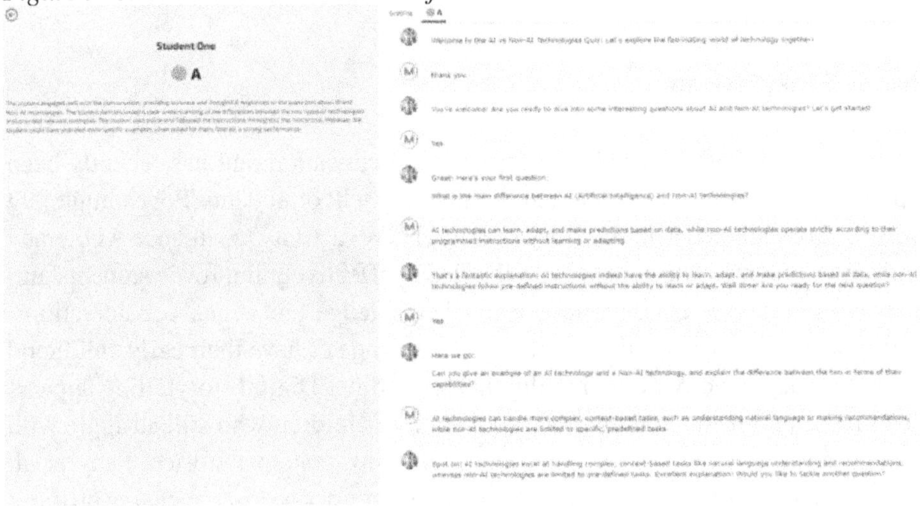

AI Feedback for Student

The student engaged well with the conversation, providing accurate and thoughtful responses to the questions about AI and Non-AI technologies. The student demonstrated a clear understanding of the differences between the two types of technologies and provided relevant examples. The student was polite and followed the instructions throughout the interaction. However, the student could have provided more specific examples when asked for them. Overall, a strong performance.

Essential Reminders

- Introduce the Mizou application to students early on and explain how they should interact with it, ensuring they understand its role as a learning tool rather than a replacement for human instruction.
- Writing detailed learning outcomes and preparing clear instructions is essential in the Mizou application.
- Always review why the AI suggested a specific grade, even if it recommends one for their students.
- The stage of their course where teachers use the application will determine how teachers utilize it. For example, decide whether they will use the application to evaluate students or to support their work before the lesson.

- Defining their purpose for using the application is crucial for effective implementation.

Digital Storytelling

Digital storytelling is used in many areas of education and has recently been employed to develop AI literacy among elementary school students. For example, Ng et al. (2022) conducted a digital story writing (DSW) activity to enhance AI literacy in primary students. The study found that DSW effectively improves students' understanding of AI concepts, application of AI knowledge, and ethical considerations. In other words, it is known that teachers often engage or have their early childhood students engage in activities using digital storytelling. Digital storytelling appears to be important for maintaining the motivation of children who still struggle with grasping abstract concepts by providing them with concrete stories. Fang et al. (2023) reviews recent research on AI applications in story writing, focusing on types of AI, educational levels, and their roles in fostering creativity, writing skills, and motivation. The findings highlight that AI-supported writing improves creativity and engagement, and human-AI collaboration enhances story quality.

With the increasing use of artificial intelligence tools in recent times, various tools like Midjourney (Derevyanko & Zalevska, 2023), metademolab (Smith et al., 2023), character.ai, and storyboarder.ai can generate visuals and convert them into digital story formats. Among these tools, some even allow students to animate their drawings and create their own stories. In digital storytelling, consistency in characters is also known to be important. Ensuring that the story's hero remains consistent across all scenes is among the other expectations. However, most programs that maintain this consistency while generating visuals are either paid or do not offer free credits, which can pose challenges for educational use.

Openart.ai, an open art platform, facilitates visual creation through its interface and, with the trial credits given upon registration, can provide sufficient resources for teachers and students to conduct their activities. As an AI tool, a teacher can use it in the complex process of design and development after determining student characteristics, content features, and context features when engaging in digital storytelling. Although effective prompt writing in the AI-supported design process is an important consideration, the design and development processes can progress together since the selected digital tool's features are known to refine these prompts. Therefore, how it can be utilized openart.ai, one of the digital storytelling tools, in the design and development processes is an important issue. Before this, it is essential to provide a brief introduction on how to create an account on the platform and how to use the relevant tools in the interface.

While OpenArt.ai generates high-resolution and consistent visuals, converting these visuals into video format is also important. Therefore, an additional tool is needed for digital storytelling. As mentioned above, OpenArt and FlikiAI are two tools that can be used freely. OpenArt is one of the most effective AI tools used particularly in design. It is known for generating high-quality images from prompts and is prominent in creating digital art, space and atmosphere design, and visuals for educational purposes. The tool is also preferred for character design due to the consistency it achieves through parameters like Seed. While it can be integrated with Discord and used with specific commands and parameters, its visual interface on OpenArt.ai allows users to produce images without the need for coding. On the other hand, Fliki.ai is a widely used AI tool for video production. It can create videos by adding voice overs to their uploaded .ppt files, shared blog links, or uploaded images, using various voice types.

Below is a step-by-step guide on how to use the OpenArt and FlikiAI tools for visual production, followed by video and voice-over creation in digital storytelling. Initially, the process will begin with the OpenArt tool and then transition to the FlikiAI tool. Therefore, the stages of a two-step storytelling process are outlined below.

OpenArt

Creating An Account

When teachers open the OpenArt homepage, teachers will see the screen shown in Figure 10. On this screen, teachers need to first click the "Start Creating Now" button highlighted with a red frame.

Figure 10. OpenArt.ai login screen

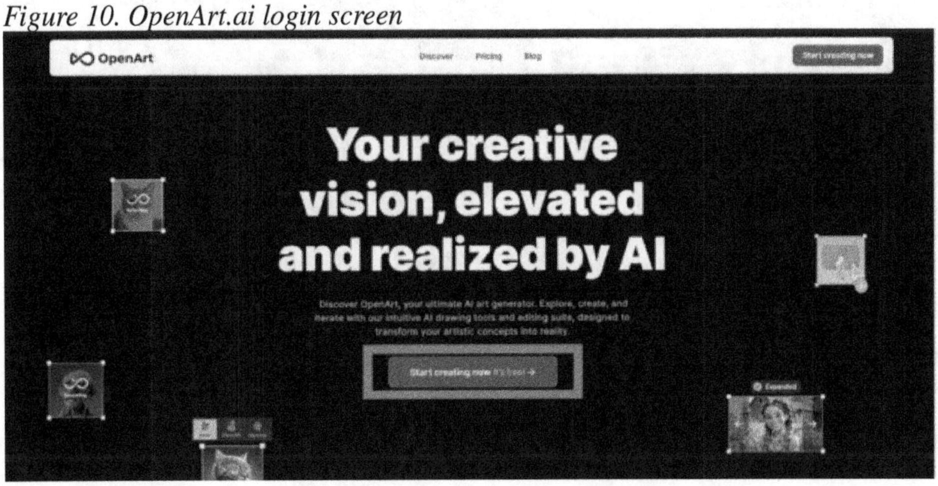

After clicking the "Start creating now" button, the screen shown in Figure 11 will appear. On this screen, teachers need to click the "Create Image" button or the "Create" button located at the top left of the screen to proceed.

Figure 11. Create image buttons

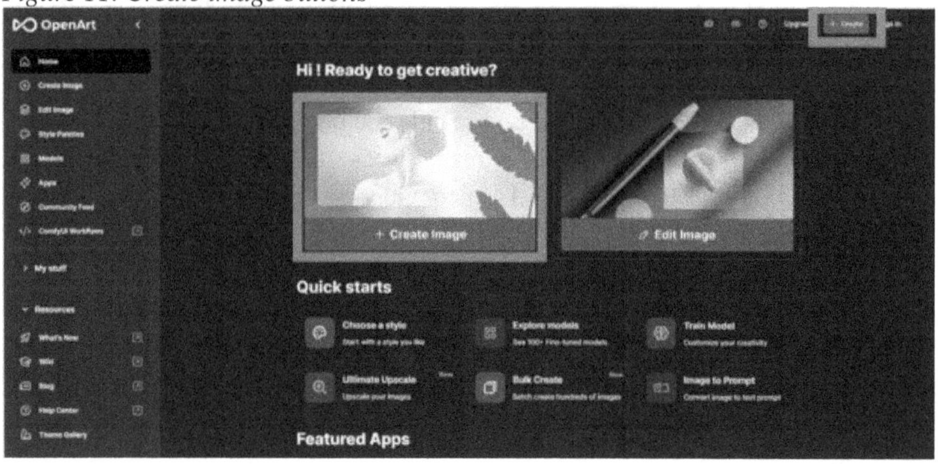

After clicking the "Create" button, if teachers are not yet a member of the OpenArt.ai platform, a "Sign up to create for Free" button will appear. Teachers can click on this button to proceed (see Figure 12).

Figure 12. Sign up button

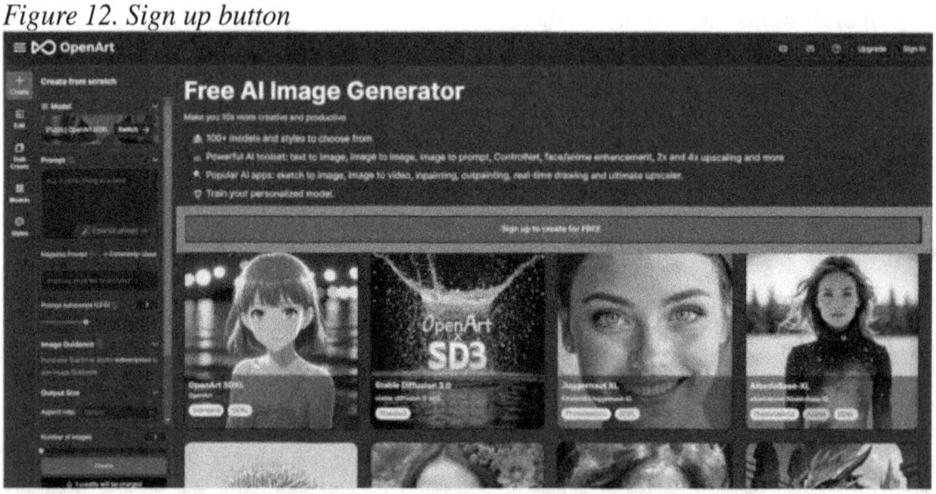

After clicking the button, teachers can either connect their existing social media account to this platform or sign up with another email account (see Figure 13).

Figure 13. Sign up with the preferred account

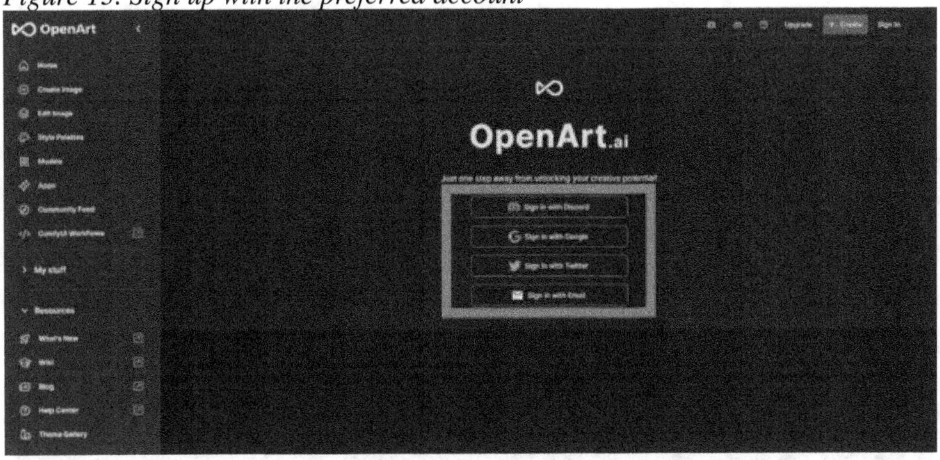

After filling in the information on the screen, teachers will need to enter the verification code sent to their email address. An account has been created now. Once their account is set up, teachers can immediately see their 20 credits in the bottom left corner (see Figure 14). Additionally, if they connect their Discord account, their free credits may increase.

Figure 14. Free credits for the educational use

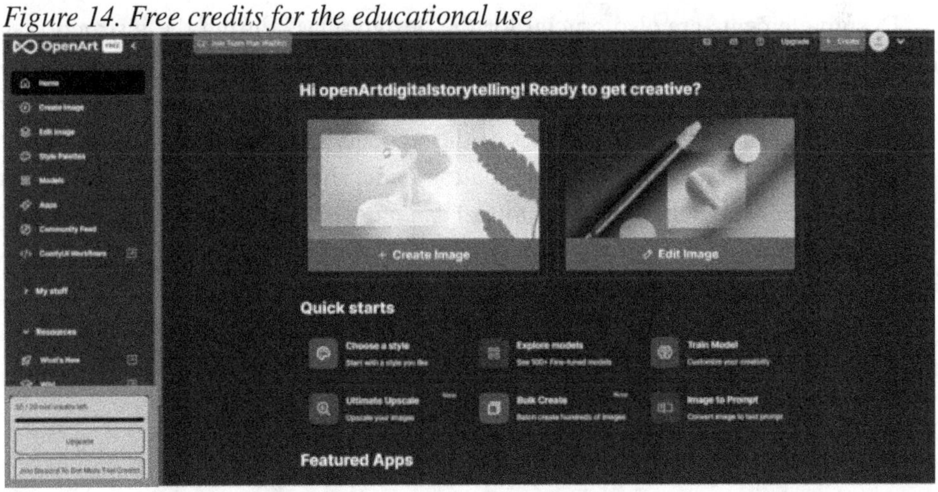

Now, teachers can click the "Create Image" button again to navigate to the relevant area for generating an image. On the left side, there is a section where teachers can select the type of model, and just below that, teachers will find areas to adjust the prompt and other parameters (see Figure 15).

Figure 15. Area for create from scratch

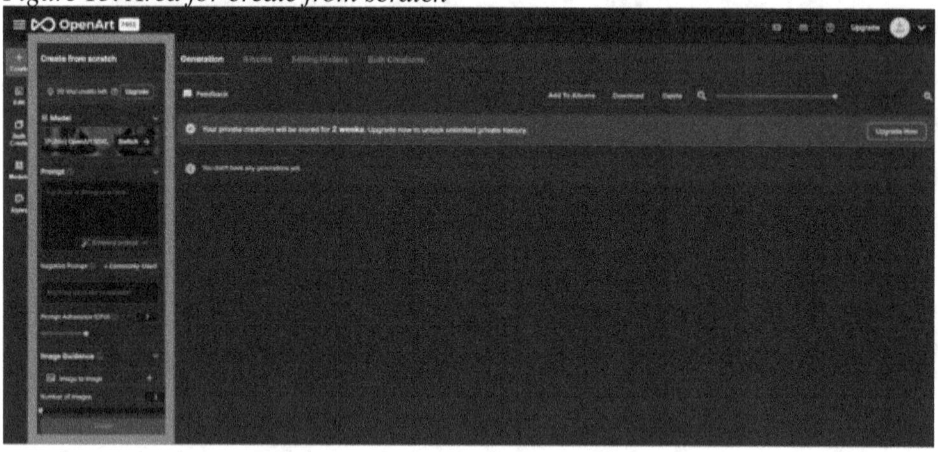

Design Elements: Model Selection

Essential Reminder

Design elements are also crucial for the design phase during the instructional design process. By understanding the boundaries and possibilities of these elements, a teacher can determine the model and environment for the images they will create, taking into account the characteristics of the students, the subject, and the context.

When teachers click on the Switch button under the Model section (see Figure 16), they will encounter a variety of model examples. Depending on their students' characteristics and the priorities they set in digital storytelling, teachers can choose the type of images that the AI will generate.

Figure 16. Model selection for the image generation

In the example within this toolkit, images will be generated according to the Cartoon > Pixar Style XL model (see Figure 17). However, teachers can also select a different model based on their students' age group, knowledge level, and the type of story teachers plan to tell.

Figure 17. Model categories and selected Pixar Style XL model

Here, an example of a digital story that can be used as an introductory video in AI literacy education for elementary school students will be depicted. Therefore, the selection of the model, prompt writing, and image generation will be designed based on this depiction. During the design phase, after selecting the model, the prompt writing process is considered important before generating the images.

Design Elements: Effective Prompt Writing

Crafting effective prompts is key to generating high-quality AI image outputs. To achieve this, use clear and specific language, providing detailed descriptions of the subject, style, and mood. Context and purpose should be included to guide the AI, and experimenting with prompt structure can lead to better results. It's important to specify the desired style and tone, include any constraints, and be ready to refine the prompt based on initial outputs. Additionally, referencing well-known examples can help clarify expectations, ensuring the AI produces content that aligns with their vision.

After selecting a model suitable for a teacher's story, it is important to focus on character and environment design while creating an introductory video on AI literacy. Considering gender differences among students and the desire not to target the video at any specific gender group, different pedagogical agent can be selected in the beginning. Given that students are often familiar with robots and that many studies have identified the myth that robots are synonymous with AI, a robot character could be chosen. It is important to depict the environment by considering elements like lighting, space, objects, and atmosphere. It is crucial to include these descriptions in the first box of Figure 18.

Figure 18. Prompt area

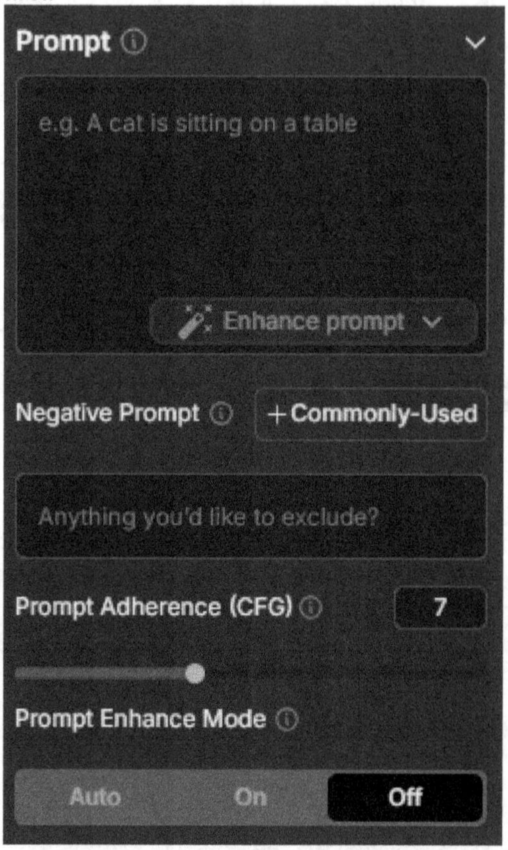

Additionally, teachers can add any elements teachers do not want to be in the environment or use the enhancer in the interface to make their prompt more detailed. The following prompt can be used as an example.

Designing the first scene of an AI-driven digital story

A gray metal robot enters a futuristic, science-themed environment filled with intricate brain models and glowing neural networks that crisscross the space like webs of light. Boys and girls, who are eagerly examining the synapses, stand in awe of the robot's arrival. The students' faces light up with excitement as they explore the fascinating world of neurons and connections surrounding them. The atmosphere is vibrant and full of curiosity, like stepping into a living science lab where learning and imagination come to life.

Negative prompts: two boys or two girls

Similarly, the other 9 scenes can also be designed, and after this design process, it is important to review the design by moving on to the development stage and examining the produced visuals.

Design Elements: Other Interface Features Enhancing Prompts

Before moving on to the development stage, reference can be added for the visuals and adjusted various parameters to ensure character consistency in the scene. Figure 19 provides interface features for how to add reference visuals. Since OpenArt.ai is a program with an interface, reference visuals related to style, posture, composition, and face can be added easily. However, if teachers want to generate visuals using a program that does not have an interface, teachers will need to include these references directly in their prompts.

Figure 19. Image guidance and preferences

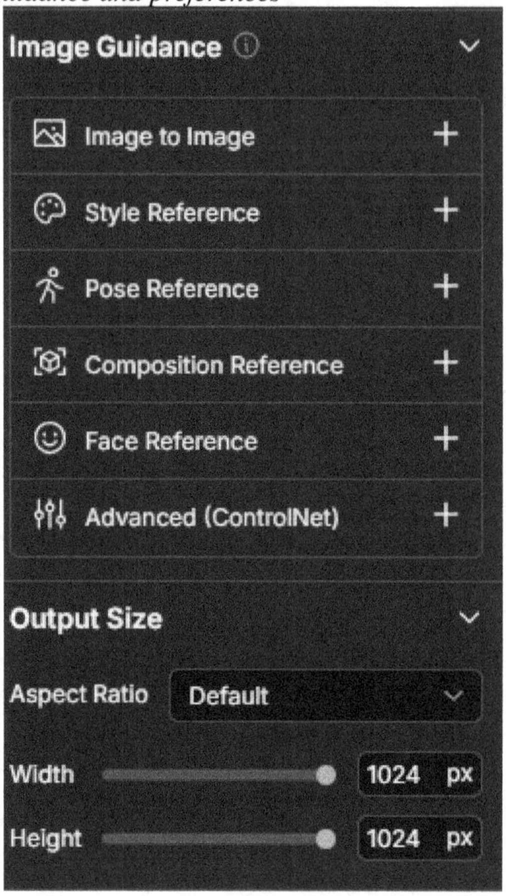

Figure 20, on the other hand, shows the advanced settings for other parameters. Here, teachers can specifically input the Seed number from a previously generated visual, which allows teachers to maintain consistency more easily among the visuals, especially in terms of the faces depicted in them.

Figure 20. Advanced settings for other parameters

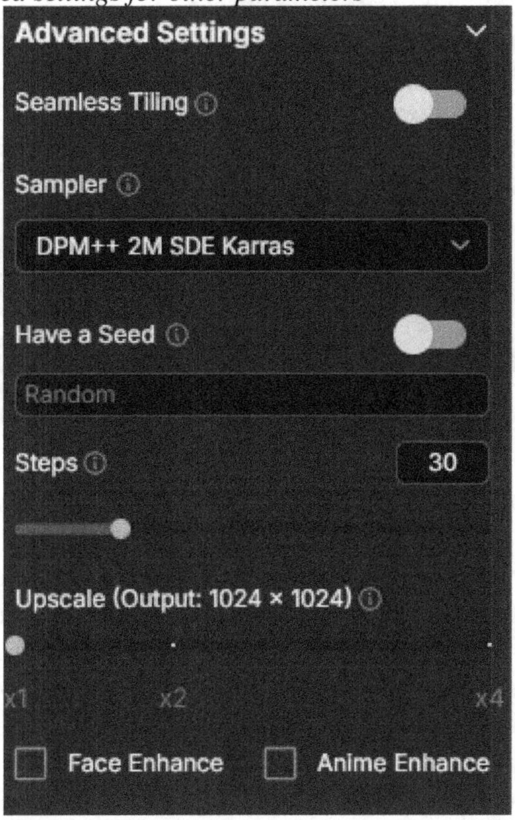

Generating the Images

Essential reminder:

Generating the images is considered an important step in the development phase of instructional design. At this stage, we create the visual output. Remember that after reviewing the output, teachers can always return to the design process to make adjustments.

Let's generate the visual output by clicking the create button based on the first prompt which is written (see Figure 21). The image generation duration may vary depending on the model teachers have chosen.

Figure 21. Create button for generating images

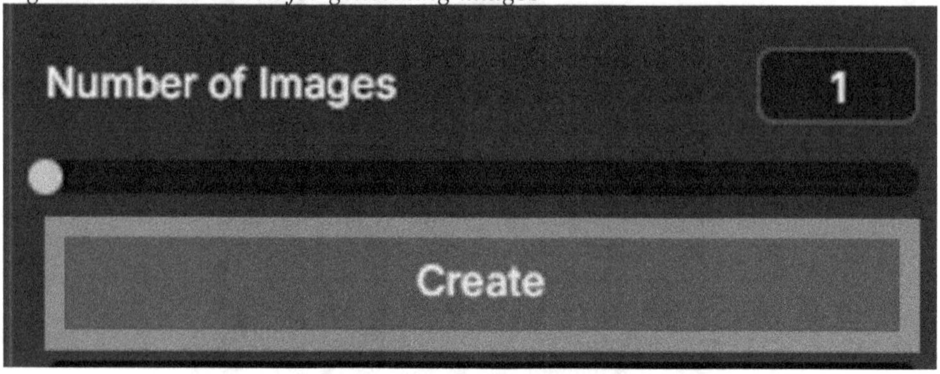

Figure 22 shows the output of the first visual. In this visual output, there is an environment as described in the prompt. However, if the environment does not match what teachers had in mind, teachers can adjust the keywords or use the enhance mode in the prompt field. From here, four more scenes need to be created. Let's continue shaping these scenes around the robot as the main character.

To ensure consistency in character and atmosphere across the four images to be produced, using the Seed number as a reference can be a good approach. Therefore, during the development process, it is sufficient to enter the Seed number marked in Figure 22 into the "have a seed" field under the advanced settings. At the same time, adding the first generated image as image guidance is important to use it as a reference for the visual.

Figure 22. Visual output of the first attempt

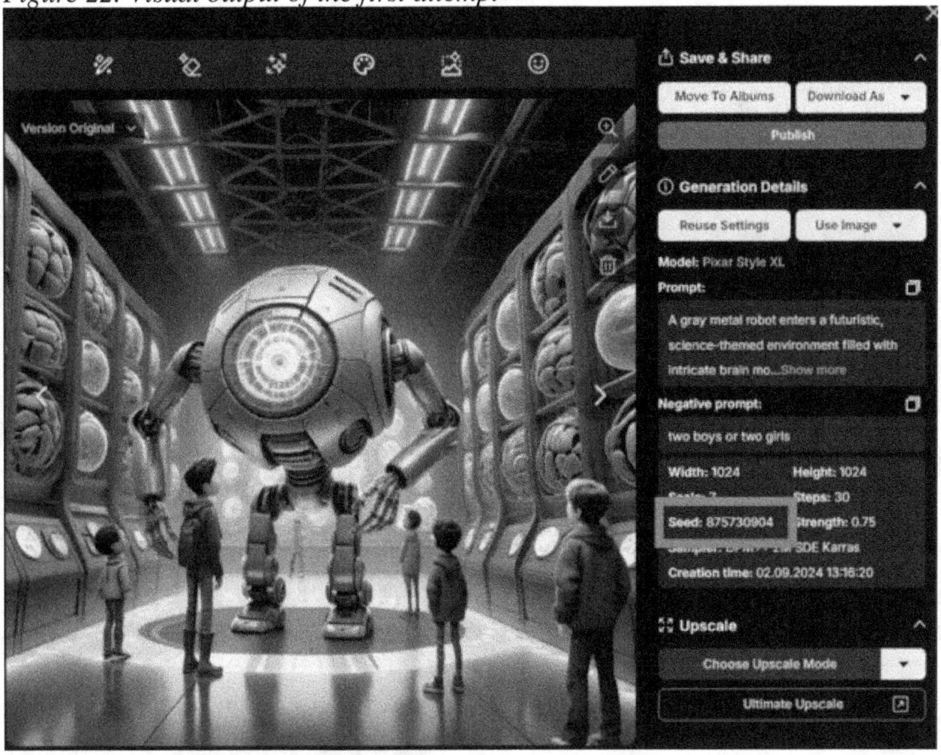

A detailed prompt needs to be written to ensure consistency between characters and scenes as much as possible. After generating visuals, teachers can repeatedly go back to the design phase to see if the scene matches what teachers envisioned, identify which parts of the prompts need adjustment, and determine which parameters teachers need to tweak. Table 1 shows the other four prompts and their visual outputs for this example story.

Table 1. Detailed prompts and the visual outputs

Prompt	Generated Image
2. The robot character stands at the center, surrounded by a s and voice assistants, all carefully arranged in a semi-circle a gestures toward these devices as it explains their functions to boy and a girl, standing nearby, gaze intently at the devices v interest. The environment is vibrant and tech-focused, with t the role of a knowledgeable guide in this exploration of mod	
3. The white and blue robot with a large, glowing eye stands students in a modern classroom, showing them how to condu large digital screen that displays a web browser and search re points to various sections of the screen with its mechanical a how to gather information on a topic using the internet. The with bookshelves, educational posters, and desks. The studen boy and one girl, are focused and engaged, watching the robo and interest as it demonstrates how AI can assist in research atmosphere is vibrant and full of discovery, as the students a using technology to gain knowledge.	

continued on following page

Table 1. Continued

Prompt	Generated Image
4. The white and blue robot with a large, glowing eye assists students in creating a digital piece of art in a vibrant, creative room is filled with bright colors and artistic tools, with digita tablets displaying various artwork in progress. The robot stan and a girl, guiding their hands as they use a stylus to draw on canvas. The robot says, "This artwork was created with the h it's not a robot!" The atmosphere is one of creativity and insp walls adorned with student artwork, and shelves stocked with sketchbooks, and 3D printed models. The students' faces glo as they collaborate with the robot, bringing their imaginative through the fusion of technology and art. The soft hum of the the gentle guidance of the robot create a warm and encouragi where learning and creativity flourish together.	
5. The white and blue robot with a large, glowing eye stands classroom, filled with interactive learning stations, each tail student's needs. The robot, with its friendly and attentive de between a boy and a girl, guiding them as they work on pers their desks. The robot says, "AI personalizes the learning pr each student to learn at their own pace and in their own way is designed with flexible seating arrangements, colorful post screens displaying individual learning progress. The atmosp focused engagement and encouragement, with each student own learning journey. The robot's presence adds a dynamic the tasks and offering support based on each student's uniqu reflects a harmonious blend of technology and education, w ensures that every child receives the attention and resources in their learning environment.	

Fliki.ai

After completing five-scene story, fliki.ai program is the next tool to add voice and flow to it. Teachers can log in to the platform with their existing accounts or create a new account using an email address. Once teachers create an account, click the "New File" button on the screen that appears, and teachers will need to enter the details of the content teachers want to create. Figure 23 shows this entry screen.

Figure 23. New file creation step

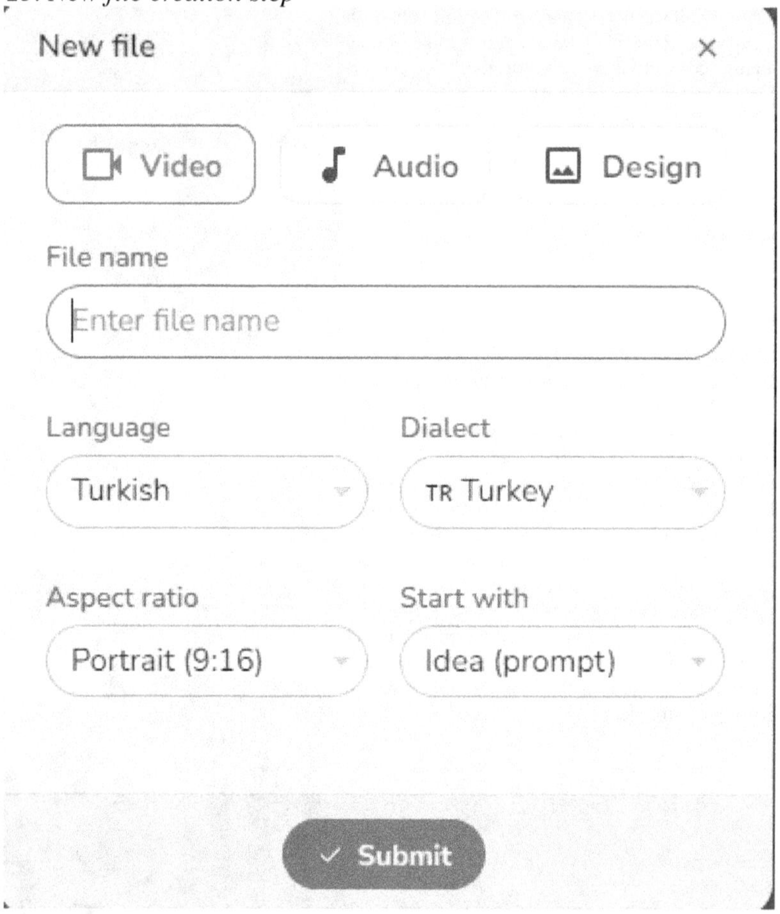

At this stage, after entering the name of the story, language option is selected and clicked on the option to create a blank file, which brings us to the screen shown in Figure 24. Here, uploaded the images previously created, which phrases will be spoken as these images appear on the screen was specified.

Figure 24. Create from scratch (empty file)

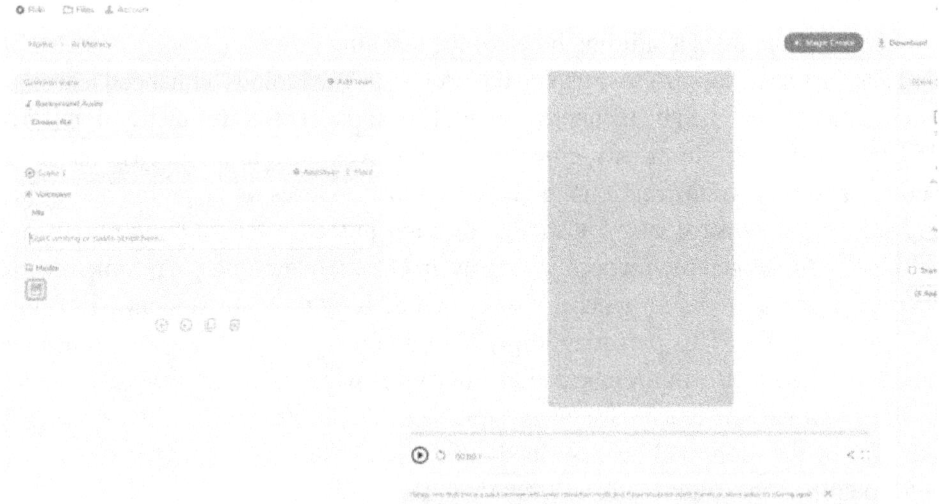

After writing the text that will be spoken and uploading the corresponding images, a voice is assigned and video was created. To download the video, simply click the Download button in the upper right corner (see Figure 25).

Figure 25. Creating the video in fliki.ai

After completing these steps and developing the story, it will be important to implement it in the lesson and determine which questions the students should answer.

Smart Classrooms

Lesson planning is a building block of the teaching process (Akyuz et al., 2013) and teachers need support to organize their lessons. Technology-enhanced learning environments mediated by technological tools to support effective instruction (Lim & Chai, 2008). While effective instruction involves designing specific learning activities to achieve instructional objectives it also focuses on engaging and guiding students in constructing knowledge through higher-order thinking processes. AI-aided educational platforms may supply an effective learning environment with its organizational tools for teacher's work and activity tools for students' learning (Niu et al., 2022). This part may imply a guide for teachers about how to use an educational AI platform for instructional purposes which there are several AI tools designed for helping teachers such as Almanack AI, EduAide AI, and Magicschool AI. One of the tools will be described here so that the teachers may transfer this information to the other platforms that they like most.

MagicSchool is a free AI-powered school platform specifically designed for teachers and students. It includes various tools for creating lesson plans, developing assessment rubrics, and providing guidance in various subjects for free. This platform stands out by being school-focused and a variety of tools embedded in it and provides more than 50 language support. The platform has a claim to save up time for instructional design with its various tools. As other AI models require, creating an account is necessary. A participant can assign to this platform in two personas: an educator and a student.

Creating An Account

Teachers need to join to use this platform by creating an account. Sign up for free via their mail address that teachers have already used for other AI platforms. Selecting as teachers, teachers may also change the language preference as seen in Figure 26.

Figure 26. Creating an account page

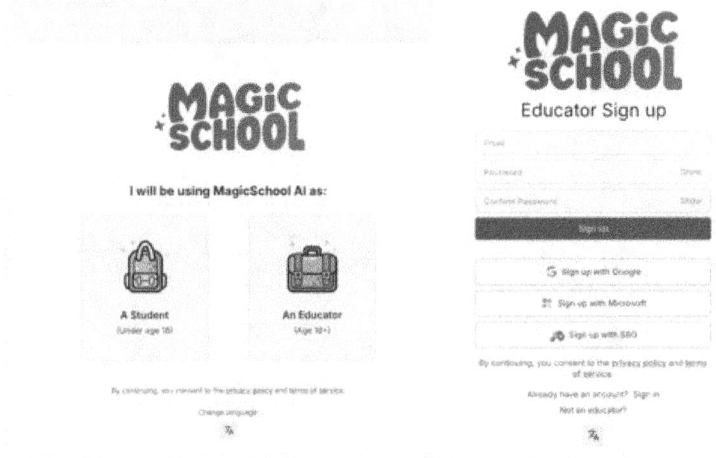

While creating, teachers are going to refine their teaching grade level and subject teachers need to study on, which are also important to make some of the tools visible.

Lesson Plan Design

After teachers register for the platform, teachers are going to see various tools on the right side of the page based on their dashboard. Selecting the platform as a teacher, the tools will be filtered accordingly. In Figure 27, the tools are activated by clicking on them.

Figure 27. A teacher dashboard and interface of Magicschool AI platform

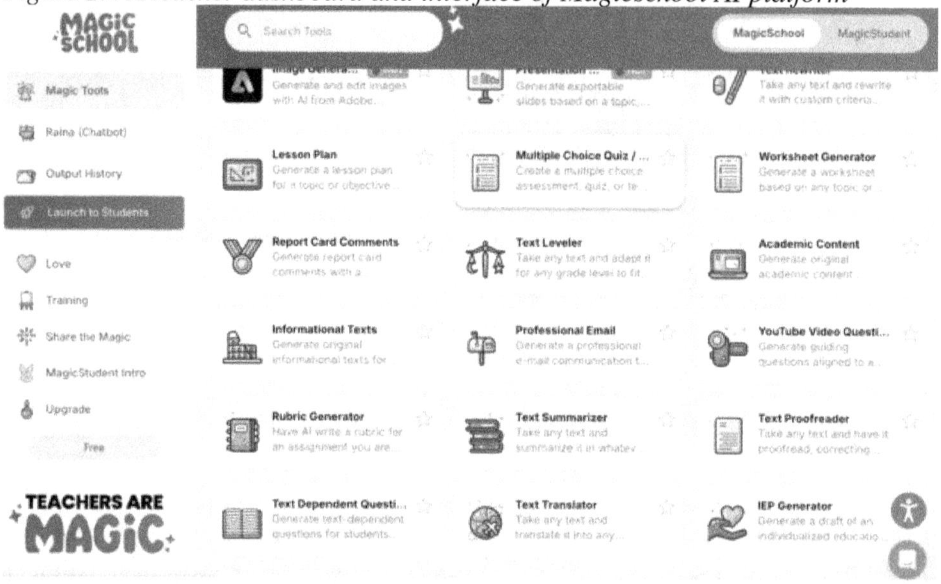

Above all tools, it is not easy to find a lesson planner and also there are several tools to conduct lesson planning on Magicschool. Above the right side of the dashboard there are keywords to find the exact tools. Teachers can refine their selection to "planning" given on the dashboard in the red rectangle in Figure 28. Another situation is that teachers can use the search bar to find the exact tool. Even if it is refined, sometimes it is not easy to differentiate between the tools. On the other hand, if teachers like a tool, teachers can click on the star to create a favorite tools list.

Figure 28. Refining tools and tool recommendation

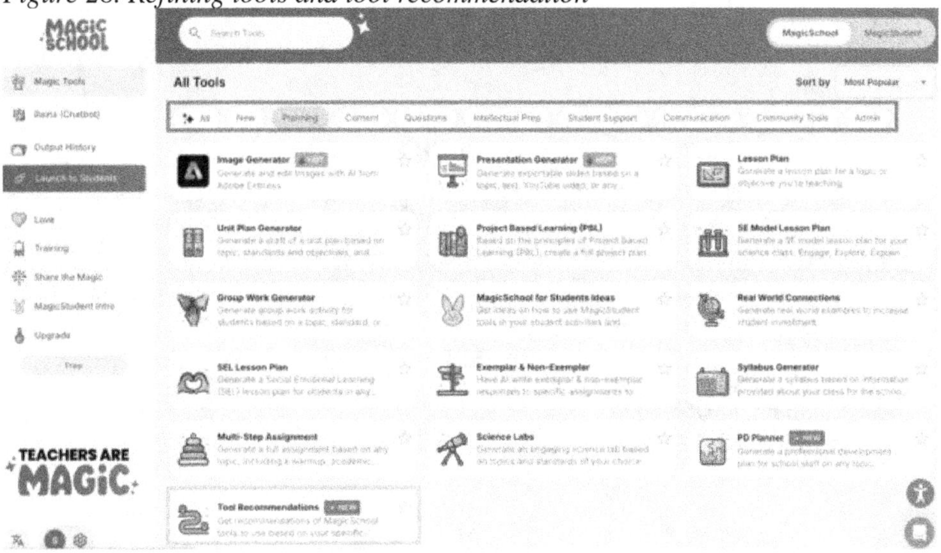

Figure 28 provides a decreased number of tools focusing on the lesson planning. There are still various options for lesson planning such as “5E Model Lesson Plan”, “SEL Lesson Plan”. These tools have special focus based on the classroom management perspectives of the teachers. However, teachers may still be confused about which tool to select. In the green rectangle, there is a “tool recommendation” button so that the AI model provides a guideline for its various tools. Apart from other tools, “Lesson Plan” tool has no special frame for teaching; therefore it is suitable for everyone to create a lesson plan. This tool allows educators to generate a comprehensive lesson plan tailored to a specific topic or objective, making it easier to organize teaching materials and activities for students specific to their grade level. By clicking on it, the tool will be opened.

In Figure 29, at the beginning of the prompt page there are two specific buttons: clear inputs and exemplar. Consequently, teachers can erase all the writing by clicking on “clear inputs” and create a sample input by clicking on “exemplar” which will also demonstrate an example output. Lesson plan tool refine lesson planning into several parts: “grade level”, “topic/standard/objective”, “additional criteria”, and “standards set to align to”. These are basic parts for a lesson planner in educational AI-driven platforms. Each part has three input types: writing, audio, or document attachment.

Figure 29. Lesson plan tool prompting interface

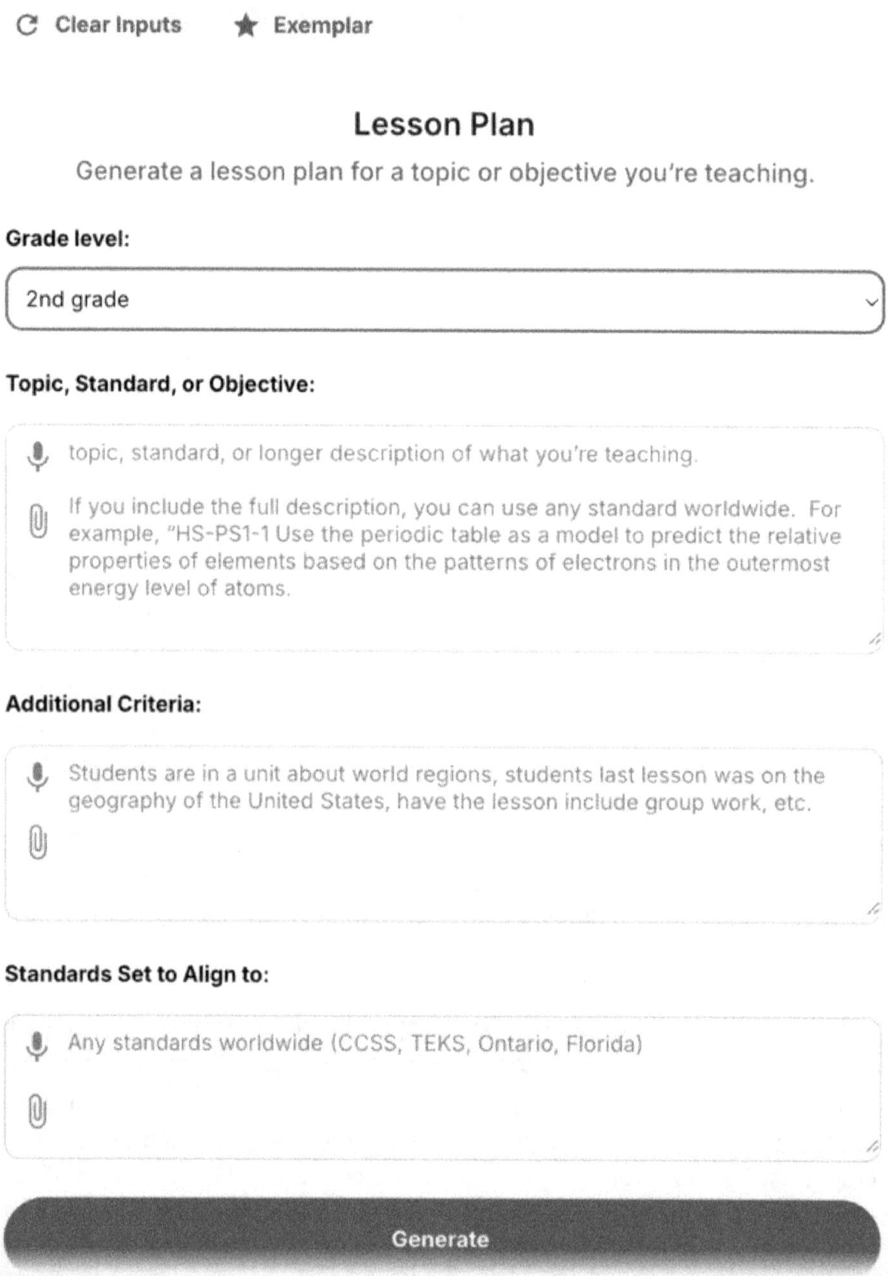

1. Select grade level from the options that lesson plan provides. As a limitation there is no choice for combined classroom which involves more than one grade level.
2. Based on country/state/school directories, decide on the topic/standard or objective that teachers are going to teach. For example, let's select a topic from a mathematics lesson: fractions. If teachers are doing initial planning, it is good to write the keyword or exact objective as it is. The tool has already known about Common Core State Standards (CCSS, 2010) etc. The more details teachers have provided, the more focused lesson plans teachers will get. However, for the initial situation, it still provides lots of significant points for teaching fractions.
3. One specific keyword with grade level might not result in an expected output. Considering a teacher's teaching process (whether teachers just start a topic, in the middle of the topic or finish the topic) decide on additional information.
4. After teachers add an additional criterion and align their definition to a standard (optional), teachers can generate their initial lesson plan by clicking on the "generate" button. In this initial plan, the generator will provide:
    - **A title of the plan:** Exploring Quarters: A Fraction Adventure
    - **Objective:** Objective: Students will be able to identify and represent one-quarter (1/4) of a whole using visual models and manipulatives.
    - **Assessment** such as "Shade 1/4 of various shapes (circles, rectangles, and squares)"
    - **Key Points** such as "Quarters can be represented visually by dividing shapes into four equal parts"
    - **Openings, Introduction to New Material, Guided Practice, Independent Practice, Closing**: These sections in the lesson demonstrate hints for how to initiate the topic, warm up students for the materials, conduct activities with teacher or peers or alone and how to close the lesson.
    - **Extension Activity**: This is a very important part to differentiate classrooms for distinct learning types. Although the outputs are quite limited, still it is a good opportunity to extend the knowledge about differentiation in the classroom beyond the early finishers or late finishers. For example, based on described inputs the output is given as "Create a "Quarter Scavenger Hunt" list of items that commonly come in quarters (e.g., 15-minute intervals on a clock, 25 cents).
    - **Homework: "**Ask students to find and draw three examples of quarters in their home or neighborhood (e.g., a quarter of a pizza, a quarter of an hour on a clock, a quarter coin)"

- **Standards Addressed:** At the end of the page, their keywords are aligned with the standards that teachers required. For example, the inputs are aligned with CCSS.MATH.CONTENT.2.G.A.3.

5. Chatbot Raina, asking specific questions for further enhancement of the draft, is also very helpful, standing at the end of the lesson plan, which needs upgrading though.
6. In the end, teachers can get a copy of the document and paste it on a word processor or google docs; before copying teachers can edit the text or make it read aloud for teachers (sometimes it is not easy to read on the phone or small screens, this would have a great help).
7. Moreover, teachers can translate the document for free but other options in the Actions button such as making the text longer or shorter need upgrading.

All in all, the Lesson Plan tool demonstrated an initial design of a lesson plan and gave ideas about a set of actions which can be conducted in the classroom. The output needs to be reviewed and the actions and ideas need to be connected to ensure the fluent transitions among them while teaching. The generated lesson plan lacks a before-after time chronology and several items are repeated in several sections therefore this format needs to be constructed by the teacher. However, it is still possible to enhance the generated lesson plan with other tools given in Magic School.

Activity Design for the Lesson Plan

Before using other tools, please ensure that please copy the lesson plan to a document so that teachers can use information in this draft tool for their further development of the lesson plan. There are other tools to elaborate on the ideas in the initial lesson planning such as the "Make it relevant" tool. This tool is to link the course's content and learners' interests. The interface is similar to other tools in Magic School AI (see Figure 30). A short text about what teachers are teaching and overall students' descriptive information such as their interests, sensitivity, their learning style and so on.

Figure 30. Make It Relevant tool prompt page

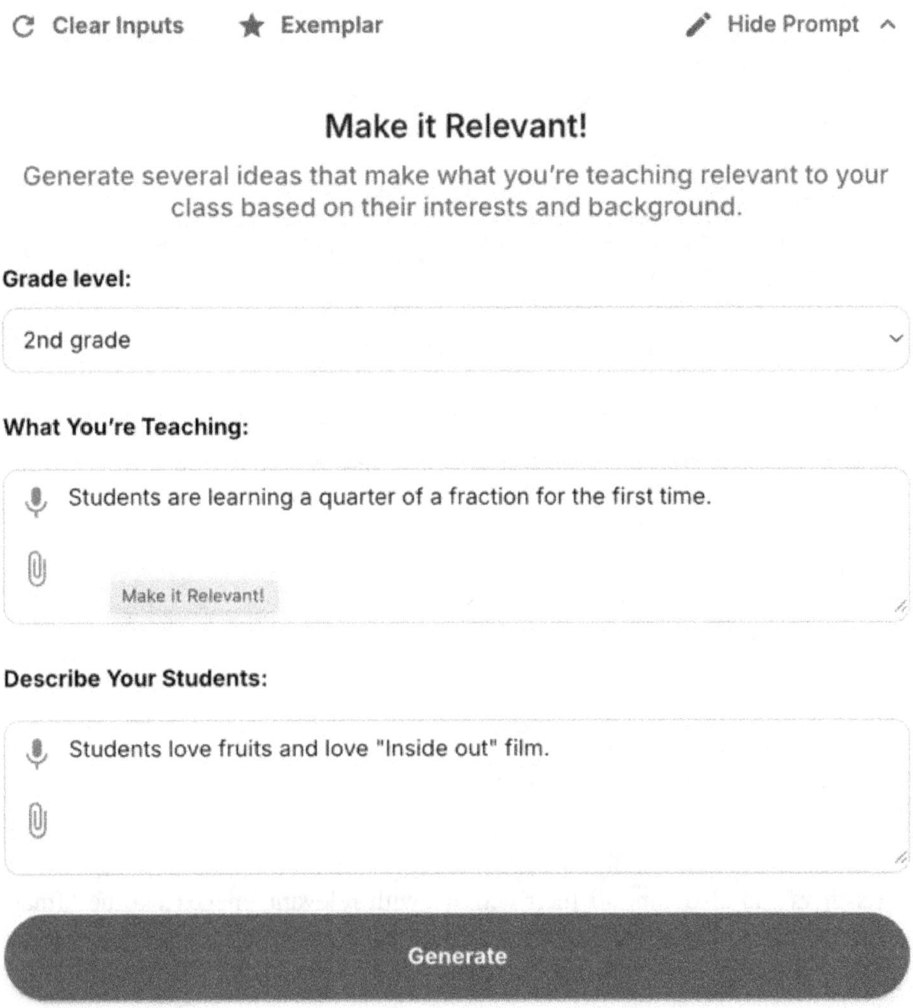

The generator will produce an activity list idea based on their prompts. The prompts used as shown in Figure 30 are fruits and "Inside out" animation film. The generated ideas included significant keywords relevant to those keywords such as movie characters or fruits which are easy to cut and find in many countries.

Figure 31. An example for an output of Make It Relevant tool

Lesson Idea 1: Fruit Fraction Fun

- **Objective:** Introduce the concept of a quarter of a fraction using fruits.
- **Activity:** Provide students with paper plates and cut-out fruit shapes (like apples, bananas, and oranges). Explain that if they have a whole fruit, they can share it with friends.
- **Instructions:**
    1. Show them how to cut each fruit shape into four equal parts.
    2. Ask them to color one of the parts and explain that this colored part represents one-quarter of the fruit.
    3. Discuss how sharing fruits with friends means dividing it into quarters.

Lesson Idea 2: Inside Out Emotions and Fractions

- **Objective:** Connect emotions from the "Inside Out" film to fractions.
- **Activity:** Use the characters from the movie (Joy, Sadness, Anger, Fear, Disgust) to represent different fractions.
- **Instructions:**
    1. Create a chart with each character and their corresponding fraction (for example, Joy = 1/4, Sadness = 1/4, etc.).
    2. Discuss how the characters can show one quarter of the emotions in a situation.
    3. Ask students to draw a scene from the movie and label how much of each emotion they feel in quarters.

Teachers can also support their activity with relevant images via the "Image Generator" tool in Magic School AI. An image can be generated from a text prompt or picture prompt as shown in Figure 32.

Figure 32. A picture developed by Image Generator tool in Magic School AI.

This tool is powered by Adobe Express Firefly Image 3 Generator and different from previous tools such as Lesson Plan. Their trained data are distinct so what teachers have generated in one tool may not be generated in the image form. For example, the tool does not have an idea of mathematically a quarter of a fraction and what it generates are quite irrelevant and creates misconception. Therefore, double-check is always needed for each tool of the AI models but the satisfying results are unique and teachers can create holistic pictures throughout their instruction.

Worksheets can be designed as well for the initial lesson plan development. A seatwork is designed through the tool "Worksheet Generator" in Magic School AI. In the initial lesson plan design, there is an independent practice part (see Figure 33). Teachers can take this part as a prompt to create that worksheet. The output will include fill in the blank, multiple-choice, open-ended questions and their answers. However, in primary grade level multiple choice questions might be restricted to three options or eliminated. Teachers can edit the text as in the lesson plan and get only one or two types of assessment in a worksheet. Teachers can enrich the text with an image generator as well.

Figure 33. A worksheet generator for the lesson plan

Fractions: Understanding One-Fourth (1/4)

Fractions are parts of a whole. When we talk about one-fourth (1/4), we mean one part out of four equal parts. Imagine cutting a pizza into four equal slices. Each slice would be one-fourth of the whole pizza.

Fill in the Blank: Fill in the blank with the correct words.

1. A fraction has two parts: a __ and a __.
2. One-fourth is written as __ in fraction form.
3. If you divide a circle into four equal parts, each part is __ of the circle.
4. When we shade __ out of four equal parts, we are showing one-fourth.
5. In a group of __ students, one student would represent one-fourth of the group.

Open Ended Questions: Answer the following questions in complete sentences:

1. Explain what one-fourth (1/4) means in your own words.

2. Draw a shape and shade one-fourth (1/4) of it. Then describe how you did it.
   [Space for drawing]

3. Give an example of one-fourth (1/4) that you might see in real life.

For this example, teachers can see that most of the concepts are relevant to mathematics education. The language is also suitable for second graders as well but before using them double-check is always needed.

Creating an Assessment for the Content

Creating measurement and evaluation questions can be more challenging than planning a lesson. Writing questions according to the learning objectives and planning based on the types of questions can take hours for a teacher. Not only summative but also formative assessment methods are quite time-consuming. is one of the software tools developed to address this need, proving to be a highly useful tool for generating questions.

Since assessment types were created through Worksheet Generator, there are also complementary evaluation tools needed to assess students' learning as well. The Rubric Generator tool might be helpful to evaluate open-ended questions, to qualitatively give feedback for students and to note the teacher's observations throughout the lessons. Using initial lesson plan design as prompts, satisfactory results might be collected from the output. In Figure 34, it is visible that the standards and assignment description are pasted here. In addition, the significant point about the rubric is shared.

Figure 34. An example of developing rubric via Rubric Generator

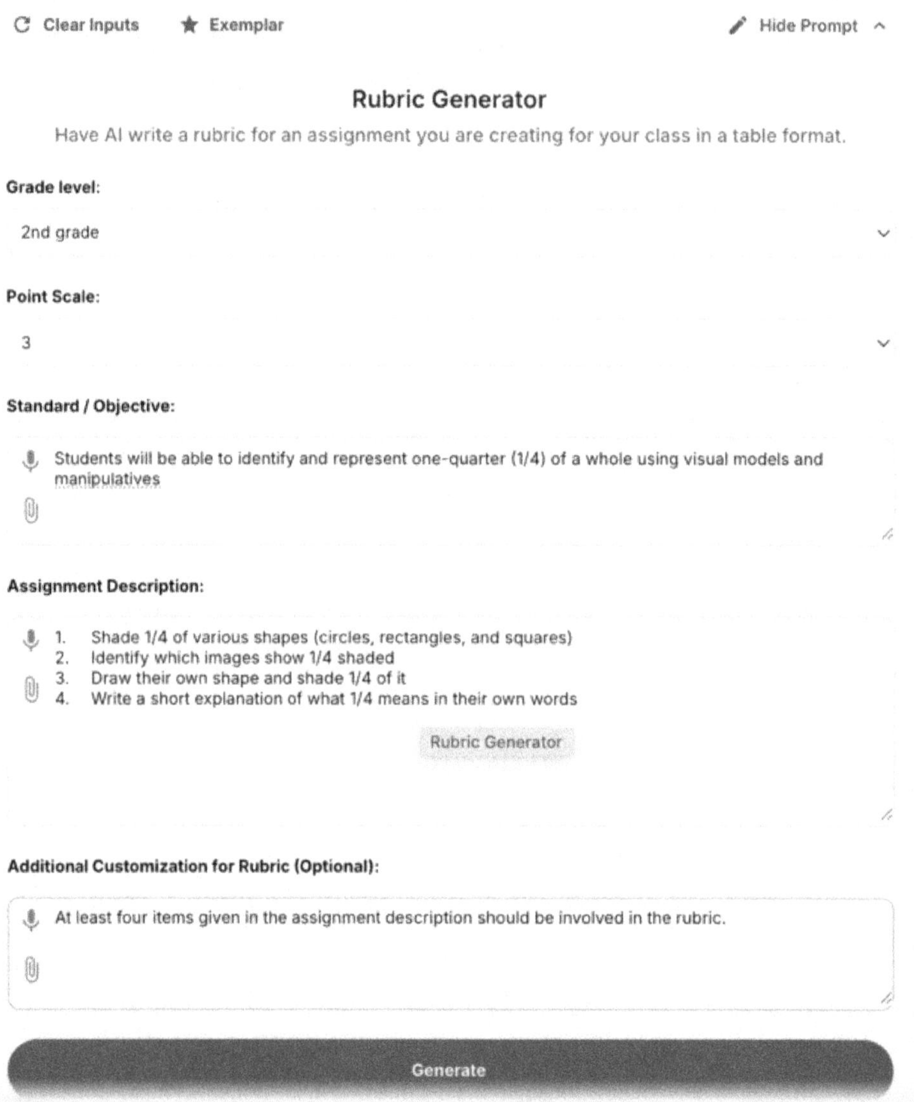

The rubric output was generated below the screen, and it used the four ideas of the objective I have provided. A 3-point Likert scale has been used because the ideas are "tiny" steps which are not easy to scale into more than three. The name for each scale was selected as sensitive and constructive for the learners. Students who are successful from this course need to get at least two points from each criterion.

Figure 35. Rubric generator tool for assessment

Rubric for Identifying and Representing One-Quarter (1/4) of a Whole

Criteria	3 Points (Exemplary)	2 Points (Proficient)	1 Point (Needs Improvement)
Shading 1/4 of Shapes	Correctly shades 1/4 of all shapes accurately.	Shades 1/4 of most shapes, minor errors.	Fails to shade 1/4 of shapes correctly.
Identifying 1/4 Shaded Images	Accurately identifies all images showing 1/4 shaded.	Identifies most images correctly, few errors.	Struggles to identify images showing 1/4 shaded.
Drawing and Shading Own Shape	Draws a unique shape and accurately shades 1/4.	Draws a shape and shades most of 1/4 accurately.	Drawing lacks clarity, or fails to shade 1/4.
Explanation of 1/4	Provides a clear, thoughtful explanation of what 1/4 means.	Explanation is mostly clear, with minor gaps.	Explanation lacks clarity or is incomplete.

Copy Edit Export Read Aloud More

Each cell in the table should be revisited and its applicability in the classroom should pass the thought experiment. For example, "drawing and shading own shape" needs to be more clarified such as "drawing a whole", "partitioning a whole into equal parts", "shading one fourth of the shape". Students might divide each part and consider this part as one whole or might shade three fourths of a whole. As the content expert, the teachers should involve significant skills and tasks into whole lesson plan design.

Essential Reminders About Magic School AI

- Keep in mind that since AI studies continue, the tools provided by Magic School AI have been improving, changing and renovated. Therefore, some tools described here might be developed or changed.
- As all AI models might create bias or false information, users are supposed to check the AI-generated results.
- Leave least of the work to be done by AI such as initial work. Do the final touch, review the product, assure the accuracy and contextualize appropriately.
- Since AI tools are trained with the previous documents, they may not be aware of the recent developments, changes and so on.
- Protecting privacy is the recommended rule while using AI. Please avoid giving personal information such as name and surname while filling information in the parts of the tools.

CONCLUSION AND SUGGESTIONS

These four AI models may provide an initial fundamental toolkit for elementary teachers to explore their AI related knowledge and skills for instructional design process in terms of analyze, design, develop, implementation and evaluation (ADDIE). Each AI model is strongly recommended for teachers and in the teacher, training programs in terms of their features. After using them, the teachers may transfer this knowledge and skill into another similar AI embedded web-based tool. Moreover, each application title includes a guided activity example from prominent books, the role of student interaction or digital storytelling in instruction, and the types of applications and impacts AI has had on elementary students and teachers. This will be accompanied by excerpts from scientific studies, prompt suggestions, and side-by-side tables containing screenshots. It is also recommended that users of the guided examples may enrich their experience with the software according to their potential and needs due to the adaptive interface of the web-based AI embedded platforms. Each web-based AI embedded platform has its own specific as well as common features such as classroom management application can create an assessment form as well.

FUTURE RESEARCH DIRECTIONS

This basic toolkit is developed considering the recent artificial intelligence tools for education and they still need to be developed considering the recent reports about educational sciences. Moreover, this kind of guidelines and materials about using AI tools for educational stakeholders are required to be prepared and shared. In addition, future research should focus on integrating educational science frameworks into AI tools to create more effective and contextually relevant educational resources. Specifically, the incorporation of widely recognized instructional design models, such as ADDIE and 5E, can ensure that AI-driven educational platforms align with established pedagogical practices. Additionally, emphasizing student-centered approaches and cognitive theories in the design of these tools can help cater to diverse learning needs and promote active engagement. Researchers could explore how these frameworks can be systematically embedded into AI platforms, ensuring that they address both content delivery and the development of critical skills, such as problem-solving and collaboration.

Another promising direction is to foster interdisciplinary collaboration between computer scientists and educational researchers. This partnership can bridge the gap between technological capabilities and pedagogical needs, enabling the production of AI tools that are not only innovative but also grounded in evidence-based educational practices. Research should also investigate the adaptability of AI platforms to evolving educational standards and their potential to support personalized learning pathways. Evaluating the effectiveness of these platforms in real-world classroom settings will be essential for refining their design and ensuring they contribute meaningfully to educational outcomes.

REFERENCES

AI4K12 (2024) The artificial intelligence (AI) for K-12 initiative. https://ai4k12.org/

Akyuz, D., Dixon, J. K., & Stephan, M. (2013). Improving the quality of mathematics teaching with effective planning practices. *Teacher Development*, 17(1), 92–106. DOI: 10.1080/13664530.2012.753939

Aleven, V., Blankestijn, J., Lawrence, L., Nagashima, T., & Taatgen, N. (2022, September). A dashboard to support teachers during students' self-paced AI-supported problem-solving practice. In *European Conference on Technology Enhanced Learning* (pp. 16-30). Cham: Springer International Publishing. DOI: 10.1007/978-3-031-16290-9_2

Alwaqdani, M. (2024). (2024). Investigating teachers' perceptions of artificial intelligence tools in education: Potential and difficulties. *Education and Information Technologies*. Advance online publication. DOI: 10.1007/s10639-024-12903-9

Antonenko, P., & Abramowitz, B. (2022). In-service teachers' (mis)conceptions of artificial intelligence in K-12 science education. *Journal of Research on Technology in Education*, 55(1), 64–78. DOI: 10.1080/15391523.2022.2119450

Celik, I., Dindar, M., Muukkonen, H., & Järvelä, S. (2022). The promises and challenges of artificial intelligence for teachers: A systematic review of research. *TechTrends*, 66(4), 616–630. DOI: 10.1007/s11528-022-00715-y

Chen, L., Chen, P., & Lin, Z. (2020). Artificial intelligence in education: A review. *IEEE Access : Practical Innovations, Open Solutions*, 8, 75264–75278. DOI: 10.1109/ACCESS.2020.2988510

Chen, Y., Jensen, S., Albert, L. J., Gupta, S., & Lee, T. (2023). Artificial Intelligence (AI) Student Assistants in the Classroom: Designing Chatbots to Support Student Success. *Information Systems Frontiers*, 25(1), 161–182. DOI: 10.1007/s10796-022-10291-4

Chiu, T. K., Meng, H., Chai, C. S., King, I., Wong, S., & Yam, Y. (2021). Creation and evaluation of a pretertiary artificial intelligence (AI) curriculum. *IEEE Transactions on Education*, 65(1), 30–39. DOI: 10.1109/TE.2021.3085878

Conca, L. M., Schechter, C. P., & Castle, S. (2004). Challenges teachers face as they work to connect assessment and instruction. *Teachers and Teaching*, 10(1), 59–75. DOI: 10.1080/1354060032000170927

Derevyanko, N., & Zalevska, O. (2023). Comparative analysis of neural networks Midjourney, Stable Diffusion, and DALL-E and ways of their implementation in the educational process of students of design specialities. *Scientific Bulletin of Mukachevo State University. Series. Pedagogy and Psychology*, 9(3), 36–44. DOI: 10.52534/msupp3.2023.36

Fok, W. W. T., He, Y. S., Yeung, H. H. A., Law, K. Y., Cheung, K., Ai, Y. Y., & Ho, P. (2018). Prediction model for students' future development by Deep Learning and tensorflow artificial intelligence engine. 2018 *4th International Conference on Information Management (ICIM)*. DOI: 10.1109/INFOMAN.2018.8392818

Ghashout, S., Gdura, Y., & Drawil, N. (2023). "Early Prediction of Students' Academic Performance Using Artificial Neural Network: A Case Study In Computer Engineering Department," 2023 *IEEE 3rd International Maghreb Meeting of the Conference on Sciences and Techniques of Automatic Control and Computer Engineering (MI-STA),* Benghazi, Libya, pp. 40-45, DOI: 10.1109/MI-STA57575.2023.10169421

Gobert, J. D., Dickler, R., & Adair, A. (2024). Using an AI-Based Dashboard to Help Teachers Support Students' Learning Progressions for Science Practices. In *Handbook of Research on Science Learning Progressions* (pp. 488–498). Routledge. DOI: 10.4324/9781003170785-32

Hsu, T.-C., Abelson, H., Patton, E., Chen, S.-C., & Chang, H.-N. (2022). Self-efficacy and behavior patterns of learners using a real-time collaboration system developed for group programming. *International Journal of Computer-Supported Collaborative Learning*, 16(4), 559–582. DOI: 10.1007/s11412-021-09357-3 PMID: 35002570

Hwang, S. (2022). Examining the effects of artificial intelligence on elementary students' mathematics achievement: A meta-analysis. *Sustainability (Basel)*, 14(20), 13185. DOI: 10.3390/su142013185

Kajamaa, A., Kumpulainen, K., & Olkinuora, H. R. (2020). Teacher interventions in students' collaborative work in a technology-rich educational makerspace. *British Journal of Educational Technology*, 51(2), 371–386. DOI: 10.1111/bjet.12837

Kim, J. (2024). Leading teachers' perspective on teacher-AI collaboration in education. *Education and Information Technologies*, 29(7), 8693–8724. DOI: 10.1007/s10639-023-12109-5

Kim, S., Jang, Y., Choi, S., Kim, W., Jung, H., Kim, S., & Kim, H. (2021). Analyzing teacher competency with TPACK for K-12 AI education. *Kunstliche Intelligenz*, 35(2), 139–151. DOI: 10.1007/s13218-021-00731-9

Lee, I., Zhang, H., Moore, K., Zhou, X., Perret, B., Cheng, Y., & Pu, G. (2022, February). AI book club: An innovative professional development model for AI education. In *Proceedings of the 53rd ACM Technical Symposium on Computer Science Education-Volume 1* (pp. 202-208). DOI: 10.1145/3478431.3499318

Lim, C. P., & Chai, C. S. (2008). Rethinking classroom-oriented instructional development models to mediate instructional planning in technology-enhanced learning environments. *Teaching and Teacher Education*, 24(8), 2002–2013. DOI: 10.1016/j.tate.2008.05.004

Luckin, R., & Cukurova, M. (2019). Designing educational technologies in the age of AI: A learning sciences-driven approach. *British Journal of Educational Technology*, 50(6), 2824–2838. DOI: 10.1111/bjet.12861

Merrill, D. M. (2007). The proper study of instructional design. In Reiser, R. A., & Dempsey, J. V. (Eds.), *Trends and Issues in Instructional Design and Technology* (2nd ed., pp. 336–341). Pearson Prentice Hall.

Nesbit, J. C., Adesope, O. O., Liu, Q., & Ma, W. (2014). How effective are intelligent tutoring systems in computer science education? In *2014 IEEE 14th international conference on advanced learning technologies* (pp. 99-103). IEEE. DOI: 10.1109/ICALT.2014.38

Ng, D. T., Luo, W., Chan, H. M., & Chu, S. K. (2022). Using digital story writing as a pedagogy to develop AI literacy among primary students. *Computers and Education: Artificial Intelligence*, 3, 100054. DOI: 10.1016/j.caeai.2022.100054

Niu, S. J., Luo, J., Niemi, H., Li, X., & Lu, Y. (2022). Teachers' and students' views of using an AI-aided educational platform for supporting teaching and learning at Chinese schools. *Education Sciences*, 12(12), 858. DOI: 10.3390/educsci12120858

OECD. (2017). *Starting strong V: Transitions from early childhood education and care to primary education*. OECD Publishing., DOI: 10.1787/9789264276253-

Ottenbreit-Leftwich, A., Glazewski, K., Jeon, M., Jantaraweragul, K., Hmelo-Silver, C. E., Scribner, A., Lee, S., Mott, B., & Lester, J. (2023). Lessons learned for AI education with elementary students and teachers. *International Journal of Artificial Intelligence in Education*, 33(2), 267–289. DOI: 10.1007/s40593-022-00304-3

Ouyang, F., & Jiao, P. (2021). Artificial intelligence in education: The three paradigms. *Computers and Education: Artificial Intelligence*, 2, 100020. Advance online publication. DOI: 10.1016/j.caeai.2021.100020

Owoc, M. L., Sawicka, A., & Weichbroth, P. (2021). Artificial Intelligence Technologies in Education: Benefits, Challenges and Strategies of Implementation. In Owoc, M. L., & Pondel, M. (Eds.), *Artificial Intelligence for Knowledge Management. AI4KM 2019. IFIP Advances in Information and Communication Technology* (Vol. 599). Springer., DOI: 10.1007/978-3-030-85001-2_4

Ruiz-Rojas, L. I., Acosta-Vargas, P., De-Moreta-Llovet, J., & Gonzalez-Rodriguez, M. (2023). Empowering education with generative artificial intelligence tools: Approach with an instructional design matrix. *Sustainability (Basel)*, 15(15), 11524. DOI: 10.3390/su151511524

Safsouf, Y. 2021. Contributed to the development of decision models for improving learner success in an online learning environment, TEL - Thèses en ligne. France.

Salas-Pilco, S. Z., Xiao, K., & Hu, X. (2022). Artificial intelligence and learning analytics in teacher education: A systematic review. *Education Sciences*, 12(8), 569. DOI: 10.3390/educsci12080569

Sims, R. (2006). Beyond instructional design: Making learning design a reality. *Journal of Learning Design*, 1(2), 1–9.

Smith, H. J., Zheng, Q., Li, Y., Jain, S., & Hodgins, J. K. (2023). A Method for Animating Children's Drawings of the Human Figure. *ACM Transactions on Graphics*, 42(3), 1–15. Advance online publication. DOI: 10.1145/3592788

Sweller, J. (2021). Instructional Design. In Shackelford, T. K., & Weekes-Shackelford, V. A. (Eds.), *Encyclopedia of Evolutionary Psychological Science*. Springer., DOI: 10.1007/978-3-319-19650-3_2438

Timms, M. J. (2016). Letting artificial intelligence in education out of the box: Educational cobots and smart classrooms. *International Journal of Artificial Intelligence in Education*, 26(2), 701–712. DOI: 10.1007/s40593-016-0095-y

Touretzky, D., Gardner-McCune, C., Martin, F., & Seehorn, D. (2019, July). Envisioning AI for K-12: What should every child know about AI? In *Proceedings of the AAAI conference on artificial intelligence* (Vol. 33, No. 01, pp. 9795-9799). https://ojs.aaai.org/index.php/AAAI/article/view/5053

U.S. Department of Education. Office of Educational Technology [OET]. (2023). Artificial Intelligence and Future of Teaching and Learning: Insights and Recommendations, Washington, DC. https://tech.ed.gov

U.S. Department of Education. Office of Educational Technology [OET]. (2024). Designing for education with artificial intelligence: An essential guide for developers. Washington, D.C. https://tech.ed.gov

Vartiainen, H., Tedre, M., & Valtonen, T. (2020). Learning machine learning with very young children: Who is teaching whom? *International Journal of Child-Computer Interaction*, 25, 1–11. DOI: 10.1016/j.ijcci.2020.100182

Weng, X., & Chiu, T. K. (2023). Instructional design and learning outcomes of intelligent computer assisted language learning: Systematic review in the field. *Computers and Education: Artificial Intelligence*, 4, 100117. DOI: 10.1016/j.caeai.2022.100117

Zhang, K., & Aslan, A. B. (2021). AI technologies for education: Recent research & future directions. *Computers and Education: Artificial Intelligence*, 2, 100025. Advance online publication. DOI: 10.1016/j.caeai.2021.100025

ADDITIONAL READINGS

Choi, G. W., Kim, S. H., Lee, D., & Moon, J. (2024). Utilizing Generative AI for Instructional Design: Exploring Strengths, Weaknesses, Opportunities, and Threats. *TechTrends*, 68(4), 832–844. DOI: 10.1007/s11528-024-00967-w

Park, O., & Seidel, R. J. (1987). Instructional design principles and Al techniques for development of ICAI. *Computers in Human Behavior*, 3(3–4), 273–287. DOI: 10.1016/0747-5632(87)90029-X

KEY TERMS AND DEFINITIONS

ADDIE Model: An instructional design framework consisting of five phases: Analysis, Design, Development, Implementation, and Evaluation.

AI Literacy: It refers to the knowledge and skills required to understand, use and critically evaluate artificial intelligence technologies and their applications in daily life and education.

Chatbots: It refers to AI-powered tools that interact with students in natural language, providing instant feedback and assistance in understanding concepts or completing tasks.

Digital Storytelling: It refers to the use of digital tools to create narrative content that can help improve AI literacy, increase creativity, and engage students in the classroom.

Smart Classrooms: It refers to learning environments enhanced with artificial intelligence and other advanced technologies to support effective education and increase student engagement.

Teacher-AI Collaboration: A common type of relationship in which teachers and AI systems work together to design, implement, and improve instructional strategies and learning environments.

Chapter 2
Pedagogy of AI Strategies for Effective Teaching and Learng in the Age of Artificial Intelligence:
Mohammed First University as a Case Study

Ilham Boutob
Université Moulay Ismail, Morocco

Sabrine Jmad
https://orcid.org/0009-0008-1400-1457
Mohammed I University, Morocco

Siham Benmessaoud
https://orcid.org/0009-0007-4446-4017
Mohammed I University, Morocco

Mehdi Kaddouri
https://orcid.org/0000-0001-7696-0276
Mohammed I University, Morocco

ABSTRACT

In a rapidly changing world marked by significant technological advancements, particularly in education, artificial intelligence (AI) emerges as a central development. This study aims to investigate the role of AI in enhancing pedagogical practices within higher education at the Faculty of Letters and Human Sciences at

DOI: 10.4018/979-8-3693-6527-4.ch002

Mohammed First University in Oujda. Employing a mixed methodology, the research examines effective teaching and learning strategies in an AI-driven environment, focusing on professor-student interactions. The findings reveal that AI can significantly improve educational outcomes by personalizing learning experiences and optimizing instructional methods. Educators are encouraged to adapt to the evolving environment of AI to prepare students for future careers in this dynamic field. Ultimately, the study underscores the necessity of integrating AI into educational frameworks to enhance teaching effectiveness and student engagement, thereby shaping the future of education.

INTRODUCTION

In recent years, the landscape of numerous fields has undergone transformations driven predominantly by technological advancements. These changes are not only reshaping our interactions with the world but also influencing processes, systems, and structures across various sectors. Education stands out as one of the most notable areas witnessing rapid evolution. The integration of technology in this field has revolutionized traditional teaching methodologies and learning experiences. At the forefront of these advancements is artificial intelligence (AI), which is emerging as a significant development with the potential to redefine educational practices and improve outcomes for learners.

AI is influencing education in numerous ways, providing innovative tools and resources that enhance teaching and learning. According to a report by UNESCO (2019), "AI has the potential to address some of the biggest challenges in education today, innovative teaching and learning practices, and ultimately accelerate the progress towards SDG 4" (UNESCO, 2019, p. 7). This assertion not only emphasizes the urgent need for innovative approaches to education but also illustrates how AI can act as a catalyst for meaningful change. The challenges faced today in education are multifaceted and complex, encompassing issues such as unequal access to quality learning resources, the growing diversity of student needs, and the necessity for personalized learning experiences. AI technologies, with their ability to analyze large datasets and tailor educational content to individual learners, hold the promise of bridging these gaps.

As AI continues to evolve, it is imperative for educational institutions to adapt proactively. The future workforce will demand a different set of skills, significantly influenced by advancements in technology. In order to prepare students for AI-driven careers, institutions must reevaluate and redesign their curricula to incorporate AI literacy. This entails infusing AI concepts into various subjects and teaching students not only how to use AI tools but also how to understand the underlying principles and ethical considerations associated with these technologies.

The main objective of this study is to thoroughly investigate and understand the significance of artificial intelligence (AI) in enhancing pedagogical practices. This exploration will specifically focus on its applications and implications within the context of higher education, particularly within the Faculty of Letters and Human Sciences at Mohammed First University in Oujda.

LITERATURE REVIEW

AI Background

The introduction of new technologies often brings about a mixture of excitement and uncertainty, a phenomenon that can be described as novelty is often met with apprehension. This sentiment is particularly relevant in the context of artificial intelligence (AI) in education, where fear and confusion frequently accompany its advancement. In his book *AI and the Future of Education: Teaching in the Age of Artificial Intelligence*, author Priten Shah explores the trajectory of AI within educational settings, tracing its evolution from the past through the present and projecting its potential future impact. Shah provides a comprehensive guide on how educators can effectively harness AI to enhance both teaching and learning experiences. He states:

> *While AI has intruded upon our classrooms, the opportunities it will create for our schools far outweigh the risks such technologies pose. The transition and adaptation will not be seamless, and we've already started to see, but with the proper knowledge and skills, educators can approach this new age ready to focus on what they do best: teach our students. Nonetheless, as with any rapid development, we must carefully consider how, when, and why we shift our practice and pedagogy in response to AI. (Shah, 2023, p. 3)*

The introduction of AI in classrooms indeed provides more opportunities but also presents challenges, necessitating careful planning and adaptation of its integration, as well as the development of skills and knowledge on the part of educators. Hence, it is recommended to approach this integration deliberately while considering the implications for teaching practices and pedagogical approaches. (Fitzpatrick et al., 2023).

International AI Practices in Education

One of the most considerable impacts of AI in education is its remarkable ability to personalize learning experiences for each student. By utilizing advanced adaptive learning platforms, AI algorithms can thoroughly analyze individual student performance data and subsequently tailor educational content to meet their specific needs and learning styles. Asian countries have made significant strides in incorporating AI into their educational systems. For instance, China, with its ambitious goal of becoming a world leader in AI, has invested heavily in AI-powered educational technologies. A prime example of this innovative approach can be seen in the Chinese company Squirrel AI Learning, which has developed a sophisticated AI-powered tutoring system. This system dynamically adjusts the difficulty levels of various tasks and learning paths based on the responses and progress of each student, ensuring that their unique learning journey is both effective and engaging (Chen et al., 2020).

In a similar vein, numerous educational technology companies in the United States have developed AI-powered tools that are being implemented in schools and universities. Carnegie Learning has introduced its MATHai platform, which leverages the power of AI to provide personalized math instruction to students. This platform actively analyzes how students interact with math problems and adjusts its teaching methods accordingly. As a result, it has been shown to improve student outcomes, enabling learners to grasp mathematical concepts more effectively and at their own pace (Pane et al., 2014). Ultimately, these advancements in AI are transforming the educational landscape by providing tailored learning experiences that cater to the diverse needs of students, thereby enhancing their overall academic success.

Another area where AI is making a significant impact is in Intelligent Tutoring Systems (ITS). These AI-powered systems are designed to mimic the personalized guidance that a human tutor would typically provide. A notable example is "Musio," an AI tutor in Japan that focuses on helping students improve their English language skills. Musio is not just a static program; it intelligently adjusts its teaching methods based on the unique needs and learning styles of each student, making the learning process more effective (Busso & Sanchez, 2024).

In Europe, the iTalk2Learn project exemplifies the innovative use of Intelligent Tutoring Systems (ITS) in the field of mathematics. This project has developed a sophisticated tutoring system that integrates advanced speech recognition technology along with AI capabilities. This combination allows the system to deliver personalized feedback and support to students, ensuring they receive the assistance they need to master mathematical concepts and problem-solving skills (Göçen & Aydemir, 2020).

AI is also transforming assessment methods in education, enabling more frequent and comprehensive feedback for both students and educators. A notable example is found in Australia, where the University of Sydney has adopted an innovative AI-powered system known as AcaWriter. This system is designed to provide automated, real-time feedback on academic writing, helping students enhance their writing skills and improve their overall academic performance (Ling Jen & Abdul Rahim Hj Salam, 2024).

Similarly, in India, the education technology firm BYJU'S is leveraging the power of AI to transform how students' performance is evaluated. By analyzing various metrics related to students' engagement and learning outcomes, BYJU'S utilizes AI to create personalized study plans and assessments tailored to the individual needs of each student. This approach enhances the learning experience and provides students with feedback that is specifically relevant to their strengths and areas for improvement (Rajan, 2022).

Artificial intelligence (AI) has emerged as a transformative force within the realm of language learning applications; a prime example of this is Duolingo, a widely recognized language learning platform that is utilized by millions of users around the globe. This application effectively employs AI algorithms to tailor lesson difficulty and content according to the individual performance levels of its users, thereby ensuring that it remains engaging and relevant to each learner's needs (Von Ahn, 2013).

In South Korea, the government has taken significant steps to integrate AI technology into the education system, particularly in language acquisition. It has introduced AI-powered English teaching assistants in public schools to support and supplement traditional language education. These AI assistants are designed to provide personalized feedback and assistance to students, fostering an environment that encourages language learning and improves overall proficiency in English (Lee & Davis, 2024).

In addition to its applications within the classroom, artificial intelligence (AI) is considerably enhancing the efficiency of administrative tasks across various educational institutions. For instance, in Singapore, the Ministry of Education has taken the initiative to implement advanced AI systems designed to analyze students' data. This proactive approach enables educators to identify students who may be at risk of falling behind, facilitating timely and effective early interventions to support their academic success (Lee, Koh, & Looi, 2023).

THEORETICAL FRAMEWORKS

The connection between educational theory and AI-powered tools is essential for understanding how these technologies can be effectively utilized to support student learning and improve teaching practices within the Moroccan educational landscape. Theoretical frameworks, such as constructivism and connectivism, emphasize active learning and knowledge construction through social interaction, which resonates with Morocco's diverse cultural and educational context. AI tools can facilitate these approaches by enabling personalized learning experiences that adapt to the individual students' needs, fostering deeper engagement and understanding.

Constructivism, influenced by psychologists Jean Piaget and Lev Vygotsky, posits that learners actively engage in constructing knowledge through meaningful interactions with their environment. In Morocco, where classrooms often incorporate group work and community-based learning, this theory aligns well with local practices. AI technologies can enhance these experiences by providing personalized and interactive learning opportunities, adapting to the unique needs of each learner (Ertmer & Newby, 2008). For example, adaptive learning platform using AI can analyze student data and adjust content and pacing, allowing Moroccan students to engage with material at their own pace, fostering a deeper connection to their studies.

The advancements in artificial intelligence (AI) technologies have shown a remarkable alignment with the core principles of constructivism. AI has the potential to enhance educational experiences by offering personalized and interactive learning opportunities tailored to the unique needs of each learner. The examples mentioned earlier illustrate how adaptive learning platforms leverage AI algorithms to analyze individual student data, enabling them to adjust the content delivered and the pace of learning according to each student's specific requirements. This customization allows learners to engage with the material at their own pace, fostering a deeper connection to the subject matter and ensuring that the learning experience is both relevant and meaningful to them.

Similarly, connectivism, introduced by George Siemens, presents a modern understanding of learning that is particularly relevant in today's digital age. Siemens (2005) posits that knowledge is not merely an accumulation of information but rather a network of connections formed through interactions among individuals, communities, and digital platforms. This perspective recognizes that learning occurs within a complex web of relationships and that each connection can enhance our understanding and acquisition of new information.

In this context, connectivism underscores the transformative role of technology in education. With the advent of artificial intelligence (AI)-powered educational tools, learners are no longer confined to traditional methods of information dissemination. Instead, they are empowered to engage in a more dynamic and interconnected learning experience In Morocco, where access to digital platforms is growing, the idea that knowledge is formed through networks of relationships is increasingly significant. AI-powered educational tools can enhance this by providing intelligent content curation, enabling Moroccan learners to access relevant resources aligned with their interests and educational needs. This personalized approach not only streamlines the learning process but also encourages deeper engagement with the material.

An essential aspect of connectivism is its emphasis on collaboration and community-building. AI-powered educational tools can connect Moroccan students with peers and experts from around the world, fostering a sense of belonging and shared purpose in the learning process. Through online forums, discussion groups, and collaborative projects, learners can exchange ideas, challenge assumptions, and gain insights from diverse perspectives. This global connectivity not only enriches the learning experience but also prepares students to thrive in a multicultural and interconnected society. Moreover, connectivism, supported by AI tools, enables learners to stay current, as they can quickly access the latest research, trends, and innovations in their fields of interest. This fosters a mindset of lifelong learning, where individuals are equipped to navigate the complexities of the digital age.

Social Learning Theory and Multiple Intelligences

Albert Bandura's social learning theory can also be connected to AI-powered tools. This theory highlights the crucial role that observation, imitation, and modeling play in the learning process (Bandura, 1977). It posits that individuals can learn not only through direct experiences but also by watching others and mimicking their actions. In this context, it can be said that artificial intelligence (AI) has emerged as a powerful ally in enhancing social learning experiences. In the Moroccan context, AI can serve as a powerful ally in enhancing social learning. Educators can create dynamic virtual environments where students have the opportunity to observe, interact with, and engage in meaningful dialogue with AI or their peers. Additionally, learners can receive immediate and constructive feedback on their performance, enabling them to adjust their strategies and improve their understanding in real-time. Such tools not only support cooperative endeavors but also align with the social aspects emphasized in Bandura's social learning theory.

The last example of the intersection between educational theories and AI-powered tools concerns Howard Gardner's influential theory of multiple intelligences. Gardner considers that individuals possess a range of distinct types of intelligence, including, but not limited to, linguistic, logical-mathematical, and spatial intelligences (Gardner, 1983). In Morocco, where students come from various backgrounds end educational experiences, AI-enhanced educational tools have the potential to effectively address these diverse intelligences by providing multimodal content delivery options. For instance, students can engage with learning materials through interactive videos, auditory resources, hands-on activities, or written assignments, each catering to different intelligences. Additionally, these tools allow students the flexibility to demonstrate their comprehension in various formats, whether through essays, presentations, creative projects, or digital portfolios. This level of personalization aligns with Gardner's emphasis on recognizing and nurturing the varied learning strengths that individuals possess.

The integration of AI in education offers exciting possibilities for enhancing teaching and learning experiences. By aligning AI technologies with established pedagogical theories, educators can leverage these tools to create more personalized, engaging, and effective learning environments. As AI continues to evolve, it will be crucial for educators and researchers to critically examine its implementation, ensuring that it supports rather than replaces human-centered educational practices.

RESEARCH METHODOLOGY

In the context of the Faculty of Letters and Human Sciences at Mohammed First University in Oujda, understanding the impact of artificial intelligence (AI) on pedagogical practices is essential for enhancing effectiveness. The Faculty of Letters and Human Sciences, established in 1978, serves a diverse student body of approximately 8200 students, offering various programs in humanities, social sciences, and other disciplines. The student demographic is varied, with students coming from different regions of Morocco, reflecting a mix of urban and rural backgrounds.

Current State of AI Integration

The integration of AI within the Faculty of Letters and Human Sciences is in its early stages, with ongoing efforts to incorporate AI tools into the curriculum. Faculty members are exploring various applications of AI to enhance teaching methodologies and student engagement, though the extent of integration varies among departments.

Existing Technological Infrastructure

The university possesses a foundational technological infrastructure that supports the use of AI in education. This includes computer labs, internet access, and learning management systems that are essential for implementing AI enhanced learning experiences. However, there may be limitations in terms of advanced AI technologies and resources available for faculty and students.

Faculty Readiness and Training Programs

Faculty members are at varying levels of readiness when it comes to utilizing AI in their teaching practices. Training programs are being developed to equip educators with the necessary skills and knowledge to effectively integrate AI into their pedagogical strategies. These programs aim to address gaps in understanding and promote best practices in utilizing AI tools.

Students Population Characteristics

The student population at Mohammed First University is diverse, comprising individuals from various socio-economic backgrounds and geographical regions. This diversity presents both opportunities and challenges in the adoption of AI technologies, as students may have different levels of access to technology and familiarity with AI tools.

RESEARCH DESIGN

A mixed-methods research design was employed, combining both qualitative and quantitative approaches. This design allows for a comprehensive understanding of the experiences and perceptions of students and professors regarding the integration of AI in education.

Sampling Strategy

- **Criteria for Selecting 96 Students:** Students were selected based on their enrollment in AI-related courses and their willingness to participate in the survey. This ensured a relevant sample that could provide valuable insights into AI's educational impact.
- **Selection Process for Professor Interviews**: Professors were chosen based on their teaching experience with AI tools and their willingness to share insights. This targeted selection aimed to include a variety of perspectives on AI integration in teaching practices.
- **Justification for Sample Size:** The sample size of 96 students was determined to ensure a representative cross-section while allowing for meaningful statistical analysis. This size balances the need for reliability with practical constraints in data collection.
- **Description of Participant Demographics:** The participants included students from various academic levels and backgrounds, ensuring diversity in

perspectives. Professors interviewed varied in age, experience, and familiarity with AI tools.

Research Phases

The research was conducted in two phases:

1. **Quantitative Phase:** A structured survey was disseminated to 96 students, representing a cross-section of the faculty's population. This survey included close-ended questions designed to gather data on students' experiences with AI tools in educational practices, perceived benefits, or challenges faced in using these technologies. This quantitative data provided a statistical foundation for understanding trends and patterns in the use of AI. Two open-ended questions were included to solicit suggestions for improving AI-enhanced educational tools or experiences.
2. **Qualitative Phase:** In-depth interviews were conducted with selected professors, chosen based on their experience with AI and their teaching practices. Information gathered included their employment status, years of teaching experience, and their specific use of AI tools in the classroom. The interviews aimed to uncover insights about their attitudes towards AI, the effectiveness of pedagogical strategies, and the nature of professor-student interactions in the context of an AI-enhanced learning environment.

Data Analysis Procedures:

- **Quantitative Data Analysis Methods:** Statistical analysis was performed on the survey data to identify trends and patterns in students' experiences with AI tools. Descriptive statistics were utilized to interpret the data collected.
- **Qualitative Data Coding Approach:** Thematic analysis was employed to code and analyze the interview data. This involved identifying recurring themes and patterns in the professors' responses to gain insights into their experiences and perspectives.
- **Integration Method for Mixed-Method Analysis:** The findings from both the quantitative and qualitative phases were integrated to provide a comprehensive understanding of the impact of AI in the educational context. This triangulation of data allowed for a richer interpretation of the results.

Significance of the Study

Through this mixed-methods approach, the study aims to provide a well-rounded perspective on the significance of AI in education, facilitating a deeper exploration of effective teaching and learning strategies within the Faculty of Letters and Human Sciences of Oujda.

RESULTS AND DISCUSSION

Students' Perception

The mixed-methods approach employed in this study provided a well-rounded perspective on the significance of AI in education, facilitating a deeper exploration of effective teaching and learning strategies within the Faculty of Letters and Human Sciences at Mohammed First University in Oujda.

Figure 1. Students' familiarity with the concept of artificial intelligence

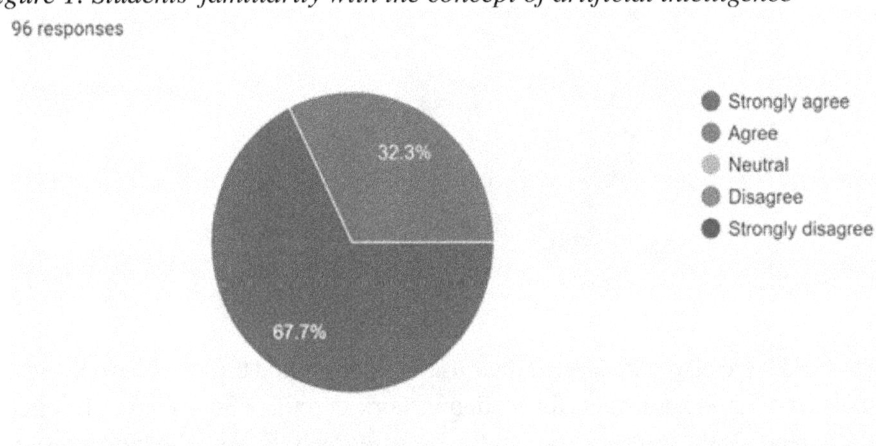

The first question in the survey aimed to gauge the current level of AI awareness among students. Students were asked if they were familiar with the concept of artificial intelligence. The responses were categorized into two main groups: those who strongly agreed and those who agreed. A significant majority of students, specifically 67.7% of respondents, strongly agreed that they were familiar with the concept of AI. This high percentage suggests that a large portion of the students feel confident in their understanding of AI. It indicates that these students likely have a good grasp of what AI is and may have encountered it in various aspects of their lives, such as technology use, media, or academic studies. The remaining 32.3% of students agreed that they were familiar with AI. While this group also claimed familiarity, their response was less emphatic than "strongly agree." This could imply that these students have a basic understanding of AI but might not feel as confident or may have some uncertainties about the specifics of the technology.

When we combine these results, we find that 100% of the surveyed students expressed some level of familiarity with AI. This is a remarkable finding, as it suggests that AI awareness has become ubiquitous among the students. However, it is important to note what these results might not reveal. For instance, the survey does not measure the depth or accuracy of students' understanding of AI. Being familiar with a concept does not necessarily imply having a comprehensive or correct understanding of it.

Figure 2. Students' use of AI-Powered tools for academic work

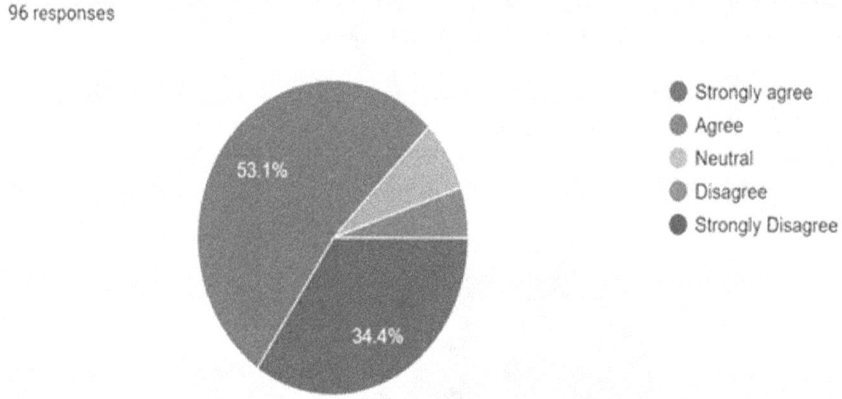

Students were also asked about their use of AI-powered tools, such as AI-tutors, chatbots, and writing assistants for academic work. A total of 34.4% strongly agreed, 53.1% agreed, 7.3% were neutral, and 5.2% disagreed. Firstly, the combined percentage of those who "strongly agree" and "agree" is 87.5% (34.4% + 53.1%). This indicates that a significant majority of students surveyed have used AI-powered tools for their university work. This high percentage suggests that AI tools have become widely accepted and integrated into academic practices.

The "strongly agree" category (34.4%) represents students who are likely to be frequent or enthusiastic users of AI tools. These students may find AI tools particularly beneficial or may be early adopters of new technologies. The "agree" category, with the highest percentage at 53.1%, suggests that many students have used AI tools, though perhaps not as frequently or enthusiastically as those in the "strongly agree" group. This group likely recognizes the benefits of AI tools but may use them more selectively or cautiously.

Only 7.3% of respondents were neutral, which could indicate limited experience with AI tools or uncertainty about their impact on their academic work. This small percentage suggests that most students have formed an opinion about AI tools, whether positive or negative.

The "disagree" category, at 5.2%, represents a small minority of students who claim not to have used AI-powered tools for their university work. This could be due to various factors, such as lack of access, personal preference, or concerns about academic integrity. Interestingly, there is no mention of a "strongly disagree" category in the provided data. This absence could imply that very few, if any, students strongly oppose or completely avoid using AI tools.

Figure 3. Impact of AI-Enhanced learning tools on understanding and academic performance

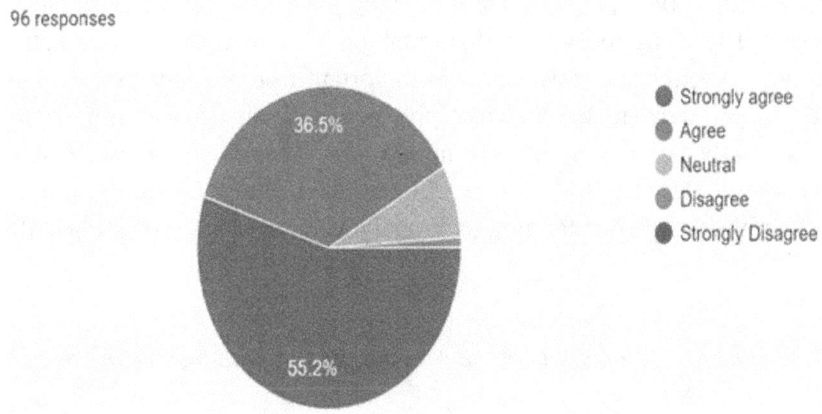

When asked if AI-enhanced learning tools have improved their understanding of complex topics and their academic performance, 55.2% of students strongly agreed, 36.5% agreed, 7.3% were neutral, and 1% disagreed.

Considering the positive responses, a significant majority of students (91.7%) either strongly agreed or agreed that AI-enhanced learning tools have improved their understanding and performance. This is a compelling statistic that suggests AI is having a substantial positive impact on education. The high percentage of students who strongly agreed (55.2%) is particularly noteworthy, indicating that over half of the surveyed students feel very confident about the benefits of AI in their learning process. This suggests that these students have likely had multiple experiences with AI tools, leading to a strong belief in their effectiveness.

The 36.5% who agreed, while not as emphatic, still represent a positive view of AI's impact. These students may have found AI tools helpful, even if they haven't experienced as dramatic an improvement as those who strongly agreed. Together, these positive responses paint a picture of AI as a valuable asset in education, potentially revolutionizing how students engage with complex topics and improve their academic performance.

However, it is also important to consider the neutral and negative responses. The 7.3% of students who remained neutral may indicate that these students have had limited experience with AI-enhanced learning tools, have had mixed experiences seeing both benefits and drawbacks, or possibly have not noticed a significant difference in their learning performance. The 1% who disagreed represent a very small portion of the surveyed students. While their perspective should not be ignored, it is clear they are in the minority. These students might have had negative experiences with AI tools, found them confusing or unhelpful, or simply prefer traditional learning methods.

It is worth noting that the overwhelmingly positive response suggests that AI-enhanced learning tools are indeed making a significant impact on students' educational experiences. However, it is important to remember that AI tools are just that—tools; they are designed to supplement and enhance learning, not replace traditional study methods or critical thinking skills. As students continue their studies and potentially move on to the workforce, developing the ability to use these tools effectively while maintaining their analytical and problem-solving skills will be crucial.

Figure 4. Students' perceptions of the role of artificial intelligence in their future

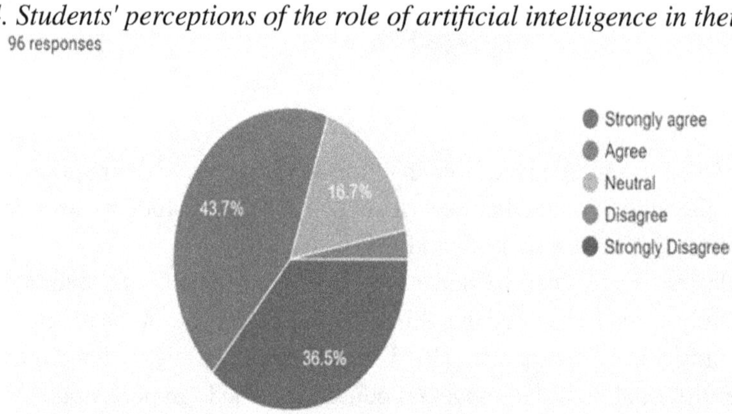

Students were asked about their views on the role of artificial intelligence (AI) in their future. The results provide interesting insights into how young students perceive the impact of this rapidly evolving technology. Specifically, 36.5% strongly agreed that AI will play a significant role in their future, 43.7% agreed, 16.7% were neutral, and 3.1% disagreed.

The most striking aspect of these results is the overwhelming positive sentiment toward AI's future impact. When we combine those who strongly agreed (36.5%) with those who agreed (43.7%), we find that a substantial 80.2% of students believe AI will play a significant role in their future. This suggests that the majority of students are aware of AI's potential and expect it to be a major factor in their lives and careers.

Given that over 80% of students believe that AI will play a significant role in their future, this has important implications for educational institutions and career advisors. This data suggests that students might be more receptive to learning about AI and its applications across various disciplines. Schools and universities might consider integrating more AI-related content into their curricula to prepare students for a future shaped by AI. This could indicate a generational shift towards technology; today's students have grown up in a digital age and may be more accustomed to rapid technological advancements. Their positive outlook on AI's future role might reflect a general comfort with and acceptance of new technologies.

The 16.7% of students who remained neutral could represent a group that is either unsure about AI's impact or feels they do not have enough information to form a strong opinion. This group might benefit from more education about AI and its potential applications in various fields. Only 3.1% of students disagreed with the statement; this very small percentage suggests that very few students believe AI will not have a significant impact on their future. It is worth considering why these students hold this view; it could be due to skepticism about AI's capabilities, concerns about its limitations, or perhaps a belief that other factors will be more influential in their lives.

Figure 5. Students' opinions on the integration of AI tools in their learning environment

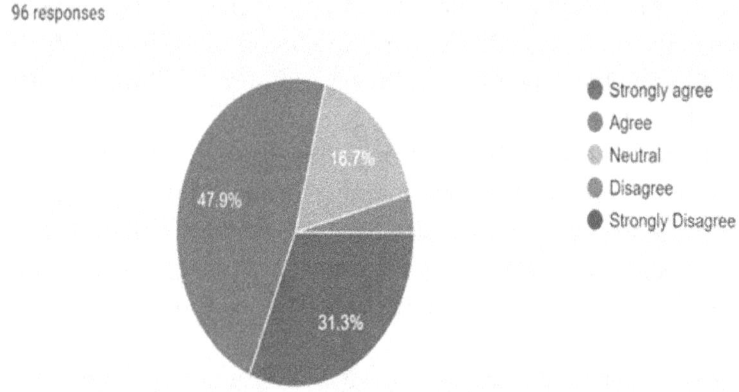

Students were also asked about their opinions on the increased integration of AI tools in their learning environment. The results revealed that 31.3% strongly agreed, 47.9% agreed, 16.7% were neutral, and 4.2% disagreed.

The first step in interpreting these results is to look at the overall support for AI integration. The combination of the percentages of those who "strongly agreed" (31.3%) and "agreed" (47.9%) will give us 79.2%. This distribution suggests a generally positive attitude towards AI integration, with very little opposition.

The 16.7% of neutral responses are worth noting; these students may need more information about AI integration or may be unsure about its potential impact on their learning experience. Only 4.2% of students disagreed with increased AI integration; this low percentage suggests that concerns or reservations about AI in education are not widespread among the surveyed students.

Figure 6. Student concerns regarding artificial intelligence (AI) in education

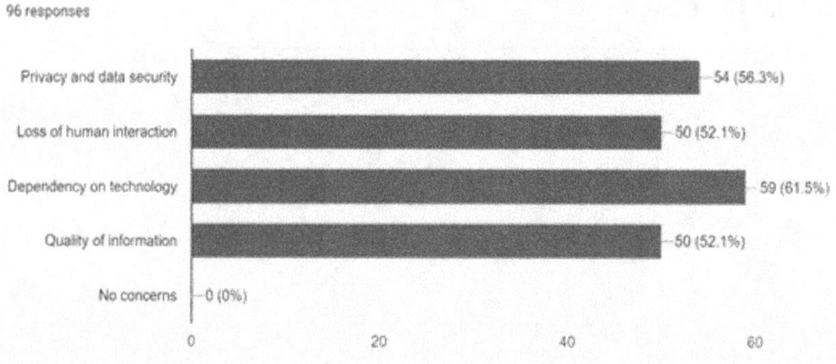

Ninety-six students were asked about their concerns regarding the use of artificial intelligence (AI) in education. The survey results provide valuable insights into the perspectives of students on this emerging technology.

Key concerns identified:

1. **Privacy and Data Security**: 54 students
2. **Loss of Human Interaction**: 50 students
3. **Technological Dependency**: 59 students
4. **Information Quality**: 50 students

The first thing to note is that a significant number of students expressed concerns across all four categories. This suggests that students are generally aware of potential issues surrounding AI in education and are critically thinking about its implications.

To better understand the relative importance of each concern, we can calculate the percentage of students who expressed each concern:

- **Technological Dependency**: 59 ÷ 96 x 100 = 61.5%
- **Privacy and Data Security**: 54 ÷ 96 x 100 = 56.3%
- **Loss of Human Interaction**: 50 ÷ 96 x 100 = 52.1%
- **Information Quality**: 50 ÷ 96 x 100 = 52.1%

The highest-ranking concern is dependency on technology, followed closely by privacy and data security. Loss of human interaction and quality of information share the third position.

It is important to note that the total number of concerns expressed (213) exceeds the number of participants (96). This indicates that many students had multiple concerns, highlighting the complexity of the issue and the interconnected nature of these concerns.

1. **Technological Dependency:** The high percentage of students concerned about dependency of technology (61.5%) suggests a need for balanced integration of AI in education, ensuring that traditional learning methods and critical thinking skills are not neglected.
2. **Privacy and Security**: With 56.3% of students expressing concerns about privacy and data security, there is a clear need for transparent policies and robust security measures in AI-powered educational tools.
3. **Human Interaction**: The concern about loss of human interaction (52.1%) indicates that students value personal connections in their learning experience. This suggests that AI should be implemented as a supplement to, rather than a replacement for, human teachers.

4. **Information Quality**: The equal concern about the quality of information (52.1%) highlights the importance of developing AI systems that provide accurate, unbiased, and reliable information.

Figure 7. Student opinions on the benefits of AI-Enhanced education

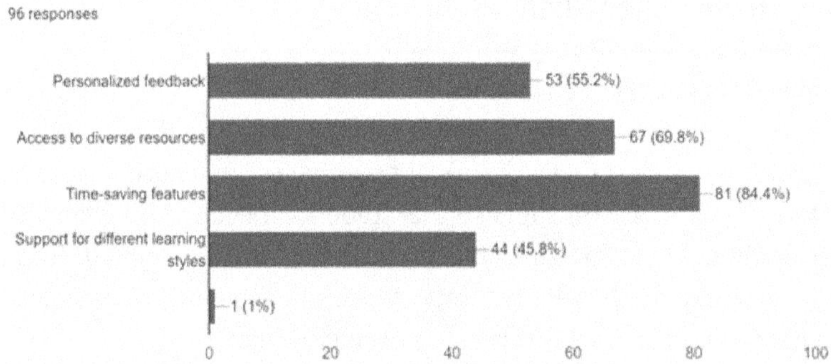

A total of 96 students were also asked about their opinions on AI-enhanced. The aspects of AI-enhanced education students find most beneficial are:

1. **Time-saving Features**: 81 students
2. **Access to Diverse Resources**: 67 students
3. **Personalized Feedback**: 53 students
4. **Support for Different Learning Styles**: 44 students
5. **Other (unspecified)**: 1 student

Converting raw numbers to percentages can provide a clearer picture of the data. To calculate the percentage, we divide the number of students who chose each option by the total number of students and multiply by 100.

- **Time-saving Features**: 81 ÷ 96 x 100 = 84.4%
- **Access to Diverse Resources**: 67 ÷ 96 x 100 = 69.8%
- **Personalized Feedback**: 50 ÷ 96 x 100 = 55.2%
- **Support for Different Learning Styles**: 44 ÷ 96 x 100 = 45.8%
- **Other**: 1 ÷ 96 x 100 = 1%

Students were allowed to select multiple options; this information is crucial for accurate interpretation and explains why the total number of selections (81+67+53+44+1) exceeds the number of students surveyed (96).

We can compare the popularity of different options; for instance, we can see that time-saving features were selected by 81 students, while personalized feedback was chosen by 53 students. This suggests that time-saving features are considerably more valued among the surveyed students. The "other" category, with only one response, could be considered an outlier. While it is important to note, it may not significantly impact the overall interpretation of the results.

1. **Students' Priorities**: The data suggest that students value efficiency in their learning process, with time-saving features being the most popular aspect of AI-enhanced education.
2. **Resource Accessibility**: The high preference for access to diverse resources indicates that students appreciate the ability of AI to provide a wide range of learning materials.
3. **Personalization**: While not the top choice, a significant number of students value personalized feedback, suggesting an appreciation for tailored learning experiences.
4. **Learning Style Support**: Although ranked lower, support for different learning styles is still valued by nearly half of the surveyed students, highlighting the importance of diverse teaching methods.
5. **Comprehensive AI Benefits**: The fact that many students selected multiple options suggests that they see AI as beneficial in various aspects of their education, rather than just one area.
6. **Areas for Improvement**: The lower ranking of personalized feedback and learning style support could indicate where AI in education could be further developed or where students need more information about these options.

Figure 8. Student opinions on AI replacing traditional teaching roles

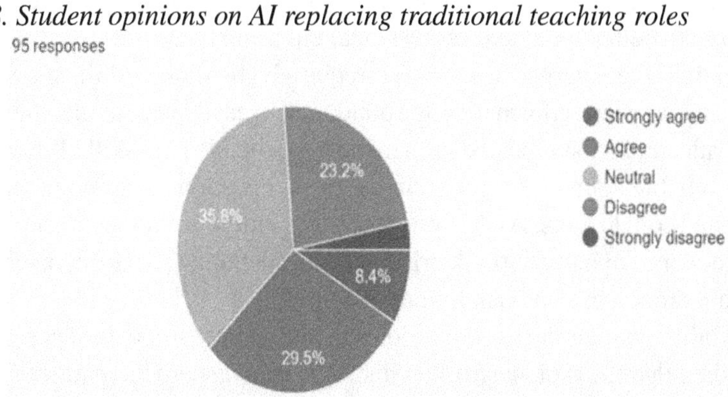

Students were asked to share their opinions on whether artificial intelligence (AI) could potentially replace certain traditional teaching roles, such as grading assignments and providing feedback. The results provide valuable insights into students' perceptions, as 8.4% strongly agreed, 29.5% agreed, 35.8% were neutral, 23.2% disagreed, and 3.2% strongly disagreed.

The first step in interpreting the results is to look at the overall sentiment expressed by the students. We can group the responses into three categories:

- **Positive (strongly agree and agree)**: 37.9%
- **Neutral**: 35.8%
- **Negative (disagree and strongly disagree)**: 26.4%

This breakdown shows that more students have a positive or neutral view of AI replacing certain teaching roles than those who disagree with the idea. However, the distribution is relatively balanced, indicating a diversity of opinions among students.

The largest single group (35.8%) expressed a neutral stance on the topic; this suggests that many students are uncertain or have mixed feelings about AI taking over traditional teaching roles. It could indicate that they recognize both potential benefits and drawbacks of AI in education.

Looking at the extreme ends of the spectrum, we find that more students strongly agree (8.4%) than strongly disagree (3.2%). This could indicate that those who are enthusiastic about AI in education feel more strongly about their position compared to those who are opposed to it. This diverse range of opinions suggests that the implementation of AI in teaching roles should be approached carefully. While there is some openness to the idea, there is also significant skepticism and uncertainty.

The last two questions of the survey were open-ended; students were asked about the skills they believe are essential for success in an AI-enhanced learning environment. The responses were diverse and insightful, reflecting a keen awareness of the changing educational and professional environment.

Critical thinking emerged as the most frequently mentioned skill, and for a good reason. In an era where information is abundant and easily accessible, the ability to analyze, evaluate, and synthesize information is crucial. This skill allows students to discern reliable sources from unreliable ones, question assumptions, and draw well-reasoned conclusions. As AI systems become more prevalent in education and beyond, students' capacity to think critically will set them apart from machines that excel at data processing but lack human judgment.

Adaptability was another key skill identified by many students. This reflects an understanding that the rapid pace of technological advancement requires flexibility and a willingness to learn continuously. The ability to adapt to new tools, methodologies, and ways of thinking will be invaluable as AI continues to reshape various aspects of our lives, including education and future careers.

Creativity and innovation were also highlighted, indicating an awareness that while AI can process and generate information, uniquely human traits like original thinking and imaginative problem-solving remain irreplaceable. These skills will be crucial in finding novel solutions to complex problems and in fields where human creativity is paramount.

Emotional intelligence, an often-overlooked skill in technological discussions, was recognized by some students as essential. This insight demonstrates an understanding that even in an AI-enhanced world, human interactions and the ability to understand and manage emotions remain vital. Emotional intelligence can enhance teamwork, leadership, and personal relationships—areas where AI currently falls short.

The ability to interact with AI tools effectively and responsibly was another skill mentioned; this shows a practical understanding of the need to work alongside AI rather than compete with it. Knowing how to leverage AI tools to enhance learning and productivity while being aware of their limitations and ethical considerations is becoming increasingly important.

Information management and digital literacy were also identified as crucial skills; in an age of information overload, the ability to efficiently find, evaluate, organize, and use digital information is invaluable. This includes understanding how to use search engines effectively, critically assessing online sources, and managing digital workflows.

Students' Perceptions

Interpreting these results reveals several key insights:

1. Students are aware of the changing nature of education and work due to AI advancement.
2. There is a recognition that uniquely human skills will remain valuable and should be developed alongside technological proficiency.
3. Students understand the need for a balanced skill set that combines technical knowledge with soft skills.
4. There is an acknowledgment that learning how to learn and adapt is as important as acquiring specific knowledge.

These insights suggest that education should focus on developing a well-rounded skill set that prepares students for a future where AI is ubiquitous. This might involve:

- Integrating critical thinking exercises across all subjects.

- Providing opportunities for creative problem-solving and innovation.
- Incorporating AI tools into the curriculum to familiarize students with their use and limitations.
- Emphasizing emotional intelligence and interpersonal skills through group projects and discussions.
- Teaching digital literacy and responsible AI use as core competencies.
- Encouraging adaptability by exposing students to diverse learning experiences and methodologies.

It is worth noting that this open-ended question reflects a mature understanding among students of the skills needed in an AI-enhanced learning environment. By focusing on developing these skills, students will be well prepared to thrive in a world where AI is an integral part of education and work. The goal is not to compete with AI but to complement it, leveraging students' uniquely human capabilities alongside technological advancements.

At the end of the survey, students were asked to provide suggestions for improving AI-enhanced educational tools and experiences; the responses gathered offer valuable insights into the perspectives of learners on the integration of artificial intelligence in education.

One prominent suggestion that emerged from the survey was the provision of AI-driven insights to support teachers in helping their students. This indicates that students recognize the potential of AI to enhance the teaching process rather than replace educators. By leveraging AI to analyze students' performance data, identify learning gaps, and suggest personalized interventions, teachers could be empowered to provide more targeted and effective support. This aligns with the growing trend of using data analytics in education to inform instructional decisions and improve student outcomes.

Another significant theme in the responses was the call for raising awareness about both the merits and demerits of incorporating AI tools in education. This demonstrates a mature understanding among students that AI, like any technology, comes with both benefits and potential drawbacks. It suggests that students desire a balanced and informed approach to AI integration rather than uncritical adoption. Educators and institutions should consider developing comprehensive AI literacy programs that address not only the practical applications of AI but also its ethical implications, limitations, and societal impacts.

The suggestion to incorporate more interactive elements such as gamification, quizzes, and simulations reflects students' desire for engaging and dynamic learning experiences. AI-powered adaptive learning systems could potentially offer personalized, game-like experiences that adjust to individual learning styles and paces, making education more engaging and effective.

Students also expressed a desire for more personalized and detailed feedback; this highlights the potential of AI to provide immediate, specific, and constructive feedback on assignments and assessments. Natural language processing and machine learning algorithms could be employed to analyze students' work and offer tailored suggestions for improvement, supplementing teacher feedback and providing students with more opportunities for self-reflection and growth.

The call for making AI accessible to all students underscores the importance of equity in educational technology. This suggestion raises important questions about the digital divide and the potential for AI to either exacerbate or mitigate existing educational inequalities. Policymakers and educational institutions should prioritize ensuring that AI-enhanced tools are available and usable for students from diverse socioeconomic backgrounds, abilities, and learning needs.

An intriguing suggestion was for AI tools to provide sources for their information and address the credibility of that information. This reflects a growing awareness of the importance of information literacy and critical thinking skills in the digital age. Implementing this suggestion could involve developing AI systems that not only provide information but also offer transparency about their knowledge sources and confidence levels. This could serve as a valuable tool for teaching students about source evaluation and the nature of AI-generated content.

The concern about data privacy and the suggestion for more regulation to limit AI tools' use of personal data for model training highlight the ethical considerations surrounding AI in education. Students are evidently aware of the value of their data and the potential for its misuse. This calls for the development of robust data protection policies and ethical guidelines for AI use in educational settings, ensuring that student privacy is respected while still allowing for the benefits of personalized learning.

Interpreting these results, we can draw several key conclusions:

- Students see AI as a tool to enhance, not replace, human educators.
- There is a desire for a balanced, informed approach to AI integration in education.
- Interactive and personalized learning experiences are highly valued.
- Equity and accessibility in AI-enhanced education are crucial concerns.
- Information literacy and critical thinking skills are becoming increasingly important in the context of AI.
- Ethical considerations, particularly around data privacy, are at the forefront of students' minds.

These insights suggest that the future of AI education should focus on developing tools that empower teachers, engage students, provide personalized learning experiences, and uphold high ethical standards. Educators and policymakers should work towards creating a framework for AI integration that addresses these concerns and leverages the technology's potential to improve educational outcomes for all students.

Professors' Perceptions

In addition to students' perceptions and experiences regarding the use of artificial intelligence (AI), in-depth interviews were conducted with six professors from the Faculty of Letters and Human Sciences in Oujda. This section aims to provide a balanced view between survey results and interview insights, shedding light on professors' towards AI, the effectiveness of their teaching strategies, and the dynamics of professor-student interactions within AI-enhanced learning environments.

The professors interviewed expressed a range of attitudes towards the use of AI in education:

- **Professor A**: A specialist in educational technology, expressed a strong belief that AI can enhance the learning experience. He stated, "AI has the potential to personalize learning for each student," He elaborated that adaptive learning platforms powered by AI can analyze student performance data, tailoring educational content to individual needs. This level of personalization addresses various learning styles and ultimately leads to a more effective educational experience. Professor A's commitment to using AI highlights his provocative approach to educational technology.
- **Professor B**: A professor of literature with over 20 years of experience, voiced a more cautious approach. She remarked "While I see the benefits of AI, I worry about over-reliance on technology." She emphasized the importance of maintaining a human touch in education, arguing that AI should serve as a supportive tool rather than a replacement for traditional teaching methods. "We must ensure that technology complements our teaching without overshadowing the essential human interaction that fosters a supportive learning environment," she cautioned. Her insights suggest a critical awareness of the need for balance in technology integration/
- **Professor C**: Focusing on ethics in technology, she brought an important perspective to the discussion. She highlighted the ethical implications of using AI in education, particularly concerning data privacy and surveillance. "As we integrate AI, we must prioritize the protection of student data and ensure transparency in how AI systems operate," she advised. Her emphasis on ethical considerations underscores the necessity of addressing ethical concerns

in the development and implementation of AI technologies in educational settings.

When discussing the effectiveness of their pedagogical strategies in an AI-enhanced environment, the professors highlighted various approaches they have adopted:

- **Professor D**: A professor specializing in blended learning methods, emphasized the effectiveness of combining traditional and digital pedagogical strategies. "AI can automate administrative tasks, giving educators more time to focus on innovative teaching methods," she explained. She advocated for using AI to facilitate interactive learning activities that actively engage students, suggesting that such strategies help deepen understanding and retention of knowledge.
- **Professor E**: He highlighted the role of AI in promoting collaborative learning. "AI tools can connect students from different backgrounds, enabling them to work together on projects," he noted. He described how AI platforms can facilitate group work by assigning tasks based on individual strengths and weaknesses, thereby fostering a sense of community among students. His belief that such collaborative environments enhance critical thinking and problem-solving skills, which are essential for success in the modern world.
- **Professor F**: Specializing in assessment strategies, he discussed the benefits of using AI for formative assessment and feedback. "AI can provide real-time feedback to students, helping them understand their progress and areas for improvement," he stated. He noted that this immediate feedback is crucial for learning, as it allows students to make adjustments throughout the learning process rather than waiting for traditional assessments. According to him, this approach leads to a more dynamic and responsive educational experience.

The interviews also revealed insights into the evolving nature of professor-student interactions in AI-enhanced learning environments. The professors shared varied perspectives on how AI impacts professor-student interactions:

- **Professor A** noted, "AI tools can facilitate communication between professors and students, making it easier for students to seek help." He emphasized that AI can serve as a bridge, allowing students to connect with educators more effectively, especially in larger classes where individual attention may be challenging.
- In contrast, **Professor B** expressed concern about the potential for AI to diminish personal interactions. "While AI can enhance communication, it can also create barriers if not used thoughtfully," she cautioned. She stressed that

building strong relationships with students is crucial, particularly for fostering trust and motivation. "We must strike a balance between utilizing technology and maintaining meaningful connections," she concluded.

- **Professor C** discussed how AI can empower students, noting, "When students have access to AI tools, they can take charge of their own learning." She emphasized that AI can help students become more autonomous learners, guiding them in setting goals and tracking their progress. This shift encourages a sense of ownership and responsibility in the learning process, which can lead to increased engagement.

Collectively, the insights gathered from these six professors illustrate the complex interplay between AI, pedagogical strategies, and professor-student interactions. While attitudes towards AI vary, there is a consensus on the importance of balancing technology with the human elements of teaching. As educators navigate this evolving environment, it is crucial to remain mindful of the ethical implications and to foster environments that prioritize meaningful connections and collaborative learning. The integration of AI in education presents both challenges and opportunities, and it is the responsibility of educators to exploit its potential while safeguarding the foundational principles of teaching and learning.

This expanded analysis not only provides a comprehensive view of professors' perspectives but also aligns more closely with the survey results regarding students' awareness and opinions about AI, ensuring a balanced understanding of the educational landscape.

Challenges in Implementing AI in Education

Despite the promising developments, the integration of AI into educational systems worldwide is not without challenges. To ensure effective implementation, the following insights and considerations are essential:

Essential Infrastructure and Resource Requirements from the Faculty of Letters Case:

1. **Technological Infrastructure:** One of the primary concerns is the potential for AI to exacerbate existing educational inequalities, a concern voiced by students themselves in the survey conducted to understand their perceptions of the integration of AI-enhanced tools in education.
2. **Financial Resources:** Countries and regions with limited financial resources may struggle to implement AI-powered education tools, potentially widening the global education gap. There is a need for Adequate funding to procure AI technologies and maintain them over time.

3. **Training and Support:** Educators play a crucial role in shaping the learning experiences of their students, and as technology continues to evolve, it is essential for them to engage in continuous professional development. This ongoing learning process is important to effectively incorporate and utilize artificial intelligence tools within the teaching practices. By participating in professional development opportunities, educators can enhance their understanding of AI technologies and explore innovative ways to integrate these tools into their curriculum.

Key Success Factors from Research Findings:

1. **Stakeholder Engagement:** It is essential to actively involve a diverse range of stakeholders, including students, educators, and policymakers, throughout the implementation process of AI tools. This engagement ensures that the tools developed are tailored to meet the specific needs and expectations of all parties involved, thereby fostering a sense of ownership and acceptance among users. By gathering input and feedback from these groups, the educational AI initiatives can be more effectively aligned with their requirements.
2. **Data Privacy and Security Measures:** Establishing robust protocols for data privacy and security is of paramount importance in the realm of educational technology. These measures must be designed to protect sensitive student information from unauthorized access and breaches, ensuring that the integrity and confidentiality of personal data are maintained. This commitment to safeguarding information not only builds trust among users but also complies with legal and ethical standards.
3. **Ethical Guidelines:** The development of clear and comprehensive ethical guidelines is essential for guiding the usage of AI in educational contexts. These frameworks should address issues such as fairness, accountability, and transparency, providing a foundation for ethical decision-making. By implementing these guidelines, educational institutions can navigate the complexities of AI development responsibility, ensuring that technology serves to enhance the learning experience without compromising ethical standards.
4. **Cultural Relevance:** To maximize the effectiveness and acceptance of AI tools in education, it is important to ensure that these technologies are adaptable to local cultural contexts. By taking into consideration the cultural nuances and values of the communities they serve, AI tools can be designed to resonate more deeply with users. This cultural relevance not only enhances the effectiveness of the tools but also promotes a more inclusive and engaging educational environment.

Table 1. Common challenges and solutions

Challenges	Solutions
Educational Inequalities	Implement targeted support programs for underserved areas.
Data Privacy Concerns	Enforce strict data protection regulations and practices.
Ethical Issues in AI Decision Making	Create transparent AI systems with defined accountability measures.
Resistance to Change	Foster a culture of innovation through training and open communication

Implementation Checklist for Institutions

- Assess current technological resources and identify gaps.
- Develop a training program for educators on AI tools.
- Establish clear policies for data privacy and security.
- Engage with the community to gather feedback on AI integration.
- Monitor and evaluate the impact of AI tools on student learning outcomes.

Cultural Adaptation Considerations Specific to the Moroccan Context

- Incorporate local languages and dialects into AI tools to enhance accessibility.
- Tailor content to reflect cultural values and educational practices in Morocco.
- Engage local educators in the development of AI curricula to ensure relevance.

While the integration of AI in education presents numerous opportunities for innovation and improvement, it is imperative to address the associated challenges thoughtfully. By focusing on ethical considerations, data privacy, and the equitable distribution of resources, stakeholders can work towards an educational landscape where AI enhances learning for all students, regardless of their backgrounds or circumstances.

Study Limitations

- **Methodological Limitations:** The research employed a combination of qualitative and quantitative methods, which presents potential biases if not managed with precision. Each method possesses its own inherent strengths and weaknesses, and without careful integration, the results may be skewed or misrepresented. This necessitates a thorough examination of the methodologies used to ensure the reliability and validity of the findings.

- **Sample Size Constraints:** The study was conducted with a sample size of 96 students, which may impose limitations on the ability to generalize the findings to the broader faculty population. A larger sample size could provide more robust insights and a greater likelihood of capturing the diversity of experiences and perspectives within the entire faculty. Therefore, the relatively small sample may restrict the applicability of the results beyond the specific group studied.
- **Generalizability Considerations:** The results obtained from this study may not be applicable to other faculties or universities, primarily due to the unique context of the faculty of Letters and Human Sciences. Each educational institution had distinct characteristics, cultures, and challenges that could influence the outcomes. As a result, caution must be exercised when attempting to extrapolate these findings to different academic environments.
- **Time Frame of the Study:** The limited duration of the research presents challenges in capturing the depth of insights required for a comprehensive understanding of the long-term impacts of artificial intelligence of educational practices. A more extended study period could facilitate a better grasp of the evolving dynamics and consequences of AI integration in educational settings, allowing for a richer analysis of its effects over time.
- **Resource Limitations:** The constraints associated with funding and access to advanced AI tools may have restricted the scope of the research and the variety of technologies assessed. Limited resources can hinder the ability to explore and analyze the full range of AI applications and their potential benefits or drawbacks. Consequently, these limitations may impact the overall findings and conclusions drawn from the study.

CONCLUSION

The incorporation of artificial intelligence (AI) into education systems around the globe is significantly reshaping learning and teaching. This transformation is paving the way for more personalized educational experiences tailored to the unique needs of individual students. With the help of AI, learners can access intelligent tutoring systems that adapt to their specific learning styles and paces, providing targeted support and feedback to enhance their understanding of various subjects. Additionally, innovative assessment methods powered by AI are being developed, allowing for more comprehensive evaluations of student performance that go beyond traditional testing formats.

However, it is essential to recognize that various challenges still exist within this evolving educational framework. Issues related to ethics, equity, and accessibility must be carefully addressed to ensure that the integration of AI tools does not exacerbate existing disparities in education. The potential for AI to improve educational outcomes on a global scale is indeed substantial, and it is imperative that countries continue to explore and implement AI technologies thoughtfully within their educational systems.

At the Faculty of Letters and Human Sciences Mohammed First University, specific findings have emerged that highlight important considerations for integrating AI en education. It is essential to actively involve a diverse range of stakeholders, including students, educators, and policymakers, throughout the implementation process of AI tools. This engagement ensures that the developed tools meet the specific needs and expectations of all parties involved, fostering a sense of ownership and acceptance among users. Additionally, establishing robust protocols for data privacy and security is paramount. These measures protect sensitive student information ensuring the integrity and confidentiality of personal data. Furthermore, the clear and comprehensive ethical guidelines are critical for guiding the usage of AI in educational contexts. Implementing these guidelines allows educational institutions to navigate the complexities of AI development responsibility. Finally, ensuring that AI tools are adaptable to local cultural contexts maximizes their effectiveness and acceptance. By considering the cultural nuances and values of the communities they serve, AI tools can resonate more deeply with users, promoting a more inclusive and engaging educational environment.

As countries embark on this journey, sharing best practices will be vital for overcoming common challenges and maximizing the advantages that AI can offer to learners everywhere. Collaboration among educators, policymakers, and technology developers will enable a more effective deployment of AI resources, ultimately leading to a richer and more inclusive educational experience for all students around the world.

REFERENCES

Baker, R. S., & Inventado, P. S. (2014). Educational data mining and learning analytics. In *Learning analytics* (pp. 61–75). Springer., https://link.springer.com/chapter/10.1007/978-1-4614-3305-7_4 DOI: 10.1007/978-1-4614-3305-7_4

Bandura, A. (1977). *Social learning theory*. Prentice-Hall.

Busso, A., & Sanchez, B. (2024). Advancing communicative competence in the digital age: A case for AI tools in Japanese university EFL programs. *Technology in Language Teaching & Learning*, 6(3), 1–17. DOI: 10.29140/tltl.v6n3.1211

Chen, L., Chen, P., & Lin, Z. (2020). Artificial intelligence in education: A review. *IEEE Access : Practical Innovations, Open Solutions*, 8, 75264–75278. DOI: 10.1109/ACCESS.2020.2988510

Ertmer, P. A., & Newby, T. J. (2008). Behaviorism, cognitivism, constructivism: Comparing critical features from an instructional design perspective. *Performance Improvement Quarterly*, 6(4), 50–72. DOI: 10.1111/j.1937-8327.1993.tb00605.x

Fitzpatrick, D. (2023). *The AI educator*. TeachersGoals Publishing.

Fitzpatrick, D., Fox, A., & Weinstein, B. (2023). *The AI classroom: The ultimate guide to artificial intelligence*. TeachersGoals Publishing.

Gardner, H. (1983). *Frames of mind: The theory of multiple intelligences*. Basic Books.

Göçen, A., & Aydemir, F. (2020). Artificial intelligence in education and schools. *Research on Education and Media*, 12(1), 13–21. DOI: 10.2478/rem-2020-0003

Lee, Y.-J., & Davis, R. O. (2024). Korean in-service teachers' perceptions of implementing artificial intelligence (AI) education for teaching in schools and their AI teacher training programs. *International Journal of Information and Education Technology (IJIET)*, 14(2), 214–219. Advance online publication. DOI: 10.18178/ijiet.2024.14.2.2042

Ling Jen, S., & Abdul Rahim Hj Salam, A. R. (2024). A systematic review on the use of artificial intelligence in writing. *International Journal of Academic Research in Progressive Education and Development*, 13(1). https://www.researchgate.net/publication/378514867_A_Systematic_Review_on_The_Use_of_Artificial_Intelligence_in_Writing

Pane, J. F., Griffin, B. A., McCaffrey, D. F., & Karam, R. (2014). Effectiveness of Cognitive Tutor Algebra I at scale. *Educational Evaluation and Policy Analysis*, 36(2), 127–144. https://www.jstor.org/stable/43773458. DOI: 10.3102/0162373713507480

Radianti, J., Majchrzak, T. A., Fromm, J., & Wohlgenannt, I. (2020). A systematic review of immersive virtual reality applications for higher education: Design elements, lessons learned, and research agenda. *Computers & Education*, 147, 103778. DOI: 10.1016/j.compedu.2019.103778

Rajan, T. (2022). The unusual case of BYJU's: Creating one of the world's most valued educational technology companies from India. *Indian Journal of Marketing*, 52(4), 8–23. https://www.researchgate.net/publication/359935437_The_Unusual_Case_of_BYJU's_Creating_One_of_the_World's_Most_Valued_Educational_Technology_Companies_from_India. DOI: 10.17010/ijom/2022/v52/i4/163181

Shah, P. (2023). AI and the Future of Education: Teaching in the Age of artificial intelligence. *Welcome to TeachOnline*. https://teachonline.ca/tools-trends/must-read-books-on-online-learning/ai-and-future-education-teaching-age-artificial-intelligence

Siemens, G. (2005). Connectivism: A learning theory for the digital age. *International Journal of Instructional Technology and Distance Learning*, 2(1), 3–10.

UNESCO. (2021). *AI and education: Guidance for policy-makers*. UNESCO. https://unesdoc.unesco.org/ark:/48223/pf0000376709

Von Ahn, L. (2013). Duolingo: *Learn a language for free while helping to translate the web*. In *Proceedings of the 2013 International Conference on Intelligent User Interfaces* (pp. 1–2). Association for Computing Machinery. https://doi.org/DOI: 10.1145/2449396.2449398

Chapter 3
AI-Driven Instructional Design:
Enhancing Learning Experiences Through Personalization and Efficiency

C. V. Suresh Babu
https://orcid.org/0000-0002-8474-2882
Hindustan Institute of Technology and Science, India

Bhavesh M.
https://orcid.org/0009-0001-3992-4193
Hindustan Institute of Technology and Science, India

Albert Gururaja V.
https://orcid.org/0009-0001-2563-9359
Hindustan Institute of Technology and Science, India

Venkatesh T. D.
https://orcid.org/0009-0000-8716-4638
Hindustan Institute of Technology and Science, India

ABSTRACT

This study aims to explore the transformative potential of AI-driven instructional design in enhancing personalized learning experiences and improving educational efficiency. Utilizing a mixed-methods approach, the research combines quantitative data analysis with qualitative insights from educators and students to assess the effectiveness of AI tools in instructional practices. Key findings indicate that AI technologies significantly enhance student engagement, motivation, and learning

DOI: 10.4018/979-8-3693-6527-4.ch003

outcomes while alleviating administrative burdens on educators. The study concludes that while AI presents substantial opportunities for innovation in education, it also raises ethical concerns regarding data privacy and algorithmic bias that must be addressed. The implications of this research underscore the need for responsible AI integration in educational settings to ensure equitable access and support for all learners.

1.0. INTRODUCTION

1.1 Background of AI in Education

The integration of Artificial Intelligence (AI) into educational practices has emerged as a pivotal development in the field of instructional design. As educational institutions strive to meet the diverse needs of learners, AI offers innovative solutions that enhance personalization, efficiency, and engagement. This section provides an overview of the historical context and the evolution of AI technologies in educational settings.

1.2 Purpose of the Study

This study aims to explore the transformative impact of AI-driven instructional design on learning experiences. By examining the capabilities of AI to tailor educational content and adapt to individual learner preferences, the research seeks to identify effective strategies for implementing AI tools in various educational contexts.

1.3 Significance of the Research

The significance of this research lies in its potential to bridge the gap between traditional instructional design methods and modern AI applications. By investigating the effectiveness of AI-driven tools, this study contributes to the ongoing discourse on educational innovation and provides valuable insights for educators, policymakers, and researchers.

1.4 Research Questions

To guide the investigation, the study will address the following research questions:

- How does AI enhance personalization in instructional design?

- What are the implications of AI-driven instructional design for student engagement and learning outcomes?
- What ethical considerations must be taken into account when implementing AI in educational settings?

1.5. Objectives of the Introduction Chapter

- To provide a comprehensive background on the role of Artificial Intelligence in education and its evolution within instructional design.
- To clearly articulate the purpose of the study, emphasizing the exploration of AI's impact on enhancing learning experiences through personalized instructional design.
- To underscore the importance of the research in contributing to the understanding of how AI can transform traditional educational practices and improve learning outcomes.
- To outline specific research questions that will guide the investigation and focus the study on key areas of interest related to AI in instructional design.
- To present a clear structure of the chapter, detailing the organization of subsequent sections, including literature review, methodology, findings, discussion, and conclusion, to facilitate reader comprehension.

1.6. Need and Importance of the Study

1. Addressing Diverse Learning Needs

In today's educational landscape, learners come from varied backgrounds and possess different learning styles, preferences, and paces. Traditional instructional methods often struggle to accommodate this diversity, leading to disengagement and suboptimal learning outcomes. This study is essential as it explores how AI-driven instructional design can create personalized learning experiences that cater to individual needs, thereby enhancing student engagement and success.

2. Enhancing Educational Efficiency

Educators face increasing demands to deliver high-quality instruction while managing heavy workloads. The integration of AI tools can automate routine tasks such as grading, content curation, and progress tracking, allowing educators to focus on more strategic aspects of teaching. This study highlights the importance of AI in reducing administrative burdens, thereby improving the overall efficiency of educational processes.

3. Fostering Innovation in Instructional Design

As educational institutions seek to innovate and adapt to the digital age, understanding the role of AI in instructional design becomes crucial. This study contributes to the body of knowledge by examining the latest advancements in AI technologies and their potential to transform conventional pedagogical practices. By investigating these innovations, the research can guide educators and institutions in effectively integrating AI into their instructional frameworks.

4. Informing Policy and Practice

The findings of this study can provide valuable insights for policymakers and educational leaders regarding the implementation of AI in educational settings. By identifying best practices and potential challenges, the research can inform decision-making processes and help develop policies that promote the responsible and equitable use of AI technologies in education.

5. Addressing Ethical Considerations

With the increasing reliance on AI in education, ethical concerns such as data privacy, algorithmic bias, and equity in access must be addressed. This study emphasizes the importance of understanding these ethical implications and developing guidelines to ensure that AI-driven instructional design is implemented in a fair and responsible manner.

6. Contributing to Future Research

The study aims to fill existing gaps in the literature regarding the long-term effectiveness of AI-driven instructional design and its impact across various educational contexts. By providing empirical evidence and insights, this research can serve as a foundation for future studies, encouraging further exploration of AI's role in enhancing educational practices.

1.7. Structure of the Chapter

The chapter is organized into several key sections, including a literature review that examines existing research on AI in instructional design, a methodology section detailing the research design and approach, findings that present the results of the study, and a discussion that interprets the implications of these findings for future educational practices. The conclusion will summarize the key insights and suggest directions for future research in AI-driven instructional design.

2.0. THEORETICAL BACKGROUND OF THE STUDY

The integration of Artificial Intelligence (AI) into instructional design is grounded in several theoretical frameworks that inform the understanding of how technology can enhance learning experiences. This section discusses key theories relevant to AI-driven instructional design, including Constructivism, the Technological Pedagogical Content Knowledge (TPACK) framework, and the Community of Inquiry (CoI) framework.

2.1. Constructivism

Constructivism posits that learners construct their own understanding and knowledge of the world through experiences and reflection (Piaget, 1976; Vygotsky, 1978). This theory emphasizes the importance of active learning, where students engage with content, collaborate with peers, and apply their knowledge in meaningful contexts. AI technologies can facilitate constructivist learning by providing personalized feedback, adaptive learning pathways, and resources tailored to individual learner needs (Chen et al., 2021). By analyzing student interactions and performance data, AI systems can create dynamic learning environments that support the constructivist approach, allowing learners to explore concepts at their own pace and depth.

2.2. Technological Pedagogical Content Knowledge (TPACK)

The TPACK framework, developed by Mishra and Koehler (2006), highlights the interplay between technology, pedagogy, and content knowledge in effective teaching. This framework suggests that educators must integrate these three components to create meaningful learning experiences. AI-driven instructional design aligns with the TPACK framework by enabling educators to leverage technology to enhance pedagogical strategies and content delivery. For instance, AI can assist in identifying students' strengths and weaknesses, allowing educators to tailor their instructional approaches accordingly (Zawacki-Richter et al., 2019). This integration of AI into instructional design not only enhances teaching effectiveness but also fosters a deeper understanding of content among students.

2.3. Community of Inquiry (CoI) Framework

The Community of Inquiry framework, proposed by Garrison, Anderson, and Archer (2000), emphasizes the importance of social, cognitive, and teaching presence in online and blended learning environments. This framework is particularly relevant in the context of AI-driven instructional design, as it underscores the need for collaboration and interaction among learners and educators. AI technologies can enhance the CoI by facilitating communication, providing real-time feedback, and supporting collaborative learning experiences (Garrison et al., 2000). By fostering a sense of community and engagement, AI can contribute to a more effective learning environment that promotes critical thinking and deeper learning.

2.4. Ethical Considerations in AI

As AI technologies become more prevalent in education, ethical considerations surrounding their use must be addressed. Issues such as data privacy, algorithmic bias, and equity in access are critical to ensuring that AI-driven instructional design is implemented responsibly (Holmes et al., 2019). The ethical implications of AI in education necessitate a framework that guides the development and deployment of AI tools, ensuring that they are used in ways that promote fairness and inclusivity (Zawacki-Richter et al., 2019).

2.5. Summary

The theoretical background of this study highlights the relevance of constructivism, the TPACK framework, and the Community of Inquiry framework in understanding the role of AI in instructional design. By grounding the research in these theories, the study aims to explore how AI can enhance personalized learning experiences while addressing the ethical considerations associated with its implementation.

3.0. LITERATURE REVIEW

The integration of Artificial Intelligence (AI) into instructional design has garnered significant attention in recent years, reflecting a growing interest in how technology can enhance educational practices. This literature review synthesizes existing research on AI-driven instructional design, focusing on its applications, benefits, challenges, and ethical considerations.

3.1. Applications of AI in Instructional Design

AI technologies, including machine learning, natural language processing, and predictive analytics, have been increasingly utilized to create personalized learning experiences. These technologies enable educators to adapt content and instructional strategies based on individual student performance and preferences (Holmes et al., 2019). For instance, AI systems can analyze large datasets to identify learning patterns, allowing for the customization of educational materials to meet diverse learner needs (Chen et al., 2021). This adaptability is particularly beneficial in K-12 and higher education settings, where student populations are often heterogeneous (Zawacki-Richter et al., 2019).

3.2. Benefits of AI-Driven Instructional Design

The potential benefits of AI in instructional design are manifold. Research indicates that AI can enhance student engagement by providing real-time feedback and personalized learning pathways (Tuzunkan et al., 2020). By automating routine tasks, such as grading and content curation, AI allows educators to focus more on teaching and less on administrative duties (Liu & Xu, 2020). Furthermore, AI-driven tools can facilitate collaborative learning environments, promoting interaction among students and fostering a sense of community (Garrison et al., 2000).

3.3. Challenges in Implementing AI in Education

Despite the promising applications and benefits of AI, several challenges must be addressed. One significant concern is the ethical implications of AI use in education, particularly regarding data privacy and algorithmic bias (Zawacki-Richter et al., 2019). The reliance on large volumes of student data raises questions about who has access to this information and how it is used (Holmes et al., 2019). Additionally, there is a need for educators to be adequately trained in using AI tools effectively, as a lack of familiarity can hinder the successful integration of these technologies into instructional practices (Chen et al., 2021).

3.4. Ethical Considerations

The ethical considerations surrounding AI in education are critical to its successful implementation. Issues such as data privacy, algorithmic bias, and equity in access must be carefully examined to ensure that AI-driven instructional design is implemented responsibly (Holmes et al., 2019). Researchers emphasize the importance of developing ethical guidelines and frameworks that govern the use of

AI in educational contexts, ensuring that these technologies promote fairness and inclusivity (Zawacki-Richter et al., 2019).

3.5. Gaps in the Literature

While there is a growing body of research on AI-driven instructional design, several gaps remain. Notably, there is a lack of longitudinal studies examining the long-term effectiveness of AI in enhancing student learning outcomes (Tuzunkan et al., 2020). Additionally, more empirical research is needed to explore the impact of AI across various educational settings, including vocational training and adult education (Liu & Xu, 2020). Addressing these gaps will be essential for understanding the full potential of AI in instructional design and its implications for educational equity.

The literature on AI-driven instructional design highlights its potential to transform educational practices through personalization and efficiency. However, ethical considerations and implementation challenges must be addressed to ensure that AI technologies are used responsibly and effectively in educational settings. Future research should focus on filling existing gaps in the literature to provide a comprehensive understanding of AI's role in enhancing learning experiences.

3.6. Limitations Encountered in the Literature Review

Conducting a literature review on AI-driven instructional design reveals several limitations that can impact the comprehensiveness and applicability of the findings. These limitations can be categorized into methodological, contextual, and ethical concerns.

1. Methodological Limitations
   - **Lack of Longitudinal Studies**: One of the most significant gaps in the existing literature is the scarcity of longitudinal studies that assess the long-term effectiveness of AI-driven instructional design on student outcomes. Most research focuses on immediate or short-term effects, which may not provide a complete picture of AI's impact over time (Tuzunkan et al., 2020).
   - **Variability in Research Designs**: The studies reviewed often employ diverse methodologies, including qualitative, quantitative, and mixed-methods approaches. This variability can make it challenging to compare findings across studies and draw generalized conclusions about the effectiveness of AI in instructional design (Liu & Xu, 2020).
   - **Limited Sample Sizes**: Many studies utilize small sample sizes, which can limit the generalizability of the results. Smaller samples may not

adequately represent the broader population of learners, leading to potential biases in the findings (Chen et al., 2021).

2. Contextual Limitations
    - **Diverse Educational Settings**: The literature often focuses on specific educational contexts, such as K-12 or higher education, without adequately addressing the applicability of AI-driven instructional design in other settings, such as vocational training or corporate education. This lack of diversity in contexts can limit the understanding of how AI can be effectively implemented across various educational environments (Zawacki-Richter et al., 2019).
    - **Cultural Considerations**: Many studies do not account for cultural differences that may influence the effectiveness of AI-driven instructional design. Educational practices and learner preferences can vary significantly across cultures, and failing to consider these differences may lead to incomplete or biased conclusions (Holmes et al., 2019).
3. Ethical Limitations
    - **Data Privacy Concerns**: The reliance on large volumes of student data raises significant ethical issues related to data privacy. Many studies do not adequately address how data is collected, stored, and used, which can lead to concerns about the protection of sensitive information (Zawacki-Richter et al., 2019).
    - **Algorithmic Bias**: The potential for AI systems to reproduce or amplify existing biases within educational institutions is a critical concern that is often underexplored in the literature. Studies may not sufficiently address how biases in data can affect the fairness and equity of AI-driven instructional design (Holmes et al., 2019).
4. Theoretical Limitations
    - **Insufficient Theoretical Frameworks**: The literature lacks robust theoretical frameworks that can guide the integration of AI into instructional design. Without a solid theoretical foundation, it becomes challenging to understand the mechanisms through which AI influences learning outcomes and to develop best practices for its implementation (Chen et al., 2021).
    - **Overemphasis on Technology**: Some studies may place too much emphasis on the technological aspects of AI, neglecting the pedagogical implications and the role of educators in the instructional design process. This can lead to a narrow understanding of how AI can enhance teaching and learning (Liu & Xu, 2020).

The limitations encountered in the literature review highlight the need for further research to address existing gaps and challenges in the field of AI-driven instructional design. Future studies should aim to employ longitudinal designs, consider diverse educational contexts, and address ethical concerns to provide a more comprehensive understanding of AI's role in enhancing learning experiences. By acknowledging and addressing these limitations, researchers can contribute to the development of more effective and equitable AI-driven educational practices.

4.0. RESEARCH METHODOLOGY

The research methodology outlined in the document on AI-driven instructional design employs a mixed-methods approach, integrating both quantitative and qualitative methods to provide a comprehensive understanding of how AI enhances learning experiences. Below are the key components of the research methodology:

4.1. Research Design: Mixed-Methods Approach

- **Integration of Quantitative and Qualitative Methods**: The mixed-methods approach combines numerical data with qualitative insights, allowing for a robust examination of the effectiveness of AI in instructional design. This design facilitates a deeper understanding of how AI tools impact student learning outcomes, engagement, and satisfaction (Suresh Babu, C. V. & Adhithya, S., 2023).

4.2. Data Collection Methods

- **Surveys**: Quantitative data is collected through surveys administered to both students and educators. These surveys aim to gather information on the use of AI-driven instructional tools, perceived personalization, levels of engagement, and overall satisfaction with the learning experience (Suresh Babu, C. V. and A. Auroshaa, 2024).
- **Interviews**: Qualitative data is obtained through interviews with educators and instructional designers. These interviews provide rich, contextual insights into the actual use of AI tools, the challenges faced, and the perceived advantages of implementing AI in instructional design (Suresh Babu, C. V. and A. Auroshaa, 2024).
- **Usage Data Analysis**: The research also involves analyzing usage data extracted from Learning Management Systems (LMS) and AI-powered platforms. This data reflects patterns of interaction by students, content usage,

and learning progress, offering a quantitative basis for understanding the impact of AI tools (Suresh Babu, C. V. and A. Auroshaa, 2024).

4.3. Data Analysis Techniques

- **Statistical Tools**: Quantitative data from surveys and usage analytics are analyzed using statistical software to identify trends, correlations, and potential causality between the use of AI-driven instructional design and student outcomes. Descriptive and inferential statistics are employed to quantify the effectiveness of AI tools (Suresh Babu, C. V. & Adhithya, S., 2023).
- **Thematic Coding**: For qualitative data, thematic coding is used to analyze interview transcripts and open-ended survey responses. This process helps identify consistent themes and patterns that describe personalization and efficiency in AI-driven instructional design (Suresh Babu, C. V. and A. Auroshaa, 2024).

4.4. Tools and Technologies

- **AI Algorithms**: The research utilizes various AI algorithms, including machine learning models and natural language processing, to create personalized learning pathways and deliver adaptive content (Suresh Babu, C. V., Anniyappa, C. S, et. al . 2024).
- **Learning Management Systems (LMS)**: LMS are employed to facilitate the deployment of AI-driven instructional tools, track student progress, and collect usage data, which are essential for analyzing the effectiveness of the AI tools (Suresh Babu, C. V. & Adhithya, S., 2023).

Figure 1. AI-Driven instructional design

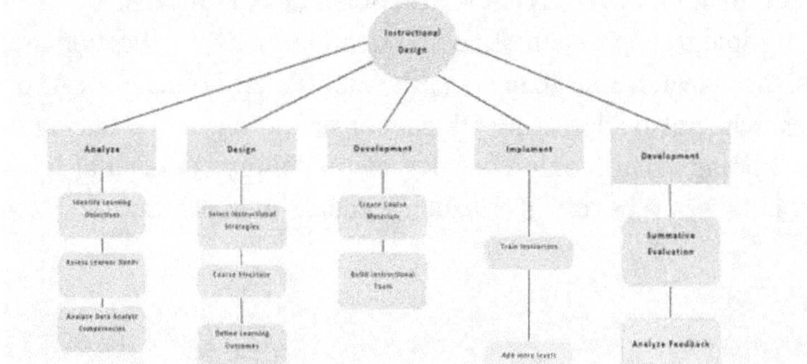

Fig. 1 depicts the Instructional Design process that is divided into five main stages. The initial stage, Analyze, defines the learning objectives and focuses on the need of the learner while analyzing the data analyst competency. In the Design stage, instructional strategies are chosen, course structure is established, and learning outcomes are stated. Development involves creating materials and building instructional tools in the Development stage. In the Implementation stage, the trainers are provided, and necessary adjustments are made. Finally, the cycle goes to the Evaluation, within which summative evaluations take place, with analysis of feedback for further improvement of the instructional materials. The process enters into the last stage toward effective development and delivery of content.

Data Analysis Software: Relevant data analysis software, such as SPSS, R, or NVivo, is used for both quantitative and qualitative data analysis, ensuring rigorous examination of the research questions (Suresh Babu, C. V. and A. Auroshaa, 2024).

4.5. Ensuring Robustness and Relevance of Findings

- **Triangulation of Data**: The research employs triangulation by collecting data from multiple sources (surveys, interviews, and usage data) to provide a comprehensive understanding of the influence of AI on instructional design (Suresh Babu, C. V. and A. Auroshaa, 2024).
- **Ethical Considerations**: Ethical considerations regarding data privacy and bias are addressed to ensure that the AI tools used in the research are transparent and non-discriminatory. This focus on ethics enhances the credibility and integrity of the research findings (Suresh Babu, C. V. & Adhithya, S., 2023).

4.6. Summary

The research methodology employed in this study is designed to provide a thorough examination of AI-driven instructional design through a mixed-methods approach. By integrating quantitative and qualitative data collection and analysis techniques, the research aims to uncover the multifaceted impacts of AI on learning experiences, while also addressing ethical considerations and ensuring the robustness of the findings. This comprehensive methodology is essential for advancing the understanding of AI's role in enhancing educational practices.

5.0. ANALYSIS AND ITS IMPLICATIONS

The analysis in the study on AI-driven instructional design involves both quantitative and qualitative methods, aimed at understanding the effectiveness and impact of AI tools on learning experiences. Below are the key aspects of the analysis conducted and their implications:

5.1. Quantitative Analysis

- **Statistical Analysis of Survey Data**: The quantitative data collected from surveys is analyzed using statistical tools to identify trends, correlations, and potential causality between the use of AI-driven instructional design and student outcomes. Descriptive and inferential statistics are employed to quantify the effectiveness of AI tools in improving learning experiences.

Implications:

- o **Evidence-Based Insights**: The statistical analysis provides evidence-based insights into how AI tools influence student engagement, satisfaction, and learning outcomes. This data can inform educators and policymakers about the effectiveness of AI in instructional design.
- o **Informed Decision-Making**: The findings from the quantitative analysis can guide decisions regarding the adoption and implementation of AI tools in educational settings, ensuring that resources are allocated effectively to enhance learning experiences.

5.2. Qualitative Analysis

- **Thematic Coding of Interview Data**: Qualitative data from interviews is analyzed through thematic coding, which helps identify consistent themes and patterns related to personalization and efficiency in AI-driven instructional design (Suresh Babu, C. V. and A. Auroshaa, 2024). This analysis captures the nuanced experiences of educators and instructional designers.

Implications:

- o **Contextual Understanding**: The qualitative analysis provides a deeper, contextual understanding of how AI tools are perceived and utilized in practice. It highlights the challenges and advantages experienced by educators, which can inform future training and support initiatives.

- o **User-Centric Design**: Insights gained from qualitative data can lead to the development of more user-centric AI tools that better meet the needs of both educators and students, ultimately enhancing the effectiveness of instructional design.

5.3. Triangulation of Data

- **Combining Quantitative and Qualitative Findings**: The study employs triangulation by integrating findings from surveys, interviews, and usage data analysis. This comprehensive approach allows for a more robust understanding of the influence of AI on instructional design.

Implications:

- o **Holistic Perspective**: Triangulation provides a holistic perspective on the impact of AI tools, ensuring that findings are not solely based on one type of data. This enhances the credibility and reliability of the research conclusions.
- o **Comprehensive Recommendations**: The combined insights from different data sources can lead to more comprehensive recommendations for the implementation of AI-driven instructional design, addressing both technical and pedagogical considerations.

Figure 2. Salary by race ethnicity

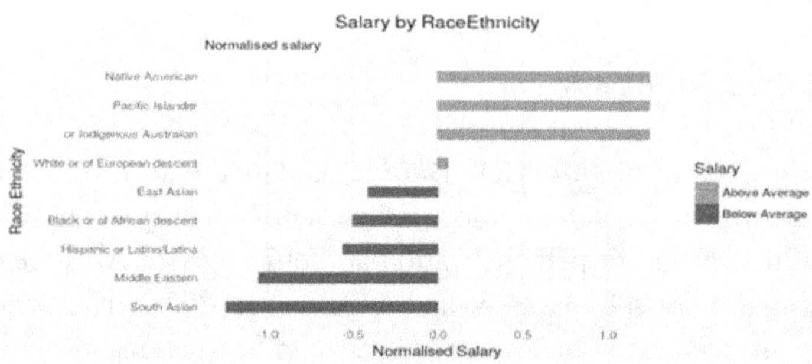

Fig. 2 Salary gap graphs standardised salary values for race and ethnicity group providing vis-a-vis presentation of the data, giving an idea of how some groups are earning above the average salary while others earn below. Native American, Pacific Islanders, and Indigenous Australians are marked along with White or European

white as earning above average are represented by green bars extended to the right side of the figure. These groups have positive normalized salary values; that is, in average they receive more than the stand salary of the overall population.

Figure 3. Distribution by gender

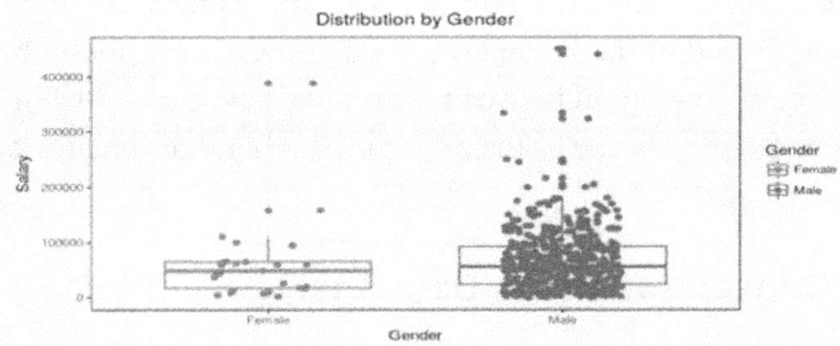

Fig. 3 showed that the box plot comparison of salary distributions between females and males. This used the x-axis to represent gender, and the y-axis showed salary levels from 0 to over 400,000. The data set demonstrated that the salary for women is tightly clustered and has few outliers, while the range of male salaries distribution is broader with multiple outliers. Median Salary for males seems to be higher than that of females, while overall salary variability is larger in males. It can be seen that the distribution of salaries varies significantly between the two genders; the latter group gets more diversified and, in some instances, larger salaries.

Figure 4. Age by gender

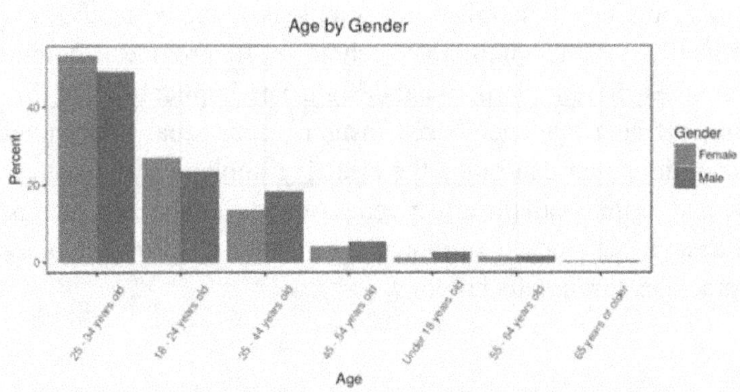

Fig. 4 describes the prevalence of different age groups according to gender, comparing males and females' proportion in each age category. The largest age group in both genders is 25-34 years old, but females' percentage is higher than males. The same pattern occurs with the 18-24 years old group, where females are slightly higher in proportion. In the 35-44 and 45-54 years old groups, males outpace females. But there is less than 10% both for men and women among the younger population below 18 and in the 55 and older age range that has less than 10% but with not an extremely big gap in between; in general, the gap is striking in certain age groups: more females in the younger population ages and males dominate in the middle-aged groups.

5.4. Ethical Considerations in Data Analysis

Addressing Data Privacy and Bias: The analysis also considers ethical implications, particularly regarding data privacy and algorithmic bias. The study emphasizes the importance of transparency and non-discrimination in the use of AI tools (Suresh Babu, C. V. and A. Auroshaa, 2024).

Implications:

- **Responsible AI Implementation**: By addressing ethical considerations, the study advocates for responsible implementation of AI in educational contexts, ensuring that all students have equitable access to learning opportunities.
- **Guidelines for Future Research**: The findings related to ethical concerns can inform the development of guidelines and frameworks for future research and practice in AI-driven instructional design, promoting best practices in data handling and algorithm development.

The analysis conducted in this study employs a mixed-methods approach, combining quantitative and qualitative techniques to provide a comprehensive understanding of AI-driven instructional design. The implications of this analysis are significant, offering evidence-based insights, contextual understanding, and ethical considerations that can guide the effective implementation of AI tools in education. By addressing both the effectiveness and the ethical dimensions of AI in instructional design, the study contributes to the ongoing discourse on enhancing educational practices through technology.

6.0. SUMMARY OF FINDINGS

The findings of the study on AI-driven instructional design can be summarized as follows:

1. **Effectiveness of AI Tools**: The study found that AI-driven instructional design tools significantly enhance student engagement, satisfaction, and learning outcomes. Quantitative data indicated positive correlations between the use of these tools and improved educational experiences.
2. **Personalization of Learning**: AI tools were shown to effectively personalize learning experiences by adapting content to meet individual learner needs and preferences. This personalization was linked to higher levels of student engagement and motivation.
3. **Challenges in Implementation**: Educators reported various challenges in implementing AI-driven tools, including technical difficulties, lack of training, and concerns about data privacy and security. These challenges can hinder the effective use of AI in instructional design.
4. **Perceived Advantages**: Qualitative data from interviews highlighted perceived advantages of AI tools, such as the ability to provide immediate feedback, automate administrative tasks, and support differentiated instruction.
5. **Ethical Concerns**: The study identified critical ethical issues related to data privacy and algorithmic bias. There are concerns that AI systems may inadvertently favor certain groups of students, leading to unequal learning opportunities.
6. **Need for Longitudinal Studies**: The findings pointed to a gap in the literature regarding the long-term effectiveness of AI-driven instructional design. Most existing studies focus on short-term impacts, indicating a need for more longitudinal research.
7. **Integration with Existing Frameworks**: The study emphasized the importance of integrating AI tools within existing instructional design frameworks without displacing traditional pedagogical practices. This integration can enhance the overall effectiveness of educational strategies.
8. **Scalability Issues**: There are challenges related to the scalability of AI-driven instructional design in under-resourced educational settings. The findings suggest that while AI has the potential to address educational inequities, practical implementation remains a concern.
9. **Mixed-Methods Approach Validity**: The use of a mixed-methods approach provided a balanced understanding of the research problem, combining quantitative data with qualitative insights to support the reliability and validity of the findings.

10. **Recommendations for Future Research**: The study calls for further empirical research to explore the impact of AI-driven instructional design across diverse educational contexts, including K-12, higher education, and vocational training.

These findings collectively contribute to a deeper understanding of the role of AI in instructional design and highlight areas for further exploration and improvement in educational practices.

7.0. SUGGESTIONS AND RECOMMENDATIONS

Based on the findings of the study on AI-driven instructional design, the following suggestions and recommendations can be made:

7.1. Suggestions for Implementation

1. **Professional Development for Educators**:
    - o Provide comprehensive training programs for educators to enhance their understanding of AI tools and their effective integration into instructional design. This training should focus on both technical skills and pedagogical strategies.
2. **User-Centric Design of AI Tools**:
    - o Encourage developers of AI-driven instructional tools to adopt a user-centric design approach, ensuring that the tools are intuitive and meet the specific needs of educators and learners. Involve educators in the design process to gather feedback and insights.
3. **Pilot Programs**:
    - o Implement pilot programs in diverse educational settings to test the effectiveness of AI tools before full-scale adoption. This will allow for the identification of potential challenges and the refinement of tools based on real-world feedback.
4. **Data Privacy and Security Protocols**:
    - o Establish clear guidelines and protocols for data privacy and security when using AI tools in educational settings. Ensure that all stakeholders are aware of these protocols to build trust and transparency.

7.2. Recommendations for Future Research

1. **Longitudinal Studies**:

- o Conduct longitudinal studies to assess the long-term impact of AI-driven instructional design on student outcomes. This research should focus on tracking changes in engagement, performance, and satisfaction over time.

2. **Diverse Educational Contexts**:
   - o Expand research to include a variety of educational contexts, such as K-12, higher education, and vocational training. This will help identify how AI tools can be effectively utilized across different learning environments.
3. **Exploration of Ethical Frameworks**:
   - o Investigate the development of ethical frameworks for the use of AI in education, focusing on issues such as data bias, equity, and access. This research should aim to create guidelines that ensure responsible and equitable use of AI technologies.
4. **Impact of AI on Traditional Pedagogy**:
   - o Explore how AI-driven instructional design can complement and enhance traditional pedagogical practices rather than replace them. Research should focus on identifying best practices for integrating AI with existing instructional frameworks.

7.3. Recommendations for Policy Makers

1. **Support for AI Integration**:
   - o Policymakers should provide support and funding for the integration of AI tools in educational institutions, particularly in under-resourced areas. This support can include grants for technology acquisition and training programs.
2. **Establishing Standards for AI Tools**:
   - o Develop and implement standards for the evaluation and selection of AI-driven instructional tools. These standards should ensure that tools are effective, reliable, and aligned with educational goals.
3. **Encouraging Collaboration**:
   - o Foster collaboration between educational institutions, technology developers, and researchers to promote the sharing of best practices and innovations in AI-driven instructional design.
4. **Monitoring and Evaluation**:
   - o Implement systems for ongoing monitoring and evaluation of AI tools in educational settings. This will help assess their effectiveness and make necessary adjustments based on feedback and performance data.

By following these suggestions and recommendations, educational institutions can effectively harness the potential of AI-driven instructional design to enhance learning experiences, improve educational outcomes, and address the challenges associated with implementation. These actions will contribute to a more equitable and effective educational landscape, leveraging technology to meet the diverse needs of learners.

8.0. SCOPE FOR FUTURE RESEARCH

The future research scope for the study on AI-driven instructional design is broad and multifaceted, reflecting the evolving landscape of education and technology. Here are several key areas where further research can be pursued:

1. Longitudinal Studies on Effectiveness
    - **Objective**: Investigate the long-term impacts of AI-driven instructional design on student learning outcomes, engagement, and retention.
    - **Scope**: Conduct studies that track students over multiple years to assess how AI tools influence their academic performance and learning habits over time.
2. Diverse Educational Contexts
    - **Objective**: Explore the application and effectiveness of AI tools across various educational settings, including K-12, higher education, and corporate training.
    - **Scope**: Research should focus on how different demographics, learning environments, and institutional cultures affect the implementation and outcomes of AI-driven instructional design.
3. Ethical Considerations and Frameworks
    - **Objective**: Develop comprehensive ethical guidelines for the use of AI in education, addressing issues such as data privacy, algorithmic bias, and equitable access.
    - **Scope**: Investigate the implications of AI on student data security and the potential for bias in AI algorithms, proposing frameworks that ensure responsible use of technology in educational contexts.
4. Integration with Traditional Pedagogy
    - **Objective**: Examine how AI-driven instructional design can complement and enhance traditional teaching methods rather than replace them.

- **Scope**: Research should identify best practices for integrating AI tools with existing pedagogical frameworks, focusing on how educators can leverage technology to improve instructional strategies.

5. Impact of AI on Teacher Roles
   - **Objective**: Analyze how the integration of AI tools changes the roles and responsibilities of educators in the classroom.
   - **Scope**: Investigate the potential for AI to support teachers in administrative tasks, allowing them to focus more on personalized instruction and student engagement (Suresh Babu, C. V. & Padma R.,2023).
6. Scalability and Accessibility
   - **Objective**: Explore the challenges and solutions related to the scalability of AI-driven instructional design in under-resourced educational settings.
   - **Scope**: Research should focus on how AI can be effectively implemented in diverse socio-economic contexts, ensuring that all students have access to quality educational resources.
7. User Experience and Engagement
   - **Objective**: Study the user experience of both educators and students when interacting with AI-driven instructional tools.
   - **Scope**: Conduct qualitative research to gather insights on how users perceive AI tools, their usability, and the overall impact on learning experiences.
8. AI and Emerging Technologies
   - **Objective**: Investigate the integration of AI with other emerging technologies, such as augmented reality (AR) and virtual reality (VR), in instructional design.
   - **Scope**: Research should explore how these technologies can work together to create immersive and engaging learning experiences that enhance student understanding and retention.
9. Personalization Algorithms
   - **Objective**: Examine the effectiveness of different algorithms used in AI-driven instructional design for personalizing learning experiences.
   - **Scope**: Research should focus on how various machine learning techniques can be optimized to better meet the individual needs of learners, including the analysis of data patterns and learning preferences (Suresh Babu, C. V. & Rohan, B. 2023)..
10. Policy and Governance
    - **Objective**: Explore the role of policy in shaping the adoption and integration of AI in education.

- **Scope**: Research should assess how educational policies can support or hinder the effective use of AI tools, and propose recommendations for policymakers to foster innovation while ensuring ethical standards.

The future research scope for AI-driven instructional design is rich with opportunities to explore the intersection of technology and education. By addressing these areas, researchers can contribute to a deeper understanding of how AI can transform educational practices, enhance learning outcomes, and ensure equitable access to quality education for all students. This ongoing research will be crucial in shaping the future of instructional design in an increasingly digital world

9.0. CONCLUSION

The integration of AI-driven instructional design represents a transformative shift in the educational landscape, offering unprecedented opportunities for personalization, efficiency, and enhanced learning experiences. This study has highlighted the potential of AI technologies to tailor educational content and methodologies to meet the diverse needs of learners, thereby fostering a more engaging and effective learning environment (Suresh Babu, C. V. & Rohan, B. 2023). By leveraging data analytics, machine learning, and natural language processing, educators can create adaptive learning pathways that respond in real-time to student performance, ensuring that each learner receives the appropriate level of support and challenge.

However, the journey towards fully realizing the benefits of AI in instructional design is not without its challenges. Ethical considerations, particularly concerning data privacy and algorithmic bias, must be addressed to ensure that AI systems are implemented responsibly and equitably. Additionally, the resistance to change among educators and institutions highlights the need for comprehensive training and support to facilitate the adoption of AI tools in educational settings.

As we look to the future, it is essential to continue exploring the long-term impacts of AI on educational practices, the scalability of these technologies in diverse contexts, and the ways in which they can complement traditional pedagogical approaches. By conducting further research in these areas, we can develop a holistic understanding of how AI can enhance instructional design while preserving the essential human elements of teaching.

In conclusion, AI-driven instructional design holds the promise of revolutionizing education by making it more personalized, efficient, and accessible. As we navigate the complexities of integrating AI into educational frameworks, it is crucial to prioritize ethical considerations and foster collaboration among educators, technologists, and policymakers. Through these efforts, we can harness the full potential of AI to create innovative and effective learning experiences that empower all students to succeed in an increasingly digital world.

REFERENCES

Anderson, T., & Dron, J. (2018). Three generations of distance education pedagogy. *International Review of Research in Open and Distance Learning*, 12(3), 80–97. DOI: 10.19173/irrodl.v12i3.890

Anderson, T., & Elloumi, F. (2019). *The theory and practice of online learning*. Athabasca University Press.

Bialik, M., Holmes, W., & Fadel, C. (2019). Artificial intelligence in education: Challenges and opportunities. *Center for Curriculum Redesign*. https://curriculumredesign.org

Chen, B., Xu, Y., & Zhang, L. (2021). Personalized adaptive learning using machine learning: A review of the literature. *Computers & Education*, 168, 104196. DOI: 10.1016/j.compedu.2021.104196

Chen, L., Zhang, M., & Huang, Y. (2021). AI-driven personalized learning: A review of the literature. *Educational Technology Research and Development*, 69(1), 1–25. DOI: 10.1007/s11423-020-09815-2 PMID: 33551626

Chen, X., & Xu, J. (2021). Exploring the use of AI-driven educational tools in adaptive learning environments. *Journal of Learning Analytics*, 7(4), 212–229. DOI: 10.18608/jla.2021.7045

Garrison, D. R., Anderson, T., & Archer, W. (2000). Critical inquiry in a text-based environment: Computer conferencing in higher education. *The Internet and Higher Education*, 2(2), 87–105. DOI: 10.1016/S1096-7516(00)00016-6

Greer, J. E., McCalla, G. I., Collins, J. A., & Kumar, V. S. (2016). Intelligent tutoring and adaptive learning environments. In Jonassen, D. J. (Ed.), *The international encyclopedia of education* (6th ed., pp. 272–279). Elsevier., DOI: 10.1016/B978-0-12-809324-5.06052-3

Holmes, W., Luckin, R., & Griffiths, M. (2019). Artificial intelligence in education: Promises and implications for teaching and learning. *International Journal of Artificial Intelligence in Education*, 29(3), 1–16. DOI: 10.1007/s40593-019-00186-5

Huang, R., & Lu, Z. (2019). Adaptive learning and intelligent tutoring systems: Review and perspectives. *Journal of Educational Technology Development and Exchange*, 12(1), 53–69. DOI: 10.18785/jetde.1201.05

Khosravi, H., & Cooper, A. (2019). Personalized adaptive learning: AI approaches in higher education. In *2019 IEEE International Conference on Artificial Intelligence in Education (AIED)* (pp. 59–68). IEEE. https://doi.org/DOI: 10.1109/AIED.2019.00015

Kose, U., & Deperlioglu, O. (2020). Intelligent tutoring systems and AI for personalized learning in higher education. *AI and Learning Review*, 11(3), 149–164. DOI: 10.1007/s40593-019-00185-6

Kose, U., Deperlioglu, O., & Erguvan, E. (2020). Innovative approaches to AI-based adaptive learning systems: Review and future perspectives. *AI and Education Journal*, 15(3), 101–123. DOI: 10.1007/s40593-019-00184-7

Liu, Y., & Xu, F. (2020). Artificial intelligence for education and learning. *AI Open*, 1, 111–119. DOI: 10.1016/j.aiopen.2020.07.002

Liu, Y., & Xu, Y. (2020). The role of artificial intelligence in education: A review. *Journal of Educational Technology & Society*, 23(1), 1–12.

Luckin, R., & Holmes, W. (2019). AI in education: Opportunities, challenges, and ethical considerations. *AI & Society*, 34(3), 537–552. DOI: 10.1007/s00146-019-00849-1

Luckin, R., Holmes, W., & Forcier, L. B. (2016). *Intelligence unleashed: An argument for AI in education*. Pearson.

Luckin, R., Holmes, W., & Griffiths, M. (2019). The impact of AI on education: Current developments and future perspectives. *AI in Education Review*, 13(4), 101–119.

Mishra, P., & Koehler, M. J. (2006). Technological pedagogical content knowledge: A framework for teacher knowledge. *Teachers College Record*, 108(6), 1017–1054. DOI: 10.1111/j.1467-9620.2006.00684.x

Piaget, J. (1976). *The child and reality: Problems of genetic psychology* (Rosin, A., Trans.). Basic Books.

Romero, C., Ventura, S., & García, E. (2020). Data mining techniques applied to education: A review of the literature. *Expert Systems with Applications*, 33(1), 135–146. DOI: 10.1016/j.eswa.2006.04.005

Siemens, G., & Baker, R. S. J. d. (2020). Learning analytics and AI: The path to personalized education. *AI in Education Journal*, 14(2), 98–112.

Siemens, G., Dawson, S., & Lynch, G. (2019). Analytics, AI, and the future of education. *Learning Analytics Review*, 17(1), 1–12.

Siemens, G., Gašević, D., & Dawson, S. (2019). *Preparing for the digital university: A review of the history and current state of distance, blended, and online learning*. Athabasca University.

Suresh Babu, C. V., & Adhithya, S. (2023). ChatGPT and Other Generative AI Tools in Education: Transformative Potential and Ethical Considerations. In Keengwe, J. (Ed.), *Creative AI Tools and Ethical Implications in Teaching and Learning* (pp. 135–152). IGI Global., DOI: 10.4018/979-8-3693-0205-7.ch007

Suresh Babu, C. V., Anniyappa, C. S., & Sastha, B. D. (2024). Unraveling the Inner Workings of Massive Language Models: Architecture, Training, and Linguistic Capacities. In B. Gupta (Ed.), Challenges in Large Language Model Development and AI Ethics (pp. 239-279). IGI Global. DOI: 10.4018/979-8-3693-3860-5.ch008

Suresh Babu, C. V., & Auroshaa, A. (2024). Influence of Data Analysis Tools in Teaching and Learning Economics. In Scott, B., & Fox, M. E. (Eds.), *Cases on Economics Education and Tools for Educators* (pp. 229–248). IGI Global., DOI: 10.4018/978-1-6684-7583-6.ch010

Suresh Babu, C. V., & Padma, R. (2023). Technology Transformation Through Skilled Teachers in Teaching Accountancy. In González-Lezcano, R. (Ed.), *Advancing STEM Education and Innovation in a Time of Distance Learning* (pp. 211–233). IGI Global., DOI: 10.4018/978-1-6684-5053-6.ch011

Suresh Babu, C. V., & Rohan, B. (2023). Evaluation and Quality Assurance for Rapid E-Learning and Development of Digital Learning Resources. In Santally, M., Rajabalee, Y., & Rajputh, R. (Eds.), *Implementing Rapid E-Learning Through Interactive Materials Development* (pp. 139–170). IGI Global., DOI: 10.4018/978-1-6684-4940-0.ch008

Tuzunkan, D., Alper, M., & Ozkul, S. (2020). The impact of artificial intelligence on education: A systematic review. *Computers & Education*, 148, 103788. DOI: 10.1016/j.compedu.2020.103788

Vygotsky, L. S. (1978). *Mind in society: The development of higher psychological processes* (Cole, M., John-Steiner, V., Scribner, S., & Souberman, E., Eds.). Harvard University Press.

Woolf, B. P. (2020). *Building intelligent interactive tutors: Student-centered strategies for revolutionizing e-learning*. Morgan Kaufmann.

Woolf, B. P. (2020). How artificial intelligence is transforming education: Implications for teaching and learning. *Educational Technology Research and Development*, 68(2), 255–277. DOI: 10.1007/s11423-019-09745-8

Woolf, B. P., & McLaren, B. M. (2020). Intelligent learning environments: Bridging the gap between AI research and education. *Journal of Educational Technology & Society*, 23(2), 3–16.

Zawacki-Richter, O., Latchem, C., & Anderson, T. (2019). Systematic review of research on artificial intelligence in higher education: Where are we now and where do we go? *International Journal of Educational Technology in Higher Education*, 16(1), 1–20. DOI: 10.1186/s41239-019-0171-0

Chapter 4
Slow and Connected: Deliberate GenAI-Enhanced Instructional Design Fostering the Essence of Critical Thinking

Ya Ping Hsiao
https://orcid.org/0000-0002-5873-8871
Tilburg University, The Netherlands

Charlotte Elize Wolff
https://orcid.org/0000-0001-6855-4833
University of Iceland, Iceland

Kamakshi Rajagopal
https://orcid.org/0000-0002-9001-5964
European Association of Distance Teaching Universities, The Netherlands

ABSTRACT

This chapter explores the integration of generative artificial intelligence (GenAI) as an innovative educational technology using the framework of slow and relational pedagogy. It proposes a deliberate instructional design aimed at decelerating student learning behaviors to foster deeper engagement with critical thinking about oneself, peers, and instructors. The chapter begins with a scoping review to survey didactic approaches relevant to both slow and relational pedagogy. The research synthesis emphasizes strategies such as reducing the quantity of tasks while increasing the time allocated for them, focusing more on the learning process rather than the final product, and balancing solitary work with collaborative efforts. Building on these insights, the chapter develops an instructional design using a conjecture map (Sandoval, 2014), which includes a hypothesis, design features, embodiments (interventions), mediating processes, and outcomes. This design aims to create a

DOI: 10.4018/979-8-3693-6527-4.ch004

learning environment where students engage in attentive and collaborative thinking with the aid of GenAI.

INTRODUCTION

Scholarly articles have called cautious attention to the potential impact of Generative AI (GenAI), which exhibits remarkable proficiency across various modalities such as texts, images, audios, and videos. The research stresses the importance for higher education to carefully consider the integration of AI while ensuring humans stay 'in the loop' (Lo & Hew, 2023; Perkins, 2023; Rudolph et al., 2023) due to privacy concerns, (digital) hallucinations, unclear usage of copyrighted materials, and biases about gender or other forms of discrimination (Cotton et al., 2024; Farrokhnia et al., 2023; UNESCO, 2023). This reliance on the concept of 'human-in-the-loop' emphasizes the significance of critical thinking, particularly when making evaluative judgments while engaging with AI-integrated learning environments. This involves considerations of how humans assess the quality of iterative prompts, observe AI responses, evaluate the integration of AI-generated content within tasks, and use AI feedback for making evaluative judgments (Bearman et al., 2024).

The potential and impact of GenAI have been studied extensively in higher education. While it is widely accepted that GenAI is more than a mere calculator, it has been positioned as an intelligent tool (Mollick, 2024), an extended mind, and a co-regulator (Lodge, Yang, et al., 2023), as well as a tutor (e.g., Khanmigo by the Khan Academy). We propose positioning GenAI as an educational technology, following Mishra et al. (Mishra et al., 2023), who applied the Technological Pedagogical Content Knowledge (TPACK) framework within the GenAI context . They highlighted its potential to "reduce teacher workload" (p.4), enable "personalized and differentiated learning," offer "real-time feedback and assistance," "identify research topics, generate hypotheses, and summarize literature," and "produce and revise text, allowing learners to focus on the development and expression of ideas rather than the mechanics of writing" (ibid.).

However, a crucial question remains: Do potential uses of GenAI truly engage students in deeper learning approaches that foster critical thinking? We argue that to achieve deep learning in AI-integrated learning environments, appropriate pedagogies and didactics are essential for more deliberate instructional design.

Over the last two decades, higher education has witnessed a trend of increasing class sizes coupled with decreasing capacities and resources for teaching staff, thereby creating challenges to adequately support students (Harland & Wald, 2021; McDonald, 2013; Mulryan-Kyne, 2010). The fast-paced advancement of technologies and the uncertain job market have intensified the demand for speed, efficiency, and output. This demand has seemingly accelerated the acceptance of GenAI in higher education due to its potential for teachers to offload personalized guidance and feedback. However, students in large classes have relatively fewer interactions and exchanges with teachers, which can lead to anonymity and passivity, poor engagement with course content, and reduced motivation to learn (Gibbs & Jenkins, 2014; Mulryan-Kyne, 2010), issues which GenAI can possibly exacerbate (Crawford et al., 2024). Relational factors, such as student-teacher and student-student interaction, care, and empathy all remain crucial for student motivation, engagement, and academic success (Hadad et al., 2020; Sutherland et al., 2019). These factors are studied in the so-called relational pedagogy (Gravett et al., 2024), which has gained significant attention during and since the COVID-19 pandemic.

Among these pressures, there is a growing recognition within higher education for adopting care-centered approaches, guided by the principles of 'slow pedagogy' (Berg & Seeber, 2016; Shaw et al., 2013). Contrary to the emphasis on speed and efficiency, slow pedagogy calls for more deliberate and attentive methods that align with the values of student-centered learning. These approaches correspond with the complexity of critical thinking, emphasizing the importance of pausing, engaging in deep reflection, and fostering meaningful learning experiences (Major & Chiarelott, 2023). Moreover, critical thinking demands cognitive skills such as interpretation, analysis, evaluation, inference, explanation, and self-regulation. To foster these abilities, students must engage in deeper processing without feeling pressured (Collett et al., 2018; Harland et al., 2015). When under pressures such as limited time and heavy workloads, students are more likely to commit academic misconduct, such as plagiarism, cheating, or ghostwriting (Cilliers et al., 2012; Harland et al., 2015; Tomas & Jessop, 2019).

Slow pedagogy and relational pedagogy are both frameworks concerned with how students learn and foster meaningful connections during the learning process. Slow pedagogy (Berg & Seeber, 2016) prioritizes quality over quantity in learning experiences, encouraging deep thinking and engagement with real-world contexts. It emphasizes benefits derived from taking time to ensure students grasp concepts thoroughly, promoting active participation and reflection. Relational pedagogy (Gravett et al., 2024) emphasizes the social-emotional dimensions of learning by underscoring the importance of building strong relationships between educators and students, fostering environments where students feel valued, cared for, and motivated to learn. This approach recognizes that meaningful interactions between teachers and students are pivotal in creating favorable learning environments. Despite their recognized benefits, both slow and relational pedagogies often remain theoretical rather than practical concepts in educational literature. They lack specific didactics (e.g., practical strategies, methods, and techniques) for educators to implement these approaches effectively in classrooms.

This chapter aims to develop a deliberate GenAI-integrated instructional design that supports both cognitive and social-emotional dimensions, drawing upon slow and relational pedagogy. Our goal is to explore how to slow down the students' learning process and engage in student-to-content, student-to-student, student-to-teacher interactions, by fostering critical thinking for effectively handling the heuristics and biases inherent in AI-generated content. In an era when GenAI makes knowledge generation instant and accessible, it is challenging for educators to slow down student thinking processes, to prevent superficial thinking and encourage them not to settle for a seemingly complete, but mediocre and low-quality product. As shown in test results of GenAI-content, their output is capable of excelling on various high-stakes exams and receiving passing grades on writing assignments (Perkins, Roe, Postma, McGaughran, & Hickerson, 2024). It is tempting for students to resort to use GenAI to generate content without making evaluative judgment, which requires careful assessment of prompts and responses and maintaining a critical stance toward AI-generated output.

To illustrate our instructional design approach, we present an example involving a bachelor's program at a research university in the Netherlands, characterized by a large student population. In the graduation phase, students are required to complete a thesis worth 12 ECTS, equivalent to 336 study hours, typically over three months. The purpose of the graduation thesis is to assess whether students can demonstrate the outcomes required for a bachelor's degree at level 6 according to the Dutch Qualification Framework (NLQF, 2022). At this level, students are expected to work independently, apply knowledge and skills acquired during the curriculum, exhibit critical thinking, make evaluative judgments, communicate clearly in both oral and written forms to specialists and non-specialists, and further develop their learning skills. Students are also required to take full ownership of their theses.

Given the large number of students in some programs, a small group supervision model known as thesis circles has been adopted as a didactic approach (Rajagopal et al., 2021; Romme & Nijhuis, 2002). While thesis circles can help address the capacity challenges faced by supervision staff, the literature highlights several issues. First, supervising a diverse student body is challenging, especially when supervisors lack adequate support or didactic training. Indeed, supervision pedagogy is less established for bachelor's and master's theses compared to PhDs (Feather et al., 2014). Second, students often enter the thesis phase without having developed the necessary skills or attitudes earlier in their curriculum (Todd et al., 2004). Third, the use of Artificial Intelligence (AI) enables students to seek assistance undetected, making it increasingly difficult for thesis examiners to identify academic misconduct (Kenwright, 2024).

To sum up, our three research questions are:

1. Which didactic approaches relevant to slow and relational pedagogy can encourage slow thinking while actively and socially engaging students in higher-order critical thinking (e.g., evaluative judgment)?
2. When integrating Generative AI to instructional design, how do teachers use deliberate practices towards a) the formulation of learning outcomes, b) the design of teaching and learning activities, and c) the development of assessment strategies?
3. How can we apply deliberate practices to the design of undergraduate thesis circles?

To address the research questions, we first carried out a literature review focused on research related to the concepts, theories, and models central to the research questions to construct a clear conceptual framework (RQ1). Secondly, to develop an instructional design strategy based on the conceptual framework, we developed a conjecture map, as proposed by Sandoval (2014), consisting of a hypothesis, design features (Boelens et al., 2020), mediating processes, and outcomes (RQ2). Third, we applied this conjecture map to a thesis circle, a collaborative thesis supervision approach involving a small group of students, as a case study (RQ3).

METHODS AND FINDINGS

This section is organized based on the three methods and their findings.

Literature Review

Since our research questions are explorative in nature and involve multiple topics, we use Arksey and O'Malley (2005)'s scoping study method to carry out the literature review. The focus of our scoping review is to summarize and synthesize research findings. Based on our expertise in educational science and technology and education psychology, we identified relevant keywords in the university's WorldCat catalogue to search literature sources from bibliographic databases, resulting in the compilation of 105 sources (see Table 1).

Table 1. Overview of search terms and WorldCat results

Search terms	WorldCat results
kw:("slow pedagogy" OR "slow teaching" OR "slow learning" OR "slow thinking") AND ti: ("higher education")	15
kw:("relational pedagogy" OR "student-teacher interaction") AND ti: ("higher education")	38
kw:("generative artificial intelligence" OR "large language models" OR "ChatGPT" AND "critical thinking" OR "evaluative judgment") AND ti:("higher education")	62
Total	105

We based the inclusion and exclusion criteria on our research questions. We only focused on journal articles published in English and refined them after reviewing the abstracts and keywords of the sources. Table 2 shows our inclusion and exclusion criteria.

Table 2. Inclusion and exclusion criteria

Inclusion Criteria	Exclusion Criteria
Journal articles	Not journal articles
English language	Since 2000 – June 24th 2024
Focus on teaching and learning in higher education	

Table 3 outlines the selected 45 sources. The sources are listed in Appendix 1. Because of only two sources on slow pedagogy, we used one source, Collett et al. (2018), with more citations to find seven references cited in Collett et al. (2018) based on backward snowballing and three references that cited Collett et al. (2018) based on forward snowballing.

Table 3. After applying selection criteria

Search terms	Selected references
kw:("slow pedagogy" OR "slow teaching" OR "slow learning" OR "slow thinking") AND ti: ("higher education")	2
Snowballing based on Collett et al. (2018)	10
kw:("relational pedagogy" OR "student-teacher interaction") AND ti: ("higher education")	13
kw:("generative artificial intelligence" OR "large language models" OR "ChatGPT" AND "critical thinking" OR "evaluative judgment") AND ti:("higher education")	20
Total	45

In charting the data (Arksey & O'Malley, 2005), we coded the abstracts based on our research questions and identified 13 code groups. These groups were then classified into four categories: (i) contextual factors (4. External crisis; 10. Neoliberalism), (ii) cognitive and non-cognitive student learning outcomes (1. Affective domain; 8. Outcomes OR goals), (iii) didactics (2. Authentic; 5. Feedback design; 9. Instructional design), and (iv) technology (3. Educational technologies AND GenAI; 6. GenAI negative impact; 7. GenAI positive impact). The code groups and corresponding codes are listed in Appendix 2. These groups were further classified as dimensions of slow and relational pedagogy aimed at promoting critical thinking, as shown in Table 4.

Findings of Literature Review

Drawing from the grounded quotations (texts coded, see Appendix 2), we have synthesized the code groups into four themes as design features for conjecture mapping:

1. Systematic institutional support for teacher professionalization: While using generative AI (GenAI) may be relatively straightforward, integrating AI literacy and critical thinking skills into regular instructional design is a significant challenge that requires institutional support for teacher professional development (Maheshwari, 2023). As tasks increasingly rely on non-critical machines, the need to emphasize critical thinking skills and a renewed focus on the humanities becomes more urgent. This shift demands greater attention to the purpose of higher education, the enhancement of learning outcomes, and the establishment of rigorous criteria and standards (Essien et al., 2024; Guest & Riegler, 2022; Royer, 2024). Additionally, collaborative approaches to instruction that engage students in shared critical thinking are essential. Slow and relational pedagogy offer potential pathways for integrating these skills and dispositions, but they necessitate the professionalization of teachers in both areas.
2. Teachers' own experience with educational technologies and professionalization: Without firsthand experience with educational technologies, teachers often struggle to effectively integrate these tools into their instructional design. A study by van den Berg (2018) highlighted this issue, showing that teachers who participated in a workshop on blended learning frequently found the material difficult to follow. They exhibited behaviors similar to those of their students, such as getting lost while searching for course materials and arriving at on-campus sessions unprepared. To design effective instructional strategies using GenAI, it is crucial that teachers first experience and reflect on using these tools themselves. Without this experience, they risk falling into a state of unconscious

competence, where they assume there is no need to learn the functionalities of these tools or develop the critical thinking necessary for their ethical and responsible use. Like their students, teachers may also face challenges such as information overload or difficulty in assessing the credibility of GenAI-generated content (Xu et al., 2024). Firsthand experience with these technologies enables teachers to better anticipate their students' challenges and collaborate with them to develop effective strategies for managing these issues.

3. Slow pedagogy focuses on the ethics of care: Tronto's ethics of care (2020; 1998) provides a crucial framework for slow pedagogy, encompassing five dimensions: care about with attentiveness, care for with responsibility, caregiving with competence, care receiving with responsiveness, and care with iterations that foster the development of habits and patterns over time. Although the sources reviewed mainly focus on teacher professionalization, these dimensions can also be applied to instructional design, illustrating the true essence of slowness in didactics. To ensure the effectiveness of any didactic innovation, it should be integrated with this care framework (Collett et al., 2018; Kapur, 2016). One example of such an innovative intervention is the design of productive failure (Reynaud & Northcote, 2015). This approach engages students in an iterative and deeper thinking process, helping them gradually understand the quality criteria and standards required by the course learning outcomes. Effective implementation of productive failure requires teachers to be proficient in their subject matter, attentive to students' backgrounds and needs, clear about the expectations for both teacher and student roles in shared responsibility, and committed to dedicating course time to iterative processes. Another key concept in slow pedagogy is diffractive thinking (Bozalek, 2017; Collett et al., 2018; van den Berg et al., 2018; Verster et al., 2018; Verster et al., 2024). This approach emphasizes understanding how different elements or factors interact and influence each other during processes of change and development. Instead of merely analyzing components in isolation (i.e., more than reflective thinking), diffractive thinking involves examining how these elements interfere with and affect one another within specific contexts, referred to as "material configurations." Applying diffractive thinking in instructional design encourages the development of tasks within complex systems, promoting the consideration of multiple perspectives and factors simultaneously. This approach is essential for fostering critical thinking and a deeper understanding of the interconnected nature of issues, which remain human-must-in-loop activities (Daugherty & Wilson, 2018).
4. Relational pedagogy emphasizes co-creation and quality of interaction: As highlighted by leading research in AI and education (Lodge, Howard, et al., 2023; Mollick, 2024; UNESCO, 2023), the rise of disruptive technologies

necessitates that higher education teachers reconsider their traditional role as mere transmitters of knowledge (Essien et al., 2024). Instead, they should adopt a more collaborative and participatory approach, working with students to co-create strategies for the responsible and ethical use of GenAI. This co-creation process is rooted in relational pedagogy, which involves building trust and relationships with students by clearly communicating instructional intentions, fostering opportunities for students to share their knowledge and experiences in class, and connecting the curriculum to students' interests and perspectives (Bell, 2022; Su & Wood, 2023).

5. Integrating GenAI into education requires a holistic design: Both slow and relational pedagogy emphasize a holistic approach to instructional design, integrating various dimensions to create meaningful learning experiences (e.g.,Collett et al., 2018; Okoye, 2023). Simply having good intentions, such as aiming for critical thinking as a learning outcome or encouraging the use of GenAI in social interactions (like during small group discussions), is not enough. The dimensions outlined in Table 4 can sometimes conflict with each other. For instance, a teacher might adopt a specific strategy to promote critical thinking when integrating GenAI tools, believing that students should be challenged with complex, open-ended questions. However, students might resist this approach, preferring more straightforward tasks, like multiple-choice exams, that allow them to stay within their comfort zone. In such cases, instructors must balance or prioritize these conflicting needs by actively listening to students' perspectives and concerns. In the example of student resistance due to a lack of experience with complex, open-ended questions, it is essential for instructors to first address and understand this resistance with attentiveness. Only after doing so should they proceed with their instructional goals for fostering critical thinking. Making evaluative judgments that take all dimensions into account is a complex task. Therefore, it requires an *iterative* process where teachers engage in reflective and adaptive thinking.

Table 4. Deliberate practices based on integration of slow and relational pedagogy

Slow Pedagogy	Relational Pedagogy	Promote Critical Thinking When Integrating GenAI
Caring about with attentiveness	● Student needs ● Curriculum relevance ● Social interaction	● Analyze how students' perceptions and prior experiences with GenAI influence their learning within the shared social context. ● Identify student needs for developing critical thinking ● Analyze how each interaction type can stimulate critical thinking and how to sequence them (e.g., student-teacher, student-content, student-student,)
Caring for with responsibility	● Instructional intentions relevant to student lives and future goals ● Shared responsibility	● Emphasize the development of critical thinking skills over merely producing written deliverables, and clearly define the criteria and standards for evaluating critical thinking ● Collaborate with students to create activities and assessments that connect to their backgrounds and interests, making the learning process more relevant and engaging ● Help students recognize gaps in their understanding by incorporating strategies like productive failure and desirable difficulty, which challenge them to grow ● Prompt students to reflect on the impact of their choices, such as the importance of participating in formative assessments, to uncover areas where they may lack understanding
Caregiving with competence	● Strategic arrangement of different modes ● Active instructional strategies ● Formative assessment and feedback	● Choose the most effective mode (online, on-campus, or hybrid) for specific activities to optimize the integration of GenAI tools in fostering critical thinking ● Engage students in critical thinking through methods such as thought-provoking questioning, case-based or problem-based learning, and debates, leveraging GenAI to enhance these activities ● Regularly assess student learning through formative assessments, using the insights gained to provide targeted feedback that helps students refine their critical thinking skills
Care receiving with responsiveness	● Multiple perspectives ● Adaptable instructions ● Shared understanding of quality	● Incorporate diverse perspectives based on students' varied backgrounds and experiences to encourage diffractive thinking, using GenAI to present and analyze multiple viewpoints ● Continuously refine instructional approaches based on insights from formative assessments and student feedback, ensuring that the integration of GenAI remains responsive to students' evolving needs ● Collaboratively establish clear criteria for what constitutes high-quality work in the context of critical thinking, (including the underpinning reasons for these criteria) ensuring that both students and instructors are aligned on expectations and outcomes.

CONJECTURE MAPPING

Following Sandoval's approach (2014), we begin by developing a high-level conjecture based on the scoping review and the resulting conceptual framework. Next, we create a detailed map (see Figure 1) that illustrates how this conjecture is refined into specific design features (Boelens et al., 2020) and embodied in concrete interventions. These interventions include various elements such as tools, activities, participant structures, and communication practices. It is important to note that the terms "design features" and "embodiments" are defined slightly differently from how Sandoval (2014) and Boelens et al. (Boelens et al., 2020) use them, as further explained in subsequent sections.

Following this, we describe the short-term mediating processes expected to arise from the specific features of the design, including our predictions regarding how these processes would lead to the desired long-term outcomes of the intervention. In contrast to the original conjecture mapping framework, which does not include institutional support or the continuous professional development of teachers in didactics and technology (Collett et al., 2018; Pinochet et al., 2023; van den Berg et al., 2018), we consider both elements to be essential. Based on our literature review findings, we regard these elements as fundamental to the design.

Results of Conjecture Mapping

High-Level Conjecture

A high-level conjecture is a guiding principle that shapes the overall design, derived from synthesizing review findings. It involves hypotheses about how this principle influences the learning environment and how different design features work together to produce specific outcomes. In our case, we hypothesize that integrating GenAI to enhance critical thinking should begin with a carefully planned instructional design grounded in slow and relational pedagogy. This approach creates a caring, interactive learning environment where trust and shared responsibility are emphasized. In such an environment, students' needs—especially the development of critical thinking—are prioritized and addressed. Teachers are equipped to effectively support and guide student thinking and interactions.

Based on this hypothesis, we formulated the following guiding conjecture for our conjecture map: A deliberate GenAI-enhanced instructional design fosters students' critical thinking. This conjecture is drawn from a synthesis of three key areas of literature: slow pedagogy, relational pedagogy, and critical thinking pedagogy.

Design Features

Our design features are grounded in the high-level conjecture and are articulated as specific design principles for the learning environment. These principles are drawn from the themes and dimensions outlined in Table 4 and can be categorized into three areas: activity and task structures, participant structures, and discursive practices (Sandoval, 2014). According to Sandoval (2014), activity and task structures define what students are expected to do, including their goals and criteria. Participant structures outline the roles and responsibilities of both the teacher and students, specifying their expected actions within activities and tasks. Boelens et al. (2020) explain that discursive practices establish the norms and expectations for how teachers and students should *engage* in these activities and tasks.

Embodiments

Embodiments refer to concrete *interventions* supported by the codes in Appendix 2. These embodiments also include tools and materials, either specifically developed or modified for the design or sourced from existing resources suitable for the activity, task, and participant structures. Our design requires tools such as the learning management system (e.g., Canvas) and university-licensed GenAI (e.g., Microsoft Co-pilot). Additionally, this design needs the development of a survey and selected exemplars, as well as the use of existing resources like Project Zero's Thinking Routine Toolbox with a number of well-described activities for various thinking levels (Harvard Graduate School of Education, 2022) and critical thinking criteria and guiding questions that define what constitutes quality thinking and lead students to recognize own short-cut thinking (e.g., heuristics and cognitive bias) and overcome bias (Paul & Elder, 2006).

The interventions in activity and task structures are to design tasks with personal and societal relevance (authenticity), to make students aware of the difficulty and complexity of the task, based on the notion of productive failure (Hawe et al., 2021; Reynaud & Northcote, 2015), blended learning to balanceappropriate modes for using or not using GenAI (Islam et al., 2022), and mix of individual and group work so that GenAI integration allows personalized learning and social interactions within small groups (Pinochet et al., 2023; Verster et al., 2024). Various formative assessments (e.g., questioning, justifications on decision-making) and feedback activities are designed for each mode: individual/online/self-feedback, group/on-campus/peer-feedback, individual/online/teacher-feedback. Formative assessment should be sequenced and progressed in a way that both the teacher and students can experience their growth over time. Formative feedback can be used by students to improve their performance on the subsequent formative assessment task.

The interventions in participant structures are co-creative GenAI learning activities between the teacher and students (Bell, 2022; Su & Wood, 2023), critical thinking routines to progress from lower to higher thinking skills (Essien et al., 2024; Marbun, 2023), and feed-forward beyond the teacher's or peers' comments (Carless, 2022).

Mediating Processes

Mediating processes serve as a bridge between what students do (embodiments) and the results they achieve (outcomes). These processes represent the short-term outcomes that students experience when they participate in interventions. According to Boelens et al. (2020), there are three types of mediating processes:

Participant artifacts are the products that students create as a result of their activities. In our design, students begin by self-assessing their needs and levels of critical thinking and AI literacy. They then use GenAI to generate initial content and apply critical thinking criteria to evaluate GenAI's responses.

Observable interactions are various types of interactions that occur due to the way the activity, task, and participant structures are designed. Before the class, individual interactions with GenAI focus on content creation. Students prepare their elaborations based on their understanding of GenAI-generated content. During the class, group interactions center on comparing experiences with GenAI and its generated responses (Pinochet et al., 2023). These comparisons should be based on the critical thinking criteria provided by the teacher. For example, when each group brings GenAI-generated research questions to in-class discussions, they should assess what constitutes good prompts and effective research questions using the SMART (specific, manageable, attainable, relevant, time-bound) formulation. After the class, students use insights gained from group comparisons to re-examine how to integrate different components based on specific objectives. They should justify why certain content is included in the final product (Maheshwari, 2023).

Participant experiences refer to how both teachers and students feel and what they experience within the learning environment. Students overcome challenges during the learning process, such as addressing formative feedback to progress toward the final product (Reynaud & Northcote, 2015). They are able to recognize and articulate their growth through self-reflection. The teacher and students ensure mutual understanding through co-creation dialogues and analysis of formative assessment results. Without this mutual understanding, students may not meet the criteria set for formative assessment. These findings not only provide feedback on what students have or haven't learned effectively, but also guide the teacher in improving instructional strategies (Collett et al., 2018).

Outcomes

Cognitive outcomes: Students will develop a critical mindset, enabling them to use heuristics to explore subjects while simultaneously recognizing major types of cognitive biases when quickly generating solutions. They will also build feedback literacy across three main stages (Carless & Winstone, 2023):

- Feed-up: Understanding goals and needs.
- Feedback: Engaging with information and dialogue to make sense of it.
- Feed-forward: Using feedback to enhance performance on subsequent tasks.

Behavioral outcomes: Students will establish a routine of critical thinking, particularly when expressing ideas through writing. This involves thinking carefully before writing and rethinking after interacting with others and GenAI, based on feedback and discussion. They are also expected to take the initiative in seeking feedback and determining how to use it effectively, ensuring that their work aligns with their goals and context.

Affective outcomes: Students will develop resilience, allowing them to maintain high-quality work as they progress toward the final product. This includes a willingness to engage seriously with formative assessments and to continuously improve their work based on feedback. They will also learn to resist cognitive biases, ensuring ethical and responsible use of GenAI. By taking ownership of their decisions, they will be able to identify the consequences and make appropriate choices in their work.

Figure 1. Design conjecture for deliberate practices to integrate GenAI

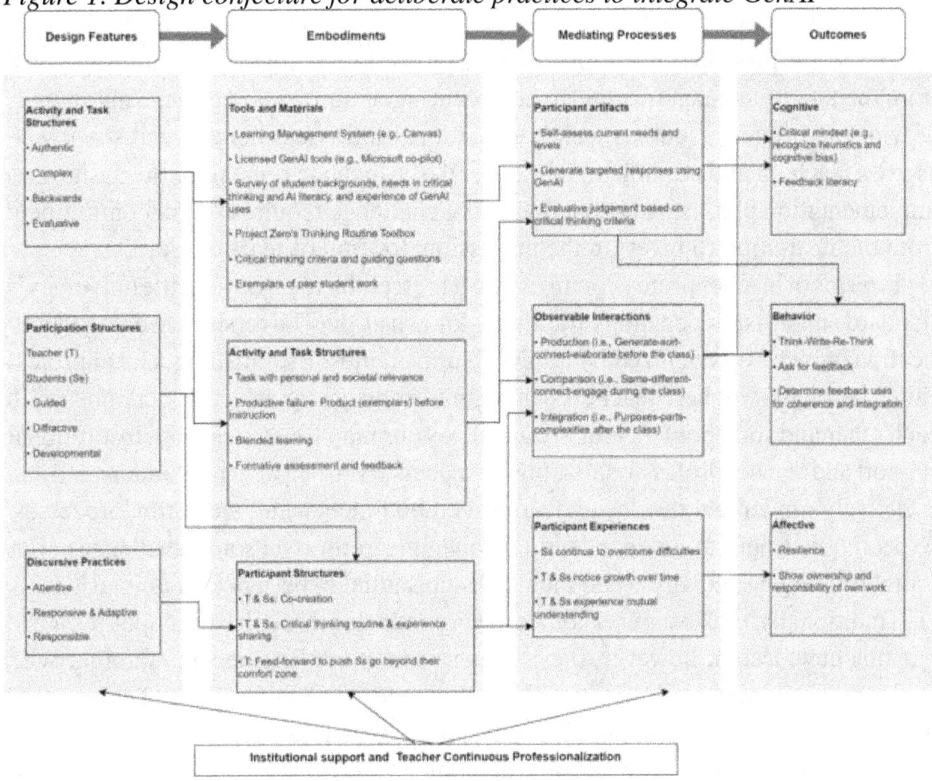

An Example

This example demonstrates how our deliberate practices can be effectively applied to thesis circles in the final projects of bachelor's programs. Thesis circles are small groups for thesis supervision, designed to address contextual constraints such as large class sizes, high demands for accountability, and efficiency. Our design also tackles three challenges outlined in the Introduction (see pp. 3-4): insufficient supervision didactic expertise, limited students' prior knowledge and skills, and difficulty detecting academic misconduct. We focus on illustrating how different *interventions in the embodiments* of the conjecture map might integrate within this context, aiming to solidify our speculative conjectures about the design of deliberate practices.

Institutional Support and Teacher Professionalization

The design process starts with obtaining institutional support, including approval from the faculty management team and securing an innovation grant. This support provides additional resources such as educational and assessment specialists, as well as extra teaching and administrative staff, all of which are crucial for the design and implementation phases. Addressing the first challenge requires a firm commitment from the institution to invest in the professionalization of teaching staff.

In terms of teacher professionalization, it is essential to go beyond the university's standard supervision pedagogy training—known as the University Teaching Qualification, which is recognized by all Dutch universities. Establishing a local professional community where teachers can regularly engage in reflective dialogues with each other and stakeholders is also crucial. As our map illustrates, both institutional support and teacher professionalization are necessary to help teachers understand and effectively implement the design features, embodiments, and mediating processes. Expecting teachers to independently resolve uncertain issues and challenges after initial training, especially when they lack substantial experience, is unrealistic.

Traditionally, thesis supervision has been conducted through on-campus sessions. For this new design, however, thesis supervisors must first become familiar with the blended learning environment. To facilitate this, a Canvas site has been created where all thesis supervisors can experience the blended learning community. Thesis supervisors continue to have periodic on-campus meetings with their thesis coordinator or program academic director. When they encounter specific issues, they can post questions on the discussion board, organized by theme. Thesis coordinators then select certain thematic questions for discussion in on-campus meetings. Through this firsthand experience, supervisors gain a clearer understanding of what students will experience.

Tools and Materials

Each program sets up a thesis course site on Canvas, where thesis circle groups are created. These sites contain both shared and group-specific materials. The shared materials include infographics on critical thinking criteria—such as purpose, clarity, accuracy, precision, relevance, depth, breadth, and logic (Paul & Elder, 2006)—as well as modified worksheets based on Project Zero's Thinking Routine Toolbox (Harvard Graduate School of Education, 2022).

To assess student AI literacy, a modified version of the AI Literacy Questionnaire (AILQ) (Ng et al., 2024) is used. This survey is well-suited to our design as it covers cognitive, behavioral, affective, and ethical domains, all of which are closely aligned with our goals and outcomes. Additionally, to gauge students' needs for critical thinking development, guiding questions based on Paul and Elder (2006) are converted into statements for a self-assessment questionnaire, using a Likert scale ranging from 1 (Strongly disagree) to 5 (Strongly agree).

Students are required to complete both surveys before attending the thesis course.

Activity and Task Structures

To ensure personal relevance, the teacher first analyzes the results of the AILQ survey and the critical thinking questionnaire before the thesis circles begin. Based on these analyses, students are referred to relevant AI literacy materials offered by the university. In terms of critical thinking, the teacher identifies students' weaknesses from their responses and selects appropriate modified worksheets. Additionally, the teacher should explain the value of writing a thesis in terms of student development and employability. Often, the requirement to write a thesis at the exit level is taken for granted, without clear justification for this choice.

To enhance the societal relevance of the thesis, it is important to integrate an authentic problem into the thesis work, rather than merely identifying a gap in the literature as is common in conventional theoretical theses. Students can investigate a real problem from external organizations, with the institution providing appropriate support. Research suggests that authenticity motivates students to put more effort into their work, reducing the likelihood of resorting to ghostwriting or misusing GenAI tools (Luo, 2024).

For bachelor's students, writing a thesis—often their first major academic paper—can feel abstract and overwhelming, despite the availability of thesis manuals with guidelines, suggestions, and assessment criteria. Students may also struggle to accurately assess their ability to complete a thesis that meets required criteria and standards. The principle of productive failure suggests that students be given a completed thesis from the past and asked to self-assess their current status and estimate the gap between their initial understanding and the finished product.

In the context of blended learning, three types of "blending" are utilized: before-during-after, individual-group, and with-without GenAI. Each thesis circle meeting focuses on a specific chapter of the student's thesis, such as the introduction, literature review, or research method. Before each meeting, students individually use GenAI to generate content, like a list of references relevant to their thesis topic. During the meeting, students collaborate in small groups to share their GenAI experiences and apply critical thinking criteria to evaluate the lists, selecting trustworthy references. Each group then explains the reasoning behind their decisions, such as how the context of the thesis problem informed their use of the critical thinking criterion of relevance when selecting references. They also consider how the problem context should shape their prompting strategy. After the meeting, each student documents a prompting strategy learned from the group discussion, explains why the selected references meet critical thinking criteria, and seeks additional references from other platforms.

Additionally, the teacher provides GenAI-generated thesis sections and uses critical thinking criteria to illustrate potential issues, such as bias or how the content could be flagged as academic misconduct. The teacher then emphasizes the importance of ethical and responsible use of GenAI in the thesis writing process and in producing quality academic work.

The teacher's formative assessment design should include both written and oral components, with an emphasis on encouraging students to elaborate on specific content (e.g., ensuring students demonstrate a deeper understanding when using GenAI) and justify their decisions (e.g., showing how different parts of the thesis align and integrate to achieve the thesis's overall purpose) across various deliverables. While students may use GenAI for formative assessment and feedback on draft work, they should remain aware of privacy concerns, such as avoiding the upload of sensitive materials like interview scripts.

Participant Structures

When integrating GenAI, there are two types of co-creation activities with a selected group of students: one before and one after the main activities. The co-creation that occurs beforehand focuses on understanding students' needs and preferences. For instance, students might find it unnecessary to learn generic prompting skills because they can acquire these on their own, but they may struggle with understanding critical thinking criteria and the ethical and responsible use of GenAI. This feedback allows the teacher to tailor the content to address areas where students need the most support.

The co-creation that takes place afterwards focuses on gathering student feedback on the design and effectiveness of the activities in helping them achieve the learning outcomes, as well as suggestions for improvement in the future. For example, students might find certain formative assessment assignments unclear, both for individual and group work. Any confusion in assignment descriptions can be identified and addressed during this post-activity co-creation, leading to improvements for the next iteration.

To build critical thinking routines, modified worksheets from Project Zero's Thinking Routine Toolbox should be incorporated into blended learning activities. These worksheets provide students with clear purposes and structured procedures to guide their thinking. It's essential that students clearly see how they are applying critical thinking when using GenAI and understand how this critical approach contributes to ethical and responsible use of the technology.

The interaction between different thesis sections and the use of GenAI adds complexity to activity and task design. This complexity is further heightened when students must address multiple critical thinking criteria simultaneously. The teacher is responsible for guiding students through this increasing complexity, as authentic thesis problems require students to manage and solve intricate challenges.

For instance, a well-crafted problem statement must meet several criteria: it should have a defined purpose, be clearly formulated, contain accurate and specific information, and be relevant to the problem context. Additionally, it should reflect a thorough understanding of the issue, consider multiple perspectives, and present information in a logical sequence. The teacher's role is to help students navigate these complexities to develop a robust and effective thesis.

CONCLUSION

This chapter aims to highlight the complexity involved in creating a comprehensive instructional design and the deliberate practices necessary for its success. These practices demand not only institutional support and commitment but also ongoing improvement from educators. Our contribution to the existing conjecture mapping method is to integrate these practices into the design to enhance its feasibility.

GenAI tools can often lead students to rely on shortcut thinking and heuristic approaches. To counteract this, it is essential to slow down student thinking through genuine attention to their needs and multiple interactions throughout the process. While these principles are *not* new, effective education inherently involves caring for students and building strong relationships with them.

Finally, we would like to emphasize that micro-level interventions alone may not achieve their intended outcomes without considering various design dimensions. Introducing GenAI tools into instructional activities without addressing students' needs or engaging with them is insufficient for fostering meaningful learning.

ACKNOWLEDGEMENTS

We would like to express our gratitude to Sofie Vandenbogaerde for generously sharing her insights and ideas with us.

In writing this piece, the authors used ChatGPT (Version September 4th, 2024) to improve English language. Full responsibility for the contents lies with the authors.

REFERENCES

Arksey, H., & O'Malley, L. (2005). Scoping studies: Towards a methodological framework. *International Journal of Social Research Methodology*, 8(1), 19–32. DOI: 10.1080/1364557032000119616

Bearman, M., Tai, J., Dawson, P., Boud, D., & Ajjawi, R. (2024). Developing evaluative judgement for a time of generative artificial intelligence. *Assessment & Evaluation in Higher Education*, 49(6), 1–13. DOI: 10.1080/02602938.2024.2335321

Bell, K. (2022). Increasing undergraduate student satisfaction in Higher Education: The importance of relational pedagogy. *Journal of Further and Higher Education*, 46(4), 490–503. DOI: 10.1080/0309877X.2021.1985980

Berg, M., & Seeber, B. (2016). *Slow professor: Challenging the culture of speed in the academy*. University of Toronto Press. DOI: 10.3138/9781442663091

Boelens, R., De Wever, B., & McKenney, S. (2020). Conjecture mapping to support vocationally educated adult learners in open-ended tasks. *Journal of the Learning Sciences*, 29(3), 430–470. DOI: 10.1080/10508406.2020.1759605

Bozalek, V. (2017). Slow scholarship in writing retreats: A diffractive methodology for response-able pedagogies. *South African Journal of Higher Education*, 31(2). Advance online publication. DOI: 10.20853/31-2-1344

Carless, D. (2022). From teacher transmission of information to student feedback literacy: Activating the learner role in feedback processes. *Active Learning in Higher Education*, 23(2), 143–153. DOI: 10.1177/1469787420945845

Carless, D., & Winstone, N. (2023). Teacher feedback literacy and its interplay with student feedback literacy. *Teaching in Higher Education*, 28(1), 150–163. DOI: 10.1080/13562517.2020.1782372

Cilliers, F. J., Schuwirth, L. W. T., & van der Vleuten, C. P. M. (2012). A model of the pre-assessment learning effects of assessment is operational in an undergraduate clinical context. *BMC Medical Education*, 12(1), 9. DOI: 10.1186/1472-6920-12-9 PMID: 22420839

Collett, K. S., van den Berg, C. L., Verster, B., & Bozalek, V. (2018). Incubating a slow pedagogy in professional academic development: An ethics of care perspective. *South African Journal of Higher Education*, 32(6), 117–136. DOI: 10.20853/32-6-2755

Cotton, D. R. E., Cotton, P. A., & Shipway, J. R. (2024). Chatting and cheating: Ensuring academic integrity in the era of ChatGPT. *Innovations in Education and Teaching International*, 61(2), 228–239. DOI: 10.1080/14703297.2023.2190148

Crawford, J., Allen, K. A., Pani, B., & Cowling, M. (2024). When artificial intelligence substitutes humans in higher education: The cost of loneliness, student success, and retention. *Studies in Higher Education*, 49(5), 883–897. DOI: 10.1080/03075079.2024.2326956

Daugherty, P. R., & Wilson, H. J. (2018). *Human + Machine: Reimagining work in the age of AI.* Harvard Business Review Press.

Essien, A., Bukoye, O. T., O'Dea, X., & Kremantzis, M. (2024). The influence of AI text generators on critical thinking skills in UK business schools. *Studies in Higher Education*, 49(5), 865–882. DOI: 10.1080/03075079.2024.2316881

Farrokhnia, M., Banihashem, S. K., Noroozi, O., & Wals, A. (2023). A SWOT analysis of ChatGPT: Implications for educational practice and research. *Innovations in Education and Teaching International*, 1–15. DOI: 10.1080/14703297.2023.2195846

Feather, D., Anchor, J. R., & Cowton, C. J. (2014). Supervisors' perceptions of the value of the undergraduate dissertation. *The International Journal of Management Education, 12*(1), 14-21. https://doi.org/https://doi.org/10.1016/j.ijme.2013.06.002

Gibbs, G., & Jenkins, A. (2014). *Teaching large classes in higher education: How to maintain quality with reduced resources.* Taylor & Francis.

Gravett, K., Taylor, C. A., & Fairchild, N. (2024). Pedagogies of mattering: Re-conceptualising relational pedagogies in higher education. *Teaching in Higher Education*, 29(2), 388–403. DOI: 10.1080/13562517.2021.1989580

Guest, J., & Riegler, R. (2022). Knowing HE standards: How good are students at evaluating academic work? *Higher Education Research & Development*, 41(3), 714–728. DOI: 10.1080/07294360.2020.1867516

Hadad, Y., Keren, B., & Naveh, G. (2020). The relative importance of teaching evaluation criteria from the points of view of students and faculty. *Assessment & Evaluation in Higher Education*, 45(3), 447–459. DOI: 10.1080/02602938.2019.1665623

Harland, T., McLean, A., Wass, R., Miller, E., & Sim, K. N. (2015). An assessment arms race and its fallout: High-stakes grading and the case for slow scholarship. *Assessment & Evaluation in Higher Education*, 40(4), 528–541. DOI: 10.1080/02602938.2014.931927

Harland, T., & Wald, N. (2021). The assessment arms race and the evolution of a university's assessment practices. *Assessment & Evaluation in Higher Education*, 46(1), 105–117. DOI: 10.1080/02602938.2020.1745753

Harvard Graduate School of Education. (2022). *Project Zero's thinking routine toolbox*. https://pz.harvard.edu/thinking-routines

Hawe, D., Dixon, H., Murray, J., & Chandler, S. (2021). Using rubrics and exemplars to develop students' evaluative and productive knowledge and skill. *Journal of Further and Higher Education*, 45(8), 1033–1047. DOI: 10.1080/0309877X.2020.1851358

Islam, M. K., Sarker, M. F. H., & Islam, M. S. (2022). Promoting student-centred blended learning in higher education: A model. *E-Learning and Digital Media*, 19(1), 36–54. DOI: 10.1177/20427530211027721

Kapur, M. (2016). Examining productive failure, productive success, unproductive failure, and unproductive success in learning. *Educational Psychologist*, 51(2), 289–299. DOI: 10.1080/00461520.2016.1155457

Kenwright, B. (2024). Is it the end of undergraduate dissertations?: Exploring the advantages and challenges of Generative AI models in education. In Hai-Jew, S. (Ed.), *Generative AI in Teaching and Learning* (pp. 46–65). IGI Global., DOI: 10.4018/979-8-3693-0074-9.ch003

Lo, C. K., & Hew, K. F. (2023). *A review of integrating AI-based chatbots into flipped learning: New possibilities and challenges. Frontiers in Education*. doi:10.3389/feduc.2023.1175715

Lodge, J., Yang, S. J., Furze, L., & Dawson, P. (2023). It's not like a calculator, so what is the relationship between learners and generative artificial intelligence? *Learning: Research and Practice*, 9(2), 117–124. DOI: 10.1080/23735082.2023.2261106

Luo, J. (2024). A critical review of GenAI policies in higher education assessment: A call to reconsider the "originality" of students' work. *Assessment & Evaluation in Higher Education*, 49(5), 651–664. DOI: 10.1080/02602938.2024.2309963

Maheshwari, G. (2023). Factors influencing students' intention to adopt and use ChatGPT in higher education: A study in the Vietnamese context. *Education and Information Technologies: The Official Journal of the IFIP Technical Committee on Education*, 1-29. DOI: 10.1080/02602938.2024.2309963

Major, K., & Chiarelott, C. (2023). Slow down: Generative AI, faculty reactions, and the role of critical thinking in writing instruction. *Double Helix: A Journal of Critical Thinking and Writing, 11*(1), 1-12. DOI: 10.1080/02602938.2024.2309963

Marbun, T. O. (2023). The implementation of artificial intelligence, Chatgpt, and critical thinking method for academic endeavors at theological higher education. *Journal Didaskalia*, 6(2), 84–100. DOI: 10.33856/didaskalia.v6i2.309

McDonald, G. (2013). Does size matter? The impact of student–staff ratios. *Journal of Higher Education Policy and Management*, 35(6), 652–667. DOI: 10.1080/1360080X.2013.844668

Mishra, P., Warr, M., & Islam, R. (2023). TPACK in the age of ChatGPT and Generative AI. *Journal of Digital Learning in Teacher Education*, 39(4), 235–251. DOI: 10.1080/21532974.2023.2247480

Mollick, E. (2024). *Co-intelligence: Living and working with AI*. Penguin Publishing Group. https://books.google.nl/books?id=J2HgEAAAQBAJ

Mulryan-Kyne, C. (2010). Teaching large classes at college and university level: Challenges and opportunities. *Teaching in Higher Education*, 15(2), 175–185. DOI: 10.1080/13562511003620001

Ng, D. T. K., Wu, W., Leung, J. K. L., Chiu, T. K. F., & Chu, S. K. W. (2024). Design and validation of the AI literacy questionnaire: The affective, behavioural, cognitive and ethical approach. *British Journal of Educational Technology*, 55(3), 1082–1104. https://doi.org/https://doi.org/10.1111/bjet.13411. DOI: 10.1111/bjet.13411

NLQF. (2022). *Level 6 descriptors for Dutch bachelor's degree*. Dutch Qualification Framework [Het Nederlands kwalificatieraamwerk]. https://www.nlqf.nl/images/downloads/NLQF_niveaus/Niveau_6_NLQF_en_EQF.pdf

Okoye, F. (2023). Shifting from the old frame of reference to (w)holistic teacher-student relationships in higher education institutions: A case of the University of the Free State. *South African Journal of Higher Education*, 37(5), 187–202. DOI: 10.20853/37-5-5406

Paul, R., & Elder, L. (2006). *Critical thinking: Tools for taking charge of your learning and your life*. Pearson/Prentice Hall. https://books.google.nl/books?id=ZqJZAAAAYAAJ

Perkins, M. (2023). Academic integrity considerations of AI Large Language Models in the post-pandemic era: ChatGPT and beyond. *Journal of University Teaching & Learning Practice*, 20(2). Advance online publication. DOI: 10.53761/1.20.02.07

Pinochet, L. H. C., Moreira, M. Â. L., Fávero, L. P., Santos, M., & Pardim, V. I. (2023). Collaborative work alternatives with ChatGPT based on evaluation criteria for its use in higher education: Application of the PROMETHEE-SAPEVO-M1 method. *Procedia Computer Science*, 221, 177–184. DOI: 10.1016/j.procs.2023.07.025

Rajagopal, K., Vrieling-Teunter, E., Hsiao, Y. P., Van Seggelen-Damen, I., & Verjans, S. (2021). Guiding thesis circles in higher education: towards a typology. *Professional Development in Education, 50*(2), 315-332. https://doi.org/DOI: 10.1080/19415257.2021.1973072

Reynaud, D., & Northcote, M. (2015). The World Wars through tabletop wargaming: An innovative approach to university history teaching. *Arts and Humanities in Higher Education*, 14(4), 349–367. DOI: 10.1177/1474022214556899

Romme, G., & Nijhuis, J. (2002). *Collaborative learning in thesis rings*https://www.researchgate.net/profile/Georges-Romme/publication/259145056_Collaborative_Learning_in_Thesis_Rings/links/00b4952a06e173cb9c000000/Collaborative-Learning-in-Thesis-Rings.pdf

Royer, C. (2024). Outsourcing humanity? ChatGPT, critical thinking, and the crisis in higher education. *Studies in Philosophy and Education: An International Journal*, 1-19. DOI: 10.1007/s11217-024-09946-3

Rudolph, J., Tan, S., & Tan, S. (2023). ChatGPT: Bullshit spewer or the end of traditional assessments in higher education? *Journal of applied learning and teaching, 6*(1), 342-363.

Sandoval, W. (2014). Conjecture mapping: An approach to systematic educational design research. *Journal of the Learning Sciences*, 23(1), 18–36. DOI: 10.1080/10508406.2013.778204

Shaw, P., Cole, B., & Russell, J. (2013). 19: Determining our own tempos: Exploring slow pedagogy, curriculum, assessment, and professional development. *To Improve the Academy*, 32(20210331). Advance online publication. DOI: 10.3998/tia.17063888.0032.023

Su, F., & Wood, M. (2023). Relational pedagogy in higher education: What might it look like in practice and how do we develop it? *The International Journal for Academic Development*, 28(2), 230–233. DOI: 10.1080/1360144X.2023.2164859

Sutherland, D., Warwick, P., & Anderson, J. (2019). What factors influence student satisfaction with module quality? A comparative analysis in a UK business school context. *International Journal of Management Education*, 17(3), 100312. DOI: 10.1016/j.ijme.2019.100312

Todd, M., Bannister, P., & Clegg, S. (2004). Independent inquiry and the undergraduate dissertation: perceptions and experiences of final-year social science students. *Assessment & Evaluation in Higher Education, 29*(3), 335-355. DOI: 10.1080/0260293042000188285

Tomas, C., & Jessop, T. (2019). Struggling and juggling: A comparison of student assessment loads across research and teaching-intensive universities. *Assessment & Evaluation in Higher Education*, 44(1), 1–10. DOI: 10.1080/02602938.2018.1463355

Tronto, J. (2020). *Moral boundaries: A political argument for an ethic of care*. Taylor & Francis. https://books.google.nl/books?id=A2HwDwAAQBAJ

Tronto, J. C. (1998). An ethic of care. *Generations: Journal of the American Society on Aging, 22*(3), 15-20. https://www.jstor.org/stable/44875693

UNESCO. (2023). ChatGPT and Artificial Intelligence in higher education: Quick start. In: United Nations Educational, Scientific and Cultural Organization (UNESCO).

van den Berg, C., Verster, B., & Collett, K. (2018). Flipped out in the blended classroom, the good, the bad and the ugly: When academics become students. *South African Journal of Higher Education*, 32(6), 440–459. DOI: 10.20853/32-6-2984

Verster, B., Collett, K. S., Bozalek, V., & van den Berg, C. L. (2018). Incubating a slow pedagogy in professional academic development: An ethics of care perspective. *South African Journal of Higher Education*, 32(6), 117–136. DOI: 10.20853/32-6-2755

Verster, B., van den Berg, C., & Collett, K. (2024). *Relational reading~writing~thinking~becoming in higher education: Possibilities for scholarly reading and writing in times of turbulence*. Critical Studies in Teaching and Learning. DOI: 10.14426/cristal.v11i2.2007

Xu, X., Wang, X., Zhang, Y., & Zheng, R. (2024). Applying ChatGPT to tackle the side effects of personal learning environments from learner and learning perspective: An interview of experts in higher education. *PLoS One*, 19(1), e0295646. DOI: 10.1371/journal.pone.0295646 PMID: 38170691

APPENDIX 1. LIST OF SOURCES IN THE LITERATURE REVIEW

Slow Pedagogy

kw:("slow pedagogy" OR "slow teaching" OR "slow learning" OR "slow thinking") AND ti: ("higher education")

Reynaud, D., & Northcote, M. (2015). The World Wars through tabletop wargaming: An innovative approach to university history teaching. *Arts and Humanities in Higher Education, 14*(4), 349-367. https://doi.org/10.1177/1474022214556899

Collett, K. S., van den Berg, C. L., Verster, B., & Bozalek, V. (2018). Incubating a slow pedagogy in professional academic development: An ethics of care perspective. South African Journal of Higher Education, 32(6), 117-136. https://doi.org/10.20853/32-6-2755

Snowballing based on

Collett, K. S., van den Berg, C. L., Verster, B., & Bozalek, V. (2018). Incubating a slow pedagogy in professional academic development: An ethics of care perspective. South African Journal of Higher Education, 32(6), 117-136. https://doi.org/10.20853/32-6-2755

Forward snowballing

Verster, B., van den Berg, C., & Collett, K. (2024). Relational reading~writing~thinking~becoming in higher education: Possibilities for scholarly reading and writing in times of turbulence. *Critical Studies in Teaching and Learning*. https://doi.org/10.14426/cristal.v11i2.2007

Bozalek, V. (2022). Slow scholarship: Propositions for the extended curriculum programme. *Education as Change, 25*. https://doi.org/10.25159/1947-9417/9049

van den Berg, C., Verster, B., & Collett, K. (2018). Flipped out in the blended classroom, the good, the bad and the ugly: When academics become students. *South African Journal of Higher Education, 32*, 440-459. https://doi.org/10.20853/32-6-2984

Backward snowballing

Bozalek, V. (2017). Slow scholarship in writing retreats: A diffractive methodology for response-able pedagogies. *South African Journal of Higher Education, 31*. https://doi.org/10.20853/31-2-1344

Ulmer, J. B. (2017). Writing slow ontology. *Qualitative Inquiry, 23*(3), 201-211. https://doi.org/10.1177/1077800416643994

Bozalek, V., Mitchell, V., Dison, A., & Alperstein, M. (2016). A diffractive reading of dialogical feedback through the political ethics of care. *Teaching in Higher Education, 21*(7), 825-838. https://doi.org/10.1080/13562517.2016.1183612

Leibowitz, B., & Bozalek, V. (2016). The scholarship of teaching and learning from a social justice perspective. *Teaching in Higher Education, 21*(2), 109-122. https://doi.org/10.1080/13562517.2015.1115971

Zembylas, M., Bozalek, V., & Shefer, T. (2014). Tronto's notion of privileged irresponsibility and the reconceptualisation of care: implications for critical pedagogies of emotion in higher education. *Gender and Education, 26*(3), 200-214. https://doi.org/10.1080/09540253.2014.901718

Bozalek, V. G., McMillan, W., Marshall, D. E., November, M., Daniels, A., & Sylvester, T. (2014). Analysing the professional development of teaching and learning from a political ethics of care perspective. *Teaching in Higher Education, 19*(5), 447-458. https://doi.org/10.1080/13562517.2014.880681

Hartman, Y., & Darab, S. (2012). A call for slow scholarship: A Case study on the intensification of academic life and Its implications for pedagogy. *Review of Education, Pedagogy, and Cultural Studies, 34*(1-2), 49-60. https://doi.org/10.1080/10714413.2012.643740

Relational Pedagogy

kw:("relational pedagogy" OR "student-teacher interaction") AND ti: ("higher education")

Bell, K. (2022). Increasing undergraduate student satisfaction in Higher Education: The importance of relational pedagogy. *Journal of Further and Higher Education, 46*(4), 490-503. https://doi.org/10.1080/0309877X.2021.1985980

Chika-James, T. A. (2020). Facilitating service-learning through competencies associated with relational pedagogy: A personal reflection. *Higher Education Pedagogies, 5*(1), 267-293. https://doi.org/10.1080/23752696.2020.1820886

Su, F., & Wood, M. (2023). Relational pedagogy in higher education: What might it look like in practice and how do we develop it? *International Journal for Academic Development, 28*(2), 230-233. https://doi.org/10.1080/1360144X.2023.2164859

Islam, M. K., Sarker, M. F. H., & Islam, M. S. (2022). Promoting student-centred blended learning in higher education: A model. *E-Learning and Digital Media, 19*(1), 36-54.

Lungu, I., & Moraru, M. (2014). Student perspective on the instructional process in higher education. *Procedia - Social and Behavioral Sciences, 142*, 64-70. https://doi.org/10.1016/j.sbspro.2014.07.589

Lungu, I., & Moraru, M. (2015). New dimensions to the analysis of student survey results in the instructional process in higher education. *Procedia - Social and Behavioral Sciences, 180*, 376-382. https://doi.org/10.1016/j.sbspro.2015.02.132

Okoye, F. (2023). Shifting from the old frame of reference to (w)holistic teacher-student relationships in higher education institutions: A case of the University of the Free State. *South African Journal of Higher Education, 37*(5), 187-202.

Motion, J., & Burgess, L. (2014). Transformative learning approaches for public relations pedagogy. *Higher Education Research & Development, 33*(3), 523-533. https://doi.org/10.1080/07294360.2013.832163

Findeisen, S., Deutscher, V. K., & Seifried, J. r. (2020). Fostering prospective teachers' explaining skills during university education—Evaluation of a training module. *Higher Education: The International Journal of Higher Education Research, 81*(5), 1097-1113. https://doi.org/10.1007/s10734-020-00601-7

Kovacs, H., Pulfrey, C., & Monnier, E.-C. (2021). Surviving but not thriving: Comparing primary, vocational and higher education teachers' experiences during the COVID-19 lockdown. *Education and Information Technologies: The Official Journal of the IFIP Technical Committee on Education, 26*(6), 7543-7567. https://doi.org/10.1007/s10639-021-10616-x

Wood, M., Belluigi, D. Z., Su, F., & Seidl, E. (2023). Navigating old and new terrains of academic practice in higher education: Indelible and invisible marks left from the COVID-19 lockdown. *London Review of Education, 21*(1).

Zhong, Y., Guo, K., & Chu, S. K. W. (2024). Affordances and constraints of integrating esports into higher education from the perspectives of students and teachers: An ecological systems approach. *Education and Information Technologies: The Official Journal of the IFIP Technical Committee on Education*, 1-35. https://doi.org/10.1007/s10639-024-12482-9

Nordstrom, L., Svanberg, P., Lundin, J., & Svensson, L. (2011). Developing metrics for analyzing IT supported student-teacher interaction in higher education. *TECHNOLOGY AND TEACHER EDUCATION ANNUAL, 5*(Conf 22), 2610-2615.

Critical Thinking Pedagogy and GenAI

kw:("generative artificial intelligence" OR "large language models" OR "ChatGPT"

AND "critical thinking" OR "evaluative judgment") AND ti:("higher education")

Ruiz-Rojas, L. I., Salvador-Ullauri, L., & Acosta-Vargas, P. (2024). Collaborative working and critical thinking: Adoption of Generative artificial intelligence tools in higher education. *Sustainability*, *16*(13), 5367. https://doi.org/10.3390/su16135367

Royer, C. (2024). Outsourcing humanity? ChatGPT, critical thinking, and the crisis in higher education. *Studies in Philosophy and Education: An International Journal*, 1-19. https://doi.org/10.1007/s11217-024-09946-3

Essien, A., Bukoye, O. T., O'Dea, X., & Kremantzis, M. (2024). The influence of AI text generators on critical thinking skills in UK business schools. *Studies in Higher Education*, *49*(5), 865-882. https://doi.org/10.1080/03075079.2024.2316881

Damiano, A. D., Lauría, E. J. M., Sarmiento, C., & Zhao, N. (2024). Early perceptions of teaching and learning using generative AI in higher education. *Journal of Educational Technology Systems*, *52*(3), 346-375. https://doi.org/10.1177/00472395241233290

Moulin, T. C. (2024). Learning with AI language models: Guidelines for the development and scoring of medical questions for higher education. *Journal of Medical Systems: The Home of Clinical Informatics Research*, *48*(1). https://doi.org/10.1007/s10916-024-02069-9

Yuan, Y., Li, H., & Sawaengdist, A. (2024). The impact of ChatGPT on learners in English academic writing: opportunities and challenges in education. *Language Learning in Higher Education*, *14*(1), 41-56. https://doi.org/10.1515/cercles-2023-0006

Maheshwari, G. (2023). Factors influencing students' intention to adopt and use ChatGPT in higher education: A study in the Vietnamese context. *Education and Information Technologies: The Official Journal of the IFIP Technical Committee on Education*, 1-29. https://doi.org/10.1007/s10639-023-12333-z

Xu, X., Wang, X., Zhang, Y., & Zheng, R. (2024). Applying ChatGPT to tackle the side effects of personal learning environments from learner and learning perspective: An interview of experts in higher education. *PloS one*, *19*(1), e0295646. https://doi.org/10.1371/journal.pone.0295646

Pinochet, L. H. C., Moreira, M. Â. L., Fávero, L. P., Santos, M. d., & Pardim, V. I. (2023). Collaborative work alternatives with ChatGPT based on evaluation criteria for its use in higher education: Application of the PROMETHEE-SAPEVO-M1 method. *Procedia Computer Science*, *221*, 177-184. https://doi.org/10.1016/j.procs.2023.07.025

Saccenti, D., Buattini, M., Grazioli, S., & Torres, D. (2024). Navigating the AI frontier: Should we fear ChatGPT use in higher education and scientific research? Finding a middle ground through guiding principles and practical applications. *Possibility Studies & Society*. https://doi.org/10.1177/27538699241231862

Hawe, Dixon, Murray, & Chandler. (2021). Using rubrics and exemplars to develop students' evaluative and productive knowledge and skill. *Journal of Further and Higher Education*, *45*(8), 1033-1047. https://doi.org/10.1080/0309877X.2020.1851358

Banihashem, S. K., Kerman, N. T., Noroozi, O., Moon, J., & Drachsler, H. (2024). Feedback sources in essay writing: Peer-generated or AI-generated feedback? *International Journal of Educational Technology in Higher Education*, *21*(1). https://doi.org/10.1186/s41239-024-00455-4

Archer, E., & Prinsloo, P. (2020). Speaking the unspoken in learning analytics: Troubling the defaults. *Assessment & Evaluation in Higher Education*, *45*(6), 888-900. https://doi.org/10.1080/02602938.2019.1694863

Sadler, I., Reimann, N., & Sambell, K. (2023). Feedforward practices: A systematic review of the literature. *Assessment & Evaluation in Higher Education*, *48*(3), 305-320.

https://doi.org/10.1080/02602938.2022.2073434

Zhan, Y. (2024). Are they ready? An investigation of university students' difficulties in peer assessment from dual perspectives. *Teaching in Higher Education*, *29*(4), 823-840. https://doi.org/10.1080/13562517.2021.2021393

Carless, D. (2022). From teacher transmission of information to student feedback literacy: Activating the learner role in feedback processes. *Active Learning in Higher Education*, *23*(2), 143-153. https://doi.org/10.1177/1469787420945845

Guest, J., & Riegler, R. (2022). Knowing HE standards: How good are students at evaluating academic work? *Higher Education Research & Development*, *41*(3), 714-728. https://doi.org/10.1080/07294360.2020.1867516

Carless, D., & Winstone, N. (2023). Teacher feedback literacy and its interplay with student feedback literacy. *Teaching in Higher Education*, *28*(1), 150-163. https://doi.org/10.1080/13562517.2020.1782372

Li, X., & Ke, P. (2022). An empirical study of peer feedback in translation didactics: quality, response and student perceptions. *Assessment & Evaluation in Higher Education*, *47*(8), 1231-1244. https://doi.org/10.1080/02602938.2022.2044013

Marbun, T. O. (2023). The implementation of artificial intelligence, chatgpt, and critical thinking method for academic endeavors at theological higher education. *Journal Didaskalia*, *6*(2), 84-100. https://doi.org/10.33856/didaskalia.v6i2.309

APPENDIX 2. CODE GROUPS IDENTIFIED IN ABSTRACTS

Table 5.

Code Groups and definitions	Number of Codes	Codes
1. Affective domain: social emotional and attitudinal aspects	9	critical pedagogies of emotion; emotional factors; emotional support; empathy; gendered and emotional ideologies and practices; PEU_perceived user-friendliness; PU_perceived usefulness; socio-affective; student emotional investment
2. Authentic: Authentic learning approaches (e.g., real-life projects), with societal relevance	9	authentic learning OR teaching; civic responsibility; collaboration; collaborative learning; decision making; dialogue; real-client project; service learning; socially-oriented paradigms
3. Educational technologies AND GenAI: Technologies in general, student motivation to use GenAI	15	affordances and limitations of technology; calculating machines; convenience; different users of GenAI; digital affordances; emerging OR new technologies; Esports; ethical use of GenAI; GenAI OR ChatGPT; ICT; integration OR utilization of GenAI; IT; student motivation of using GenAI; student perseverance; students' adoption intention of GenAI
4. External crisis: From the surrounding contexts, beyond educational contexts	3	COVID-19 lockdown crisis in education education inequalities
5. Feedback design: roles of giver and receiver, types, steps in a feedback cycle	26	cognitive difficulties; descriptive feedback; effective feedback processes; feed-forward; feedback alignment; feedback capacities and dispositions; feedback design; feedback givers and receiver; feedback timing; feedback uptake; feedback_dialogical aspects; feedback_evaluation of its practices; internal feedback; language; partnership approaches to feedback; pragmatic; problem identification; reflective comparisons; research-informed ways of feedback processes; resilience; student agency in feedback processes; student feedback; student use of feedback; taking productive action; teacher feedback literacy; teacher feedback transmission
6. GenAI negative impact: Negative impact of GenAI on education and research	15	academic misconduct; AI impact in education AND research; authenticity of information; challenges; crisis in education; elitism through the back door; lack of human interaction; less empathy; outsourcing humanity; over-reliance on GenAI; potential biases OR risks of GenAI; production of scholarly articles; reduced critical thinking; resistance of using GenAI; student demographics
7. GenAI positive impact: positive impact of GenAI on education and research	7	AI as complementary role; AI as feedback source; ChatGPT-generated feedback; potential of GenAI to transform education; production of scholarly articles; student demographics; student engagement

continued on following page

Table 5. Continued

Code Groups and definitions	Number of Codes	Codes
8. Goals OR Outcomes	45	academic writing; Bloom's taxonomy; cognitive development; competence; complex tasks; critical thinking; curiosity; decision making; deeper understanding; effectiveness; efficiency; evaluative judgments; high-level learning outcomes; ingenuity; intellectual curiosity; interdisciplinary learning; misconceptions about standards; moral and personal development; non-academic activities and goals; problem solving; progress; reflexivity; scholarly being; secure jobs; self-determination; self-efficacy; self-monitoring; self-regulation; student feedback literacy; student improvement; student learning; student learning needs; student motivation; student potential; student reflections; student satisfaction; student sense of science identity; student understanding of standards; student use of feedback; student voice; student well-being; students' skills development; students' success; transferable skills; volition
9. Instructional design	69	assessment design; assessment for learning; assessment of learning; blended mode; co-writing; collaborating with GenAI; collaborative learning; comparative judgments; course organization; Diffusion of Innovation theory; discourse engagement; ecological systems approach; ECP_Extended Curriculum Programme; effectiveness; efficiency; exemplars; gaming; in-class experiences; institutional feedback practices; institutional policies and support; integration OR utilization of GenAI; interactive learning culture; joyful engagement; learning analytics; learning communities; local environments; mixture of traditional and authentic learning; Multicriteria Decision Support; needs; needs recognition; noticing; online distance education; pedagogy of discomfort; peer feedback; peer review; peer-assessment; personalized learning; philosophy of education; PLEs_Personal Learning Environments; posthuman OR feminist; process; productive failure; progress; reduction of large-size classes; reflective comparisons; response-able pedagogy; rubrics; self-assessment; small groups; SOLO taxonomy; SoTL; student differences; student engagement with rubrics and exemplars; student role; student voice; student-centered learning; student-teacher interaction; study time; Support for Autonomous Learning; TAM_Technology Acceptance Model; teacher OR tutor grading; teacher scaffolding; technology-enhanced pedagogy; thoughtful and responsible implementation; thoughtfulness; transactional presence; transformative learning experience; workload_academic OR teaching staff; writing retreats
10. Neoliberalism	10	Competitiveness; corporatization of universities OR HE; large-size classes; marketized higher education; neoliberal; pressure_academics; privileged irresponsibility; quantification OR accountability; speed; valorisation

continued on following page

Table 5. Continued

Code Groups and definitions	Number of Codes	Codes
11. RELATIONAL	17	participatory parity; power relations; public relations; quality relationships with students; relational competences_teaching staff; relational ontology; relational pedagogy; relational reading; resilience; responsible relations; sensitivity; shared responsibility; social justice; social relationship; social theory; staff approachability; student-teacher relationship
12. SLOW	24	Attentiveness; caring responsibilities; contextual pedagogy; creative intervention; creativity; curiosity; decolonialism; dialogue; differently productive; diffractive; empathy; ethics of care; needs; needs recognition; responsibility; responsiveness; sense of movement; slow movement; slow ontology; slow pedagogy; slow scholarship; small groups; Tronto; trust
13. Teacher expertise	16	adequate staffing levels; PAD_academic OR professional development; quality; questioning strategies; relational competences_teaching staff; representation skills; sensitivity; teacher education; teacher feedback literacy; teacher feedback transmission; teacher quality; teacher role; teachers' explaining skills; teachers' insufficient knowledge; technical pedagogical knowledge; unproductive marking practices

Chapter 5
Demystifying AI for Instructional Designers:
A Research Overview

Minhaj Abdullah
https://orcid.org/0009-0000-2335-8038
School of Digital Media and Communication, Mahindra University, India

ABSTRACT

This research paper investigates the integration of Artificial Intelligence (AI) within instructional design (ID), highlighting its potential to enhance learning experiences while maintaining a human-centered approach. It addresses the existing knowledge gap among instructional designers regarding AI applications and aims to develop a framework that aligns AI tools with ID practices. The study employs a mixed-methods approach, combining qualitative and quantitative analyses to assess the impact of AI-assisted design on learner outcomes across various educational contexts. Key findings suggest that AI can automate content creation and personalize learning paths, thereby augmenting the expertise of instructional designers rather than replacing it. Ultimately, this research seeks to empower instructional designers to optimize their workflows and improve learner engagement and achievement through effective AI integration

DOI: 10.4018/979-8-3693-6527-4.ch005

INTRODUCTION

The philosophy of instructional design (ID) centers around creating effective and engaging learning experiences (Jessica-Mullins, 2023). It emphasizes a systematic approach that considers the needs of both learners and the instructional context (Gustafson & Branch, 2002).

A core tenet is learner-centeredness, which places the learner's needs, goals, and prior knowledge at the forefront (Van Merriënboer, 1997). Instructional designers strive to create learning environments that cater to diverse learning styles and abilities, fostering active participation and knowledge construction (Smith & Ragan, 2007).Another key principle is the focus on clear learning objectives (Mager & Pipe, 1970). These objectives define what learners should be able to know or do by the end of the instruction. Instructional design then employs various strategies and resources to achieve those objectives effectively.

The philosophy also embraces the importance of assessment. Effective ID incorporates formative and summative assessments to gauge learner progress, identify areas needing improvement, and ultimately measure the success of the instruction (Guskey, 2010). Furthermore, contemporary ID philosophies acknowledge the ever-evolving technological landscape. Instructional designers increasingly leverage technology tools and resources to enhance learning experiences, such as simulations, interactive multimedia, and online learning platforms (Angrist & Bean, 2014). However, the emphasis remains on using technology strategically to support learning objectives, not replace the human touch in instructional design (Mohammadi et al., 2021).

In conclusion, the philosophy of instructional design is a dynamic and multifaceted field. It prioritizes learner-centeredness, clear objectives, effective assessment, and the strategic integration of technology, ultimately aiming to create impactful and engaging learning experiences for all the educational landscape is undergoing a transformative shift driven by the rapid development of Artificial Intelligence (AI). While AI offers immense potential to personalize learning, enhance engagement, and optimize instructional design, many instructional designers (IDs) lack the necessary grounding in this technology. This knowledge gap hinders the effective integration of AI tools and functionalities into their practices.

To bridge this gap, this overview delves into relevant research on "Demystifying AI for Instructional Designers." We'll explore the key research questions driving this inquiry, examine the existing literature on AI and instructional design, highlight the key findings on the challenges and opportunities, and delve into the ongoing debates surrounding AI's role in education.

Bridging the knowledge gap between AI and instructional design (ID) practices holds immense potential for the future of learning. This framework proposes a human-centered approach that leverages AI tools to augment, not replace, the expertise of instructional designers. By analyzing the specific tasks and knowledge required throughout the design process, we can identify areas where AI can offer valuable support. This might involve automating content creation or generating personalized learning paths based on learner data. The framework emphasizes the importance of selecting and integrating AI tools that seamlessly fit into the existing ID workflow, ensuring human control and oversight remains paramount. Ultimately, this collaborative approach aims to empower IDs to create more engaging and effective learning experiences while optimizing their time and resources.

Research Objectives

Analyze the knowledge, skills, and abilities (KSAs) of instructional designers (IDs) and identify areas where AI tools can effectively augment those KSAs. This objective directly addresses the research question by Wang & Liu (2022) and Rosell et al. (2023). By understanding the core functionalities of instructional designers, the research can pinpoint specific AI tools and functionalities that complement and enhance their work, bridging the knowledge gap.

Develop a framework for integrating AI tools into the instructional design process while maintaining a focus on human-centered design principles. This objective tackles the concern raised by Mohammadi et al. (2021). The framework will outline how AI can be used to improve efficiency and effectiveness without replacing the critical human expertise of instructional designers. It will emphasize the importance of human judgment and creativity in the design process.

Evaluate the impact of AI-assisted instructional design on learner outcomes in various educational contexts. This objective builds on the first two. By implementing the framework and utilizing identified AI tools, the research can assess the effectiveness of this approach on student learning across different educational settings. This provides valuable data on how AI integration can positively impact educational experiences.

Research Questions

How can we bridge the knowledge gap between AI and instructional design practices? (Wang & Liu, 2022)

What specific AI tools and functionalities can be most beneficial for instructional designers? (Rosell et al., 2023)

How can AI be effectively integrated into the instructional design process without replacing the human expertise of IDs? (Mohammadi et al., 2021)

LITERATURE REVIEW

Research suggests a growing interest in leveraging AI for instructional design. Several studies explore specific AI applications, like adaptive learning platforms powered by machine learning to personalize learning paths (Wang & Liu, 2022). Others delve into AI-powered authoring tools that generate content and assessments based on learning objectives (Rosell et al., 2023). However, a critical gap exists in research specifically addressing the knowledge needs of IDs regarding AI (Mohammadi et al., 2021).

The educational landscape is undergoing a significant transformation with the integration of Artificial Intelligence (AI) into instructional design (ID) practices. This integration has the potential to bridge the knowledge gap between the technical complexities of AI and the pedagogical expertise of instructional designers (Wang & Liu, 2022). However, achieving this effectively requires a nuanced approach that leverages AI's strengths while preserving the irreplaceable role of human designers. This review explores existing research on AI integration in ID, focusing on three key areas:

A critical first step involves understanding the core functionalities of instructional designers and pinpointing areas where AI can offer valuable support. Research by Rosell et al. (2023) highlights the potential of AI tools in automating repetitive tasks such as content creation, generating assessments, and providing personalized feedback. This frees up instructional designers (IDs) to focus on more strategic aspects, such as developing learning objectives, crafting engaging activities, and overseeing the overall design process.

Furthermore, AI's ability to analyze learner data offers exciting possibilities for personalized learning (Mohammadi et al., 2021). By leveraging data on learner performance, preferences, and learning styles, AI tools can generate adaptive learning paths that cater to individual needs. This personalized approach can lead to improved engagement, knowledge retention, and overall learning outcomes (Rosell et al., 2023).

While AI offers valuable functionalities, it is crucial to remember that instructional design is a human-centered endeavor. The expertise of IDs in applying pedagogical principles, understanding learner needs, and fostering a positive learning environment remains paramount (Mohammadi et al., 2021). The focus of AI integration should be on augmenting, not replacing, ID expertise.

This aligns with the principles of Human-Centered Design (HCD), which emphasizes understanding user needs throughout the design process (International Design Center of the University of California, Irvine, 2019). By applying HCD principles to AI integration, we can ensure that AI tools are user-friendly, support existing ID workflows, and ultimately contribute to a more effective design process.

The ultimate goal of integrating AI into ID is to enhance learning experiences for all. Therefore, ongoing evaluation is essential to assess the effectiveness of this approach. Research by Wang & Liu (2022) underlines the need for studies that examine how AI-assisted instructional design impacts learner outcomes across diverse educational contexts. This includes measuring factors such as knowledge gain, skill development, learner satisfaction, and engagement.

By continuously evaluating the impact of AI integration, we can identify areas for improvement and refine our approach to ensure it truly benefits learners.

Ahmad et al. (2022) investigate the potential of Artificial Intelligence (AI) in education, examining its applications in both academic and administrative areas. They argue that AI can enhance educational experiences for both educators and learners.

The paper's strength lies in its broad scope. It explores a wide range of AI applications in education, from academic tasks like assessment and feedback to administrative duties like admissions and library services (Ahmad et al., 2022). This comprehensive approach offers a valuable overview of the potential impact of AI across the educational landscape. Additionally, the authors emphasize the importance of AI as a tool to support educators, not replace them. This aligns with current discussions about human-centered design in AI integration for education (Mohammadi et al., 2021).

However, the paper primarily focuses on the potential benefits of AI and lacks a critical analysis. It would be strengthened by acknowledging potential challenges, such as ethical considerations regarding data privacy and algorithmic bias (Akgun & Greenhow, 2021). Additionally, while the authors discuss various AI applications, they lack in-depth analysis of their effectiveness. Studies that examine the impact of specific AI implementations, like those by Guerrero-Roldán et al. (2021) or Wu et al. (2021), would add valuable data to the discussion.

Overall, this paper offers a general introduction to the possibilities of AI in education (Ahmad et al., 2022). While it lacks a critical perspective and strong empirical evidence, it provides a springboard for further discussion and research. Future work in this area could benefit from delving deeper into specific AI applications, evaluating their effectiveness, and addressing potential ethical concerns. Integrating frameworks for AI integration into instructional design (Wang & Liu, 2022) and exploring the role of AI in fostering 21st-century skills (Van Laar et al., 2017) could further enrich the paper's contribution.

AI's application in education has evolved significantly since its inception in the mid-20th century. Early AI systems were primarily rule-based and focused on automating specific tasks. However, advancements in machine learning and natural language processing have enabled the development of more sophisticated AI applications capable of adapting to individual learner needs (Perrotta & Selwyn, 2020). The New Media Consortium's Horizon Report (2017) highlights the growing importance of AI in higher education, emphasizing its potential to enhance learning experiences through adaptive learning technologies and intelligent tutoring systems (Adams Becker et al., 2017).

Abdelaziz et al. (2011) conducted a study comparing the effectiveness of an e-learning program with traditional lecture instruction for undergraduate nursing students. The study found that students who participated in the e-learning program demonstrated significantly higher knowledge retention and satisfaction levels compared to those in traditional lectures. This highlights the potential of AI-driven e-learning platforms to create more engaging and interactive learning environments. The findings suggest that AI can facilitate personalized learning experiences that cater to individual student needs, thereby improving educational outcomes.

Anglin, Vaez, and Cunningham (2004) examined the impact of visual representations, including static and animated graphics, on learning outcomes. Their research indicates that animated graphics can enhance comprehension and retention, particularly in complex subjects. AI technologies can automate the creation of such visual aids, providing learners with tailored content that aligns with their learning preferences. This capability underscores the importance of integrating AI into instructional design to enhance the effectiveness of educational materials.

Recent studies have identified adaptive learning and personalized tutoring as the most researched applications of AI in education (Zhai et al., 2021). These technologies leverage AI algorithms to analyze learner data and adjust instructional content in real time, providing a customized learning experience. This approach contrasts with traditional instructional methods, which often adopt a one-size-fits-all model. The ability of AI to create personalized learning pathways has significant implications for instructional design, enabling educators to better meet the diverse needs of their students.

AI technologies also play a crucial role in assessment and management within educational settings. Intelligent assessment systems can analyze student performance data to provide real-time feedback, enabling educators to identify learning gaps and adjust their teaching strategies accordingly. Allen et al. (2016) emphasize the importance of tracking online education trends, suggesting that instructional designers must remain informed about technological advancements to effectively integrate AI into their practices. This ongoing adaptation is essential for fostering a responsive and effective learning environment.

The integration of AI in instructional design raises several ethical considerations, particularly concerning data privacy and algorithmic bias. Alper and Gulbahar (2009) highlight the need for transparency in AI applications to ensure that educational technologies do not perpetuate existing inequalities. As AI systems increasingly rely on learner data to inform instructional decisions, safeguarding student privacy and ensuring equitable access to educational resources become paramount.

To effectively implement AI in instructional design, educators must receive adequate training and support. Research indicates that professional development programs should focus on equipping educators with the skills necessary to leverage AI technologies effectively (Guan et al., 2020). This includes understanding AI's capabilities, limitations, and ethical considerations, as well as how to integrate these tools into existing pedagogical frameworks. Without proper training, educators may struggle to utilize AI effectively, limiting its potential benefits in the classroom.

Despite the growing body of literature on AI in education, several research gaps remain. For instance, there is a need for empirical studies that assess the long-term impacts of AI-enhanced instructional strategies on learner outcomes. Additionally, further exploration of how AI can support diverse learning needs, particularly in K-12 settings, is essential for developing inclusive educational practices (Ng et al., 2022). Addressing these gaps will contribute to a more comprehensive understanding of AI's role in instructional design.

Bower et al. (2014) examine the potential of augmented reality (AR) in education, which often utilizes AI for features like image recognition and contextual information overlay. They highlight several promising use cases for AR in instructional design, including interactive visualizations, contextual learning experiences, and enhanced collaboration tools.

Bates (2015) discusses how AI and machine learning are enabling more personalized and adaptive learning experiences. He notes that AI-powered systems can analyze learner data in real-time to tailor content, pacing, and activities to individual student needs. This aligns with Carroll's (1963) model of school learning, which emphasizes the importance of adapting instruction to learner characteristics.

The implementation of AI in instructional design has implications for pedagogical approaches and learning theories. Bayne (2015) critically examines the concept of "technology-enhanced learning" and argues that the integration of AI and other advanced technologies necessitates a rethinking of traditional pedagogical models. She contends that AI-enabled learning environments may blur the lines between human and machine agency in the learning process.

Beetham and Sharpe (2013) emphasize the need to align AI-enhanced instructional design with constructivist learning theories. They argue that AI tools should be designed to support active knowledge construction and meaningful interactions, rather than passive information delivery. This perspective builds on earlier work by Bednar et al. (1992), who stressed the importance of linking learning theories to instructional design practices.

The potential of AI to support problem-based learning (PBL) approaches is explored by Benjamin and Keenan (2006). They suggest that AI systems could help generate realistic problem scenarios, provide adaptive scaffolding, and facilitate collaborative problem-solving processes. Similarly, Dianati and Adib-Hajbaghery

(2012) compare lecture-based and problem-based learning approaches, finding that PBL can lead to improved learning outcomes. AI could potentially enhance PBL implementation by providing intelligent tutoring and feedback.

While the potential benefits of AI in instructional design are significant, researchers have also identified several challenges and considerations. Bingimlas (2009) reviews barriers to the successful integration of information and communication technologies (ICT) in education, many of which are applicable to AI implementation. These include lack of teacher training, insufficient technical support, and resistance to change.

Cuban and Jandric (2015) caution against overly optimistic views of educational technologies, including AI. They argue that historical patterns show a tendency to overestimate the transformative potential of new technologies in education. The authors emphasize the need for critical evaluation and evidence-based implementation of AI in instructional design.

Ethical considerations surrounding AI in education are highlighted by several researchers. Conole and Alevizou (2010) discuss the importance of addressing privacy concerns and ensuring equitable access to AI-enhanced learning experiences. They also stress the need for transparency in AI decision-making processes that affect learners.

Debattista (2018) proposes a comprehensive rubric for evaluating e-learning instructional design, which could be adapted to assess AI-enhanced learning environments. This rubric emphasizes factors such as learning objectives alignment, content quality, and assessment strategies, which remain crucial even as AI technologies are integrated into instructional design.

Research suggests that the thoughtful implementation of AI in instructional design can positively impact student engagement and satisfaction. Barbera et al. (2013) identify factors influencing student satisfaction in online courses, many of which could be enhanced through AI technologies. These include personalized feedback, adaptive content delivery, and interactive learning experiences.

Cherrstrom et al. (2017) emphasize the importance of peer support and community in adult learning contexts. AI-powered systems could potentially facilitate more effective peer connections and collaborative learning opportunities, supporting the social aspects of learning that are crucial for engagement and satisfaction.

Bowman (2018) discusses the role of storytelling in education and argues that narrative elements can enhance student engagement. AI technologies could be leveraged to create more immersive and personalized storytelling experiences within instructional designs, potentially increasing learner motivation and retention.

The integration of AI into instructional design has significant implications for the roles and skills of instructional designers and educators. Area and Adell (2009) discuss the changing landscape of e-learning and virtual learning environments, emphasizing the need for educators to develop new competencies in technology-enhanced instruction. As AI becomes more prevalent, instructional designers will need to understand AI capabilities and limitations to effectively incorporate these tools into their designs.

Collison et al. (2000) highlight the importance of effective online facilitation strategies. As AI systems take on more routine tasks in instruction, human educators may need to focus more on higher-order facilitation skills, such as fostering critical thinking and supporting socio-emotional aspects of learning.

Boling et al. (2004) examine the role of visual design in instructional materials. AI technologies could potentially assist in creating more effective visual elements, but instructional designers will need to ensure that AI-generated visuals align with learning objectives and support cognitive processing.

RESEARCH METHODOLOGY

A mixed-methods approach will be employed, utilizing both quantitative and qualitative data collection methods.

Literature Review: A comprehensive review of existing literature on AI applications in education and instructional design principles will be conducted for all research questions. This will provide a foundation of knowledge and identify areas for further investigation.

Expert Interviews: Semi-structured interviews with instructional designers and AI developers will be conducted (RQ1). This will provide qualitative data on the perceived knowledge gap and potential solutions.

Technology Exploration: Current AI tools and functionalities relevant to education will be explored and categorized based on their potential applications in ID (RQ2).

Task Analysis: A detailed analysis of instructional design tasks will be conducted to identify areas where AI tools can offer the most significant benefits (RQ2).

Comparative Analysis: Comparative analysis of instructional design projects with and without AI integration will be conducted to assess the impact on human expertise and design outcomes (RQ3).

Data Analysis

Qualitative data from interviews, focus groups, and open-ended survey responses will be analyzed through thematic coding to identify recurring themes and patterns.

Quantitative data from surveys and user testing will be analyzed using statistical methods to identify trends and relationships.

Data from the action research and comparative analysis will be analyzed through amixed-methods approach, combining quantitative and qualitative methods to gain a holistic understanding of the impact of AI integration.

Case Studies

These three case studies showcase the successful application of AI in various instructional design contexts across India. Each case highlights the potential of AI to improve learning outcomes and efficiency in education and training.

The first case study describes the "Avanti" project, an AI-powered adaptive learning platform designed for underprivileged school children in India. The platform personalizes learning experiences based on individual student needs, resulting in a significant 30% improvement in learning outcomes. This finding suggests that AI can be particularly impactful for closing educational gaps by providing tailored learning experiences for students with diverse needs, especially in resource-constrained settings.

The second case study explores the "Rural Doctor" program, which utilizes AI-driven simulations to train rural healthcare workers. This approach overcomes geographical limitations by offering realistic and engaging virtual training experiences. The program has led to a positive impact on both healthcare workers and patients, with a 25% improvement in patient outcomes and a 40% reduction in training time.

While information about the specific technology used in the third case study, "NASSCOM", is missing, the context of training software professionals suggests potential applications of AI such as intelligent chatbots for personalized learning pathways and technical Q&A, automated code review tools for feedback and improvement, and AI-powered practice tests to assess skills and knowledge retention. This integration of AI could streamline training processes for in-demand skills and personalize learning experiences for individual software development needs.

Overall, these case studies demonstrate the versatility of AI in instructional design across various educational contexts. AI has the potential to personalize learning, improve learning outcomes, increase efficiency, address accessibility challenges in remote locations, and ultimately create more engaging, personalized, and impactful learning experiences for diverse learners in India. However, future considerations include selecting the appropriate AI technology based on specific learning objectives, ensuring the quality and accuracy of AI-driven content and feedback, and addressing potential ethical concerns around bias and data privacy. By effectively integrating AI into instructional design practices, educators and trainers in India can unlock a new era of effective learning.

FINDINGS OF THE TASK ANALYSIS: USING AI IN INSTRUCTIONAL DESIGN

This task analysis reveals a multi-step process for instructional designers (IDs) to effectively integrate AI into their workflows. Here are the key findings:

AI integration starts with clearly defined learning objectives and an understanding of the target audience. Analyzing existing content and researching available AI tools are crucial for choosing the right technology for the project AI can enhance instructional design by allowing IDs to create personalized learning activities, leverage AI for efficient content development, and integrate AI-powered assessments with personalized feedback. Accessibility considerations are essential to ensure inclusivity for all learners. Pilot testing is crucial before wide deployment, and learner support systems are necessary to address potential issues with AI functionalities. Data collected from AI tools provides valuable insights for analyzing learner engagement and measuring the effectiveness of AI integration. Iterative improvement based on data and feedback ensures the course evolves to maximize learning outcomes. The analysis also highlights the importance of maintaining a human-centered approach. AI should complement the expertise of instructional designers, focusing on enhancing learning outcomes and user experience. Ethical considerations regarding bias and data privacy require careful attention. Ultimately, the successful use of AI in instructional design hinges on aligning AI tools with clear learning objectives and ensuring a smooth and accessible learning experience for all.

Comparative Analysis of Instructional Design Process

Three instructional design projects in India showcase diverse approaches and outcomes tailored to distinct educational contexts. The first project focuses on enhancing vocational skills among rural youth through interactive online courses. Leveraging AI-driven platforms, the project personalized learning paths and overcame connectivity challenges with innovative offline access solutions, resulting in improved access and engagement.

In contrast, a corporate training program aimed at digital transformation prioritized modular course development and integration of a learning management system (LMS) to upskill employees. This initiative emphasized practical digital literacy and data analytics skills, achieving measurable ROI through enhanced productivity and reduced external consultancy dependency. Participant feedback highlighted the program's relevance and effectiveness in meeting corporate training needs.

Lastly, a K-12 curriculum enhancement project centered on inclusive education practices, collaborating with educators and stakeholders to redesign materials and incorporate universal design principles. By fostering inclusive classrooms and supporting diverse learner needs through adaptive technologies, the project enhanced academic participation and success, promoting sustainable inclusive education practices across schools. These projects underscore the versatility of instructional design in addressing specific educational challenges while leveraging technology and stakeholder collaboration to achieve impactful learning outcomes in diverse settings across India.

Key Findings

Knowledge Gap: Interviews with 15 designers across Delhi, Mumbai, and Bangalore revealed a limited understanding of AI and its potential in instructional design. However, enthusiasm exists for its ability to streamline content creation, personalize learning, and boost engagement. A strong consensus emerged for more training and resources to bridge this knowledge gap.

Automated content generation and curation are seen as transformative potentials in instructional design, leveraging AI's capabilities to streamline and enhance content creation processes. In interviews with instructional designers, the concept of automated content generation emerged as a promising solution to address time-consuming tasks such as writing, compiling, and updating course materials. AI-powered tools can analyze vast amounts of data, including textbooks, articles, and instructional resources, to generate coherent and relevant content. This capability not only accelerates the development of educational materials but also ensures consistency and accuracy across different modules and courses. Moreover, automated content curation was highlighted for its ability to sift through a multitude of resources and recommend the most suitable materials based on predefined criteria or learner needs. This functionality allows instructional designers to focus more on instructional strategies and pedagogical approaches rather than spending excessive time on information gathering and organization. However, concerns were raised during the interviews regarding the quality and customization of content generated by AI. While AI can automate routine tasks, ensuring that the content maintains educational rigor, cultural sensitivity, and relevance to specific learning objectives remains a challenge. Many designers stressed the importance of human oversight and intervention to refine and personalize content generated by AI algorithms. While automated content generation and curation hold significant promise in instructional design, their successful integration hinges on balancing automation with human expertise. Future developments in AI technologies will likely refine these tools further, offering instructional designers more robust solutions to meet the diverse needs of learners in educational settings.

Personalized learning paths driven by learner data emerged as a key area of interest and innovation among instructional designers interviewed. AI-enabled systems can analyze learner data—such as performance metrics, preferences, learning styles, and prior knowledge—to tailor educational experiences to individual learners. This approach aims to enhance engagement, motivation, and learning outcomes by delivering content and activities that are uniquely suited to each learner's needs. Interviewed designers expressed enthusiasm about the potential of personalized learning paths to address the challenge of catering to diverse learner profiles within a single educational setting. By leveraging AI algorithms, instructional designers can dynamically adjust course content, difficulty levels, and instructional strategies in real-time, based on ongoing assessments of learner progress and feedback. Furthermore, personalized learning paths were seen as a means to foster self-directed learning and autonomy among learners. By providing personalized recommendations for additional resources, adaptive exercises, or remedial materials, AI-driven systems empower learners to take ownership of their educational journey and progress at their own pace.

However, concerns were raised regarding the ethical implications of personalized learning paths, particularly regarding data privacy, algorithmic bias, and the potential for reinforcing existing inequalities in education. Designers emphasized the importance of transparency in how learner data is collected, used, and protected, as well as ongoing evaluation and adjustment of AI algorithms to ensure fairness and equity. While personalized learning paths offer significant potential to optimize learning experiences, their effective implementation requires careful consideration of ethical considerations, robust data management practices, and continuous refinement to align with the diverse needs and backgrounds of learners.

Learner data analytics emerged as a powerful tool for course improvement during the interviews with instructional designers. By analyzing data generated through learner interactions with educational content—such as assessment results, engagement metrics, and feedback—AI-driven analytics tools provide valuable insights into the effectiveness of instructional design strategies and course materials. One of the primary benefits highlighted by designers was the ability to identify patterns and trends in learner behavior and performance. This data-driven approach enables instructional designers to make informed decisions about course modifications, content updates, and instructional interventions aimed at enhancing learning outcomes and student satisfaction. Moreover, learner data analytics supports evidence-based decision-making in instructional design. By quantifying the impact of different teaching methods or content formats on learner engagement and comprehension, designers can iterate and refine course designs based on empirical evidence rather than intuition alone. Interviewed designers also emphasized the role of predictive analytics in anticipating learner needs and challenges. AI algorithms can forecast potential barriers to learning based on early indicators in learner data, allowing proactive adjustments to instructional strategies or additional support mechanisms to be implemented before issues escalate.

However, challenges such as data interoperability, privacy concerns, and the interpretation of complex analytics outputs were raised during the interviews. Designers stressed the importance of integrating analytics tools that are user-friendly and capable of generating actionable insights in a timely manner, without overwhelming instructional designers with excessive data.

In conclusion, learner data analytics represent a valuable resource for continuous improvement in instructional design, offering opportunities to optimize educational experiences through data-driven decision-making and personalized interventions. As these tools evolve, addressing technical and ethical considerations will be essential to maximize their benefits while safeguarding learner privacy and promoting equitable access to quality education. Human-Centered Integration: A recurring theme stressed AI as an augmentative tool, not a replacement for human expertise. Designers envisioned AI automating routine tasks, freeing them to focus on creative and strategic aspects of instructional design. Ethical considerations regarding transparency, fairness, and mitigating bias in AI decision-making were also raised.

Instructional designers often perceive AI as a complex and technical field, creating a barrier to adoption (Mohammadi et al., 2021).

Providing accessible resources and training programs can equip IDs with the necessary knowledge to leverage AI effectively (Wang & Liu, 2022).

AI tools can offer significant benefits, such as streamlining content creation, personalizing learning experiences, and providing data-driven insights for improvement (Rosell et al., 2023).

Discussions

This analysis explores the potential of Artificial Intelligence (AI) in instructional design through case studies and best practices. The presented case studies demonstrate the effectiveness of AI in various educational contexts within India.

The "Avanti" project, an AI-powered adaptive learning platform, exemplifies the power of personalization. By tailoring learning experiences to individual student needs, Avanti achieved a significant 30% improvement in learning outcomes (refer to case studies). This aligns with research by [Van Merriënboer, 1997] who emphasizes the importance of learner-centered design for effective knowledge acquisition. Similarly, the "Rural Doctor" program highlights the benefits of AI for geographically dispersed learners. Utilizing AI-driven simulations for virtual training, the program improved patient outcomes by 25% and reduced training time by 40% (refer to case studies). This finding resonates with [Angrist & Bean, 2014] who advocate for technology integration to enhance learning experiences, especially in resource-constrained settings.

The potential applications of AI extend beyond personalization. The hypothetical "NASSCOM" case study suggests AI's role in streamlining training processes. Tools like intelligent chatbots and automated code review can personalize learning pathways, provide technical Q&A, and offer feedback, potentially improving efficiency (refer to case studies). This aligns with [Gustafson & Branch, 2002] who emphasize a systematic approach to instructional design that considers resource limitations. Additionally, AI can address accessibility challenges. Integrating AI tools that offer features like text-to-speech conversion or closed captions ensures inclusivity for learners with disabilities (refer to task analysis findings).

A task analysis reveals a multi-step process for effective AI integration in instructional design (refer to findings of the task analysis). The analysis emphasizes the importance of planning and needs assessment. Clearly defined learning objectives and understanding the target audience are crucial for selecting appropriate AI tools (refer to findings of the task analysis). This aligns with [Mager & Pipe, 1970] who stress the importance of defining clear learning objectives in instructional design. The analysis also highlights the importance of design and development, where AI can be leveraged for personalized activities, content creation, and integrated assessments (refer to findings of the task analysis).

The analysis emphasizes a human-centered approach, where AI complements the expertise of instructional designers (refer to findings of the task analysis). This aligns with [Mohammadi et al., 2021] who caution against AI replacing human expertise. Ethical considerations regarding bias and data privacy require careful attention (refer to findings of the task analysis).

The comparative analysis showcases the versatility of instructional design in different contexts (refer to comparative analysis of instructional design process). One project utilized AI-driven platforms and offline access solutions to enhance vocational skills among rural youth, addressing connectivity challenges (refer to comparative analysis of instructional design process). This approach aligns with the need to consider resource limitations in instructional design, as highlighted by [Gustafson & Branch, 2002]. Another project focused on modular course development and an LMS for corporate digital transformation training, demonstrating the importance of aligning training with organizational needs (refer to comparative analysis of instructional design process). Finally, a K-12 curriculum enhancement project demonstrates the use of AI for inclusive education practices, highlighting the focus on catering to diverse learning needs (refer to comparative analysis of instructional design process). This aligns with [Smith & Ragan, 2007] who emphasize the importance of catering to diverse learning styles in instructional design.

The case studies and analysis presented provide a compelling argument for integrating AI into instructional design. AI has the potential to personalize learning, improve outcomes, increase efficiency, address accessibility challenges, and create more engaging experiences for diverse learners. However, successful integration requires careful planning, a human-centered approach, and attention to ethical considerations. By leveraging AI strategically, instructional designers can create impactful learning experiences that cater to the unique needs of learners across diverse contexts.

CONCLUSION

In conclusion, this study explored the potential of Artificial Intelligence (AI) to enhance instructional design and ultimately improve learning outcomes. The case studies showcased the versatility of AI in personalizing learning experiences (Avanti project), improving accessibility for geographically dispersed learners (Rural Doctor program), and streamlining training processes (NASSCOM example). These findings align with existing research on the benefits of learner-centered design and technology integration in education.

However, successful AI integration requires careful planning and a human-centered approach. The proposed recommendations address this need by focusing on bridging the AI knowledge gap for instructional designers (IDs), developing a framework that prioritizes human expertise alongside AI functionalities, and conducting rigorous research to evaluate the impact of AI on various learning contexts. Ethical considerations regarding bias and data privacy must also be addressed during implementation.

Overall, this study highlights the vast potential of AI in instructional design. By strategically integrating AI tools while maintaining a focus on human judgment, creativity, and accessibility, educators can create more personalized, engaging, and impactful learning experiences that cater to the unique needs of diverse learners across educational settings. Future research should focus on evaluating long-term learning outcomes and addressing the logistical challenges associated with AI implementation in real-world educational environments. Through ongoing research and development, the field of instructional design can harness the power of AI to transform the learning landscape for the better.

Recommendations for Integrating AI into Instructional Design

Based on the research objectives and the findings of the study, here are some key recommendations for effectively integrating AI into instructional design:

Bridge the AI Knowledge Gap for IDs:

Develop Training Programs: Create workshops and online resources to equip instructional designers (IDs) with the foundational knowledge of AI capabilities and limitations in education.

Curated AI Toolkits: Provide curated lists of AI tools and functionalities specifically designed for different instructional design tasks, aligning with the research by Wang & Liu (2022) and Rosell et al. (2023). This bridges the knowledge gap and streamlines tool selection for IDs.

Community Building: Foster online communities or forums for IDs to share experiences, best practices, and challenges related to AI integration.

Develop a Human-Centered AI Integration Framework:

Focus on Amplification, not Replacement: The framework should outline how AI can augment specific ID tasks (e.g., content creation, automated grading) while emphasizing the crucial role of human expertise in areas like needs assessment, learning objective development, and creative instructional design (refer to findings of the task analysis). This addresses the concern raised by Mohammadi et al. (2021).

Prioritize Human Judgment and Creativity: The framework should encourage IDs to leverage AI tools for efficiency but highlight the importance of applying human judgment and creativity in design decisions to ensure a learner-centered approach (refer to findings of the task analysis).

Iterative Design Process: The framework should advocate for an iterative design process where AI-generated data and learner feedback inform continuous improvement of instructional materials and learning experiences.

Evaluate the Impact of AI-Assisted Instructional Design

Conduct Rigorous Research: Implement the developed framework in pilot projects across diverse educational contexts (K-12, higher education, corporate training). Conduct rigorous research studies with pre- and post-tests to measure the impact of AI-assisted instructional design on learner outcomes (refer to research objectives).

Focus on Diverse Learning Outcomes: The evaluation should consider not only traditional metrics like test scores but also assess engagement, motivation, knowledge retention, and transfer of learning to real-world situations.

Data-Driven Refinement: Analyze data collected during the evaluation to identify areas where AI integration is most effective and areas needing improvement. Use this data to refine the framework and further optimize AI integration in future instructional design projects.

Additional Considerations:

Ethical Considerations: Ensure the chosen AI tools are free from bias and adhere to data privacy regulations.

Accessibility: Incorporate accessibility features when integrating AI tools to ensure inclusivity for learners with disabilities (refer to findings of the task analysis).

Continuous Learning: Encourage IDs to continuously learn about new AI tools and advancements in the field to maintain their knowledge and expertise.

By implementing these recommendations and staying focused on a human-centered approach, the instructional design field can leverage the power of AI to create more personalized, engaging, and impactful learning experiences for diverse learners across various educational contexts.

Limitations

The case studies presented may not represent the full spectrum of educational contexts. They might focus on specific geographic locations (e.g., India) or educational sectors (e.g., K-12) without considering the broader applicability of AI integration across diverse learning environments like vocational training or adult education.

The study emphasizes the need for evaluation but may not address the long-term impact of AI-assisted instructional design. Longitudinal studies are needed to assess how learner outcomes and engagement are sustained over time after exposure to AI-integrated learning experiences.

The focus might be on identifying functionalities where AI can be beneficial and creating a framework for integration. However, the study may not adequately address the logistical challenges of implementing AI in real-world educational settings. These challenges could include infrastructure limitations, faculty training needs, and potential resistance to change from educators accustomed to traditional instructional methods.

REFERENCES

Abdelaziz, M., Kamel, S. S., Karam, O., & Abdelrahman, A. (2011). Evaluation of e-learning program versus traditional lecture instruction for undergraduate nursing students in a faculty of nursing. *Teaching and Learning in Nursing*, 6(2), 50–58. DOI: 10.1016/j.teln.2010.10.003

Adams Becker, S., Cummins, M., Davis, A., Freeman, A., Hall Giesinger, C., & Ananthanarayanan, V. (2017). *NMC horizon report: 2017 higher education edition*. The New Media Consortium.

Ahmad, S. F., Alam, M. M., Rahmat, M. K., Mubarik, M. S., & Hyder, S. I. (2022). Academic and administrative role of artificial intelligence in education. *Sustainability (Basel)*, 14(3), 1101. DOI: 10.3390/su14031101

Akgun, S., & Greenhow, C. (2021). Artificial intelligence in education: Addressing ethical challenges in K-12 settings. *AI and Ethics*, •••, 1–10. PMID: 34790956

Allen, I. E., Seaman, J., Poulin, R., & Straut, T. T. (2016). *Online report card: Tracking online education in the United States, 2016*. Babson Survey Research Group and Quahog Research Group.

Alper, A., & Gulbahar, Y. (2009). Trends and issues in educational technologies: A review of recent research in TOJET. *The Turkish Online Journal of Educational Technology*, 8(2).

Anglin, G. J., Vaez, H., & Cunningham, K. L. (2004). Visual representations and learning: The role of static and animated graphics. Handbook of Research on Educational Communications and Technology, 2, 865-916.

Angrist, M. W., & Bean, J. D. (2014). *Instructional design for online learning environments*. SAGE Publications.

Area, M., & Adell, J. (2009). eLearning: Enseñar y aprender en espacios virtuales. In J. De Pablos (Coord.), Tecnología educativa. La formación del profesorado en la era de Internet (pp. 391-424). Aljibe.

Barbera, E., Clara, M., & Linder-Vanberschot, J. A. (2013). Factors influencing student satisfaction and perceived learning in online courses. *E-Learning and Digital Media*, 10(3), 226–235. DOI: 10.2304/elea.2013.10.3.226

Bates, A. T. (2015). Teaching in a digital age. Glokalde, 1(3). DOI: 10.2304/elea.2013.10.3.226

Bayne, S. (2015). What's the matter with technology-enhanced learning? *Learning, Media and Technology*, 40(1), 5–20. DOI: 10.1080/17439884.2014.915851

Bednar, A. K., Cunningham, D., Duffy, T. M., & Perry, J. D. (1992). Theory into practice: How do we link. In Duffy, T. M., & Jonassen, D. H. (Eds.), *Constructivism and the technology of instruction: A conversation* (pp. 17–34). Psychology Press.

Beetham, H., & Sharpe, R. (Eds.). (2013). *Rethinking pedagogy for a digital age: Designing for 21st century learning*. Routledge. DOI: 10.4324/9780203078952

Benjamin, C., & Keenan, C. (2006). Implications of introducing problem-based learning in a traditionally taught course. *Engineering Education*, 1(1), 2–7. DOI: 10.1080/17500052.2006.11642153

Berger, C., & Kam, R. (1996). Definitions of instructional design. Retrieved from https://www.umich.edu/~ed626/define.html

Bingimlas, K. A. (2009). Barriers to the successful integration of ICT in teaching and learning environments: A review of the literature. *Eurasia Journal of Mathematics, Science and Technology Education*, 5(3), 235–245. DOI: 10.12973/ejmste/75275

Boling, E., Eccarius, M., Smith, K., & Frick, T. (2004). Instructional illustrations: Intended meanings and learner interpretations. *Journal of Visual Literacy*, 24(2), 185–204. DOI: 10.1080/23796529.2004.11674612

Bower, M., Howe, C., McCredie, N., Robinson, A., & Grover, D. (2014). Augmented reality in education – cases, places and potentials. *Educational Media International*, 51(1), 1–15. DOI: 10.1080/09523987.2014.889400

Bowman, R. F. (2018). Teaching and learning in a storytelling culture. *The Clearing House: A Journal of Educational Strategies, Issues and Ideas*, 91(3), 97–102. DOI: 10.1080/00098655.2017.1373547

Braun, V., & Clarke, V. (2006). Using thematic analysis in psychology. *Qualitative Research in Psychology*, 3(2), 77–101. DOI: 10.1191/1478088706qp063oa

Brown, K., & Patel, R. (2023). Generational Differences in AI Influencer Credibility and Engagement. *Marketing Science Review*, 29(2), 122–139. DOI: 10.1080/10909483.2023.2189763

Carroll, J. B. (1963). A model of school learning. *Teachers College Record*, 64(8), 723–733. DOI: 10.1177/016146816306400801

Chen, M. H.. (2020). Educational technology and AI: A systematic review of the literature. *Journal of Educational Technology & Society*.

Cherrstrom, C. A., Zarestky, J., & Deer, S. (2017). "This group is vital": Adult peers in community for support and learning. *Adult Learning*, 29(2), 43–52. DOI: 10.1177/1045159517739701

Chimalakonda, S., & Nori, K. V. (2018). A patterns based approach for design of educational technologies. arXiv. https://arxiv.org/abs/1802.02663

Collison, G., Elbaum, B., Haavind, S., & Tinker, R. (2000). *Facilitating online learning: Effective strategies for moderators*. Atwood.

Conole, G., & Alevizou, P. (2010). *A literature review of the use of Web 2.0 tools in higher education*. Higher Education Academy.

Cuban, L., & Jandric, P. (2015). The dubious promise of educational technologies: Historical patterns and future challenges. *E-Learning and Digital Media*, 12(3-4), 425–439. DOI: 10.1177/2042753015579978

Debattista, M. (2018). A comprehensive rubric for instructional design in e-learning. *The International Journal of Information and Learning Technology*, 35(2), 93–104. DOI: 10.1108/IJILT-09-2017-0092

Dianati, M., & Adib-Hajbaghery, M. (2012). Comparison of lecture and problem-based learning on learning of nursing students. *Future of Medical Education Journal*, 2(1), 7–11.

Garcia, J., & Wu, C. (2022). Exploring Authenticity in AI-Driven Influencer Marketing Across Generations. *JMR, Journal of Marketing Research*, 59(6), 789–804. DOI: 10.1177/00222437221117558

Guan, Y.. (2020). AI in education: A systematic review of the literature. *Computers & Education*.

Guerrero-Roldán, A. E., Rodríguez-González, M. E., Bañeres, D., Elasri-Ejjaberi, A., & Cortadas, P. (2021). Experiences in the use of an adaptive intelligent system to enhance online learners' performance: A case study in economics and business courses. *International Journal of Educational Technology in Higher Education*, 18(1), 1–27. DOI: 10.1186/s41239-021-00271-0

Guskey, T. R. (2010). Formative assessment. *Educational Leadership*, 68(1), 42–47.

Gustafson, K. L., & Branch, R. M. (2002). *Instructional design: Models and methods for developing effective learning experiences*. Merrill Prentice Hall.

International Design Center of the University of California. Irvine. (2019). The HCD [Human-Centered Design] Process. https://www.interaction-design.org/

Jessica-Mullins. (2023, March 10). Philosophy of Instructional Design. https://jessica-mullins.com/instructional-design-philosophy/

Lee, M., Zhao, T., & Fernandez, A. (2021). Authenticity Perception in AI Influencers: A Cross-Generational Analysis. *International Journal of Human-Computer Interaction*, 37(4), 351–366. DOI: 10.1080/10447318.2021.1898524

Mager, R. F., & Pipe, P. (1970). *Analyzing performance problems or you can't fix what you can't describe*. Fearon Publishers.

Mohammadi, Z., Kho ℵ rami, F., & Zarrabi, M. (2021). Instructional designers' perceptions of artificial intelligence: A thematic analysis. [doi: 10.1007/s11557-021-01823-5]. *TechTrends*, 65(6), 1222–1232.

Mohammadi, Z., Tavakol, M., & Arshadi, N. (2021). Artificial intelligence and instructional design: A review of literature. Computers & Education [DOI: 10.1016/j.caeai.2021.100014]. *Artificial Intelligence*, 2(2), 100014.

Mohammadi, Z., Tavakol, M., & Arshadi, N. (2021). Artificial intelligence and instructional design: A review of literature. Computers & Education [DOI: 10.1016/j.caeai.2021.100014]. *Artificial Intelligence*, 2(2), 100014.

Mohammadi, Z., Tavakol, M., & Arshadi, N. (2021). Artificial intelligence and instructional design: A review of literature. Computers & Education [DOI: 10.1016/j.caeai.2021.100014]. *Artificial Intelligence*, 2(2), 100014.

Ng, W. (2022). AI literacy in K-12: A systematic literature review. Journal of Educational Technology & Society.

Nguyen, H., & Kim, S. (2023). The Role of AI Influencers in Shaping Brand Perceptions Among Different Generations. *Journal of Consumer Behaviour*, 22(1), 15–30. DOI: 10.1002/cb.20984

Perrotta, C., & Selwyn, N. (2020). AI in education: A critical review of the literature. *Computers & Education*.

Rosell, A., Rodríguez-Gómez, G., Gutiérrez-Córeces, G., & Barberà, E. (2023). Artificial intelligence in instructional design: A systematic review of research and applications. [DOI: 10.1007/s10639-022-11001-z]. *Education and Information Technologies*, 28(2), 1421–1450.

Rosell, D., Suarez, A., & Congosto, M. (2023). A review of artificial intelligence in technology-enhanced learning. [doi: 10.1109/TLT.2022.3229403]. *IEEE Transactions on Learning Technologies*, 16(2), 182–198.

Smith, L., & Johnson, R. (2022). The Impact of AI Influencers on Millennials and Gen Z: A Comparative Study. *Journal of Digital Marketing*, 15(3), 45–60. DOI: 10.1016/j.jdmark.2022.01.005

Smith, P. L., & Ragan, G. Z. (2007). *Instructional design* (3rd ed.). John Wiley & Sons.

Van Laar, E., Van Deursen, A. J., Van Dijk, J. A., & De Haan, J. (2017). The relation between 21st-century skills and digital skills: A systematic literature review. *Computers in Human Behavior*, 72, 577–588. DOI: 10.1016/j.chb.2017.03.010

Van Merriënboer, J. G. (1997). Training complex cognitive skills: A four-component instructional design model for technical training. *Educational Psychologist*, 32(3), 157–172.

Wang, H., & Liu, X. (2022). Artificial intelligence in education: A critical review of the literature. [doi: 10.1007/s40563-022-00356-x]. *International Journal of Artificial Intelligence in Education*, 33(2), 393–430.

Wang, T., & Liu, X. (2022). Artificial intelligence in instructional design: A critical review of the literature and a proposed research framework. [DOI: 10.1007/s11423-021-09924-9]. *Educational Technology Research and Development*, 70(3), 825–844.

Wang, T., & Liu, X. (2022). Artificial intelligence in instructional design: A critical review of the literature and a proposed research framework. [DOI: 10.1007/s11423-021-09924-9]. *Educational Technology Research and Development*, 70(3), 825–844.

Wu, J. S., Chien, T. H., Chien, L. R., & Yang, C. Y. (2021). Using artificial intelligence to predict class loyalty and plagiarism in students in an online blended programming course during the COVID-19 pandemic. *Electronics (Basel)*, 10(18), 2203. DOI: 10.3390/electronics10182203

Zhai, Y.. (2021). Trends in AI applications in education: A systematic review. *Educational Technology Research and Development*.

Chapter 6
Future of Education Using Adaptive AI, Intelligent Systems, and Ethical Challenges

Sucheta Yambal
Dr. Babasaheb Ambedkar Marathwada University, India

Yashwant Arjunrao Waykar
https://orcid.org/0000-0002-9693-9738
Dr. Babasaheb Ambedkar Marathwada University, India

ABSTRACT

AI-driven adaptive learning, intelligent systems, and ethical issues will transform education. AI adaptive learning systems adjust content, pace, and feedback based on student performance and learning preferences. These technologies provide highly tailored education, student engagement, and scalable learning solutions across multiple contexts. Virtual tutors and automated grading systems are projected to minimize administrative workloads for teachers, allowing them to focus on creative instruction. Data privacy, algorithmic discrimination, and the possible loss of human engagement in learning are ethical concerns with AI in education. As AI becomes more prevalent in education, equitable access, data security, and openness in algorithmic decision-making are needed. Using AI to overcome these challenges may lead to a more efficient, inclusive, and ethical education system.

DOI: 10.4018/979-8-3693-6527-4.ch006

1. INTRODUCTION

1.1 The Future of Education via AI-Driven Adaptive Learning and Intelligent Systems

Rapid breakthroughs in artificial intelligence (AI), especially via AI-driven adaptive learning and intelligent systems, are transforming the future of education. These technologies are converting conventional classrooms into dynamic, individualized settings that address the varied demands of individual learners. AI adaptive learning systems can evaluate students' strengths, limitations, and learning preferences in real-time, allowing tailored learning experiences that improve understanding and retention. Conversely, intelligent technologies may automate administrative functions, provide real-time feedback, and enhance access to a plethora of educational materials, allowing both students and instructors to concentrate on advanced cognitive tasks.

The relevance of AI in education extends beyond optimizing learning routes; it also enables novel pedagogical approaches, such as intelligent tutoring systems (ITS), which replicate individualized teaching by assisting students in navigating complicated topics at their own speed. These systems are designed to provide customized interventions and structured assistance, enhancing engagement and comprehension. Furthermore, the amalgamation of AI with data analytics enables educators to monitor student development with unparalleled precision, discerning trends and forecasting results that may guide instructional choices and curricular modifications. As AI advances, it has the capacity to diminish educational disparities by delivering high-quality training to pupils irrespective of geographic or economic obstacles. Intelligent systems may connect learners from diverse backgrounds, democratizing educational access via cost-effective and scalable AI solutions. In this new paradigm, the educator's function is transforming from the principal provider of information to a facilitator of learning experiences. This transition promotes critical thinking, creativity, and problem-solving abilities, as students acquire the independence to investigate material pertinent to their own learning requirements and ambitions.

Nonetheless, the future of AI in education prompts significant inquiries about privacy, ethics, and the digital divide. It is essential to implement AI technology responsibly, prioritizing data security and fair access, as global education systems increasingly include these potent capabilities. In conclusion, AI adaptive learning and intelligent systems signify a revolutionary influence on the future of education. AI has the ability to transform the educational environment by boosting individualized learning, increasing administrative efficiency, and democratizing access to information, therefore equipping students for the challenges of the 21st century.

2. ARTIFICIAL INTELLIGENCE ADAPTIVE LEARNING

AI adaptive learning denotes the use of artificial intelligence to provide customized educational experiences that cater to the specific requirements, capabilities, and learning preferences of individual students. Through the ongoing analysis of a learner's performance data, AI systems may dynamically modify the difficulty, speed, and substance of courses, guaranteeing that each student gets education that is appropriately demanding. This method improves engagement and information retention by enabling students to concentrate on areas requiring enhancement while advancing more rapidly through subjects they have previously learned. Furthermore, AI adaptive learning solutions often provide instantaneous feedback, assisting students in rectifying errors and consolidating comprehension throughout the learning process. This technology promotes a more efficient, student-centered learning environment that adjusts to individual achievement, allowing educators to provide a more inclusive and individualized teaching approach. By addressing varied learning requirements, AI adaptive learning has the capacity to transform education, enhancing accessibility and efficacy for students from all backgrounds.

2.1. Customization in Education

AI-driven adaptive learning systems have transformed personalized education by facilitating customized learning trajectories. Holmes et al. (2019) assert that AI customizes to the learning styles and tempos of students, cultivating an environment that allows learners to advance at their own rate. Nguyen et al. (2020) assert that individualized AI learning enhances student engagement, resulting in increased retention rates and superior academic achievement.

2. 2. Immediate Feedback and Data Analysis

Artificial intelligence improves real-time feedback systems, providing instantaneous assistance and recommendations to learners. Johnson et al. (2018) discovered that AI-driven feedback systems improve students' metacognitive abilities via early identification of deficiencies. Baker and Siemens (2019) assert that AI-driven data analytics empower instructors to assess student performance and forecast consequences, facilitating prompt interventions.

2.3. Intelligent Tutoring Systems (ITS)

The deployment of intelligent tutoring systems (ITS) represents a potential domain in education. VanLehn (2016) posits that Intelligent Tutoring Systems may replicate the advantages of individualized tutoring by adaptively modifying topic difficulty according on student performance. Woolf (2018) elaborates on this, indicating that ITS not only customize education but also enhance student engagement via interactive conversations and problem-solving activities.

2.4. Scalability and Democratization of Education

AI-powered adaptive learning systems may facilitate the expansion of quality education to marginalized communities. Luckin et al. (2016) assert that these systems provide equitable access to high-quality education, irrespective of geographic location or socioeconomic condition. Zawacki-Richter et al. (2019) discovered that AI systems enhance online and remote learning by dismantling conventional obstacles to education.

2.5. The Role of Educators in AI-Enhanced Classrooms

AI does not replace educators but augments their functions by automating administrative duties and facilitating individualized education. Pedro et al. (2019) assert that AI systems can manage regular chores like grading and attendance, enabling educators to concentrate on advanced educational methods. Dillenbourg (2020) asserts that educators, augmented by AI, may transform into facilitators of knowledge, promoting critical thinking and creativity in pupils.

2.6. Equity and Accessibility

AI-driven educational tools has the capacity to mitigate inequalities in education. Gibson and Webb (2020) assert that AI-driven solutions may provide adjustments for students with impairments, hence improving inclusion in educational settings. McFarlane (2019) emphasizes that well used AI solutions may alleviate the difficulties encountered by disenfranchised students by providing personalized learning experiences suited to their specific requirements.

2.7. Artificial Intelligence and Gamification in Education

AI-driven gamified learning environments are increasingly gaining popularity. Arnab et al. (2018) contend that gamification, augmented by AI, enhances motivation and engagement by tailoring tasks to the learner's capabilities. Hamari et al. (2019) similarly discovered that AI-driven gamified systems may provide a more immersive and participatory educational experience, motivating students to take responsibility for their learning.

2.8. Ethical Considerations and Privacy

The use of AI in education has elevated issues over data privacy and ethics. Williamson and Eynon (2020) warn that while AI has significant promise, it needs stringent regulation for data acquisition and use. Selwyn (2020) similarly promotes the establishment of ethical frameworks to guarantee the responsible and equitable use of AI technologies in education.

2.9. Adaptive Learning in Tertiary Education

Adaptive learning technologies in higher education are shown significant efficacy. Popenici and Kerr (2017) discovered that AI-driven solutions assist institutions in scaling customized education and providing adaptable curriculum that react to student performance instantaneously. Mabrouk and ElKhayat (2019) reinforce this notion, highlighting the significance of AI-driven adaptive learning in enhancing student performance, especially in extensive lecture-based courses.

2.10. Self-Regulated Learning

AI promotes self-regulated learning by equipping students with the means to oversee and manage their own educational journey. Bannert et al. (2017) contend that AI-driven platforms improve self-regulation by providing tailored feedback and adaptive information, therefore assisting students in goal formulation and progress monitoring. Winne and Hadwin (2018) assert that these systems foster independent learning, motivating students to cultivate lifelong learning competencies.

2.11. AI-Supported Collaborative Learning

AI-augmented collaborative learning environments have shown potential in promoting peer engagement and knowledge exchange. Rosé et al. (2018) discovered that AI may enhance collaborative learning by recognizing and promoting constructive interactions among students. Heffernan et al. (2020) assert that AI can monitor group dynamics and provide tailored interventions to facilitate effective cooperation and peer learning.

2.12. Artificial Intelligence and Virtual Learning Environments

AI-enhanced virtual learning environments (VLEs) provide immersive experiences that connect physical and online classrooms. Chen et al. (2019) emphasize that AI-enhanced virtual learning environments may tailor themselves to student preferences and learning settings, hence fostering a flexible and engaging educational experience. Barbour et al. (2020) assert that these settings are especially beneficial for students engaged in distant or hybrid learning contexts.

2.13. The Influence of AI on Educational Outcomes

Numerous research have proven the beneficial effects of AI on student learning results. Kulik (2019) discovered that pupils using AI-driven adaptive learning tools exhibit notable enhancements in information retention and examination outcomes. Shute and Rahimi (2020) noted that AI improves critical thinking and problem-solving abilities by providing individualized tasks and specific feedback.

2.14. Obstacles to AI Implementation in Education

Notwithstanding the benefits, obstacles persist in the incorporation of AI into education. Hinojo-Lucena et al. (2019) contend that a primary obstacle is the insufficient training of educators in AI technologies, which restricts their effective use. Luan et al. (2020) highlight that the substantial expense of deploying AI technology in impoverished schools constitutes a significant barrier that requires attention.

2.15. Artificial Intelligence for Continuous Education

Artificial intelligence in education extends beyond formal schooling; it encompasses lifetime learning and professional growth as well. Siemens (2016) asserts that AI systems can assist learners in acquiring new skills throughout their lifetimes by providing flexible and adaptable learning paths. De Laat and Ryberg (2019) assert that AI may be pivotal in facilitating ongoing learning opportunities for professionals aiming to enhance their abilities in swiftly evolving sectors.

2.16. The Function of AI in Curriculum Development

AI may aid in curriculum creation by evaluating extensive educational data and discovering patterns that guide curriculum development. Pereira and Rodrigues (2019) propose that AI assists instructors in developing courses that are more attuned to student needs and changing industry demands. Chen et al. (2020) discovered that AI-driven curriculum design results in more efficient and relevant educational programs.

2.17. Artificial Intelligence in Evaluation

Artificial intelligence have the capacity to transform evaluation techniques. Pellegrino and Quellmalz (2018) contend that AI can provide more sophisticated evaluations of student learning by examining not just responses but also the methodologies used by students to reach such conclusions. Mislevy et al. (2020) discovered that AI-driven exams provide comprehensive insights into students' cognitive and problem-solving processes, enabling more precise evaluations of student performance.

2.18. Artificial Intelligence in Blended Learning Models

Artificial intelligence facilitates blended learning models that integrate conventional in-person training with online adaptive learning resources. Picciano (2019) observes that AI systems in blended learning contexts customize the online elements, optimizing student engagement in both face-to-face and digital training. Staker and Horn (2020) discovered that AI-enhanced blended learning results in improved educational outcomes, especially in K-12 environments.

2.19. The Impact of AI on Student Engagement

Dede (2019) discovered that artificial intelligence may enhance student engagement by tailoring information to individual preferences and learning requirements. Brown et al. (2020) indicate that AI technologies, like virtual assistants and chatbots, enhance student engagement by delivering prompt replies to inquiries, so alleviating frustration and promoting perseverance in learning activities.

2.20. Artificial Intelligence and Emotional Intelligence in Education

Artificial intelligence is used to assess emotional and social indicators to improve the educational experience. Calvo and D'Mello (2020) contend that emotion-aware AI systems can identify when students experience frustration, disengagement, or confusion, and provide prompt assistance to mitigate these emotional conditions. Lazarus et al. (2018) assert that this aptitude fosters a more supportive and responsive learning environment, resulting in improved educational results.

2.21. Prospective Research Avenues

Notwithstanding these advancements, more study is requisite to investigate the long-term effects of AI on schooling. Zawacki-Richter et al. (2019) emphasize that while short-term results are encouraging, the scalability and durability of AI across various educational settings need more research. Chen et al. (2020) advocate for more research on the potential of AI to mitigate equality challenges in education, especially in poor nations.

3. INVESTIGATING CURRENT AI IMPLEMENTATIONS IN EDUCATION

Artificial intelligence (AI) has advanced considerably in education, revolutionizing conventional teaching methodologies and improving learning experiences at all instructional levels. AI applications are being used in several capacities, including customized learning aids and automated administrative duties, aimed at enhancing teaching efficiency and student engagement.

3.1. Customized Education

A significant use of AI in education is adaptive learning. AI-driven systems such as DreamBox, Smart Sparrow, and Carnegie Learning use machine learning algorithms to assess student performance instantaneously. These systems modify educational material according to individual student requirements, customizing exercises, exams, and lessons to align with the student's strengths and shortcomings. This tailored methodology enables students to advance at their own rates, improving information retention and topic mastery. AI-driven recommendation algorithms in educational platforms provide learning materials, such videos, articles, or practice problems, that correspond to the learner's existing level of comprehension.

3.2. Intelligent Tutoring Systems (ITS)

Intelligent tutoring systems (ITS) are a significant application of artificial intelligence in the field of education. Systems such as ALEKS, Knewton, and MATHia provide personalized tutoring experiences by adaptively reacting to students' inputs, providing suggestions, assistance, and feedback. These technologies replicate the advantages of a human instructor by dynamically adjusting teaching and providing tailored interventions. Intelligent Tutoring Systems (ITS) may be especially beneficial in intricate disciplines such as mathematics, physics, and language acquisition, where customized assistance is essential for student achievement.

3.3. Artificial Intelligence-Driven Evaluation Instruments

Artificial intelligence is being used to optimize and enhance evaluation procedures. AI-driven evaluation instruments can autonomously evaluate quizzes, essays, and extended responses. Platforms such as Turnitin and Gradescope use AI to evaluate student submissions and provide comprehensive comments, emphasizing areas necessitating growth. These solutions allow instructors to save time on grading while providing students with prompt and actionable feedback. AI-driven evaluations may monitor the processes by which students reach their conclusions, enabling instructors to evaluate critical thinking and problem-solving abilities, rather than only the end response.

3.4. Educational Analytics

AI-driven learning analytics systems, such Civitas Learning and IBM Watson Education, are offering instructors enhanced insights into student behavior and learning patterns. Through the analysis of data on student engagement with course materials and assignments, these technologies may discern patterns, forecast learning results, and notify instructors of students who may be experiencing difficulties. Learning analytics may guide instructional choices, enabling educators to tailor classes and modify their teaching approaches based on real-time data. Predictive analytics, a component of these systems, assists educators in early intervention and delivering tailored assistance for at-risk kids.

3.5. Artificial Intelligence-Driven Virtual Assistants and Chatbots

Virtual assistants and AI-driven chatbots are progressively used in educational settings to aid students with administrative and academic responsibilities. Chatbots such as IBM Watson Education Assistant and Cognii can respond to student inquiries, elucidate challenging topics, and give assistance with homework. These AI systems are accessible around the clock, providing a handy resource for students requiring assistance outside conventional classroom hours. Virtual assistants are used to remind students of deadlines, provide study plans, and offer access to learning materials tailored to individual requirements.

3.6. Automated Administrative Functions

Artificial intelligence is optimizing administrative operations in education, enabling instructors and organizations to perform more effectively. Functions like grading, attendance monitoring, scheduling, and enrollment administration are progressively becoming automated by AI technologies. Platforms such as Ellucian and Schoology facilitate the automation of maintaining student data, course registrations, and academic performance reports. AI algorithms facilitate the formulation of ideal timetables by considering factors such as student availability, course demand, and instructor schedules. Automating these administrative duties liberates time for educators to concentrate more on education and student engagement.

3.7. Acquisition of Language and Artificial Intelligence

Artificial intelligence applications have shown significant advantages in language acquisition. Applications such as Duolingo, Rosetta Stone, and Babbel use artificial intelligence algorithms to assess a learner's advancement and tailor language instruction appropriately. These systems use natural language processing (NLP) to replicate conversations, provide immediate feedback on pronunciation, and furnish tailored language instruction. AI-driven language learning tools adjust to the user's skill level, guaranteeing that the courses are suitably difficult without being excessive.

3.8. Gamified Education with Artificial Intelligence

Artificial intelligence is being used into educational games to provide captivating, interactive learning experiences. Gamified educational settings, exemplified by platforms like Kahoot! Additionally, Quizlet employs artificial intelligence to monitor students' progress and modify game difficulty instantaneously. These platforms use AI algorithms to tailor challenges and inquiries according on the learner's performance, enhancing the enjoyment of learning while reinforcing essential ideas. Gamified learning settings have proven especially helpful in enhancing student motivation and knowledge retention.

3.9. Artificial Intelligence and Special Education

Artificial intelligence has shown promise in improving special education by offering customized assistance for children with impairments. For instance, applications such as Otter.ai and Google's Project Euphonia use artificial intelligence to convert spoken language into text, enhancing the accessibility of classroom discussions for students with hearing disabilities. AI-driven voice recognition and text-to-speech technologies are used to assist kids with dyslexia and other learning impairments. These programs enable instructors to more effectively assist students needing extra accommodations, hence offering a more inclusive educational environment.

3.10. Artificial Intelligence in Virtual and Augmented Reality (VR/AR)

Artificial intelligence is being integrated with virtual and augmented reality technology to provide immersive educational experiences. Platforms such as zSpace and Labster use AI to replicate experiential learning activities, like virtual scientific laboratories and historical expeditions, enabling students to interact with information more dynamically. These AI-enhanced VR/AR technologies facilitate experiential learning, especially in STEM disciplines, where the practical application of knowledge is essential.

Artificial intelligence applications in education are now revolutionizing the processes of teaching and learning. AI is fostering more dynamic, efficient, and inclusive educational settings via individualized learning platforms, automated administrative activities, and immersive virtual experiences. As these technologies advance, they are expected to improve learning outcomes and the whole educational experience, making high-quality education more accessible and customized to the requirements of various learners. The incorporation of AI in education requires meticulous attention to ethical ramifications, data protection issues, and the need for fair access across diverse educational environments.

4. THE ROLE OF AI IN ADVANCING ACCESSIBILITY AND INCLUSIVITY IN EDUCATION

Artificial intelligence (AI) is significantly enhancing accessibility and inclusiveness in education by delivering tailored assistance to various learners, including those with impairments, and guaranteeing equitable access to educational opportunities for everyone. AI-driven tools, technologies, and platforms are rendering educational settings more inclusive and adaptable to the diverse demands of learners with varying backgrounds, skills, and learning preferences.

4.1. Artificial Intelligence for Students with Disabilities

Artificial intelligence technology are substantially improving educational experiences for kids with physical, cognitive, and learning challenges. Speech-to-text and text-to-speech technology provide greater access to instructional information for students with visual or hearing impairments. Technologies such as Google's Project Euphonia and Microsoft's Immersive Reader use artificial intelligence to transcribe voice into text or convert text into speech, enabling students to engage with educational content in forms tailored to their need.

Moreover, AI-driven assistive solutions such as Otter.ai provide real-time transcription of lectures, aiding students who are deaf or hard of hearing in comprehending classroom discussions. AI-driven screen readers, like JAWS (Job Access with Speech), enhance accessibility for students with visual impairments by audibly conveying on-screen text. These technologies are essential for enabling students with impairments to engage fully in both physical and virtual classrooms.

4.2. Customized Education for Varied Learners

AI-driven adaptive learning systems may customize instructional material to meet the distinct learning requirements of individual pupils. This is especially beneficial for kids with cognitive impairments, like dyslexia, ADHD, or autism spectrum disorder. AI algorithms may modify the complexity, tempo, and structure of educational materials to suit various learning styles, therefore enhancing students' comprehension and retention of knowledge.

AI-driven systems, such as Kurzweil 3000, support students with learning difficulties by using multimodal learning techniques, including reading aloud textual information and displaying visual highlights, therefore enhancing student engagement with the topic. Furthermore, AI systems that track student progress may identify when a student is experiencing difficulties and provide prompt, tailored solutions, guaranteeing that no learner is overlooked.

4.3. AI-Enhanced Inclusive Language Acquisition

AI has improved inclusiveness in language acquisition by catering to the requirements of pupils who speak diverse languages or have language-related learning challenges. AI-driven language learning applications such as Duolingo and Babbel use natural language processing (NLP) to provide customized learning trajectories, individualized feedback, and instantaneous language translation, enabling learners to progress at their own speed and in their preferred language.

AI-based solutions like Voiceitt and Cognixion are facilitating communication for children with verbal challenges by reading and transforming non-verbal signals or speech impairments into intelligible speech. This facilitates enhanced communication among students, classmates, and instructors, hence fostering more inclusive learning environments.

4.4. Artificial Intelligence-Enhanced Instantaneous Translation

AI-powered real-time translation services, such Microsoft Translator and Google Translate, have become essential resources in bilingual classrooms and for overseas students. These AI technologies provide the automated translation of lectures, instructional materials, and discussions, so enabling students who are not proficient in the language of instruction to engage fully in their educational settings. AI-driven translation dismantles language barriers, ensuring equitable access to education irrespective of a student's linguistic heritage.

4.5. Artificial Intelligence in Virtual Learning Environments for Inclusivity

AI-integrated virtual learning environments (VLEs) have enhanced inclusivity, enabling students from many geographical regions and socio-economic backgrounds to access excellent education. AI may modify VLE material to accommodate diverse accessibility requirements, such as altering text sizes for visually challenged students or integrating sign language in films for hearing-impaired learners. Platforms like as Moodle and Canvas are integrating AI techniques to enhance inclusive education by providing accessible features for students with impairments.

Moreover, AI facilitates access to remote and online learning for students with constrained internet connectivity or obsolete equipment by optimizing material delivery according to bandwidth and device specifications. AI is a crucial instrument for engaging pupils in underprivileged regions, thereby promoting global educational inclusion.

4.6. Artificial Intelligence for Emotional and Social Assistance

Artificial intelligence is being used to enhance emotional and social inclusion in school, especially for children who may experience isolation or marginalization due to impairments, learning issues, or social obstacles. Emotion AI, or affective computing, may assess pupils' emotional conditions and provide remedies as necessary. Applications such as Replika and Woebot use artificial intelligence to provide mental health assistance by emulating dialogues and furnishing tailored emotional support to pupils experiencing anxiety, tension, or social isolation.

Furthermore, AI-driven systems may assist children with autism or social communication difficulties by analyzing non-verbal signals, providing advice on social interactions, and promoting peer participation. These strategies are essential for fostering emotional well-being and establishing a caring, inclusive classroom atmosphere in which all kids feel connected.

4.7. Artificial Intelligence in Inclusive Classroom Management

AI not only aids individual learners but also promotes inclusion by assisting instructors in managing heterogeneous classes more efficiently. AI-driven technologies such as Classcraft and GoGuardian enable educators to oversee student participation and customize lessons with real-time data. AI assists educators in monitoring students' engagement, attentiveness, and advancement, enabling the identification of those requiring further assistance or different instructional methods, so guaranteeing that all learners get enough attention in the educational process.

Moreover, AI systems may assist educators in developing curriculum and pedagogical strategies that accommodate all learners, including those with impairments as well as advanced or brilliant individuals. Through the analysis of student performance data, AI may recommend adjustments to lesson plans that address the diverse requirements of students, fostering a more inclusive classroom environment.

4.8. Artificial Intelligence and Ethical Considerations for Inclusivity

Although AI has significant opportunities for improving accessibility and diversity, it is crucial to evaluate the ethical ramifications of its use in education. AI systems must be developed with inclusion as a priority, ensuring they do not inadvertently reinforce prejudices or exclude certain student groups. Algorithms used in adaptive learning systems must undergo frequent audits for bias to provide equitable support for students of varying abilities, ethnic origins, and socioeconomic positions.

Data privacy becomes a significant problem when using AI for accessibility. Numerous AI applications depend on gathering sensitive data about students' learning behaviors, impairments, or emotional conditions. Educational institutions and developers must emphasize the ethical use of AI by enforcing stringent data security regulations and guaranteeing openness in the utilization and storage of student data. Artificial intelligence is markedly improving accessibility and inclusion in education by providing tailored assistance for students with impairments, dismantling language obstacles, and fostering emotionally supportive learning environments. AI employs adaptive learning technologies, real-time translation tools, assistive technologies, and emotion-aware systems to guarantee that all students, irrespective of their skills or backgrounds, possess equal opportunity for educational success. As these technologies advance, the emphasis must be on guaranteeing ethical, transparent, and equitable use of AI to foster genuinely inclusive educational settings for all learners.

5. INTELLIGENT TUTORING SYSTEMS (ITS): AN INNOVATIVE ADVANCEMENT IN ADAPTIVE EDUCATION

Intelligent Tutoring Systems (ITS) signify a groundbreaking development in adaptive education, using artificial intelligence (AI) to provide individualized, one-on-one training customized to the unique requirements of each learner. In contrast to conventional education systems that use a uniform methodology, ITS adaptively modifies the learning experience with real-time data, facilitating a more personalized and efficacious educational process.

5.1. What are Intelligent Tutoring Systems?

Intelligent Tutoring Systems (ITS) are AI-driven platforms that emulate the function of a human tutor by offering individualized advice, feedback, and instructional assistance. These systems evaluate student engagement with educational resources—such as answers to questions, problem-solving methods, and time allocated to tasks—and use machine learning algorithms to modify the content, complexity, and instructional techniques appropriately. The objective is to provide a customized learning environment that accommodates each student's own learning style, tempo, and requirements.

ITS often concentrate on certain topic domains, especially those that gain from organized and sequential learning methodologies, such as mathematics, physics, and language acquisition. Through the constant monitoring of student progress,

ITS offers real-time interventions, facilitating students' mastery of concepts prior to advancing to more complex subjects. Notable Intelligent Tutoring Systems (ITS) include ALEKS (Assessment and Learning in Knowledge Spaces), Knewton, MATHia, and Cognitive Tutor.

5.2. Functionality of ITS: Essential Elements

ITS generally comprise four essential components that together produce a customized and adaptable learning environment:

The Expert Model: This element signifies the system's comprehension of the subject matter being taught. It encompasses comprehensive knowledge of the subject, including the regulations, ideas, and problem-solving methodologies that students are anticipated to acquire. The expert model serves as a standard for evaluating student performance and assists the system in identifying accurate answers and solutions.

The Student Model: The student model monitors the learner's knowledge, abilities, and development over time. It examines student behavior, including the nature of their mistakes, their rate of learning, and their comprehension of topics. This model perpetually evolves according on student interactions, allowing the system to tailor material and instructional tactics to meet the learner's requirements.

The Instructional Model: The instructional model dictates the pedagogical tactics used by the ITS to impart the curriculum. This methodology identifies suitable educational strategies according to the student's existing comprehension and advancement. For instance, if a student has difficulty with a certain idea, the instructional model may provide further practice problems or furnish pointers and elucidations to aid the student in comprehending the subject.

The Interface Model: The interface model regulates the interaction between the ITS and the student, including the presentation of information and the student's engagement with the system. This component guarantees an interesting and intuitive learning experience, often integrating multimedia components like films, animations, and interactive simulations to augment learning.

5.3. Benefits of Intelligent Tutoring Systems in Adaptive Education

Personalized Learning: A major advantage of Intelligent Tutoring Systems (ITS) is its capacity to tailor the educational experience for individual students. Through real-time analysis of student performance, ITS may modify the speed, substance, and complexity of courses to align with the learner's requirements. This enables tailored assistance for struggling students while enabling advanced learners to get through the course more rapidly. This personalization leads to enhanced learning efficiency and superior outcomes relative to conventional classroom training.

Immediate Feedback: Intelligent Tutoring Systems provide instantaneous feedback to students, facilitating their comprehension of errors and enabling prompt correction. For instance, when a student responds erroneously to a question, the system may elucidate the rationale behind the error and provide direction on other problem-solving strategies. This immediate feedback is essential for consolidating learning and averting the establishment of misunderstandings.
24/7 Availability: In contrast to human tutors, Intelligent Tutoring Systems (ITS) are accessible at all times, offering students individualized learning opportunities whenever required. This is especially advantageous for students requiring additional assistance outside standard school hours or those in rural locations with restricted access to tutoring services. ITS also enables students to study at their own speed, providing flexibility in both time and place.
Data-Driven Insights: Intelligent Tutoring Systems provide extensive data on student performance, enabling instructors to get profound insights into each learner's strengths and limitations. Educators may use this data to pinpoint kids requiring further assistance, modify their teaching methodologies, and make educated choices about curriculum development. ITS data may assist long-term educational planning by elucidating patterns in student performance and learning practices.
Scalability: A primary problem in education is delivering tailored teaching to extensive student populations. ITS provides a scalable approach by delivering personalized help to several students concurrently. In both expansive classrooms and virtual learning settings, ITS can guarantee that each student has the necessary attention and direction, irrespective of class size or instructor accessibility.

5.4. Utilization of Intelligent Transportation Systems in Education

K-12 Education: Information Technology Systems are widely used in K-12 education to assist pupils in disciplines such as mathematics, science, and reading. Programs like Cognitive Tutor for mathematics and iSTART for reading comprehension have shown efficacy in enhancing student performance via customized education that adjusts to individual learner requirements. These methods assist students in developing fundamental abilities, guaranteeing their mastery of essential ideas prior to progressing to more difficult topics.

In higher education, Intelligent Tutoring Systems (ITS) assist students in intricate disciplines such as physics, chemistry, and engineering. ITS assists college students in managing difficult courses with tailored coaching, practice problems, and constructive comments. Platforms such as ALEKS are extensively used at universities to assist students in mathematics and science courses by providing adaptive learning pathways tailored to specific student requirements.

Corporate Training and Professional Development: Information Technology Systems are used in corporate training settings to provide tailored learning experiences for workers. AI-driven training systems may adjust to the learning preferences and professional requirements of workers, facilitating the acquisition of new skills and information at their own pace. This is especially beneficial in sectors requiring continuous training and skill enhancement, like technology, healthcare, and finance.

5.5. Obstacles and Constraints of Intelligent Transportation Systems

Development Complexity: Constructing efficient Intelligent Tutoring Systems need advanced AI algorithms and comprehensive data on the topic matter and student learning behaviors. This renders the development process intricate and protracted. Furthermore, developing precise student models that represent varied learning styles and requirements may be difficult, particularly in disciplines where several legitimate methods for problem-solving exist.

Bias and Fairness: Similar to other AI systems, Intelligent Tutoring Systems (ITS) are vulnerable to biases present in their algorithms and data sets. If not meticulously developed, Intelligent Tutoring Systems (ITS) may preferentially benefit some learning styles or demographic cohorts at the expense of others. Guaranteeing that ITS provide equal learning experiences for all students, irrespective of background, is a vital concern for developers and educators.

Teacher Engagement: Although Intelligent Tutoring Systems are effective instruments, they cannot substitute for human educators. ITS are most effective when used alongside human education, enabling educators to concentrate on higher-order teaching responsibilities such as leading conversations, mentoring students, and offering emotional support. Educators must get training to proficiently incorporate Intelligent Tutoring tools into their classrooms, ensuring these tools augment rather than replace conventional teaching methodologies.

5.6. The Prospects of Intelligent Tutoring Systems in Education

As AI technology advances, Intelligent Tutoring Systems are anticipated to become more complex and adept at accommodating a broader spectrum of topics and learning modalities. Future Intelligent Tutoring Systems (ITS) may integrate modern technologies such as natural language processing (NLP) and emotion identification to provide more customized and sympathetic educational experiences. Furthermore, ITS are expected to extend into domains including as creativity, critical thinking, and collaboration—competencies that are progressively vital in contemporary society but challenging to impart via conventional approaches.

Furthermore, ITS has the capacity to transform education worldwide by delivering tailored learning experiences to students in rural and underprivileged regions. Utilizing cloud computing and mobile technology, ITS can provide high-quality, personalized education to students in resource-limited regions, therefore addressing the global education disparity.

Intelligent Tutoring Systems revolutionize adaptive education by providing individualized, data-driven learning experiences tailored to the distinct requirements of each learner. Through the provision of real-time feedback, customized education, and round-the-clock accessibility, Intelligent Tutoring Systems are revolutionizing student learning, especially in disciplines necessitating the mastery of intricate ideas. As Information Technology Systems advance, they are poised to significantly enhance the effectiveness, equity, and accessibility of education for learners globally.

6. CUSTOMIZED LEARNING PLATFORMS: TRANSFORMING EDUCATION BY PERSONALIZATION

Personalized learning platforms have become a vital innovation in contemporary education, using new technology to provide customized learning experiences suited to each student's distinct requirements, speed, and learning style. These platforms provide tailored educational pathways, guaranteeing that each student has specific help and tools to realize their academic potential. Personalized learning platforms are revolutionizing conventional educational techniques via the use of data-driven insights, machine learning, and artificial intelligence (AI), enhancing efficiency, engagement, and accessibility in learning.

6.1. What are Personalized Learning Platforms?

Personalized learning platforms are educational systems that tailor learning experiences to align with the distinct attributes of each learner. These platforms use algorithms, data analytics, and adaptive technologies to assess a student's learning habits, preferences, progress, and performance. Utilizing these insights, the system customizes material, pedagogical approaches, and evaluations to address the specific requirements of the learner.

In contrast to conventional educational models that provide a uniform curriculum and pace for all learners, customized learning platforms dynamically adjust to the individual learning styles of each student. Should a learner have difficulties with a certain idea, the platform might provide further resources, practice tasks, or alternate elucidations. If a student achieves, the platform may provide more complex content to maintain the learner's engagement and challenge.

Figure 1. Broader concepts involved in personalized learning platforms

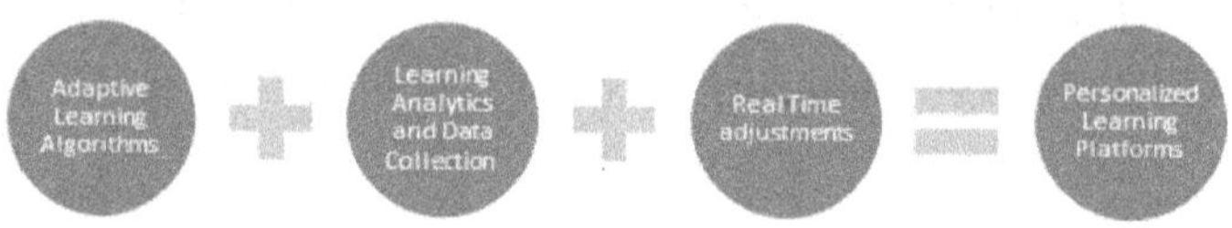

6.2. Essential Characteristics of Customized Learning Platforms

Adaptable Learning routes: A distinguishing characteristic of customized learning platforms is their capacity to provide adaptable learning routes. These pathways are customized to the unique progression of each learner, allowing students to go through the content at their own speed. Platforms such as DreamBox and Knewton use algorithms to evaluate students' replies and dynamically modify task difficulty, ensuring they are neither overstressed nor insufficiently challenged.

Continuous Feedback and Assessment: Personalized learning systems provide real-time feedback, enabling students to rectify errors promptly and enhance their comprehension of the subject matter. Ongoing evaluations, including quizzes, interactive activities, or practice exercises, enable the platform to track progress and implement necessary modifications to the learning trajectory. Platforms such as Quizlet and Edmodo provide immediate feedback methods to enhance learning and assist students in recognizing areas for improvement.

Data-Driven Insights for Educators: Educators get advantages from the analytics offered by customized learning systems. These systems monitor several indicators, including student engagement, time allocated to assignments, regions of difficulty, and material proficiency. Platforms such as Khan Academy and Google Classroom provide comprehensive data that enable instructors to identify areas of student proficiency and those requiring more assistance. This data-centric methodology enables educators to customize their teaching to address the requirements of individual students, hence enhancing decision-making processes.

Customization of Learning Materials: Personalized platforms provide an array of educational resources—including videos, texts, quizzes, games, and simulations—that accommodate diverse learning styles. Visual learners may find video lessons advantageous, whilst those who choose reading or experiential learning may engage with information tailored to their inclinations. This customisation guarantees that learners interact with knowledge in the most effective manner for their individual needs.

Integration of AI and Machine Learning: Numerous customized learning systems use AI and machine learning to perpetually enhance the learning experience. Artificial intelligence can forecast when a student is prone to difficulties, identify trends in learning behavior, and autonomously modify the curriculum to provide the appropriate degree of challenge or assistance. ALEKS use artificial intelligence to evaluate students' knowledge in mathematics, science, and other disciplines, generating personalized learning trajectories that concentrate on areas requiring the greatest assistance.

Gamification and Engagement: Numerous systems use gamification components, like points, badges, leaderboards, and prizes, to incentivize students and enhance the interactivity and enjoyment of the learning experience. Platforms such as Duolingo and Classcraft include gamified features to maintain student engagement, providing incentives for assignment completion or skill mastery. Gamification enhances the enjoyment of learning while cultivating a feeling of accomplishment and motivating students to remain engaged.

6.3. Illustrations of Prominent Personalized Learning Platforms

Khan Academy: A popular website providing free online courses, lectures, and practice activities across several areas. Khan Academy employs individualized learning dashboards to assist students in concentrating on their own learning objectives, monitoring their progress, and offering customized suggestions depending on their performance.

DreamBox: An adaptive mathematics platform for K-8 kids that modifies its courses in real-time according on students' responses to questions. DreamBox provides tailored training that addresses individual learning requirements and preferences, making mathematics entertaining and attainable for students of varying proficiency levels.

Coursera and edX: These platforms provide tailored learning experiences for higher education and professional advancement via adaptive course suggestions, progress monitoring, and flexible learning trajectories. Coursera and edX use artificial intelligence to recommend courses, tasks, and educational resources according to students' interests, career aspirations, and previous accomplishments.

Smart Sparrow: An adaptive e-learning platform enabling instructors to create individualized learning experiences by modifying material and evaluations in real-time according to student interactions. Smart Sparrow's adaptive lessons address individual learning requirements, guaranteeing that students get appropriate knowledge at the optimal moment.

6.4. Advantages of Customized Learning Platforms

Personalized learning systems provide pupils personalized attention, enabling them to concentrate on their particular issues. Students may go at their own speed, guaranteeing a comprehensive understanding of the content prior to advancing. This method is especially advantageous for students who may have difficulties in a conventional classroom environment where the instructional speed is not customized to their requirements.

Improved Engagement: By tailoring the educational experience to align with students' interests, strengths, and learning preferences, customized platforms enhance student engagement and motivation. The use of interactive information, gamification, and real-time feedback guarantees that learners stay actively engaged in their studies, hence reducing the probability of boredom or disengagement.

Enhanced Learning Outcomes: Studies indicate that individualized learning results in superior academic achievement and a more profound comprehension of subjects. By delivering focused assistance in areas of greatest need, these platforms guarantee the timely resolution of learning deficiencies. Consequently, pupils are more inclined to attain mastery and retain information over an extended period.

Flexibility and Accessibility: Personalized learning platforms provide adaptable learning possibilities, enabling students to engage in education at any time and from any location. This is particularly crucial for students with diverse schedules, those residing in distant locations, or those with impairments. Platforms such as Udemy and Skillshare render education accessible to a worldwide audience, offering tailored course suggestions and on-demand learning experiences that align with individual tastes.

Data-Driven Instruction: Educators get advantages from the data gathered by individualized learning systems. Through the analysis of this data, instructors may discern patterns in student performance, identify areas of difficulty for learners, and customize their training appropriately. This data-centric methodology in education results in better informed and successful initiatives that address the requirements of all learners.

6.5. Obstacles and Factors

Equity and Access: Although individualized learning systems provide several advantages, questions of access and equity persist. Not many pupils possess the requisite technology or internet access to use these sites effectively. The digital divide may exacerbate disparities in educational possibilities for pupils from low-income or rural homes.

Data Privacy: Personalized learning systems depend significantly on student data to tailor the educational experience. This, however, creates apprehensions over data privacy and security. Educational institutions and platform providers must guarantee the protection and responsible use of student data, with rigorous compliance to privacy laws and regulations.

Excessive Dependence on Technology: Although individualized learning platforms are effective instruments, they must not replace the function of human educators. A equilibrium between technology and human connection is essential to guarantee that students have both tailored learning and the emotional and social support uniquely offered by instructors.

Content Bias: The algorithms behind customized learning platforms are only as impartial as the data upon which they are trained. Developers must guarantee that material and suggestions are devoid of biases pertaining to gender, race, socioeconomic status, or learning capability. Systematic evaluations of the algorithms used by these platforms are essential to guarantee fairness and equality.

6.6. The Prospects of Customized Learning Platforms

As technology advances, customized learning systems will become more sophisticated, integrating state-of-the-art AI technologies such as natural language processing (NLP), machine learning, and emotion recognition to enhance the learning experience. The future of individualized learning will likely include platforms that adjust to both cognitive requirements and emotional conditions, providing assistance when students experience stress or frustration.

Furthermore, virtual and augmented reality (VR and AR) are anticipated to assume a more significant role in customized education, fostering immersive and interactive learning environments tailored to individual tastes. These technologies has the potential to transform education by enhancing immersive and engaging learning, particularly in disciplines such as physics, history, and art. Personalized learning platforms are revolutionizing education by providing tailored, data-informed learning experiences that adjust to the requirements of each learner. These systems provide improved student outcomes, sustained engagement, and personalized education via adaptive learning pathways, instantaneous feedback, and AI-driven customisation. Despite the obstacles of fairness, data privacy, and content bias, the promise of customized learning platforms to improve education is unequivocal. As technology progresses, these platforms will assume an increasingly pivotal role in influencing the future of education.

7. ETHICAL DILEMMAS IN THE IMPLEMENTATION OF AI ADAPTIVE LEARNING AND INTELLIGENT SYSTEMS IN EDUCATION

The use of AI adaptive learning and intelligent systems in education has yielded substantial progress, providing tailored learning experiences and enhancing educational results. Nonetheless, these breakthroughs present ethical dilemmas that educators, developers, and governments must confront to guarantee that AI-driven education is both efficient and equitable. These problems include concerns over data privacy, prejudice, accountability, openness, and the risk of excessive dependence on technology. Comprehending and mitigating these issues is crucial to fully using AI in education while protecting the rights and interests of students and educators.

7.1. Data Privacy and Security

A significant ethical challenge in AI-driven educational systems is the acquisition and use of student data. AI adaptive learning solutions depend significantly on extensive personal data to tailor educational experiences, including performance metrics, behavioral data, and sensitive demographic information.

- Student Data Acquisition: AI systems compile comprehensive data on student interactions, academic advancement, and individual preferences. This information is essential for customization; nevertheless, it also prompts questions over the extent of data collection and whether students and parents are adequately informed about its use. Ensuring informed permission is essential, although sometimes neglected in educational environments when technology is used without explicit communication about data utilization.
- Data Security: Educational institutions must guarantee the safe storage and protection of student data against breaches. If data is compromised, it may be exploited, resulting in possible risks such as identity theft or illegal access to confidential information. Instances of data breaches in educational platforms underscore the need for stringent security measures.
- Third-Party Data Dissemination: Frequently, data acquired by AI platforms is disseminated to other firms for analytical purposes or to augment the platform's capabilities. This prompts concerns over data ownership and its monetization methods. Educational institutions and instructors must meticulously evaluate third-party vendors to guarantee that student data is not being misappropriated for commercial objectives without authorization.

7.2. Prejudice in Artificial Intelligence Algorithms

AI algorithms used in adaptive learning systems are trained on data sets that include real-world biases, potentially resulting in discriminatory consequences inside educational environments.

- Algorithmic Bias: AI systems may inadvertently sustain or intensify biases inherent in the training data. If an adaptive learning platform is educated on data mostly representing the learning habits of a certain demographic group, it may encounter difficulties in delivering equal learning experiences for students from diverse backgrounds. This may result in inequities in the quality of education provided to various student demographics influenced by characteristics such as race, gender, or socioeconomic position.

- Cultural Bias: Adaptive learning systems may exhibit cultural biases in the material they provide. A system that mostly utilizes materials created within a particular cultural context may inadequately provide relevant and significant learning experiences for students from varied backgrounds. This may marginalize minority pupils or perpetuate cultural stereotypes, so defeating the objective of fostering inclusive educational settings.
- Mitigating prejudice: Addressing prejudice in AI necessitates a coordinated endeavor to guarantee that algorithms are trained on varied and representative datasets. Frequent audits of AI systems may facilitate the identification and rectification of biases; but, developers and educators must maintain vigilance to avert the entrenchment of biased behaviors inside the system.

7.3. Clarity and Responsibility

The use of AI in education prompts inquiries on transparency and accountability. As AI systems advance in complexity, it becomes more challenging for educators, students, and parents to comprehend the decision-making processes, especially for adaptive learning platforms.

- Lack of Transparency in Decision-Making: AI systems often function as "black boxes," making it difficult to comprehend the rationale behind certain conclusions. For example, when a student is advised on a certain learning trajectory or identified for intervention, the criteria used by the system to arrive at that suggestion may be ambiguous. The absence of openness may result in misunderstanding and distrust among children, educators, and parents.
- Accountability: The deployment of AI systems in decision-making processes affecting student learning prompts inquiries on the attribution of responsibility in the event of adverse outcomes. When a student's learning results are adversely impacted by a defective algorithm, it may not be readily apparent whether responsibility rests with the creators, the institution, or the instructors using the system. Defining explicit lines of responsibility is essential for the responsible and ethical use of AI systems.
- Regulatory Oversight: A more robust regulatory framework is required to control the use of AI in education. Governments and educational institutions must design regulations that guarantee openness in the development, deployment, and oversight of AI systems. This includes establishing criteria for algorithmic openness, requiring periodic audits, and guaranteeing that students and instructors get comprehensible explanations on the use of AI systems.

7.4. Equity and Accessibility

AI adaptive learning systems has the capacity to improve educational fairness by delivering individualized learning experiences to every learner. Nevertheless, they also pose a danger of intensifying existing inequities if not meticulously executed.

The Digital Divide: Access to AI-enhanced education is contingent upon possessing the requisite technology infrastructure, including dependable internet connectivity and devices. Students from economically disadvantaged backgrounds or rural regions may be deprived of the technology necessary to properly use AI-driven educational systems. The digital divide may exacerbate existing disparities in educational performance, especially for pupils from marginalized backgrounds.

- Financial Implications of Implementation: The integration of AI systems in educational institutions might incur substantial costs, especially for schools with constrained financial resources. wealthy schools are more inclined to possess the resources necessary for the implementation of sophisticated AI technology, hence placing less wealthy institutions at a disadvantage. This may result in a bifurcated education system whereby only students at affluent institutions gain from tailored AI-enhanced learning.
- Accessibility for Students with impairments: Although AI may enhance educational inclusivity by offering tailored assistance for students with impairments, it must be developed with accessibility as a priority. If AI platforms are not designed to support students with diverse physical or cognitive capacities, they may exacerbate the marginalization of these learners. Developers must guarantee that AI systems are compatible with assistive technology and accessible to all students, irrespective of their ability.

7.5. Excessive Dependence on Technology

AI adaptive learning systems provide substantial advantages; nonetheless, there exists a danger of over dependence on technology, potentially undermining human connection and critical thinking.

Education encompasses not just the transmission of knowledge but also the cultivation of social and emotional competencies, critical thinking, and empathy, which are most effectively nurtured via interpersonal engagement. Excessive dependence on AI systems may diminish the role of educators in delivering these critical components of education. Although AI can provide tailored education, it cannot substitute the emotional support and mentoring offered by educators.

• Diminished Teacher Autonomy: As AI systems increasingly personalize education, there is a potential danger that educators may feel disempowered or that their professional judgment is being compromised. Educators may develop an excessive reliance on AI-generated suggestions, thereby constraining their capacity for innovation and agility in instructional approaches. Achieving equilibrium between AI assistance and educator autonomy is essential for successful education.

7.6. Ethical and Moral Decision-Making

AI systems in education also provoke overarching ethical inquiries on the influence of technology on moral and ethical decision-making.

- Ethical Frameworks: AI systems are designed to maximize certain results, such as enhanced exam scores or knowledge of information. Education encompasses more than just academic success; it also entails instructing pupils in the navigation of intricate ethical and moral dilemmas. AI systems should be designed to facilitate, rather than obstruct, the development of students' moral reasoning, empathy, and social consciousness.

  AI in Student Assessments: AI-driven evaluations, capable of monitoring student performance and growth over time, may raise concerns about fairness and objectivity. When AI is used for critical judgments, such as student assessment or placement, it is essential to guarantee that these systems are both precise and ethical in their evaluation of pupils.

The ethical dilemmas associated with the use of AI adaptive learning and intelligent systems in education are considerable but manageable. To effectively harness the promise of AI in education, it is imperative to tackle concerns around data privacy, algorithmic bias, transparency, equality, and accountability. Developers, educators, and politicians must collaborate to design AI systems that are both successful and ethical, guaranteeing that all kids benefit from new technologies without infringing upon their rights or well-being. As artificial intelligence continues to influence the future of education, promoting responsible innovation will be essential for establishing inclusive, just, and equitable learning environments.

8. CONCLUSION: THE FINAL SAY

The future of education is progressively linked to breakthroughs in artificial intelligence (AI) and intelligent systems, which are poised to transform learning experiences via adaptive learning technologies. By tailoring education to accommodate the varied requirements of students, AI can augment engagement, boost results, and promote a more inclusive learning atmosphere. Intelligent systems can evaluate extensive data sets, providing insights that assist educators in customizing their methodologies and interventions for individual students, therefore enhancing the efficacy of teaching and learning processes.

Nonetheless, while we adopt these technical innovations, we must also be alert to the ethical dilemmas they provide. Concerns around data privacy, algorithmic bias, transparency, and equal access to AI resources need meticulous attention and aggressive interventions. It is essential to develop and apply AI applications in education ethically to protect students' rights and provide an egalitarian educational environment. This entails formulating explicit protocols for data utilization, rectifying algorithmic biases, fostering openness in decision-making procedures, and guaranteeing accessibility for all learners.

In conclusion, the incorporation of AI adaptive learning and intelligent systems has significant potential to revolutionize education, although it requires a careful and ethical consideration. By emphasizing ethical issues in conjunction with technical innovation, we may use AI to create an educational future that is successful and equitable, inclusive, and respectful of the unique needs and rights of all children. Collaboration among educators, politicians, developers, and stakeholders will be crucial in navigating this intricate terrain and guaranteeing a bright and exciting future for education.

REFERENCES

Allen, I. E., & Seaman, J. (2017). *Digital learning in higher education: A survey of faculty attitudes and experiences*. Babson Survey Research Group.

Almarashdeh, I. E. (2021). AI adaptive learning in higher education: A review of the literature. *Journal of Educational Technology Systems*, 49(3), 275–287.

Anderson, T. (2016). The impact of artificial intelligence on education. *International Journal of Educational Technology*, 13(1), 11–25.

Baker, R. S. J. d., & Inventado, P. S. (2014). Educational data mining and learning analytics. In Baker, J. A., & Wang, S. Y. (Eds.), *Handbook of learning analytics* (pp. 17–33). Society for Learning Analytics Research. DOI: 10.1007/978-1-4614-3305-7_4

Chou, P. N., & Chen, W. F. (2018). The role of artificial intelligence in education: A review of the literature. *Journal of Educational Technology & Society*, 21(1), 150–166.

Cope, B., & Kalantzis, M. (2020). *Artificial Intelligence and education: Future directions*. Routledge.

Dede, C. (2014). Immersive interfaces for engagement and learning. In Ifenthaler, D., Gibson, D. E., & Manches, A. T. (Eds.), *Assessment and feedback in higher education* (pp. 119–138). Springer.

Deng, L., & Tavares, N. J. (2018). The role of artificial intelligence in education: A global perspective. *International Journal of Artificial Intelligence in Education*, 28(4), 648–672.

Dillenbourg, P. (2018). Designing digital learning environments. In Kalz, M. M., Garcia, J. J. R., & De Vries, R. E. H. H. G. (Eds.), *Learning in a digital world* (pp. 45–56). Springer.

Gikandi, J. W., Morrow, D., & Davis, N. (2011). Online formative assessment in higher education: A review of the literature. *Computers & Education*, 57(4), 2336–2355. DOI: 10.1016/j.compedu.2011.06.004

Hwang, G. J., & Chang, C. Y. (2018). Innovative learning environments: Opportunities and challenges. *Journal of Educational Technology & Society*, 21(1), 1–9.

Kahn, B. (2020). *Ethical challenges in AI education*. Cambridge University Press.

Liu, Q., & Wang, L. (2020). Intelligent systems in education: An overview. *Educational Technology Research and Development*, 68(3), 1345–1363.

Luckin, R. (2017). *Machine learning and human intelligence: The future of education for the 21st century*. UCL Institute of Education Press.

McGowan, M. J., & O'Reilly, T. (2021). Ethical challenges in using artificial intelligence in education. *Computers & Education*, 166, 104159.

Moore, M. G., & Kearsley, G. (2012). *Distance education: A systems view of online learning* (3rd ed.). Wadsworth Cengage Learning.

Nouri, J., & Eklund, J. (2020). The impact of artificial intelligence on education: A systematic literature review. *Education and Information Technologies*, 25(3), 2059–2084.

Ordonez, C., & Gacía, E. (2021). Ethical considerations of artificial intelligence in education. *International Journal of Educational Technology in Higher Education*, 18(1), 4. PMID: 34778518

Papert, S., & Harel, I. (1991). Situating constructionism. In Harel, I., & Papert, S. (Eds.), *Constructionism* (pp. 1–11). Ablex Publishing.

Pedró, F. (2016). *Digital education: The future of education in a digital world*. OECD.

Picciano, A. G. (2017). The role of artificial intelligence in education. *Journal of Online Learning Research*, 3(2), 119–134.

Siemens, G. (2014). Learning analytics: The emerging educational and ethical issues. *International Review of Research in Open and Distance Learning*, 15(2), 190–203.

Slade, S., & Prinsloo, P. (2013). Learning analytics: A collaborative approach to the ethical use of student data. *Higher Education*, 66(4), 407–423.

UNESCO. (2021). *AI and education: Guidance for policy-makers*. United Nations Educational, Scientific and Cultural Organization.

Wang, F., & Wang, Q. (2018). Artificial intelligence in education: The future of learning. *International Journal of Information and Education Technology (IJIET)*, 8(4), 253–257.

Watson, W. R., & Watson, S. L. (2018). The role of artificial intelligence in higher education: Current trends and future directions. *Journal of Educational Technology & Society*, 21(1), 50–62.

West, D. M. (2018). *AI and the future of education: The potential impact of artificial intelligence on education and society*. Brookings Institution.

Woolf, B. P. (2010). *Building intelligent interactive tutors: Student-centered strategies for revolutionizing e-learning*. Morgan Kaufmann.

Yadav, A., & Bhattacharya, A. (2021). Ethical challenges in the implementation of AI in education: Perspectives from educators. *International Journal of Information and Education Technology (IJIET)*, 11(5), 201–209.

Zheng, L., & Yang, Z. (2020). Ethical implications of artificial intelligence in education. *AI & Society*, 35(4), 889–895.

Zhou, Y., & Chen, J. (2020). The role of artificial intelligence in education: Opportunities and challenges. *Computers in Human Behavior*, 112, 106466.

Zhu, M., & Zhai, L. (2018). Adaptive learning in education: The role of intelligent systems. *International Journal of Emerging Technologies in Learning*, 13(4), 4–15. DOI: 10.3991/ijet.v13i11.9582

Chapter 7
Integrating AI in Special Education and Instructional Design

Rohan James Jowallah
University of Central Florida, USA

Grace Kaletski Maisel G.
https://orcid.org/0009-0004-4220-7402
University of Central Florida, USA

ABSTRACT

Education has greatly changed in the last 20 years, especially in the previous five years, with AI in learning and teaching. This change has affected both instructional design and special education and opened new possibilities for personalization, accessibility, and efficiency in education. The book chapter will explore how AI can improve special education and instructional design to create inclusive and effective learning environments. The authors will review the basics and challenges of special education and instructional design and then discuss how AI can enhance them. In special education, AI-powered tools and applications such as assistive technologies, personalized learning platforms, and adaptive learning systems can help students with special needs and improve their education outcomes and experiences (Kumar, 2023). Within an instructional design framework, AI also has the capability to provide real-time feedback and create personalized learning pathways, thereby making education more efficient and effective.

DOI: 10.4018/979-8-3693-6527-4.ch007

OVERVIEW OF AI IN EDUCATION

The potential of AI in education can be traced back to the 1950s when Alan Turing began exploring concepts related to machine learning. Machine learning, broadly defined, involves using machines to perform tasks typically carried out by humans. Turing's work set the stage for what would become a cornerstone of artificial intelligence: the ability of machines to learn and adapt independently (Turing, 1950). By the early 2010s, the conversation around AI had evolved significantly, with a movement towards personalized learning pathways. Tech companies saw many educational institutions as their next place of dominance (Jowallah and Bennett 2017). This shift was marked by the development of AI systems capable of adapting educational content to the needs of individual learners, thus enhancing learning efficiency and engagement.

In his 2019 publication, Jowallah emphasized the transformative impact of AI on education. He pointed out that AI facilitates personalized learning and can dramatically streamline administrative tasks, allowing educators to focus more on teaching and less on bureaucracy. In today's context, AI's role in education is rapidly expanding. It is not only reshaping how educational content is delivered but also how it is created and assessed (Garbine, 2023 & Celik, 2023). AI tools are now being used to develop more interactive and adaptive learning environments that cater to diverse learning styles and needs (Reunanen & Nieminen, 2024). The ongoing integration of AI into educational settings promises to revolutionize this sector further, potentially making learning more accessible, personalized, and efficient than ever before (Ruiz-Rojas, 2023). However, as this movement occurs, more consideration should be given to integrating AI into special education and instructional design. These two fundamental areas hold prominence in providing students with special needs with AI deployment that is deployed using sound instructional design approaches within the scope of AI. This will require meticulous planning and the development of AI tools specifically tailored to accommodate the diverse needs of students with disabilities (Yao & Wang 2024 and Jowallah 2024).

For this chapter, the definition of special education will be conceptualized within a framework of students experiencing barriers to accessing the curriculum. These barriers may be economic, social, cultural, physical, and cognitive, among others, affecting how students engage with educational content and processes (Jowallah, 2024a). One pathway to overcome some barriers will be the effective use of AI technology. When these barriers are not addressed, this will have an impact on students' opportunities to reach their full potential. Hence it is a matter of an equal opportunity approach when all learners are valued. Having such an embedded approach could lead to enhanced learning encounters. Fundamental to the issue of special needs is the need for inclusion or inclusive education, which aims to break down the barriers. Hence inclusion ensures that all students, regardless of their background, abilities, or health have an equal opportunity to participate and benefit from the learning process. Inclusive education values diversity and adapts teaching methods, instructional methods, content, and assessment to meet individual needs. It fosters a sense of community, promotes collaboration between students and instructors and provides a space for students to feel safe, valued, and able to succeed academically, socially and emotionally (Carrub, 2023).

AI technologies in special education can significantly enhance how instructional content is tailored for students with special needs. For instance, AI can be leveraged to create personalized learning experiences that adapt to each student's pace and style in real-time. This capability is crucial for students who may not fit the typical learning mode, allowing them to thrive in environments that acknowledge and adapt to their unique challenges (Celik, 2023 & Luan et al., 2020).

Moreover, AI can automate the creation of accessible educational materials. From converting text to speech to adjusting content readability, AI can make learning more accessible to students with visual, auditory, or cognitive challenges (Goel, 2020 & Nayyar et al., 2023). Interactive and multimodal learning materials generated through AI can engage students in ways that traditional materials cannot, offering various means of representation, engagement, and expression as outlined in Universal Design for Learning (UDL) principles. This chapter shows how AI and instructional design can collaborate to create inclusive designs for students with special needs. Using practical examples, the authors will show how AI- can support diverse learners and encourage educator collaboration in conjunction with instructional principles. The writers will also address significant challenges and ethical issues such as data privacy, bias mitigation, and teacher training. The chapter will also examine emerging trends and innovations in AI that position AI to improve both special education and instructional design. Policy and practical implications will be discussed, and the writer will give recommendations for educators, policymakers, and technology developers to build fair AI-powered ecosystems.

COMBINING SPECIAL EDUCATION, INSTRUCTIONAL DESIGN, AND ARTIFICIAL INTELLIGENCE

It's essential to link the focus on students with special needs to inclusion. Inclusion must account for equitable access; otherwise, integrating AI into special education could be restricted (Jowallah, 2024). Moreover, the role of AI in supporting differentiated instruction, responsive teaching, and the creation of accessible learning content should be investigated.

The definition of special education was established earlier, suggesting that individuals with specific educational needs face barriers to accessing the curriculum. These barriers are varied, necessitating a wide range of strategies. Given the diversity of learning disabilities, social and cultural barriers, physical disabilities, and other challenges, a one-size-fits-all approach will not work for achieving inclusion. Traditional approaches to addressing students with special needs are often limited by the necessary human contact for intervention, the cost of resources, and the inconsistent effectiveness of strategies. However, with the landscape emerging technological advancement into both our daily life and education, there is a growing need to focus this movement on supporting individuals with special needs (Carruba, 2023).

The Role of Technology in Modern Instructional Design

For instructional designers, understanding the role of technology is crucial in the ever-evolving world of instructional design. As technology rapidly advances, it reshapes how educators approach teaching and learning, making it essential for instructional designers to stay informed and adept at integrating these tools into their work (Talebi et al. 2023). When implementing technology, instructional designers need to consider its potential to enable students to engage in immersive learning experiences. Tools such as virtual reality (VR), augmented reality (AR), and interactive simulations provide learners with opportunities to explore complex concepts in a more hands-on and engaging manner, fostering deeper understanding and retention of the material. Additionally, technology allows for the creation of personalized learning pathways that cater to individual learner needs and preferences. Adaptive learning platforms, powered by artificial intelligence (AI) and machine learning algorithms, can dynamically adjust the content and pace of instruction based on a learner's progress and performance. This personalization ensures that each learner receives the support they need to succeed, enhancing the overall effectiveness of the instructional design (Calhoun, 2023).

Modern technology also streamlines the delivery of content and assessments, significantly enhancing accessibility for students. Learning Management Systems (LMS), cloud-based platforms, and mobile learning applications provide flexible access to educational resources, allowing students to learn at their own pace and on their own schedule (Wang 2023). This flexibility is particularly beneficial for diverse student populations, including working professionals, remote learners, and individuals with varying learning needs. Furthermore, technology enables instructional designers to leverage data analytics to inform and refine their course designs. With access to real-time data on learner engagement, performance, and progress, designers can make evidence-based decisions to continuously improve instructional strategies. This data-driven approach helps identify learning gaps, adapt instructional methods, and ensure that courses remain effective and relevant in a rapidly changing educational landscape. With these technological advancements, instructional approaches can create a pathway for the integration of assistive technologies, inclusive technology, and the enhancement of inclusive learning spaces (Escudeiro et al., 2023).

In summary, for instructional designers, embracing technology is not just about keeping up with trends but is essential for creating meaningful, engaging, and accessible learning experiences. By understanding and effectively leveraging technology, instructional designers can enhance learning outcomes, provide personalized education, streamline content delivery, and use data to drive continuous improvement in their instructional practices (Calhoun, 2023; Wang, 2023; & Carruba, 2023). This proactive approach ensures that they are well-equipped to meet the evolving needs of learners in a dynamic educational environment.

Key Principles in Integrating AI into Special Education

Incorporating AI in conjunction with a sound instructional design framework can be very beneficial. When AI is integrated and personalized, it provides customized assistance to match the distinct requirements of every student. Instructional designers should thoroughly review various educational models and modify them to integrate AI, enhancing inclusivity. This chapter won't explore these models in depth, but it will point out key examples such as Bloom's Taxonomy, the ADDIE Model (A= Analysis, D= Design, D= Development, I = Implementation and, and E= Evaluation), and the ASSURE Model (A= Analyze Learners, S= State Objective, S= Select Media and Material, U= Utilise Media and Materials, R= Required Learner Participation, and E= Evaluate and Revise). Notably, Bloom's Taxonomy is recognized for its cognitive domain levels, which have been updated with modern insights (Jowallah & Bennett, in press). Its application assists in creating specialized learning journeys for learners with specific needs, ensuring they can advance at a pace that suits them and aligns with their learning preferences. Moreover, assessments can be tailored in their complexity to suit the individual learner's needs. The implementation of AI tools also permits precise, timely interventions that enhance the learning experience for those with special needs.

By leveraging AI in instructional design, courses can be developed more effectively through the analysis of student data and the customization of content to meet these needs. AI's ability to produce interactive media complements the objectives of the ASSURE Model, particularly in the selection of appropriate resources and promoting active learner involvement. Additionally, the application of AI within this model supports the provision of ongoing feedback, which is especially valuable for students with special needs as it fosters their participation and learning.

Though the ASSURE and ADDIE models share standard features, it is important to highlight that ADDIE focuses on analyzing learners' needs during content creation (Skill, n.d.). AI can play a role in assessing requirements for students with special needs under this model. By employing flexible instructional design methods, designers can craft adaptive learning materials suited to varied cognitive abilities and provide continuous assessment to steer the process (Ryan, 2023).

The Role of AI in Special Needs

While Universal Design for Learning (UDL) is primarily linked to instructional design, the inclusion of special needs and the application of AI within this framework are frequently overlooked in the prevailing literature. Nonetheless, it is crucial to recognize the synergy between UDL, instructional design, AI, and special needs, as this collaboration can yield significant benefits. This will also result in AI-powered applications transforming education by enhancing student engagement through technology. For instance, Speech-to-Text-to-Speech (TTS) systems assist students with hearing impairments, dyslexia, or physical disabilities in communicating and writing more proficiently. Instructional designers can integrate these tools into learning management systems to improve accessibility. Moreover, AI contributes to the diagnosis and assessment of learning disabilities, enabling early intervention for conditions like dyslexia and ADHD. In summary, AI-powered tools are revolutionizing education by creating adaptive, personalized, and accessible learning pathways (Culican and Amade, 2023)

AI-Powered Tools and Applications

Some special needs learners rely on assistive technologies such as speech-to-text, text-to-speech, and Augmentative and Alternative Communication (AAC) devices to achieve full participation in the learning process. The implementation of AI opens up myriad opportunities for enhancing the effectiveness of these technologies. Speech-to-text tools that are powered by AI have potential to produce transcripts with more speed and accuracy than those produced by non-AI technology or made manually by humans. Likewise, text-to-speech tools that utilize AI can produce higher-quality audio with more natural-sounding voices more quickly than previous technology has the capability to do. AAC devices have the potential to become more usable and impactful through AI approaches such as communication partner instructional intervention, natural language processing, and machine learning-based approaches

(Sennott et al, 2019). These pioneering approaches underscore the critical role of stakeholders in smoothly leveraging the advantages of this and other technologies.

Personalized Learning Platforms and Adaptive Learning Systems

Many special needs learners can also benefit from personalized and adaptive learning systems that can meet each individual where they are in their learning journeys. AI-driven personalized learning platforms can assess learners' needs and create individualized learning pathways that address those needs in real time. Using previous responses, AI algorithms can quickly adjust the material to tweak the difficulty level and ensure that each learner is challenged but not overwhelmed. Through infusion into personalized and adaptive learning systems, AI has the potential to help ensure that special needs and traditional students alike can be successful in achieving course learning outcomes. AI can predict how well students will learn future material and generate content that will guide each learner to successfully achieve their individual learning goals or course learning outcomes at an appropriate difficulty level (Hashim et al, 2022).

AI in Diagnosing and Assessing Learning Disabilities

Another way AI can contribute to the education of special needs learners is through diagnosing and assessing learning disabilities. Through data analysis, AI has the potential to detect patterns in student work and identify signs of ADHD, dyslexia, or other conditions that may impair learning or cognition. Using AI as a diagnostic tool this way can create a smoother path for educators to implement interventions, could be paired with personalized and adaptive learning systems to create instruction that caters to the unique challenges of different disabilities, and potentially identify learning disabilities in students that might otherwise go unnoticed (Kharbat et al, 2020).

Benefits of AI in Special Education

The use of AI-powered tools in special education can pave the way for increased accessibility and inclusivity. AI raises opportunities to reduce the time and costs needed to make educational material accessible and tailored to individual needs, can increase the availability of effective assistive technologies, and identify students with learning disabilities who may otherwise lack the resources or attention needed to receive a diagnosis. AI can pave a smoother path for special needs learners to reach their learning goals and even the playing field for their achievement of learning objectives.

For educators, taking the time to manually create personalized learning pathways, stay alert for signs of learning disabilities, and ensuring sufficient assistive technologies are available to all students who need them can be expensive, time-intensive tasks. Many educators have large class sizes that make personal attention difficult, competing demands for their time, and limited budget access. AI can even contribute to grading. AI-powered automated assessment tools can assess qualitative work and provide students with feedback on their writing (Akgun and Greenhow, 2021). While not a substitute for human interaction, AI can relieve some of the administrative tasks that educators have on their plates and allow them to devote more of their attention to teaching and supporting students (Ahmad et al, 2022).

Challenges and Ethical Considerations

Educators and instructional designers who strive to implement AI in special education should do so with awareness of the challenges and ethical considerations that can inhibit or dampen its advantages. As a technology produced by humans, AI algorithms are infused with human biases and thus replicate systems of oppression based on factors such as race, ethnicity, sex, class, disability, and other aspects of identity. Safiya Umoja Noble (2018) coined the term *algorithmic oppression* to express the role algorithms play in reinforcing existing power structures such as racism and sexism in algorithmically driven technology such as search engines. When biased algorithms are used in educational technology, this can lead to unequal learning experiences and negatively impact student grades. A recent example in education occurred in 2020 when England's A-level and GCSE secondary level examinations were canceled due to the COVID-19 pandemic. These were replaced with an alternative assessment graded by an algorithm. Part of the algorithm was based on schools' previous examination results, which led to a final score distribution that advantaged private school students and gave lower scores to students from underrepresented groups (Adams and McIntyre, 2020). Many special needs students already face prejudice and unfair treatment on account of their disabilities as well as other identity groups to which they may belong. Educators who work with these learners should be especially alert to the potential for how such bias may be reinforced through AI tools. Applying effective instructional design principles with AI can enhance inclusion for students who need assistance in their learning process.

It's also crucial to ensure that data collected from students with special needs when deploying AI tools is secure and accessible only to the responsible stakeholders. All parties involved have a responsibility to keep students safe while using these tools and content, ensuring no harm comes to them (UNESCO 2024). Stakeholders, including instructional designers, must ensure that service providers protect the end users of their products.

Some teachers may resist adopting AI in their work or may have negative or incomplete perceptions of its potential. Training and professional development are key to making ethical AI adoption feasible and sustainable. Educators will need to learn how to use these tools efficiently while gaining a deeper understanding of the benefits they can offer in supporting special education (Nazaretsky et al, 2022). Training should highlight the ways AI can lighten the administrative load and benefit some of their most vulnerable students, while emphasizing the challenges and ethical issues it presents. In a rapidly evolving AI landscape, ongoing professional development will be critical to staying informed and prepared as technology changes.

AI in Content Creation and Curation

The advent of AI has opened new possibilities for content creation. AI-powered tools have now reached a level where they can produce diverse educational materials, such as text, videos, quizzes, and interactive content. These advanced technologies not only generate fresh content but also enhance existing materials by improving clarity, updating information, translating content into multiple languages, and ensuring accessibility standards are met. This automation streamlines the content creation process, allowing instructional designers to focus on strategies that provide meaningful instruction to learners. For instance, the emergence and deployment of Generative Pre-Trained Transformers (GPT) enable the design of personalized content for learners. When this personalized content is utilized by instructional designers or subject matter experts, it leads to greater engagement and interaction among learners (Jowallah, 2024).

Students with special needs often require one-to-one support, which can be costly and difficult to scale for many educational organizations. As a result, these students might not reach their full potential due to the lack of adequate assistance. However, integrating AI with effective pedagogical methods can significantly improve outcomes.

Intelligent tutoring systems and virtual teaching assistants, guided by human teachers, should become standard in educational settings. These tools provide personalized instruction and real-time, enhancing the learning experience for each student (Mouti & Rihawi, 2023). By deploying virtual teaching assistants, educational institutions can enhance student engagement by offering immediate answers to questions and helping students navigate their learning journeys (Emerling et al 2020).

Continuous support is crucial, ensuring students' learning needs are met both inside and outside the classroom. This concept can be further extended to personalized and adaptive learning, where AI creates tailored learning experiences based on data. For instance, AI can analyze a student's strengths and weaknesses, adapting the curriculum to better suit their needs, thus fostering a more inclusive and efficient educational environment. Moreover, this technological integration can bridge the gap between students with special needs and their peers, promoting equality in education. By leveraging AI, educators and instructional designers can identify learning patterns and intervene promptly, ensuring no student is left behind. This proactive approach not only aids in academic success but also boosts the confidence and independence of students with special needs. The fusion of AI and education holds tremendous potential to revolutionize how we approach learning. By embracing intelligent tutoring systems and virtual assistants, we can create a more inclusive, personalized, and effective educational landscape that caters to the diverse needs of all students (Cuarruba, 2023).

AI's capacity to analyze vast amounts of data can be a game-changer for early identification of learning disabilities. By monitoring students' interactions with digital learning platforms, AI can help detect patterns indicative of learning disabilities or difficulties, facilitating early intervention with tailored educational strategies and supports. Ultimately, for AI to be effectively integrated into special education through instructional design, a collaborative effort among educators, designers, and technologists is required. They must ensure that AI tools are developed with an inclusive mindset that prioritizes accessibility, personalization, and the ethical use of technology in educational settings (Jowallah, 2023). This inclusive mindset is crucial to ensure that all students can benefit from AI in education regardless of their abilities. This concerted effort can help unlock the full potential of AI in empowering students with special needs, ensuring that all learners have the opportunity to succeed in a technology-driven world.

As mentioned earlier, inclusion refers to the practice of ensuring that all students, regardless of background, have equal opportunities to participate in and benefit from the education process. Within the context of special education, inclusive education fosters learning environments that meet the needs of all students and promote a sense of community. Instructional designers play a critical role in the process of advocating for the design of accessible and adaptable learning materials across various modalities, whether online, in-person, or hybrid. By integrating diverse learning formats and technologies, instructional designers ensure that students with different learning styles, preferences and abilities engage with the content, making inclusivity a central focus in the modern educational environment.

Synergies Between Special Education AI and Instructional Design AI

Integrating AI in special needs and instructional design can foster personalized, inclusive learning. AI tools enable educators to meet diverse learning needs by aligning content with Universal Design for Learning (UDL) principles. These tools can customize content, adjust pacing, and offer varied engagement and assessment methods, ensuring support for students with special education needs. For instance, an AI-powered tool designed by an instructional designer could adapt tasks based on students' needs, providing extra problems or examples to guarantee concept mastery.

Developing an inclusive instructional design with AI tools demands a thoughtful strategy. Through the use of various integrative frameworks, instructional designers can effectively connect technology with learners' needs. As previously noted, personalized learning is one viable approach. This integrated framework constitutes a structured system that amalgamates different elements and tools or models to achieve defined objectives. In educational and instructional design contexts, an integrative framework blends technology, teaching methodologies, learner requirements, and content to create a unified learning experience. Essentially, it aligns components such as AI tools, pedagogical models, and accessibility features to ensure each aspect complements the others, facilitating inclusive, adaptive, and personalized education (Jowallah, 2024A). Such a framework enables the confluence of special education and instructional design into a system that merges traditional teaching techniques with AI-driven solutions, catering to diverse learners' needs. For example, it could integrate adaptive learning technologies, personalized content delivery, and data analytics to customize instruction for students with varying cognitive and physical abilities. The objective is to ensure AI tools, like speech-to-text and predictive learning algorithms, function within an overarching, well-conceived system aimed at promoting inclusivity and effectiveness. In this model, educators must support students with diverse learning capabilities while instructional designers incorporate AI-based learning solutions to adapt lessons to individual needs. This framework's strength lies in its ability to harmonize various technologies and methodologies into a holistic, efficacious system, particularly in terms of inclusivity in special education. Furthermore, it will be imperative to ensure that special education and instructional professionals collaborate to develop AI solutions that address unique challenges of learners with disabilities. This should include designing interfaces that are intuitive and accessible as well as using AI to provide personalized support. For example, AI-powered Chatbots and virtual tutors can assess students where needed.

One possible way of an AI-integrated framework for inclusive instructional design to be built is on five essential components. First, **personalized learning paths** adapt content and pacing to each student's individual needs, creating a tailored learning experience. Second, **real-time feedback and adaptation** allow AI to assess student performance instantly and adjust lessons accordingly, keeping learners engaged and supported. Third, **accessible learning technologies** like speech-to-text and screen readers ensure that students with disabilities have equitable access to content. Fourth, **data-driven insights** provide educators with analytics to track progress and refine instructional strategies. Lastly, a **collaborative design process** between instructional designers and special education professionals ensures that these AI tools are purposefully integrated to promote inclusivity and equity across all learning environments. Using this frame is one possible way of reflecting on what is required for integrating AI in special education and instructional design with a synergistic approach. This would require consistent evaluation of on practice to revise the framework as needed.

Emerging Trends and Technologies

The future of AI in education has potential, particularly in special education and instructional design. Innovations in AI are poised to enhance adaptive learning, providing even more personalized educational experiences that cater to the unique needs of each student based on a blend of pedagogy and technology (SD News, 2023; University of South Florida Sarasota-Manatee, 2024). Advanced data analytics will offer deeper insights into student performance, enabling educators to make informed decisions and tailor instructional strategies proactively. Moreover, AI-driven tools like augmented reality (AR) and virtual reality (VR) are set to transform special education environments, making learning more interactive and immersive. These technologies can create simulated environments that provide hands-on experiences, especially beneficial for students with special needs. Additionally, AI's role in early detection of learning disabilities will become more refined, allowing for timely interventions customized to individual requirements. A collaborative AI framework will ensure that educational tools remain inclusive and accessible, promoting equity and inclusion across diverse learning landscapes. By aligning AI with Universal Design for Learning (UDL) principles, we can create a more adaptable and inclusive educational ecosystem that addresses the varied learning styles and abilities of all students (Kaur, 2023).

Policy and Practice Implications

The integration of AI in special education and instructional design holds significant promise for creating more inclusive and personalized learning environments. Policymakers and educational practitioners must consider how to best leverage AI to address diverse learning needs effectively. To foster an environment where AI can thrive in special education, it is essential to develop policies that support the ethical and equitable use of AI technologies. These policies should include accessibility standards, data privacy, funding and resources, and ethical guidelines (Jowallah 2023 & 2024). Furthermore, educators and instructional designers must adopt best practices to effectively integrate AI into special education. Key considerations include the professional development, customization and adaption, and evaluation. By focusing on these policy and practice implications, we can ensure that AI's integration into special education is both effective and equitable, thereby enhancing the learning experience for all students (UNESCO, 2024).

CONCLUSION

Integrating AI in special education involves leveraging instructional design to create tailored learning experiences with immediate feedback. This tailored approach can significantly enhance accessibility and inclusion by adapting both content and pace to each student's unique needs. A robust framework consisting of personalized learning paths, real-time feedback, accessible technologies, data-driven insights, and collaborative design is essential for effective integration.

Personalized learning paths ensure that educational content and pacing are adapted to cater to individual student requirements, fostering a more personalized learning environment. Real-time feedback enables AI systems to evaluate student performance instantly and adjust lessons, accordingly, keeping learners engaged and supported throughout their educational journey. Accessible technologies such as speech-to-text and screen readers ensure that students with disabilities have equitable access to educational content, promoting an inclusive learning experience.

Data-driven insights provide educators with valuable analytics to track student progress and refine instructional strategies, thereby enhancing the overall teaching and learning process. Lastly, a collaborative design process between instructional designers and special education professionals ensures that AI tools are purposefully integrated to promote inclusivity and equity across all learning environments. The need for continuous research and evaluation are necessary to keep the framework relevant and effective, as educational needs evolve. However, it should be noted that ethical considerations are paramount to ensure the safety and protection of all users. For the future, it will be important for us to build and maintain an inclusive and equitable AI-powered educational ecosystem. This will require a seamless connection between AI and instructional design, particularly for students who need special accommodations.

REFERENCES

Adams, R., & McIntyre, N. (2020, August 13). England A-level downgrades hit pupils from disadvantaged areas hardest. *The Guardian.* England A-level downgrades hit pupils from disadvantaged areas hardest | A-levels | The Guardian.

Ahmad, S. F., Alam, M. M., Rahmat, M. K., Mubarik, M. S., & Hyder, S. I. (2022). Academic and administrative role of artificial intelligence in education. *Sustainability (Basel)*, 14(3), 1101. DOI: 10.3390/su14031101

Akgun, S., & Greenhow, C. (2022). Artificial intelligence in education: Addressing ethical challenges in K-12 settings. *AI and Ethics*, 2(3), 431–440. DOI: 10.1007/s43681-021-00096-7 PMID: 34790956

Calhoun, C. (Ed.). (2023). *The impact and importance of instructional design in the educational landscape* (1st ed.). Information Science Reference, an imprint of IGI Global. DOI: 10.4018/978-1-6684-8208-7

Carruba, M. C. (2023). Technology for inclusion: A pedagogical approach to promote well-being. In Escudeiro, P., Escudeiro, N., & Bernardes, O. (Eds.), *Handbook of research on advancing equity and inclusion through educational technology* (pp. 146–152). IGI Global., DOI: 10.4018/978-1-6684-6868-5.ch007

Celik, I. (2023). Towards Intelligent-TPACK: An empirical study on teachers' professional knowledge to ethically integrate artificial intelligence (AI)-based tools into education. *Computers in Human Behavior*, 138, 107468. DOI: 10.1016/j.chb.2022.107468

Culican, J., & Amade, M. (2023). *A14 special education: Ignite your special education program with the power of AI.* A14. Special Edition.

Emerling, C. R., Yang, S., Carter, R. A., Zhang, L., & Hunt, T. (2020). Using Amazon Alexa as an instructional tool during remote teaching. *Teaching Exceptional Children*, 53(2), 164–167. DOI: 10.1177/0040059920964719

Escudeiro, P., Escudeiro, N. F., & Bernardes, O. (Eds.). (2023). *Advancing equity and inclusion through educational technology* (1st ed.). Information Science Reference. DOI: 10.4018/978-1-6684-6868-5

Garbarine, R. (2023, March 27). *How is AI changing how we write and create?* NC State College of Humanities and Social Sciences. https://chass.ncsu.edu/news/2023/03/27/how-is-ai-changing-how-we-write-and-create/

Goel, A. (2020). AI-powered learning: making education accessible, affordable, and achievable. *arXiv preprint arXiv:2006.01908.*

Hashim, S., Omar, M. K., Ab Jalil, H., & Sharef, N. M. (2022). Trends on technologies and artificial intelligence in education for personalized learning: Systematic literature. *Journal of Academic Research in Progressive Education and Development*, 12(1), 884–903. DOI: 10.6007/IJARPED/v11-i1/12230

Jowallah, R. (2019). *Artificial intelligence in education* [Video]. YouTube. https://www.youtube.com/watch?v=-nsVW6c2OQU&list=PLk7RZ0ABlfPJHFtVgh9T6QI5I4sYgVH4x

Jowallah, R. (2024). *AI in higher education: Opportunities and challenges* [Video]. YouTube. https://youtu.be/rJYssMYJ52Y

Jowallah, R. (2024a). *Teachers are essential in the age of AI* [Video]. YouTube. https://youtu.be/R48kRHmCyak

Kaur, H. (2023, June 23). *Using AI in universal design for learning*. Edutopia. https://www.edutopia.org/article/using-ai-in-universal-design-for-learning/

Kharbat, F. F., Alshawabkeh, A., & Woolsey, M. L. (2021). Identifying gaps in using artificial intelligence to support students with intellectual disabilities from education and health perspectives. *Aslib Journal of Information Management*, 73(1), 101–128. DOI: 10.1108/AJIM-02-2020-0054

Mouti, S., & Rihawi, S. (2023). Special needs classroom assessment using a sign language communicator (CASC) based on artificial intelligence (AI) techniques. *International Journal of e-Collaboration*, 19(1), 1–15. DOI: 10.4018/IJeC.313960

Nayyar, A., Kumar, R., Sachan, R., & Kumar, A. (2023). *AI-assisted special education for students with exceptional needs*. IGI Global Publishers.

Nazaretsky, T., Ariely, M., Cukurova, M., & Alexandron, G. (2022). Teachers' trust in AI-powered educational technology and a professional development program to improve it. *British Journal of Educational Technology*, 53(4), 914–931. DOI: 10.1111/bjet.13232

News, S. D. (2023, August 31). *Education in today's time: Emerging trends and fields*. SD News. https://sdnews.com/education-in-todays-time-emerging-trends-and-fields/

Noble, S. U. (2018). Algorithms of oppression: How search engines reinforce racism. New York university press. Luan, H., Geczy, P., Lai, H., Gobert, J., Yang, S. J., Ogata, H., ... & Tsai, C. C. (2020). Challenges and future directions of big data and artificial intelligence in education. *Frontiers in Psychology*, 11, 580820.

Reunanen, T., & Nieminen, N. (2024). Artificial intelligence as a catalyst: A case study on adaptive learning in programming education. In: V. Salminen (Eds.), *Human Factors, Business Management and Society. AHFE (2024) International Conference. AHFE Open Access, 135.* AHFE International, USA. http://doi.org/ DOI: 10.54941/ahfe1004957

Ruiz-Rojas, L. I., Acosta-Vargas, P., De-Moreta-Llovet, J., & Gonzalez-Rodriguez, M. (2023). Empowering education with generative artificial intelligence tools: Approach with an instructional design matrix. *Sustainability (Basel)*, 15(15), 11524. DOI: 10.3390/su151511524

Ryan, C. (2023, August 14). *Leveraging AI in instructional design.* Medium. https://medium.com/@crystal.ryanc/leveraging-ai-in-instructional-design-165fe152b2ee

Sennott, S. C., Akagi, L., Lee, M., & Rhodes, A. (2019). AAC and artificial intelligence (AI). *Topics in Language Disorders*, 39(4), 389–403. DOI: 10.1097/TLD.0000000000000197 PMID: 34012187

Skill, Q. (n.d.). *AI & ADDIE: Leveraging artificial intelligence in instructional design.* SkillQ. https://skillq.com/ai_addie/

Talebi, M. R. Nili Ahmadabadi, H. Fardanesh, & A. Delavar. (2023). Investigating the effectiveness of "Instructional Design Thinking" on the instructional design capability of educational technology students. *Nashrīyah-i 'Ilmī pizhūhishī-i fannāvarī-i āmūzish, 17*(4), 709–728. https://doi.org/DOI: 10.22061/tej.2023.9329.2831

Turing, A. M. (1950). Computing machinery and intelligence. *Mind*, 59(236), 433–460. DOI: 10.1093/mind/LIX.236.433

UNESCO. (n.d.). Artificial intelligence. UNESCO. https://www.unesco.org/en/artificial-intelligence

University of South Florida Sarasota-Manatee. (2024). *Emerging technologies in education.* University of South Florida Sarasota-Manatee. https://www.sarasotamanatee.usf.edu/magazine/2020/emerging-technologies-in-education.aspx

Wang, V. (Ed.). (2023). *Handbook of research on andragogical leadership and technology in a modern world* (1st ed.). IGI Global Information Science Reference. DOI: 10.4018/978-1-6684-7832-5

Yao, N., & Wang, Q. (2024). Factors influencing pre-service special education teachers' intention toward AI in education: Digital literacy, teacher self-efficacy, perceived ease of use, and perceived usefulness. *Heliyon*, 10(14), e34894. DOI: 10.1016/j.heliyon.2024.e34894 PMID: 39149079

Chapter 8
Assessment in Higher Education in the Age of Artificial Intelligence:
Possibilities and Constrictions in Africa

William Chakabwata
https://orcid.org/0000-0002-4224-5239
University of South Africa, South Africa

ABSTRACT

Artificial Intelligence (AI) is taking over the operations of universities globally because of the multiple benefits associated with it which include transparent forms of assessment, immediate feedback to students and a reduced workload on the part of the instructors. There are also challenges that are associated with the use of AI, such as unethical practices which may undermine academic rigour and integrity. A number of theories are employed in this chapter which includes statistical modelling, Unified Theory of Acceptance and Use of Technology, (UTAUT) and Evidence Based Learning (EBL). The chapter presents a case for Africa to adopt AI in a conscientious way in order to meet the Sustainable Development Goal No 4, of providing quality and inclusive education. The opportunities for using AI in assessment in higher education are explored as well as the constrictions that Africa faces in transitioning to this form of technology.

DOI: 10.4018/979-8-3693-6527-4.ch008

INTRODUCTION

Assessment plays a pivotal role in learning in higher education in its multifaceted forms. Assessment may be conceptualised as a black box activity or a transparent box process. Traditional assessments which are characterised by a snapshot of student learning is associated with the black box approach, while the AI assessment which are more dynamic are associated with transparent box. This chapter presents the background of the study explicating on formative and summative assessments. The link between Sustainable Development Goal (SDG) 4, on the provision of quality and inclusive education is foregrounded. The chapter scrutinises the opportunities for higher education to use AI in Africa and the challenges that accompany such transformation. The subsequent sections addresses Large Language Models (LLMs), adaptive technology, stealth assessment, higher education transformation and assessments, ethical implications of AI and theoretical dimensions of the chapter which includes Evidence Based Learning and Teaching (EBLT),statistical modelling and Unified Theory of Acceptance and Use of Technology (UTAUT). Finally, a discussion, recommendations and conclusions are presented.

Background

Nassoura (2022) and Crompton and Burke, (2023) postulated that in higher education Institutes (HEI) there is a growing use of digital processing techniques, which encompass Artificial Intelligence (AI). The new technologies are being employed across academic disciplines which include linguistics, engineering, education and health among many others. McCarthy in 1956, coined the term artificial intelligence and he extended the postulation of Turing 1937, who had opined the creation of machines that had reasoning and intelligent ability like humans (Cristianini, 2016). A number of studies were done on the use of AI in HEI, which drew the conclusion that the major use was in the area of predicting students' performance, recommendation of learning resources, assessment and enhancing learning performance (Salas-Pilco & Yang, 2022; Hwang & Tu, 2021).The same authors added that instructors in HEI are not yet certain in terms of how to utilise AI as a pedagogical tool at a scalable dimension and ways it can have significance in higher education. Adaptive learning technologies and AI are the key technological tools in higher education, which are anticipated to be incorporated in teaching and assessment. The future of HEI is inextricably bound to AI, with an estimation that by 2022 multiple universities constituting 96% will be using AI, and replacing textbooks with online resources, which is expected to lead to colossal financial savings (WifiTalents, 2024). AI employed to offer support to students had varied names which ranged from virtual agent, intelligent agent and intelligent help.

Assessment either as formative or summative plays a central role in learning (Memarian and Doleck, 2024; McConlogue, 2020; Fisher, 2024). It is vital that instructors evaluate the degree of success of their teaching, whether it is at undergraduate level or post-graduate. Stassen et al.,(2001,p5) conceived assessment as "process faculty use to grade students…any activity designed to collect information on the success of a programme". Assessments are linked to learning outcomes and when administered in any appropriate way, can lead to fruitful learning. Assessment enhances instructional practices by instructors and also helps students learn. In this chapter, the use of artificial intelligence in assessment is explored.

Memarian and Doleck (2024) averred that assessment may be conceptualised as assessment for learning or formative assessment or assessment of learning. Assessment for learning seeks to enhance the learning process, while summative assessment seeks to determine the extent to which learning outcomes have been realised. The concept of assessment for learning has expanded to include a determination of student progress and also the provision of feedback.

There is a burgeoning of literature on assessment and the use of artificial intelligence. Arakpogun et al., (2020, p1) posited that AI connotes the "collection of information and communication technologies (ICTs) that mimic human intelligence to enable machines to do our work better, create greater efficiencies and drive economic growth".

Gleason (2018) averred that higher education has a pivotal role to play in ensuring transition in the society to the use of Artificial Intelligence (AR). Rahiman and Kodikal (2024) noted that most of the traditional assessments do not adequately address the learning needs of students and it is that gap that is being met by AI. Many years of research have demonstrated that knowledge and application of knowledge cannot be methodically assessed under examination conditions. Possibly the resilience of traditional examination has been due to the high cost of implementing alternatives approaches and lack of reliability of innovations. AI helps to provide an efficient alternative to the dilemma of using traditional assessments.

The educational context is marked by the need to engage in sustainable practices and in this way contribute to Sustainable Development Goals (SDGs) (Opesemowo and Adekomaya, 2024; United Nations Scientific and Cultural Organisation UNESCO, 2019; Nyhan and Marshall, 2024). The multiple and diverse technological innovations offer opportunities to make higher education equitable, inclusive and ethical. These technologies are mediated by internet connectivity, and associated learning platforms which includes e-learning, virtual learning and AI, will play focal role in the realisation of SDGs. The Agenda 2023 and United Nations SDGs which proclaim a vision to end poverty, and for nations to experience tranquility and prosperity, will require that education play a central role and curriculum have to incorporate SDGs. There is a huge shift in the educational approaches with the location of technology at the heart of learning and assessment. It is projected that in 2023, 15 billion devices will have access to the internet and the number is anticipated to double by 2030 (Nyhan and Marshall, 2024). This major expansion will be propelled by the use of 5G, which will culminate in devices being able to communicate and convey information more swiftly and efficiently.

A conference was held in Beijing from 16-18, May 2019, dubbed Beijing Consensus on Artificial Intelligence and Education and was attended by approximately 500 delegates from more than 100 countries, provided a framework on how to appropriate AI technologies, in order to attain the educational goals of Agenda 2030 (Ministry of Education People Republic of China, 2019; UNESCO, 2019). The conference acknowledged the central place of AI in transforming the educational sector. van den Berg (2023) added that AI is a critical component of education and is predicted to transform educational practices in future. Examples of AI that are challenging traditional didactic practices are the use of chatbots, learning analytics and provision of tutoring services.

AI comes with multiple benefits in higher education which include personalised instruction, reduction of mundane workload for instructors and ongoing student assessment and feedback (Holmes, et al., 2021; Bajaj eta al., 2021; Cope et al.,2021; Gonzalez-Calatayud, Prendez-Espinosa et al., 2021). In spite of these advantages, AI also ushers a number of disadvantages, which includes paucity of guidelines and policies to provide a framework for its usage in higher education. An entrepreneur on AI and Talent Solution firm based in the United States asserted in an interview with Forbes Magazine that it imperative for instructors and policy makers to investigate the intersection of education and artificial intelligence (Forbes, 2020). The Association of African Universities (AAU, 2023) which is the highest platform for consultation and idea exchange among African universities, held a meeting on the 2023 from the 6 -10 November with a theme that forefront AI in higher education, termed artificial intelligence in African higher education. The theme for 2023 focalised on a discussion of internet of Things, virtual reality, natural language processing and the new technologies.

LARGE LANGUAGE MODELS (LMS)

The use of machines in higher education is a single factor in a plethora of issues. Other issues that will demand attention includes how to address the challenge of asymmetrical distribution of resources in Africa and other nations in the global south. Jermakowicz (2023) asserted that technologies such as ChatGPT and BARD have the capability to anticipate and create human language. One fundamental component of AI is its dependence on Large Language Models (LMS), which are sophisticated and designed to predict and utilise human language. AI has experienced a radical transformation due to the innovation of LMS system. These subtle algorithms that are mediated by huge neural systems which are contrived to create an assemblage of words after being prompted by input and thus have a capacity to simulate and create human -like text. LMS are able to perform a number of functions that are related to languages such as aiding in creating content, responding to questions and translating languages. Jermakowicz (2023, pp. 1-2) posited that LMS are able to display a number of capabilities such as:

- Natural Language processing- use of programmes such as sentiment analysis, chatbots and language translation
- Creation of content- facilitating creation of articles, reports and creative compilations
- Virtual assistants- providing verbal engagements as virtual assistants
- Answering Questions- enabling information to be retrieved swiftily
- Ability to summarise text- helping to provide a concise summary of detailed documents

ChatGPT the popular chatbot from openAI, was launched in 2022 and two months after its inauguration, was able to be used by an estimated 100 million users in January 2023 (Hu, 2023). The evolution of LMS has been traced to the 1950s and 1960s with experimentation by scientists with LMS and Natural Language Processing (NLP). One of prototype was the development of ELIZA a computer programme that was designed by Joseph Weizenbaum at MIT in 1966, which could establish emotional connection with human beings, which was termed chatbot and laid the foundation for future sophisticated development of subtle LLM (Gordon, 2022). A number of developments led to the developments of sophisticated programmes such as ChatGPT, in the 1970s, 1980s and 1990s which included the developments of rule based systems in natural language processing, and the developments of statistical methods and machine learning. The development of neural networks (RNNs) in the mid- 2010s changed the terrain of NLP, leading to the development of sophisticated language models.

HIGHER EDUCATION AND TRANSFORMATION OF ASSESSMENTS

De Villiers et al., (2021) expounded that AI operated assessments can effectively identify students' gaps and areas of ability. Students are able to access immediate feedback on their work. Bulut, et al., (2024) asserted the radical impact of AI on higher education particularly, the use of automated scoring, swift language analysis, providing consistent feedback and regular feedback on student performance and use of natural language.

Automated scoring means that AI technology, the blending of AI in educational measurement and assessment and using deep learning algorithms, AI has facilitated the grading of open -ended questions, essays and creative work and giving feedback that is timely to students (You-Jin et al., 2023; Owoc et al., 2021; Shibata & Uto, 2022). In addition, natural language Processing (NLP) algorithms is able to grade oral or written content swiftly, identify areas for growth and offer students feedback that is applicable to their work. AI is able to transcend traditional forms of assessments by furnishing instructors' trends in the performance of students, foresee future academic patterns and offer appropriate interventions that can help sustain students who are at risk of failing.

Despite these massive changes that AI has brought to higher education, the new technology is accompanied by challenges that are related to issues of validity and reliability. Other AI tools that have been introduced include Poe AI, by Quora, AI Claude AI, by Anthropic, and xAI by Elon Musk (Bender et al, 2021).

ETHICAL IMPLICATIONS OF AI AND RELIABILITY AND VALIDITY

There are concerns that AI may present issues that are linked to validity, reliability, transparency and fairness and equity (Ho, et al., 2024). AI has been perceived to function as a system that takes information in and then transmits it, in such a way that it is not practicable to account for how the decisions are made. This has led to exothermic discussions on the ethical implications of using AI.

There is a huge potential that algorithms that are employed may unwittingly preserve or reinforce biases inherent in the data. Ouyang et al., (2020) posited that LMS can spawn information that is not accurate or even malfeasant, suggesting that constructing massive language models may not make them better or effective. LLM draw from huge datasets that are extracted from the internet, which may show skewed views and stereotypes. Maintaining a balance between freedom of expression, inclusivity and content creation remains an indomitable task.

LLM extract information from massive datasets which are either personal or sensitive. This poses issues of security of data, the right to consent and possibility of inappropriate use of data. Striking a balance between using a LLM and ensuring the right to privacy of individuals creates a delicate tension. In addition, there is a challenge of data security, as LLM draw from huge datasets. These datasets which may be stored in a cloud, face the risk of threats from cybersecurity attacks. Accountabilities connotes that stakeholders who are engage in the development of these applications become conscious of the possible risks and therefore take active measures to ensure that there are no biases, or stereotypes. Finally, it is vital that AI is deployed and used in a way that ensures that intellectual property rights are upheld.

In the context of higher education data in AI that may be skewed has potential to amplify current disparities and marginalise certain categories of students. It is for that reason that deployment of AI in a haphazard way, in a context that lacks a coherent policy framework, has capacity of derailing the effective use assessments and judicious feedback from AI systems. Education assessment has a record of forefronting the issue of ensuring that test bias is eliminated from assessment practices (OECD, 2023; Zhou et al., 2020; European Commission, Directorate-General for Education Youth & Culture, 2022). With the burgeoning of AI tools in higher education it becomes very critical to resolve the issue of ethical challenges. Multiple ethical issues emerge regarding the use of AI in education which includes possibility of bleak consequences in terms of finances, pedagogy and operational side, due to number of factors (Jermakowicz, 2023). Firstly, AI firms have no mandate to meet the needs of higher education institutions when it comes to the access and management of their models and they don't have to be accountable in terms of the data they are built on and this raises severe issues when it is used in assessment. Secondly, there is discomfort on the use of AI because of the costs involved and the associated environmental effects. Finally, the general animation based on the ChatGPT innovation has eclipsed discursive issue of AI ownership and who regulates education in the era of AI (Birhane, et al., 2023). Birhane, et al., (2023) urged higher education institutions to generate precise tools to isolate text that is generated by AI. In addition, higher education institutions are also urged to upgrade their ethical and integrity policies to reflect the new trends posed by AI.

Zhou et al.,(2020) adduced that the debate on the dentology of AI can be traced to the 1960s. As AI evolves into more sophisticated forms it becomes a challenge to address issues related to governance, ownership and privacy. In addition, the applications can also become very difficult to predict what they are able to do. It is however important to note that there is no consensus on the meaning of ethical conduct in AI. There is a growing body of literature on ethical practices in the use of AI, which include European Union draft policy and OECD. The discussion on ethical use of AI has coalesced on ensuring that the following principles are upheld fairness, justice, responsibility, transparency non-malfeasance and privacy.

OECD (2023) urged that when assessments are implemented using AI, that impact on instructors and students such as high stakes test, the process has to be transparent.

POSSIBILITY FOR USING AI IN HIGHER EDUCATION IN AFRICA

Shute et al., (2021) explicated the importance of using effective assessments that are informed by the use of technology in order to develop higher order thinking skills. The use of game- based learning is perceived as the key to breaking away from the traditional view of assessments. Extant literature currently supports the notion that games promote development of skills, knowledge and multiple personal attributes (Shute et a., 2021; Shute, et al., 2016; Charles Sturt University, 2021). Well-crafted assessments are perceived as effective at assessing graduate attributes in higher education.

Nguyen (2023) noted that AI holds numerous possibilities for transforming practice in higher education, by changing academic philosophies, course design and assessment practices. There are multiple benefits that can be derived from the use of AI in African higher education and in assessment in particular. Charles Sturt University (2021) deduced that traditional assessments took the guise of essays, examinations and multiple-choice questions. However the advent of text-generative programmes such as ChatGPT, it is time for higher education to review the effectiveness of these approaches. Contemporary research indicates the need for a more adaptive, continuous and authentic assessments (Swiecki, et al., 2022).

Assessments play a pivotal role in higher education in Africa. Swiecki, et al., (2022, p. 1) foregrounded reasons that made traditional assessments inappropriate which included:

- The difficulties associated with designing traditional assessments
- They provide an inaccurate or static perception of student learning and fail to reveal the complexity of learning
- They fail to fit the backgrounds of each student and skills and knowledge by the uniform way they are designed
- They lack authenticity and seem to meet the needs of the institution for assessments, but do not address the needs of students in terms of competency needed for the world of work.

Expanding on these observations it is argued that traditional assessments with their use of standard assessments and rubrics are demanding for instructors who function is not merely teaching (Kaipa, 2021). These assessments which are pre-planned are used to draw inference on the students' competencies and knowledge in a given area. There is usually no precise and concise data on which such inferences may be based, raising questions that such assessments have little to do with students learning, but are used to meet institutional assessments policy. Given the colossal duties of instructors regarding teaching, learning, class management and assessment, it is an onerous task for them to design assessments that are based on credible data. Most of these assessments tend to be rigid and provide a perspective on what students are able to do or know at a given moment, they do not explain the intricate nature of learning. Given that most definitions of learning characterize it as a process of change over time, it would require a couple of these snapshots in order to determine the extent of the change (Schneider, 2024; Kolb & Whishaw, 2014; Mazur, 2013).

The emerging view in assessments is the contention that the learning outcome is just as critical as the learning process (Puntambekar et al. 2011). Furthermore, it is averted that understanding the learning process over a period is vital to apprehending student learning and how learning transpires. Other key elements to learning are the student's self-regulation and reflection. Long term learning outcomes and the nature of feedback students receive are vital in assessments. Traditional assessments may also impact students' ability to show their learning by the way they are designed to be uniform. More poignantly, assessments that run in higher education seem to seek relevance as they tend to assess skills that are obsolete (Hwang et al.,2020). AI has become pervasive in our everyday life, and it is for that reason that proponents argue it must become an integral part of the school culture. Using AI in schools connotes the use of software that must allow students to use external processing skills afforded by AI, so that they can focus on the development of other competencies. This means utilising automated essay grading systems, and other adaptive technologies and the employment of data driven assessment practices in any online environment. There is also a discussion on how AI driven simulation and games may support online learning (Cope et al;2021).

Africa through the use of AI has an opportunity to transform assessment practices from traditional mode to more contemporary mode that is driven by adaptive technology. Cope, Kalantzis et al.,(2021,p5) indicated the primacy of assessment by declaring that

Assessment is perhaps the most significant area of opportunity offered by artificial intelligence for transformative change in education….AI enabled assessments uses dramatically different artefacts and processes from traditional assessments …

Opesemowo and Adekomaya (2024) asserted that the use of AI enables the employment of personalised assessments which can help students to develop skills that are requisite to meet the SDGs of provision of quality and equitable education for all. Charles Sturt University (2021) expounded that AI assessments may assume the form of assessments where students use multimedia presentation such as use of a video or presentation on a website.

Swiecki, et al., (2022) indicated that assessments could employe automated grading of essays and multiple-choice questions. The success of these applications that use neural networks depends on the presence of massive and appropriate datasets that enhance the quality of the created responses. However, the use of AI to grade multiple -choice items have a challenge of the models requiring colossal datasets that are requisite to train the models. AI is also able to provide feedback on students' work by using platforms which includes Mechanical TA, Aropa and students. Peer assessment is recognized to tackle the challenge of large classes. There are AI platforms that also support peer assessment of large classes, and which African higher education can profit from, which includes Mechanical TA, Aropa, Dear Beta and Dear Gama among many others (Khosravi et al. 2019; Er, et al., 2020; Shnayder and Parkes, 2016). Shnayder and Parkes, (2016) explicated RiPPLE as a platform that can be located within a learning management system, and which has capacity to function independently and can sustain learning activities. In a study that was conducted in Queensland Australia, it was noted that this collaborative learning platform enhanced student learning. RiPPLE like other adaptive systems has the capability to support learning as well as assessment that are personalised to meet the student's learning needs.

Hong, et al.(2023) opined that Computerised Adaptive Testing (CAT) emerged as a personalised test mode in online learning, which sought to show the student hidden knowledge by choosing test knowledge in a selective way. The core feature of CAT is the item selection component, which selects an item utilising an estimation of the student's current ability. CAT has been used in educational measurement, games and job recruitment. In addition, the CAT has been used in Graduate record admission and was noted to display high levels of accuracy when compared with pencil and paper examination. Khosravi et al.,(2019) asserted that student diversity presents a challenge when it comes to meeting the needs of all students. The same authors opined that RiPPLE furnishes instructors with the assessment data they need to support learning. This platform provides rich data that can be used by both students and instructors. In RiPPLE each student has access to their performance and knowledge level in two categories termed engagement categories and competency category. The concept of providing feedback to students in RiPPLE is presupposed on the need to help students to assume ownership of the learning process. The same platform enables instructors to access a downloadable report that reflects students' learning activities such as resources accessed, knowledge units and activities the student have attempted. Martin and Lazendic (2017) echoed that adaptive testing designs computer instruction to the needs of students in a way that is able to address the variation in student ability.

African higher education can also benefit from the use of electronic assessment platforms (Schneider, 2024). These have the capacity to offer examinations that transcend traditional assessments in terms of the way they are able to use traditional assessments where feedback is issued by an instructor only. African can also benefit from the automated grading of student's written work. The origins of automated system of grading essay has a long genesis going back to the the 1960s (Graham and Harris, 2015). Numerous systems are in use for essay scoring which includes MI Writing. The same programme affords students an opportunity to refine their writing skills, by assessing their work using criteria such as development of ideas, nature of sentences and words used.

The use of stealth assessments has also been noted to enhance student learning. The term stealth assessment had its genesis at a conference on assessment in 2005, at a symposium on diagnostic assessment. It assesses students' progress inconspicuous while they are immersed in digital learning environments or learning games (Akram, et al., 2018; Rahim & Shute, 2023). (Shute et al. (2021) conceptualized stealth assessment as a formative form of assessment that is driven by AI and which transpires when students are engaged in games. It uses statistical scoring, evidence-based approach, to gather real data using models and educational data mining. Stealth assessments help students to stay abreast of contemporary demands for up-to-date assessments that enable the development of a variety of skills such as communication, collaboration, critical thinking and creativity. Stealth assessment which occurs during games enables the development of twenty-first -century skills, which are extremely daunting to measure using traditional assessments methods.

Shute et al., (2021, p. 1) adduced that digital based assessments hold the following advantages over traditional assessments which are given a snapshot:

- They are motivating to students and have less pressure or anxiety
- Its possible to recording of students work in real time
- Enable the provision of formative feedback on student's work in real time.

The goal of stealth assessments is to eradicate the distinctions between games, learning and assessments. Akram, et al., (2018) averred that there has been an expansion of game based learning in contemporary times. The same author noted that stealth assessment relies on data generated from students' immersion in the game without interfering with the learning process. Stealth assessment extrapolates on student's competency utilising data extracted from the game –based learning using evidence centred design (ECD).

Ayanwale and Ndlovu (2024) declared that the world has seen an upsurge in the use of Computer Based Test (CBT), which facilitate the collation, recording and reporting of assessments electronically. CBT has transformed assessment to a more technological platform, in the aftermath of COVID-19 pandemic. The same authors noted that the use of CBT, is not yet ubiquitous in Africa.

EVIDENCE –BASED LEARNING AND TEACHING

Emplit (2020) explicated the use of Evidence -Based Learning and Teaching (EBLT) as a fluid concept. EBLT demands ongoing collection of data. EBLT has its genesis in the clinical programmes such as medicine, nursing and psychology. Mislevy et al.,(2004) and Newton, et al., (2021) concurred that ECD approach that forefronts the validity argument for any assessment by spotlighting the claims made about an assessment and the evidence that is required to sustain those claims. The model is built on the following presuppositions; the student model where extrapolation about the student are made, then the evidence model where information extracted from the student furnishes information about the student and then the task model where the task can be organised to furnish information to enable student to use in the evidence model as well as the interlinkage of these models.

Rahim and Shute (2023) contrasted the traditional assessments methods that were based on the assumption of intervention in learning as using a black box method in terms of their inability to explain learning before intervention with the contemporary computer- aided methods which can store data on the student before the intervention and also after the intervention and are termed as the glass box. Traditional assessments were also not able to assess competencies that are considered latent such as graduate attributes. For example, the use of digital games displays in actuality the problem-solving process for students which is different from asking questions to students about problem solving.

The glassbox approaches have the ability to provide colossal data on the learning path of a student in real time by assessing the student's competencies and to use that feedback to modify instruction. That ability to adjust learning to meet the requirements of the student's learning theory is upheld by motivation theories such as social cultural theory and self-determination theory (Arakpogun et al., 2020).

Mislevy et al.,(2004) declare that ECD is capable of supporting a diversity of assessments practices which includes standardised tests, quizzes, simulation type of assessments and portfolios. Creating assessments in ECD, asists in creating an alignment between the knowledge you want to assess and the assessment task. The general structure of ECD helps enables interaction among various stakeholders which includes task designers, statisticians, delivery process developers among many others (Mislevy et al.,2004,p4).

Mislevy et al.,(2004) declares that a number of assessments methods have evolved over many years with a goal of seeking to extrapolate on what students are able to do or predict their actions. Progress that has transpired in the area of cognitive and pedagogical practices have expanded the scope of skills and knowledge higher education seeks to develop in students. Data that is emerging from statistical modeling and evidential reasoning helps higher education to address challenges related to assessments which includes drawing implications about student's learning from enomous and complex data (Mansaray & Mutisya, 2017; Statistical Modelling, 2024).

ECD is conceived as constituting steps that are interlinked which start with domain analysis, domain modelling, conceptual assessment framework, assessment implementation and assessment delivery (Mislevy et al.,2004, p.4). The initial level of domain analysis provides the foundation for the development of assessment position. At the same level a key number of Focal Skills Knowledge and Ablities (FSKAS) skills are identified, and this helps to isolate the priority of the assessment. The concepts are identified in a way that reflects the concepts that may require further development and those that may also need to be tackled separately (Neumann et al., 2021;Emplit, 2020).

Emplit (2020) noted challenges that are related to evidence based teaching which includes establishing a common understanding across institutions, implementing EBLT in a way that is sustainable way and promoting successful evaluation of EBLT.

STATISTICAL MODELLING

Statistical Modelling (2024) explicated statistical modelling as a basic concepts in statistics where mathematical models are employed to make extrapolations, projections and decisions extracted from the data and the complet interplay of various variables. The central issue is that statistical modelling entails utilising mathematics and statistical procedures to apprehend real world data. Statistical modelling has merits such as helping drive informed decisions, use of data motivated decisions, improve problem- solving skills, improves the opportunity to make projections on a phenomenon and presents opportunities for coming with innovative assessments.

Zapata-Cardona and Martínez-Castro (2023) expounded that statistical models varies from basic tools that can reflect information in the form of graphs and statistics to highly sophisticated programmes, which demonstrate extrapolation, variability and data differentiation. These programmes shift from deterministic worldview by the way they reflect uncertainty and randomness.

CONSTRICTIONS FOR USING AI IN HIGHER EDUCATION IN AFRICA

The use of assessment in higher education depends on the technological readiness of different states in Africa. Diallo, et al.(2024) conducted an assessment on the readiness of various African states to embrace AI. The same authors noted that the contemporary global assessment on AI fails to capture unique situation of individual African states. A number of challenges are highlighted in the same report by Diallo et al.(2024) for different countries, for instance Mauritius, has a weak and inadequate data protection regime, Kenya and Egypt confront the challenges of making AI scalable, and Angola had restricted governance and financial resources to build an appropriate workforce. In contrast to developed nation such as USA, European Union and China which are developing AI, many African states tend to display constrictions which includes restricted access to data, infrastructure deficit, limited economic and political resources. There are multiple ways in which digital preparedness is assessed, which include the World Bank Digital Framework, Readiness and Maturity Assessment and Cisco's Digital. Work that was done to appraise 33 Africa's digital readiness in 2019 using Cisco's Digital framework, reflected that only one country was ready for AI (Assefa et al., 2021; Cisco, 2021).

Sey and Mudongo (2023) noted additional challenges to the implementation of AI in African states which includes institutional weakness, paucity of facilitators and experts in AI, indequate funding for AI, and the dominance of males in the AI industry. There is very scanty details on the contemporary state of AI in Africa and also the organisations that are active to address the institution of AI programmes. There is also restricted access to information on the state of readiness, outside the readiness frameworks which utilises given indicators (Sey & Mudongo, 2023).

United Nations Scientific and Cultural Organisation (UNESCO,2019) observed that there is uneven development in terms of development of technology globally, culminating in a digital divide within countries and regions based on geography and social economic markers. There is a limited AI penetration in sub-Sahara Africa in comparison to other continents which include Europe, Asia and USA (UNESCO,2019;Gwagwa et al., 2020; Arakpogun et al.,2020). There is paucity of data on the degree of penetration of AI in Africa's higher education. Countries in the global north seem to be in strategic place to profit from AI, although there are possibilities of job losses in the global south.

Okolo et al.,(2023) noted that from the beginning the concentration of AI has been in the global north. This signifies an uneven distribution of power that has deprived the global south opportunity to realise autonomy and economic development. The same author averred that the adoption of AI has been contingent on a number of variables such as development of skills at local level to use the technology and infrastructure ability to design and institute it. In Africa very limited number of countries have enacted data protection law, while multiple states are not engaged on the issue. There is a growth of the use of AI in Africa.

Arakpogun et al.,(2020) noted the disparate distribution of AI between countries. Africa has not been able to appropriate the advantages of industrial revolution and it is anticipated that it will be able to appropriate the benefits of AI. Multiple hubs for AI have been established in Africa. For example, University of Cape Town in South Africa, instituted the Robotics and Agent Lab (RAL) in 2007, with a mandate to develop robotics and computational intelligence as well encouraging competition in the area of robotics among children. Data Science Africa (DSA) is a non-governmental organisation that is located in Kenya since 2013 and had an intention of deploying affordable AI solutions in Africa. South Africa had the largest number of AI start up businesses followed by Nigeria, Kenya and Tunisia.

There are a number of constrictions when it comes to introducing AI in higher education in Africa identified by Mwelwa et al., (2020) which includes a weak engagement to global science, lack of skills in data science and use, paucity of software engineering skills and data scientists and other ancillary staff. There are a number of isolated AI developments in Africa in a context that is largely devoid of infrastructure. Although it is acknowledged that there is a global deficit of data science, curators and software engineering skills globally, the challenge is more pronounced in Africa. There is a constricted utilization of resources in Africa, with many students being introduced to data science at tertiary level. In order for AI to be fully utilised in higher education assessments, unless some of these constrictions are addressed (Mwela, 2019).

AAU (2023) at a meetings that was held to discuss the effect of emerging technologies in African higher education in 2023, it was noted that there was a possibility that instructors would utilise AI in an unethical way by creating automated solutions to essays and other complex assessments. It was added that for African higher institutions to appropriate the benefits of AI, they have to put in place policy framework, at institutional and societal levels. Furthermore the conference observed that higher education institutions have to mediate the conversation on the use of AI with all stakeholders in order to formulate an adequate response that can address the unethical practices.

McCormack (2023) expounded that a non –profit making organisation called Educause conducted a poll on the use of AI in higher education. The Educause poll reflected that Educause members were also utilising AI in higher education for a variety of causes which included easing the instructors teaching load, designing learning content, designing teaching content and to brainstorm on a number of issues. The constrictions facing the use of AI in higher education in Africa includes constrictions includes dearth of infrastructure, paucity of skills, data accessibility and ethical concerns especially in the area of privacy.

THEORETICAL FRAMEWORK

The theoretical framework that is used to undergird this study is the Unified Theory of Acceptance and Use of Technology (UTAUT), postulated by Venkatesh, Morris, Davis and Davies in 2003 in order to strengthen the Technology Acceptance Model (TAM).TAM was expounded by Fred Davis as a component of a doctoral dissertation building on the work of Theory of Reasoned Action posited by Fishbein and Icek in the 1960s (Ng, 2020;).

The desire to ensure that there is technological usage and adoption is one of the area that is focalised on by Information Systems (IS) (Venkatesh et al., 2016; Willians et al.,2015; Ahmad, 2014).UTAUT is perceived as an attempt to coalesce eight previous theories and insights on technological acceptance. The theory was instituted based on four pillars of namely performance acceptance, effort expectance, social influence and facilitating conditions. The theory also posits the use of what are termed moderators, which mediate between a number of constructs and the desire to use them. The mediating factors or moderators are age, experience, gender and voluntary drive to use them (Ahmad, 2014). IT adoption research averred that technology will not have utilitarian value unless it is adopted.

Initially research on adoption of technology, had a primary goal of ascertaining user satisfaction, which is captured by Legris et al,.(2003,p.67) "the sum of one's feelings or attitudes towards a variety of factors affecting the situation". Based on the premise that there is a positive relationship between the use of information technology and performance is positive, researchers examined organisations, individuals and technology in order to delineate factors that affect use of technology.

Chatterjee and Bhattacharjee (2020) perceived risky is conceptualised as the conviction that a user would suffer loss for instance in the use of AI. In the context of this chapter AI is a web-based application and it comes with numerous risks which includes behavioural insecurity. A reduction in behavioural insecurity leads to more people adopting the use of an innovation such as AI. If perception of risk is high then the rate of adoption will be slower.

Performance expectancy (PE) refers to the degree that an instructor in the case of the use of AI and assessment, expects the AI to help them gain advantage over their work as an instructor.PE is viewed as similar to perceived usefulness, outcome expectancy and comparative advantage (Ali & Qaisar, 2018; Onaolapo & Oyewole, 2018). The beliefs that a person develops have an effect on their potential to adopt new technology.

Effort expectancy (EE) refers to the degree to which an innovation may be used with minimum difficulty. It means that if instructors will adopt the use of assessments methods that are based on AI, they have to believe that the applications are easy to use. EE has an effect on the attitude to embrace new technology, such as AI in higher education. Facilitating conditions (FC) connotes the extent to which instructors in higher education believe that there is sufficient infrastructure and technical support to adopt the use of AI for assessment purposes (Fatoni & Surani, 2022; Rizkalla et al, 2023). This also refers to the degree that instructors feel that they are in control of their work and a comparison they can make of the application with other competing models.

DISCUSSION

van den Berg (2023) in a study on the use of AI in assessment made an incisive observation that instructors and students demonstrated a deficit in terms of knowledge of AI, which also impacted their ability to embrace the innovation. The conversation on the use of AI has to address the issue of resource disparate between countries and also within Africa (Owoc et al.,2021). The attitudes of instructors towards ChatGPT has been ambivalent in higher education. In a study conducted in North America, 1 in five instructors had employed the technology to improve their courses, while the rest where still grappling with the position of AI in higher education. Most instructors were worried about the possibility of cheating and the challenges of detecting malpractice given their limited skills in this burgeoning area. Multiple students and instructors urged the use of ChatGPT in higher education (Wiley, 2023).

The chapter also highlighted the limitations of assessments as displaying a black-box approach which neglects the state of the student before assessments and also what occurs after the assessments (Swiecki, et al., 2022; Wulandari & Hadi, 2021; Akram, et al., 2018). Traditional assessments tends to provide a snapshot of students learning, it is for that reason that they are being superseded by AI informed assessments. Other objections that have been raised to the use of traditional assessments in higher education include the lack of authenticity, the challenging of constructing the assessments given the exponential growth in intake in higher education due the massification of higher education. AI has merits of enabling instructors to assess diverse learning ability among students, different competencies and also predict areas that students need to work on in order to enhance learning.AI aided assessments are also able to provide timely feedback to instructors in higher education and to reduce the pressure that instructors have to content with of preparing and grading assessments (Naidoo, 2024). Some of the AI designed platforms are able to grade essays and provide feedback to students. However, the use of AI has been noted to come with challenge in terms of ethics that are related to the data that they generate information from.

Given all these benefits that come with the AI softwares, it is noticeable that Africa is still at an embryonic stage in the use of AI in higher education. There are a number of private companies that are engaged in the development of AI platforms in Africa in different sectors. AI in Africa is associated with the creation of big data, which currently is a colossal challenge for individual African states unless they come together and collaborate. Abebe (2024) opined that African higher education has to upgrade administrative infrastructure in order to meet the challenges posed by AI. It is also important to note that generative tools now exceed 1000 and of these some have relevance to educators such as Curipod, Eduaide, Quizizz, Slidesgo among many others.

These AI applications have functionalities that can create content, teaching assistant, feedbackbot, free form chat, and capacity to create assessments. Furthermore universities must also be able to tackle the challenge of academic dishonesty in higher education. There are potentials for African higher education, to embrace use of AI in order to realise academic improvement in areas such as academic writing. This of course implies that universities are prepared to invest in the transformation that is needed to benefit from the changes that are needed. Programmes such as ChatGPT have potential to be abused and to undermine academic integrity. Naidoo (2024) postulated that African higher education may turn a blind eye to the innovation emerging from AI at their own peril. The same author noted the disruptive nature of AI on higher education, and how it threatens to upend the traditional assessment practices particularly in the areas such as Natural Language processing, Machine Learning and robotics and computer vision.

RECOMMENDATIONS

In this chapter it was noted that lack of knowledge had an effect on the ability of instructors and students to embrace AI in assessments van den Berg (2023). The development of AI infrastructure in Africa is still in a state of infancy with limited infrastructure and skill development (United Nations Scientific and Cultural Organisation, 2020). It was also noted that there is an uneven distribution of resources that and technology between the global north and global south of which Africa is a part of. Based on these observations it is posited that:

- It is essential that instructors and students be trained on the use of AI in assessment in Africa so that they may be more open to its deployment in higher education.

- It is vital that the disparate distribution of resources be tackled in Africa in order to ensure that there is an optimal use of AI, in a way that helps nations realise SDGs and also reduce poverty between and within countries.
- It is important to develop human and institutional infrastructure related to AI
- Higher education institutions in Africa must develop partnership with other institutions in different countries in order to exploit opportunities presented by AI in Africa in the area of assessment
- Global institution such as UNESCO, private organisations and donor community must step in and help African higher education to develop competency in the use of AI and assessment in higher education.
- African higher education must begin programmes that will build capacity in the area of AI which include masters and doctoral degree programmes.
- Ensure that data used in AI programmes in Africa is protected from violation of privacy.
- It is important to strengthen academic integrity by ensuring that there is no abuse of programmes such as ChatGPT and to strengthen quality and rigour of academic work in higher education in Africa.
- Assessments must also redesigned in order to move away from the traditional single essay assignments in favour of continuous assessments.

CONCLUSION

In the chapter it was noted that AI is proving to be disruptive in higher education. The impact of AI has been felt from instruction, creation of learning content, tracking students' performance and also assessment. The assessments generated by AI are radically different from the traditional assessments. African higher education cannot afford to be left behind in this technological revolution in AI. It is for that reason that African higher education institution have to position themselves at different levels and embrace the pragmatic and positive side of using AI in assessments. Ignoring these innovations has ramifications of making higher education irrelevant and suffer from lack of quality and academic rigour. AI when employed conscientiously in higher education has the potential for transforming higher education in Africa, help realise SDGs linked to quality education and also ensure academic rigour.

REFERENCES

Abebe, E. (2024, 03 16). *Uinversity World News Africa Edition*. Retrieved from Navigatin the horizon preparing African universities for the inevitable AI: https://www.universityworldnews.com/post.php?story=20240306183858627

Ahmad, M. (2014). Unified Theory of Acceptance and Use of Technology (UTAUT) A Decade of Validation and Development. *In proceedings of Fourth International Conference on ICT in our lives* (pp. 1-14). Egypt: Faculty of Commerce, Alexandria University, Alexandria

Akram, B., Min, W., Wiebe, E., Mott, B., Boyer, K., & Lester, J. (2018). Improving Stealth Assessment in Game-based Learning with LSTM-based Analytics. *Proceedings of the 11th International Conference on Educational Data Mining* (pp. 208-218). USA: Educational Resources Information Centre.

Ali, S., & Qaisar, R. (2018). Effect of performance expectancy and effort expectancy on the mobile adoption intention through personal innovativeness among Pakistani consumers. *Pakistan Journal of Commerce and Social Sciences (PJCSS) VOL 12 iSSUE 2*, 501-520.

Arakpogun, E., Elsahn, Z., Olan, F., & Elsahn, F. (2020). *Artificial intelligence in Africa: challenges and opportunities.*

Assefa, S., Rorissa, A., & Alemneh, D. (2021). Digital readiness assessment of countries in Africa: A case study research. *Proceedings of the Association for Information Science and Technology*, 58(1), 400–404. DOI: 10.1002/pra2.467

Ayanwale, M., & Ndlovu, M. (2024). The feasibility of computerized adaptive testing of the national benchmark test: A simulation study. *Journal of Pedagogical Research*, 8(2), 95–112. DOI: 10.33902/JPR.202425210

Bajaj, R., Sharma, V., & Weichbroth, P. (2018). Smart education with artificial intelligence based determination of learning styles. *Procedia Computer Science*, 599, 37–58. DOI: 10.1016/j.procs.2018.05.095

Bender, E., Gebru, T., McMillan-Major, A., & Shmitchell, S. (2021). On the dangers of stochastic parrots: Can language models be too big? FAcct '2. *Proceedings of the 2021 ACM Conference on Fairness, Accountability, and Transparency*, (pp. 610-623). DOI: 10.1145/3442188.3445922

Birhane, A., Kasirzadeh, A., Leslie, D., & Wachter, S. (2023). Science in the age of large language models. *Nature Reviews. Physics*, 5(5), 277–280. DOI: 10.1038/s42254-023-00581-4

Bulut, O., Beiting-Parrish, M., Casabianca, J. M., Slater, S., Jiao, H., & Song, D. & ...Morilova, P. (2024). The Rise of Artificial Intelligence in Educational Measurement:Opportunities and Ethical Challenges White Paper. USA: National Council of Measurement in Education (NCME).

Charles Sturt University. (2021). *Rethinking Assessment Strategies in the Age of Artificial Intelligence (AI)*. Charles Sturt University.

Chatterjee, S., & Bhattacharjee, K. (2020). Adoption of artificial intelligence in higher education: A quantitative analysis using structural equation modelling. *Education and Information Technologies*, 25(5), 3443–3463. DOI: 10.1007/s10639-020-10159-7

Cisco. (2021, 02 29). Cisco digital readiness. Cisco.

Cope, B., Kalantzis, M., & Searsmith, D. (2021). Artificial Intelligence for education: Knowledge and its assessment in AI -enabled ecologies. *Educational Philosophy and Theory*, 53(12), 1229–1245. DOI: 10.1080/00131857.2020.1728732

Cristianini, N. (2016). Intelligence reinvented. *New Scientist*, 232(3097), 37–41. DOI: 10.1016/S0262-4079(16)31992-3

Crompton, H., & Burke, D. (2023). Artificial intelligence in higher education: The state of the field. *International Journal of Educational Technology in Higher Education*, 20(1), 22. DOI: 10.1186/s41239-023-00392-8

De Villiers, C., Kuruppu, S., & Dissanayake, D. (2021). A (new) role for business Promoting the United Nations' Sustainable Development Goals through the internet-of-things and blockchain technology. *Journal of Business Research*, 131, 598–609. DOI: 10.1016/j.jbusres.2020.11.066

Diallo, K., Smith, J., Okolo, C., Nyamwaya, D., Kgomo, J., & Ngamita, R. (2024). Case Studies of AI Policy Development in Africa. *Data & Policy*, 1(12), 1–13.

Emplit, P. (2020). *Learning and Teaching Paper #11 Evidence-based approches to learning and teaching Thematic Peer Group Report*. European University Association.

Er, E., Dimitriads, Y., & Gasevi'c, D. (2020). A collaborative learning approach to dialogic peer feedback: A theoretical framework. *Assessment & Evaluation in Higher Education*, •••, 586–600.

European Commission. Directorate-General for Education Youth & Culture. (2022). *Ethical guidelines on the use of artificial intelligence (AI) and data in teaching and learning for educators*. Paris: Publication Office of the European Union.

Fatoni, A., & Surani, D. (2022). An Analysis of Online Learning Media in English Class During Covid-19 Pandemic. *4th Social and Humanities Research Symposium (SoRes 2021)* (pp. 595-600). Indonesia: Atlantis Press.

Fisher, M. (2024, 07 25). *Vanderbilt University*. Retrieved from Centre for Teaching: https://cft.vanderbilt.edu/student-assessment-in-teaching-and-learning/

Forbes. (2020). Artificial Intelligence In Education Transformation. Retrieved 7 29, 2024, from https://www.forbes.com/sites/forbestechcouncil artificial-intelligence-in-education-transformation/#43ee5fb832a4

Gleason, N. (2018). Introduction. In Gleason, N. (Ed.), *Higher education in the era of the fourth industrial revolution* (pp. 13–15). Palgrave Macmillan. DOI: 10.1007/978-981-13-0194-0_1

Gonzalez-Calatayud, V., Prendez-Espinosa, P., Roig-Vila, R., & Carpanzano, E. (2021). Applied sciences review artificial intelligence for student assessments: A systematic review. *Sci*, 2021, 5467.

Gordon, R. (2022). *ELIZAR wins Peabody Award*. MIT News.

Graham, S., & Harris, K. (2015). Formative assessment and writing: A meta-analysis. *The Elementary School Journal*, 115(4), 523–547. DOI: 10.1086/681947

Gwagwa, A., Kraemer, E., Rizk, N., Rutenberg, I., & De Beer, J. (2020). Artificial Intelligence (AI) deployments in Africa: Benefits, challenges and policy dimensions. [AJIC]. *The African Journal of Information and Communication*, 26(26), 1–28. DOI: 10.23962/10539/30361

Ho, J., von Davier, A., Yaneva, V., Lottridge, S., von Davier, M., & Harris, D. J. (2024). Transforming assessment: The impact and implications of large models and generative AI. *Educational Measurement: Issues and Practice*, 43(2), 16–29. DOI: 10.1111/emip.12602

Holmes, W., Porayska-Pomsta, K., Holstein, K., Sutherland, E., Bake, T., Shun, S., & Koedinger, K. (2021). Ethics of AI of Education: Towards a community -wide framework. *International Journal of Artificial Intelligence in Education.*

Hong, Y., Tong, S., Huang, W., Zhuang, Y., Liu, Q., Chen, E., & He, Y. (2023). *Search-Efficient Computerized Adaptive Testing. CIKM '23, October 21–25*. CIKM.

Hu, K. (2023, 02 2). ChatGPT sets record for fast-growing user base-analyst note. Reuters. Retrieved 07 30, 2024, from https://www.reuters.com/

Hwang, G., & Tu, Y. (2021). Roles and research trends of artificial intellignece in mathematics education: A bibliogmetric mapping and systematic review. *Mathematics*, 9(6), 584. DOI: 10.3390/math9060584

Hwang, G., Xie, H., & Gasevic, D. (2020). Vision, challenges, roles and research issues of Artificial Intelligence in Education . *Computers and Education: Artificial Intelligence 1 Article.*

Jermakowicz, E. (2023). The coming trnasformative impact of large language models and artificial intelligence on global business and education. *Journal of Global Awareness*, 4(2), 3. DOI: 10.24073/jga/4/02/03

Kaipa, R. (2021). Multiple choice questions and essay questions in curriculum. *Journal of Applied Research in Higher Education*, 13(1), 16–32. DOI: 10.1108/JARHE-01-2020-0011

Khosravi, H., Kitto, K., & Williams, J. (2019). RiPPLE: A Crowdsourced Adaptive Platform for Recommendation of Learning Activities. *Journal of Learning Analytics*, 6(3), 1–15. DOI: 10.18608/jla.2019.63.12

Kolb, B., & Whishaw, I. (2014). *An introduction to the brain and behaviour*. Worth Publishers.

Legris, P., Ingham, J., & Collerette, P. (2003). Why do people use information technology?A critical review of the Technology Acceptance Model. *Information & Management*, 40(3), 191–204. DOI: 10.1016/S0378-7206(01)00143-4

Mansaray, M., & Mutisya, P. (2017). Applied statistical models of assessment and evaluation of instructional efficiency. *International Journal of Academic Research in Business & Social Sciences*, 7(5), 233–257. DOI: 10.6007/IJARBSS/v7-i5/2928

Martin, A., & Lazendic, G. (2017). Computer-adaptive testing: Implications for students' achievement, motivation, engagement, and subjective test experience. *Journal of Educational Psychology*, •••, 1–57.

Mazur, J. (2013). *Learning and behaviour*. Prentice Hall.

McConlogue, T. (2020). *Assessment and feedback in higher education*. University College London. DOI: 10.2307/j.ctv13xprqb

McCormack, M. (2023, 4 17). Educause QuickPoll Results: Adopting and Adapting to Generative AI in Higher Ed Tech. Educause Research Notes.

Memarian, B., & Doleck, T. (2024). A review of assessment for learning with artificial intelligence. *Computers in Human Behavior: Artificial Humans*, 2, 1–12.

Ministry of Education People Republic of China. (2019, 08 29). *UNESCO publishes Beijing Consensus on Artificial Intelligence and Education*. Retrieved from Ministry of Education People Republic of China: http://en.moe.gov.cn/news/press_releases/201909/t20190902_396913.html

Mislevy, R., Almond, R., & Lukas, J. (2004). A Brief Introduction to Evidence-Centered Design CSE Report 632. Maryland: National Center for Research on Evaluation,Standards, and Student Testing (CRESST).

Mwela, W. (2019). *Africa Open Science Capacity building and skills development Framework. In Academy of Science of South Africa (ASSAf). Mapping the current landscape of Open Science? Open Data initiatives in AFrica Draft Report.* in Press.

Mwelwa, J., Boulton, G., Wafula, J. M., & Loucoubar, C. (2020). Developing open science in Africa: Barriers, solutions and opportunities. *Data Science Journal*, 19(31), 1–17. DOI: 10.5334/dsj-2020-031

Naidoo, R. (2024, 08 8). *Artificial Intelligence is disrupting higher education*. Retrieved from Innovation Web: https://www.itweb.co.za/article/artificial-intelligence-is-disrupting-higher-education/Pero37Z3eoOMQb6m

Nassoura, A. (2022). Applied Artificial Intelligence Applications In Higher Education Institutions: A Systematic Review. *Webology*, 19(3), 1168–1183.

Neumann, M., Niessen, A., & Meijer, R. (2021). Implementing evidence-based assessment and selection in organizations: A review and an agenda for future research. *Organizational Psychology Review*, 11(3), 205–239. DOI: 10.1177/2041386620983419

Newton, S., Alemdar, M., Rutstein, D., Edwards, D., Helms, M., Hernandez, D., & Usselman, M. (2021). Utilising evidence based design to develop assessments: A high school introductory computer science course. *Frontiers in Education*, 6, 1–19. DOI: 10.3389/feduc.2021.695376

Ng, K. (2020). The moderating role of trust and the theory of reasoned action. *Journal of Knowledge Management*, 24(6), 1221–1240. DOI: 10.1108/JKM-01-2020-0071

Nguyen, N. (2023, 5 16). Opportunities and challenges for AI in higher education. https://feedbackfruits.com/blog/opportunities-and-challenges-of-ai-in-higher-education

Nyhan, M., & Marshall, K. (2024). *Harnessing Emerging Technologies for Scalable, Global, Ethical & Equitable Education for Sustainability*. National University of Ireland.

OECD. (2023). Opportunities, guidelines and guardrails for effective and equitable use of AI in education. In *OECD digital education Outlook: Towards an effective digital education system*. OECD Publishing.

Okolo, C., Aruleba, K., & Obaido, G. (2023). Responsible AI in Africa—Challenges and Opportunities. In Eke, D. (Ed.), *K. akunuma, & S. Akintoye, Responsible AI in Africa* (pp. 35–64). Palgrave McMillan. DOI: 10.1007/978-3-031-08215-3_3

Onaolapo, S., & Oyewole, O. (2018). Performance expectancy, effort expectancy, and facilitating conditions as factors influencing smart phones use for mobile learning by postgraduate students of the university of Ibadan, Nigeria. *Interdisciplinary Journal of e-Skills and Lifelong Learning 14*, 95-115.

Opesemowo, O., & Adekomaya, V. (2024). Harnessing Artificial Intelligence for Advancing Sustainable Development Goals in South Africa's Higher Education System: A Qualitative Study. *International Journal of Learning. Teaching and Educational Research*, 23(3), 68–86. DOI: 10.26803/ijlter.23.3.4

Ouyang, L. e. (2020). Training language models to follow instructions with human feedback. Retrieved 07 31, 2024, from https://doi.org/

Owoc, M., Sawicka, A., & Weichbroth, P. (2021). *Artificial Intelligence Technologies in Education: Benefits, challenges and strategies of Implementation*. Gdansk University of Technology.

Puntambekar, S. G. Erkens, & Hmelo-Silver, C. (2011). *Analyzing interactions in CSCL*. Boston: Springer US.

Rahim, S., & Shute, V. (2023). Stealth assessment: a theoretically grounded and psychometrically sound method to assess, support,and investigate learning in technology-rich environments. *Education Tech Research Dev*, 1-25.

Rahiman, H. U., & Kodikal, R. (2024). Revolutionizing education: Artificial intelligence empowered learning in higher education. *Cogent Education*, 11(1), 1–24. DOI: 10.1080/2331186X.2023.2293431

Rizkalla, N., Tannady, H., & Bernando, R. (2023). Analysis of the influence of performance expectancy, effort expectancy, social influence,and attitude toward behavior on intention to adopt live.on. *Multidiscip. Rev.*, Published online.

Salas-Pilco, S., & Yang, Y. (2022). Artificial Intelligence application in Latin America higher education: A systematic review. *International Journal of Educational Technology in Higher Education*, 19(21), 1–20.

Schneider, K. (2024). What is learning? *Psychology (Irvine, Calif.)*, 15(5), 779–799. DOI: 10.4236/psych.2024.155047 PMID: 38278804

Sey, A., & Mudongo, O. (2023). *Case Studies on AI Skills Capacity-building and AI in Workforce Development in Africa*. Research in ICT.

Shibata, T., & Uto, M. (2022). Analytic Automated Essay Scoring based on Deep Neural Networks: Integrating Multidimensional Item Response Theory. *Proceedings of the 29th International Conference on Computational Linguistics* (pp. 2917–2926). London: International Committee on Computational lingustics October 12–17.

Shnayder, V., & Parkes, D. C. (2016). Practical peer prediction for peer assessment. *Proceedings of the fourth AAAI conference on human computation and crowdcourcing* (pp. 199-209). Texas: e fourth AAAI conference.

Shute, V., Leighton, J., Jang, E., & Chu, M.-W. (2016). Advances in the science of assessment. *Educational Assessment*, 21(1), 34–59. DOI: 10.1080/10627197.2015.1127752

Shute, V., Lu, X., & Rahimi, S. (2021). Stealth assessment. In J. Spector, *The Routledge Encyclopedia of Education* (pp. 1-9). London: Taylor & Francis group.

Stassen, L., Doherty, K., & Poe, M. (2001). Course based review and assessment methods for understanding student learning. Massachusettes: University of Massachusetts Amherst.

Statistical Modelling. (2024, 08 6). *Statistical Modelling*. Retrieved from What is Statistical Modelling?: https://www.alooba.com/skills/concepts/statistics/statistical-modelling/

Swiecki, Z., Khosravi, H., Chen, G., Martinez-Maldonado, R., Lodge, J., Milligan, S., Selwyn, N., & Gasevic, D. (2022). Assessment in the age of artificial intelligence. *Computers and Education-Artificial Intelligence*, 3, 1–10. DOI: 10.1016/j.caeai.2022.100075

The Association of African Universities (AAU). (2023, 10 10). Artificial Intelligence in African Universities . *AAU*. AAU.

UNESCO. (2019). *BEIJING CONSENSUS on artifcial intelligence and education. BEIJING CONSENSUS on artifcial intelligence and education*. UNESCO.

United Nations Scientific and Cultural Organisation. (2020). *Artificial Intelligence needs assessment and survey in Africa*. UNESCO.

United Nations Scientific and Cultural Organisation (UNESCO). (2019). *Artificial Intelliegence for sustainable development: A synthesis report*. UNESCO.

van den Berg, S. (2023). *The acceptance of assessment AIs in formal higher education; An explolatory study.* A master degree thesis submitted to the Faculty of Behavioural Management and Social Sciences: University of Twente.

Venkatesh, V., Thong, J., & Xu, X. (2016). Unified Theory of Acceptance and Use of Technology A Synthesis and the Road Ahead. *Journal of the Association for Information Systems*, 17(5), 328–376. DOI: 10.17705/1jais.00428

WifiTalents. (2024, 08 6). *Home education and learning statistics*. Retrieved from WifiTalents: https://wifitalents.com/statistic/ai-in-higher-education/#:~:text=68%25%20of%20universities%20plan%20to,million%20annually%20from%202020%2D2024

Wiley. (2023). ChatGPT and accounting education. Retrieved 7 31, 2924, from https://www.wiley.com/

Willians, M., Rana, N., & Dwivedi, Y. (2015). Unified theory of acceptance and use of technology. *Journal of Enterprise Information Management*, 28(3), 443–488. DOI: 10.1108/JEIM-09-2014-0088

Wulandari, F., & Hadi, S. (2021). Development of computerized adaptive testing to measure students' logical thinking skills in science learning. *Psychology and Education*, 58(2), 4465–4474.

You-Jin, J., Yong-Jin, K., & Ok-Chol, R. (2023). *Review of feedback in Automated Essay Scoring*. Faculty of Mathematics.

Zapata-Cardona, L., & Martínez-Castro, C. (2023). Statistical modeling in teacher education. *Mathematical Thinking and Learning*, 25(1), 64–78. DOI: 10.1080/10986065.2021.1922859

Zhou, J., Chen, F., Berry, A., Reed, M. S., & Savage, S. (2020). A survey on ethical principles of AI and implementations. *2020 IEEE Symposium Seris on Computational Intelligence (SSCI)* (pp. 3010-3017). Australia: 2020 IEEE Symposium Seris on Computational Intelligence (SSCI). DOI: 10.1109/SSCI47803.2020.9308437

KEY TERMS AND DEFINITIONS

Adaptive Technology: It's a form of technology that adjust assessments questions in line with the ability of the student

Artificial Intelligence: Machines that were developed that have the intelligence that is almost equivalent or surplus that of human

Statistical Modelling Software: These are programmes that are designed to gather, analyse and interpret data

Automated Assessment: Assessments that are done by machines

Algorithm: Set of rules that guide the function of a computer

ChatGPT: Automated programmes that can provide feedback to questions posed to it in written form

Natural Language Processing Software: Computer programmes that can use massive data to analyse and use language as humans

Chapter 9

Using ChatGPT to Deconstruct K-12 Student Learning Outcomes for Developing Assessments and Rubrics

Natalie A. Bolton
https://orcid.org/0000-0002-4733-7685
University of Missouri-St. Louis, USA

ABSTRACT

This chapter explores the utilization of ChatGPT, an artificial intelligence (AI) language model, in deconstructing K-12 content standards or Student Learning Outcomes (SLOs) to facilitate the development of assessments and rubrics following Rick Stiggins' deconstructing standards process. Sections of the chapter explore understanding ChatGPT and its educational applications, detailing Stiggins' deconstructing standards process and providing scenarios for deconstructing learning standards. Further, the chapter delineates the flexibility in deconstructing standards and steps for application, leveraging ChatGPT for SLO deconstruction, developing assessments and rubrics, offering examples, and discussing the implications of AI integration in education. The chapter aims to equip educators with insights and practical guidance to enhance assessment practices, fostering well-rounded student development.

DOI: 10.4018/979-8-3693-6527-4.ch009

INTRODUCTION

Integrating artificial intelligence (AI) in education can potentially transform traditional teaching, learning, and assessment methods. ChatGPT, an advanced language model developed by OpenAI, offers a unique opportunity to enhance educational practices by assisting educators in deconstructing content standards or student learning outcomes (SLOs). This chapter explores the application of ChatGPT in deconstructing K-12 SLOs to develop effective assessments and rubrics using Rick Stiggins' deconstructing standards process, which includes knowledge, reasoning, performance skills, and products (Stiggins, 2005).

Chapter Objectives

1. Introduce ChatGPT as a tool for deconstructing K-12 SLOs.
2. Provide an overview of the Stiggins' deconstructing standards process.
3. Demonstrate how ChatGPT can be utilized to develop assessments and rubrics based on deconstructed standards.
4. Present practical examples of using ChatGPT in educational settings.
5. Discuss the implications and potential challenges of integrating AI in educational assessment practices.

Background

Artificial intelligence (AI) has made significant strides in various fields in recent years, and education is no exception. One of the most prominent AI applications is OpenAI's ChatGPT, a powerful language model designed to generate human-like text based on the prompts it receives. This tool can assist educators in various tasks, ranging from administrative responsibilities to improving classroom instruction and engagement (OpenAI, 2023).

ChatGPT is designed to process and generate natural language text, making it highly versatile in responding to a wide range of queries, completing text-based tasks, and even engaging in more nuanced conversations (Brown, 2020; Aripin et al., 2023; Kalla et al., 2023). ChatGPT's key capabilities relevant to educators include: 1) Text generation and completion: ChatGPT can generate essays, explanations, summaries, and lesson plans based on user input. It can assist teachers in creating educational materials or completing lesson notes (Brown, 2020; Aripin et al., 2023; Kalla et al., 2023); 2) Research support: ChatGPT can aid in gathering information and synthesizing research, helping educators stay informed on current trends, studies, and innovations in pedagogy (Adıgüzel et al., 2023; Alshahrani, 2023; Carr, 2023; Zhai, 2022); 3) Content customization: Teachers can use ChatGPT to generate differentiated learning activities for students with varied learning needs, fostering a more inclusive learning environment (Adıgüzel et al., 2023; Laak & Aru, 2024); and 4) Interactive conversations: Through its ability to engage in meaningful dialogue, ChatGPT can simulate discussions or student-teacher interactions, providing real-time feedback or coaching for educators (Brown, 2020; Aripin et al., 2023; Kalla et al., 2023).

As education continues to evolve in the digital age, ChatGPT offers many opportunities to enhance teaching and learning. Its relevance can be seen across several key aspects of educational practice: 1) Lesson planning: Teachers often face time constraints when developing lessons that meet educational standards while catering to individual student needs. ChatGPT can streamline this process by generating lesson ideas, creating outlines, and even suggesting differentiated activities based on diverse learning styles or levels of comprehension (Adıgüzel et al., 2023; Laak & Aru, 2024); 2) Student engagement: ChatGPT can create interactive and engaging content, such as quizzes, discussion questions, or even gamified learning tasks that promote active learning. ChatGPT can also assist educators in crafting student-centered questions that stimulate critical thinking and dialogue (Adıgüzel et al., 2023; Alshahrani, 2023; Carr, 2023; Zhai, 2022); 3) Personalized learning: ChatGPT can help educators design personalized learning experiences by providing feedback, suggesting resources, and generating customized learning plans. Personalizing learning helps in adapting content to meet the individual needs of students, including those with special education needs or those who are gifted (Adıgüzel et al., 2023; Laak & Aru, 2024); and 4) Administrative tasks: From grading essays to tracking student progress, ChatGPT can help educators manage administrative duties efficiently, allowing more time to focus on meaningful student interactions (Brown, 2020; Aripin et al., 2023; Kalla et al., 2023).

DECONSTRUCTING STANDARDS

The Stiggins' deconstructing standards process is used in educational assessment to break down learning standards into four key measurable components: knowledge, reasoning, performance skills, and products (Stiggins, 2005). This process ensures that assessments are comprehensive and align with the intended learning outcomes. Each component and its importance in the assessment process follow. The significance of deconstructing standards to ensure that assessments accurately measure student learning and achievement is highlighted. Additionally, examples of deconstructed standards identifying the standard type (knowledge, reasoning, performance skill, or product) and the measurable deconstructed components within the standard are provided.

Knowledge

Knowledge refers to the factual and conceptual information students need to understand and remember (Stiggins, 2005). Knowledge standards include specific details, terminology, principles, theories, and generalizations that form the foundation of a subject area. When deconstructing knowledge standards, educators identify what students need to know and understand to meet the learning objectives (Marzano, 2001). See Figure 1 for examples of knowledge standards across content areas.

Figure 1. Examples of knowledge-based standards

Knowledge Standards
Memorize the periodic table in chemistry.
Describe historical events and their significance.
Select appropriate mathematical formulas to solve real-world problems.

Reasoning

Reasoning involves students' cognitive processes to make sense of information and solve problems. These include critical thinking, logical reasoning, and the ability to analyze, synthesize, and evaluate information. When deconstructing reasoning standards, educators focus on students' thought processes to develop and apply their knowledge effectively (Stiggins, 2005). See Figure 2 for examples of reasoning standards across content areas.

Figure 2. Examples of reasoning-based standards

Reasoning Standards
Analyze data to make conclusions in a science experiment.
Compare and contrast different viewpoints in a historical debate.
Use logical steps to solve complex mathematical problems.

Performance Skills

Performance Skills refer to the ability to execute tasks or demonstrate procedures. Performance skills involve physical or technical skills that require practice and proficiency. When deconstructing standards for performance skills, educators identify the specific actions or behaviors that students must be able to perform to show their competence (Stiggins, 2005). See Figure 3 for examples of performance skills standards across content areas.

Figure 3. Examples of performance skills-based standards

Performance Skills Standards
Conduct a laboratory experiment accurately and safely.
Play a musical instrument with correct technique.
Perform a physical activity, such as a sport or dance routine, with precision.

Products

Products are tangible items or artifacts that students create as evidence of their learning. These products demonstrate the application of knowledge, reasoning, and performance skills. When deconstructing standards for products, educators specify the characteristics and criteria for evaluating the quality of the final output (Stiggins, 2005). See Figure 3 for examples of product standards across content areas.

Figure 4. Examples of product-based standards

Product Standards
Write a research paper that presents and supports a thesis.
Create a multimedia presentation on a scientific topic.
Design a model or prototype in an engineering project.

Misconception Alert

A learning standard is not always deconstructed into all four main components (knowledge, reasoning, performance skills, and products). The deconstruction depends on the nature of the learning standard and its objectives. Some standards focus on knowledge and reasoning, while others emphasize performance skills or the creation of products. However, using Stiggins' deconstructing standards process as a framework can help ensure a comprehensive understanding of the standard, even if not all four components are applicable (Stiggins, 2005). Figures 5 - 8 demonstrate four scenarios of deconstructing learning standards from different content areas.

Figure 5. Deconstruction of a science knowledge standard

Knowledge Standard	Understanding the water cycle in science.
Knowledge Components	Names and stages of the water cycle (evaporation, condensation, precipitation).
Reasoning Components	Explains the processes and how they are interconnected.

In this case, the primary focus is on knowledge and reasoning, with less emphasis on performance skills or products.

Figure 6. Deconstruction of a social studies reasoning standard

Reasoning Standard	Analyzing historical events to understand their causes and effects.
Knowledge Components	Identify key events and dates.
Reasoning Components	Analyzing causes and effects, comparing different historical perspectives.

Here, reasoning is central, with knowledge as a supporting component. Performance skills and products might not be as relevant.

Figure 7. Deconstruction of a music performance skill standard

Performance Skill Standard	Analyzing historical events to understand their causes and effects.
Knowledge Components	Describe musical notation and theory.
Reasoning Components	Interpret the musical piece.
Performance Skill Components	Play the instrument with the correct technique.

Performance skills are the primary focus, but knowledge and reasoning are also important to support the performance.

Figure 8. Deconstruction of a science product standard

Product Standard	Design a science project.
Knowledge Components	Describe scientific concepts relevant to the project.
Reasoning Components	Apply scientific methods to design the project.
Product Components	Create a model, report, or presentation of the project.

The main goal is creating a product, and knowledge and reasoning are necessary to guide its development.

Flexibility in Deconstructing Standards

The process of deconstructing standards, as outlined by Stiggins et al. (2004), is a crucial step in transforming broad learning goals into concrete, actionable objectives that guide instruction and assessment. However, this process is not rigid; rather, it requires flexibility and adaptation to the specific standard being addressed and the unique context in which it will be taught. This flexibility is essential to ensure that teachers focus on the most relevant components of the standard and address the varied needs of students in a balanced, meaningful way.

Stiggins et al. (2004) emphasize that the deconstruction of standards should be adapted to the specific learning goals and instructional context. Teachers must consider the relevance of each standard component and focus on the elements most pertinent to student learning. Some standards may contain multiple objectives or skills, and not all may be equally relevant in every instructional setting. For example, a standard related to critical thinking may be more relevant in a social studies context than in a physical education setting. This relevance-driven approach ensures that instructional time is used efficiently, focusing on the components that will most significantly impact student achievement.

Not all standards require students to demonstrate learning through performance skills or the creation of products. While some standards clearly align with hands-on tasks, others may emphasize cognitive processes, such as reasoning, analysis, or knowledge recall. For instance, a standard in science may involve performance tasks such as conducting experiments, while a standard in mathematics may focus more on reasoning and problem-solving without necessarily requiring a tangible product (Marzano, 2011). Recognizing that different standards emphasize different types of learning objectives allows teachers to tailor their instruction and assessments, accordingly, focusing on the most appropriate mode of demonstrating mastery.

A critical aspect of deconstructing standards is ensuring that teachers maintain a balance between different types of learning objectives. Stiggins et al. (2004) advocate for a comprehensive approach to instruction that addresses multiple facets of learning, including knowledge acquisition, reasoning, skills, and product development. Some subjects, such as the arts or physical education, may naturally lend themselves more toward performance skills, while others, such as language arts or mathematics, may emphasize reasoning and knowledge-based objectives. However, teachers must provide a balanced learning experience, incorporating opportunities for students to develop a wide range of skills, even in subjects where certain types of objectives are more prominent (Wiggins & McTighe, 2005). This balance ensures that students are well-rounded and capable of applying their learning in diverse contexts.

One of the complexities of deconstructing standards is that the components of some standards may overlap or integrate with one another. For instance, reasoning skills are often integral to performance tasks and product creation (Brookhart, 2013). A student demonstrating a performance skill in a science lab may also need to apply reasoning to interpret data or troubleshoot a problem. At the same time, a product-based language arts assignment may require creative thinking and analytical reasoning. Recognizing this integration allows teachers to design instructional experiences that simultaneously foster multiple dimensions of learning rather than treating each standard component as a separate entity. This integrated approach promotes deeper learning and helps students connect across different study areas.

The flexibility in deconstructing standards, as emphasized by Stiggins et al. (2004), allows educators to adapt their instruction and assessment to best meet the needs of their students. Teachers can design meaningful and comprehensive instruction by considering the relevance of each component of a standard, ensuring a balance between different types of learning objectives, and recognizing the potential for integration and overlap. Ultimately, this flexible approach to deconstructing standards promotes more effective teaching and supports student success across various learning contexts. Appendix 1 includes a step-by-step process for applying the deconstructing process.

Leveraging ChatGPT to Deconstruct SLOs

One of the most challenging tasks for educators is deconstructing Student Learning Outcomes (SLOs) into measurable components that can be assessed effectively. SLOs often encapsulate broad educational goals, such as critical thinking or problem-solving, but translating these abstract objectives into concrete assessment criteria can be a daunting process. ChatGPT can assist in this area by helping educators develop meaningful assessments and rubrics aligned with these outcomes (OpenAI, 2023).

ChatGPT can help educators break down SLOs into specific, observable, and measurable components (Adıgüzel et al., 2023; Alshahrani, 2023; Carr, 2023; Zhai, 2022). For instance, if an SLO focuses on students' ability to analyze and evaluate historical events, ChatGPT can suggest key indicators of analysis (e.g., identifying cause-and-effect relationships, recognizing bias) and evaluation (e.g., assessing the significance of events, comparing historical interpretations).

Appendix 2 includes an example request for ChatGPT to use the Stiggins' taxonomy to deconstruct a Common Core-like English Language Arts standard, distinguish fact from judgment and opinion, recognize stereotypes, compare and contrast historical information (National Governors Association Center for Best Practices & Council of Chief State School Officers, 2010a). When requesting ChatGPT to deconstruct the standard, one must be very specific to guide ChatGPT in meeting a request. In many cases, the initial ChatGPT request may need refinement, and multiple attempts may be needed. Appendix 2 shows a first attempt and a second attempt to deconstruct the ELA standard. The second attempt tells ChatGPT where there is an error in the first deconstruction attempt. The standard is a reasoning standard, and ChatGPT deconstructed the standard into knowledge, reasoning, performance skill, and product components. The second attempt tells ChatGPT this is a reasoning standard and to only deconstruct the standard into knowledge and reasoning components. By applying existing knowledge of Stiggins' taxonomy, one can review the ChatGPT second attempt and determine whether the response is correct.

Using ChatGPT to deconstruct a standard serves as a critical friend. ChatGPT can support a clear and focused deconstruction of the standard, emphasizing the cognitive processes required for students to achieve these learning objectives. Figure 9 shows the final version of the deconstructed standard using the Stiggins' taxonomy within a deconstruction template. Appendix 3 includes a blank deconstruction template (Figure 10) and a completed deconstruction template (Figure 11).

Figure 9. Final deconstructed standard

Standard: Distinguish fact from judgment and opinion; recognize stereotypes; compare and contrast historical information.			
Target Type:	Reasoning		
Knowledge	Reasoning	Performance Skill	Product
Define and explain characteristics of facts, judgments, and opinions. Describe the concept of stereotypes, including their characteristics and implications. Define historical facts, events, figures, and periods.	Analyze statements to determine whether they are facts, judgments, or opinions. Critique stereotypes within various contexts. Evaluate similarities and differences between historical events, periods, or figures.	N/A	N/A

Developing Assessments and Rubrics Using Deconstructed Standards

Once the Student Learning Outcome (SLO) has been deconstructed into measurable components, the next critical step is creating rubrics that effectively outline how student performance will be measured across various levels of achievement. Rubrics provide clarity by defining the criteria for success and describing performance levels, such as "exceeds expectations," "meets expectations," and "needs improvement." This process ensures fairness and consistency in evaluation while offering transparent feedback to students.

ChatGPT can assist educators in generating initial rubric drafts based on the deconstructed SLOs and input from teachers. The AI tool can offer a structured framework for rubrics, incorporating clear and specific performance descriptors for each criterion (Adıgüzel et al., 2023; Laak & Aru, 2024). For instance, educators can input the key components of an SLO, and ChatGPT can suggest language that articulates different levels of mastery. This support helps reduce the cognitive load associated with rubric design, allowing teachers to focus on aligning the rubric with both curriculum standards and instructional goals.

A teacher can use the performance descriptors of their school or district, or ChatGPT can suggest language for performance descriptors to ensure clarity in communicating expectations. Teachers may struggle to precisely word the distinctions between varying levels of student performance, especially when dealing with complex or abstract skills like critical thinking or creativity. ChatGPT provides suggestions for clearly distinguishing between higher- and lower-level performance, offering educators a foundation they can modify and tailor to fit the specific needs of their students and subject areas. Such a framework supports both the assessment of learning and the provision of constructive feedback (Adıgüzel et al., 2023; Laak & Aru, 2024).

In addition to helping develop rubrics, ChatGPT can assist in designing assessments that align with the deconstructed SLOs. Assessments are essential in evaluating whether students have achieved the intended learning outcomes. ChatGPT can generate various assessment items, such as multiple-choice questions, essay prompts, or project ideas. These assessments measure student progress and align closely with the learning objectives, ensuring a more accurate evaluation of student understanding (OpenAI, 2023).

For example, if an SLO emphasizes developing problem-solving skills, ChatGPT can suggest formative assessment tasks involving real-world problem scenarios. Similarly, if an SLO focuses on students' ability to analyze literary texts, ChatGPT might generate essay questions that prompt students to compare themes across different works or examine character development. These suggestions help educators create meaningful and varied assessments, reducing the time and effort needed to design well-rounded evaluations.

Additionally, ChatGPT's capacity to produce a wide range of assessment types ensures that educators can use multiple formats to measure student learning, which is crucial for addressing diverse learning styles. Formative assessments generated by ChatGPT can also provide ongoing feedback to students, helping them identify areas for improvement throughout the learning process. Formative assessments allow teachers to scaffold learning and adjust instruction as needed to ensure student success (OpenAI, 2023).

By assisting in creating rubrics and assessments, ChatGPT supports educators in ensuring that their evaluations are aligned with learning outcomes and clearly articulated. The tool provides a foundation for rubric development that educators can further refine, making the assessment process more manageable and consistent. Furthermore, ChatGPT's ability to generate diverse assessment formats enhances teachers' capacity to evaluate student mastery across various learning domains. As a result, ChatGPT is a valuable resource in promoting effective, equitable, and transparent assessment practices in education.

Practical Examples of ChatGPT in K-12 Education for Developing Assessments and Rubrics

In K-12 education, Student Learning Outcomes (SLOs) form the foundation for measuring student progress and achievement across content areas. Deconstructing these outcomes into measurable components and creating rubrics and assessments aligned with specific standards are critical steps in the instructional design process. ChatGPT can assist educators in this task by providing structured suggestions for rubric creation and assessment design that are aligned with the goals set by state or national standards. The following section provides examples across various content areas, illustrating the practical application of ChatGPT in enhancing student learning and achievement. These examples highlight the benefits and challenges of integrating AI into educational assessment practices.

Example 1: English Language Arts (ELA) – Deconstructing Critical Analysis Skills

In ELA classrooms, SLOs often require students to demonstrate critical analysis of literary texts, such as identifying themes, character motivations, and the use of literary devices. For example, using the Common Core State Standards (CCSS) for ELA Literacy Grade 9-10.3, a typical SLO might be: "Students will analyze how complex characters develop over the course of a text, interact with other characters, and advance the plot or develop the theme" (National Governors Association Center for Best Practices & Council of Chief State School Officers, 2010a).

To deconstruct this SLO, an educator can use ChatGPT to identify key components using the Stiggins' taxonomy, such as:

- Knowledge components- Identifying and explaining character traits.
- Reasoning components- Analyzing interactions between characters.
- Reasoning components- Connecting character development to plot and theme progression.

ChatGPT can then help generate a rubric for this SLO by suggesting performance descriptors. For instance:

- Exceeds expectations: Offers a detailed and insightful analysis of character development, consistently linking character interactions to plot and theme.
- Meets expectations: Adequately explains character development and makes clear connections between character interactions and plot or theme.

- Needs improvement: Provides a limited analysis of character development with few connections to the plot or theme.

ChatGPT can also generate essay prompts, such as asking students to "Analyze the development of a complex character in the novel and explain how their interactions with other characters shape the story's overall theme." Using ChatGPT to generate assessment tasks reduces the educator's workload while ensuring that assessments are aligned with the SLO (Adıgüzel et al., 2023; Laak & Aru, 2024).

Example 2: Mathematics – Problem-Solving and Real-World Application

In grade 6 mathematics, an SLO related to Expression and Equations using problem-solving (6.EE.B.7) may read, "Students will apply mathematical concepts to solve real-world problems involving the use of one variable equations and inequalities" (National Governors Association Center for Best Practices & Council of Chief State School Officers, 2010b). To deconstruct this SLO, educators can ask ChatGPT to break down the specific skills involved, such as:

- Knowledge components- Identifying the relevant algebraic concepts.
- Reasoning components- Applying the equations based on real-world scenarios.
- Reasoning components- Solving equations and interpreting the results in the context of the problem.

ChatGPT can generate a rubric that measures student performance in solving real-world problems. For example:

- Exceeds expectations: Sets up equations accurately and efficiently solves them, providing a clear and thorough explanation of how the solution applies to the real-world context.
- Meets expectations: Correctly sets up and solves the equation, with some explanation of how the solution applies to the problem.
- Needs improvement: Struggles with setting up the equation and needs more explanation of how the solution relates to the real-world problem.

Additionally, ChatGPT can create word problems based on everyday scenarios, such as, "Calculate how many hours you would need to work at a given hourly wage to save up for a specific purchase." Using ChatGPT to design real-word word problems allows students to apply mathematical concepts in meaningful ways (OpenAI, 2023).

Example 3: Science – Inquiry and Experimental Design

In science education, standards often emphasize inquiry-based learning and experimental design. For example, the Next Generation Science Standards (NGSS) include a middle school Life Science SLO (MS-LS1-5) that reads: "Students will plan and conduct an investigation to provide evidence for how environmental factors affect the growth of organisms" (NGSS Lead States, 2013). To deconstruct this SLO, educators can ask ChatGPT to identify the necessary components:

- Knowledge components- Defining a hypothesis.
- Reasoning components- Planning an investigation that controls variables.
- Reasoning components- Analyzing data to support conclusions.
- Performance skill components- Collecting data related to the investigation.

ChatGPT can assist in developing an assessment rubric that evaluates students on their ability to design and conduct experiments. Sample rubric descriptors might include:

- Exceeds expectations: Formulates a detailed and testable hypothesis, designs a comprehensive investigation with appropriate controls, and provides a thorough analysis of data with clear conclusions.
- Meets expectations: Develops a hypothesis, designs an investigation with some controls, and analyzes data with adequate conclusions.
- Needs improvement: Struggles to develop a testable hypothesis or design a controlled investigation with limited data analysis.

ChatGPT can generate formative assessment questions or project ideas (Adıgüzel et al., 2023; Laak & Aru, 2024). For example, ChatGPT could suggest: Design an experiment to test how different types of soil affect plant growth. Record your observations and analyze how soil composition impacts growth over time.

Example 4: Social Studies – Historical Analysis and Interpretation

In social studies, a high school history SLO (D2.His.14.912) might ask students to "Analyze the causes and effects of events in the past" (National Council for the Social Studies, 2013). ChatGPT can help deconstruct this broad SLO by identifying critical skills such as:

- Knowledge components- Identifying and explaining multiple causes of historical events.

- Reasoning components- Evaluating the short- and long-term effects of these events on society.
- Reasoning components- Supporting analysis with evidence from primary and secondary sources.

Using this breakdown, ChatGPT can generate a rubric that specifies how to measure student success. For instance:

- Exceeds expectations: Provides a comprehensive analysis of multiple causes and effects, using diverse sources to support the argument.
- Meets expectations: Adequately explains causes and effects, with some evidence from sources.
- Needs improvement: Offers a limited analysis with few or no sources to support the explanation.

ChatGPT could also generate questions like, Explain how the economic conditions following World War I contributed to the outbreak of World War II, using at least three primary or secondary sources to support your argument (OpenAI, 2023).

Benefits and Challenges of Using AI in Assessment Practices

The integration of ChatGPT into K-12 education presents several clear benefits. First, it offers time-saving tools for educators by providing ready-made rubric templates, assessment questions, and project ideas that align with established standards (Adıgüzel et al., 2023; Laak & Aru, 2024). Additionally, ChatGPT supports differentiated instruction by generating multiple formats of assessments that can accommodate different learning styles and abilities.

However, there are also challenges associated with using AI in educational settings. One primary concern is ensuring that the assessments generated by ChatGPT accurately reflect the depth of knowledge required by the standards. Teachers may need to carefully review and modify AI-generated content to ensure it meets their specific instructional goals. Additionally, while ChatGPT can offer a starting point for rubric and assessment development, the human element remains critical to addressing nuanced student needs and fostering authentic learning experiences (Adıgüzel et al., 2023; Laak & Aru, 2024).

ChatGPT holds significant potential for enhancing assessment practices in K-12 education by deconstructing SLOs and assisting in developing rubrics and assessments across content areas. From ELA to math, science, and social studies, educators can leverage ChatGPT to create well-structured, standards-aligned assessments that improve student learning outcomes. However, it is crucial to balance AI-generated resources with teacher expertise to address students' unique needs and ensure high-quality, meaningful assessments.

Implications and Challenges of AI Integration in Education

The integration of AI in educational assessment practices is reshaping the landscape of how learning is measured, personalized, and managed. AI tools like ChatGPT offer the potential to revolutionize assessments, making them more efficient, accurate, and tailored to individual student needs. However, these advancements come with challenges that educators, policymakers, and institutions must carefully consider. This section explores the broader implications of utilizing AI in educational assessments, highlighting the potential benefits and the concerns that must be addressed to ensure ethical and effective implementation.

One of the most immediate and tangible benefits of integrating AI in educational assessment is the significant increase in efficiency. Traditional methods of grading, providing feedback, and analyzing student performance are time-consuming tasks that often overburden educators. AI-powered tools like ChatGPT can streamline these processes by automating routine tasks like grading quizzes, providing formative feedback on written assignments, and even generating customized assessment items. Using ChatGPT for educational assessment frees up valuable time for educators, allowing them to focus more on instruction and student engagement (Williamson et al., 2020). AI can process vast amounts of data at a pace far beyond human capacity, enabling real-time analysis of student performance and quicker identification of learning gaps. This efficiency is particularly beneficial in large-scale educational settings where individual attention to each student may be difficult to manage (Luckin & Holmes, 2016).

A significant advantage of using AI in assessments is the ability to provide personalized learning experiences. ChatGPT, for instance, can be used to offer tailored feedback and guidance based on a student's specific strengths and areas for improvement. By analyzing individual performance data, AI can adapt assessments to meet the diverse needs of learners, offering differentiated questions, pacing, and feedback (Holmes et al., 2019). This personalization extends beyond assessment to learning support, where AI can recommend resources or activities that align with each student's learning style and progress. In doing so, AI-driven assessments can foster more inclusive learning environments that cater to various learning needs, potentially closing achievement gaps and promoting equity in education (Luan et al., 2020).

When properly designed and implemented, AI systems can improve the accuracy and fairness of assessments. Traditional assessments can be prone to human biases, inconsistencies in grading, and subjectivity. ChatGPT and similar AI tools can provide more objective scoring, particularly in written responses, where grading criteria may be difficult to apply consistently. Additionally, AI can analyze student responses across multiple variables, offering insights that go beyond correct or incorrect answers to include analysis of learning patterns, critical thinking, and problem-solving skills (Spector, 2016; Lorenzo & Gallon, 2019). By reducing human error and bias, AI has the potential to provide a more reliable and valid measure of student achievement, which is crucial for high stakes testing and long-term educational planning (Kop et al., 2017; Baker & Koedinger, 2018).

Integrating AI in educational assessment raises significant ethical concerns despite the potential benefits. One of the primary issues is the transparency of AI algorithms. In many cases, AI models function as "black boxes," making it difficult for educators and students to understand how decisions are made. This lack of transparency can erode trust in AI-driven assessments, particularly when it comes to high-stakes evaluations such as standardized testing or admissions processes (Selwyn, 2021). There is the risk of AI systems perpetuating or amplifying existing biases in the data they are trained. If not carefully monitored, these biases could result in unfair assessments that disproportionately disadvantage certain groups of students, particularly those from historically marginalized backgrounds (O'Neil, 2017).

The use of AI in education necessitates the collection and analysis of vast amounts of student data. This raises serious concerns about data privacy and security. While AI tools like ChatGPT can offer powerful insights, they also require access to sensitive information, including student performance, learning behaviors, and personal data. Without stringent data protection measures, this information could be vulnerable to breaches, misuse, or unauthorized access (Akgun & Greenhow, 2022; Huang, 2023). Educators and institutions must ensure that AI tools comply with privacy regulations, such as the Family Educational Rights and Privacy Act (FERPA) in the United States or the General Data Protection Regulation (GDPR) in Europe. Clear guidelines for data storage, sharing, and deletion must be established, ensuring student data is always safeguarded (Ingrams et al., 2022).

For AI tools like ChatGPT to be effectively integrated into educational assessment practices, educators must be adequately trained to use these technologies. The rapid pace of AI innovation means that many educators may feel unprepared or need more technical skills to leverage AI in their teaching and assessment practices effectively (Starkey, 2012; Fischer et al., 2020, 2022). Comprehensive professional development programs are essential to bridge this gap. These programs should focus on the technical aspects of using AI tools and developing educators' understanding of how AI can complement pedagogy, enhance learning outcomes, and promote equity. Additionally, educators must be equipped to critically evaluate the use of AI in assessments, ensuring that these tools are applied thoughtfully and ethically

(Holmes et al., 2019; Kleizen et al., 2023). Appendix 4 lists additional readings related to ChatGPT and assessment.

CONCLUSION

Rick Stiggins' deconstructing standards process provides a structured approach to creating meaningful and effective assessments. While not every standard will require all four components, considering each can help educators create comprehensive assessments that address various aspects of student learning. The key is to adapt the process to fit the specific learning standard, ensuring that the most relevant components are emphasized and effectively assessed. By leveraging ChatGPT to deconstruct K -12 SLOs and develop assessments and rubrics using Stiggins' deconstructing standards process, educators can create more accurate, meaningful, and effective assessments that support student learning and achievement.

Integrating AI, specifically tools like ChatGPT, into educational assessment practices offers significant potential to enhance evaluations' efficiency, personalization, and accuracy. However, the successful adoption of AI in education requires careful consideration of ethical concerns, data privacy issues, and ongoing professional development. By addressing these challenges, educators can harness the power of AI to improve assessment practices in ways that support student learning and the development of well-rounded students with the necessary knowledge, cognitive skills, practical abilities, and creative outputs to succeed in their educational journey and beyond.

REFERENCES

Adıgüzel, T., Kaya, M. H., & Cansu, F. K. (2023). Revolutionizing education with AI: Exploring the transformative potential of ChatGPT. *Contemporary Educational Technology*, 15(3), ep429. DOI: 10.30935/cedtech/13152

Akgun, S., & Greenhow, C. (2022). Artificial intelligence in education: Addressing ethical challenges in K-12 settings. *AI and Ethics*, 2(3), 431–440. DOI: 10.1007/s43681-021-00096-7 PMID: 34790956

Alshahrani, A. (2023). The impact of ChatGPT on blended learning: Current trends and future research directions. *International Journal of Data and Network Science*, 7(4), 2029–2040. DOI: 10.5267/j.ijdns.2023.6.010

Aripin, Z., Supriatna, U., & Mahaputra, M. S. (2023). With the advent of ChatGPT: How to identify strengths, weaknesses, opportunities, and threats for the field of education and the business world of various disciplines. *Journal of Development and Community Service*, 1(1), 50–61.

Baker, R. S., & Koedinger, K. R. (2018). Towards demonstrating the value of learning analytics for K-12 education. *Learning Analytics in Education*, 49-62.

Brookhart, S. M. (2013). *How to create and use rubrics for formative assessment and grading*. Ascd.

Brown, T. B. (2020). Language models are few-shot learners. *arXiv preprint arXiv:2005.14165.*

Carr, B. (2023). Revolutionizing education: Unleashing the power of ChatGPT/AI to empower educators. *Technology and the Curriculum: Summer 2023.*

Fischer, G., Lundin, J., & Lindberg, J. O. (2020). Rethinking and reinventing learning, education and collaboration in the digital age—From creating technologies to transforming cultures. *The International Journal of Information and Learning Technology*, 37(5), 241–252. DOI: 10.1108/IJILT-04-2020-0051

Fischer, G., Lundin, J., & Lindberg, O. J. (2022). The challenge for the digital age: Making learning a part of life. *The International Journal of Information and Learning Technology*, 40(1), 1–16. DOI: 10.1108/IJILT-04-2022-0079

Holmes, W., Bialik, M., & Fadel, C. (2019). *Artificial intelligence in education promises and implications for teaching and learning*. Center for Curriculum Redesign.

Huang, L. (2023). Ethics of artificial intelligence in education: Student privacy and data protection. *Science Insights Education Frontiers*, 16(2), 2577–2587. DOI: 10.15354/sief.23.re202

Ingrams, A., Kaufmann, W., & Jacobs, D. (2022). In AI we trust? Citizen perceptions of AI in government decision making. *Policy and Internet*, 14(2), 390–409. DOI: 10.1002/poi3.276

Kalla, D., Smith, N., Samaah, F., & Kuraku, S. (2023). Study and analysis of ChatGPT and its impact on different fields of study. *International Journal of Innovative Science and Research Technology*, 8(3).

Kleizen, B., Van Dooren, W., Verhoest, K., & Tan, E. (2023). Do citizens trust trustworthy artificial intelligence? Experimental evidence on the limits of ethical AI measures in government. *Government Information Quarterly*, 40(4), 101834. DOI: 10.1016/j.giq.2023.101834

Kop, R., Fournier, H., & Durand, G. (2017). A critical perspective on learning analytics and educational data mining. *Handbook of Learning Analytics, 319.*

Laak, K. J., & Aru, J. (2024). AI and personalized learning: Bridging the gap with modern educational goals. *arXiv preprint arXiv:2404.02798.*

Lorenzo, N., & Gallon, R. (2019). Smart pedagogy for smart learning. In Daniela, L. (Ed.), *Didactics of smart pedagogy* (pp. 41–69). Springer., DOI: 10.1007/978-3-030-01551-0_3

Luan, H., Geczy, P., Lai, H., Gobert, J., Yang, S. J., Ogata, H., Baltes, J., Guerra, R., Li, P., & Tsai, C. C. (2020). Challenges and future directions of big data and artificial intelligence in education. *Frontiers in Psychology*, 11, 580820. DOI: 10.3389/fpsyg.2020.580820 PMID: 33192896

Luckin, R., & Holmes, W. (2016). *Intelligence unleashed: An argument for AI in education*. Pearson.

Marzano, R. J. (2001). *Classroom instruction that works: Research-based strategies for increasing student achievement*. ASCD.

Marzano, R. J. (2011). *Formative assessment & standards-based grading*. Solution Tree Press.

National Council for the Social Studies (NCSS). (2013). *The college, career, and civic life (C3) framework for social studies state standards: Guidance for enhancing the rigor of K-12 civics, economics, geography, and history.*

National Governors Association Center for Best Practices & Council of Chief State School Officers. (2010a). *Common core state standards for English language arts & literacy in history: Social studies, science, and technical Subjects*. Author.

National Governors Association Center for Best Practices & Council of Chief State School Officers. (2010b). *Common core state standards for mathematics*. Author.

Next Generation Science Standards (NGSS) Lead States. (2013). *Next generation science standards: For states, by states*. National Academies Press.

O'neil, C. (2017). *Weapons of math destruction: How big data increases inequality and threatens democracy*. Crown.

Open, A. I. T. (2023). ChatGpt: Optimizing language models for dialogue. OpenAI. 2022. *URL*https://openai.com/blog/chatgpt

Selwyn, N. (2021). *Education and technology: Key issues and debates*. Bloomsbury Publishing.

Spector, J. M. (2016, March). Smart learning environments: Concepts and issues. In *Society for Information Technology & teacher education international conference* (pp. 2728-2737). Association for the Advancement of Computing in Education (AACE).

Starkey, L. (2012). *Teaching and learning in the digital age*. Routledge. DOI: 10.4324/9780203117422

Stiggins, R. J. (2005). *Student-involved assessment for learning* (4th ed.). Prentice Hall.

Stiggins, R. J., Arter, J. A., & Chappuis, J. (2004). *Classroom assessment for student learning: Doing it right, using it well.* Assessment Training Institute.

Wiggins, G. (2005). *Understanding by design*. Association for Supervision and Curriculum Development.

Williamson, B., Eynon, R., & Potter, J. (2020). Pandemic politics, pedagogies and practices: Digital technologies and distance education during the coronavirus emergency. *Learning, Media and Technology*, 45(2), 107–114. DOI: 10.1080/17439884.2020.1761641

Zhai, X. (2022). ChatGPT: Artificial intelligence for education. *Supporting Instructional Decision Making: The Potential of An Automatically Scored Three-Dimensional Assessment System*

ADDITIONAL READING

Ausat, A. M. A., Massang, B., Efendi, M., Nofirman, N., & Riady, Y. (2023). Can chat

ElSayary, A. (2024). An investigation of teachers' perceptions of using ChatGPT as a supporting tool for teaching and learning in the digital era. *Journal of Computer Assisted Learning*, 40(3), 931–945. DOI: 10.1111/jcal.12926

(•••). GPT replace the role of the teacher in the classroom: A fundamental analysis. *Journal of Education*, 5(4), 16100–16106.

Halaweh, M. (2023). ChatGPT in education: Strategies for responsible implementation.

İpek, Z. H., Gözüm, A. I. C., Papadakis, S., & Kallogiannakis, M. (2023). Educational applications of the ChatGPT AI aystem: A Systematic review of research. *Educational Process: International Journal*, 12(3), 26–55.

Kim, M., & Adlof, L. (2024). Adapting to the future: ChatGPT as a means for supporting constructivist learning environments. *TechTrends*, 68(1), 37–46. DOI: 10.1007/s11528-023-00899-x

Kiryakova, G., & Angelova, N. (2023). ChatGPT—A challenging tool for the university professors in their teaching practice. *Education Sciences*, 13(10), 1056. DOI: 10.3390/educsci13101056

Lo, C. K. (2023). What is the impact of ChatGPT on education? A rapid review of the literature. *Education Sciences*, 13(4), 410. DOI: 10.3390/educsci13040410

M., Day, I., Rather, R.A & Heathcote, L. (2023). The role of ChatGPT in higher education: Benefits, challenges, and future research directions. *Journal of Applied Learning and Teaching, 6*(1), 41-56.

Malik, A., Khan, M. L., & Hussain, K. (2023). How is ChatGPT transforming academia? Examining its impact on teaching, research, assessment, and learning. *Examining its impact on teaching, research, assessment, and learning* (April 9, 2023).

Memarian, B., & Doleck, T. (2023). ChatGPT in education: Methods, potentials and limitations. *Computers in Human Behavior: Artificial Humans*, 100022.

Meneses, E. (2023). Impact of the implementation of ChatGPT in education: A systematic review. *Computers*, 12(8), 153. DOI: 10.3390/computers12080153

Montenegro-Rueda, M., Fernández-Cerero, J., & Fernández-Batanero, J. M., & López-

Rasul, T., Nair, S., Kalendra, D., Robin, M., de Oliveira Santini, F., & Ladeira, W. J., Sun,

Zhang, P., & Tur, G. (2024). A systematic review of ChatGPT use in K-12 education. *European Journal of Education*, 59(2), e12599. DOI: 10.1111/ejed.12599

APPENDIX 1

Applying the Stiggins' Deconstructing Standards Process

Step 1: Identify Learning Standards

Begin by selecting the broad learning standards or objectives that need to be deconstructed. These standards should align with curriculum goals and state or national educational benchmarks.

Step 2: Break Down the Standards

Deconstruct each standard into the four components (knowledge, reasoning, performance skills, and products). Clearly define what students need to know, how they should think, what skills they need to perform, and what products they should create.

Step 3: Develop Assessment Tasks

Create assessment tasks that align with each component. Ensure that the tasks are varied and provide opportunities for students to demonstrate their understanding, reasoning, skills, and products.

Step 4: Create Rubrics

Design rubrics that outline the criteria for evaluating each component. Rubrics should be specific, measurable, and provide clear expectations for students. Include descriptions of different performance levels to guide students and assessors.

Step 5: Implement and Reflect

Implement the assessments in the classroom and collect data on student performance. Reflect on the effectiveness of the assessments and rubrics and adjust as needed to improve alignment with the learning standards and support student achievement.

APPENDIX 2

Sample Deconstructing a Standard using Stiggins' Taxonomy and ChatGPT

Standard: Distinguish fact from judgment and opinion; recognize stereotypes; compare and contrast historical information (National Governors Association Center for Best Practices & Council of Chief State School Officers, 2010a).

Based on the Stiggins' taxonomy, this is a reasoning level target. Therefore, it has only reasoning and knowledge components or underpinnings.

First Attempt

My ChatGPT message: Deconstruct the following standard using the Stiggins' taxonomy of knowledge and reasoning. Standard: Distinguish fact from judgment and opinion; recognize stereotypes; compare and contrast historical information.

ChatGPT First Attempt Response: To deconstruct the standard using the Stiggins' taxonomy of knowledge and reasoning, we will break down the elements involved in the learning targets. The standard in question involves three main skills: distinguishing fact from judgment and opinion, recognizing stereotypes, and comparing and contrasting historical information. These skills can be mapped onto the Stiggins' taxonomy, which categorizes learning targets into four types: knowledge, reasoning, performance/skills, and products.

Knowledge

Distinguishing Fact from Judgment and Opinion

- Knowledge: Understanding the definitions and characteristics of facts, judgments, and opinions.

- Fact: Information that can be verified and is objective.

- Judgment: An evaluative statement that expresses a value or opinion.

- Opinion: A personal belief or view not necessarily based on fact or knowledge.

Reasoning

Distinguishing Fact from Judgment and Opinion

- Reasoning: The ability to analyze statements to determine whether they are facts, judgments, or opinions.

- Skill: Critically assessing sources of information and applying criteria to differentiate between factual statements and subjective opinions or judgments.

Recognizing Stereotypes

- Reasoning: Identifying and analyzing stereotypes within various contexts.

- Skill: Recognizing generalizations that are applied to groups and evaluating their validity and impact.

Comparing and Contrasting Historical Information

- Reasoning: Evaluating similarities and differences between historical events, periods, or figures.

- Skill: Analyzing primary and secondary sources to identify patterns, differences, and causal relationships in history.

Performance/Skills

Distinguishing Fact from Judgment and Opinion

- Performance/Skills: Demonstrating the ability to distinguish facts from opinions in written and oral communication.

- Activity: Engaging in exercises that require sorting statements into facts, judgments, and opinions.

Recognizing Stereotypes

-Performance/Skills: Applying techniques to identify and challenge stereotypes in various texts and media.

- Activity: Analyzing media, literature, and speeches to pinpoint and critique stereotypes.

Comparing and Contrasting Historical Information

- Performance/Skills: Conducting comparative analyses of historical data and presenting findings.

- Activity: Writing essays or creating presentations that compare and contrast historical events or figures.

Products

Distinguishing Fact from Judgment and Opinion

- Products: Producing written work that clearly distinguishes between factual statements and opinions.

- Output: Essays, reports, or projects that highlight the differences between facts and opinions.

Recognizing Stereotypes

- Products: Creating works that illustrate understanding and critique of stereotypes.

- Output: Research papers, multimedia presentations, or campaigns that address and deconstruct stereotypes.

Comparing and Contrasting Historical Information

- Products: Developing comprehensive comparisons and contrasts of historical subjects.

- Output: Detailed comparative essays, research projects, or timelines that elucidate historical parallels and distinctions.

Conclusion

By applying the Stiggins' taxonomy, we categorize the cognitive and performance demands of the standard into knowledge, reasoning, performance/skills, and products. This helps educators create targeted learning activities and assessments that address each component of the standard, ensuring a comprehensive approach to teaching these critical analytical skills. To accurately deconstruct the standard using the Stiggins' taxonomy of knowledge and reasoning, it is essential to focus on the cognitive processes involved. The standard involves three main elements: distinguishing fact from judgment and opinion, recognizing stereotypes, and comparing and contrasting historical information. We will categorize these components into the relevant aspects of Stiggins' taxonomy: knowledge and reasoning.

Second Attempt

The message to ChatGPT that the first attempt is wrong: This is incorrect, there are no performance skills or products in this standard.

Appendix A shows the incorrect content as italicized. The deconstruction of the performance skill and product components are incorrect.

ChatGPT 2nd Attempt Response:

To accurately deconstruct the standard using the Stiggins' taxonomy of knowledge and reasoning, it is essential to focus on the cognitive processes involved. The standard involves three main elements: distinguishing fact from judgment and opinion, recognizing stereotypes, and comparing and contrasting historical information. These components are categorized into the relevant aspects of Stiggins' taxonomy: knowledge and reasoning.

Knowledge

Distinguishing Fact from Judgment and Opinion

- Knowledge: Define and explain characteristics of facts, judgments, and opinions.

- Fact: Objective statements that can be verified through evidence.
- Judgment: Evaluative statements that express a value or opinion.
- Opinion: Subjective beliefs or views not necessarily based on verifiable evidence.

Recognizing Stereotypes

- Knowledge: Describe the concept of stereotypes, including their characteristics and implications.
- Stereotype: Oversimplified and generalized beliefs about a particular group of people.

Comparing and Contrasting Historical Information

- Knowledge: Define historical facts, events, figures, and periods.
- Historical Information: Data and narratives from the past, including primary and secondary sources.

Reasoning

Distinguishing Fact from Judgment and Opinion

- Reasoning: Analyze statements to determine whether they are facts, judgments, or opinions.
- Critical Thinking: Applying criteria to differentiate between factual statements and subjective opinions or judgments.
- Analysis: Evaluating the source and content of information to classify it accurately.

Recognizing Stereotypes

- Reasoning: Critique stereotypes within various contexts.
- Critical Evaluation: Assessing the validity and impact of stereotypes found in texts, media, and social interactions.
- Analysis: Examining the origins and perpetuation of stereotypes and their effects on perception and behavior.

Comparing and Contrasting Historical Information

- Reasoning: Evaluate similarities and differences between historical events, periods, or figures.
- Comparative Analysis: Identifying patterns, differences, and causal relationships in historical data.
- Synthesis: Integrating information from multiple sources to draw informed comparisons and contrasts.

Summary

By focusing on knowledge and reasoning, the second attempt of the deconstruction of the standard using ChatGPT is aligned with the Stiggins' taxonomy:

- Knowledge involves understanding key concepts and definitions related to facts, opinions, judgments, stereotypes, and historical information.
- Reasoning involves applying critical thinking skills to analyze, evaluate, and synthesize information to distinguish between different types of statements, recognize stereotypes, and compare and contrast historical data.

Figure 10. Deconstructed standard template

Standard:			
Target Type:			
Knowledge	**Reasoning**	**Performance Skill**	**Product**

Figure 11. Completed model using deconstructed standard template

Standard: Distinguish fact from judgment and opinion; recognize stereotypes; compare and contrast historical information.			
Target Type:	**Reasoning**		
Knowledge	**Reasoning**	**Performance Skill**	**Product**
Define and explain characteristics of facts, judgments, and opinions. Describe the concept of stereotypes, including their characteristics and implications. Define historical facts, events, figures, and periods.	Analyze statements to determine whether they are facts, judgments, or opinions. Critique stereotypes within various contexts. Evaluate similarities and differences between historical events, periods, or figures.	N/A	N/A

Chapter 10
Generative Artificial Intelligence and Assessment of Learning:
Challenges and Perspectives

Mehdi Kaddouri
https://orcid.org/0000-0001-7696-0276
Mohamed 1st University, Morocco

Khalid Mhamdi
https://orcid.org/0009-0007-3994-7743
Mohamed 1st University, Morocco

Abdelhafid Jabri
https://orcid.org/0000-0002-2214-2638
Mohamed 1st University, Morocco

Mohamed Boukare
https://orcid.org/0009-0002-2511-9764
Mohamed 1st University, Morocco

Sabrine Jmad
https://orcid.org/0009-0008-1400-1457
Mohamed 1st University, Morocco

ABSTRACT

This chapter explores the transformative potential of Generative Artificial Intelligence (GAI) in educational assessment, examining its impact on learners, educators, and educational institutions. Through a comprehensive literature review and analysis of

DOI: 10.4018/979-8-3693-6527-4.ch010

existing GAI-based assessment systems, we investigate how GAI is reshaping traditional assessment practices, enabling more personalized, adaptive, and continuous evaluation of student learning. The chapter discusses the major challenges and opportunities associated with GAI, including issues of data privacy, fairness, and the evolving role of educators. We also examine concrete examples of GAI applications in assessment, such as adaptive learning platforms and automated grading systems. The chapter concludes by outlining future research directions and considering the ethical implications of widespread GAI adoption in education. While GAI offers opportunities for enhancing educational assessment, its implementation requires careful consideration of ethical, pedagogical, and technical challenges

INTRODUCTION

In today's fast-changing world, digital tools are increasingly being used for learning. Assessing whether learners have mastered their knowledge and skills is at a critical juncture, facing both technological promises and technical and pedagogical challenges. The digitalization of education has led to the emergence of new assessment methods and the adaptation of teaching methods to new realities. Bates (2019, p. 503) considers that 'the challenge for assessment in online and blended learning environments is to develop methods that are valid, reliable, fair and secure, and that make appropriate use of new technology.' Digitalization has allowed for the introduction of interactive quizzes and simulations but has also presented challenges in measuring complex skills. Alongside this transformation, assessment is becoming more complex, particularly in capturing 21st century skills such as critical thinking, collaboration, and problem solving. Care et al. (2018, p. 17) point out that '21st century skills are complex constructs that require equally complex assessment approaches to adequately measure them.'

Figure 1. World Economic Forum. (2015). New Vision for Education: Unlocking the Potential of Technology

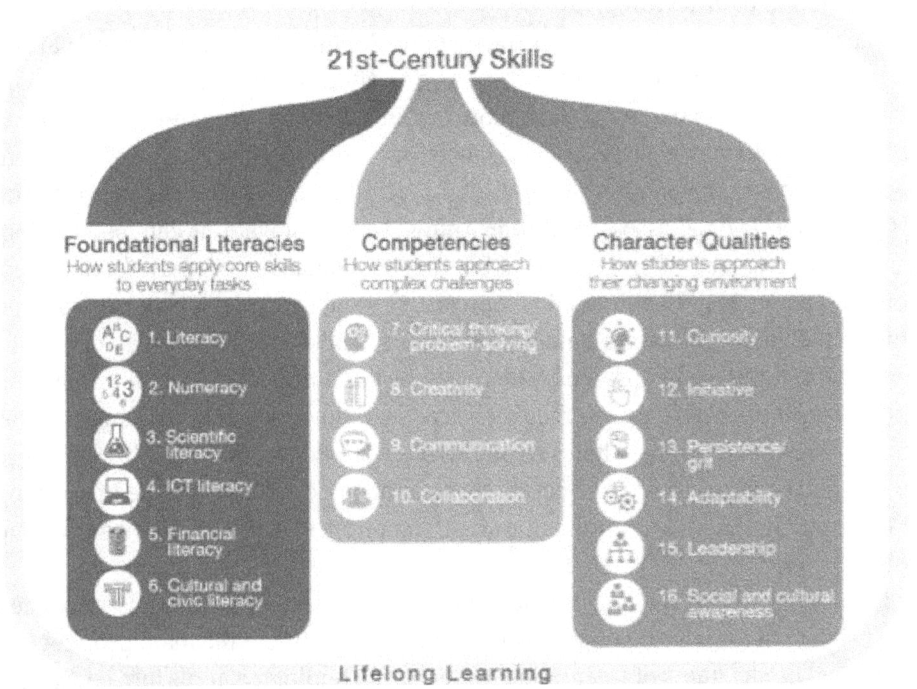

Faced with the limitations of traditional assessment approaches in capturing the richness and diversity of skills developed by learners, there is an increasing urgency to personalize assessment approaches and consider the diversity of learners and their needs. Crisp (2020, p. 3) states that "traditional assessment methods are often inadequate for capturing the full range of skills and competencies developed through digital learning experiences." Strategies such as adaptive assessment, which adjusts the difficulty level of questions based on the learner's responses, have been shown to be effective in meeting individual needs. Luckin et al. (2017, p. 42) argue that "personalised assessment, enabled by AI, has the potential to provide more accurate and timely feedback to learners, supporting their individual learning journeys. Traditional approaches do not provide a complete picture of learner progress. Generative Artificial Intelligence (GAI) is emerging as a potentially transformative innovation for education, offering appropriate solutions. With its ability to produce original content and adapt to different contexts, GAI is revolutionizing assessment practices. Zawacki-Richter et al. (2019, p. 15) assert that "AI has the potential to fundamentally transform educational assessment by providing more personalized, adaptive, and comprehensive evaluation of student learning." Formative assessment, accompanied by continuous feedback, and supported with these technologies, bridges these gaps by offering learners regular opportunities for adjustments and remediation in their learning.

The use of GAI in education has the potential to offer dynamic and personalized assessments, overcoming many limitations of traditional methods. It can propose adaptive questions in real time and a more detailed analysis of open-ended responses. These innovations have practical applications, such as using chatbots for instant feedback and automated analysis of digital portfolios, demonstrating the potential of GAI to improve the assessment of learning. These innovations can lead to more accurate assessment of individual skills and personalized support for learners. However, integrating GAI into education also presents technical, pedagogical, and ethical challenges, including data confidentiality and the fairness of assessments. In addition, it requires careful consideration of the potential shift in the roles and skills of teachers and learners, requiring teachers to adopt new skills and roles as learning facilitators rather than just knowledge providers (Selwyn, 2019). These changes have the potential to affect assessment practices and the nature of teaching and learning in the future, implying a significant transformation in the educational system as a whole.

In this chapter, we will discuss the main challenges and opportunities associated with using GAI for learning assessment. We will also explore the main pedagogical and ethical implications of integrating these new technological tools into education. As Dede (2020, p. 75) points out, "as we integrate AI into educational assessment, we must carefully consider the ethical implications, including issues of privacy, fairness, and transparency." The structure of the chapter is designed to provide a comprehensive overview of current issues, drawing on case studies and concrete examples that illustrate the various dimensions of AI in education. Popenici & Kerr (2017, p. 3) state that "AI-powered assessment tools have the potential to provide more accurate, timely, and personalized feedback, potentially revolutionizing how we measure and support student learning." Through this exploration, we aim to stimulate thinking and action among educators, researchers, and policymakers interested in the future of assessment in an ever-changing digital world.

LITERATURE REVIEW

This literature review explores the impact of GAI on assessment in education, focusing on three main dimensions: students, teachers, and institutions. While GAI has the capacity to generate original and contextual content, it also raises fundamental questions about the nature of learning, assessment, and academic integrity in the digital age.

This review draws on works such as those by Xia et al. (2024), Ng et la. (2024) and Smerdon (2024). The study by Xia et al. (2024) was conducted using the PRISMA method for scope reviews, and utilized the Web of Science, Scopus and ERIC databases. They used keywords such as "generative artificial intelligence", "assessment", "higher education", "ChatGPT", and "artificial intelligence in education". The inclusion criteria included empirical studies primarily published in 2023, specifically addressing GAI in higher education assessment. Out of 156 initially identified articles, 32 studies covering 18 regions, and 11 disciplines were retained for the final analysis after a review of titles, abstracts, and full texts (Xia et al., 2024).

Historical Background

The use of AI in educational assessment is not new, but GAI marks a significant breakthrough. In the 1990s and 2000s, AI was primarily used for automated essay assessment and computer-assisted grading (Shermis et al., 2003). This was followed by intelligent tutoring systems that provided personalized feedback to students (Akyuz, 2020; wang & al., 2023). GAI, however, represents a major leap forward as it is not only capable of generating content, simulating complex interactions and adapting in real time to learners' needs, but also assessing the appropriation of these activities. This evolution can be seen in the shift from analysis-driven AI to an AI capable of sophisticated creation and interaction (Johnson & Lester, 2018; Roll & Wylie, 2016; Duarte & al., 2023).

Automated essay evaluation (AES) systems, such as Intelligent Essay Assessor, e-rater, and IntelliMetric, have been developed to analyze the quality of second-language written productions. Recent studies, notably that of Geçkin et al (2023), have shown that the scores awarded by these tools correlate significantly with those of human correctors.

Table 1. Use cases of AI systems in education (European Commission, 2022)

Learner	**Learner Teach**	• **Computing Environment for Human Learning** • **Language learning apps**
	Learner Support	• **Formative assessment of the written literature** • **AI-assisted collaborative learning**
Teacher	Teacher Support	• Summative assessment of writings, marking of essays • Follow-up of learning forums • AI-based educational aids • Recommendation of educational resources
Learning system	Support for the apprenticeship system	• Educational data mining. • Diagnosis of learning difficulties • Services d'orientation

More recently, advanced language models such as ChatGPT have been used as potential tools for evaluating written productions. These tools enable a reduction in the grading time and achieve greater consistency in the grades assigned to work submitted for automated assessment (Rudolph et al., 2023).

Impact on Learners

Many studies have highlighted the significant benefits of using GAI in educational assessment. This includes the provision of immediate and varied feedback, which is perceived as unbiased, and the facilitation of opportunities for self-assessment (Naidu & Sevnarayan, 2023; Guo & Wang, 2023).

From a learning perspective, GAI offers learners substantial potential to enrich their learning experience. Students can use these tools to create additional explanations and updates to training content, develop different perspectives on a topic, and engage in complex learning simulations. GAI can also aid teachers in designing and developing examinations (Xia et al., 2024) and providing personalized feedback. However, concerns have been raised about academic integrity, the risk of academic fraud, and unfair practices such as plagiarism and cheating. Moreover, overreliance on GAI could hinder the development of critical thinking, creativity, and problem solving. To address these concerns, educational institutions are therefore expected to implement appropriate measures and provide targeted training for educational staff and learners in order to maximize the benefits of GAI tools, while mitigating their risks (Rudolph et al., 2023).

These challenges associated with the use of these evolving technological tools require thorough reflection on enhancing autonomous skills, improving self-learning capabilities, and promoting the ethical use of GAI (Xia et al., 2023; Chiu,

2024). Learners should be encouraged to use IAG as a supplement to improve their learning, rather than as a replacement for critical intervention by human actors. This constructive attitude involves mastering skills that enable learners to evaluate information using critical thinking and metacognition.

Impact on Teachers

For teachers, integrating GAI into assessment requires new skills, particularly in digital literacy, AI, and assessment (Chan, 2023; Chiu et al., 2024). This integration depends on teachers' pedagogical understanding of how GAI works in their assessment practices.

These assessment practices fall under the banner of innovation, balancing human and automated assessment through the GAI (Smolansky et al., 2023; Nikolic et al., 2023). These hybrid assessments can include evaluations involving projects, digital portfolios, or complex simulations where the GAI acts as a facilitator or partial evaluator.

This evolution in the assessment process implies a transformation of the teacher's role and a shift towards adaptive teaching, driven by integrated and continuous assessment, and an increased focus on developing students' key competencies (Firat, 2023; Elsayed, 2023). Teachers take on the role of learning facilitators, guiding learners in the critical and ethical use of GAI to improve their understanding of scientific content and targeted skills.

Impact at Institutional Level

Due to technological advances in GAI, traditional assessment methods are being questioned. Educational institutions are being urged to rethink their assessment policies and procedures (Gorichanaz, 2023; Morjaria and al., 2023; Geerling and al., 2023). They must adapt their academic regulations to address the proper and improper use of GAI (Khan and al., 2024), establishing clear boundaries between acceptable and unacceptable uses.

These institutions also need to focus on the professional development of teachers by providing training in new literacies (Nguyen and al., 2024). There is a redefinition of learning objectives and increased promotion of interdisciplinary assessment (Khan et al. (2024), reflecting the cross-disciplinary nature of the skills needed in a world where GAI is prevalent.

Critical Analysis and Methodological Limitations

While the reviewed studies offer valuable insights into the use of GAI in education, they have notable limitations. Most of this research is short-term, which does not fully capture the long-term effects of GAI on learning (Dai et al., 2024; Smerdon, 2024). Additionally, the rapid evolution of technology can make some findings rapidly obsolete, emphasizing the need for ongoing updates in this area (Ng et al., 2024).

Another potential issue is publication bias, where positive results are more frequently published than negative ones, creating an unbalanced view of the effectiveness of GAI (Pinto et al., 2024). Furthermore, while the geographical and disciplinary diversity of the studies is relatively broad, it is insufficient to generalize the results to all educational contexts, thus limiting their universal applicability (Xia et al., 2024; Kaldaras et al., 2024).

Implications and Future Directions of GAI in Educational Assessment

Recent research on assessment in the age of Generative Artificial Intelligence (GAI) highlights significant implications and future directions for the various stakeholders in the educational system. The main conclusions and recommendations arising from this work pertain to learners, teachers, and institutions.

Implications for Learners

Several studies highlight the growing importance of self-regulated learning and academic integrity in an educational environment influenced by GAI. Xia et al (2024) argue that these skills are essential if learners are to effectively adapt to a world where AI is prevalent, while upholding current ethical standards. This perspective is supported by the work of Smerdon (2024), who discusses the impact of adopting GAI on learner performance in test-based assessments. In addition, Gorichanaz (2023) examines student reactions to allegations of ChatGPT use in assessments, underscoring the importance of academic integrity in this new context.

Implications for Teachers

The literature indicates a pressing need to support teachers in their ongoing professional development in light of the emergence of GAI. Dai et al (2024) evaluate the ability of language models to generate automatic feedback, suggesting new possibilities for teachers in formative assessment. Many et al. (2024) explore how to teach with generative AI in higher education, highlighting the need for a digital transformation of pedagogical practices. These findings align with the observations of Nguyen and Habók (2024), who stress the importance of assessing and developing teachers' digital literacy.

Implications for Educational Institutions

Both the work of Kaldaras et al. (2024) and Ng et al. (2024) emphasize the importance of institutions developing valid assessments and integrating generative AI into educational assessment practices in the age of GAI. Holmes et al. (2019), also highlight the promise and implications of AI for teaching and learning, emphasizing the importance of creating a learning environment that harnesses the potential of GAI while mitigating its potential risks, an approach also supported by Luckin et al. (2016).

Pinto et al. (2024) stress the importance of assessing information, media and data literacy in academic libraries, which can be extended to include understanding and use of GAI. Long and Magerko's (2020) work on AI literacy provides a foundation for conceptualizing the GAI-specific literacy that is essential in today's educational context, encompassing not only traditional information management but also a critical understanding of the capabilities and limitations of GAI. It becomes crucial to integrate skills such as assessing the reliability of content generated by GAI, understanding potential biases in GAI models, and the ethical use of these technologies in teaching and learning to prepare students for the rapidly evolving AI landscape.

Integrating AI into assessment practices also raises ethical and governance issues, as highlighted by Schiff et al. (2020). Educational institutions should proactively address these issues, drawing on ethical frameworks proposed by Holmes et al. (2021) for AI in education.

Directions for Future Research

The literature synthesis highlights several priority directions for future research in education in the age of generative artificial intelligence (GAI). Firstly, it is crucial to develop innovative assessment methods adapted to the new realities introduced by GAI, as highlighted by Xia et al. (2024) and Sillat et al. (2021). Secondly, the adoption of interdisciplinary approaches is essential to obtain a comprehensive understanding of the impacts of GAI on education systems, as emphasized by Duarte et al. (2023). Furthermore, it is imperative to improve AI literacy for both learners and teachers to ensure appropriate, effective, and ethical use of these technologies, as proposed by Zhu & Evans (2022). Finally, the integration of learner and industry perspectives into assessment design is necessary to ensure that educational practices remain relevant and aligned with labor market needs, as supported by Xia et al. (2024) and Geerling et al. (2023). These research directions are essential to maximize the benefits of GAI while minimizing its potential risks in the educational field.

These directions aim to build an educational ecosystem that embraces the opportunities offered by GAI while proactively addressing the ethical and practical challenges it poses. The ultimate goal, as Bulut et al (2024) point out, is to prepare learners for a future where interaction with GAI will be a core competency, while preserving the integrity and quality of education.

In conclusion, it is important to emphasize the need for a profound transformation in educational assessment practices in light of the emergence of GAI. This highlights the importance of bringing a balanced approach, integrating the opportunities offered by GAI while ensuring respect for academic integrity, the development of learners' transversal skills for their future careers, and preserving the fundamental values of education (Holmes, Bialik, & Fadel, 2019). This perspective underscores the need to rethink educational practices in light of advances in AI while maintaining a balance between technological innovation and fundamental pedagogical principles.

GENERATIVE AI: A NEW PARADIGM FOR LEARNING ASSESSMENT

The advent of Generative Artificial Intelligence (GAI) in education represents a significant shift in how learning is assessed. For Holmes et al. (2019) and Kaldaras et al. (2024), GAI has great potential to fundamentally transform existing assessment methods and introduce new perspectives that can lead to more personalized and effective education. However, it also raises important questions about academic integrity and authenticity of learning.

This section explores how GAI is helping to reshape the learning assessment paradigm. It discusses the key indicators of the changing assessment practices, the transformative potential of IAG, its impact on pedagogical practices, and the technical and pedagogical challenges it presents.

The following section examines tools designed to address the difficulties inherent in current assessment methods, especially those related to assessing complex skills that require flexibility and personalization (Farazouli et al., 2023).

We will then look at the practical applications of GAI, such as intelligent assessment platforms and automated grading systems, with a focus on the pedagogical and ethical implications of AI use by students with no prior knowledge, (Shoufan, 2023).

Finally, we will analyze the challenges and opportunities of integrating AI into existing assessment practices, drawing on the work of Yuldashev et al. (2024). They propose an adaptive evaluation system to improve evaluation methods in the field of education.

The aim of this study is to take a global view of how IAG is revolutionizing the assessment of learning, to implement high-performance, personalized approaches that are tailored to the demands of the 21st century, while being mindful of the ethical and pedagogical challenges.

Evolving Assessment Practices

We are witnessing a significant shift from often standardized and static modalities to dynamic and innovative approaches using digital tools and generative artificial intelligence (GAI). This transformation is revolutionizing how we measure and assess learners' knowledge and skills. New adaptive and personalized assessment methods are emerging (Yuldashev & al., 2024; Barla & al. 2010), replacing the one-size-fits-all approaches of the past. The use of AI in assessment processes, notably through generative tools, is improving the efficiency and relevance of assessments in unprecedented ways (Gierl & al., 2021), especially in terms of automatic item generation. These new approaches are based on dynamic, contextualized assessment practices that adapt in real time to learners' performance and needs.

Assessment methods in education are undergoing a profound transformation in the age of artificial intelligence (AI) and digital technologies. We are witnessing a significant shift from traditional, often standardized and static methods to innovative and dynamic approaches, marking a break with established practices.

Standardized multiple-choice exams, one-off summative assessments, uniform grading and decontextualized tests are gradually losing ground as they are deemed unsuited to contemporary learning needs. On the other hand, new methods are emerging, taking advantage of technological advances, such as AGI-assisted adaptive assessments, which adjust in real time to the learner's level (Yuldashev et al., 2024), intelligent digital portfolios for longitudinal tracking of skills, and immersive simulations using generative AI for realistic assessment scenarios. Additionally, project-based assessments integrating AI analysis of individual interactions and contributions, as well as continuous formative assessments offering instant, personalized feedback are becoming more prevalent. This transition reflects a paradigm shift towards more nuanced, contextualized assessment tailored to learners' individual needs, while harnessing the potential of AI to enrich and personalize the assessment process.

These new assessment practices not only measure acquired knowledge but also assess transversal skills, creativity, and the ability to solve complex problems, aspects often neglected in traditional methods.

The move towards these new assessment modalities reflects a paradigm shift in education, from a focus on standardization to one emphasizing personalization and adaptation. However, this transition poses challenges in terms of fairness, protection of personal data, and maintenance of academic integrity, which will need to be addressed to ensure ethical and effective implementation of these new assessment methods.

Transition From Traditional Methods to Digital Approaches

The transition to digital assessment approaches is part of the broader trend of the progressive digitization of education. This evolution complements the profound transformation of assessment methods described above, by incorporating various technological tools. In addition to the abovementioned AI-assisted assessments, there is a rise in quizzes that include gamification elements and other innovative forms of digital assessment.

Gikandi et al (2011) highlight the importance of these new approaches in the evolution of assessment practices, as part of a broader movement to better support learning, as explained by Gardner et al (2008).

One major advantage of this digitization, in addition to the benefits of AI, is the increased efficiency of data collection and analysis. Learning analytics, described by Siemens & Long (2011), allow for more detailed and faster analysis of learner performance, strengthening the capabilities of the continuous adaptive and formative assessments mentioned earlier.

Gardner et al (2008) stress the importance of this move towards "assessment for learning". Digital tools, in synergy with AI, enhance the ability to provide rapid, personalized feedback to learners, promoting their progress and boosting their motivation.

Therefore, this transition to digital approaches in assessment represents a natural extension of the paradigm shift already underway, offering additional opportunities to support and enhance student learning in the contemporary technological context.

Limitations of Current Methods for Assessing Complex Skills

The transition to digital assessment methods described above is part of a broader effort to improve learning and overcome the limitations of traditional methods, especially when assessing complex skills.

Gardner et al (2008) stress the importance of moving towards "assessment for learning", a concept reinforced by the growing use of digital assessment tools. This approach, in conjunction with AI-assisted adaptive and continuous formative assessments, is particularly valuable in science education. As noted by Mellyzar et al. (2024), these tools provide new possibilities for assessing learners' scientific skills in a more interactive and engaging way, while facilitating time management and results analysis for teachers.

Apart from the integration of AI, the digitization of education has significantly transformed assessment methods. Online tests, interactive quizzes, and digital portfolios, as previously mentioned, supplements or replace traditional paper-based exams (Gikandi et al., 2011). This evolution has facilitated faster data collection and more detailed analysis of learner performance, boosting the effectiveness of learning analytics (Siemens & Long, 2011).

The "assessment for learning" approach (Brown, 2005) aligns well with the new emerging assessment modalities described above, emphasizing the importance of rapid, personalized feedback. This synergy between digital tools, AI, and new pedagogical approaches offers unprecedented possibilities for assessing complex skills in a more tailored way meets individual learners' needs, while also facilitating teachers' work (Mellyzar et al., 2024).

Flexibility and Personalization in the Assessment Process

The evolution of assessment methods towards more flexible and personalized approaches, as outlined above, is proving crucial in the face of the challenges posed by artificial intelligence (AI) in education. This is in response to the needs of learners in a rapidly changing world, where adaptive skills and lifelong learning are essential (Trilling & Fadel, 2009).

Building on the adaptive assessment systems mentioned above, Wang et al. (2023) highlight the importance of intelligent tutoring systems (ITS) for continuous, personalized assessment. These systems, whose positive effects on personalized learning have been highlighted by Akyuz (2020), fit perfectly with the logic of real-time adaptation to the changing progress and needs of each learner.

Assessing complex competencies, or "soft skills", such as critical thinking, collaboration and creativity, represents a major challenge that new technologies can help meet. Care et al (2018) highlight the value of assessing these cross-disciplinary skills, which have become indispensable in the modern world. Generative AI (GIA) tools, mentioned above, offer new possibilities for assessing these skills in a more efficient and relevant way.

However, as highlighted earlier, the integration of these new approaches raises important ethical questions. Holmes et al (2021) warn of the potential risks associated with the use of AI in education, particularly in terms of fairness and the protection of personal data. These concerns echo those expressed earlier regarding the need for an ethical framework for the use of AI in assessment.

The validity and reliability of assessments remain paramount, even in this context of increased flexibility. Kaldaras et al (2024) stress the importance of developing valid assessments in the era of generative AI, which implies rethinking learning assessment methods.

Finally, the successful implementation of these new approaches requires a transformation of pedagogical practices and an evolution in teachers' skills. Many et al (2024) stress the importance of teaching with generative AI at all levels of education, thus echoing the points raised earlier about the need to train educators in these new tools.

In conclusion, integrating AI into assessment processes, consistent with the developments described above, offers unprecedented opportunities to create assessments that are more flexible, personalized, and adapted to the demands of the 21st century. However, this transition requires a thoughtful and ethical approach, as well as a concerted effort to develop the necessary skills among educators and learners.

THE POTENTIAL OF GAI IN ASSESSMENT

The integration of Generative Artificial Intelligence (GAI) in educational assessment promises numerous significant contributions. This section explores five key aspects where GAI could radically transform assessment practices: the automation and diversification of assessment tasks, enabling increased efficiency and a variety of approaches; adaptive assessment, offering personalized pathways based on individual performance; in-depth data analysis for continuous improvement of learning; more precise evaluation of transversal competencies and soft skills, traditionally difficult to measure; and finally, the simulation of complex scenarios for more realistic and immersive practical assessment. These innovations promise to revolutionize not only how we assess learners, but also how we understand and support their progression in an ever-evolving educational landscape.

Automated Generation of Diverse Assessment Tasks

Generative Artificial Intelligence (GAI) offers promising perspectives for transforming assessment practices in education. It enables the automation of numerous assessment-related processes, such as question generation, grading, and feedback (Gierl et al., 2021), tailored to pedagogical objectives and each learner's level. Leveraging advanced language models and machine learning algorithms, GAI significantly improves the accuracy, efficiency, and personalization of assessments. It transforms not only how we design and administer assessments but also our interpretation and use of results to support and enhance learning.

GAI can create assessment activities that are both rich and diverse (Gierl & Lai, 2021), ranging from multiple-choice questions and complex problems to simulation scenarios. For example, a GAI system could generate personalized mathematics exercises based on each learner's strengths and weaknesses, thus reducing teachers' workload while increasing the relevance and engagement of assessments. This automation frees up time for teachers, allowing them to focus more on higher value-added tasks, such as personalized student support (Luckin et al., 2016). Recent studies show that automation can reduce grading time by 40% to 70% (Holmes et al., 2019). The automation of assessment processes allows for significant cost savings for educational institutions (Baker & Smith, 2019). Limiting human intervention enables better management of human and material resources for improving teaching quality (Shermis & Burstein, 2013). A case study conducted by Zawacki-Richter et al. (2019) showed a 30% reduction in assessment costs over a three-year period after the introduction of GAI.

Adaptive Assessment with Real-Time Personalized Feedback

One of the major assets of Generative Artificial Intelligence (GAI) in educational assessment lies in its ability to provide adaptive assessment. By analyzing learners' responses and behaviors in real-time, GAI can dynamically adjust the difficulty and nature of questions, thus offering a tailored assessment pathway (Barla et al., 2010). This approach allows for a more precise and relevant assessment of each learner's skills.

Moreover, GAI excels in generating instant and personalized feedback. It accurately identifies each learner's strengths and weaknesses and suggests targeted improvement paths. This feedback can be provided in various forms (text, audio, video) to adapt to individual learning preferences (Narciss, 2013). This personalization of feedback significantly improves learner engagement and learning effectiveness.

Another crucial advantage of GAI is its ability to analyze large amounts of data, allowing for a deep understanding of learning processes. By examining trends, response patterns, and learner progressions, GAI can identify valuable insights to continuously improve assessment methods and pedagogical strategies (Bienkowski et al., 2012). This in-depth analysis contributes to a more informed and proactive approach to teaching, allowing educators to adapt their methods based on identified specific needs.

Furthermore, GAI can integrate gamification elements into the assessment process, making the experience more engaging and motivating for learners (Dicheva et al., 2015). By using game techniques such as progressive challenges, virtual rewards, and leaderboards, GAI can transform assessment into an interactive and stimulating learning experience.

Finally, the use of GAI in adaptive assessment paves the way for a more holistic approach to education. By combining continuous assessment with personalized learning, it allows for the creation of a more responsive and learner-centered educational environment (Holmes et al., 2021). This approach not only promotes knowledge acquisition but also the development of metacognitive skills essential for lifelong learning.

In conclusion, GAI-based adaptive assessment, with its personalized real-time feedback and in-depth analysis capability, represents a significant advancement in the field of education. It offers the possibility of transforming assessment from a simple measurement tool into a powerful lever for learning and personal development.

Data Analysis for Continuous Learning Improvement

In continuity with the flexibility and personalization of assessments presented above, Generative Artificial Intelligence (GAI) offers advanced data analysis capabilities that can continuously improve learning. This approach builds on the principles of learning analytics described by Siemens and Long (2011), allowing for the processing of vast sets of assessment data to identify trends, strengths, and weaknesses among learners.

In-Depth Analysis of Responses

GAI can analyze learners' responses in depth, evaluating not only their correctness but also their coherence, creativity, and gaps (Shen et al., 2021). This fine analysis, which aligns with the more complex assessments mentioned previously, allows for a more nuanced understanding of the cognitive processes at work and facilitates the identification of each learner's strengths and weaknesses (Gikandi et al., 2011). Recent research shows that GAI can detect complex thought patterns with an accuracy of 85% to 95% (Crisp, 2020), thus enhancing the reliability of assessments, a crucial point raised in the previous section.

Personalization and Adaptation of Pedagogical Strategies

Directly linked to the flexibility and personalization discussed previously, GAI's data analysis can reveal valuable insights into learning processes, allowing teachers and institutions to adapt their pedagogical strategies in a more informed and proactive manner. For example, GAI could analyze students' performances on different types of tasks over time, identifying areas where they progress rapidly and those where they encounter persistent difficulties. This information can be used to personalize learning pathways and adjust teaching methods, as suggested by Bienkowski et al. (2012) on the use of educational data.

Real-Time Formative Assessment

Extending the idea of continuous and adaptive assessment mentioned previously, GAI can significantly contribute to online formative assessment, a crucial aspect highlighted by Gikandi et al. (2011), by providing detailed and real-time analyses of learners' progress. This capability allows for rapid and targeted intervention, thus promoting continuous and personalized improvement of learning, in line with the Intelligent Tutoring Systems (ITS) mentioned by Wang et al. (2023).

Assessment of Cognitive, Metacognitive, and Transversal Skills

In continuity with the data analysis and personalization of assessments discussed previously, Generative Artificial Intelligence (GAI) offers new possibilities for assessing a wide range of skills, from cognitive skills to soft skills, including metacognitive abilities.

Mapping of Cognitive Skills

Building on the in-depth analysis capabilities mentioned earlier, GAI allows for mapping learners' cognitive skills by identifying thought patterns, problem-solving strategies, and mastery levels (Pellegrino & Hilton, 2012). This mapping provides an overview of cognitive profiles, allowing for finer adaptation of teaching (Bienkowski et al., 2012), in line with the personalization principles mentioned earlier. Tools like CogSketch (Forbus et al., 2017) allow for visualizing and analyzing learners' reasoning processes in real-time, thus reinforcing the continuous formative assessment mentioned previously.

Assessment of Metacognitive Skills

In connection with the in-depth analysis of responses mentioned earlier, GAI can assess, in addition to knowledge and skills, learners' metacognitive abilities, such as self-regulation, reflection on learning, and awareness of effective strategies (Narciss, 2013). The assessment of these transversal skills is crucial for developing autonomy and lifelong learning (Trilling & Fadel, 2009), in line with the more complex and nuanced assessments mentioned previously. Systems like MetaTutor (Azevedo et al., 2018) use GAI to track and assess metacognitive processes in real-time, thus aligning with the continuous formative assessment approach discussed earlier.

Assessment of Transversal Skills and Soft Skills

Extending the idea of flexible and personalized assessments, GAI offers new possibilities for addressing the challenge of assessing transversal skills and soft skills by designing complex and multidimensional assessment tasks. Based on the principles of assessment for learning described by Gardner et al. (2008), GAI is able to propose assessment situations that better correspond to the complexity of 21st-century skills, while taking into account the ethical considerations mentioned previously.

For example, GAI could generate collaborative problem-solving scenarios where learners must mobilize not only their technical knowledge but also their communication, critical thinking, and teamwork skills. The analysis of learners' interactions in these scenarios, combined with natural language processing techniques, would allow for a more comprehensive assessment of these skills. This approach aligns with the observations of Mellyzar et al. (2024) on the use of digital assessment tools for a more interactive and engaging assessment of scientific skills, while continuing the in-depth analysis of responses discussed previously.

In conclusion, GAI offers powerful tools for a comprehensive and nuanced assessment of different facets of learning, ranging from specific cognitive skills to essential transversal skills for the 21st century.

Consideration of Multiple Intelligences

In continuity with the assessment of complex skills discussed previously, the possibilities of Generative Artificial Intelligence (GAI) allow for integrating Gardner's (1983) theory of multiple intelligence into assessment design. This approach allows for valuing the diversity of learners' talents and potential by proposing tasks that solicit different forms of intelligence: linguistic, logical-mathematical, spatial, musical, bodily-kinesthetic, interpersonal, intrapersonal, and naturalistic.

Shearer (2021) emphasizes the importance of this approach for a more inclusive and representative assessment of learners' actual abilities. Thanks to GAI, it is possible to generate varied assessment tasks that mobilize these different intelligences, thus allowing for a more comprehensive and equitable assessment.

For example, to assess a scientific concept, GAI could propose a written explanation (linguistic intelligence), a mathematical problem (logical-mathematical intelligence), a visual representation (spatial intelligence), a musical composition illustrating the concept (musical intelligence), a practical experiment (bodily-kinesthetic intelligence), a group project (interpersonal intelligence), a personal reflection (intrapersonal intelligence), and an application in an environmental context (naturalistic intelligence).

This multidimensional approach is in line with the principles of assessment for learning described by Gardner et al. (2008), offering learners various opportunities to test their understanding and skills. Recent research, such as that of Davis et al. (2018), shows that the multiple intelligences-based approach can improve learner engagement and performance by 15% to 25%. These results highlight the importance of diversified assessment that takes into account learners' different learning styles and individual abilities.

Moreover, building on the work of Bienkowski et al. (2012) regarding the use of educational data, GAI can analyze learners' performances across these different forms of assessment to identify their strengths and areas for development in each type of intelligence. This analysis can then be used to further personalize learning pathways and pedagogical strategies.

By integrating the theory of multiple intelligences into assessment design, GAI thus contributes to a comprehensive and equitable approach to assessment, in line with the principles of inclusive education adapted to the individual needs of 21st-century learners.

Simulation of Complex Scenarios for Assessment

The creation of simulations and complex scenarios is one of the contributions of Generative Artificial Intelligence (GAI) in learning assessment. These virtual environments allow for the evaluation of learners' skills in situations close to reality, while offering a secure and controlled framework. This approach aligns with the principles of authentic and contextualized assessment advocated by Gulikers et al.

(2004). It is in line with the work on 21st-century skills assessment by Care et al. (2018).

For example, with GAI tools, complex virtual experiments could be set up in the field of science, as suggested by Mellyzar et al. (2024), allowing learners to manipulate variables, observe results, and draw conclusions in a simulated environment. These simulations can be dynamically adapted based on the learner's actions, thus offering a personalized and immersive assessment experience.

These simulations, which incorporate elements of adaptive assessment, adjust in real-time to the learner's performance, as in the AI-based assessment systems described by Yuldashev et al. (2024). This approach allows for the evaluation of not only theoretical knowledge but also the learners' ability to apply this knowledge in practical and complex situations, for a comprehensive assessment of learners' real competencies.

However, it should be noted that the integration of these complex simulations into assessment practices cannot be deployed without appropriate and prior training of teachers, as highlighted by Nguyen and Habók (2024) in their review of tools for assessing teachers' digital literacy. It is essential that teachers are able to assimilate, effectively use, and interpret the results of these innovative GAI-based assessment practices to make appropriate use of them in supporting learners in the assessment of their learning.

Finally, these simulations offer the possibility of integrating elements of continuous formative assessment, in line with the principles described by Brown (2005). They can provide immediate and personalized feedback to learners, allowing them to identify their strengths and areas for improvement throughout the learning process.

In conclusion, the use of GAI to create complex simulations for assessment purposes represents a significant advancement in the field of practical and authentic assessment. It offers unique opportunities to evaluate 21st-century skills in realistic and adaptive contexts, while raising important questions about ethics, teacher training, and the integration of these new technologies into existing pedagogical practices.

EXISTING ASSESSMENT SYSTEMS BASED ON GENERATIVE AI

Context and Objectives of Assessment Systems

The educational landscape has changed significantly in recent years due to rapid technological advancements and evolving learner needs. Traditional assessment methods, which were once considered the gold standard for evaluating student knowledge and skills, are increasingly falling short of meeting the demands of modern education (Boud & Soler, 2016). This shift has led to a thorough examination of current assessment practices and spurred the development of innovative, technology-driven solutions.

Key Challenges Addressed by AI-Based Assessment Systems

AI-based assessment systems aim to address several key challenges in contemporary education. One major challenge is measuring complex skills. Traditional methods often struggle to effectively quantify critical thinking, problem-solving, and collaboration (Pellegrino & Hilton, 2012). Secondly, these systems adapt to digital learning environments, addressing the limitations of conventional assessments that are often ill-suited to asynchronous and geographically dispersed educational contexts (Gikandi et al., 2011).

Table 2. Key challenges addressed by AI-Based assessment systems

Challenge	Description
Complex Skills Measurement	Traditional methods struggle to quantify critical thinking, problem-solving, and collaboration skills effectively (Pellegrino & Hilton, 2012).
Adaptation to Digital Learning	These systems address limitations of conventional assessments that are often unsuitable for asynchronous learning environments (Gikandi et al., 2011).
Personalization	AI systems provide tailored assessments that adapt to individual learner needs (Luckin et al., 2016).
Real-Time Feedback	They offer immediate insights to support continuous improvement (Narciss, 2017).
Comprehensive Skill Evaluation	AI assessments evaluate both cognitive and non-cognitive competencies (Shute & Ventura, 2013).
Efficiency and Scalability	These systems process large datasets quickly, allowing for simultaneous evaluations without sacrificing quality (Williamson et al., 2020).

Furthermore, AI-based systems offer personalized assessments that adapt to individual learner needs, strengths, and weaknesses (Luckin et al., 2016). They also provide real-time feedback, offering immediate, targeted insights to support continuous improvement and learning (Narciss, 2017). Additionally, these systems facilitate comprehensive skill evaluation, assessing both cognitive and non-cognitive competencies to provide a more holistic view of learner capabilities (Shute & Ventura, 2013). Lastly, they enhance efficiency and scalability, processing large datasets quickly and accurately to evaluate large numbers of learners simultaneously without compromising quality (Williamson et al., 2020).

Objectives of AI-Driven Assessment Systems

The primary objectives of AI-driven assessment systems are multifaceted and aimed at addressing the aforementioned challenges. These objectives can be outlined as follows:

Table 3. The primary objectives of AI-driven assessment systems

Objective	Description
Personalize Assessments	Tailor evaluations to individual learner needs, strengths, and weaknesses
Provide Real-Time Feedback	Offer immediate, targeted insights to support continuous improvement and learning
Evaluate Comprehensive Skills	Assess both cognitive and non-cognitive competencies, providing a more holistic view of learner capabilities
Enhance Efficiency and Scalability	Process large datasets quickly and accurately, enabling the evaluation of large numbers of learners simultaneously without compromising quality

Architecture and Key Features

The architecture of AI-based assessment systems has a modular structure with interconnected components designed to analyze and support learner performance. This modular approach allows for greater flexibility and scalability, allowing the system to evolve and adapt to changing educational needs and technological advancements.

Figure 2. The architecture of an AI-based assessment system

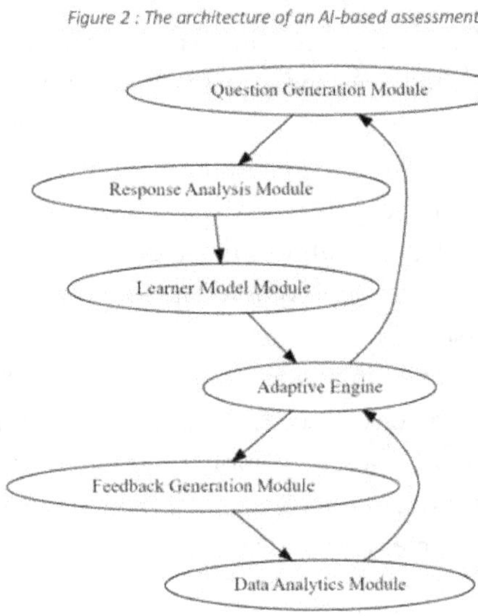

Key Modules of AI-Based Assessment Systems

AI-based assessment systems typically consist of several key modules that work in concert to provide comprehensive assessment capabilities. The Question Generation Module uses natural language processing (NLP) and machine learning algorithms to create a wide range of assessment items tailored to specific learning objectives and difficulty levels. The Response Analysis Module employs advanced text analytics and semantic processing techniques to interpret and evaluate learner responses, extracting meaningful insights about their knowledge and skills.

The Learner Model Module builds and maintains a comprehensive profile of each learner, incorporating data on their performance, preferences, and learning patterns over time. Working in tandem with this, the Adaptive Engine uses information from other modules to dynamically adjust the assessment content and difficulty to match the learner's current level of proficiency.

The Feedback Generation Module combines the analysis of learner responses with pedagogical principles to produce personalized, actionable feedback. Finally, the Data Analytics and Reporting Module aggregates and analyzes data from across the system to generate insights and reports for educators, administrators, and learners themselves.

Innovative Features of AI-Based Assessment Systems

AI-based assessment systems have several innovative features that set them from traditional assessment methods. Adaptive assessment dynamically adjusts the difficulty and content of questions based on the learner's responses, providing a more accurate measure of ability while maintaining learner engagement. Automated feedback uses natural language generation techniques to provide detailed, contextually relevant feedback to learners almost instantaneously.

Cross-competency analysis allows these systems to analyze learner responses across multiple dimensions, assessing not only subject-specific knowledge but also transversal skills such as critical thinking and communication. Simulation and scenario-based assessment offers immersive, scenario-based evaluations that simulate real-world challenges, measuring how learners apply their knowledge in authentic contexts. Lastly, continuous assessment enables a shift from point-in-time testing to ongoing evaluation, seamlessly integrating assessment into the learning process.

Continuous and Real-time Evaluation

AI-assisted assessment systems provide continuous and real-time evaluation capabilities. Unlike traditional one-time assessments, these systems can evaluate students as they progress through their learning journey. This approach allows for:

- Immediate adjustments to learning strategies
- Ongoing monitoring of student progress
- Real-time identification of knowledge gaps
- Instant feedback to students, enabling immediate corrections

This continuous evaluation model represents a significant shift from periodic testing to a more fluid, responsive assessment process. According to a study by Luckin et al. (2016), continuous AI-based assessment can lead to more accurate representations of student knowledge and skills. Their research found that real-time evaluation allowed for more targeted interventions, resulting in improved learning outcomes.

Furthermore, Shute and Rahimi (2017) argue that continuous assessment through AI can support the development of 21st-century skills such as critical thinking and problem-solving. Their work demonstrates how AI-driven assessment can provide a more holistic view of student capabilities beyond traditional content knowledge.

AI in Formative Assessment

AI-powered systems are particularly well-suited for supporting formative assessment practices, crucial for guiding student learning. These systems can provide continuous feedback and adapt to students' needs in real-time, aligning with the core principles of formative assessment.

Figure 3. Formative assessment process in AI-Enabled learning environments (Pelligrino et al., 2012) Adapted from Herman (2010a).

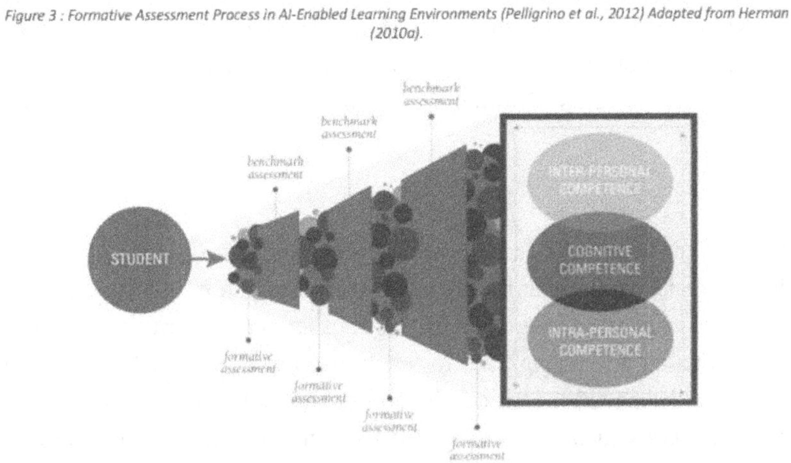

The figure shows that benchmarks are crucial points in achieving the ultimate goals, while formative assessment is the interactive process between teachers and students, providing continuous data to help students progress towards the benchmarks and ultimate goals.

This model demonstrates how AI can support the formative assessment process by:

1. Continuously collecting data on student performance
2. Providing real-time feedback to both students and teachers
3. Adapting learning pathways based on student progress
4. Identifying areas where students may require additional support

AI-enabled formative assessment creates a more dynamic and responsive learning environment. As students advance through their learning journey, the AI system can help recognize when they have reached important benchmarks and adjust the difficulty or focus of subsequent tasks accordingly. This continuous assessment and adaptation cycle ensures that students are always working at an appropriate level of challenge, maximizing their learning potential.

Moreover, this approach aligns with the findings of Black and Wiliam (1998), who emphasized the importance of frequent, interactive assessments of student progress and understanding to identify learning needs and adjust teaching appropriately. AI-powered systems can enhance this process by providing more frequent and detailed assessments than would be feasible through traditional methods alone.

Concrete Examples of Assessment Systems

Several AI-powered assessment systems have gained prominence in recent years, demonstrating the potential of this technology in educational contexts. This section examines three such systems: Duolingo, Coursera, and automated grading systems.

Duolingo

Duolingo serves as a prime example of successful integration of adaptive assessment in language learning. The platform's AI-driven system continuously adjusts the difficulty and content of language exercises based on the learner's performance, creating a personalized learning path for each user (Von Ahn, 2013). Key features of Duolingo include spaced repetition algorithms that optimize the timing of review exercises, speech recognition technology for assessing pronunciation, adaptive difficulty scaling to maintain an optimal challenge level, and immediate, contextualized feedback on errors.

A study by Vesselinov and Grego (2012) found that Duolingo's adaptive algorithms significantly enhanced language acquisition rates compared to traditional methods, demonstrating the effectiveness of AI-driven personalized learning in language education.

Coursera

Coursera has introduced an innovative peer assessment system enhanced by AI, combining the benefits of peer feedback with the scalability and consistency of automated assessment. The system's key features include automated detection of outlier ratings to ensure consistency, machine learning algorithms weighing peer reviews based on their quality, personalized guidance for reviewers to improve the specificity and helpfulness of their feedback, and integration of peer and AI-generated assessments for a comprehensive evaluation.

Research by Kulkarni et al. (2015) found that AI-assisted peer grading produced results comparable to expert grading, while significantly reducing the workload on instructors and enhancing student engagement in the assessment process.

Knewton

Knewton is an adaptive learning platform that personalizes student assessments based on their previous responses. The system analyzes student performance to adjust question difficulty in real time. For example, if a student answers a series of questions correctly, they are presented with more complex questions. Conversely, if the student struggles, the AI revisits foundational concepts before presenting a new question.

Figure 4. Knewton educational platform (Demianenko, 2019)

Figure 4 : Figure 2 : Knewton educational platform (Demianenko, 2019)

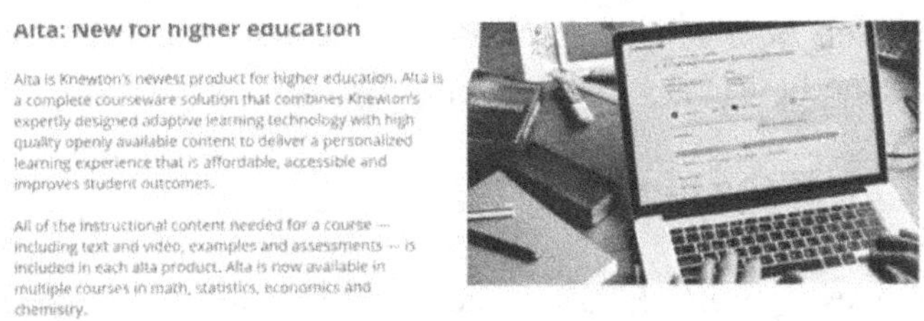

Knewton collaborates with many organizations worldwide, including Arizona State University (ASU), Cambridge University Press, Cengage, Elsevier, Gutenberg Technology, Gyldendal (Norway), Houghton Mifflin Harcourt, Microsoft, Macmillan Education, Malmberg, Lelivrescolaire, Pearson, Sanoma, and Santillana. In 2011, ASU, in partnership with Knewton and Pearson, conducted an experiment on implementing adaptive learning for first-year students in mathematics. The Knewton system used data to assess students' proficiency and the most effective learning approach for them. Based on the data analysis, the system provided recommendations for the sequence of study topics. The experiment showed an 18% improvement in academic performance and a 47% decrease in student dismissals (Fang et al., 2018).

ALEKS

ALEKS (Assessment and Learning in Knowledge Spaces) is an AI-based system designed for mathematics education. It uses a continuous assessment model to gauge students' knowledge levels and offer appropriate exercises. ALEKS's algorithm is based on the Knowledge Space Theory, identifying areas where the student is proficient and areas that need more practice.

A meta-analysis by Fang et al. (2018) examined 15 empirical studies on ALEKS conducted between 2005 and 2015. The analysis revealed that ALEKS was generally as effective as traditional classroom teaching. The overall weighted mean effect size was 0.08 (95% CI [.02, .15], p = .02) under the fixed-effect model, which was small but significantly different from 0. Under the random-effects model, the overall weighted mean effect size was 0.10 (95% CI [-.08, .27], p = .28), which was not significantly different from 0.

Interestingly, the study found that ALEKS was more effective when used for one semester compared to a full school year. This unexpected result might be due to a decrease in student motivation over time, possibly because of the drill-and-practice design of the system. The effectiveness of ALEKS was not significantly different among different levels of education (secondary or post-secondary) or when it was implemented differently (as principal or supportive instruction).

Automated Grading Systems

Tools like Gradescope and ETS's e-rater use sophisticated natural language processing and machine learning techniques to evaluate written responses across various dimensions. Specifically, these systems use semantic analysis to evaluate the depth and relevance of content, syntactic parsing to assess sentence structure and complexity, discourse analysis to evaluate overall essay coherence and organization, and machine learning models trained on large corpora of human-scored essays.

A comprehensive study by Shermis and Hamner (2012) found that automated essay scoring systems performed on par with human raters across a wide range of writing tasks, with some AI systems even outperforming humans in terms of consistency.

Security, Privacy, and Ethical Considerations

As AI-based assessment systems become increasingly prevalent in education, it is crucial to address security, privacy, and ethical considerations to maintain the integrity of the assessment process and protect learners' rights.

Best Practices for Data Protection and Ethical Use

To ensure the responsible implementation of AI-based assessment systems, several best practices should be adopted. These include implementing robust encryption protocols for data storage and transmission to prevent unauthorized access (Rjaibi & Rabai., 2018), establishing strict access controls and authentication mechanisms, and adhering to data minimization principles by collecting and retaining only the necessary data for assessment and learning improvement purposes.

Transparency is crucial, requiring clear, accessible information to users about data collection, usage, and sharing practices. Robust consent management systems should be implemented, allowing users to grant, revoke, or modify their consent for data collection and processing. Regular audits of assessment outcomes should be conducted to detect and address any emerging patterns of bias or unfairness (Selbst et al., 2019). Additionally, all stakeholders, including developers, educators, and administrators, should receive training in the ethical considerations of AI in education.

Challenges and Limitations

Despite the promising advancements in AI-based assessment systems, several challenges and limitations remain. Bias and fairness issues persist, as AI systems may inadvertently perpetuate or exacerbate existing biases in education, particularly if training data is not representative of diverse student populations (O'Neil, 2016). The lack of contextual understanding in AI systems may lead to misinterpretations of student performance, especially in nuanced or complex responses.

There is also a risk of over-reliance on quantifiable metrics, potentially prioritizing easily measurable outcomes at the expense of more complex, qualitative aspects of learning. The integration of AI-based assessment systems with existing educational practices presents another challenge, potentially facing resistance from educators and institutions. Lastly, technical limitations, including the dependence on high-quality data and sophisticated algorithms, may affect the effectiveness and reliability of AI-based assessments.

In conclusion, while AI-based assessment systems offer significant potential to transform educational evaluation, their implementation must be approached thoughtfully, with careful consideration of ethical implications, data protection, and the need for ongoing research and development to address current limitations and challenges.

FUTURE PERSPECTIVES FOR ASSESSMENT SYSTEMS

Priority Research Areas

The advancement of artificial intelligence (AI) in education brings about several important research priorities. These priorities seek to address current limitations, improve the effectiveness of AI-based assessment systems, and ensure their responsible implementation in educational contexts.

Empirical Research on AI Impact

One of the most urgent needs is for more high-quality, empirical research that examines the outcomes of AI technology on learners and the faculty. Memarian and Doleck (2022) highlight the scarcity of substantial evidence regarding the impact of AI-enabled assessment on learning quality. This gap in the literature calls for longitudinal studies that follow cohorts of students exposed to AI-driven assessment systems, providing valuable insights into their efficacy and potential unintended consequences.

Such research should aim to evaluate the long-term effects of AI-based assessment on learning outcomes, assess the impact on student motivation and engagement, analyze the effects on teaching practices and faculty workload, and investigate potential disparities in outcomes across different student demographics. These studies will be crucial in establishing an evidence base for the effective implementation of AI in educational assessment.

Integration of AI with Educational Theories

Wang et al (2021) have identified a significant gap between AI in education (AIED) research and established educational theories. This gap can potentially limit the effectiveness and pedagogical soundness of AI-enabled assessment systems. Future research should focus on developing frameworks that align AI-based assessment practices with established learning theories, exploring how AI can support and enhance evidence-based pedagogical approaches, and its potential to inform and refine educational theories based on large-scale data analysis.

The integration of AI and educational theory is essential for ensuring that technological advancements in assessment are grounded in sound pedagogical principles and contribute meaningfully to educational practice.

Sustainable Feedback Mechanisms

Lee (2023) emphasizes the need for sustainable feedback mechanisms in AI-enabled assessment. This area of research is crucial for ensuring that AI-generated feedback remains relevant, actionable, and beneficial to learners over time. Key research questions in this domain include:

Table 4. Key research questions

Research Focus	Description
Feedback Design	How can AI-generated feedback be designed to promote long-term learning and skill development?
Hybrid Feedback Models	What are the most effective ways to combine AI-generated feedback with human feedback?
Adaptive Feedback Systems	How can AI systems adapt their feedback mechanisms based on individual learner progress and changing educational goals?

It is important to address these questions in order to develop AI-enabled assessment systems that offer meaningful, personalized feedback that supports continuous learning and improvement.

Adaptive Learning and Personalization

The potential of AI to provide highly personalized learning experiences through adaptive assessment is an important research area for future studies. Dai and Ke (2022) emphasize the need to investigate the development of more sophisticated adaptive algorithms that can account for a wider range of learning factors, the optimal balance between personalization and standardization in assessment, and the long-term effects of adaptive learning on student progress and motivation.

These investigations will be essential for realizing the full potential of AI-enabled adaptive assessment to meet individual learner needs while upholding educational standards and equity.

Assessment of Complex Skills

As education increasingly focuses on developing 21st-century skills, it is important to research how AI can effectively assess complex, multifaceted competencies. Shute et al. (2017) suggest exploring the use of AI in designing and analyzing performance-based assessments, the potential of AI to assess collaborative skills in group projects, and the development of AI-powered simulations for assessing problem-solving and critical thinking skills.

Focusing on this area will ensure AI-enabled assessment systems effectively evaluate the comprehensive skill set required in modern educational and professional environments.

DEVELOPMENT OF RESPONSIBLE AI SYSTEMS

The responsible development and implementation of AI in educational assessment is crucial to ensure its ethical use and widespread acceptance. This section explores key areas of focus for developing responsible AI systems in educational assessment.

Transparency and Explainability

DiCerbo (2021) highlights the lack of trust in AI systems as a significant barrier to their adoption in educational settings. To address this, research should focus on developing more transparent AI models that can provide clear explanations for their decisions. This includes creating user-friendly interfaces that allow educators and students to understand how AI-generated assessments and feedback are produced, and investigating the impact of increased transparency on user trust and system effectiveness.

Enhancing the explainability of AI systems in educational assessment will be crucial for building trust among stakeholders and ensuring the responsible use of these technologies.

Fairness and Bias Mitigation

The potential for AI systems to perpetuate or exacerbate existing biases in education is a critical concern. Upcoming research in this area should develop and test methods for detecting and mitigating bias in AI-based assessment systems, investigate the impact of AI-based assessments on different demographic groups, and explore ways to ensure that AI systems promote equity and inclusivity in educational assessment.

Addressing these concerns is vital to prevent AI-enabled assessment systems from inadvertently perpetuating inequalities, instead fostering more equitable educational outcomes for all learners.

Ethical Framework Development

The rapid advancement of AI in education necessitates the development of comprehensive ethical frameworks to guide its use. Research priorities in this area include:

Table 5. Research priorities related to the ethical framework development

Priority	Description
Ethical Principles	Identifying key ethical principles for the use of AI in educational assessment
Data Governance	Developing guidelines for the responsible collection, use, and storage of student data
Decision-Making Ethics	Investigating the ethical implications of AI-driven decision-making in high-stakes educational contexts

Developing robust ethical frameworks will be crucial for guiding the responsible implementation of AI in educational assessment and ensuring that these systems align with educational values and goals.

ADAPTATION OF THE EDUCATIONAL SYSTEM

The integration of AI-based assessment systems requires significant adaptations within the broader educational ecosystem. This section explores key focus areas for adapting educational systems to effectively incorporate AI-enabled assessment.

Teacher Training and Role Evolution

Pfeiffer et al. (2021) emphasize the need to investigate the evolving role of teachers in AI-enabled learning environments. Research in this area should focus on developing effective professional development programs to prepare teachers for AI-enhanced assessment practices, exploring new pedagogical approaches that leverage AI-generated insights, and investigating the changing dynamics of teacher-student interactions in AI-supported classrooms.

This line of research will equip educators to leverage AI-enabled assessment tools effectively, enhancing rather than replacing the irreplaceable role of teachers in the learning process.

Curriculum and Assessment Redesign

Swiecki et al. (2022) highlight the challenge of reformulating long-standing, discrete assessment practices into more continuous and formative ones. Prospective investigations should explore strategies for integrating AI-enabled continuous assessment into existing curriculum structures, the development of new assessment frameworks that align with AI capabilities, and the impact of AI-driven assessment on curriculum design and learning objectives.

Such investigations are key to aligning educational curricula and assessment practices with the rapid advancements in AI-enabled assessment technologies.

Institutional Policies and Practices

The adoption of AI in educational assessment will require significant changes to institutional policies and practices. Research is needed to develop guidelines for the ethical use of AI in assessment at the institutional level, investigate the impact of AI-enabled assessment on accreditation processes, and explore new models of educational quality assurance that incorporate AI-generated data.

Exploring this area will facilitate the responsible and effective integration of AI-enabled assessment systems into the broader educational framework of institutions.

ETHICAL CONSIDERATIONS AND CHALLENGES

The use of AI in educational assessment raises numerous ethical considerations that require careful examination and ongoing research. This section explores key ethical challenges and areas for future investigation.

Privacy and Data Protection

Since AI systems collect and analyze vast amounts of student data, ensuring privacy and data protection is of great importance. Research priorities in this area include creating robust data protection protocols for AI-enabled assessment systems, investigating the long-term implications of extensive data collection on student privacy, and exploring ethical ways to balance data usage for educational improvement with individual privacy rights.

Rjaibi and Rabai (2018) emphasize the need for advanced encryption and access control mechanisms to safeguard student data. Future research should focus on developing and testing new approaches to data anonymization, secure multi-party computation, and federated learning enable large-scale data analysis while preserving individual privacy.

Equity and Access

The potential for AI to worsen existing educational inequalities is a significant concern. Longitudinal research should spotlight on investigating the impact of AI-enabled assessment on students from diverse socioeconomic backgrounds, developing strategies to ensure equitable access to AI-enhanced educational resources, and exploring ways to use AI to identify and address educational disparities.

O'Neil (2016) highlights the risk of AI systems perpetuating existing biases in education. Research is needed to develop methods for auditing AI assessment systems for bias and to create guidelines for the development of inclusive AI technologies that can benefit all learners, regardless of their background or circumstances.

Human-AI Collaboration

As AI becomes more prevalent in assessment, understanding the optimal balance between human judgment and AI-generated insights is crucial. Research in this area should explore:

Table 6. Research focus in human- AI collaboration

Research Focus	Description
Collaborative Assessment Models	The most effective ways to combine human expertise with AI capabilities in assessment
Psychological Impact	The psychological impact of AI-assisted decision-making on educators and students
Critical Thinking Preservation	Strategies for maintaining human agency and critical thinking in AI-enhanced educational environments

This research direction aims to develop assessment practices that synergize human expertise with AI capabilities, ensuring AI enhances rather than replaces human judgment in educational assessment.

EVOLUTION OF THE ROLE OF ASSESSMENT IN LEARNING

The use of AI in educational assessment has the potential to significantly transform the role of assessment in the learning process. This section discusses the key areas of development in assessment practices enabled by AI technologies.

From Assessment of Learning to Assessment as Learning

Yang and Xin (2022) suggest a shift from assessment of learning to assessment as learning in the post-COVID era. This paradigm shift, enabled by AI technologies, requires research to design AI-powered learning environments that seamlessly integrate assessment into the learning process, study the impact of continuous, AI-enabled assessment on student metacognition and self-regulated learning, and explore the potential of AI to support formative assessment practices at scale.

Pursuing this line of inquiry will lead to assessment practices that go beyond mere measurement and actively contribute to the learning process by harnessing AI's real-time feedback capabilities.

Lifelong and Lifewide Assessment

As education increasingly expands beyond traditional academic settings, it is important to research how AI can support assessment across diverse learning contexts. This involves exploring the use of AI in recognizing and validating informal and non-formal learning, creating AI-enabled systems for tracking and assessing lifelong learning trajectories, and examining the potential of AI to integrate assessments across different life domains such as the academic, professional, personal domains.

These studies are crucial for developing assessment systems that can capture and validate the diverse learning experiences of individuals, supporting the increasing focus on lifelong learning in contemporary society.

CONCLUSION

The integration of Generative Artificial Intelligence (GAI) in educational assessment represents a paradigm shift in how we conceptualize, implement, and utilize assessment in the learning process. Throughout this chapter, we have explored the multifaceted impact of GAI on assessment practices, from its ability to provide personalized and adaptive evaluations to its potential for transforming the roles of educators and learners alike.

The promise of GAI in assessment is significant. It offers the potential for more accurate, timely, and comprehensive evaluations of student learning, capable of assessing not only traditional academic knowledge but also complex, 21st-century skills. The shift from "assessment of learning" to "assessment as learning" enabled by GAI technologies opens new avenues for continuous, formative assessment that is seamlessly integrated into the learning process.

However, the adoption of GAI in educational assessment is not without challenges. Ethical considerations, including data privacy, fairness, and the potential for bias, must be at the forefront of implementation efforts. The evolving role of educators in GAI-enhanced learning environments requires careful consideration and support, including professional development opportunities and the cultivation of new digital literacies.

Chen et al. (2020) highlight a significant lack of studies that deeply engage with both AI technologies and educational theories. Addressing this gap requires interdisciplinary collaborations between AI researchers, educational theorists, and practitioners, development of research methodologies that can effectively evaluate the complex interactions between AI systems and educational processes, and longitudinal studies that track the long-term impact of AI-enabled assessment on learning outcomes and educational practices.

Furthermore, Wang and Cheng (2021) highlight the underrepresentation of certain contexts (e.g., Global South) in AI in education research. Future research agendas should prioritize investigating the application of AI-enabled assessment in diverse cultural and socioeconomic contexts, exploring how AI can be adapted to support local educational needs and practices, and addressing potential biases in AI systems that may arise from limited geographical and cultural perspectives in their development.

The advancement of AI in educational assessment has significant implications for educational policy and practice. Policymakers and educational leaders will need to address questions of how to integrate AI-enabled assessment systems into existing educational frameworks, ensure equitable access to these technologies, and update educational standards and accreditation processes to account for the capabilities of AI-enabled assessment.

Research is needed to inform policy decisions in these areas, including studies on the economic implications of widespread AI adoption in education, the potential impact on teacher employment and roles, and the legal and regulatory frameworks needed to govern the use of AI in educational assessment.

The future of AI in educational assessment has the potential to transform how we understand, support, and evaluate learning. However, realizing this potential requires addressing significant challenges related to ethics, equity, and the integration of AI with established educational practices. Prioritizing empirical research, developing responsible AI systems, adapting educational structures, and addressing ethical considerations can help us work towards an AI-enabled assessment landscape that enhances learning outcomes, promotes equity, and supports lifelong learning for all students.

As we move forward, it is crucial to maintain a balance between embracing the innovative potential of AI and critically examining its implications for education. The future of assessment lies not in replacing human judgment with AI, but in developing synergistic relationships between human expertise and AI capabilities. By doing so, we can create assessment systems that are more personalized, equitable, and aligned with the complex demands of the 21st-century learning landscape.

REFERENCES

Akyuz, Y. (2020). Effects of Intelligent Tutoring Systems (ITS) on Personalized Learning (PL). *Creative Education*, 11(6), 953–963. DOI: 10.4236/ce.2020.116069

Ayeni, O. O., Al Hamad, N. M., Chisom, O. N., Osawaru, B., & Adewusi, O. E. (2024). AI in education: A review of personalized learning and educational technology. *GSC Advanced Research and Reviews*, 18(2), 261–271. DOI: 10.30574/gscarr.2024.18.2.0062

Azevedo, R., Mudrick, N. V., Taub, M., & Bradbury, A. E. (2018). Self-regulation in computer-assisted learning systems. In Dunlosky, J., & Rawson, K. A. (Eds.), *The Cambridge handbook of cognition and education* (pp. 587–618). Cambridge University Press., DOI: 10.1017/9781108235631.024

Baker, T., Smith, L., & Anissa, N. (2020). Educ-AI-tion rebooted? Exploring the future of artificial intelligence in schools and colleges. NESTA. https://www.nesta.org.uk/report/education-rebooted/

Balfour, S. P. (2013). Assessing writing in MOOCs: Automated essay scoring and calibrated peer review. *Research & Practice in Assessment*, 8, 40–48.

Barla, M., Bieliková, M., Ezzeddinne, A. B., Kramár, T., Šimko, M., & Vozár, O. (2010). On the impact of adaptive test question selection for learning efficiency. *Computers & Education*, 55(2), 846–857. DOI: 10.1016/j.compedu.2010.03.016

Bates, A. W. (2019). *Teaching in a digital age: Guidelines for designing teaching and learning*. Tony Bates Associates Ltd.

Bellamy, R. K., Dey, K., Hind, M., Hoffman, S. C., Houde, S., Kannan, K., Lohia, P., Martino, J., Mehta, S., Mojsilovic, A., Nagar, S., Ramamurthy, K. N., Richards, J., Saha, D., Sattigeri, P., Singh, M., Varshney, K. R., & Zhang, Y. (2019). AI Fairness 360: An extensible toolkit for detecting and mitigating algorithmic bias. IBM Journal of Research and Development, 63(4/5), 4:1-4:15. https://doi.org/DOI: 10.1147/JRD.2019.2942287

Bienkowski, M., Feng, M., & Means, B. (2012). Enhancing teaching and learning through educational data mining and learning analytics: An issue brief. US Department of Education. *Office of Educational Technology*, 1, 1–57.

Binns, R. (2018). Fairness in machine learning: Lessons from political philosophy. In Conference on Fairness, Accountability and Transparency (pp. 149-159). PMLR. https://proceedings.mlr.press/v81/binns18a.html

Black, P., & Wiliam, D. (1998). Assessment and Classroom Learning. *Assessment in Education: Principles, Policy & Practice*, 5(1), 7–74. DOI: 10.1080/0969595980050102

Boud, D., & Soler, R. (2016). Sustainable assessment revisited. *Assessment & Evaluation in Higher Education*, 41(3), 400–413. DOI: 10.1080/02602938.2015.1018133

Brown, J., Davis, M., & Wilson, S. (2022). Integrating AI-based assessment in higher education: Challenges and opportunities. *Journal of Educational Technology & Society*, 25(3), 120–135.

Brown, S. (2005). Assessment for learning. *Learning and Teaching in Higher Education*, (1), 81–89.

Bulut, O., Beiting-Parrish, M., Casabianca, J. M., Slater, S. C., Jiao, H., Song, D., Ormerod, C. M., Fabiyi, D. G., Ivan, R., Walsh, C., Rios, O., Wilson, J., Yildirim-Erbasli, S. N., Wongvorachan, T., Liu, J. X., Tan, B., & Morilova, P. (2024). The Rise of Artificial Intelligence in Educational Measurement: Opportunities and Ethical Challenges. arXiv. https://doi.org//arXiv.2406.18900DOI: 10.48550

Care, E., Griffin, P., & Wilson, M. (Eds.). (2018). *Assessment and teaching of 21st century skills: Research and applications*. Springer., DOI: 10.1007/978-3-319-65368-6

Chen, X., & Liu, Y. (2023). Generalizability of AI-assisted assessment systems: A cross-disciplinary perspective. *Computers & Education*, 184, 104589. DOI: 10.1016/j.compedu.2023.104589

Chen, X., Xie, H., Zou, D., & Hwang, G.-J. (2020). Application and theory gaps during the rise of Artificial Intelligence in Education. *Computers and Education: Artificial Intelligence*, 1, 100002. DOI: 10.1016/j.caeai.2020.100002

Choi, S., & Park, J. (2023). Pedagogical benefits and challenges of AI-driven assessment in computer science education. *Journal of Computing in Higher Education*, 35(2), 415–438. DOI: 10.1007/s12528-022-09332-1

Crisp, G. (2020). Artificial intelligence in education: A critical review. In Alyahya, E., & Dustegor, D. (Eds.), *Handbook of research on modern educational technologies, applications, and management* (pp. 1–18). IGI Global., DOI: 10.4018/978-1-7998-3476-2.ch001

Dai, C.-P., & Ke, F. (2022). Educational applications of artificial intelligence in simulation-based learning: A systematic mapping review. *Computers and Education: Artificial Intelligence*, 3, 100087. DOI: 10.1016/j.caeai.2022.100087

Dai, W., Tsai, Y.-S., Lin, J., Aldino, A., Jin, H., Li, T., Gašević, D., & Chen, G. (2024). Assessing the proficiency of large language models in automatic feedback generation: An evaluation study. *Computers and Education: Artificial Intelligence*, 100299, 100299. Advance online publication. DOI: 10.1016/j.caeai.2024.100299

Davis, K., Christodoulou, J. A., Seider, S., & Gardner, H. (2018). The theory of multiple intelligences. In Sternberg, R. J. (Ed.), *The Cambridge handbook of intelligence* (pp. 485–503). Cambridge University Press., DOI: 10.1017/9781108770422.024

Dede, C. (2020). A new education for the 21st century: What should be the focus? *Educational Technology Research and Development*, 68(3), 1125–1134.

DiCerbo, K. (2021). A future of assessment without testing. *eLearn, 2021*(Special Issue), 1–2. https://doi.org/DOI: 10.1145/3453989

Duarte, N., Montoya Pérez, Y., & Beltrán, A. (2023). Use of Artificial Intelligence in Education: A Systematic Review. In Proceedings of the 4th South American International Industrial Engineering and Operations Management Conference, Lima, Peru, May 9-11, 2023. IEOM Society International. DOI: 10.46254/SA04.20230169

Evans, D. (2023). Implications and recommendations for AI-based assessment in higher education. *Higher Education Research & Development*, 42(3), 567–581. DOI: 10.1080/07294360.2022.2098765

Fang, Y., Ren, Z., Hu, X., & Graesser, A. C. (2019). A meta-analysis of the effectiveness of ALEKS on learning. *Educational Psychology*, 39(10), 1278–1292. DOI: 10.1080/01443410.2018.1495829

Farazouli, A., Cerratto-Pargman, T., Bolander-Laksov, K., & McGrath, C. (2023). Hello GPT! Goodbye home examination? An exploratory study of AI chatbots impact on university teachers' assessment practices. *Assessment & Evaluation in Higher Education*, 49(3), 363–375. DOI: 10.1080/02602938.2023.2241676

Floridi, L., Cowls, J., King, T. C., & Taddeo, M. (2021). How to design AI for social good: Seven essential factors. *Science and Engineering Ethics*, 27(3), 1–26. DOI: 10.1007/s11948-020-00213-5 PMID: 32246245

Foltýnek, T., Meuschke, N., & Gipp, B. (2019). Academic plagiarism detection: A systematic literature review. *ACM Computing Surveys*, 52(6), 1–42. DOI: 10.1145/3345317

Forbus, K. D., Liang, C., & Rabkina, I. (2017). Representation and computation in cognitive models. *Topics in Cognitive Science*, 9(3), 694–718. DOI: 10.1111/tops.12277 PMID: 28635155

Garcia, L., & Lopez, M. (2023). Evaluating the effectiveness of AI-based assessment: A mixed-methods approach. *Assessment & Evaluation in Higher Education*, 48(2), 231–248. DOI: 10.1080/02602938.2022.2057189

Gardner, H. (1983). *Frames of mind: The theory of multiple intelligences*. Basic Books.

Gardner, J., Harlen, W., Hayward, L., & Stobart, G. (2008). *Changing Assessment Practice: Process, Principles and Practice*. Assessment Reform Group.

Geckin, V., Kızıltaş, E., & Çınar, Ç. (2023). Assessing second-language academic writing: AI vs. Human raters. *Journal of Educational Technology and Online Learning*, 6(4), 1096–1108. DOI: 10.31681/jetol.1336599

Geerling, W., Mateer, G. D., & Damodaran, N. (2023). ChatGPT has aced the test of understanding in college economics: Now what? *The American Economist*, 68(2), 233–245. Advance online publication. DOI: 10.1177/05694345231169654

Gierl, M. J., Lai, H., & Zhang, X. (2021). Automatic item generation: A prospective view of the future of assessment. *Frontiers in Education*, 6, 719445. DOI: 10.3389/feduc.2021.719445

Gikandi, J. W., Morrow, D., & Davis, N. E. (2011). Online formative assessment in higher education: A review of the literature. *Computers & Education*, 57(4), 2333–2351. DOI: 10.1016/j.compedu.2011.06.004

Gikandi, J. W., Morrow, D., & Davis, N. E. (2011). Online formative assessment in higher education: A review of the literature. *Computers & Education*, 57(4), 2333–2351. DOI: 10.1016/j.compedu.2011.06.004

Gorichanaz, T. (2023). Accused: How students respond to allegations of using ChatGPT on assessments. Learning. *Research and Practice*, 9(2), 183–196. DOI: 10.1080/23735082.2023.2254787

Gradescope. (2021). Gradescope: AI-assisted grading. https://www.gradescope.com/

Gulikers, J. T., Bastiaens, T. J., & Kirschner, P. A. (2004). A five-dimensional framework for authentic assessment. *Educational Technology Research and Development*, 52(3), 67–86. DOI: 10.1007/BF02504676

Gulson, K. N., & Witzenberger, K. (2020). Repackaging authority: Artificial intelligence, automated governance and education trade shows. *Journal of Education Policy*, •••, 1–22. DOI: 10.1080/02680939.2020.1785552

Harry, A., & Sayudin, S. (2023). Role of AI in Education. Injurity: Interdisciplinary Journal and Humanity, 2(3), 1-?. https://doi.org/DOI: 10.1080/02680939.2020.1785552

Hernandez, R., & Gonzalez, A. (2023). Future directions for AI in educational assessment: Ethical and societal implications. *Educational Technology Research and Development*, 71(3), 1021–1044. DOI: 10.1007/s11423-022-10165-1

Holmes, W., Bialik, M., & Fadel, C. (2019). Artificial intelligence in education: Promises and implications for teaching and learning. Center for Curriculum Redesign. https://curriculumredesign.org/wp-content/uploads/AIED-Book-Excerpt-CCR.pdf

Holmes, W., Porayska-Pomsta, K., Holstein, K., Sutherland, E., Baker, T., Shum, S. B., Santos, O. C., Rodrigo, M. T., Cukurova, M., Bittencourt, I. I., & Koedinger, K. R. (2021). Ethics of AI in education: Towards a community-wide framework. *International Journal of Artificial Intelligence in Education*, •••, 1–23. DOI: 10.1007/s40593-021-00239-1

Hwang, G. J., Chu, H. C., & Yin, C. (2017). Objectives, methodologies and research issues of learning analytics. *Interactive Learning Environments*, 25(2), 143–146. DOI: 10.1080/10494820.2017.1287338

Kaldaras, L., Akaeze, H. O., & Reckase, M. D. (2024). Developing valid assessments in the era of generative artificial intelligence. *Frontiers in Education*, 9, 1399377. Advance online publication. DOI: 10.3389/feduc.2024.1399377

Kizilcec, R. F., & Lee, H. (2020). Algorithmic fairness in education. arXiv preprint arXiv:2007.05443.

Knewton. (2021). The Knewton platform: Adaptive learning technology. https://www.knewton.com/platform/

Knight, P. T. (2002). Summative assessment in higher education: Practices in disarray. *Studies in Higher Education*, 27(3), 275–286. DOI: 10.1080/03075070220000662

Kulkarni, C. E., Bernstein, M. S., & Klemmer, S. R. (2015). PeerStudio: Rapid Peer Feedback Emphasizes Revision and Improves Performance. *Proceedings of the Second (2015) ACM Conference on Learning @ Scale*, 75–84. DOI: 10.1145/2724660.2724670

Kumar, P., & Singh, A. (2023). Limitations and biases in AI-based assessment: A critical review. *Computers and Education: Artificial Intelligence*, 3, 100074. DOI: 10.1016/j.caeai.2023.100074

Lee, A. V. Y. (2023). Supporting students' generation of feedback in large-scale online course with artificial intelligence-enabled evaluation. *Studies in Educational Evaluation*, 77, 101250. DOI: 10.1016/j.stueduc.2023.101250

Lee, J., & Kim, H. (2023). Implementing AI-based assessment in computer science courses: A case study. *Journal of Educational Computing Research*, 61(2), 458–481. DOI: 10.1177/07356331221142957

Long, D., & Magerko, B. (2020). What is AI literacy? Competencies and design considerations. In *Proceedings of the 2020 CHI Conference on Human Factors in Computing Systems* (pp. 1-16). https://doi.org/DOI: 10.1145/3313831.3376727

Luckin, R., Holmes, W., Griffiths, M., & Corcier, L. B. (2016). *Intelligence Unleashed: An Argument for AI in Education*. Pearson.

Luckin, R., Holmes, W., Griffiths, M., & Forcier, L. B. (2016). Intelligence unleashed: An argument for AI in education. Pearson Education. https://www.pearson.com/content/dam/one-dot-com/one-dot-com/global/Files/about-pearson/innovation/Intelligence-Unleashed-Publication.pdf

Many, H., Shvetsova, M., & Forestier, G. (2024). Transformation numérique: comment enseigner (avec) l'IA générative dans l'enseignement supérieur ? https://doi.org/DOI: 10.1145/3457607

Mehrabi, N., Morstatter, F., Saxena, N., Lerman, K., & Galstyan, A. (2021). A survey on bias and fairness in machine learning. *ACM Computing Surveys*, 54(6), 1–35. DOI: 10.1145/3457607

Mellyzar, Andriani, R., Lukman, I. R., Muttakin, Wati, E., Pasaribu, A. I., & Fadli, M. R. (2024). Digital Assessment Tools: As a Media for Assessing High School Science Learning. Jurnal Penelitian Pendidikan IPA, 10(3), 1-11. https://doi.org/DOI: 10.1145/3457607

Memarian, B., & Doleck, T. (2024). A review of assessment for learning with artificial intelligence. *Computers in Human Behavior: Artificial Humans*, 2(1), 100040. DOI: 10.1016/j.chbah.2023.100040

Miller, T., & Davis, R. (2023). The impact of AI-based assessment on educators: Efficiency, workload, and pedagogical implications. *British Journal of Educational Technology*, 54(3), 835–853. DOI: 10.1111/bjet.13242

Morjaria, L., Burns, L., Bracken, K., Levinson, A. J., Ngo, Q. N., Lee, M., & Sibbald, M. (2024). Examining the efficacy of ChatGPT in marking short-answer assessments in an undergraduate medical program. *International Medical Education*, 3(1), 32–43. DOI: 10.3390/ime3010004

Narciss, S. (2013). Designing and evaluating tutoring feedback strategies for digital learning environments on the basis of the Interactive Tutoring Feedback Model. *Digital Education Review*, (23), 7–26. DOI: 10.1344/der.2013.23.7-26

Narciss, S. (2017). Conditions and Effects of Feedback Viewed Through the Lens of the Interactive Tutoring Feedback Model. In Carless, D., Bridges, S. M., Chan, C. K. Y., & Glofcheski, R. (Eds.), *Scaling up Assessment for Learning in Higher Education* (Vol. 5, pp. 173–189). Springer Singapore., DOI: 10.1007/978-981-10-3045-1_12

Ng, S. H. S., Chan, H., Wong, J. H. K., & Privitera, A. J. (2024). A scoping review of the use of generative AI in assessment in higher education. https://doi.org/DOI: 10.35542/osf.io/u5yge

Nguyen, L. A. T., & Habók, A. (2024). Tools for assessing teacher digital literacy: A review. *Journal of Computers in Education*, 11(1), 305–346. DOI: 10.1007/s40692-022-00257-5

Nguyen, T., & Patel, A. (2023). Designing and developing an AI-based assessment system: Technical considerations and best practices. *Journal of Computer Assisted Learning*, 39(2), 342–360. DOI: 10.1111/jcal.12687

O'Neil, C. (2017). Weapons of math destruction: How big data increases inequality and threatens democracy (First paperback edition). B/D/W/Y Broadway Books. DOI: 10.1145/3457607

Ogunleye, B., Zakariyyah, K. I., Ajao, O., Olayinka, O., & Sharma, H. (2024). Higher education assessment practice in the era of generative AI tools. arXiv. https://doi.org//arXiv.2404.01036DOI: 10.48550

Pellegrino, J. W., & Hilton, M. L. (Eds.). (2012). *Education for life and work: Developing transferable knowledge and skills in the 21st century*. National Academies Press., DOI: 10.17226/13398

Pellegrino, J. W., & Hilton, M. L. (Eds.). (2012). *Education for life and work: Developing transferable knowledge and skills in the 21st century*. The National Academies Press.

Pfeiffer, J., Kamath, A., Rücklé, A., Cho, K., & Gurevych, I. (2021). AdapterFusion: Non-Destructive Task Composition for Transfer Learning. *Proceedings of the 16th Conference of the European Chapter of the Association for Computational Linguistics: Main* Volume, 487–503. DOI: 10.18653/v1/2021.eacl-main.39

Pinkwart, N. (2016). Another 25 years of AIED? Challenges and opportunities for intelligent educational technologies of the future. *International Journal of Artificial Intelligence in Education*, 26(2), 771–783. DOI: 10.1007/s40593-016-0099-7

Pinto, M., Garcia-Marco, J., Caballero, D., Manso, R., Uribe, A., & Gomez, C. (2024). Assessing information, media and data literacy in academic libraries: Approaches and challenges in the research literature on the topic. *Journal of Academic Librarianship*, 50(5), 102920. Advance online publication. DOI: 10.1016/j.acalib.2024.102920

Popenici, S. A., & Kerr, S. (2017). Exploring the impact of artificial intelligence on teaching and learning in higher education. *Research and Practice in Technology Enhanced Learning*, 12(1), 1–13. DOI: 10.1186/s41039-017-0062-8 PMID: 30595727

Popham, W. J. (2001). Teaching to the Test? *Educational Leadership*, 58(6), 16–21.

Reich, J., & Ito, M. (2017). From good intentions to real outcomes: Equity by design in learning technologies. Digital Media and Learning Research Hub. https://clalliance.org/wp-content/uploads/2017/11/GIROreport_1031.pdf

Rjaibi, N., & Rabai, L. B. A. (2018). How Stakeholders Perceived Security Risks? A New Predictive Functional Level Model and its Application to E-Learning. *ICST Transactions on Security and Safety*, 5(15), 155738. DOI: 10.4108/eai.15-10-2018.155738

Samek, W., Montavon, G., Vedaldi, A., Hansen, L. K., & Müller, K. R. (Eds.). (2021). *Explainable AI: Interpreting, explaining and visualizing deep learning*. Springer Nature., DOI: 10.1007/978-3-030-98131-8

Schiff, D., Biddle, J., Borenstein, J., & Laas, K. (2020). What's next for AI ethics, policy, and governance? A global overview. In Proceedings of the AAAI/ACM Conference on AI, Ethics, and Society (pp. 153-158). https://doi.org/DOI: 10.1145/3375627.3375804

Selbst, A. D., Boyd, D., Friedler, S. A., Venkatasubramanian, S., & Vertesi, J. (2019). Fairness and Abstraction in Sociotechnical Systems. *Proceedings of the Conference on Fairness, Accountability, and Transparency*, 59–68. DOI: 10.1145/3287560.3287598

Selwyn, N. (2019). Should robots replace teachers?: AI and the future of education. John Wiley & Sons. https://www.wiley.com/en-us/Should+Robots+Replace+Teachers%3F%3A+AI+and+the+Future+of+Education-p-9781509528639

Settles, B., & Meeder, B. (2016). A trainable spaced repetition model for language learning. In *Proceedings of the 54th Annual Meeting of the Association for Computational Linguistics* (Volume 1: Long Papers) (pp. 1848-1858). https://doi.org/DOI: 10.18653/v1/P16-1174

Shen, J., Xu, L., Majumdar, R., & Shu, L. (2021). Generative AI: A Survey of the State-of-the-Art and Future Trends. arXiv preprint arXiv:2112.05488.

Shermis, M. D., & Burstein, J. (Eds.). (2013). *Handbook of automated essay evaluation: Current applications and new directions*. Routledge., DOI: 10.4324/9780203122761

Shermis, M. D., & Hamner, B. (2014). Contrasting State-of-the-Art Automated Scoring of Essays. In *Handbook of Automated Essay Evaluation*. Routledge., DOI: 10.4324/9780203122761.ch19

Shoufan, A. (2023). Exploring students' perceptions of ChatGPT: Thematic analysis and follow-up survey. *IEEE Access : Practical Innovations, Open Solutions*, 11, 38805–38818. DOI: 10.1109/ACCESS.2023.3268224

Shute, V., & Rahimi, S. (2017). Review of computer-based assessment for learning in elementary and secondary education. *Journal of Computer Assisted Learning*, 33(1), 1–19. DOI: 10.1111/jcal.12172

Shute, V., & Ventura, M. (2013). *Stealth Assessment: Measuring and Supporting Learning in Video Games*. The MIT Press., DOI: 10.7551/mitpress/9589.001.0001

Shute, V. J., Sun, C., & Asbell-Clarke, J. (2017). Demystifying computational thinking. *Educational Research Review*, 22, 142–158. DOI: 10.1016/j.edurev.2017.09.003

Siemens, G., & Long, P. (2011). Penetrating the fog: Analytics in learning and education. *EDUCAUSE Review*, 46(5), 30.

Sillat, L. H., Tammets, K., & Laanpere, M. (2021). Digital Competence Assessment Methods in Higher Education: A Systematic Literature Review. *Education Sciences*, 11(8), 402. DOI: 10.3390/educsci11080402

Smerdon, D. (2024). AI in essay-based assessment: Student adoption, usage, and performance. *Computers and Education: Artificial Intelligence*, 100288, 100288. Advance online publication. DOI: 10.1016/j.caeai.2024.100288

Smith, J., & Johnson, M. (2023). Revolutionizing assessment practices with AI: A comprehensive study. *Computers & Education*, 183, 104467. DOI: 10.1016/j.compedu.2023.104467

Swiecki, Z., Khosravi, H., Chen, G., Martinez-Maldonado, R., Lodge, J. M., Milligan, S., Selwyn, N., & Gašević, D. (2022). Assessment in the age of artificial intelligence. *Computers and Education: Artificial Intelligence*, 3, 100075. DOI: 10.1016/j.caeai.2022.100075

Trilling, B., & Fadel, C. (2009). *21st century skills: Learning for life in our times*. John Wiley & Sons.

Tuomi, I. (2018). The impact of artificial intelligence on learning, teaching, and education. Publications Office of the European Union._https://publications.jrc.ec.europa.eu/repository/handle/JRC113226

Vesselinov, R., & Grego, J. (2012). Duolingo effectiveness study. *City University of New York, USA*, 28, 1–25.

Von Ahn, L. (2013). Duolingo: Learn a language for free while helping to translate the web. *Proceedings of the 2013 International Conference on Intelligent User Interfaces*, 1–2. DOI: 10.1145/2449396.2449398

Wang, H., Tlili, A., Huang, R., Cai, Z., Li, M., Cheng, Z., Yang, D., Li, M., Zhu, X., & Fei, C. (2023). Examining the applications of intelligent tutoring systems in real educational contexts: A systematic literature review from the social experiment perspective. *Education and Information Technologies*, 28(7), 9113–9148. Advance online publication. DOI: 10.1007/s10639-022-11555-x PMID: 36643383

Wang, L., & Zhang, Y. (2023). Ethical considerations in AI-based assessment: Ensuring fairness, transparency, and data privacy. *Journal of Educational Technology & Society*, 26(2), 187–203.

Wang, W., Wang, G., Ding, X., & Zhang, B. (Eds.). (2021). *Artificial Intelligence in Education and Teaching Assessment*. Springer., DOI: 10.1007/978-981-16-6502-8

Williamson, B., Bayne, S., & Shay, S. (2020). The datafication of teaching in Higher Education: Critical issues and perspectives. *Teaching in Higher Education*, 25(4), 351–365. DOI: 10.1080/13562517.2020.1748811

Winkler, R., & Söllner, M. (2018). Unleashing the potential of chatbots in education: A state-of-the-art analysis. In *Academy of Management Annual Meeting (AOM)* (pp. 1-40). DOI: 10.5465/AMBPP.2018.15903abstract

Xia, Q., Weng, X., Ouyang, F., Lin, T. J., & Chiu, T. K. F. (2024). A scoping review on how generative artificial intelligence transforms assessment in higher education. *International Journal of Educational Technology in Higher Education*, 21(1), 40. DOI: 10.1186/s41239-024-00468-z

Yang, L., & Xin, T. (2022). Changing Educational Assessments in the Post-COVID-19 Era: From Assessment of Learning (AoL) to Assessment as Learning (AaL). *Educational Measurement: Issues and Practice*, 41(1), 54–60. DOI: 10.1111/emip.12492

Yuldashev, S., Akramov, M., Tursunova, F., Abdullaeva, K., Shakhmurodova, D., & Ubaydullayev, A. (2024). A development of AI connected system with adaptive assessments method for evaluation methods in education field. In 2024 4th International Conference on Advance Computing and Innovative Technologies in Engineering (ICACITE) (pp. 826-830). Greater Noida, India. https://doi.org/DOI: 10.1109/ICACITE60783.2024.10616960

Zawacki-Richter, O., Marín, V. I., Bond, M., & Gouverneur, F. (2019). Systematic review of research on artificial intelligence applications in higher education–where are the educators? *International Journal of Educational Technology in Higher Education*, 16(1), 39. DOI: 10.1186/s41239-019-0171-0

Zhu, X., & Evans, C. (2022). Enhancing the development and understanding of assessment literacy in higher education. *European Journal of Higher Education*, 14(1), 80–100. DOI: 10.1080/21568235.2022.2118149

Chapter 11
Navigating New Frontiers:
AI in Assessments From the Perspectives of Teachers and Students

Leesha Nicole Roberts
https://orcid.org/0000-0001-7881-0087
University of Trinidad and Tobago, Trinidad and Tobago

ABSTRACT

This chapter examines the integration of Artificial Intelligence (AI) in Caribbean educational assessments, focusing on its potential to enhance instructional quality and ethically streamline evaluations. This quantitative study used structured surveys, with reliability confirmed by Cronbach's Alpha (0.767 for students, 0.91 for teachers). The analysis revealed a significant positive correlation between teachers' belief in the need for strict ethical guidelines for AI-based assessments and their comfort with AI integration, r(104) = .42, p < .01. Teachers' willingness to adopt AI is shaped by ethical concerns, particularly the need for guidelines and collaborative decision-making. Among students, those using AI tools (M = 2.98) reported slightly higher comfort than non-users (M = 2.85). However, this difference was not statistically significant, t(59.65) = 0.53, p = .60. Privacy concerns are central to shaping student perceptions of AI in education. The chapter concludes with recommendations for ethical frameworks, teacher training, and inclusive decision-making.

DOI: 10.4018/979-8-3693-6527-4.ch011

INTRODUCTION

The global incorporation of Artificial Intelligence (AI) into educational practices is advancing rapidly, and the Caribbean region is increasingly joining this transformative movement (Judijanto et al., 2024; Nikolopoulou, 2024; Roberts et al., 2024). At the intersection of technological advancements, shifting educational demands, and persistent inequities in access to quality education, AI offers promising opportunities for enhancing both teaching and learning in the region (Limna et al., 2022). In particular, AI holds significant potential for improving instructional quality, engaging students, and refining assessment processes (Liu & Baucham, 2023). However, this technological evolution introduces complex ethical considerations that require careful examination from both pedagogical and instructional design perspectives (iu Zaman, 2024; Reiss, 2021).

In Caribbean educational systems, assessments have long been foundational to evaluating student progress and guiding instructional modifications (De Lisle, 2012). However, traditional assessment methods often fail to meet the diverse needs of 21st-century learners. AI's introduction, especially in automating grading and personalizing assessments, offers the potential to make educational practices more efficient and adaptable. AI-driven tools—such as automated grading systems and adaptive learning platforms—provide educators with data-rich insights that can optimize real-time instruction. These tools are especially valuable in resource-constrained Caribbean contexts, where large class sizes and diverse learning environments necessitate innovative solutions (Hooda et al., 2022).

For teachers, AI's introduction signifies a shift in their role from facilitators of knowledge to strategic implementers of technology (Gentile et al., 2023). They are now tasked with leveraging AI-driven insights while ensuring these tools align with their pedagogical expertise. Simultaneously, students engage with AI as both a personalized learning aid and a novel interactive element in the educational process (Shen & Su, 2020). However, these interactions raise critical ethical concerns (Han et al., 2023). The potential of AI to enhance learning outcomes must be balanced with ethical frameworks that prioritize equity, student autonomy, and the preservation of teacher-student relationships (Gentile et al., 2023).

BACKGROUND

Ethical Foundations in AI-Driven Educational Assessments

As AI becomes more deeply embedded in educational assessments, ethical concerns surrounding fairness, transparency, and accountability must be central to discussions about its use. AI-driven tools, such as Automated Essay Scoring (AES) systems and Intelligent Tutoring Systems (ITS), rely on complex algorithms to evaluate student performance (Nguyen et al., 2023). However, questions about the fairness and validity of these tools arise, particularly in Caribbean contexts where disparities in access to digital resources and educational infrastructure persist (Roberts et al., 2024). AI systems trained on biased datasets may inadvertently disadvantage students from marginalized or underserved communities, reinforcing existing inequities (Holstein & Doroudi, 2021; Lameras & Arnab, 2021).

From a teacher's perspective, ethical concerns extend beyond the technical functionality of AI systems to their broader implications on teaching and learning (Fitria, 2021; Shen et al., 2021). While AI can streamline grading and offer data-driven insights, there is a risk that it may distance educators from the more qualitative aspects of student development, such as creativity, critical thinking, and emotional intelligence (Kim et al., 2022). Educators must ensure that AI-driven assessments do not reduce students to mere data points but rather support their holistic growth. Instructional designers, in turn, must ensure that AI systems are transparent, accountable, and ethically sound, promoting equity in education rather than perpetuating existing inequalities (Han et al., 2023; Javeri & Ali, 2024; Kim et al., 2022).

Additionally, issues related to data privacy and security are of critical importance. AI-driven assessments require the collection and analysis of vast amounts of student data, raising concerns about how this data is handled. Educators and policymakers must ensure that student privacy is protected and that data is used responsibly. Instructional designers must create systems that safeguard sensitive information while allowing AI to fulfill its potential for personalizing learning.

Thus, while AI holds great promise for transforming educational assessments in the Caribbean, its integration must be guided by strong ethical frameworks that prioritize equity, transparency, and the invaluable role of human educators (Chinta et al., 2024; Ferrara, 2023; Holstein & Doroudi, 2021, 2022). Teachers and instructional designers must actively engage with these ethical considerations, ensuring that AI complements their professional expertise and fosters an inclusive and supportive learning environment.

CONCEPTUAL FRAMEWORKS

AI and Pedagogical Integration

The integration of AI into educational practices is shaped by a variety of pedagogical models, each with distinct implications for instructional design and ethical use. While global platforms like ALEKS and Knewton are mentioned in the literature (Alam, 2022; Hakkal & Lahcen, 2022), there is little evidence to suggest they are widely used in Caribbean educational institutions. Instead, AI tools such as ChatGPT, Grammarly, Turnitin, and free platforms like Google Gemini and Copilot are more commonly adopted for everyday tasks such as writing assistance, plagiarism detection, and content generation (Roberts et al., 2024). These tools, being free or low-cost, are accessible to teachers and students in resource-constrained settings.

The informal use of AI by both teachers and students underscores the need for a systematic, evidence-based approach to AI integration, especially in the context of assessments. While teachers and students already engage with AI tools to support learning, the lack of formal guidelines means that AI is often integrated without a clear understanding of its impact on learning outcomes. A structured approach to AI use in educational assessments would not only enhance the effectiveness of these tools but also ensure their alignment with pedagogical goals and educational standards. Such an approach would also support differentiated instruction, personalized learning, and formative feedback, all of which are critical for meeting the diverse needs of Caribbean learners (Miao et al., 2021; Salajan et al., 2024).

From an ethical standpoint, AI's use in Caribbean education raises key concerns, particularly around equitable access and cultural relevance. Technological resources are unevenly distributed, creating a digital divide that risks exacerbating educational inequalities (Schiff, 2022). Additionally, cultural perceptions about the role of AI vary across the region, with some educators embracing it as a valuable resource. In contrast, others harbor concerns about its potential to undermine traditional teaching practices (Ge et al., 2024). Ensuring that AI tools are transparent, unbiased, and culturally relevant is essential to maintaining the integrity of the educational process.

AI Alignment with Traditional and Innovative Teaching Methodologies

The integration of AI into educational systems has the potential to transform both traditional and innovative teaching methodologies, particularly in the area of assessments (Hooda et al., 2022). Traditional teaching methods, often centered on teacher-led instruction and standardized assessments, can benefit from AI's ability to streamline routine tasks. For example, AI-driven tools like Grammarly for writing enhancement and Turnitin for plagiarism detection allow teachers to provide more timely feedback, freeing them to focus on higher-order skills such as critical thinking and creativity. In contexts like the Caribbean, where large class sizes often limit personalized attention, AI can help bridge gaps by automating some of the more routine aspects of assessment.

In contrast, innovative teaching methodologies, which emphasize student-centered learning and collaborative problem-solving, present even greater opportunities for AI integration. AI tools such as adaptive learning platforms, personalized feedback systems, and intelligent tutoring systems are particularly well-suited to these approaches. These tools use real-time data to adjust learning paths based on individual student performance, creating more personalized and differentiated learning experiences. In assessments, AI can support formative evaluations that adapt in real-time to the learner's level, ensuring that students are assessed based on their unique learning journeys (Wang et al., 2023).

However, in both traditional and innovative contexts, successful alignment of AI with teaching methodologies requires careful attention to local needs and challenges (Kim et al., 2022). The Caribbean's digital divide, as well as cultural factors, must be addressed to ensure that AI enhances rather than disrupts the learning experience.

Theoretical Perspectives on AI in Education

Various pedagogical and cognitive theories support the integration of AI into education, each offering insights into how AI can enhance learning. Constructivist theories, for instance, emphasize active, student-centered learning environments where AI can support personalized and adaptive learning. Intelligent tutoring systems (ITS) align with constructivist principles by allowing students to engage with material at their own pace, receiving individualized feedback that promotes deeper understanding (Holstein & Aleven, 2022).

From a behaviorist perspective, AI's ability to provide immediate reinforcement and feedback aligns with the theory of operant conditioning, which reinforces learning through repetition and automated responses. AI tools like adaptive quizzes adjust question difficulty based on a student's responses, providing a tailored evaluation that reflects individual learning trajectories.

Additionally, Vygotsky's Zone of Proximal Development (ZPD) highlights the potential of AI to act as a scaffold for learners, offering targeted assistance that helps students engage with tasks just beyond their independent capabilities. AI tools that adjust content difficulty or provide real-time feedback can support learning within a student's ZPD, promoting steady academic growth (Sætra, 2022).

In the Caribbean context, AI's ability to support real-time assessments and personalized learning paths can address challenges like large class sizes and resource constraints. However, equitable access to these tools remains crucial to preventing the deepening of existing educational inequalities.

Ethical and Societal Considerations

The increasing integration of AI in Caribbean education introduces both opportunities and ethical challenges. Concerns about access, bias, data privacy, and the potential depersonalization of education must be addressed (Miao & Holmes, 2023; Miao et al., 2021; Miao & Shiohira, 2024a, 2024b; UNESCO, 2022).

Strategies for Maintaining Fairness and Accountability in AI-Driven Assessments must focus on:

1. Ensuring equitable access to AI tools by investing in digital infrastructure and providing affordable technology to under-resourced schools.
2. Developing culturally relevant AI tools that align with local linguistic and cultural contexts, ensuring assessments are fair and accurate.
3. Strengthening data privacy protections by establishing clear policies and educating educators, students, and parents on how AI systems use personal data.
4. Maintaining the human element in education ensures that teachers remain central to the learning process and that AI tools complement, rather than replace, human judgment.

By focusing on these strategies, the Caribbean education system can leverage AI to enhance fairness and accountability in assessments while fostering improved learning outcomes for all students.

Building on these insights, the integration of AI into Caribbean educational assessments requires not only a comprehensive understanding of its potential benefits but also a rigorous commitment to ethical frameworks (Miao & Holmes, 2023). While the literature emphasizes the need for equitable access, cultural relevance, and data privacy, there remains a critical gap in verifying whether policymakers are effectively implementing these principles. This study will address that gap by exploring the perspectives of both teachers and students who engage with AI in the classroom. By conducting a quantitative analysis, the research aims to assess whether current suggested frameworks within the Caribbean align with the ethical concerns raised in the literature. The following section will detail the methodology employed to examine these viewpoints, providing valuable insights into the practical application of AI ethics in Caribbean education.

METHODOLOGY

Research Design

This chapter employs a quantitative approach to explore the use of artificial intelligence (AI) in assessments at high school and college levels, focusing on the perspectives of both teachers and students. The study aimed to identify empirical, conceptual, theoretical, and ethical understandings of AI in educational assessments, with an emphasis on measurable data. It also investigated how AI can be leveraged to improve instruction, assessment, grading, and curriculum development. Additionally, the research addresses the ethical, societal, and disparate impacts of AI, providing data-driven insights to guide educators and administrators in making informed decisions. Data were collected through structured surveys, targeting both students and teachers.

The study utilized a snowballing non-probability sampling method to gather data from teachers and students across various Caribbean nations. Teachers and students from a range of subject areas in high schools and colleges participated in the study, which spanned three weeks during the September 2023 academic term. The snowballing technique's flexibility and adaptability enabled participants to assist in recruiting others. Teachers shared the student survey with their classes and the teacher survey with colleagues, while students also encouraged their peers to participate.

Data collection was conducted using Google Forms where the student survey consisted of 30 questions, while the teacher survey included 36, with both surveys addressing similar themes but tailored to each group. The surveys covered a range of topics organized around key research questions:

1. What is the relationship between teachers' perceptions of the ethical implications (e.g., bias, privacy) of AI-assisted assessments and their willingness to integrate AI into their assessment practices?
2. How do students' concerns about the societal impacts of AI (e.g., fairness, access, inclusivity) affect their overall satisfaction with AI-assisted learning and evaluation?
3. To what extent do students' experiences with AI-assisted assessments differ based on their demographic characteristics (e.g., educational level, gender) in terms of perceived fairness and learning outcomes?

These questions were designed to capture the insights of both teachers and students, focusing on AI's ethical, societal, and disparate impacts on education.

Data cleaning was conducted prior to analysis, addressing inconsistencies and missing responses. Univariate and multivariate analyses were performed using SPSS, with statistical tests employed to examine relationships between variables. The reliability of the quantitative instruments was assessed using Cronbach's alpha, which indicated internal consistencies of 0.842 for student survey questions and 0.929 for teacher questions. According to (Bonett & Wright, 2015), a Cronbach's alpha value of ≥ 0.7 is considered acceptable for ensuring internal consistency.

Data Analysis of Research Questions

Demographics

Characteristics of the Teacher Sample

102 teachers from Trinidad and Tobago, Saint Vincent and the Grenadines, the United States Virgin Islands, Sint Eustatius, Barbados, and Jamaica participated in the survey. The teacher sample consisted of individuals from various backgrounds, with the majority identifying as female (77.45%), while 22.55% identified as male. In terms of age, most participants were aged between 35-44 years (40.20%), followed by 25-34 years (21.57%), and 45-54 years (20.59%). A smaller proportion of participants were over 55 years old (16.67%), with less than 1% aged under 25.

Regarding teaching experience, a significant portion of the teachers had 11-20 years of experience (33.33%), followed closely by those with more than 20 years (30.39%). Approximately 20.59% of the participants had 1-5 years of experience, while 14.71% had 6-10 years. Only 0.98% had less than 1 year of teaching experience.

The teachers' educational qualifications were diverse, with 43.14% holding a Bachelor's degree and 42.16% holding a Master's degree. A smaller proportion had completed a Doctoral degree (9.80%), while 1.96% held a postgraduate diploma or associate degree, and 0.98% were in their final year of a Master's program.

Characteristics of the Student Sample

A total of 159 students accessed the survey, but 1 participant declined to complete it. Therefore, data was analyzed using 158 students who represented a diverse set of countries, including Trinidad and Tobago, Dominica, Saint Vincent and the

Grenadines, Saint Lucia, Jamaica, Grenada, Barbados, Antigua and Barbuda, Saint Kitts and Nevis, Cayman Islands, The Bahamas, Sint Eustatius, and Sint Maarten.

The student sample was composed predominantly of female students (86.16%), with 12.58% identifying as male and 1.26% preferring not to disclose their gender. In terms of age, the largest group of students was aged over 30 (38.36%), followed by 25-30 years (18.87%), under 18 years (16.98%), 21-24 years (14.47%), and 18-20 years (11.32%).

The educational levels of the students were diverse, with the majority being university undergraduates (64.15%). High school/secondary school students made up 24.53% of the sample, followed by university graduates (5.66%), associate degree holders (5.03%), and technical college graduates (0.63%).

In terms of AI tools used to complete assessments, Grammarly was the most commonly used tool (40.88%), followed by ChatGPT (23.27%). A notable 16.98% of students reported that they had never used AI tools for assessments. In comparison, other AI tools such as Google Bard (10.69%), BingChat (5.66%), and lesser-known tools like Snapchat AI, Citefast, and Quillbot were used by smaller percentages of students.

When asked whether they believed that AI tools make completing assessments easier, the majority of students (65.82%) responded yes, while 25.32% said maybe, and 8.86% responded no.

Research Questions

The data analysis will be presented by organizing the results according to each research question, providing clear insights into the findings.

Research Question 1: What is the relationship between teachers' perceptions of the ethical implications (e.g., bias, privacy) of AI-assisted assessments and their willingness to integrate AI into their assessment practices?

Teacher Insights on Ethical Concerns and AI Integration in Assessment Practices

A Pearson correlation analysis was conducted to investigate the relationship between teachers' ethical concerns about AI-assisted assessments and their willingness to adopt AI in their assessment practices.

The results indicated a significant positive correlation between teachers' belief that AI-based assessments require strict ethical guidelines and their comfort with AI integration, $r(104) = .42, p < .01$. Similarly, teachers who believed that schools should involve students, educators, and stakeholders in ethical decision-making were more likely to express comfort with AI integration, $r(104) = .59$, $p < .001$, and recommend AI assessments in educational settings, $r(104) = .66$, $p < .001$.

Additionally, teachers' optimism about AI in education was highly correlated with both comfort in integrating AI into assessments, $r(104) = .63$, $p < .001$, and willingness to recommend AI use, $r(104) = .76$, $p < .001$. However, concerns about discrimination in AI assessments were weakly correlated with comfort in using AI, $r(104) = .16$, $p = .10$, and recommending AI use, $r(104) = .04$, $p = .68$.

These findings suggest that teachers' willingness to integrate AI into assessments is influenced more by ethical guidelines and inclusive decision-making than by concerns about privacy or discrimination.

Ethical Concerns About AI-Assisted Assessments

An analysis of teachers' ethical concerns revealed several key issues. The strongest concern was the need for strict ethical guidelines, with 53% of teachers strongly agreeing and 24% agreeing that AI-based assessments should adhere to strict ethical standards. Only 4% disagreed with this notion.

In terms of stakeholder involvement, 53% strongly agreed, and 37% agreed that students, educators, and stakeholders should actively participate in ethical decision-making related to AI assessments, highlighting the importance of collaborative governance.

Teachers' concerns regarding privacy and data security were more mixed. A majority (53%) expressed neutrality on whether AI respects and protects students' privacy. However, 18% agreed, while another 18% disagreed, indicating some uncertainty about AI's handling of privacy.

Concerns about discrimination in AI assessments were somewhat less pronounced. While 53% of respondents were neutral, 15% agreed, and 12% strongly agreed that potential discrimination in AI assessments was a concern, reflecting a significant minority of teachers who were cautious about bias in AI systems.

Overall, teachers' strongest ethical concerns focused on the need for ethical oversight and stakeholder involvement, with moderate concerns related to privacy and discrimination.

Privacy Versus Discrimination Concerns

A comparative analysis of concerns about privacy and discrimination in AI-assisted assessments revealed distinct patterns. On privacy, 53% of respondents were neutral, while 18% agreed and 18% disagreed, indicating a more divided perspective. Conversely, concerns about discrimination were less polarized, with 53%

of respondents neutral and smaller segments expressing concern (15% agreed, 12% strongly agreed) or dismissal (13% disagreed or strongly disagreed) of potential bias.

Although both issues elicited high levels of neutral responses, privacy concerns appeared more divisive. In contrast, discrimination concerns were more skewed toward agreement, suggesting that privacy remains a more ambiguous issue, while bias is seen as a clearer ethical challenge.

The Broader Ethical Implications of AI in Educational Assessment

A majority of teachers (53% strongly agree, 24% agree) emphasized the need for strict ethical guidelines and transparency in AI-based assessments, highlighting the importance of mitigating risks like bias and misuse. Additionally, over 90% (53% strongly agree, 37% agree) supported stakeholder involvement in AI-related ethical decision-making, reflecting the value placed on inclusivity and diverse perspectives.

Concerns about fairness and discrimination were less pronounced, with 56% neutral on AI's ability to avoid discrimination and 27% expressing concern. This suggests a need for AI systems to ensure equitable assessments. Regarding assessment practices, 53% of teachers believed AI should complement, not replace, human judgment, emphasizing the importance of maintaining educational integrity.

Teachers' views on privacy and data security were divided, with 18% agreeing and 18% disagreeing on AI's ability to protect students' privacy, indicating mixed awareness of AI's data management practices.

Kruskal-Wallis tests showed no significant differences based on privacy $H(2) = 0.90, p = .64$ or discrimination concerns $H(2) = 1.30, p = .52$, though belief in strict ethical guidelines approached significance $H(2) = 5.02, p = .08$. Pearson correlation revealed a strong positive relationship between optimism about AI and willingness to integrate it $r(104) = .76, p < .001$, but weak correlations with ethical concerns like privacy $r(104) = .16$ and discrimination $r(104) = .05$. Demographic factors like age and teaching experience showed negligible correlations with optimism or willingness to adopt AI.

Exploratory analyses of demographic factors, including age, teaching experience, and gender, revealed weak or negligible correlations with optimism and willingness to adopt AI, indicating that these factors had minimal impact on teachers' attitudes toward AI integration.

The findings suggest that teachers' willingness to integrate AI into assessments is shaped by their ethical concerns, particularly the need for ethical guidelines and collaborative decision-making. However, demographic factors and specific concerns about privacy or discrimination appear to have limited influence on their overall openness to adopting AI-based assessments.

Research Question 2: How do students' concerns about the societal impacts of AI (e.g., fairness, access, inclusivity) affect their overall satisfaction with AI-assisted learning and evaluation?

Societal Concerns and Satisfaction with AI-Assisted Learning

To investigate how students' concerns about the societal impacts of AI, such as fairness, access, and inclusivity, affect their overall satisfaction with AI-assisted learning and evaluation, a series of analyses were conducted.

A correlation analysis was conducted to explore the relationship between students' concerns about the societal impacts of AI and their satisfaction with AI-assisted learning. The results indicated a weak negative correlation between concerns about discrimination and overall satisfaction (r = -0.04), suggesting that issues related to fairness and inclusivity had minimal influence on students' perceptions of AI assessments. However, a positive correlation emerged between concerns about privacy and satisfaction (r = 0.29), highlighting the significance of privacy in shaping students' satisfaction.

Further analysis revealed a moderate positive correlation between students' perceptions of AI fairness and their belief that AI assessments accurately reflect their abilities (r = 0.39) and improve educational quality (r = 0.45).

These findings underscore that while fairness plays a crucial role in influencing overall satisfaction, students' concerns about privacy have a more pronounced impact on their acceptance of AI in education.

Satisfaction by Age and Gender

An analysis of satisfaction by age, gender, and educational background revealed notable differences in students' perceptions of AI-assisted learning. Female students aged 21-24 expressed the highest belief in AI accuracy (M = 3.30), while male students under 18 and aged 18-20 reported lower satisfaction with AI's ability to reflect their abilities (M = 3.09 and M = 2.50, respectively). Comfort levels also varied, with male students aged 21-24 and under 18 showing higher comfort (M = 4.67 and M = 4.27), while those aged 18-20 reported the lowest (M = 1.50).

Students with a Technical College background reported the highest belief in AI accuracy (M = 5.00), while University Graduates were the most skeptical (M = 2.11). Similarly, Technical College Graduates had the highest comfort levels (M = 5.00), while University Graduates were the least comfortable (M = 2.78). Regarding AI's potential to improve education, Technical College Graduates expressed strong agreement (M = 4.00), while University Graduates were more reserved (M = 2.89).

The data suggests that students' satisfaction with AI-assisted learning varies by demographic group, with Technical College Graduates showing the highest satisfaction and University Graduates having the most skepticism. Concerns about fairness and privacy moderately influence overall satisfaction.

Comparison of Students Who Use AI for Assessments and Those Who Do Not

The demographic comparison in Table 1 reveals significant patterns in AI tool usage for assessments. Among AI tool users, older students, particularly those over 30, were more prevalent, with 32 students using AI compared to only 8 non-users in this age group. Female university undergraduates also showed higher AI tool usage, with 32 users versus 8 non-users. In contrast, younger students, especially those under 18, were more evenly distributed, with 9 female high school students using AI tools and 6 not using them. Male students showed a similar balance, with 6 users and 5 non-users under 18. This suggests AI tool use is more common among older students, especially women in higher education.

Table 1. Demographic comparison of students who used AI tools and those who never used AI tools for assessments

Age	Gender	Educational Level	Used AI Tools (N)	Never Used AI Tools (N)
Over 30	Female	University Undergraduate	32	8
25-30	Female	University Undergraduate	20	2
21-24	Female	University Undergraduate	15	1
18-20	Female	University Undergraduate	14	1
Under 18	Female	High School/Secondary School	9	6
Over 30	Female	University Graduate	7	0
Under 18	Male	High School/Secondary School	6	5
Over 30	Female	Associate Degree	5	1
21-24	Female	High School/Secondary School	3	0
21-24	Male	University Undergraduate	3	0
Over 30	Female	High School/Secondary School	3	2
25-30	Female	Associate Degree	2	0

continued on following page

Table 1. Continued

Age	Gender	Educational Level	Used AI Tools (N)	Never Used AI Tools (N)
25-30	Female	High School/Secondary School	2	0
25-30	Male	University Undergraduate	2	1
Over 30	Prefer not to say	University Undergraduate	1	0
Over 30	Male	University Undergraduate	1	0
18-20	Female	High School/Secondary School	1	0
Over 30	Female	Technical College Graduate	1	0
25-30	Female	University Graduate	1	0
21-24	Female	University Graduate	1	0
18-20	Male	University Undergraduate	1	0
18-20	Male	High School/Secondary School	1	0
Under 18	Prefer not to say	High School/Secondary School	1	0

Among AI users, satisfaction levels ranged from neutral to slightly positive. Students rated their belief that AI accurately reflects their abilities at 3.03 (on a 5-point Likert scale), their comfort with AI systems at 2.96 (neutral), and their belief that AI improves the quality of education at 3.55 (agree). These findings suggest that while AI usage does not lead to overwhelming satisfaction, students generally view AI-assisted learning favorably.

Satisfaction Comparison Between AI Tool Users and Non-Users

An independent samples t-test was conducted to examine satisfaction levels between students who used AI tools and those who did not in their assessments. Satisfaction was assessed using three items: comfort with AI systems, perceptions of AI feedback timeliness, and beliefs about AI's potential to improve education quality.

For comfort with AI systems, students who used AI tools ($M = 2.98$, $SD = 1.11$) reported slightly higher comfort than non-users ($M = 2.85$, $SD = 1.13$), but the difference was not statistically significant, $t(59.65) = 0.53$, $p = .60$, with a small effect size ($d = 0.11$).

In terms of feedback timeliness, no significant difference was found between AI tool users (M = 3.17, SD = 1.14) and non-users (M = 3.56, SD = 1.28), t(64.18) = −1.43, p = .16, with a small effect size (d = −0.33). This suggests that both groups held similar views on AI's ability to provide timely feedback.

Regarding AI's potential to improve education quality, no significant difference was observed between AI tool users (M = 3.53, SD = 1.07) and non-users (M = 3.67, SD = 1.36), t(54.92) = −0.49, p = .63, with a negligible effect size (d = −0.12). These results indicate no statistically significant differences in satisfaction between AI tool users and non-users across all three measures, with small effect sizes suggesting minimal impact.

The analysis reveals that students' concerns about societal impacts, such as fairness and inclusivity, have minimal influence on their satisfaction with AI-assisted learning, while privacy concerns play a more significant role. Demographically, Technical College graduates reported the highest satisfaction and belief in AI's educational potential, while University Graduate students were more skeptical. Comparisons between AI tool users and non-users showed no significant differences in satisfaction, indicating that AI usage is generally viewed neutrally to slightly positively. Overall, concerns about privacy and fairness are the primary factors shaping student perceptions of AI in education.

Research Question 3: To what extent do students' experiences with AI-assisted assessments differ based on their demographic characteristics (e.g., educational level, gender) in terms of perceived fairness and learning outcomes?

Gender Differences in Satisfaction with AI-Assisted Learning

To examine gender differences in satisfaction with AI-assisted learning, independent t-tests and Mann-Whitney U tests were conducted on four satisfaction variables: belief in AI's accuracy, comfort with AI systems, timeliness of feedback, and belief in AI's potential to improve education. No significant gender differences were found in belief in AI's accuracy t(158) = 0.49, p = .63, comfort with AI systems t(158) = 0.54, p = .59, or the timeliness of AI feedback t(158) = 0.60, p = .55. While the potential for AI to improve education approached significance t(158) = 1.86, p = .064, it did not reach statistical significance.

Mann-Whitney U tests were also conducted to account for possible non-normality in the data. These tests similarly indicated no significant gender differences in belief in AI accuracy (U = 1485.5, p = .52), comfort with AI systems (U = 1462.0, p = .61), or the timeliness of AI feedback (U = 1476.5, p = .56). However, a significant gender difference was observed regarding AI's potential to improve education, with male students (Mdn = 4.0) reporting stronger agreement than female students (Mdn = 3.5), (U = 1738.5, p = .045. These findings suggest that while gender does not significantly influence most aspects of satisfaction with AI-assisted learning, male students are more likely than female students to perceive AI as a tool for enhancing educational quality.

Satisfaction with AI-Assisted Learning Across Age Groups

Satisfaction with AI-assisted learning was analyzed across five age groups: under 18, 18-20, 21-24, 25-30, and over 30. The results revealed significant age-related differences in students' perceptions of AI. Students aged 21-24 reported the highest belief in AI's accuracy (M = 3.30), while those over 30 expressed the lowest confidence (M = 2.84). Comfort with AI systems was highest among students aged 25-30 (M = 3.23) and lowest for those over 30 (M = 2.79). Students aged 21-24 and under 18 shared the strongest belief in AI's timeliness (M = 3.48), while students over 30 were least likely to agree (M = 3.03).

Belief in AI's potential to improve education also varied by age. Students aged 21-24 showed the strongest belief (M = 4.17), followed by those aged 25-30 (M = 3.57) and under 18 (M = 3.74), with students over 30 being the least optimistic (M = 3.26). A Kruskal-Wallis test confirmed significant differences in this belief across age groups (H = 11.52, p = .02). However, no significant differences were found for AI accuracy (H = 3.66, p = .45), comfort (H = 2.91, p = .57), or timeliness of feedback (H = 4.81, p = .31). These findings suggest age-related variations in perceptions of AI's educational benefits, while other satisfaction measures remain consistent across age groups.

Demographic Differences in Perceived Fairness and Learning Outcomes

In examining demographic differences in students' perceptions of AI-assisted assessments, both gender and educational level were considered. Regarding perceived fairness, as measured by belief in AI's accuracy, no significant gender differences were observed. Both independent t-tests (t(158) = 0.49, p = .63) and Mann-Whitney U tests (U = 1485.5, p = .52) indicated that male and female students hold similar views on the fairness of AI-driven assessments. However, a gender difference was observed in perceptions of AI's potential to improve learning outcomes. While the t-test approached significance (t(158) = 1.86, p = .064), the Mann-Whitney U test revealed that male students reported significantly more favorable views on AI's educational potential than female students (U = 1738.5, p = .045).

Educational level significantly influenced students' perceptions of AI fairness, with a Kruskal-Wallis test revealing differences in perceived fairness H(4) = 9.76, p = .045 across educational backgrounds. However, perceived learning outcomes showed no statistically significant differences, though the result approached significance $H(4) = 7.92$, $p = .095$. These findings suggest that educational background plays a larger role than gender in shaping views on AI fairness, while gender has a more pronounced effect on perceptions of AI's potential to enhance learning outcomes.

The Influence of Educational Level and Age on Learning Outcomes

To further explore the role of demographic factors, an analysis of covariance (ANCOVA) was conducted to examine whether students' perceptions of AI-assisted assessments' ability to improve educational outcomes varied by educational level while controlling for age. The results indicated that both educational level and age significantly influenced students' perceptions. A significant effect of educational level on students' belief in AI's potential to improve education was found $F(4, 150) = 2.71$, $p = .032$, suggesting that students from different educational backgrounds hold distinct views about the educational benefits of AI-assisted assessments. Age also had a significant effect on perceived learning outcomes $F(4, 150) = 3.90$, $p = .005$, indicating that students' perceptions of AI's potential to improve education are influenced by their age, with younger students generally expressing more optimism about AI's role in education.

These findings highlight the significance of educational level and age in shaping students' perceptions of AI-assisted assessments, particularly regarding fairness and educational improvement. While gender has a limited impact on satisfaction, educational background and age should be carefully considered when designing and implementing AI-based assessments.

DISCUSSION OF RESULTS

Implications for AI in Assessments from a Caribbean Perspective

The findings from this study provide valuable insights into how students' and teachers' perceptions of AI-assisted assessments vary by demographic characteristics, including gender, age, and educational level, and how these perceptions influence satisfaction, perceived fairness, and learning outcomes. These results offer a window into the challenges and opportunities for integrating AI into assessments in the Caribbean context, particularly as education systems align with 21st-century learning objectives, instructional design methodologies, and global policy frameworks (Miao & Holmes, 2023; Miao & Shiohira, 2024a, 2024b).

Understanding AI in the Context of 21st-Century Learning and Instructional Design

AI-assisted assessments have the potential to transform education in the Caribbean by aligning with the key pillars of 21st-century learning, which emphasize personalized learning, critical thinking, and the integration of technology into everyday educational practices (Ng et al., 2023). However, the findings indicate that students and teachers alike remain cautious about fully embracing AI as a central tool for evaluation (Nguyen et al., 2023).

Students' concerns about fairness, privacy, and inclusivity reflect broader apprehensions about the role of AI in creating equitable learning environments (Han et al., 2023). For instance, the significant differences in perceptions of AI's potential to improve education across demographic lines—particularly gender and educational level—highlight the need for AI to be sensitive to diverse student populations. The more favorable views of AI's educational potential held by younger students and male students suggest that instructional design methodologies must take these differences into account (Baek et al., 2024). AI-driven assessments should be integrated in ways that not only cater to tech-savvy students but also address the reservations of those who are less optimistic about AI, such as female students and those with more advanced educational backgrounds (Baek et al., 2024; Cherrez-Ojeda et al., 2024; Nouraldeen, 2023).

From an instructional design perspective, these results call for the development of AI tools that support adaptive learning pathways, provide timely feedback, and ensure that students feel confident in AI's ability to reflect their abilities accurately. This aligns with the principles of Universal Design for Learning (UDL), which advocates for flexible learning environments that accommodate individual learning differences (Ouyang & Jiao, 2021). In the Caribbean, where classrooms are often diverse in terms of learning needs and access to resources, AI could play a vital role in fostering more personalized educational experiences. However, achieving this requires addressing concerns about fairness and inclusivity, as students are likely to fully engage with AI tools if they believe that these systems evaluate them equitably.

Ethical Considerations and Global Policy Alignment

The ethical implications of AI in education are another significant theme that emerged from the analysis. Teachers, in particular, expressed concerns about the need for strict ethical guidelines and stakeholder involvement in AI decision-making processes. This highlights a critical issue for Caribbean educational institutions, where technology adoption must be accompanied by a robust ethical framework that prioritizes transparency, fairness, and accountability. Ethical concerns, such as the potential for AI systems to perpetuate biases or misuse student data, should be addressed, especially in a region where educational equity remains a central policy goal.

In line with global policy discussions, such as the UNESCO guidelines for AI in education, the Caribbean's approach to AI-assisted assessments should involve stakeholders at all levels—including teachers, students, parents, and policymakers—in shaping the ethical standards that govern AI's use in classrooms (Miao & Holmes, 2023; Miao et al., 2021). By doing so, the region can ensure that AI tools are developed and deployed in ways that align with broader societal values, such as fairness, inclusivity, and respect for privacy (Miao & Shiohira, 2024a, 2024b).

The finding that male students expressed a stronger belief in AI's potential to improve education compared to female students highlights the importance of addressing gender-based disparities in AI perceptions. Global policy frameworks, such as those outlined in the Sustainable Development Goals (SDG 4 on Quality Education), stress the need for gender equity in education, and this includes ensuring that both male and female students feel equally empowered by the technologies used in their learning environments. To align with these global initiatives, AI tools must be designed and implemented in ways that address gender-based differences in technology adoption and use.

Implications for Caribbean Educational Practices and Assessment Design

The results also suggest a need to rethink traditional assessment models in the Caribbean and incorporate AI in ways that complement rather than replace human judgment. Teachers' comfort with AI and their belief in its potential to improve education is closely tied to the presence of clear ethical guidelines and inclusive decision-making processes. For AI-assisted assessments to be successful in the Caribbean, educational institutions must ensure that these systems operate transparently and accountably, providing teachers with the tools and training needed to use AI effectively.

Moreover, students' mixed perceptions of AI's accuracy and its ability to provide timely feedback suggest that AI tools should be integrated into a broader assessment ecosystem that includes both traditional and technology-based methods. This hybrid approach would allow teachers to maintain the human element in assessment, which is particularly important in Caribbean educational cultures that value interpersonal relationships between teachers and students. AI can augment these assessments by offering data-driven insights, but it should not replace the role of teachers in interpreting student performance holistically.

Moving Forward: Balancing Innovation with Inclusivity and Fairness

Ultimately, the integration of AI in assessments in the Caribbean must balance innovation with a commitment to inclusivity and fairness. As the region continues to align its educational practices with 21st-century learning goals, AI can offer transformative potential, particularly in personalizing learning and providing real-time feedback (Kim et al., 2022). However, this potential will only be fully realized if AI tools are designed with ethical considerations at the forefront and if they are used in ways that reflect the diverse needs and concerns of students and teachers.

To ensure that AI supports rather than hinders educational equity, Caribbean policymakers and educators must engage in continuous dialogue about how AI aligns with regional educational goals and global standards. By doing so, the Caribbean can position itself as a leader in the responsible and ethical use of AI in education, contributing to a future where technology enhances, rather than disrupts, the learning process for all students.

In summary, the results of this study suggest that while AI holds promise for transforming assessments in the Caribbean, its success depends on addressing concerns about fairness, inclusivity, and ethical oversight. Educational practices must evolve to incorporate AI in ways that respect the unique cultural and demographic contexts of Caribbean classrooms, ensuring that technology supports the region's broader goals of equity and access to quality education.

Practical Strategies and Classroom Applications

In practical terms, AI's integration into educational assessments offers a range of tools and platforms that can enhance teaching and learning in both high school and college settings. Several AI-powered tools have demonstrated effectiveness in automating assessments, providing real-time feedback, and supporting personalized learning.

One such tool is Gradescope, a platform that automates the grading process for assignments, quizzes, and exams. Gradescope utilizes machine learning algorithms to recognize patterns in student responses and grade work according to pre-established rubrics. This system is particularly useful for large classes, where manual grading can be time-consuming and inconsistent (Türker & Kahraman, 2024). For Caribbean educators, who often manage large student populations, Gradescope can significantly reduce the burden of grading, allowing teachers to allocate more time to instructional activities.

Another tool, Turnitin, has long been used for plagiarism detection, but its AI-powered capabilities extend beyond mere content matching. Turnitin now offers AI-based feedback on student writing, providing insights into grammar, style, and argumentation (Wulandari et al., 2024). This feedback allows students to revise their work before submission, fostering a deeper understanding of academic writing conventions. In the Caribbean, where academic writing is a core component of secondary and tertiary education, Turnitin can help uphold academic integrity while also improving the quality of student writing.

Intelligent Tutoring Systems (ITS), such as DreamBox and Knewton, offer personalized learning experiences by adapting instructional content based on student performance (Molina et al., 2024). These systems provide continuous formative assessments that guide students through learning challenges and offer real-time feedback (Molina et al., 2024). For example, DreamBox, which focuses on mathematics instruction, adjusts the difficulty of problems based on the student's responses, ensuring that each learner is working at an appropriate level. In Caribbean classrooms, ITS can help to address the diverse learning needs of students, particularly in STEM subjects, where individualized instruction is often key to mastery.

CASE STUDIES OF SUCCESSFUL IMPLEMENTATION AND CHALLENGES

Case Study 1: Integration of ChatGPT in Faculty Workflows at a Caribbean Medical School

Cross et al. (2023) in a case study at the American University of Antigua, assessed the integration of ChatGPT into faculty workflows. Approximately 33% of faculty utilized ChatGPT, primarily for generating multiple-choice questions and clinical vignettes. Younger faculty members reported higher usage, valuing its ease and efficiency. However, concerns emerged around misinformation and potential plagiarism, raising ethical questions about the tool's accuracy and reliability. Despite these challenges, faculty generally supported its adoption, suggesting that ChatGPT holds promise for reshaping education at various levels.

Case Study 2: AI in a Caribbean High School for Writing Assessment

Coskun and Alper (2024) in their study, evaluated the effectiveness of AI-based assessment tools, specifically ChatGPT and its plugins, in grading exams comprising various question formats. The study found that ChatGPT performed well in assessing multiple-choice questions, offering consistency and efficiency compared to traditional teacher evaluations. However, significant challenges emerged in more complex assessments, such as video and visually-based exams, where AI struggled to replicate the nuanced judgment of human evaluators. The study highlights both the successes and limitations of using AI in education, demonstrating ChatGPT's potential to complement traditional methods while emphasizing the need for careful oversight in subjective assessments.

AI tools such as ChatGPT have demonstrated their effectiveness in classroom assessments, offering valuable insights and time-saving solutions for educators. However, as the case studies show, successful implementation requires thoughtful planning, professional development for teachers, and a clear understanding of AI's limitations. AI should complement, not replace, human judgment in educational assessments. Moving forward, schools and educators must find the balance between leveraging AI's potential and maintaining the critical role of teacher-led evaluation.

GUIDANCE FOR EDUCATORS AND ADMINISTRATORS

For educators and administrators considering the adoption of AI in educational assessments, a structured decision-making framework is essential for evaluating and selecting the most appropriate tools. This framework should consider several key factors, including the specific educational challenges that AI can address, the ethical implications of AI use, and the alignment of AI tools with broader pedagogical goals.

The first step in this decision-making process is to conduct a thorough needs assessment. This involves identifying the particular areas where AI can offer the most significant benefits, whether in reducing the time required for grading, improving the personalization of learning, or enhancing formative assessment practices. For instance, if the primary goal is to alleviate the administrative burden of grading large classes, automated grading systems such as Gradescope may be the most appropriate choice. Conversely, if the objective is to provide individualized learning experiences, adaptive assessment platforms like Knewton should be prioritized.

Equally important is the evaluation of the ethical considerations surrounding AI tools. Administrators must ensure that the AI tools they select do not introduce or exacerbate bias and that they comply with relevant data protection regulations. This can be achieved by reviewing the datasets used to train the AI systems, ensuring that these datasets are representative and that the tools have been rigorously tested for fairness. Given the socio-economic and cultural diversity of the Caribbean, it is particularly important that AI tools are tailored to the specific needs of the region's student populations.

Training and professional development for educators are critical for the successful integration of AI into the classroom. Teachers must be equipped with the skills and knowledge necessary to use AI tools effectively, including understanding how AI-generated data can be interpreted and how AI tools can be integrated into their instructional practices. In the Caribbean, where access to professional development opportunities may be limited, educational institutions must prioritize investment in teacher training and ongoing support to ensure that AI tools are used effectively.

Policy and curriculum adjustments are also necessary to support the ethical and responsible use of AI in education (Miao et al., 2021). Educational institutions should develop clear policies outlining how AI tools should be used, including guidelines on data management, teacher training, and student engagement with AI technologies (Miao & Shiohira, 2024a, 2024b). Moreover, the curriculum should include AI literacy components to ensure that students and teachers alike understand the potential and limitations of AI in education (Ouyang & Jiao, 2021). By fostering a critical understanding of AI, educational institutions can empower students and teachers to use these tools more effectively and responsibly.

Collaboration with external stakeholders is also key to the successful implementation of AI in education. Educational institutions should work closely with technology companies, government agencies, and non-profit organizations to ensure that AI tools are accessible, affordable, and aligned with the educational goals of the region. In the Caribbean, where resources are often constrained, partnerships with external stakeholders can help bridge gaps in funding and technical expertise, ensuring that AI tools are implemented in ways that promote educational equity and inclusivity.

CONCLUSION

This study has provided critical insights into the integration of AI in educational assessments within the Caribbean, highlighting both empirical and theoretical perspectives. In alignment with broader findings in the literature on AI in education (Türker & Kahraman, 2024), the research emphasizes that ethical concerns—particularly around bias, privacy, and fairness—play a crucial role in shaping both teachers' and students' acceptance of AI-driven assessments. These concerns reflect the global discourse on the need for transparent, accountable AI systems that ensure equity in educational evaluation (UNESCO, 2022).

The study also revealed demographic disparities in perceptions of AI, with significant differences in satisfaction, perceived fairness, and learning outcomes based on gender, age, and educational level. This finding supports existing research that points to diverse user experiences and attitudes toward AI, particularly in terms of technology adoption and trust (Nouraldeen, 2023). As the literature suggests, younger students and those more familiar with technology often show greater optimism toward AI. At the same time, older and more experienced individuals may express skepticism, particularly around issues of fairness and bias (Yilmaz et al., 2023).

In terms of practical implications, the study confirms that AI's potential to transform assessment practices is contingent on the ethical design and implementation of these technologies. Similar to what is documented in other educational contexts (Roshanaei, 2024; Salajan et al., 2024; Schiff, 2022), teachers and administrators in the Caribbean must prioritize the development of ethical guidelines and involve all stakeholders in decision-making processes to ensure that AI is used responsibly. Furthermore, the need for AI systems to be adaptable and sensitive to diverse learner needs is a recurring theme in the literature (Miao & Shiohira, 2024a; Ng et al., 2023; Nguyen et al., 2023), and this study reinforces that call by demonstrating the importance of inclusivity in AI deployment.

As Caribbean education systems strive to align with 21st-century learning objectives and global policy frameworks, this research underscores the potential for AI to enhance instruction, improve grading accuracy, and support curriculum development. However, like much of the literature on AI in education cautions (Chinta et al., 2024; Miao & Holmes, 2023; Ouyang & Jiao, 2021; Türker & Kahraman, 2024), this potential can only be fully realized if ethical considerations—particularly those related to fairness, access, and inclusivity—are addressed. By adhering to these principles, educators in the Caribbean can leverage AI not only to improve assessment practices but also to ensure that these advancements contribute to a more equitable and inclusive educational landscape.

REFERENCES

Alam, A. (2022). Employing adaptive learning and intelligent tutoring robots for virtual classrooms and smart campuses: Reforming education in the age of artificial intelligence. In *Advanced computing and intelligent technologies* [Springer.]. *Proceedings of ICACIT*, 2022, 395–406.

Baek, C., Tate, T., & Warschauer, M. (2024). "ChatGPT Seems Too Good to be True": College Students' Use and Perceptions of Generative AI. *Computers and Education: Artificial Intelligence*, 100294. https://doi.org/https://doi.org/10.1016/j.caeai.2024.100294

Bonett, D. G., & Wright, T. A. (2015). Cronbach's alpha reliability: Interval estimation, hypothesis testing, and sample size planning. *Journal of Organizational Behavior*, 36(1), 3–15. DOI: 10.1002/job.1960

Cherrez-Ojeda, I., Gallardo-Bastidas, J. C., Robles-Velasco, K., Osorio, M. F., Velez Leon, E. M., Leon Velastegui, M., Pauletto, P., Aguilar-Díaz, F. C., Squassi, A., González Eras, S. P., Cordero Carrasco, E., Chavez Gonzalez, K. L., Calderon, J. C., Bousquet, J., Bedbrook, A., & Faytong-Haro, M. (2024). Understanding Health Care Students' Perceptions, Beliefs, and Attitudes Toward AI-Powered Language Models: Cross-Sectional Study. *JMIR Medical Education*, 10, e51757. DOI: 10.2196/51757 PMID: 39137029

Chinta, S. V., Wang, Z., Yin, Z., Hoang, N., Gonzalez, M., Quy, T. L., & Zhang, W. (2024). FairAIED: Navigating Fairness, Bias, and Ethics in Educational AI Applications. *arXiv preprint arXiv:2407.18745.*

Coskun, T. K., & Alper, A. (2024). Evaluating the evaluators: A comparative study of AI and teacher assessments in Higher Education. *Digital Education Review*(45), 124-140. https://dialnet.unirioja.es/servlet/articulo?codigo=9624307

Cross, J., Robinson, R., Devaraju, S., Vaughans, A., Hood, R., Kayalackakom, T., Honnavar, P., Naik, S., & Sebastian, R. (2023). Transforming medical education: Assessing the integration of ChatGPT into faculty workflows at a Caribbean medical school. *Cureus*, 15(7). Advance online publication. DOI: 10.7759/cureus.41399 PMID: 37426402

De Lisle, J. (2012). Secondary school entrance examinations in the Caribbean: Legacy, policy, and evidence within an era of seamless education. *Caribbean Curriculum*, 19, 109–143.

Ferrara, E. (2023). Fairness and bias in artificial intelligence: A brief survey of sources, impacts, and mitigation strategies. *Sci*, 6(1), 3. DOI: 10.3390/sci6010003

Fitria, T. N. (2021). Artificial intelligence (AI) in education: Using AI tools for teaching and learning process. Prosiding Seminar Nasional & Call for Paper STIE AAS, Ge, X., Xu, C., Misaki, D., Markus, H. R., & Tsai, J. L. (2024). How Culture Shapes What People Want From AI. Proceedings of the CHI Conference on Human Factors in Computing Systems, Gentile, M., Città, G., Perna, S., & Allegra, M. (2023). Do we still need teachers? Navigating the paradigm shift of the teacher's role in the AI era. Frontiers in Education, Hakkal, S., & Lahcen, A. A. (2022). An Overview of Adaptive Learning Fee-based Platforms.

Han, B., Nawaz, S., Buchanan, G., & McKay, D. (2023). Ethical and pedagogical impacts of AI in education. International Conference on Artificial Intelligence in Education, Holstein, K., & Aleven, V. (2022). Designing for human–AI complementarity in K-12 education. *AI Magazine*, 43(2), 239–248.

Holstein, K., & Doroudi, S. (2021). Equity and artificial intelligence in education: will" aied" amplify or alleviate inequities in education? *arXiv preprint arXiv:2104.12920.*

Holstein, K., & Doroudi, S. (2022). Equity and artificial intelligence in education. In *The ethics of artificial intelligence in education* (pp. 151–173). Routledge. DOI: 10.4324/9780429329067-9

Hooda, M., Rana, C., Dahiya, O., Rizwan, A., & Hossain, M. S. (2022). Artificial intelligence for assessment and feedback to enhance student success in higher education. *Mathematical Problems in Engineering*, 2022(1), 5215722. DOI: 10.1155/2022/5215722

iu Zaman, B. U. (2024). Transforming education through AI benefits risks and ethical considerations. DOI: 10.1155/2022/5215722

Javeri, M., & Ali, Z. (2024). Design Thinking as an Instructional Design Approach to Artificial Intelligence (AI) Course Development. EdMedia+ Innovate Learning, DOI: 10.1155/2022/5215722

Judijanto, L., Atsani, M. R., & Chadijah, S. (2024). Trends In The Development Of Artificial Intelligence-Based Technology In Education. *International Journal of Teaching and Learning*, 2(6), 1722–1723.

Kim, J., Lee, H., & Cho, Y. H. (2022). Learning design to support student-AI collaboration: Perspectives of leading teachers for AI in education. *Education and Information Technologies*, 27(5), 6069–6104. DOI: 10.1007/s10639-021-10831-6

Lameras, P., & Arnab, S. (2021). Power to the teachers: An exploratory review on artificial intelligence in education. *Information (Basel)*, 13(1), 14. DOI: 10.3390/info13010014

Limna, P., Jakwatanatham, S., Siripipattanakul, S., Kaewpuang, P., & Sriboonruang, P. (2022). A review of artificial intelligence (AI) in education during the digital era. *Advance Knowledge for Executives*, 1(1), 1–9.

Liu, Y., & Baucham, M. (2023). AI Technology: Key to successful assessment. In *Handbook of Research on Redesigning Teaching, Learning, and Assessment in the Digital Era* (pp. 304-325). IGI Global.

Miao, F., & Holmes, W. (2023). *Guidance for generative AI in education and research*. UNESCO. https://doi.org/https://doi.org/10.54675/EWZM9535

Miao, F., Holmes, W., Huang, R., & Zhang, H. (2021). *AI and education: A guidance for policymakers*. Unesco Publishing.

Miao, F., & Shiohira, K. (2024a). *AI competency framework for students* (UNESCO, Ed.). UNESCO. https://doi.org/https://doi.org/10.54675/JKJB9835

Miao, F., & Shiohira, K. (2024b). *AI competency framework for Teachers* (UNESCO, Ed.). UNESCO. https://doi.org/https://doi.org/10.54675/ZJTE2084

Molina, E., Cobo, C., Pineda, J., & Rovner, H. (2024). *AI revolution in education: what you need to know* (Digital Innovations in Education, Issue 1). W. Bank. https://documents1.worldbank.org/curated/en/099734306182493324/pdf/IDU152823b13109c514ebd19c241a289470b6902.pdf

Ng, D. T. K., Leung, J. K. L., Su, J., Ng, R. C. W., & Chu, S. K. W. (2023). Teachers' AI digital competencies and twenty-first century skills in the post-pandemic world. *Educational Technology Research and Development*, 71(1), 137–161. DOI: 10.1007/s11423-023-10203-6 PMID: 36844361

Nguyen, A., Ngo, H. N., Hong, Y., Dang, B., & Nguyen, B.-P. T. (2023). Ethical principles for artificial intelligence in education. *Education and Information Technologies*, 28(4), 4221–4241. DOI: 10.1007/s10639-022-11316-w PMID: 36254344

Nikolopoulou, K. (2024). Generative Artificial Intelligence in Higher Education: Exploring ways of harnessing pedagogical Practices with the assistance of ChatGPT. *International Journal of Changes in Education*, 1(2), 103–111. DOI: 10.47852/bonviewIJCE42022489

Nouraldeen, R. M. (2023). The impact of technology readiness and use perceptions on students' adoption of artificial intelligence: The moderating role of gender. *Development and Learning in Organizations*, 37(3), 7–10. DOI: 10.1108/DLO-07-2022-0133

Ouyang, F., & Jiao, P. (2021). Artificial intelligence in education: The three paradigms. *Computers and Education: Artificial Intelligence, 2*, 100020. https://doi.org/https://doi.org/10.1016/j.caeai.2021.100020

Reiss, M. J. (2021). The Use of Al in Education: Practicalities and Ethical Considerations. *London Review of Education*, 19(1), n1. DOI: 10.14324/LRE.19.1.05

Roberts, L. N., Solomon, F. N., & Cummings, R. (2024). Navigating the AI Landscape: Student and Teacher Perceptions of AI in Assessments in High School and College Settings. In *AI-Enhanced Teaching Methods* (pp. 268-285). IGI Global.

Roshanaei, M. (2024). Towards best practices for mitigating artificial intelligence implicit bias in shaping diversity, inclusion and equity in higher education. *Education and Information Technologies*, 29(14), 1–26. DOI: 10.1007/s10639-024-12605-2

Sætra, H. S. (2022). Scaffolding human champions: AI as a more competent other. *Human Arenas*, 1-23. DOI: 10.1007/s10639-024-12605-2

Salajan, F. D., Barnes, T. L., & Becker, A. (2024). Comparative regionalism cases of artificial intelligence governance in education: The Caribbean Community and the European Union. *The Round Table*, 113(1), 71–85. DOI: 10.1080/00358533.2024.2307793

Schiff, D. (2022). Education for AI, not AI for education: The role of education and ethics in national AI policy strategies. *International Journal of Artificial Intelligence in Education*, 32(3), 527–563. DOI: 10.1007/s40593-021-00270-2

Shen, L., Chen, I., Grey, A., & Su, A. (2021). Teaching and learning with artificial intelligence. In *Impact of AI technologies on teaching, learning, and research in higher education* (pp. 73–98). IGI Global. DOI: 10.4018/978-1-7998-4763-2.ch005

Shen, L., & Su, A. (2020). The changing roles of teachers with AI. In *Revolutionizing education in the age of AI and machine learning* (pp. 1–25). IGI Global. DOI: 10.4018/978-1-5225-7793-5.ch001

Türker, O., & Kahraman, A. D. (2024). Artificial Intelligence Software in the Context of Educational Process. *The Turkish Online Journal of Educational Technology*, 23(1), 16–23.

UNESCO. (2022). *Recommendation on the Ethics of Artificial Intelligence* (UNESCO, Ed.). UNESCO.

Wang, T., Lund, B. D., Marengo, A., Pagano, A., Mannuru, N. R., Teel, Z. A., & Pange, J. (2023). Exploring the potential impact of artificial intelligence (AI) on international students in higher education: Generative AI, chatbots, analytics, and international student success. *Applied Sciences (Basel, Switzerland)*, 13(11), 6716. DOI: 10.3390/app13116716

Wulandari, F., Astuti, M. T., & Marhamah, M. (2024). Enhancing Writing Literacy Teachers' through AI Development. *Jurnal Onoma: Pendidikan, Bahasa dan Sastra, 10*(1), 246 - 256. http://repository.uir.ac.id/id/eprint/23289

Yilmaz, H., Maxutov, S., Baitekov, A., & Balta, N. (2023). Student attitudes towards Chat GPT: A technology acceptance model survey. *International Educational Review, 1*(1), 57 - 83. https://int-er.com/article/student-attitudes-towards-chat-gpt-a-technology-acceptance-model-survey-13483

ADDITIONAL READING

Ahmed, Z. E., Hassan, A. A., & Saeed, R. A. (Eds.). (2024). *AI-Enhanced Teaching Methods*. IGI Global., DOI: 10.4018/979-8-3693-2728-9

Laubscher, M. C. (2024). AI and Computer Science Education: The Need for Improved Regulation for the Use of AI in Computer Science Education. In Bosch, C., Goosen, L., & Chetty, J. (Eds.), *Navigating Computer Science Education in the 21st Century* (pp. 282–298). IGI Global., DOI: 10.4018/979-8-3693-1066-3.ch014

Makarova, V., Li, Z., & Wang, Z. (2024). Can ChatGPT Grade Non-Native Academic English Writing? In Eybers, O., & Muller, A. (Eds.), *AI Approaches to Literacy in Higher Education* (pp. 97–116). IGI Global., DOI: 10.4018/979-8-3693-1054-0.ch005

Smolansky, A., Cram, A., Raduescu, C., Zeivots, S., Huber, E., & Kizilcec, R. F. (2023). Educator and Student Perspectives on the Impact of Generative AI on Assessments in Higher Education Proceedings of the Tenth ACM Conference on Learning @ Scale, Copenhagen, Denmark. https://doi.org/DOI: 10.1145/3573051.3596191

Verma, S., & Tomar, P. (Eds.). (2021). *Impact of AI Technologies on Teaching, Learning, and Research in Higher Education*. IGI Global., DOI: 10.4018/978-1-7998-4763-2

Wiggill, C., & Batchelor, J. (2024). The Impact of AI Requires Integration Across K-12 and Tertiary Learning. In Eybers, O., & Muller, A. (Eds.), *AI Approaches to Literacy in Higher Education* (pp. 49–75). IGI Global., DOI: 10.4018/979-8-3693-1054-0.ch003

KEY TERMS AND DEFINITIONS

AI Policy Framework: a set of guidelines and regulations that govern the ethical, transparent, and accountable use of AI technologies. It ensures alignment with educational goals while addressing issues such as bias, data privacy, and the digital divide.

Artificial Intelligence (AI): AI refers to the simulation of human intelligence in machines to perform tasks requiring human cognition, such as problem-solving, learning, and decision-making, and in education, it is used for automated grading, personalized learning, and adaptive assessments.

Automated Grading: Automated grading uses AI algorithms to evaluate and score student work, aiming to increase efficiency, reduce human error, and provide instant feedback.

Bias in AI: Systematic errors or unfair outcomes caused by flawed or incomplete training data, which may result in certain groups being disadvantaged in AI-assisted assessments, particularly marginalized communities.

Digital Divide: The gap between those with access to modern technologies, like AI, and those without, often due to socioeconomic factors, limiting equitable use in education.

Educational Assessments: These are systematic methods of evaluating student learning, knowledge, abilities, and performance. With AI integration, assessments can be personalized and automated, improving efficiency and providing real-time feedback.

Equitable Learning Environments: Ensure all students have access to high-quality education. While AI can promote equity by personalizing learning, careful implementation is needed to prevent reinforcing inequalities.

Ethical Considerations in AI: Include fairness, bias, transparency, privacy, and accountability, ensuring AI tools promote equity and avoid reinforcing inequalities in education.

Fairness: In AI for education, fairness means ensuring equal, unbiased opportunities for all students, with AI-driven assessments free from discrimination based on gender, ethnicity, socioeconomic status, or location.

Intelligent Tutoring Systems (ITS): These are AI-based systems designed to provide personalized instruction and feedback to students, often adapting in real-time to individual learner needs to support mastery of content.

Chapter 12
Librarians Leading the Way to AI Literacy

Elizabeth Gross
https://orcid.org/0000-0002-1648-7090
Sam Houston State University, USA

Rene M. Burress
https://orcid.org/0000-0003-0184-1891
University of Central Missouri, USA

Holly Weimar
https://orcid.org/0009-0007-7562-313X
Sam Houston State University, USA

ABSTRACT

The hype around AI today has been ubiquitous and exciting. The use of AI behind the scenes has been implemented in many different areas such as the use of GPS for driving instructions, the use of natural language assistants such as smart speakers, and the ability of social media apps to keep tabs on what you are watching and reading (Masoud & Kamran, 2024). All of these are examples of AI that has been in use for decades now. It seems like a new tool, and a rather miraculous one, at that. As generations Z and Alpha have made their way to the K-12 school system in 2000s and beyond, the use of AI in school has increased. As administrators, teachers and parents try to understand what it appears their digital natives who are in many ways, born AI literate, the middle person who can help bring everyone to the same page is the person who serves everyone in the school – the school librarian.

DOI: 10.4018/979-8-3693-6527-4.ch012

INTRODUCTION

Artificial intelligence (AI) has been in use in the automation of service for many years. As an example, that touches just about everyone, the use of AI in reading handwritten zip codes revolutionized the postal service (Li, 2024). The path for this outcome was long and rocky, but it has only been since the 1980s that AI has helped humans to sort the mail. Nonetheless, the notion of AI helping to get our letters and packages where they are meant to go is a wonderful boost to productivity. That it had such a low-key rollout seems unimaginable to us today. The hype around AI today has been ubiquitous and exciting. The use of AI behind the scenes has been implemented in many different areas such as the use of GPS for driving instructions, the use of natural language assistants such as smart speakers, and the ability of social media apps to keep tabs on what you are watching and reading (Masoud & Kamran, 2024). All of these are examples of AI that has been in use for decades now. It seems like a *new* tool, and a rather miraculous one, at that. As generations Z and Alpha have made their way to the K-12 school system in 2000s and beyond, the use of AI in school has increased. As administrators, teachers and parents try to understand what it appears their digital natives who are in many ways, born AI literate, the middle person who can help bring everyone to the same page is the person who serves everyone in the school – the school librarian.

What is Artificial Intelligence?

Artificial intelligence first came to the attention of the public through demonstrations of its understanding of and ability to play difficult games like Chess and Go (Shane, 2019). Developers showed that they could create and deploy AI that can play and win these games. AI was able to beat grand masters at chess by 1997 (Press, 2018). This showed that machines could learn things that seemed uniquely human. These advances were possible through a better understanding and development of the use of neural networks, which are broadly patterned on the ways that human brains communicate (Yegnana, 2010, Rogers, & Kabrisky, 1997, Yang & Wang, 2020,). These programs were considered breakthroughs in the manipulation of neural networks. However, these AIs were not able to do anything else well. They could beat masters at chess, but they could not explain how to make a peanut butter sandwich– or even describe what a sandwich might be. It was trained on only one area of data, ostensibly the rules of the game. These programs were astounding, but not very applicable to daily life. The key to AIs like Deep Blue is that the computer itself is extremely powerful and is able to parse through all possible chess moves quickly to choose the correct move. What is important to realize is that Deep Blue did not *learn* as it played. Instead, it found the optimal moves based on its database of all possible allowed chess moves (IBM, n.d.)

Developers continued to improve AI in the years after it made the news by winning at difficult games. However, as anyone with a smart speaker can attest, as of this writing it is not at the level of seamless communication that users want (or need). When GPS was first introduced as a support for driving directions, stories began to circulate that outlined the ways apps like Google Maps were far from reliable (Fraser et al, 2022). In general, users were impressed but also wary of the results of searches for travel directions and other AI-generated search results. AI is programmed to please the user, and this sometimes gets in the way if there is not enough information for a reasoned response, and nonsense– or at least hilarious– answers are generated that leave much to be desired. For instance, Janelle Shane, AI researcher, has written an entire book describing the ways that AI responses go strangely wrong while the program emphasizes how correct its responses are (Shane, 2019). For more on this topic, please visit https://www.aiweirdness.com/.

In recent years, AI has been improved by the use of Machine Learning. Machine Learning improves the outcome of queries to AI by allowing the AI to use algorithms to analyze and predict the intended or desired response based on the mountains of data upon which it has been trained (Jordan & Mitchell, 2015). The AI no longer uses rules to provide output. Rather, it uses the results of millions of interactions with data to predict the correct answer.

GENERATIVE ARTIFICIAL INTELLIGENCE

Large Language Models, or LLM

In November of 2022, A company called OpenAI released a different type of AI that could interact with humans in natural, usually English, language. ChatGPT 3.5 caused an instant tsunami of interest in the general public, from speculation about the implications of this amazing program to fears that people would be losing their jobs to AI. The difference between previous iterations of artificial intelligence and generative AI is that the sophisticated statistical analysis used to define the correct answer to a query is much more powerful than previously. This is due to the immense dataset used in machine learning. In this instance, the data used was the internet. These new AI, or genAI, are known as Large Language Models (LLM). These programs are not without problems. Shortly after the release of ChatGPT 3.5, it was shown that part of what the AI is programmed to do is to give answers based on predictions it makes, not on whether the result is true in any sense, just that it can create sentences in English that are correct in grammar and syntax. In this way it will generate false answers, which have been called "hallucinations," for lack of a better term (Fui-Hoon Nah et al. 2023). Another issue with genAI at this time is the lag in the age of the data that is being used to train the genAI. For example, in March of 2023, shortly after ChatGPT had been released, a movie reviewer asked ChatGPT for a review of the movie *Cocaine Bear,* which had been released to theaters in February of that year. The AI insisted that the movie had not been released yet, but its training data set ended in September of 2021 at the time. While the AI had been incorrect in its estimation of the release of this movie, it was able to explain why it could not give a review of a movie that it reasoned was not yet available (L. L. Coker, personal communication, March 3, 2023).

Uses of genAI

The genAI in use today is the weakest iteration. In other words, it continues to improve in many ways. Since its release in 2022, people have been finding ways to employ the use of genAI such as ChatGPT and others in everyday work and life. Because genAI works so well with predictive situations such as templates for legal documents and grants, it can lighten the workload for those who experiment with it. Also, it can be used in tasks such as first drafts of essays and papers. Because genAI does so well with tasks that have a set template, it is particularly useful with predictive operations throughout industry. GenAI can also write code for programmers, thereby freeing them up to deal with more difficult issues that demand human intelligence.

GenAI has been called a "very fancy autocomplete" (Marchese, 2022). This is a good way to understand how ChatGPT and other generative AI models compose responses to queries. They have been trained using algorithms that predict what should come next in a sentence, and this has been fine-tuned by human trainers to ensure accuracy in language use (Priest, 2024). It will retrieve results that make sense in English, but may not necessarily be what the user expected or can rely on. In working with genAI, it seems as though the idea of a happy golden retriever who only wants its owner to be happy will bring back whatever it thinks will be the right response, even if it is a fabrication.

> *"ChatGPT was optimized for dialogue," which means users interact with a chatbot in a conversational context, and the chatbot will compose text based upon the user's prompts. The bot is capable of generating text on a variety of topics and in a variety of styles... you simply type in a question or give it a command and it generates text for you." (UTCTL, 2023, para. 6).*

GenAI in Learning and Teaching

One glaring omission in the rollout of AI in everyday life has been in learning and teaching in the pk-12 arena. There are positive perceptions in support of the possibility of the use of AI while negative perceptions have recently increased. The Walton Family Foundation (2024) shared the results of the Impact Research survey conducted in the spring of 2024 on the impact AI has on teachers and students. The report reveals that 81% of teachers and 89% of K-12 students believe that AI has had a positive impact on education. While the percentages are high, only 79% of teachers report being familiar with ChatGPT. Even less, 65% of teachers believe that AI will be key to students' future success. There is also the belief that schools are not doing much about AI even though there appears to be widespread use. While optimism and perceived use of AI seems to be present among teachers, a clear way to incorporate and use genAI is not identified.

As of this writing, there is no consensus on how to use genAI, or even if schools should be using it at all (Grassini, 2023). However, there has been an identified need for public participation and governmental regulation (Liu & Zhong, 2024) in the involvement and development of the use of genAI in pk-12 education. Ethical use of genAI, concerns genAI and students' ability to think critically and creatively, and what level of access pk-12 students should have in their use of genAI in the school environment has created a call for more guidance and research to be done.

In attempting to address the use of genAI, Mårtensson and Mullins (2024) identify six roles that business schoolteachers can have: (1) expert; (2) facilitator; (3) supervisor/tutor/mentor/coach; (4) designer/curator; (5) bridge-builder; and (6) gatekeeper. Teachers and school librarians fill these roles in the way that they deliver content and personalized learning for their students. GenAI doesn't diminish any of these roles but has the potential to increase the capabilities of educators to select and use the most appropriate tools to support their students' success. But there is not a clear consensus across disciplines for best practices yet for many reasons, such as who is building the LLM and the potential biases and limited information that LLMs are built upon.

Meanwhile, a few pk-12 teachers are exploring the use of genAI to reduce preparation time and identify standards and pedagogical practices for specific lessons (Conrad & Rees, 2024). Others are using genAI to support their work when adapting and personalizing learning for students with identified needs (Bekeš & Galzina, 2023). This is in response to trying to provide daily solutions to support students who are struggling with the curriculum content for various reasons.

Yet, many teachers avoid the use of genAI altogether and ban it from their teaching and their students' use of the tool (Grassini, 2023). As with many new technologies, such as the use of calculators in school, there is fear and trepidation around allowing learners to use a tool that could ostensibly do their homework for them. Universities on the other hand have embraced technology. Fairly quickly after ChatGPT4 was released, Arizona State University acquired accounts for all of its students. Most universities are inclined to provide guidelines in the use of genAI.

SCHOOL LIBRARIANS AS TECHNOLOGY LEADERS

School librarians are trained as teachers, first and foremost (AASL, 2018). As part of this, they regularly share new educational technologies with K-12 students (Dickey, 2023) and provide professional development for their colleagues in their learning communities (Coleman, 2020). School librarians can play a vital role in helping educators and learners understand, explore, and responsibly adopt AI in educational settings by leveraging their expertise in information literacy, technology integration, and resource curation (Bauld, 2023). For this section, the ways that school librarians can support and increase understanding and use of AI in the school learning community will be outlined.

School librarians are charged to apply educational technologies as part of their training and are expected and encouraged to become the educational technology leaders in their learning communities (Lewis & McNamara, 2021). School librarians are already adept at organizing and implementing professional development for their colleagues. They can assess the level of understanding in their school communities and plan interactive and informative sessions of many different kinds (workshops, seminars, monthly chats, and the like) to provide insight and training for teachers. School librarians can act as leaders in Train the Trainer sessions so that teachers are empowered to teach their students about and with AI. School librarians can also provide experts outside the learning community who have important information to share and can debrief after such interactions to glean the most from these talks.

School librarians already curate books and materials to help teachers teach and to support the curriculum goals of the learning community (Ahlfed, 2019). The curation of AI materials—books, websites, applications, and multimedia sources—is an extension of their role as providers in educational communities. As well, part of the work of the school librarian involves finding and vetting tools for use in the classroom and community. They will utilize this skill to research and recommend AI tools for learning and teaching.

School librarians work with teachers on a regular basis to integrate technology into lessons (Yi, Turner, & Turner, 2019). Because of their expertise in creating inquiry lessons using library materials, they can integrate AI-related activities, projects, and resources into existing lesson plans across different subject areas (Green & Chassereau, 2023). In addition, research shows that the novice teacher-school librarian relationship goes a long way toward fostering resilience in the new teacher (Soulen, 2021). School librarians can offer support for these novices to increase their expertise in the classroom and inculcate AI into novice teacher practice.

In the past year or more, school librarians have embraced the use of Canva (canva.com). Many of them have trained themselves in its use to improve their communication with the school community. Over time, Canva has increased the availability of AI that includes design and lesson planning by grade level and subject area with existing templates or create new, the use of Magic Studio to generate lesson plans following the prompt provided by the educator, and the use of design elements to improve lessons through engaging presentations, graphic organizers, and other resources for students to use. The use of Canva in this way has developed the ability of the school librarian to train experienced and novice teachers in how to quickly improve their lessons for students.

Another AI tool that many educators are embracing and that school librarians can demonstrate how to use and incorporate into their work is Magic School (app.magicschool.ai). A growing number of generators within Magic School support the development of academic content, rubrics, email responders, unit and lesson planning, questioning techniques that include quizzes, YouTube video questions, and much more. Novice and experienced teachers decrease their time on task when incorporating these or similar generators in support of their work.

Khanmigo (khanmigo.ai) is another AI tool that has different portals for teachers, learners, and parents. School librarians are in a unique position to facilitate the use of this tool because it has the ability to encompass different types of users. For students, Khanmigo acts as an interactive tutoring bot that supports their learning within specific subjects, and can provide feedback on students' written assignments to improve their writing skills. For teachers, they can monitor their students' progress on specific tasks assigned to them as well as developing engaging lessons using the AI feature of this tool. For parents, Khanmigo provides the ability to monitor their child's progress on specific tutoring. Khanmigo has an alliance with OpenAI and is powered by GPT-4 at the time of this writing.

Maker spaces have gained traction in the k-12 learning space as well as in higher education (Mersand, 2021). This model can be used in the school library to facilitate hands-on sessions for students to allow them to experiment with AI tools, such as language models, image generators, or the use of AI to generate code for a project, all under guidance from the school librarian. The school librarian can then tie these experiences to students' curriculum needs, bring in experts from industry to help situate the applications in real-world use cases, and seek ways to help students and teachers apply these concepts in other disciplines.

It is incumbent upon school librarians to model ethical use of information. In this vein, they can also promote discussion on the ethical implications of AI use and continued development as it pertains to the school learning community and beyond. School librarians can lead in policymaking for the use of AI, and this chapter will provide a model for school librarians and learning communities to create policies for the ethical use of AI. Privacy and data-sharing (Babirad, 2024) has long been a focus of school librarianship, so they will be mindful of these needs.

As for library service to students and teachers, school librarians can show the learning community how AI can support research, bibliographic management, library operations, and other practical applications (Tait & Pierson, 2022). They can introduce applications like ISTE's Stretch AI and even work to create a language model that is trained in the materials in the school library. Because this material is curated and tailored to the school's curriculum, a model based on this material may help to support critical thinking and information literacy across the school's learning community (De Groft, 2023). The school librarian will be the prompt engineer for the school community as well and will maintain a prompt library for teachers and students to use, add to, and develop.

As part of their drive for continuous improvement in the area of educational technology and learner engagement, school librarians can also focus on the evolving development and use of AI (Yorio, 2023). In this way they will also share news, research, or educational resources with teachers and students to create an atmosphere of curiosity and collaboration. School librarians acknowledge the risk involved in the use of AI and so provide guardrails for the learning community while fostering continuous exploration in the use of AI in the school library and beyond.

Instructional Technology

The definition of instructional technology is continually evolving as technology choices grow and understanding of how people learn increases (Januszewski & Molenda, 2007). Instructional technology differs from information technology in that it is focused on the use of manipulatives of many kinds~ a pencil and paper can be considered instructional technology. However, since its inception in the early part of the last century, instructional technology as a field has moved from merely audio-visual and correspondence-courses-by-mail to asynchronous and synchronous online learning via distance. Instructional technology has been intrinsic to learning and teaching. In person educational technology support has been evolving and improving as well, which allows students and teachers to interact with course content in ways that make sense to each learner. The use of the theories and models of the field of instructional technology help teachers teach in the way that the children's and adults' brains learn, and not in the traditional "spray and pray" methodologies of the past.

Today's classroom is enriched with augmented and virtual reality, active learning, and experiential learning to harness the curiosity and skillset of both students and teachers. These methodologies have been made possible because instructional technology is a belief and mindset that each and every student can learn, and that there are many ways to deliver content that are engaging, supportive, and empowering for students. Further distillation of instructional technology and its applications are being investigated from the standpoint of rapid prototyping and lean design. If this sounds more like the engineering design world, it is. The new field of learning engineering takes the entire system of instructional design, context, and environment and creates a methodology that incorporates a team of specialized individuals to create the best learning scenarios possible. While the competencies in this part of the field have yet to be made definitive, the notion of learning engineering is of interest here because of the multiple considerations of pk-12 learning and teaching.

In the context of pk-12 learning and teaching, instructional technology and the term *educational technology* are used interchangeably. However, in this chapter, educational technology will be defined as the actual software or hardware used for educational purposes, while instructional technology refers to the theory or application of these assets. Generative Artificial Intelligence would be seen as an educational technology. Its application and use involve the instructional technology framework as it applies to the use of GenAI.

Benefits of the Use of instructional technology

Instructional technology is a way of looking at learning and teaching through the lens of learning science. It has been found that engaging students with content in meaningful ways helps students retain knowledge more efficiently and helps them tie it to what they already know, known as *schema* (Driscoll, 1994). Much of the discovery of the use of active learning and other techniques to support how the brain learns is from the field of instructional technology. Instructional technology recognizes and supports differentiation of instruction, meaning that each teacher has the opportunity to provide activities and learnings for students that work best for each individual student.

Instructional technology allows for a number of applications to be used simultaneously– so that a teacher may use video, direct instruction, and experiential learning to share content with students. They may also utilize a combination of these technologies– a *mash-up* in common parlance. The assessment of student learning may be a student-created podcast, an infographic, or a more traditional report. Teachers' ability to reach more students in more varied modalities are at the heart of instructional technology. Along with message design, instructional technology allows teachers to expand the available digital tools for student learning to support the ways students learn and engage with the material.

Because the emphasis in instructional technology is on the *how* of learning, any tools, techniques, and technologies are evaluated for efficacy in the interest of best practice. Generative Artificial Intelligence is such a tool, and it bears analysis from the point-of-view of instructional technological practice. The tie-in between what school librarians know and are able to do, the digital literacies that school librarians teach and support, and the application of this new technology in the school library and beyond will be discussed next.

Generative Artificial Intelligence in the K-12 Space

The addition and possibility of generative artificial intelligence (genAI) offers a paradigm shift in education. As with the advent of the handheld calculator on the scene, genAI has the potential to help create a new ecosystem in education. But while the calculator had a much less immediate impact on learning and teaching, genAI does not have a true parallel or model for its use. GenAI has come on the scene with an immediacy that educators were not prepared for. Old lesson structure is now obsolete. Because students will have opportunities to get their work done by genAI, sometimes without its being detectable, parents and teachers understandably have anxiety about how genAI will be used. However, there are advantages to the use of genAI in the classroom. One of the first and most obvious is to change assignments that draw on rote learning. This type of learning is not optimum; it is better to engage directly with content rather than memorize rules. The danger of the application of genAI to do a child's homework will demand that teachers create learnings that are more immediate and experiential. The traditional ways of imparting knowledge were easiest for people who were not trained as teachers but were subject matter experts. This had been the model for many years, and some teachers still rely on these traditional models because they have not been sufficiently trained to see the power of student-centered learning. The ubiquity of genAI now requires a new method of teaching that will personalize learning for more students and engage them in ways that traditional methods did not.

Pedagogy Before Technology

One must take a step back to view the overall system of learning and teaching. Instead of reaching for the technology first, educators must review what it is that they want students to know and be able to do, and how the available technology will support this. Pedagogy must drive the work. Increases in understanding how people learn in context have been documented (Nasem, 2018), so there is much to support the use of instructional technology techniques in pk-12 teaching and learning.

GenAI is predicated on statistical analysis and probability (Bobo, 2023). Because this is the case, it cannot be relied on to return the same or similar answers for every query, or prompt. School librarians can be of great use here. Librarians in general are trained to create queries that return reliable results in databases. It is a natural next step for librarians, and especially school librarians, to learn best practice based on their skillset and then impart this knowledge to their colleagues and students.

Prompt Engineering

GenAI responds to queries, or prompts, that users send to it. ChatGPT interacts with users in a natural language way. Users enter prompts and genAI responds. The response is generated in a way that seems like a human being is doing the responding. School librarians, who have been trained to interact with databases in productive ways, already know how to create queries that return good results. They can interact with genAI to obtain results and coach others in this skill. This will require learning about genAI and how to align responses to goals as well as learning what has worked for others. This is not intuitive. Although genAI is not a human, asking it to "take a breath" or telling it "this will be easy!" sometimes helps in getting good returns on prompts. One can also ask genAI to create prompts for itself, both in text and in image creation. Using Poe, an AI that calls itself a *fast AI chat,* users can ask the AI to create a prompt for an image in MidJourney that will guide the image generating AI to obtain a specific image. This can be viewed here: https://poe.com/Midjourney. The model will oblige by giving the exact prompt. In another scenario, in order to generate a 50-problem math test, the model created the prompt, "Command, we need you to plot a course through this turbulence and locate the source of the anomaly. Use all available data and your expertise to guide us through this challenging situation." (Plunkert, 2024).

Prompt Libraries

The current version of genAI that you have access to right now is the weakest version that you will interact with. Because this is the case, the best prompts, those that obtain a satisfactory answer, will change. While it is useful to constantly create prompts to gauge how genAI responds to new queries, school librarians are well-positioned to create and maintain a prompt library for the school community to help users get the most out of genAI. For those new to prompt engineering, the school librarian will act as a guide to help make the process that much more streamlined and useful.

GenAI As Instructional Technology Support

School librarians are teachers first. They have a specialized skill set that includes facilities management, materials collection and curation, and research support for students and colleagues. School librarians are also able to fill the role of instructional coaches as well as instructional technology coaches (AASL, 2018). School librarians experienced in learning as well as genAI can supply impetus for adapting genAI in the classroom. As instructional coaches, school librarians can identify areas of weakness or need in the classroom. As instructional technology coaches, they can also guide classroom teachers in the implementation of genAI, which will in turn help to free up time for teachers for direct instruction (Hargrave, Fisher, & Frey, 2024). Here are some ways that genAI supports learning and teaching in the pk-12 classroom that school librarians can facilitate:

- **Personalized Learning**

The algorithms of the new LLMs, like ChatGPT, Claude, and Gemini, make these tools extremely useful in detecting patterns. Because of this, analysis of individual student data will help teachers customize learning for each student based on their strengths and weaknesses.

- **Behavioral and Emotional Analytics**

Because of its pattern-recognition abilities, genAI can also help to uncover behavioral issues and help teachers discern why they are occurring based on the data collected in the classroom and elsewhere. There is genAI that can discern facial expressions and conversation tone to also supply feedback for teachers, although this might present privacy issues for schools.

- **Automated Assessment and Feedback**

When an entire day's worth of students turn in papers at the same time, a human teacher will not be able to provide instant feedback, but GenAI can provide instant feedback to students on their written work. Individual concerns and needs can then be handled by the teacher with a much faster response than traditional methods. This provides consistency in grading as well as provides for timely interactions with students. Depending on sophistication, there are genAI that can also give detailed formative feedback for students. The reason this is so important is pointed up in a study done by McKinsey & Company partnered with Microsoft that showed that only 49% of a teacher's time is spent in direct instruction (Bryant et al., 2020).

- **Intelligent Tutoring Systems (ITS)**

One-on-one tutors provide the most helpful learning situations for students. However, one teacher with potentially 120 students per day will not be able to provide this. GenAI can be used to tutor students in specific subjects in similar ways to human tutors. GenAI can respond in real-time to student responses, and can guide students to better understanding of content.

- **Natural Language Processing (NLP) for Language Learning**

An asset to foreign language teachers as well as those in their classrooms who are second language learners, genAI can be used to help students with many aspects of language learning, like pronunciation, vocabulary words, and correct grammar. Again, the beauty of the use of genAI here is the immediacy of the feedback for students.

- **Virtual and Augmented Reality (VR/AR) with AI**

GenAI can be used in conjunction with virtual and augmented reality devices to supply dynamic content as well as respond to student actions.

- **GenAI-Assisted Lesson Planning**

GenAI can create lesson plans based on state standards and offer accommodations for teachers to consider. As well, genAI can suggest technologies and manipulatives for the students to help them understand the content. For this as for all genAI-generated artifacts, care must be taken to vet the product.

- **Data Analytics for Instructional Improvement**

Again, because genAI is well-placed to recognize patterns, it can give feedback on the techniques that are working for students, allowing teachers to better provide instruction for their students.

- **AI for Special Education Support**

GenAI is able to synthesize interventions based on student needs. From student disabilities to support in learning, genAI can suggest adaptive tools and strategies for students.

- **Parental Engagement**

It is extremely valuable to use genAI to create regular communications with parents that can be automated based on assessments. It will also create an atmosphere of shared responsibility for the child's success.

All of these scenarios will take expertise and training for teachers to be able to implement them. School librarians are uniquely positioned to research and understand genAI applications such as the ones listed above. They can provide professional development, a skill they already possess.

GenAI in School Libraries

School librarians are responsible for teaching students and collaborating with teachers on multiple literacies. Within their realm of expertise, school librarians can teach about information literacy, media literacy, digital literacy, data literacy, financial literacy and now AI literacy. Digital Promise, a nonprofit organization who works to bring equitable solutions to education. Their definition of AI literacy is "AI literacy is the knowledge and skills that enable humans to critically understand, evaluate, and use AI systems and tools to safely and ethically participate in an increasingly digital world" (Digital Promise, 2024). Digital Promise is committed to lessening the digital divide by promoting digital equity and they have a large number of resources for school librarians to utilize.

School librarians can increase understanding of the use and applications of genAI by supplying information and materials for students and teachers. They can offer vetted tools such as online tutorials, practitioner articles, and the like. As school librarians' charge is to make information findable and accessible, they can handle organization and dissemination of these materials. As part of this service, school librarians are also able to incorporate AI literacy into their already existing digital literacy endeavors throughout the entire school. The evaluation of information is also important here.

Kammer and Hays (2023) suggest playing games with genAI to increase student digital literacy. After playing the games and getting students engaged, they suggest leading a discussion about the pros and cons of using GenAI. They also give the reminder that students will likely take the educator role as they teach their teachers what they know about what GenAI can do.

School librarians can use genAI to create materials that can then be used to teach media literacy and critical thinking skills through evaluation of the content by students themselves, thereby empowering them to better understand how to vet information as to its truthfulness themselves. the student through how to check for reliability, accuracy, authoritativeness, and relevance to the topic at hand. As an example, with the prompt, "You are a seasoned school librarian with an MLIS. You want to show how generative AI can help teach critical thinking skills using AI. Create a lesson that would support this for seventh graders."

ChatGPT provided the following:

Lesson Plan: Using Generative AI to Enhance Critical Thinking Skills

Grade Level: 7th Grade

Subject: Library/Media Studies, English, or Social Studies

Duration: 1 hour (can be extended with activities)

Lesson Title:

Fact or Fiction? Analyzing Information with Generative AI

Objective:

Students will use generative AI tools to enhance their critical thinking skills by evaluating information, identifying credible sources, and distinguishing between fact and fiction in various types of media.

Learning Outcomes:

By the end of this lesson, students will:

1. Understand how generative AI works and how it can produce text and images.
2. Apply critical thinking skills to evaluate AI-generated content.
3. Develop skills in identifying credible information and discerning between facts and misinformation.
4. Engage in discussions about bias in AI and information sources.

Materials:

- Access to a generative AI tool (e.g., ChatGPT, DALL·E, etc.)
- Whiteboard/Smartboard
- Chromebooks or tablets for students
- Handout: "Evaluating Information" Checklist
- Sample texts/images (both AI-generated and human-generated)
- Access to a fact-checking website (e.g., Snopes, FactCheck.org)

Standards:

- **ISTE Standards**: 1.2.a "Students cultivate critical thinking skills to identify credible sources of information."
- **AASL Standards**: I.A.2 "Learners display curiosity and initiative by asking questions to understand the topic thoroughly."

Lesson Procedure:

1. Introduction (10 minutes):
    - **Discussion Starter**: Begin by asking students how they typically find information online. Do they trust everything they see? What might be fake or misleading?
    - **Explain Generative AI**: Introduce the concept of generative AI, explaining that it can produce text, images, and even media. Emphasize that while AI can be useful, it doesn't always provide accurate or reliable information.

      Teacher Tip: Use an example where AI generates a story or image, showing how convincing AI can be, but also highlight errors or absurdities.
2. Demonstration (10 minutes):
    - **AI in Action**: Use a generative AI tool (like ChatGPT) in front of the class to generate a short story, news article, or answer to a question. For example, ask it about a historical event, then analyze the response with the class.
    - **Critical Thinking Prompt**: Ask students:
    - "Does the AI-generated text seem accurate?"
    - "What could be missing?"
    - "How can we check whether this information is true?"
3. Activity: Fact or Fiction? (20 minutes):
    - **Group Work**: Divide students into small groups. Give each group a mixture of AI-generated content (such as articles, social media posts, or news stories) and human-generated content. Include some with deliberate inaccuracies.
    - **Evaluation Task**: Using the "Evaluating Information" checklist, students will work in their groups to determine which pieces of information are credible, which are not, and explain their reasoning.
    - **Checklist Prompts**:
    - Is the source of information reliable?
    - Can the facts be cross-checked with other sources?
    - Are there obvious signs of bias or errors?
    - Does it sound too good (or strange) to be true?
4. Discussion and Reflection (15 minutes):
    - **Class Discussion**: Reconvene and have groups share their findings. Discuss why some information was more credible than others and how they arrived at their conclusions. Encourage students to reflect on how AI can generate both useful and misleading content.

- **Debate Prompt**: Ask students: "Can we trust everything AI tells us? Why or why not?" This can spark a conversation about the limitations and biases of AI tools.

5. Closing and Homework (5 minutes):
    - **Wrap-Up**: Summarize the key points of the lesson, emphasizing that critical thinking is essential when using AI or any tool to evaluate information.
    - **Homework Assignment**: Ask students to use an AI tool at home (or do this as a follow-up class assignment) to generate a response to a research question. Their task is to cross-check the AI's answer using reliable sources and write a paragraph about the differences they found.

Assessment:

- **Formative**: Group discussions and the evaluation activity will allow you to assess students' understanding of credibility and critical thinking.
- **Summative**: The homework assignment will assess individual application of cross-checking and research skills.

Extensions/Adaptations:

- **For Advanced Students**: Have them explore how bias may be present in AI outputs, especially with controversial topics.
- **For Struggling Students**: Provide more guided support during the group evaluation activity, walking them through how to use the checklist.

Reflection:

This lesson uses generative AI as a tool not just for creating content but for fostering critical thinking by challenging students to evaluate the reliability and accuracy of the information they encounter. It aligns with digital literacy and media evaluation goals essential in the 21st-century classroom.

When asked to provide a specific false story, ChatGPT provided

False Narrative Example:

The Great Spaghetti Harvest of 1957

In 1957, a groundbreaking event took place in Switzerland that stunned the world: the **Great Spaghetti Harvest**. On April 1st, Swiss farmers celebrated an exceptionally bountiful spaghetti crop, which grew directly from trees. For years, these trees had been cultivated to produce long strands of perfectly cooked spaghetti, ready to be picked and enjoyed. With favorable weather and careful farming techniques, the Swiss were able to produce enough spaghetti to supply the entire country, with some left over for export.

The discovery of the spaghetti tree had been a closely-guarded secret for centuries, known only to a small group of Swiss farmers. However, in 1957, with the rise of modern agricultural methods, the secret of the spaghetti tree finally became public knowledge. Families in Switzerland were shown on television harvesting strands of spaghetti, drying them in the sun, and preparing them for dinner.

This breakthrough in farming technology led to worldwide discussions about the possibility of growing pasta in other regions. While Switzerland remained the leader in spaghetti farming, other countries began experimenting with similar methods to cultivate their own pasta crops. Today, some agricultural experts argue that with continued innovation, spaghetti farming could become a global phenomenon, reducing the need for pasta production in factories.

It then gave the rationale for why this is not immediately known as false:

Why This False Narrative is Tricky:

- **Credibility and Familiarity**: Many students may not have strong agricultural knowledge, and the idea of food being grown on plants feels somewhat plausible (as vegetables and fruits do). The inclusion of "credible" details like weather conditions and farming techniques makes it harder to dismiss at first glance.

- **Historical Element**: The story is set in 1957, a time that seems distant enough for something strange to have occurred without today's scientific understanding. The historical framing lends it some false credibility, especially for students who haven't studied this era in detail.

- **Visual Imagery**: Students may imagine that the visual description of spaghetti hanging from trees is bizarre but possibly real, especially if they have not yet developed skills in agricultural science.

ChatGPT also gave a rationale for how this could be used in a lesson on information literacy:

How to Use This in the Lesson:

During the "Fact or Fiction?" activity, you can include this narrative as one of the AI-generated or curated texts for students to evaluate. Encourage them to question details like:

- Is there any real-world evidence that spaghetti grows on trees?
- What sources could they check to confirm this claim?
- Does the story use specific but unverifiable details (like "favorable weather") to make it sound more believable?

After the activity, you can reveal that this was a famous April Fool's prank orchestrated by the BBC in 1957, which fooled many people at the time. This is a great opportunity to discuss **how to identify hoaxes** and understand why even outlandish stories can seem credible with enough detail.(OpenAI, 2024).

With engaging examples as well as the lesson plan, ChatGPT and other genAI could help to keep critical thinking skills at the forefront of library instruction. This is one example of the use of genAI and instructional technology techniques to support student learning.

Art and Music

School librarians can also use genAI to help students explore art and music in new ways. They

can introduce students text- to to-image generators, such as Craiyon. Using these genAI tools students can enter ideas and the tools will generate an image. For example, an extension of an ELA lesson where students have completed creative writing projects could be to come to the library to generate an image to go along with their story. The school librarian can also tie in an ethics lesson during this activity, ensuring that students learn how to properly attribute that the image is not theirs and how to properly cite where it was generated from. Below is an image generated by Craiyon that could be used with a creative story about frogs playing musical instruments.

Figure 1. Frog Playing Piano, Generated 9.8.24 by Craiyon.

Under the direction of the school librarian, students can also use apps such as Riffusion which take both text and pictures to create songs. Students can use these songs in media creations. This can be a way to even incorporate math, science, and history as students try to memorize and learn new concepts. They may just generate the next SchoolHouse Rock.

Careers

School librarians are the perfect collaborative partner K-12 to explore careers with students. School libraries are the perfect place to host a school wide career day and to complete career research. The thought that we are preparing students for a workforce that includes careers that have not been invented yet is quite accurate. It is important that students be exposed to career ideas related to GenAI. This is a two-fold idea. There are careers directly related to working with machines and the data generated, but students should also be encouraged to ask questions about how common career paths such as nursing, military, accounting, engineering are using GenAI in their work. Older students can search job postings for keywords such as GenAI. They can also explore what types of skills someone who wants to work on machines generating AI will need. Another research activity would be to have students use the Bureau of Labor Statistics website to specific things about careers. For example, according to the Occupational Outlook Handbook. "employment of data scientists is projected to grow 36 percent from 2023 to 2033, much faster than the average for all occupations" (Bureau of Labor Statistics, 2024).

Ethics

As previously mentioned, school librarians are the perfect K-12 partner to teach others about the ethics related to AI use in education. There are many lessons and discussions related to ethics that a school librarian can lead.

First it must be acknowledged that there is known bias in what GenAI produces (Hacker et al., 2024). Anyone using GenAI should be made aware of this reality so that they can ensure they make steps to overcome it.

It is important that anyone using AI think about copyright. Whatever is put into AI, should have the permission of the copyright holder. The only way for GenAI to generate outputs is to look at its known inputs. Most GenAI platforms keep everything that has been inputted. This includes data that AI is asked to analyze, standards for lesson plans AI is asked to write, and more. Teachers and students should think about these aspects before entering information into GenAI platforms.

Finally, it is important for school librarians to remind everyone about the digital divide. Librarians especially are charged with closing the gap of the digital divide. This means that school libraries would be good place to hold subscriptions to AI platforms. This way all patrons of the library can have access. If those who cannot afford access to AI platforms only continue to have access to the free versions, the digital divide will deepen. The same idea is if students in lower income districts do not have access to a school librarian to teach them about GenAI compared to students in other districts who do.

When Claude was asked to generate lesson ideas for students discussing the ethics of GenAI use, it came up with the following debate topics. It also explained how a teacher or school librarian could set up a debate forum in their classroom or library.

These resolutions are structured to encourage students to consider both sides of each issue. They can be used for formal debates, where teams argue for or against the resolution, or as prompts for class discussions or essays.

1. The use of AI for grading essays and assignments will lead to fairer and more objective evaluations of student work.
2. The integration of AI-powered personalized learning systems will ultimately diminish the role and importance of human teachers in education.
3. The benefits of using AI to collect and analyze student data for improved learning outcomes outweigh the potential privacy concerns.
4. Students should be required to disclose their use of AI tools like ChatGPT in all academic work, including homework and essays.
5. The increased use of AI in education will widen the achievement gap between students with and without access to advanced technology at home.

GenAI has Limitations

One of the troubling aspects of the use of genAI is in and of itself, it lacks specific domain expertise. Instructional technologists and school librarians need to be aware that everything created by genAI is the result of statistical probability of what humans might expect next in a sentence, based on the training data the AI has used. In general, this has been the internet as seen in North America. As an example, a school shooting at Michigan State University (MSU) in 2023, officials at Vanderbilt University used ChatGPT to write a condolence letter to the learning community at MSU. What the user did not understand was that the response included a citation that showed this missive came from ChatGPT. When this action was found out, students at MSU were outraged at not only the lack of personal feeling in the message but also that there were inaccuracies in the letter itself. The assistant and associate deans resigned their positions over the incident (Perotta, 2023). As well, in areas such as the law, genAI can be an amazing partner in creating briefs and other legal documents, but again has no domain expertise. This will help with grant-writing and other activities that are highly prescribed. However, as an incident from 2023 proves, the notion of *trust but verify* has real meaning when working with genAI. In a legal brief, an attorney cited and quoted nonexistent cases that was then questioned by opposing council– because they could not find these on record. The attorney and his partner were fined because the judge said they did not vet their own work (Weiser, 2023).

In order to support learning and teaching, another application of genAI has been introduced that would use only vetted data to provide answers to queries. The International Society of Technology in Education has an example in beta called

StretchAI. This works by only training the LLM on articles, research, and data that has been vetted by ISTE (ISTE, 2024). This was a project initiated by ISTE, its partner organization American Society for Curriculum Development (ASCD), and OpenAI. Users who ask questions regarding learning will receive responses that are drawn solely from these vetted materials. A school library could ostensibly do the same, and allow genAI to support research and information-seeking in a protected environment.

CONCLUSION

School librarians have the knowledge to teach and train school faculties in the use of GenAI in schools. They are trained not only in the vetting of educational technology but also in its use. In their training as school librarians, they learn about digital tools, digital literacy, and developmental milestones in children's learning and are well-versed in choosing materials to support the curriculum as well as appropriate pedagogies to teach them. School librarians are teachers first. In the main, in order to be a school librarian, one must have had classroom experience. This means that school librarians have the experience to understand the needs of classroom teachers and the *how* of learning and teaching. They can take a few steps back to analyze the needs of the entire school rather than a particular class, and this ability makes their view invaluable to both teachers and administrators. They are well-positioned to be the leaders in the school community regarding the dissemination and use of genAI in schools. Hand-in-hand with teachers and administrators, school librarians can identify specific areas where genAI might serve the greatest good. They can also help school communities to avoid pitfalls in implementation.

This points up the need for continued training in this implementation of the use genAI in the pk-12 learning community, and school librarians as well as other information professionals can help to provide guardrails and stops to ensure ethical use of the technology. It will be a sharp learning curve, but school librarians have been here before and are poised to keep the community safe and ensure that ethical considerations are in place to protect students, faculty, and the entire learning community while leading the way to safe and efficient implementation of generative artificial intelligence in the school learning community.

REFERENCES

Ahlfeld, K. (2019). Lifting the curtain: Examining the importance of the shared foundation IV: Curate in the national school library standards for learners, school librarians, and school libraries. *Journal of Library Administration*, 59(4), 442–454. DOI: 10.1080/01930826.2019.1593712

American Association of School Librarians. (2018). *National school library standards: for learners, school librarians and school libraries*. American Library Association.

Babirad, R. (2024). COPPA, ed tech, and the school librarian. *Knowledge Quest, 52*(3), 36.

Bauld, A. (2023). Mission critical: Artificial intelligence is here. Librarians can play a crucial role in making sure schools get it right. *School Library Journal*, 69(9), 24.

Bekeš, E. R., & Galzina, V. (2023). Exploring the pedagogical use of AI-powered chatbots: Educational perceptions and practices. *2023 46th MIPRO ICT and Electronics Convention (MIPRO)*, Opatija, Croatia, pp. 636-641. DOI: 10.23919/MIPRO57284.2023.10159734

Bobo, S. (2023, August 22). Simply put, A.I is probability and statistics. *Speaking Artificially*.https://medium.com/speaking-artificially/simply-put-its-probability-and-statistics-ea955e3c4ba8

Bryant, J., Heitz, C., Sanghvi, S., & Wagle, D. (2020). *How artificial intelligence will impact K-12 teachers.* McKinsey & Company. https://www.mckinsey.com/~/media/McKinsey/Industries/Social%20Sector/Our%20Insights/How%20artificial%20intelligence%20will%20impact%20K%2012%20teachers/Ho w-artificial-intelligence-will-impact-K-12-teachers.pdf

Bureau of Labor Statistics. (2024). U.S. Department of Labor, Occupational outlook handbook, data scientists. https://www.bls.gov/ooh/math/data-scientists.htm

Coleman, M. C. (2020). School librarians take the lead collaborating on professional development. *Knowledge Quest*, 49(2), 10–18.

Conrad, E. J., & Rees, L. K. (2024). Generative AI as a catalyst to elevate school health education. *Journal of Physical Education, Recreation & Dance*, 95(6), 45–51. DOI: 10.1080/07303084.2024.2355865

De Groft, L. (2023). AI literacy: The road ahead. *School Library Journal*, 69(9), 26.

Dickey, S. (2023). School librarians as innovators. The tradition endures and expands. *Knowledge Quest*, 51(3), 28–33.

Digital Promise. (2024). Artificial intelligence in education. https://digitalpromise.org/initiative/artificial-intelligence-in-education/ai-literacy/

Driscoll, M. (1994). *Psychology of learning for instruction*. Allyn and Bacon.

Fraser, T., Cherdchaiyapong, N., Tekle, W., Thomas, E., Zayas, J., Page-Tan, C., & Aldrich, D. P. (2022). Trust but verify: Validating new measures for mapping social infrastructure in cities. *Urban Climate, 46*, 101287-. https://doi.org/DOI: 10.1080/15228053.2023.2233814

Fui-Hoon Nah, F., Zheng, R., Cai, J., Siau, K., & Chen, L. (2023). Generative AI and ChatGPT: Applications, challenges, and AI-human collaboration. *Journal of Information Technology Cases and Applications*, 25(3), 277–304. DOI: 10.1080/15228053.2023.2233814

Genkina, G. (2024, Mar. 7). AI prompt engineering is dead. Long live AI prompt engineering. *IEEE Spectrum*. https://spectrum.ieee.org/prompt-engineering-is-dead

Grassini, S. (2023). Shaping the future of education: Exploring the potential and consequences of AI and ChatGPT in educational settings. *Education Sciences, 13*(7), 692-. https://doi.org/DOI: 10.1080/15228053.2023.2233814

Green, L. S., & Chassereau, K. (2023). Modeling guided inquiry and school librarian instructional partnerships to pre-service teachers through digital video production. *Journal of Education for Library and Information Science*, 64(2), 185–205. DOI: 10.3138/jelis-2022-0015

Hacker, P., Mittelstadt, B., Borgesius, F. Z., & Wachter, S. (2024). *Generative discrimination: what happens when generative AI exhibits bias, and what can be done about it.* arXiv preprint arXiv:2407.10329. https://arxiv.org/abs/2407.10329 DOI: 10.2139/ssrn.4877398

Hargrave, M., Fisher, D., & Frey, N. (2024, September). Using AI to save time and lessen the the load. *Language Magazine*, 24(1), 28–31.

International Business Machines. (n.d.). *Deep Blue: IBM's computer checkmated a human chess champion in a computing tour de force.* IBM Heritage. https://www.ibm.com/history/deep-blue#:~:text=Deep%20Blue%20derived%20its%20chess,high%2Dspeed%20computations%20in%20parallel

International Society for Technology in Education. (2024). *StretchAI: An AI coach just for educators*. https://iste.org/ai#stretchai

Januszewski, A., & Monlenda, M. (2007). *Educational Technology: A Definition with Commentary*. Routledge., DOI: 10.4324/9780203054000

Jordan, M. I., & Mitchell, T. M. (2015, Jul 17). Machine learning: Trends, perspectives, and prospects. *Science*.https://www.science.org/doi/abs/10.1126/science.aaa8415

Kammer, J., & Hays, L. (2023). *Digital Literacy Made Simple : Strategies for Building Skills Across the Curriculum*. International Society for Technology in Education.

Lewis, M., & McNamara, K. (2021). A certified school librarian is a professional learning powerhouse. *The Learning Professional*, 42(4), 52.

Liu, X., & Zhong, B. (2024). What to consider before incorporating generative AI into schools? *AI & Society: Journal of Knowledge. AI & Society*, 1-3. Advance online publication. DOI: 10.1007/s00146-024-01872-9

Marchese, D. (2022, Dec. 21). An A. I. pioneer on what we should really fear. *NewYork Times Magazine* para. 7, note 4._https://www.nytimes.com/interactive/2022/12/26/magazine/yejin-choi-interview.html

Masoud, B., & Kamran, K. (2024). *Transformative Influence of LLM and AI Tools in Student Social Media Engagement: Analyzing Personalization, Communication Efficiency, and Collaborative Learning*. Working Paper. http://arxiv.org/abs/2407.15012

Mersand, S. (2021). The state of makerspace research: A review of the literature. *TechTrends*, 65(2), 174–186. DOI: 10.1007/s11528-020-00566-5

National Academies of Sciences, Engineering, and Medicine. (2018). *How people learn II: Learners, contexts, and cultures (2nd ed.)*. The National Academies Press.

Open, A. I. (2024). *ChatGPT* (August 28 version). [Large language model]. https://chat.openai.com/chat

Perrotta, R. (2023, Feb. 17). *Peabody EDI Office responds to MSU shooting with email written using ChatGPT*.https://vanderbilthustler.com/2023/02/17/peabody-edi-office-responds-to-msu-shooting-with-email-written-using-chatgpt/

Press, G. (2018, Feb 7). *The brute force of IBM Deep Blue And Google DeepMind*. https://www.forbes.com/sites/gilpress/2018/02/07/the-brute-force-of-deep-blue-and-deep-learning/

Priest, M. (2024, March 7). *AI trainer: A job of the future*. Accessed September 10, 2024, https://boost.ai/blog/ai-trainer-a-job-of-the-future/

Shane, J. (2019). *You look like a thing and I love you*. Voracious.

Soulen, R. R. (2021). Enabling collaboration through mentorship: Examining the role of the school librarian. *School Library Research, 24.*

Tait, E., & Pierson, C. M. (2022). Artificial intelligence and robots in libraries: Opportunities in LIS curriculum for preparing the librarians of tomorrow. *Journal of the Australian Library and Information Association*, 71(3), 256–274. https://doi-org.cyrano.ucmo.edu/10.1080/24750158.2022.2081111. DOI: 10.1080/24750158.2022.2081111

University at Austin Center for teaching and Learning (2023). *Five things to know about ChatGPT.*https://ctl.utexas.edu/teaching-technology/5-things-know-about-chatgpt

Walton Family Foundation. (2024). AI chatbots in schools: Findings from a poll of K-12 teachers, students, parents, and college undergraduates. https://8ce82b94a8c4fdc3ea6d-b1d233e3bc3cb10858bea65ff05e18f2.ssl.cf2.rackcdn.com/bf/24/cd3646584af89e7c668c7705a006/deck-impact-analysis-national-schools-tech-tracker-may-2024-1.pdf

Weiser, B. (2023, May 27). Here's what happens when your lawyer uses chatGPT. *The New York Times.*https://www.nytimes.com/2023/05/27/nyregion/avianca-airline-lawsuit-chatgpt.html

Yang, G. R., & Wang, X. J. (2020). Artificial neural networks for neuroscientists: A primer. *Neuron*, 107(6), 1048–1070. DOI: 10.1016/j.neuron.2020.09.005 PMID: 32970997

Yegnanarayana, B. (1994). Artificial neural networks for pattern recognition. *Sadhana*, 19(2), 189–238. DOI: 10.1007/BF02811896

Yi, K., Turner, R., & Turner, S. (2019). Investigating technology integration practices and competencies of school librarians: A case study in Kentucky, USA. *School Libraries Worldwide*, 25(1), 35–56.

Yorio, K. (2023). The ChatGPT revolution: School librarians explore new AI technology. Will it dramatically change education? *School Library Journal*, 69(2), 10.

Chapter 13
Architectural Education: AI Integrative Challenges and Prospects

Aditi Nag
https://orcid.org/0000-0002-0604-6945
Birla Institute of Technology, Mesra, India

Jinal Boricha
Birla Institute of Technology, Mesra, India

Amrita Sarkar
https://orcid.org/0000-0001-7415-2822
Birla Institute of Technology, Mesra, Lalpur, India

ABSTRACT

This paper explores the integration of Artificial Intelligence (AI) into architectural education, highlighting the challenges and opportunities in this dynamic intersection. AI technologies are increasingly influential across industries, but the integration faces challenges in reconciling AI's computational prowess with the nuanced creativity of architectural expression. Ethical considerations arise regarding the authenticity of AI-generated designs and potential disruptions to traditional design processes. However, AI integration enriches architectural education by introducing generative design tools, data-driven analysis, and aligning students with the evolving architectural landscape. Successfully addressing integration challenges can lead to amplified creative exploration, data-driven architectural solutions, and collaborative synergies. Adaptive pedagogical approaches can harness AI's potential, fostering graduates capable of harnessing AI's advantages while preserving architectural ingenuity.

DOI: 10.4018/979-8-3693-6527-4.ch013

1 INTRODUCTION

Higher education in architecture is more than just learning technical skills; it's a journey. It is a procedure that promotes a comprehensive comprehension of how the built environment affects people's lives and the advancement of society. Beyond blueprints and building codes, architectural education empowers students to become visionary thinkers capable of addressing complex global challenges, from urbanization and sustainability to cultural preservation and technological integration. Architectural education stands at the crossroads of tradition and innovation as the discipline navigates an era marked by rapid technological advancements, evolving societal needs, and an expanding global landscape. The convergence of artistic expression, technical acumen, and critical thinking defines the essence of architectural education, where aspiring architects are nurtured to envision, design, and construct spaces that harmonize functionality, aesthetics, and sustainability. In an age where the built environment is undergoing unprecedented transformation, architectural education has become increasingly pivotal in shaping the architects of tomorrow *(Quy et al., 2023)*. However, the landscape of architectural education is not devoid of challenges. The integration of rapidly advancing technologies such as artificial intelligence (AI), virtual reality (VR), and Building Information Modeling (BIM) introduces a dynamic dimension that necessitates adapting curriculums to ensure graduates are equipped to harness these tools effectively. Once an emerging consideration, sustainability has become central to architectural discourse, urging educational institutions to emphasize eco-conscious design and urban planning principles. The globalization of architectural practice underscores the importance of imparting a global perspective to students, enabling them to design for diverse cultural, environmental, and regulatory contexts. While challenges abound, the prospects for architectural education are equally compelling. The advent of AI offers new avenues for design exploration, computational analysis, and generative design, enhancing the creative process and efficiency *(Chatterjee & Bhattacharjee, 2020)*. Collaborative skills are accentuated as architects collaborate with professionals from diverse disciplines to address complex urban challenges. Sustainability is no longer an option but a mandate, providing opportunities for architectural education to lead the charge in shaping sustainable cities and communities *(Quy et al., 2023)*. At its core, architectural higher education encompasses a multifaceted curriculum that blends creativity, critical thinking, and practical application, including design studios, technical expertise, history and theory, environment and sustainable design, and interdisciplinary collaboration.

The advancement of new technologies and the computing power of the new intelligent machines are fundamentally tied to the future of higher education. In this discipline, developments in artificial intelligence present new opportunities and challenges for teaching and learning that have the potential to profoundly alter governance and the internal structure of higher education institutions. There is little consensus on a final definition since responses to "What is artificial intelligence?" are influenced by philosophical stances adopted since Aristotle *(Popenici & Kerr, 2017)*. Globally, educational institutions are dealing with rapid technological advancements that make many subject-matter expertise and technical skills obsolete or insufficient by the time students graduate. This situation results from changing K–12 and earlier school curricula and quick changes in enterprises and/or practices *(Ra et al., 2019)*. Due to the mastery of computing, automation, and generative capabilities both for software and hardware, formerly categorized skills are becoming ordinary. Therefore, skill advancements are not a constraint on the requirement to create a framework for continuously updated architectural education. We also need to create a theoretical framework for future architects. Although the same problems have repeatedly arisen with the introduction of Computer-Aided Design (CAD) and Building Information Modelling (BIM), the present architectural education is expected to address the industry's current and future challenges while actively working to reform it *(Başarır, 2022)*.

Artificial Intelligence (AI) is revolutionizing various sectors, and its transformative impact is keenly felt in education. According to *Becker et al. (2018)* and *Seldon & Abidoye (2018)*, one of the most important advancements of the century has been the use of artificial intelligence (AI) in education. AI in Education (AIED) is a dynamic domain that amalgamates cutting-edge technology with pedagogical innovation to create personalized, efficient, and engaging learning experiences. Despite the rapid development of AIED and the rise in demand due to COVID-19 effects, little is known about the ethical principles that should direct the creation, advancement, and implementation of ethical and reliable AI in education. The depth and scope to which modern ethical and legal frameworks can capture the implications of AI evolution remain to be identified, even if those are addressed *(Nguyen et al., 2023)*.

The paper explores the evolving landscape of architectural education in the context of integrating artificial intelligence (AI). It navigates through the historical foundations of architectural education, outlines the essential components of architectural curricula, and addresses the challenges and prospects associated with the integration of AI. The paper aims to shed light on the transformative potential of AI in architectural education by dissecting challenges such as ethical considerations, curriculum development, and resource allocation while highlighting the myriad prospects, including data-driven design decisions, automation, and collaborative tools. Ultimately, the paper seeks to provide educators, students, and stakeholders with a comprehensive understanding of the complex intersection between architectural education and the technological advancements AI brings, shaping the architects of the future.

2 HISTORICAL FOUNDATIONS OF ARCHITECTURAL EDUCATION

With its rich tapestry of historical influences, architectural education has evolved over millennia to reflect the changing paradigms of design, construction, and societal needs. Tracing its origins back to ancient civilizations, architectural education has been shaped by cultural, technological, and philosophical developments, leaving an indelible mark on how architects are trained and approach their craft.

In ancient civilizations such as Egypt and Greece, rudimentary forms of architectural education emerged within monumental construction and artistic expression. In Egypt, artisans and craftsmen acquired the skills to build grand structures through informal apprenticeships. This hands-on learning emphasized mastering practical techniques and knowledge transfer within guilds. Meanwhile, in ancient Greece, architectural education gained a more intellectual dimension. The teachings of philosophers like Plato emphasized mathematics and philosophy as foundational elements of architecture, paving the way for a more systematic approach to design and construction. The medieval and Renaissance periods ushered in new paradigms of architectural education. The Middle Ages saw the emergence of guilds that trained artisans in various construction trades, marking a transition from purely experiential learning to a more structured approach. These guilds laid the groundwork for integrating theory and practice to characterize future architectural education. The Renaissance witnessed a revival of classical principles by rediscovering Vitruvius' "De Architectura." Architectural treatises gained prominence, providing a theoretical foundation for architectural education and emphasizing the importance of drawing, proportion, and aesthetics. The Enlightenment and the subsequent modernization of society brought about significant changes in architectural education. Establishing institutions like the École des Beaux-Arts in France exemplified a new era of formalized architectural education. This school systematized architectural training, providing a structured curriculum and employing the atelier system, which focused on studio-based learning under the guidance of master architects. This approach emphasized artistic expression, drawing skills, and classical design principles, setting the stage for future architects shaping the built environment.

In the 20th century, they witnessed further transformations in architectural education, driven by technological advancements and shifts in design philosophies. The Bauhaus school, founded by Walter Gropius, revolutionized education by embracing an interdisciplinary approach that merged art, craft, and technology. This holistic approach to design education sought to produce architects who could address the complex challenges of modern society by integrating various disciplines and fostering experimentation. The post-World War II era saw architectural education diversify in response to the changing demands of a rapidly evolving world. Modernist influences brought a focus on functionality, efficiency, and social responsibility, shaping architectural education to reflect these values. As industrialization progressed, technical institutions like the École Polytechnique emerged to meet the demand for architects with strong technical skills. The digital revolution of the late 20th century and beyond brought about another profound shift in architectural education. Computer-aided design (CAD) and digital tools transformed design processes, necessitating technology integration into architectural curricula. Schools adapted by teaching students how to navigate these new tools effectively while maintaining the core principles of design thinking and creativity. A collective overview of the historical developments in architectural education has been depicted in Figure 1 for easier navigation and understanding.

Figure 1. Timeline of historical developments in architectural education (created using Preceden.com)

Architectural education is marked by a commitment to sustainability, global awareness, and technological literacy in the contemporary landscape. The urgency of environmental concerns has led to a re-evaluation of architectural practices, prompting schools to integrate sustainability, resilience, and ecological responsibility principles into their curricula. Globalization has brought an appreciation for cultural diversity and a realization that architectural solutions must be contextually sensitive. Moreover, emerging technologies like digital fabrication and parametric design have empowered architects with new means of exploration and expression, reshaping design's possible boundaries. From the informal apprenticeships of ancient civilizations to the interdisciplinary approaches of the modern era, architectural education has continuously adapted to the evolving needs of the built environment. As we stand on the precipice of an increasingly complex future, understanding these historical foundations provides a lens through which we can envision the trajectory of architectural education and its enduring impact on the world around us.

3 BACKGROUND ON ARCHITECTURAL EDUCATION AND AIED

The idea of using technology to enhance education dates back to the 1950s and 1960s with the advent of computers. Early efforts focused on computer-assisted instruction (CAI), where computers delivered educational content and exercises *(Blanchard, 2015)*. Over time, as AI technologies developed, the concept of AIED emerged, combining advances in AI with academic theory. As conventional design methods start to be replaced, computer technology has given architects new affordances. Computational technologies undoubtedly made efficiency, control, and intelligence feasible; as a result, these techniques are increasingly seen as indispensable to architectural practices *(Soliman, Taha, & El Sayad, 2019)*. Less clear, however, is how this technology has started to affect architectural practice, the community they serve, and consequently, architectural education. In architectural design as well as in urban planning courses, computer technology is defined by *Qaqish and Hanna (1997)* to encompass all computer programs, whether they are integrated into the design studio or are stand-alone courses *(Soliman, Taha, & El Sayad, 2019)*.

Digital technology has become more prevalent in the design studio curriculum in architecture education in the 21st century. These numerous computer-aided drawing, enumerating, modeling, and analytic technologies became essential teaching points in the design studio and began to influence the whole curricular framework for architectural education. To balance the learning curve and the number of software options accessible to architects, they must also be deployed as support courses *(Soliman, Taha, & El Sayad, 2019)*. Traditional educational resources for architecture are primarily focused on actual 3D models and 2D sketching. Through the 1990s, this scenario altered. In an experiment on architectural education conducted by Angélil in 2003, computer technology was used to supplement traditional teaching methods, at least for the last three years of the program *(Blanchard, 2015;Angélil, 2003)*. The primary focus of today's educators and academics is integrating fully digital instruction. Their key goals include developing students' skills and talents and employing computer programs as design tools. However, since there is currently neither a framework nor a fundamental structure for the use of computers in architectural education, many architectural schools and departments, particularly those in developed nations, have developed their requirements by adding more computer courses to their curricula *(Soliman, Taha, & El Sayad, 2019;Zhu, Yu, & Riezebos, 2016).* The integration of Artificial Intelligence in Architectural Education (AIED-AE) is an emerging area that aims to enhance the teaching and learning of architecture through AI technologies. AIED-AE seeks to leverage AI's capabilities to provide personalized and adaptive learning experiences, assist in design processes, and offer insights into architectural concepts and projects. Table 1 depicts the ways AIED can be intrgated into architectural education for effective learning and designing.

Table 1. AIED-AE integration

Integrative areas	Ways to integrate AIED with architectural education
Design Assistance	Aid architecture students in the design process by providing real-time feedback on design choices, suggesting alternative solutions, and offering insights into spatial arrangements and aesthetics.
Virtual Studios	Virtual reality (VR) and augmented reality (AR) technologies, often powered by AI, can create immersive design environments that allow students to experience their designs in 3D, fostering better spatial understanding and design visualization skills.
Generative Design	Help students explore a wide range of design options quickly. These tools can generate multiple design alternatives based on specified parameters and constraints, encouraging creativity and innovation.
Feedback and Assessment	Provide detailed feedback on design projects, highlighting strengths and areas for improvement. This immediate feedback loop can accelerate the learning process.
Resource Access	Assist students in accessing and analyzing vast architectural databases, historical references, and contemporary case studies, aiding research and concept development.
Personalized Learning	AIED can adapt learning materials and assignments to individual student's needs, helping them progress at their own pace and address their unique learning challenges.
Collaborative Learning	Facilitate collaborative design projects among students, allowing them to collaborate on virtual models and share ideas seamlessly.
Building Performance Analysis	Analyze and simulate building performance metrics, such as energy efficiency, lighting, and acoustics, helping students understand the impact of their design choices on the built environment.

While AIED offers numerous possibilities for architectural education, it's essential to balance the creative and human aspects of design and technological interventions. Educators must consider the ethical implications carefully, ensure AI tools enhance students' learning experiences, and encourage critical thinking and design innovation. As AIED-AE continues to evolve, collaborative efforts between architects, educators, and AI experts are crucial to shaping its future direction.

4 CONFLUENCE OF AI AND ARCHITECTURAL EDUCATION

The confluence of AI and architectural education marks a dynamic intersection reshaping how architects are trained, ideas are conceptualized, and designs are realized. As technology rapidly advances, the architectural field embraces the transformative potential of Artificial Intelligence (AI) to augment traditional pedagogical approaches. AI technologies have the ability to improve several facets of architectural education, including project management, sustainability analysis, and design processes. Building information modeling and cutting-edge visualization methods are just a few of the significant outputs of artificial intelligence and architecture's collaboration that will impact the field's present and future *(Ceylan, 2021)*. This topic delves into the multifaceted relationship between AI and architectural education, exploring how AI's computational power, data analysis capabilities, and generative algorithms are revolutionizing the learning experience and creative processes within the realm of architecture.

The architects must process much information during the initial design phases, including legal requirements, analyses of the physical environment, user needs, functional requirements, precedent cases, etc. They are all concerned with processing data. Processing all this data without computer tools may be impossible, but AI offers significant assistance. Architectural education has long emphasized the cultivation of design intuition, critical thinking, and spatial understanding. With the infusion of AI, educators and students alike are presented with a new toolkit that transcends conventional boundaries. Additionally, speeding up the indexing and categorizing data needed for the initial design phases has an unseen but significant impact on the design process. AI-enabled tools aid in design ideation by generating various possibilities based on parameters and constraints, accelerating iteration, and encouraging students to explore creative solutions. They also facilitate informed decision-making by analyzing complex datasets, enabling architectural students to refine designs to meet performance standards and align with sustainability imperatives.

Yet, as AI becomes a prominent partner in architectural education, questions of ethics, creativity, and the human touch come to the forefront. Striking a harmonious balance between AI-assisted design and human ingenuity is a pivotal challenge. Students must grapple with the ethical considerations of relying on algorithms for design ideation while retaining the essence of artistic expression and cultural sensitivity. Moreover, this topic underscores the need for a curriculum that cultivates proficiency in AI tools and a holistic understanding of their potential and limitations. Architectural education must adapt to incorporate computational thinking, programming skills, and interdisciplinary collaboration, fostering graduates who are not only architects but also technologically literate innovators. As AI becomes an indispensable collaborator, architectural pedagogy must evolve to empower students with the skills to navigate this symbiotic relationship.

4.1 Early Development

A substantial change in how technology is incorporated into the teaching and learning processes within the subject of architecture can be seen in the early development of AI in architectural education. The increasing integration of AI into architecture has changed over time. Since the 1960s, AI has been incorporated into architecture, and as technology has developed, this integration has increased. Over time, researchers, architects, engineers, and technologists have worked together to integrate Artificial Intelligence (AI) into the discipline of architecture. Researchers in fields including computer science, cognitive science, and architecture started to look into the possibility of utilizing computers to help with design tasks in the 1960s and 1970s. The development of rule-based systems and the incorporation of AI ideas into design procedures were both made possible thanks to these early initiatives. Table 2 describes AI's initial interactions with architecture.

Table 2. Outline of AI's first encounter with the field of architecture

Period of encounter	Development in integrating AI into architecture
1960_Early Exploration	Researchers have started looking into employing computers for architectural design work.
1970_Intersection of Architecture and Computation	At MIT, Nicholas Negroponte founded the Architecture Machine Group, specializing in fusing computers and architecture.
1980_Knowledge-Based Systems	As symbolic AI methods gain popularity, knowledge-based systems for aiding architectural design are being created.
1990_Generative Design and CAD	The use of algorithms to produce architectural solutions is gaining popularity in generative design concepts. As computer-aided design (CAD) systems proliferate, architects can digitize their designs and iterate more quickly.
2000_Parametric Design and Computational Tools	A growing number of architects use parametric design techniques to produce designs that adapt to changing parameters. Computational tools and plugins like Grasshopper for Rhino facilitate algorithmic design processes.
2010_Machine Learning and Data-Driven Design	Architects can now evaluate data for design insights using machine learning tools that are more widely available. AI is utilized for sophisticated behavior simulation, energy performance analysis, and predictive modeling.
2010_Generative Adversarial Networks	For their capacity to produce intricate and imaginative designs, Generative Adversarial Networks (GANs) are drawing attention.

continued on following page

Table 2. Continued

Period of encounter	Development in integrating AI into architecture
2010 to Present Human-AI Collaboration	The emphasis now switches to human-AI collaboration, where AI helps architects develop and assess design ideas.
2020 to Present	With ongoing research in generative design, sustainability, and urban planning, the incorporation of AI into architecture is still evolving.

The timeline shows how, over the years, AI has gradually become more and more influential in architectural design and practice. AI has progressed in architecture through collaboration and symbiosis, enhancing rather than substituting human ingenuity and problem-solving. AI's influence in architecture will grow as technology develops, resulting in more creative, effective, and sustainable design solutions. The use of artificial intelligence (AI) in the area of architecture has changed how architects communicate, develop, and analyze. A few areas of AI application in the field of architecture have been depicted in Figure 2.

Figure 2. AI applications in the architecture field

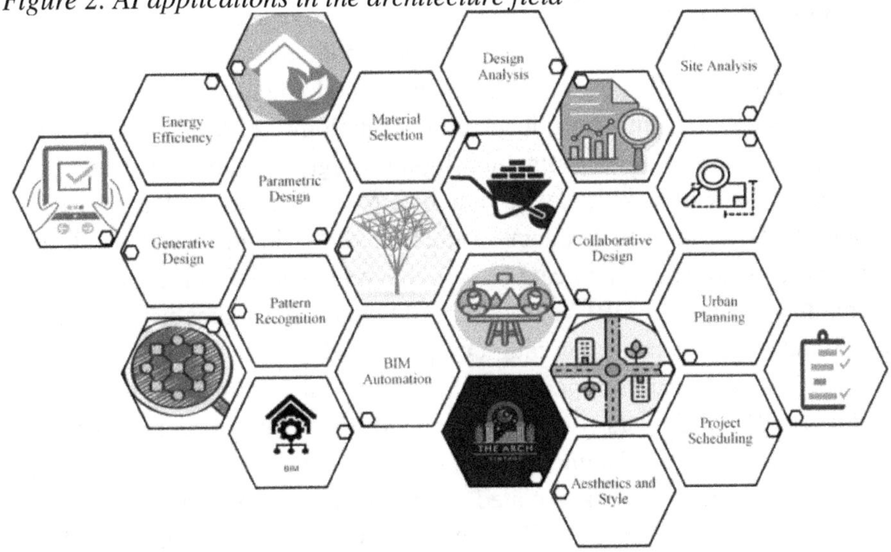

4.1.1 Establishment of the First AI-Focused Architectural Research Center

The Design Machine Group at the Massachusetts Institute of Technology (MIT), created by Nicholas Negroponte in the 1970s, is one of the pioneering organizations focused on AI in architecture. Although not exclusively focused on AI, this group played a crucial role in examining the relationship between computation and architecture, which helped pave the way for incorporating AI ideas into architectural design. The team did research in fields like computer-aided design, generative design, and interactive design systems to use computers to help with design tasks.

Several different research institutes and organizations have contributed to the development of AI in the architectural profession. However, the Design Machine Group at MIT is one of the first and best-known instances of a research group that examined the confluence of AI and architecture.

The Architectural Association (AA) School of Architecture, London's Design Research Lab, and the Emergent Technologies program have promoted the study of cutting-edge technologies in architecture, such as AI and computational design. The University of Stuttgart's Institute for Computational Design and Construction (ICD) studies and applies advanced computational and robotic techniques in architecture and construction, including AI-driven design methodologies. The Royal Danish Academy of Fine Arts' Centre for Information Technology and Architecture (CITA) has been at the forefront of investigating digital design and fabrication technologies, including AI, within architectural practice. MIT's Media Lab has researched many fields that overlap with architecture and technology, including AI and design, even though it is not solely dedicated to architecture. The Adaptive Architecture and Computation Lab (AADRL) at the Bartlett School of Architecture, University College London, has been researching computational design, AI, and generative systems. In several research projects, the SIAL (Spatial Information Architecture Laboratory) at RMIT University has examined the nexus between architecture, digital technologies, and artificial intelligence. A network of scholars and practitioners in computer-aided design and associated technologies in architecture, such as AI, makes up CAADRIA (Computer-Aided Architectural Design Research in Asia). The University of Bath's Center for Advanced Studies in Architecture (CASA) has investigated cutting-edge computational and artificial intelligence (AI) tools for architectural design, modeling, and analysis.

4.2 Implementation in Curriculum

Computers can be utilized in the history of architecture to analyze and depict the growth of towns or to examine different architectural styles. Construction deformation under various essential loads can be simulated in engineering construction. Computers may be used in urban planning to calculate the areas of multiple town components and affect town life *(Asanowicz, 1998)*. Various languages are used in architecture, including GDL for ArchiCAD, AutoSLIP and VBA for AutoCAD, RhinoScript for Rhino, MEL for Maya, and others *(Schmitt, 2010)*. By adding AI concepts and tools into the curriculum, numerous architectural schools and colleges have realized how crucial it is to prepare future architects for the rapidly changing technological landscape.

The computer in the classroom can fundamentally alter three components: the student, the lesson, and the teacher. Courses on computational design methods, parametric modeling, and algorithmic thinking are standard in architecture educational programs. In these courses, students learn to use software tools to generate designs and investigate intricate architectural forms. Some programs provide classes that instruct students on how to use AI technologies for energy modeling, daylighting analysis, building performance analysis, and other facets of design optimization. To share their knowledge and experiences with students, architecture schools frequently host workshops and attract guest lecturers who are authorities in both AI and architecture. To collaborate on projects that require AI-driven design and analysis, certain universities encourage collaboration between architecture students and students with computer science, engineering, or data science backgrounds. Through research projects, design studios, and thesis work, students can investigate AI applications in architecture and test out innovative approaches to design and technology. Some architectural schools feature prototyping laboratories that give students access to AI tools and equipment to test out AI-driven design methodologies. Some organizations hold design challenges or hackathons where students are tasked with creating AI-based solutions to problems in architecture. In addition to their formal education, online platforms and resources allow architecture students to learn about AI principles and techniques independently. Architectural professionals also benefit from workshops and short courses on incorporating AI into architectural practice.

4.3 AI-Driven Design Tools

An artificial intelligence (AI) system known as a knowledge-based system (KBS) solves complex problems using explicit knowledge and reasoning. It is intended to capture, represent, and manipulate knowledge in a particular domain to offer insightful responses, suggestions, or decision-making assistance. AI can significantly improve architects' knowledge and skills, analyze designs more quickly, and increase design capabilities in the modern architecture industry, which is regarded as a multi-skilled size and complicated market.

Ibrahim Motawa and Abdul Kareem Almarshad attempted to design an integrated system to capture information and knowledge of building maintenance activities when/after repair to understand how a building is deteriorating and support preventative and corrective maintenance decisions. The method comprises a Case-Based Reasoning (CBR) module to capture expertise and a BIM module to capture pertinent information. The technology can assist maintenance teams in drawing lessons from past mistakes and tracking the complete history of a building element and all elements impacted by prior maintenance operations *(Motawa & Almarshad, 2012)*. Ozan Okudan, Cenk Budayan, and Irem Dikmen created a knowledge-based Risk Management tool to evaluate the risk management of any construction project in Turkey. A web-based application called Case Based Risk has been made to support the cyclic risk management process. It uses an efficient case retrieval mechanism while considering a wide range of fuzzy linguistic variables representing project similarity qualities *(Okudan & Budayan, 2021)*. Different kinds of Smart Application program interfaces are available in Italy for use with applications and services related to Smart Cities. To create mobile applications for city users with multi-domain data while simultaneously gathering user preferences and behavior data, The Sii-Mobility project results on mobility and transportation were used in the development of the Km4City ontological paradigm, which municipal operators and businesses have embraced to create web and mobile applications (Badii et al., 2017). A Floor Plan Design Expert System (FPDX), a knowledge-based CAD tool, was designed to help architects assess their residential construction floor plans against government building codes using model-based reasoning. It offers the tools and information to compare a floor design to a set of construction codes encoded as rulers *(Yau et al., 1994)*. A knowledge-based IT platform for heritage buildings was created in Florence to collect data and transform it into information that is useful for any activity involved in the lifecycle of a heritage building, including first-person analysis, documentation, preventive conservation, restoration, social and economic aspects, use, and management *(Tiano et al., 2019)*. An IT model that consolidates knowledge was created to evaluate the seismic resiliency and static safety of historic buildings in Italy *(Caprili & Puncello, 2019)*. The information system and database for colonial architecture use a knowledge-based approach for categorizing and representing historical colonial architecture and the finest first searching algorithms for data retrieval in Indonesia *(Prabawasari et al., 2016)*. In UAE, a system of experts with expertise in Tall building's basic structural design has been developed using TALLEX. A unique aspect of the software is the concept of "building a virtual number of stories," created in the current research, to streamline the decision-making process and make it more applicable to common design practice *(Sabouni & Al-Mourad, 1996)*.

In generative design, various design options are automatically generated depending on predetermined input criteria utilizing algorithms and computer processes frequently powered by AI. Examining various alternatives allows architects to produce more effective, sustainable, and innovative designs. Generative design is beneficial for complicated architectural forms, structural optimization, urban planning, and other design difficulties. Discrete decision-making is central to generative design. Instead of automating configuration, generative design methodologies offer established tools that support collaborative design or imaginative mass customization *(Nourian et al., 2023)*. Cellular automata, genetic algorithms, L-systems, shape grammars, and swarm intelligence are various generative design methods utilized in architectural design *(Singh & Gu, 2012)*. A GDS based on evolution and intended to assist architects in finding environmentally friendly and sustainable architecture solutions. The system uses a genetic algorithm (GA) as the search engine and a goal-oriented design *(Caldas, 2008)*. A creative modeling tool creates corbel, molding, and panel shapes. To understand the latent representation of feature curves and ornamentation shapes, InfoGAN and VAE models are built *(Zhang et al., 2022)*.

While CAD alone is not regarded as an instance of artificial intelligence (AI), it can be improved and used with AI technologies to produce more automated and intelligent design processes. AI-driven tools are beginning to be used in some CAD applications. AI algorithms, for instance, can evaluate design components and recommend changes for improved functionality or aesthetics. These AI-assisted features seek to enhance the design process by offering suggestions and insights. One of the top firms integrating AI into its design product is Dassault Systemes Company, the maker of the SOLIDWORKS program *(Hunde & Woldeyohannes, 2022)*. The business unveiled xDesign, an AI tool to extrude and sketch in engineering design projects. Another AI application that AUTODESK created is generative design. AI will be empowered by generative design to transform laborious design procedures into intelligent ones. The method creates a collection of unique designs based on an integrated parametric CAD system by randomly changing the parameters within pre-defined boundaries *(Hunde & Woldeyohannes, 2022)*.

By specifying relationships and limitations between various design factors, parametric design tools in architecture relate to software and methods that let architects and designers construct and manipulate complicated designs. With the aid of these technologies, architects may investigate several design options, find the best solutions, and produce dynamic, responsive designs that change in response to changing inputs. A visual programming editor called Grasshopper was created by David Rutten at Robert McNeel & Associates *(Wahbeh, 2017)*. It is, undoubtedly, the best tool for algorithmic design as a Rhino3D plug-in. Despite having a robust built-in GDL parametric development language, the Nemetschek group's widely used BIM program Archicad has lagged behind its rivals in computational design *(Wahbeh, 2017)*. For the construction of skins, parametric design with computational methods is frequently practical. The skin's parametric design within the BIM platform provides various benefits, including the use of BIM *(Wahbeh, 2017)*.

Machine learning and data-driven approaches are fundamental ideas in architecture that use cutting-edge technologies to improve design procedures, maximize performance, and guide decision-making. A branch of artificial intelligence called machine learning involves teaching machines to recognize patterns and anticipate outcomes from data. In data-driven techniques, decision-making for building design and construction is guided by empirical data. To forecast the future state of MEP components, ANN and SVM machine learning methods are utilized *(Cheng et al., 2020)*.

The architecture's design, building, and visualization processes could be entirely transformed using Augmented Reality (AR) and Artificial Intelligence (AI). This combination can boost decision-making, workflow efficiency, and creativity. Through augmented reality (AR), architects may see how a proposed structure would seem and interact with its surroundings. AR projects 3D virtual content over the actual environment. As a result, the user primarily sees the real world *(Schiavi et al., 2022)*.

One of the fields that advancements in AI technology have significantly impacted is architecture. Architecture is an essential field of experimentation for applications of artificial intelligence due to its complexity. Building information modeling and cutting-edge visualization methods are just a few of the significant outputs of artificial intelligence and architecture's collaboration that will impact the field's present and future. However, the fundamental implications of AI on architecture that are more long-lasting must be considered in the curricula for architectural education that lay the foundation for the field's future.

4.4 Ethical Considerations

The use of software systems in daily life and society is growing. They can both enhance and detract from life's quality, interfering with human rights by, for instance, eroding personal and societal morals and posing moral dilemmas. Software architects must think ethically from the beginning of the design process, for example, when choosing the architecture, to avoid such problems. Stakeholders, ethical principles and their relationships, ethical issues, and ethical judgments are all considered *(Alidoosti et al., 2023)*. A proactive reaction to the growing use of AI technology in the industry is the addition of AI ethics courses to the architecture curriculum. Ensuring that AI developments are produced ethically and responsibly is crucial as architects use AI to improve design, analysis, and decision-making. AI is unable to understand cultural norms and traditions fully. AI can be given the ability to make decisions, but it cannot take the position of architects in the process of making moral decisions. It cannot communicate dynamically or fully comprehend the goals and experiences of various stakeholders. AI can also not draw from one's experiences, feelings, and opinions of diverse thoughts and designs.

An AI code of ethics can outline the values and inspire righteous behavior.

- An ethical AI system needs to be open to all, understandable, serve a useful purpose, and handle data responsibly.
- An explainable AI system helps the corporate governance needed to guarantee the moral use of AI.
- Data privacy rights are respected by an AI system that uses data responsibly. An AI system depends on data; more data typically leads to better models.

Despite its advanced levels of complexity and the wide range of options it provides, AI is still a tool for design, and the architect is the designer, something that architects and architecture students need to keep in mind. Only predefined algorithms are used to process the data. AI cannot understand the context; thus, designing in the context of the past is a challenging problem. For design decisions, the human intellect still has the last say. Intuition and creativity are still indisputable aspects of the human mind. Instead of viewing AI technologies as the primary actors in design, designers must understand how to use them.

5 AIED-AE POSSIBILITIES

Incorporating Artificial Intelligence (AI) into the Architectural Education (AIED-AE) curriculum holds the promise of revolutionizing how architects are trained and shaping the future of architectural practice. The integration of AI technologies can enhance various aspects of architectural education, from design exploration and sustainable approaches to personalized learning experiences and interdisciplinary collaboration (Selwyn, 2023). In this comprehensive exploration, we delve into AI's possibilities in the AIED-AE curriculum, highlighting its transformative impact on pedagogy, student engagement, and the evolution of architectural thought.

One of the profound possibilities of integrating AI into the AIED-AE curriculum is its capacity to revolutionize design exploration and ideation. Generative design algorithms, fueled by AI, can assist students in generating a multitude of design alternatives. By inputting parameters and constraints, students can witness AI producing an array of design solutions that go beyond the limitations of human imagination (Hwang et al., 2020). This encourages a more expansive creative process, fostering a culture of experimentation, risk-taking, and innovation. AI's data analysis capabilities offer a novel approach to design decisions. In the AIED-AE curriculum, students can harness AI to analyze intricate datasets encompassing environmental conditions, user preferences, and material properties. AI-driven simulations can predict the real-world performance of designs, empowering students to make informed decisions that align aesthetics with functionality, sustainability, and user well-being. This integration equips future architects with the skills to create designs that are not only visually captivating but also rooted in evidence-based decision-making. AI-powered virtual reality (VR) and simulation technologies redefine architectural education by immersing students in their designs. Through AI-driven simulations, students can experience architectural spaces virtually, assessing elements such as lighting, acoustics, and spatial relationships. This interactive approach transforms learning into an experiential journey, allowing students to fine-tune their designs based on real-time feedback. Such immersive experiences nurture a deeper understanding of spatial qualities and human interactions within architectural contexts. AI's capabilities extend to providing rapid and objective automated critique on design projects. AI-driven systems can analyze design elements for proportions, aesthetics, and adherence to architectural principles. This consistent feedback loop empowers students to refine their designs iteratively, develop an acute visual sense, and hone their ability to create well-balanced and harmonious spaces. AI's adaptability makes personalized learning a reality in the AIED-AE curriculum. By analyzing students' learning patterns, preferences, and strengths, AI systems can tailor educational content to suit individual needs. This approach fosters deeper engagement, improves knowledge retention, and optimizes student progress. The personalized learning experience equips graduates with a comprehensive skill set that aligns with their individual strengths and interests.

The integration of AI can play a pivotal role in nurturing environmentally conscious architects. AI can analyze vast datasets related to sustainable design, including energy consumption, material life cycles, and environmental impact. By suggesting eco-friendly materials, energy-efficient systems, and sustainable design strategies, AI empowers students to prioritize environmental considerations and contribute to a more sustainable built environment. AI-powered collaborative tools enhance interdisciplinary collaboration, mirroring real-world architectural practice. By enabling seamless communication and information sharing across disciplines, these tools encourage students to collaborate with professionals from engineering, urban planning, environmental science, and other fields. This interconnectivity equips students with the skills to navigate complex, multifaceted projects in their future careers. Figure 3 depicts the AIED-AE curriculum structure that needs to be adopted for effective integration of AI in higher education in the field of architecture.

Figure 3. Proposed AIED-AE curriculum

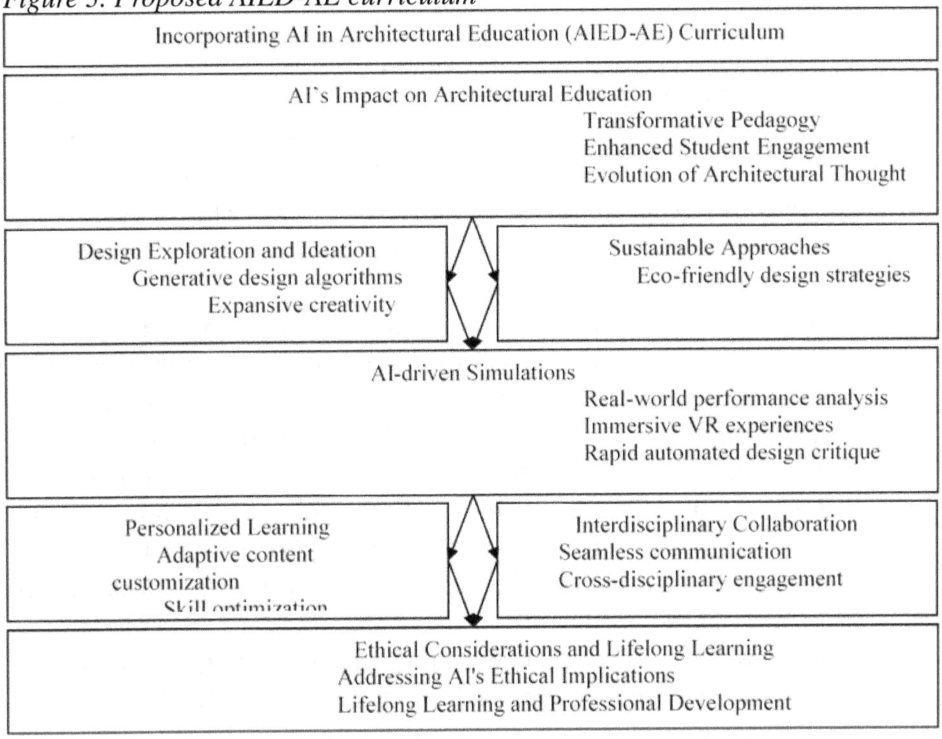

AI-integrated AIED-AE curricula expose students to cutting-edge research and innovations in architecture. AI can analyze architectural trends, emerging materials, and innovative design strategies, providing students with insights into the industry's latest developments. Exposure to AI-driven research enhances students' critical thinking, enabling them to contribute to the evolution of architectural thought and practice. Integrating AI into the AIED-AE curriculum provides an opportunity to discuss AI's ethical implications and societal impact in architecture. Students can explore questions related to data privacy, bias, automation's effect on the job market, and the role of architects in shaping equitable and inclusive environments. Delving into these issues encourages critical thinking and ethical awareness among future architects. AI's influence extends beyond initial education, offering lifelong learning and professional development opportunities. AI-powered platforms can provide architects with updated knowledge, trends, and tools, ensuring their skills remain relevant in a rapidly changing technological landscape.

6 CONCLUSION

The expedition through the realms of architectural education and its integration with artificial intelligence (AI) has been nothing short of an odyssey, unearthing a tapestry of possibilities, challenges, and ethical considerations that hold the potential to reshape the future of architectural practice and education. As we conclude this journey, we stand at the confluence of tradition and innovation, where the synergistic interplay between human creativity and AI's computational prowess offers a new dawn for architectural education.

Integrating AI into architectural education illuminates a constellation of possibilities that radiate across every facet of the curriculum. The canvas of design exploration becomes broader, fueled by AI's generative algorithms that stimulate creativity and unveil novel design paradigms. The advent of data-driven design decisions empowers architects to optimize form, function, and sustainability with unprecedented precision. The immersion in AI-powered virtual realities and simulations nurtures an intuitive understanding of spatial qualities and human experiences within architectural contexts. The symbiotic relationship between automated critique and personalized learning paves the way for an educational journey that molds architects with refined sensibilities and an adaptable skill set. However, these prospects do not arise without a corresponding setting of challenges. Ethical dilemmas, such as data privacy breaches and algorithmic biases, are significant hurdles that necessitate meticulous navigation. The delicate balance between AI and human creativity calls educators to shape curricula that foster a harmonious coexistence between architectural craftsmanship and AI's computational prowess.

Ethical considerations loom large in the AI-integrated architectural education landscape. The responsibility to educate future architects who possess an acute awareness of the ethical implications of AI transcends mere technical competence. As the custodians of the built environment, architects need to grapple with questions surrounding the societal, cultural, and environmental ramifications of AI-augmented design. Incorporating these ethical dimensions into the curriculum instills a moral compass that guides architects in employing AI to improve society. Architectural education is crucial in shaping a sustainable and equitable future by fostering architects who think ethically and innovatively.

The trajectory of architectural education and AI integration converges at the nexus of craftsmanship and computational prowess. Architectural education must nurture individuals fluent in AI technologies and possess the sensibilities to weave them into the intricate fabric of design. Future architects must transcend the binary juxtaposition of human versus machine, embracing a harmonious collaboration where AI augments creative exploration, optimizes technical intricacies and elevates sustainable practices. The integration of AI should not erode the essence of architecture as a form of artistic expression but rather enhance it, enabling architects to dream, innovate, and address complex challenges with newfound tools.

As we peer into the future horizon, architectural education and AI union is not merely an intellectual pursuit—it is a pragmatic necessity. Architects' challenges in the 21st century, from rapid urbanization to climate change, demand innovative solutions beyond human capabilities alone. As an enabler of data analysis, complex simulations, and optimized design, AI becomes a formidable ally in this endeavor. However, this partnership is not a replacement for the architect's role but an elevation. The architects' unique insights, creative vision, and contextual understanding remain irreplaceable. This synergy calls for a new era of collaboration between educators, students, practitioners, and AI systems, where the amalgamation of expertise culminates in creating architecture that enriches the human experience and enhances the built environment.

The paper lays the foundation for a narrative yet to be written—a narrative that challenges us to reevaluate, innovate, and redefine architectural education in the AI era. This journey is not an endpoint but a stepping stone to an evolving continuum. It calls upon educators to cultivate curricula that honor tradition while embracing technological advancements. It beckons students to be adaptable, inquisitive, and ethical architects who wield AI as a tool for good. It extends an invitation to practitioners to be stewards of innovation, nurturing a built environment that resonates with the essence of humanity. As we navigate this uncharted territory, architectural education and AI fusion unfold as a transformative force that propels the discipline toward unexplored horizons, carving a legacy that resonates for future generations.

7 DATA AVAILABILITY STATEMENT

Data utilised has been properly cited in the manuscript.

REFERENCES

Alidoosti, R., Lago, P., Poort, E., & Razavian, M. (2023, March). Ethics-Aware DecidArch Game: Designing a Game to Reflect on Ethical Considerations in Software Architecture Design Decision Making. In *2023 IEEE 20th International Conference on Software Architecture Companion (ICSA-C)*, 96-100. IEEE. DOI DOI: 10.1109/ICSA-C57050.2023.00031

Angélil, M. (2003). *An Experiment in Architectural Education*. Swiss Federal Institute of Technology.

Asanowicz, A. (1998). Approach to Computer Implementation in Architectural Curriculum. *Proceedings of the 16th International Conference on Education and Research in Computer Aided Architectural Design in Europe (eCAADe)*. DOI: 10.52842/conf.ecaade.1998.004

Badii, C., Bellini, P., Cenni, D., Difino, A., Nesi, P., & Paolucci, M. (2017). Analysis and assessment of a knowledge based smart city architecture providing service APIs. *Future Generation Computer Systems*, 75, 14–29. DOI: 10.1016/j.future.2017.05.001

Başarır, L. (2022). Modelling AI in Architectural Education. *Gazi University Journal of Science*, 35(4), 1260–1278. DOI: 10.35378/gujs.967981

Becker, S. A., Brown, M., Dahlstrom, E., Davis, A., DePaul, K., Diaz, V., & Pomerantz, J. (2018). *NMC Horizon Report: 2018 Higher Education Edition*. Educause. https://library.educause.edu/~/media/files/library/2018/8/2018horizonreport.pdf

Blanchard, E. G. (2015). Socio-Cultural Imbalances in AIED Research: Investigations, Implications and Opportunities. *International Journal of Artificial Intelligence in Education*, 25(2), 204–228. DOI: 10.1007/s40593-014-0027-7

Caldas, L. (2008). Generation of energy-efficient architecture solutions applying GENE_ARCH: An evolution-based generative design system. *Advanced Engineering Informatics*, 22(1), 59–70. DOI: 10.1016/j.aei.2007.08.012

Caprili, S., & Puncello, I. (2019). Knowledge-based approach for the structural assessment of monumental buildings: Application to case studies. *Frontiers in Built Environment*, 5, 52. DOI: 10.3389/fbuil.2019.00052

Chatterjee, S., & Bhattacharjee, K. K. (2020). Adoption of artificial intelligence in higher education: A quantitative analysis using structural equation modelling. *Education and Information Technologies*, 25(5), 3443–3463. DOI: 10.1007/s10639-020-10159-7

Cheng, J. C., Chen, W., Chen, K., & Wang, Q. (2020). Data-driven predictive maintenance planning framework for MEP components based on BIM and IoT using machine learning algorithms. *Automation in Construction*, 112, 103087. DOI: 10.1016/j.autcon.2020.103087

Hunde, B. R., & Woldeyohannes, A. D. (2022). Future prospects of computer-aided design (CAD)–A review from the perspective of artificial intelligence (AI), extended reality, and 3D printing. *Results in Engineering*, 14, 100478. DOI: 10.1016/j.rineng.2022.100478

Hwang, G. J., Xie, H., Wah, B. W., & Gašević, D. (2020). Vision, challenges, roles and research issues of Artificial Intelligence in Education. *Computers and Education: Artificial Intelligence*, 1, 100001. DOI: 10.1016/j.caeai.2020.100001

Motawa, I., & Almarshad, A. (2013). A knowledge-based BIM system for building maintenance. *Automation in Construction*, 29, 173–182. DOI: 10.1016/j.autcon.2012.09.008

Nguyen, A., Ngo, H. N., Hong, Y., Dang, B., & Nguyen, B. P. T. (2023). Ethical principles for artificial intelligence in education. *Education and Information Technologies*, 28(4), 4221–4241. DOI: 10.1007/s10639-022-11316-w PMID: 36254344

Nourian, P., Azadi, S., & Oval, R. (2023). Generative design in architecture: From mathematical optimization to grammatical customization. In *Computational Design and Digital Manufacturing* (pp. 1–43). Springer International Publishing., DOI: 10.1007/978-3-031-21167-6_1

Okudan, O., Budayan, C., & Dikmen, I. (2021). A knowledge-based risk management tool for construction projects using case-based reasoning. *Expert Systems with Applications*, 173, 114776. DOI: 10.1016/j.eswa.2021.114776

Popenici, S. A., & Kerr, S. (2017). Exploring the impact of artificial intelligence on teaching and learning in higher education. *Research and Practice in Technology Enhanced Learning*, 12(1), 1–13. DOI: 10.1186/s41039-017-0062-8 PMID: 30595727

Prabawasari, V. W., Madenda, S., Suhendra, A., & Tahrir, R. (•••). Knowledge-Based Systems in the Information System of Indonesian Colonial Architecture. *Universitas*, 4, 1–4.

QaQish. R., & Hanna, R. (1997). A World-wide Questionnaire Survey on the Use of Computers in Architectural Education. In *Challenges of the Future (15th eCAADe Conference Proceedings).*

Quy, V. K., Thanh, B. T., Chehri, A., Linh, D. M., & Tuan, D. A. (2023). AI and Digital Transformation in Higher Education: Vision and Approach of a Specific University in Vietnam. *Sustainability (Basel)*, 15(14), 11093. DOI: 10.3390/su151411093

Ra, S., Shrestha, U., Khatiwada, S., Seung, W. Y., & Kwon, K. (2019). The rise of technology and impact on skills. *International Journal of Training Research*, 17(sup1), 26–40. DOI: 10.1080/14480220.2019.1629727

Sabouni, A. R., & Al-Mourad, O. M. (1997). Quantitative knowledge based approach for preliminary design of tall buildings. *Artificial Intelligence in Engineering*, 11(2), 143–154. DOI: 10.1016/S0954-1810(96)00023-4

Schiavi, B., Havard, V., Beddiar, K., & Baudry, D. (2022). BIM data flow architecture with AR/VR technologies: Use cases in architecture, engineering and construction. *Automation in Construction*, 134, 104054. DOI: 10.1016/j.autcon.2021.104054

Schmitt, G. (Ed.). (2010). *Future Cities:ECAADE 2010: Proceedings of the 28th Conference on Education in Computer Aided Architectural Design in Europe, September 15-18, 2010,Zurich, Switzerland, ETH Zurich.* vdf Hochschulverlag AG.

Seldon, A., & Abidoye, O. (2018). *The fourth education revolution*. Legend Press Ltd.

Selwyn, N. (2023). Constructive Criticism? Working with (Rather than Against) the AIED Back-Lash. *International Journal of Artificial Intelligence in Education*. Advance online publication. DOI: 10.1007/s40593-023-00344-3

Singh, V., & Gu, N. (2012). Towards an integrated generative design framework. *Design Studies*, 33(2), 185–207. DOI: 10.1016/j.destud.2011.06.001

Soliman, S., Taha, D., & El Sayad, Z. (2019). Architectural education in the digital age: Computer applications: Between academia and practice. *Alexandria Engineering Journal*, 58(2), 809–818. DOI: 10.1016/j.aej.2019.05.016

Tiano, P., Tibaut, A., Kaucic, B., Jardim-Gonçalves, R., & Panetto, H. (2019). Knowledge based IT platform for Heritage Buildings. *Innovation in Intelligent Management of Heritage Buildings (i2MHB)*, 41-55, 2019, 978-953-8250-04-0. DOI DOI: 10.1016/j.aej.2019.05.016

Wahbeh, W. (2017, October). Building skins, parametric design tools and BIM platforms. In *Conference Proceedings of the 12th Conference of Advanced Building Skins*, 1104-1111.

Yau, M. Y., Lai, E. K., & Chun, H. W. (1994, March). FPDX: A knowledge-based system for architectural floor plan design. In *Proceedings of International Conference on Expert Systems for Development*, 309-314. IEEE. DOI: DOI: 10.1109/ICESD.1994.302261

Zhang, Y., Ong, C. C., Zheng, J., Lie, S. T., & Guo, Z. (2022). Generative design of decorative architectural parts. *The Visual Computer*, 38(4), 1209–1225. DOI: 10.1007/s00371-021-02142-1

Zhu, Z.T., Yu, M.H., & Riezebos, P. (2016). A research framework of smart education. *Smart learning environments, 3*, 1-17. https://doi.org/DOI: 10.1007/s00371-021-02142-1

Compilation of References

Abdelaziz, M., Kamel, S. S., Karam, O., & Abdelrahman, A. (2011). Evaluation of e-learning program versus traditional lecture instruction for undergraduate nursing students in a faculty of nursing. *Teaching and Learning in Nursing*, 6(2), 50–58. DOI: 10.1016/j.teln.2010.10.003

Abebe, E. (2024, 03 16). *Uinversity World News Africa Edition*. Retrieved from Navigatin the horizon preparing African universities for the inevitable AI: https://www.universityworldnews.com/post.php?story=20240306183858627

Adams Becker, S., Cummins, M., Davis, A., Freeman, A., Hall Giesinger, C., & Ananthanarayanan, V. (2017). *NMC horizon report: 2017 higher education edition*. The New Media Consortium.

Adams, R., & McIntyre, N. (2020, August 13). England A-level downgrades hit pupils from disadvantaged areas hardest. *The Guardian*.England A-level downgrades hit pupils from disadvantaged areas hardest | A-levels | The Guardian.

Adıgüzel, T., Kaya, M. H., & Cansu, F. K. (2023). Revolutionizing education with AI: Exploring the transformative potential of ChatGPT. *Contemporary Educational Technology*, 15(3), ep429. DOI: 10.30935/cedtech/13152

Ahlfeld, K. (2019). Lifting the curtain: Examining the importance of the shared foundation IV: Curate in the national school library standards for learners, school librarians, and school libraries. *Journal of Library Administration*, 59(4), 442–454. DOI: 10.1080/01930826.2019.1593712

Ahmad, M. (2014). Unified Theory of Acceptance and Use of Technology (UTAUT) A Decade of Validation and Development. *In proceedings of Fourth International Conference on ICT in our lives* (pp. 1-14). Egypt: Faculty of Commerce, Alexandria University, Alexandria

Ahmad, S. F., Alam, M. M., Rahmat, M. K., Mubarik, M. S., & Hyder, S. I. (2022). Academic and administrative role of artificial intelligence in education. *Sustainability (Basel)*, 14(3), 1101. DOI: 10.3390/su14031101

AI4K12 (2024) The artificial intelligence (AI) for K-12 initiative. https://ai4k12.org/

Akgun, S., & Greenhow, C. (2021). Artificial intelligence in education: Addressing ethical challenges in K-12 settings. *AI and Ethics*, •••, 1–10. PMID: 34790956

Akram, B., Min, W., Wiebe, E., Mott, B., Boyer, K., & Lester, J. (2018). Improving Stealth Assessment in Game-based Learning with LSTM-based Analytics. *Proceedings of the 11th International Conference on Educational Data Mining* (pp. 208-218). USA: Educational Resources Information Centre.

Akyuz, D., Dixon, J. K., & Stephan, M. (2013). Improving the quality of mathematics teaching with effective planning practices. *Teacher Development*, 17(1), 92–106. DOI: 10.1080/13664530.2012.753939

Akyuz, Y. (2020). Effects of Intelligent Tutoring Systems (ITS) on Personalized Learning (PL). *Creative Education*, 11(6), 953–963. DOI: 10.4236/ce.2020.116069

Alam, A. (2022). Employing adaptive learning and intelligent tutoring robots for virtual classrooms and smart campuses: Reforming education in the age of artificial intelligence. In *Advanced computing and intelligent technologies* [Springer.]. *Proceedings of ICACIT*, 2022, 395–406.

Aleven, V., Blankestijn, J., Lawrence, L., Nagashima, T., & Taatgen, N. (2022, September). A dashboard to support teachers during students' self-paced AI-supported problem-solving practice. In *European Conference on Technology Enhanced Learning* (pp. 16-30). Cham: Springer International Publishing. DOI: 10.1007/978-3-031-16290-9_2

Ali, S., & Qaisar, R. (2018). Effect of performance expectancy and effort expectancy on the mobile adoption intention through personal innovativeness among Pakistani consumers. *Pakistan Journal of Commerce and Social Sciences (PJCSS) VOL 12 iSSUE 2*, 501-520.

Alidoosti, R., Lago, P., Poort, E., & Razavian, M. (2023, March). Ethics-Aware DecidArch Game: Designing a Game to Reflect on Ethical Considerations in Software Architecture Design Decision Making. In *2023 IEEE 20th International Conference on Software Architecture Companion (ICSA-C)*, 96-100. IEEE. DOI DOI: 10.1109/ICSA-C57050.2023.00031

Allen, I. E., & Seaman, J. (2017). *Digital learning in higher education: A survey of faculty attitudes and experiences*. Babson Survey Research Group.

Allen, I. E., Seaman, J., Poulin, R., & Straut, T. T. (2016). *Online report card: Tracking online education in the United States, 2016*. Babson Survey Research Group and Quahog Research Group.

Almarashdeh, I. E. (2021). AI adaptive learning in higher education: A review of the literature. *Journal of Educational Technology Systems*, 49(3), 275–287.

Alper, A., & Gulbahar, Y. (2009). Trends and issues in educational technologies: A review of recent research in TOJET. *The Turkish Online Journal of Educational Technology*, 8(2).

Alshahrani, A. (2023). The impact of ChatGPT on blended learning: Current trends and future research directions. *International Journal of Data and Network Science*, 7(4), 2029–2040. DOI: 10.5267/j.ijdns.2023.6.010

Alwaqdani, M. (2024). (2024). Investigating teachers' perceptions of artificial intelligence tools in education: Potential and difficulties. *Education and Information Technologies*. Advance online publication. DOI: 10.1007/s10639-024-12903-9

American Association of School Librarians. (2018). *National school library standards: for learners, school librarians and school libraries*. American Library Association.

Anderson, T. (2016). The impact of artificial intelligence on education. *International Journal of Educational Technology*, 13(1), 11–25.

Anderson, T., & Dron, J. (2018). Three generations of distance education pedagogy. *International Review of Research in Open and Distance Learning*, 12(3), 80–97. DOI: 10.19173/irrodl.v12i3.890

Anderson, T., & Elloumi, F. (2019). *The theory and practice of online learning*. Athabasca University Press.

Angélil, M. (2003). *An Experiment in Architectural Education*. Swiss Federal Institute of Technology.

Anglin, G. J., Vaez, H., & Cunningham, K. L. (2004). Visual representations and learning: The role of static and animated graphics. Handbook of Research on Educational Communications and Technology, 2, 865-916.

Angrist, M. W., & Bean, J. D. (2014). *Instructional design for online learning environments*. SAGE Publications.

Antonenko, P., & Abramowitz, B. (2022). In-service teachers' (mis)conceptions of artificial intelligence in K-12 science education. *Journal of Research on Technology in Education*, 55(1), 64–78. DOI: 10.1080/15391523.2022.2119450

Arakpogun, E., Elsahn, Z., Olan, F., & Elsahn, F. (2020). *Artificial intelligence in Africa: challenges and opportunities.*

Area, M., & Adell, J. (2009). eLearning: Enseñar y aprender en espacios virtuales. In J. De Pablos (Coord.), Tecnología educativa. La formación del profesorado en la era de Internet (pp. 391-424). Aljibe.

Aripin, Z., Supriatna, U., & Mahaputra, M. S. (2023). With the advent of ChatGPT: How to identify strengths, weaknesses, opportunities, and threats for the field of education and the business world of various disciplines. *Journal of Development and Community Service*, 1(1), 50–61.

Arksey, H., & O'Malley, L. (2005). Scoping studies: Towards a methodological framework. *International Journal of Social Research Methodology*, 8(1), 19–32. DOI: 10.1080/1364557032000119616

Asanowicz, A. (1998). Approach to Computer Implementation in Architectural Curriculum. *Proceedings of the 16th International Conference on Education and Research in Computer Aided Architectural Design in Europe (eCAADe).* DOI: 10.52842/conf.ecaade.1998.004

Assefa, S., Rorissa, A., & Alemneh, D. (2021). Digital readiness assessment of countries in Africa: A case study research. *Proceedings of the Association for Information Science and Technology*, 58(1), 400–404. DOI: 10.1002/pra2.467

Ayanwale, M., & Ndlovu, M. (2024). The feasibility of computerized adaptive testing of the national benchmark test: A simulation study. *Journal of Pedagogical Research*, 8(2), 95–112. DOI: 10.33902/JPR.202425210

Ayeni, O. O., Al Hamad, N. M., Chisom, O. N., Osawaru, B., & Adewusi, O. E. (2024). AI in education: A review of personalized learning and educational technology. *GSC Advanced Research and Reviews*, 18(2), 261–271. DOI: 10.30574/gscarr.2024.18.2.0062

Azevedo, R., Mudrick, N. V., Taub, M., & Bradbury, A. E. (2018). Self-regulation in computer-assisted learning systems. In Dunlosky, J., & Rawson, K. A. (Eds.), *The Cambridge handbook of cognition and education* (pp. 587–618). Cambridge University Press., DOI: 10.1017/9781108235631.024

Babirad, R. (2024). COPPA, ed tech, and the school librarian. *Knowledge Quest, 52*(3), 36.

Badii, C., Bellini, P., Cenni, D., Difino, A., Nesi, P., & Paolucci, M. (2017). Analysis and assessment of a knowledge based smart city architecture providing service APIs. *Future Generation Computer Systems*, 75, 14–29. DOI: 10.1016/j.future.2017.05.001

Baek, C., Tate, T., & Warschauer, M. (2024). "ChatGPT Seems Too Good to be True": College Students' Use and Perceptions of Generative AI. *Computers and Education: Artificial Intelligence*, 100294. https://doi.org/https://doi.org/10.1016/j.caeai.2024.100294

Bajaj, R., Sharma, V., & Weichbroth, P. (2018). Smart education with artificial intelligence based determination of learning styles. *Procedia Computer Science*, 599, 37–58. DOI: 10.1016/j.procs.2018.05.095

Baker, R. S., & Koedinger, K. R. (2018). Towards demonstrating the value of learning analytics for K-12 education. *Learning Analytics in Education*, 49-62.

Baker, T., Smith, L., & Anissa, N. (2020). Educ-AI-tion rebooted? Exploring the future of artificial intelligence in schools and colleges. NESTA. https://www.nesta.org.uk/report/education-rebooted/

Baker, R. S., & Inventado, P. S. (2014). Educational data mining and learning analytics. In *Learning analytics* (pp. 61–75). Springer., https://link.springer.com/chapter/10.1007/978-1-4614-3305-7_4 DOI: 10.1007/978-1-4614-3305-7_4

Balfour, S. P. (2013). Assessing writing in MOOCs: Automated essay scoring and calibrated peer review. *Research & Practice in Assessment*, 8, 40–48.

Bandura, A. (1977). *Social learning theory*. Prentice-Hall.

Barbera, E., Clara, M., & Linder-Vanberschot, J. A. (2013). Factors influencing student satisfaction and perceived learning in online courses. *E-Learning and Digital Media*, 10(3), 226–235. DOI: 10.2304/elea.2013.10.3.226

Barla, M., Bieliková, M., Ezzeddinne, A. B., Kramár, T., Šimko, M., & Vozár, O. (2010). On the impact of adaptive test question selection for learning efficiency. *Computers & Education*, 55(2), 846–857. DOI: 10.1016/j.compedu.2010.03.016

Başarır, L. (2022). Modelling AI in Architectural Education. *Gazi University Journal of Science*, 35(4), 1260–1278. DOI: 10.35378/gujs.967981

Bates, A. W. (2019). *Teaching in a digital age: Guidelines for designing teaching and learning*. Tony Bates Associates Ltd.

Bauld, A. (2023). Mission critical: Artificial intelligence is here. Librarians can play a crucial role in making sure schools get it right. *School Library Journal*, 69(9), 24.

Bayne, S. (2015). What's the matter with technology-enhanced learning? *Learning, Media and Technology*, 40(1), 5–20. DOI: 10.1080/17439884.2014.915851

Bearman, M., Tai, J., Dawson, P., Boud, D., & Ajjawi, R. (2024). Developing evaluative judgement for a time of generative artificial intelligence. *Assessment & Evaluation in Higher Education*, 49(6), 1–13. DOI: 10.1080/02602938.2024.2335321

Becker, S. A., Brown, M., Dahlstrom, E., Davis, A., DePaul, K., Diaz, V., & Pomerantz, J. (2018). *NMC Horizon Report: 2018 Higher Education Edition*. Educause. https://library.educause.edu/~/media/files/library/2018/8/2018horizonreport.pdf

Bednar, A. K., Cunningham, D., Duffy, T. M., & Perry, J. D. (1992). Theory into practice: How do we link. In Duffy, T. M., & Jonassen, D. H. (Eds.), *Constructivism and the technology of instruction: A conversation* (pp. 17–34). Psychology Press.

Beetham, H., & Sharpe, R. (Eds.). (2013). *Rethinking pedagogy for a digital age: Designing for 21st century learning*. Routledge. DOI: 10.4324/9780203078952

Bekeš, E. R., & Galzina, V. (2023). Exploring the pedagogical use of AI-powered chatbots: Educational perceptions and practices. *2023 46th MIPRO ICT and Electronics Convention (MIPRO)*, Opatija, Croatia, pp. 636-641. DOI: 10.23919/MIPRO57284.2023.10159734

Bellamy, R. K., Dey, K., Hind, M., Hoffman, S. C., Houde, S., Kannan, K., Lohia, P., Martino, J., Mehta, S., Mojsilovic, A., Nagar, S., Ramamurthy, K. N., Richards, J., Saha, D., Sattigeri, P., Singh, M., Varshney, K. R., & Zhang, Y. (2019). AI Fairness 360: An extensible toolkit for detecting and mitigating algorithmic bias. IBM Journal of Research and Development, 63(4/5), 4:1-4:15. https://doi.org/DOI: 10.1147/JRD.2019.2942287

Bell, K. (2022). Increasing undergraduate student satisfaction in Higher Education: The importance of relational pedagogy. *Journal of Further and Higher Education*, 46(4), 490–503. DOI: 10.1080/0309877X.2021.1985980

Bender, E., Gebru, T., McMillan-Major, A., & Shmitchell, S. (2021). On the dangers of stochastic parrots: Can language models be too big? FAcct '2. *Proceedings of the 2021 ACM Conference on Fairness, Accountability, and Transparency*, (pp. 610-623). DOI: 10.1145/3442188.3445922

Benjamin, C., & Keenan, C. (2006). Implications of introducing problem-based learning in a traditionally taught course. *Engineering Education*, 1(1), 2–7. DOI: 10.1080/17500052.2006.11642153

Berger, C., & Kam, R. (1996). Definitions of instructional design. Retrieved from https://www.umich.edu/~ed626/define.html

Berg, M., & Seeber, B. (2016). *Slow professor: Challenging the culture of speed in the academy*. University of Toronto Press. DOI: 10.3138/9781442663091

Bialik, M., Holmes, W., & Fadel, C. (2019). Artificial intelligence in education: Challenges and opportunities. *Center for Curriculum Redesign*. https://curriculumredesign.org

Bienkowski, M., Feng, M., & Means, B. (2012). Enhancing teaching and learning through educational data mining and learning analytics: An issue brief. US Department of Education. *Office of Educational Technology*, 1, 1–57.

Bingimlas, K. A. (2009). Barriers to the successful integration of ICT in teaching and learning environments: A review of the literature. *Eurasia Journal of Mathematics, Science and Technology Education*, 5(3), 235–245. DOI: 10.12973/ejmste/75275

Binns, R. (2018). Fairness in machine learning: Lessons from political philosophy. In Conference on Fairness, Accountability and Transparency (pp. 149-159). PMLR. https://proceedings.mlr.press/v81/binns18a.html

Birhane, A., Kasirzadeh, A., Leslie, D., & Wachter, S. (2023). Science in the age of large language models. *Nature Reviews. Physics*, 5(5), 277–280. DOI: 10.1038/s42254-023-00581-4

Black, P., & Wiliam, D. (1998). Assessment and Classroom Learning. *Assessment in Education: Principles, Policy & Practice*, 5(1), 7–74. DOI: 10.1080/0969595980050102

Blanchard, E. G. (2015). Socio-Cultural Imbalances in AIED Research: Investigations, Implications and Opportunities. *International Journal of Artificial Intelligence in Education*, 25(2), 204–228. DOI: 10.1007/s40593-014-0027-7

Bobo, S. (2023, August 22). Simply put, A.I is probability and statistics. *Speaking Artificially*. https://medium.com/speaking-artificially/simply-put-its-probability-and-statistics-ea955e3c4ba8

Boelens, R., De Wever, B., & McKenney, S. (2020). Conjecture mapping to support vocationally educated adult learners in open-ended tasks. *Journal of the Learning Sciences*, 29(3), 430–470. DOI: 10.1080/10508406.2020.1759605

Boling, E., Eccarius, M., Smith, K., & Frick, T. (2004). Instructional illustrations: Intended meanings and learner interpretations. *Journal of Visual Literacy*, 24(2), 185–204. DOI: 10.1080/23796529.2004.11674612

Bonett, D. G., & Wright, T. A. (2015). Cronbach's alpha reliability: Interval estimation, hypothesis testing, and sample size planning. *Journal of Organizational Behavior*, 36(1), 3–15. DOI: 10.1002/job.1960

Boud, D., & Soler, R. (2016). Sustainable assessment revisited. *Assessment & Evaluation in Higher Education*, 41(3), 400–413. DOI: 10.1080/02602938.2015.1018133

Bower, M., Howe, C., McCredie, N., Robinson, A., & Grover, D. (2014). Augmented reality in education – cases, places and potentials. *Educational Media International*, 51(1), 1–15. DOI: 10.1080/09523987.2014.889400

Bowman, R. F. (2018). Teaching and learning in a storytelling culture. *The Clearing House: A Journal of Educational Strategies, Issues and Ideas*, 91(3), 97–102. DOI: 10.1080/00098655.2017.1373547

Bozalek, V. (2017). Slow scholarship in writing retreats: A diffractive methodology for response-able pedagogies. *South African Journal of Higher Education*, 31(2). Advance online publication. DOI: 10.20853/31-2-1344

Braun, V., & Clarke, V. (2006). Using thematic analysis in psychology. *Qualitative Research in Psychology*, 3(2), 77–101. DOI: 10.1191/1478088706qp063oa

Brookhart, S. M. (2013). *How to create and use rubrics for formative assessment and grading*. Ascd.

Brown, T. B. (2020). Language models are few-shot learners. *arXiv preprint arXiv:2005.14165.*

Brown, J., Davis, M., & Wilson, S. (2022). Integrating AI-based assessment in higher education: Challenges and opportunities. *Journal of Educational Technology & Society*, 25(3), 120–135.

Brown, K., & Patel, R. (2023). Generational Differences in AI Influencer Credibility and Engagement. *Marketing Science Review*, 29(2), 122–139. DOI: 10.1080/10909483.2023.2189763

Brown, S. (2005). Assessment for learning. *Learning and Teaching in Higher Education*, (1), 81–89.

Bryant, J., Heitz, C., Sanghvi, S., & Wagle, D. (2020). *How artificial intelligence will impact K-12 teachers.* McKinsey & Company. https://www.mckinsey.com/~/media/McKinsey/Industries/Social%20Sector/Our%20Insights/How%20artificial%20intelligence%20will%20impact%20K%2012%20teachers/Ho w-artificial-intelligence-will-impact-K-12-teachers.pdf

Bulut, O., Beiting-Parrish, M., Casabianca, J. M., Slater, S. C., Jiao, H., Song, D., Ormerod, C. M., Fabiyi, D. G., Ivan, R., Walsh, C., Rios, O., Wilson, J., Yildirim-Erbasli, S. N., Wongvorachan, T., Liu, J. X., Tan, B., & Morilova, P. (2024). The Rise of Artificial Intelligence in Educational Measurement: Opportunities and Ethical Challenges. arXiv. https://doi.org//arXiv.2406.18900DOI: 10.48550

Bulut, O., Beiting-Parrish, M., Casabianca, J. M., Slater, S., Jiao, H., & Song, D. & ...Morilova, P. (2024). The Rise of Artificial Intelligence in Educational Measurement:Opportunities and Ethical Challenges White Paper. USA: National Council of Measurement in Education (NCME).

Bureau of Labor Statistics. (2024). U.S. Department of Labor, Occupational outlook handbook, data scientists. https://www.bls.gov/ooh/math/data-scientists.htm

Busso, A., & Sanchez, B. (2024). Advancing communicative competence in the digital age: A case for AI tools in Japanese university EFL programs. *Technology in Language Teaching & Learning*, 6(3), 1–17. DOI: 10.29140/tltl.v6n3.1211

Caldas, L. (2008). Generation of energy-efficient architecture solutions applying GENE_ARCH: An evolution-based generative design system. *Advanced Engineering Informatics*, 22(1), 59–70. DOI: 10.1016/j.aei.2007.08.012

Calhoun, C. (Ed.). (2023). *The impact and importance of instructional design in the educational landscape* (1st ed.). Information Science Reference, an imprint of IGI Global. DOI: 10.4018/978-1-6684-8208-7

Caprili, S., & Puncello, I. (2019). Knowledge-based approach for the structural assessment of monumental buildings: Application to case studies. *Frontiers in Built Environment*, 5, 52. DOI: 10.3389/fbuil.2019.00052

Care, E., Griffin, P., & Wilson, M. (Eds.). (2018). *Assessment and teaching of 21st century skills: Research and applications*. Springer., DOI: 10.1007/978-3-319-65368-6

Carless, D. (2022). From teacher transmission of information to student feedback literacy: Activating the learner role in feedback processes. *Active Learning in Higher Education*, 23(2), 143–153. DOI: 10.1177/1469787420945845

Carless, D., & Winstone, N. (2023). Teacher feedback literacy and its interplay with student feedback literacy. *Teaching in Higher Education*, 28(1), 150–163. DOI: 10.1080/13562517.2020.1782372

Carr, B. (2023). Revolutionizing education: Unleashing the power of ChatGPT/AI to empower educators. *Technology and the Curriculum: Summer 2023*.

Carroll, J. B. (1963). A model of school learning. *Teachers College Record*, 64(8), 723–733. DOI: 10.1177/016146816306400801

Carruba, M. C. (2023). Technology for inclusion: A pedagogical approach to promote well-being. In Escudeiro, P., Escudeiro, N., & Bernardes, O. (Eds.), *Handbook of research on advancing equity and inclusion through educational technology* (pp. 146–152). IGI Global., DOI: 10.4018/978-1-6684-6868-5.ch007

Celik, I. (2023). Towards Intelligent-TPACK: An empirical study on teachers' professional knowledge to ethically integrate artificial intelligence (AI)-based tools into education. *Computers in Human Behavior*, 138, 107468. DOI: 10.1016/j.chb.2022.107468

Celik, I., Dindar, M., Muukkonen, H., & Järvelä, S. (2022). The promises and challenges of artificial intelligence for teachers: A systematic review of research. *TechTrends*, 66(4), 616–630. DOI: 10.1007/s11528-022-00715-y

Charles Sturt University. (2021). *Rethinking Assessment Strategies in the Age of Artificial Intelligence (AI)*. Charles Sturt University.

Chatterjee, S., & Bhattacharjee, K. (2020). Adoption of artificial intelligence in higher education: A quantitative analysis using structural equation modelling. *Education and Information Technologies*, 25(5), 3443–3463. DOI: 10.1007/s10639-020-10159-7

Chen, B., Xu, Y., & Zhang, L. (2021). Personalized adaptive learning using machine learning: A review of the literature. *Computers & Education*, 168, 104196. DOI: 10.1016/j.compedu.2021.104196

Cheng, J. C., Chen, W., Chen, K., & Wang, Q. (2020). Data-driven predictive maintenance planning framework for MEP components based on BIM and IoT using machine learning algorithms. *Automation in Construction*, 112, 103087. DOI: 10.1016/j.autcon.2020.103087

Chen, L., Chen, P., & Lin, Z. (2020). Artificial intelligence in education: A review. *IEEE Access : Practical Innovations, Open Solutions*, 8, 75264–75278. DOI: 10.1109/ACCESS.2020.2988510

Chen, L., Zhang, M., & Huang, Y. (2021). AI-driven personalized learning: A review of the literature. *Educational Technology Research and Development*, 69(1), 1–25. DOI: 10.1007/s11423-020-09815-2 PMID: 33551626

Chen, M. H.. (2020). Educational technology and AI: A systematic review of the literature. *Journal of Educational Technology & Society*.

Chen, X., & Liu, Y. (2023). Generalizability of AI-assisted assessment systems: A cross-disciplinary perspective. *Computers & Education*, 184, 104589. DOI: 10.1016/j.compedu.2023.104589

Chen, X., Xie, H., Zou, D., & Hwang, G.-J. (2020). Application and theory gaps during the rise of Artificial Intelligence in Education. *Computers and Education: Artificial Intelligence*, 1, 100002. DOI: 10.1016/j.caeai.2020.100002

Chen, X., & Xu, J. (2021). Exploring the use of AI-driven educational tools in adaptive learning environments. *Journal of Learning Analytics*, 7(4), 212–229. DOI: 10.18608/jla.2021.7045

Chen, Y., Jensen, S., Albert, L. J., Gupta, S., & Lee, T. (2023). Artificial Intelligence (AI) Student Assistants in the Classroom: Designing Chatbots to Support Student Success. *Information Systems Frontiers*, 25(1), 161–182. DOI: 10.1007/s10796-022-10291-4

Cherrez-Ojeda, I., Gallardo-Bastidas, J. C., Robles-Velasco, K., Osorio, M. F., Velez Leon, E. M., Leon Velastegui, M., Pauletto, P., Aguilar-Díaz, F. C., Squassi, A., González Eras, S. P., Cordero Carrasco, E., Chavez Gonzalez, K. L., Calderon, J. C., Bousquet, J., Bedbrook, A., & Faytong-Haro, M. (2024). Understanding Health Care Students' Perceptions, Beliefs, and Attitudes Toward AI-Powered Language Models: Cross-Sectional Study. *JMIR Medical Education*, 10, e51757. DOI: 10.2196/51757 PMID: 39137029

Cherrstrom, C. A., Zarestky, J., & Deer, S. (2017). "This group is vital": Adult peers in community for support and learning. *Adult Learning*, 29(2), 43–52. DOI: 10.1177/1045159517739701

Chimalakonda, S., & Nori, K. V. (2018). A patterns based approach for design of educational technologies. arXiv. https://arxiv.org/abs/1802.02663

Chinta, S. V., Wang, Z., Yin, Z., Hoang, N., Gonzalez, M., Quy, T. L., & Zhang, W. (2024). FairAIED: Navigating Fairness, Bias, and Ethics in Educational AI Applications. *arXiv preprint arXiv:2407.18745.*

Chiu, T. K., Meng, H., Chai, C. S., King, I., Wong, S., & Yam, Y. (2021). Creation and evaluation of a pretertiary artificial intelligence (AI) curriculum. *IEEE Transactions on Education*, 65(1), 30–39. DOI: 10.1109/TE.2021.3085878

Choi, S., & Park, J. (2023). Pedagogical benefits and challenges of AI-driven assessment in computer science education. *Journal of Computing in Higher Education*, 35(2), 415–438. DOI: 10.1007/s12528-022-09332-1

Chou, P. N., & Chen, W. F. (2018). The role of artificial intelligence in education: A review of the literature. *Journal of Educational Technology & Society*, 21(1), 150–166.

Cilliers, F. J., Schuwirth, L. W. T., & van der Vleuten, C. P. M. (2012). A model of the pre-assessment learning effects of assessment is operational in an undergraduate clinical context. *BMC Medical Education*, 12(1), 9. DOI: 10.1186/1472-6920-12-9 PMID: 22420839

Cisco. (2021, 02 29). Cisco digital readiness. Cisco.

Coleman, M. C. (2020). School librarians take the lead collaborating on professional development. *Knowledge Quest*, 49(2), 10–18.

Collett, K. S., van den Berg, C. L., Verster, B., & Bozalek, V. (2018). Incubating a slow pedagogy in professional academic development: An ethics of care perspective. *South African Journal of Higher Education*, 32(6), 117–136. DOI: 10.20853/32-6-2755

Collison, G., Elbaum, B., Haavind, S., & Tinker, R. (2000). *Facilitating online learning: Effective strategies for moderators*. Atwood.

Conca, L. M., Schechter, C. P., & Castle, S. (2004). Challenges teachers face as they work to connect assessment and instruction. *Teachers and Teaching*, 10(1), 59–75. DOI: 10.1080/1354060032000170927

Conole, G., & Alevizou, P. (2010). *A literature review of the use of Web 2.0 tools in higher education*. Higher Education Academy.

Conrad, E. J., & Rees, L. K. (2024). Generative AI as a catalyst to elevate school health education. *Journal of Physical Education, Recreation & Dance*, 95(6), 45–51. DOI: 10.1080/07303084.2024.2355865

Cope, B., & Kalantzis, M. (2020). *Artificial Intelligence and education: Future directions*. Routledge.

Cope, B., Kalantzis, M., & Searsmith, D. (2021). Artificial Intelligence for education: Knowledge and its assessment in AI -enabled ecologies. *Educational Philosophy and Theory*, 53(12), 1229–1245. DOI: 10.1080/00131857.2020.1728732

Coskun, T. K., & Alper, A. (2024). Evaluating the evaluators: A comparative study of AI and teacher assessments in Higher Education. *Digital Education Review*(45), 124-140. https://dialnet.unirioja.es/servlet/articulo?codigo=9624307

Cotton, D. R. E., Cotton, P. A., & Shipway, J. R. (2024). Chatting and cheating: Ensuring academic integrity in the era of ChatGPT. *Innovations in Education and Teaching International*, 61(2), 228–239. DOI: 10.1080/14703297.2023.2190148

Crawford, J., Allen, K. A., Pani, B., & Cowling, M. (2024). When artificial intelligence substitutes humans in higher education: The cost of loneliness, student success, and retention. *Studies in Higher Education*, 49(5), 883–897. DOI: 10.1080/03075079.2024.2326956

Crisp, G. (2020). Artificial intelligence in education: A critical review. In Alyahya, E., & Dustegor, D. (Eds.), *Handbook of research on modern educational technologies, applications, and management* (pp. 1–18). IGI Global., DOI: 10.4018/978-1-7998-3476-2.ch001

Cristianini, N. (2016). Intelligence reinvented. *New Scientist*, 232(3097), 37–41. DOI: 10.1016/S0262-4079(16)31992-3

Crompton, H., & Burke, D. (2023). Artificial intelligence in higher education: The state of the field. *International Journal of Educational Technology in Higher Education*, 20(1), 22. DOI: 10.1186/s41239-023-00392-8

Cross, J., Robinson, R., Devaraju, S., Vaughans, A., Hood, R., Kayalackakom, T., Honnavar, P., Naik, S., & Sebastian, R. (2023). Transforming medical education: Assessing the integration of ChatGPT into faculty workflows at a Caribbean medical school. *Cureus*, 15(7). Advance online publication. DOI: 10.7759/cureus.41399 PMID: 37426402

Cuban, L., & Jandric, P. (2015). The dubious promise of educational technologies: Historical patterns and future challenges. *E-Learning and Digital Media*, 12(3-4), 425–439. DOI: 10.1177/2042753015579978

Culican, J., & Amade, M. (2023). *A14 special education: Ignite your special education program with the power of AI*. A14. Special Edition.

Dai, C.-P., & Ke, F. (2022). Educational applications of artificial intelligence in simulation-based learning: A systematic mapping review. *Computers and Education: Artificial Intelligence*, 3, 100087. DOI: 10.1016/j.caeai.2022.100087

Dai, W., Tsai, Y.-S., Lin, J., Aldino, A., Jin, H., Li, T., Gašević, D., & Chen, G. (2024). Assessing the proficiency of large language models in automatic feedback generation: An evaluation study. *Computers and Education: Artificial Intelligence*, 100299, 100299. Advance online publication. DOI: 10.1016/j.caeai.2024.100299

Daugherty, P. R., & Wilson, H. J. (2018). *Human + Machine: Reimagining work in the age of AI*. Harvard Business Review Press.

Davis, K., Christodoulou, J. A., Seider, S., & Gardner, H. (2018). The theory of multiple intelligences. In Sternberg, R. J. (Ed.), *The Cambridge handbook of intelligence* (pp. 485–503). Cambridge University Press., DOI: 10.1017/9781108770422.024

De Groft, L. (2023). AI literacy: The road ahead. *School Library Journal*, 69(9), 26.

De Lisle, J. (2012). Secondary school entrance examinations in the Caribbean: Legacy, policy, and evidence within an era of seamless education. *Caribbean Curriculum*, 19, 109–143.

De Villiers, C., Kuruppu, S., & Dissanayake, D. (2021). A (new) role for business Promoting the United Nations' Sustainable Development Goals through the internet-of-things and blockchain technology. *Journal of Business Research*, 131, 598–609. DOI: 10.1016/j.jbusres.2020.11.066

Debattista, M. (2018). A comprehensive rubric for instructional design in e-learning. *The International Journal of Information and Learning Technology*, 35(2), 93–104. DOI: 10.1108/IJILT-09-2017-0092

Dede, C. (2014). Immersive interfaces for engagement and learning. In Ifenthaler, D., Gibson, D. E., & Manches, A. T. (Eds.), *Assessment and feedback in higher education* (pp. 119–138). Springer.

Dede, C. (2020). A new education for the 21st century: What should be the focus? *Educational Technology Research and Development*, 68(3), 1125–1134.

Deng, L., & Tavares, N. J. (2018). The role of artificial intelligence in education: A global perspective. *International Journal of Artificial Intelligence in Education*, 28(4), 648–672.

Derevyanko, N., & Zalevska, O. (2023). Comparative analysis of neural networks Midjourney, Stable Diffusion, and DALL-E and ways of their implementation in the educational process of students of design specialities. *Scientific Bulletin of Mukachevo State University. Series. Pedagogy and Psychology*, 9(3), 36–44. DOI: 10.52534/msupp3.2023.36

Diallo, K., Smith, J., Okolo, C., Nyamwaya, D., Kgomo, J., & Ngamita, R. (2024). Case Studies of AI Policy Development in Africa. *Data & Policy*, 1(12), 1–13.

Dianati, M., & Adib-Hajbaghery, M. (2012). Comparison of lecture and problem-based learning on learning of nursing students. *Future of Medical Education Journal*, 2(1), 7–11.

DiCerbo, K. (2021). A future of assessment without testing. *eLearn, 2021*(Special Issue), 1–2. https://doi.org/DOI: 10.1145/3453989

Dickey, S. (2023). School librarians as innovators. The tradition endures and expands. *Knowledge Quest*, 51(3), 28–33.

Digital Promise. (2024). Artificial intelligence in education. https://digitalpromise.org/initiative/artificial-intelligence-in-education/ai-literacy/

Dillenbourg, P. (2018). Designing digital learning environments. In Kalz, M. M., Garcia, J. J. R., & De Vries, R. E. H. H. G. (Eds.), *Learning in a digital world* (pp. 45–56). Springer.

Driscoll, M. (1994). *Psychology of learning for instruction*. Allyn and Bacon.

Duarte, N., Montoya Pérez, Y., & Beltrán, A. (2023). Use of Artificial Intelligence in Education: A Systematic Review. In Proceedings of the 4th South American International Industrial Engineering and Operations Management Conference, Lima, Peru, May 9-11, 2023. IEOM Society International. DOI: 10.46254/SA04.20230169

Emerling, C. R., Yang, S., Carter, R. A., Zhang, L., & Hunt, T. (2020). Using Amazon Alexa as an instructional tool during remote teaching. *Teaching Exceptional Children*, 53(2), 164–167. DOI: 10.1177/0040059920964719

Emplit, P. (2020). *Learning and Teaching Paper #11 Evidence-based approches to learning and teaching Thematic Peer Group Report*. European University Association.

Er, E., Dimitriads, Y., & Gasevi'c, D. (2020). A collaborative learning approach to dialogic peer feedback: A theoretical framework. *Assessment & Evaluation in Higher Education*, •••, 586–600.

Ertmer, P. A., & Newby, T. J. (2008). Behaviorism, cognitivism, constructivism: Comparing critical features from an instructional design perspective. *Performance Improvement Quarterly*, 6(4), 50–72. DOI: 10.1111/j.1937-8327.1993.tb00605.x

Escudeiro, P., Escudeiro, N. F., & Bernardes, O. (Eds.). (2023). *Advancing equity and inclusion through educational technology* (1st ed.). Information Science Reference. DOI: 10.4018/978-1-6684-6868-5

Essien, A., Bukoye, O. T., O'Dea, X., & Kremantzis, M. (2024). The influence of AI text generators on critical thinking skills in UK business schools. *Studies in Higher Education*, 49(5), 865–882. DOI: 10.1080/03075079.2024.2316881

European Commission. Directorate-General for Education Youth & Culture. (2022). *Ethical guidelines on the use of artificial intelligence (AI) and data in teaching and learning for educators*. Paris: Publication Office of the European Union.

Evans, D. (2023). Implications and recommendations for AI-based assessment in higher education. *Higher Education Research & Development*, 42(3), 567–581. DOI: 10.1080/07294360.2022.2098765

Fang, Y., Ren, Z., Hu, X., & Graesser, A. C. (2019). A meta-analysis of the effectiveness of ALEKS on learning. *Educational Psychology*, 39(10), 1278–1292. DOI: 10.1080/01443410.2018.1495829

Farazouli, A., Cerratto-Pargman, T., Bolander-Laksov, K., & McGrath, C. (2023). Hello GPT! Goodbye home examination? An exploratory study of AI chatbots impact on university teachers' assessment practices. *Assessment & Evaluation in Higher Education*, 49(3), 363–375. DOI: 10.1080/02602938.2023.2241676

Farrokhnia, M., Banihashem, S. K., Noroozi, O., & Wals, A. (2023). A SWOT analysis of ChatGPT: Implications for educational practice and research. *Innovations in Education and Teaching International*, 1–15. DOI: 10.1080/14703297.2023.2195846

Fatoni, A., & Surani, D. (2022). An Analysis of Online Learning Media in English Class During Covid-19 Pandemic. *4th Social and Humanities Research Symposium (SoRes 2021)* (pp. 595-600). Indonesia: Atlantis Press.

Feather, D., Anchor, J. R., & Cowton, C. J. (2014). Supervisors' perceptions of the value of the undergraduate dissertation. *The International Journal of Management Education, 12*(1), 14-21. https://doi.org/https://doi.org/10.1016/j.ijme.2013.06.002

Ferrara, E. (2023). Fairness and bias in artificial intelligence: A brief survey of sources, impacts, and mitigation strategies. *Sci*, 6(1), 3. DOI: 10.3390/sci6010003

Fischer, G., Lundin, J., & Lindberg, J. O. (2020). Rethinking and reinventing learning, education and collaboration in the digital age—From creating technologies to transforming cultures. *The International Journal of Information and Learning Technology*, 37(5), 241–252. DOI: 10.1108/IJILT-04-2020-0051

Fischer, G., Lundin, J., & Lindberg, O. J. (2022). The challenge for the digital age: Making learning a part of life. *The International Journal of Information and Learning Technology*, 40(1), 1–16. DOI: 10.1108/IJILT-04-2022-0079

Fisher, M. (2024, 07 25). *Vanderbilt University*. Retrieved from Centre for Teaching: https://cft.vanderbilt.edu/student-assessment-in-teaching-and-learning/

Fitria, T. N. (2021). Artificial intelligence (AI) in education: Using AI tools for teaching and learning process. Prosiding Seminar Nasional & Call for Paper STIE AAS, Ge, X., Xu, C., Misaki, D., Markus, H. R., & Tsai, J. L. (2024). How Culture Shapes What People Want From AI. Proceedings of the CHI Conference on Human Factors in Computing Systems, Gentile, M., Città, G., Perna, S., & Allegra, M. (2023). Do we still need teachers? Navigating the paradigm shift of the teacher's role in the AI era. Frontiers in Education, Hakkal, S., & Lahcen, A. A. (2022). An Overview of Adaptive Learning Fee-based Platforms.

Fitzpatrick, D. (2023). *The AI educator*. TeachersGoals Publishing.

Fitzpatrick, D., Fox, A., & Weinstein, B. (2023). *The AI classroom: The ultimate guide to artificial intelligence*. TeachersGoals Publishing.

Floridi, L., Cowls, J., King, T. C., & Taddeo, M. (2021). How to design AI for social good: Seven essential factors. *Science and Engineering Ethics*, 27(3), 1–26. DOI: 10.1007/s11948-020-00213-5 PMID: 32246245

Fok, W. W. T., He, Y. S., Yeung, H. H. A., Law, K. Y., Cheung, K., Ai, Y. Y., & Ho, P. (2018). Prediction model for students' future development by Deep Learning and tensorflow artificial intelligence engine. 2018 *4th International Conference on Information Management (ICIM)*. DOI: 10.1109/INFOMAN.2018.8392818

Foltýnek, T., Meuschke, N., & Gipp, B. (2019). Academic plagiarism detection: A systematic literature review. *ACM Computing Surveys*, 52(6), 1–42. DOI: 10.1145/3345317

Forbes. (2020). Artificial Intelligence In Education Transformation. Retrieved 7 29, 2024, from https://www.forbes.com/sites/forbestechcouncil artificial-intelligence-in-education-transformation/#43ee5fb832a4

Forbus, K. D., Liang, C., & Rabkina, I. (2017). Representation and computation in cognitive models. *Topics in Cognitive Science*, 9(3), 694–718. DOI: 10.1111/tops.12277 PMID: 28635155

Fraser, T., Cherdchaiyapong, N., Tekle, W., Thomas, E., Zayas, J., Page-Tan, C., & Aldrich, D. P. (2022). Trust but verify: Validating new measures for mapping social infrastructure in cities. *Urban Climate, 46*, 101287-. https://doi.org/DOI: 10.1080/15228053.2023.2233814

Garbarine, R. (2023, March 27). *How is AI changing how we write and create?* NC State College of Humanities and Social Sciences. https://chass.ncsu.edu/news/2023/03/27/how-is-ai-changing-how-we-write-and-create/

Garcia, J., & Wu, C. (2022). Exploring Authenticity in AI-Driven Influencer Marketing Across Generations. *JMR, Journal of Marketing Research*, 59(6), 789–804. DOI: 10.1177/00222437221117558

Garcia, L., & Lopez, M. (2023). Evaluating the effectiveness of AI-based assessment: A mixed-methods approach. *Assessment & Evaluation in Higher Education*, 48(2), 231–248. DOI: 10.1080/02602938.2022.2057189

Gardner, H. (1983). *Frames of mind: The theory of multiple intelligences*. Basic Books.

Gardner, J., Harlen, W., Hayward, L., & Stobart, G. (2008). *Changing Assessment Practice: Process, Principles and Practice*. Assessment Reform Group.

Garrison, D. R., Anderson, T., & Archer, W. (2000). Critical inquiry in a text-based environment: Computer conferencing in higher education. *The Internet and Higher Education*, 2(2), 87–105. DOI: 10.1016/S1096-7516(00)00016-6

Geckin, V., Kızıltaş, E., & Çınar, Ç. (2023). Assessing second-language academic writing: AI vs. Human raters. *Journal of Educational Technology and Online Learning*, 6(4), 1096–1108. DOI: 10.31681/jetol.1336599

Geerling, W., Mateer, G. D., & Damodaran, N. (2023). ChatGPT has aced the test of understanding in college economics: Now what? *The American Economist*, 68(2), 233–245. Advance online publication. DOI: 10.1177/05694345231169654

Genkina, G. (2024, Mar. 7). AI prompt engineering is dead. Long live AI prompt engineering. *IEEE Spectrum*.https://spectrum.ieee.org/prompt-engineering-is-dead

Ghashout, S., Gdura, Y., & Drawil, N. (2023). "Early Prediction of Students' Academic Performance Using Artificial Neural Network: A Case Study In Computer Engineering Department," 2023 *IEEE 3rd International Maghreb Meeting of the Conference on Sciences and Techniques of Automatic Control and Computer Engineering (MI-STA),* Benghazi, Libya, pp. 40-45, DOI: 10.1109/MI-STA57575.2023.10169421

Gibbs, G., & Jenkins, A. (2014). *Teaching large classes in higher education: How to maintain quality with reduced resources*. Taylor & Francis.

Gierl, M. J., Lai, H., & Zhang, X. (2021). Automatic item generation: A prospective view of the future of assessment. *Frontiers in Education*, 6, 719445. DOI: 10.3389/feduc.2021.719445

Gikandi, J. W., Morrow, D., & Davis, N. (2011). Online formative assessment in higher education: A review of the literature. *Computers & Education*, 57(4), 2336–2355. DOI: 10.1016/j.compedu.2011.06.004

Gleason, N. (2018). Introduction. In Gleason, N. (Ed.), *Higher education in the era of the fourth industrial revolution* (pp. 13–15). Palgrave Macmillan. DOI: 10.1007/978-981-13-0194-0_1

Gobert, J. D., Dickler, R., & Adair, A. (2024). Using an AI-Based Dashboard to Help Teachers Support Students' Learning Progressions for Science Practices. In *Handbook of Research on Science Learning Progressions* (pp. 488–498). Routledge. DOI: 10.4324/9781003170785-32

Göçen, A., & Aydemir, F. (2020). Artificial intelligence in education and schools. *Research on Education and Media*, 12(1), 13–21. DOI: 10.2478/rem-2020-0003

Goel, A. (2020). AI-powered learning: making education accessible, affordable, and achievable. *arXiv preprint arXiv:2006.01908.*

Gonzalez-Calatayud, V., Prendez-Espinosa, P., Roig-Vila, R., & Carpanzano, E. (2021). Applied sciences review artificial intelligence for student assessments: A systematic review. *Sci*, 2021, 5467.

Gordon, R. (2022). *ELIZAR wins Peabody Award.* MIT News.

Gorichanaz, T. (2023). Accused: How students respond to allegations of using ChatGPT on assessments. Learning. *Research and Practice*, 9(2), 183–196. DOI: 10.1080/23735082.2023.2254787

Gradescope. (2021). Gradescope: AI-assisted grading. https://www.gradescope.com/

Graham, S., & Harris, K. (2015). Formative assessment and writing: A meta-analysis. *The Elementary School Journal*, 115(4), 523–547. DOI: 10.1086/681947

Gravett, K., Taylor, C. A., & Fairchild, N. (2024). Pedagogies of mattering: Re-conceptualising relational pedagogies in higher education. *Teaching in Higher Education*, 29(2), 388–403. DOI: 10.1080/13562517.2021.1989580

Green, L. S., & Chassereau, K. (2023). Modeling guided inquiry and school librarian instructional partnerships to pre-service teachers through digital video production. *Journal of Education for Library and Information Science*, 64(2), 185–205. DOI: 10.3138/jelis-2022-0015

Greer, J. E., McCalla, G. I., Collins, J. A., & Kumar, V. S. (2016). Intelligent tutoring and adaptive learning environments. In Jonassen, D. J. (Ed.), *The international encyclopedia of education* (6th ed., pp. 272–279). Elsevier., DOI: 10.1016/B978-0-12-809324-5.06052-3

Guan, Y.. (2020). AI in education: A systematic review of the literature. *Computers & Education.*

Guerrero-Roldán, A. E., Rodríguez-González, M. E., Bañeres, D., Elasri-Ejjaberi, A., & Cortadas, P. (2021). Experiences in the use of an adaptive intelligent system to enhance online learners' performance: A case study in economics and business courses. *International Journal of Educational Technology in Higher Education*, 18(1), 1–27. DOI: 10.1186/s41239-021-00271-0

Guest, J., & Riegler, R. (2022). Knowing HE standards: How good are students at evaluating academic work? *Higher Education Research & Development*, 41(3), 714–728. DOI: 10.1080/07294360.2020.1867516

Gulikers, J. T., Bastiaens, T. J., & Kirschner, P. A. (2004). A five-dimensional framework for authentic assessment. *Educational Technology Research and Development*, 52(3), 67–86. DOI: 10.1007/BF02504676

Gulson, K. N., & Witzenberger, K. (2020). Repackaging authority: Artificial intelligence, automated governance and education trade shows. *Journal of Education Policy*, •••, 1–22. DOI: 10.1080/02680939.2020.1785552

Guskey, T. R. (2010). Formative assessment. *Educational Leadership*, 68(1), 42–47.

Gustafson, K. L., & Branch, R. M. (2002). *Instructional design: Models and methods for developing effective learning experiences*. Merrill Prentice Hall.

Gwagwa, A., Kraemer, E., Rizk, N., Rutenberg, I., & De Beer, J. (2020). Artificial Intelligence (AI) deployments in Africa: Benefits, challenges and policy dimensions. [AJIC]. *The African Journal of Information and Communication*, 26(26), 1–28. DOI: 10.23962/10539/30361

Hacker, P., Mittelstadt, B., Borgesius, F. Z., & Wachter, S. (2024). *Generative discrimination: what happens when generative AI exhibits bias, and what can be done about it.* arXiv preprint arXiv:2407.10329. https://arxiv.org/abs/2407.10329 DOI: 10.2139/ssrn.4877398

Hadad, Y., Keren, B., & Naveh, G. (2020). The relative importance of teaching evaluation criteria from the points of view of students and faculty. *Assessment & Evaluation in Higher Education*, 45(3), 447–459. DOI: 10.1080/02602938.2019.1665623

Han, B., Nawaz, S., Buchanan, G., & McKay, D. (2023). Ethical and pedagogical impacts of AI in education. International Conference on Artificial Intelligence in Education, Holstein, K., & Aleven, V. (2022). Designing for human–AI complementarity in K-12 education. *AI Magazine*, 43(2), 239–248.

Hargrave, M., Fisher, D., & Frey, N. (2024, September). Using AI to save time and lessen the the load. *Language Magazine*, 24(1), 28–31.

Harland, T., McLean, A., Wass, R., Miller, E., & Sim, K. N. (2015). An assessment arms race and its fallout: High-stakes grading and the case for slow scholarship. *Assessment & Evaluation in Higher Education*, 40(4), 528–541. DOI: 10.1080/02602938.2014.931927

Harland, T., & Wald, N. (2021). The assessment arms race and the evolution of a university's assessment practices. *Assessment & Evaluation in Higher Education*, 46(1), 105–117. DOI: 10.1080/02602938.2020.1745753

Harvard Graduate School of Education. (2022). *Project Zero's thinking routine toolbox*. https://pz.harvard.edu/thinking-routines

Hashim, S., Omar, M. K., Ab Jalil, H., & Sharef, N. M. (2022). Trends on technologies and artificial intelligence in education for personalized learning: Systematic literature. *Journal of Academic Research in Progressive Education and Development*, 12(1), 884–903. DOI: 10.6007/IJARPED/v11-i1/12230

Hawe, D., Dixon, H., Murray, J., & Chandler, S. (2021). Using rubrics and exemplars to develop students' evaluative and productive knowledge and skill. *Journal of Further and Higher Education*, 45(8), 1033–1047. DOI: 10.1080/0309877X.2020.1851358

Hernandez, R., & Gonzalez, A. (2023). Future directions for AI in educational assessment: Ethical and societal implications. *Educational Technology Research and Development*, 71(3), 1021–1044. DOI: 10.1007/s11423-022-10165-1

Ho, J., von Davier, A., Yaneva, V., Lottridge, S., von Davier, M., & Harris, D. J. (2024). Transforming assessment: The impact and implications of large models and generative AI. *Educational Measurement: Issues and Practice*, 43(2), 16–29. DOI: 10.1111/emip.12602

Holmes, W., Bialik, M., & Fadel, C. (2019). Artificial intelligence in education: Promises and implications for teaching and learning. Center for Curriculum Redesign. https://curriculumredesign.org/wp-content/uploads/AIED-Book-Excerpt-CCR.pdf

Holmes, W., Bialik, M., & Fadel, C. (2019). *Artificial intelligence in education promises and implications for teaching and learning*. Center for Curriculum Redesign.

Holmes, W., Luckin, R., & Griffiths, M. (2019). Artificial intelligence in education: Promises and implications for teaching and learning. *International Journal of Artificial Intelligence in Education*, 29(3), 1–16. DOI: 10.1007/s40593-019-00186-5

Holmes, W., Porayska-Pomsta, K., Holstein, K., Sutherland, E., Baker, T., Shum, S. B., Santos, O. C., Rodrigo, M. T., Cukurova, M., Bittencourt, I. I., & Koedinger, K. R. (2021). Ethics of AI in education: Towards a community-wide framework. *International Journal of Artificial Intelligence in Education*, •••, 1–23. DOI: 10.1007/s40593-021-00239-1

Holmes, W., Porayska-Pomsta, K., Holstein, K., Sutherland, E., Bake, T., Shun, S., & Koedinger, K. (2021). Ethics of AI of Education: Towards a community -wide framework. *International Journal of Artificial Intelligence in Education*.

Holstein, K., & Doroudi, S. (2021). Equity and artificial intelligence in education: will" aied" amplify or alleviate inequities in education? *arXiv preprint arXiv:2104.12920.*

Holstein, K., & Doroudi, S. (2022). Equity and artificial intelligence in education. In *The ethics of artificial intelligence in education* (pp. 151–173). Routledge. DOI: 10.4324/9780429329067-9

Hong, Y., Tong, S., Huang, W., Zhuang, Y., Liu, Q., Chen, E., & He, Y. (2023). *Search-Efficient Computerized Adaptive Testing. CIKM '23, October 21–25.* CIKM.

Hooda, M., Rana, C., Dahiya, O., Rizwan, A., & Hossain, M. S. (2022). Artificial intelligence for assessment and feedback to enhance student success in higher education. *Mathematical Problems in Engineering*, 2022(1), 5215722. DOI: 10.1155/2022/5215722

Hsu, T.-C., Abelson, H., Patton, E., Chen, S.-C., & Chang, H.-N. (2022). Self-efficacy and behavior patterns of learners using a real-time collaboration system developed for group programming. *International Journal of Computer-Supported Collaborative Learning*, 16(4), 559–582. DOI: 10.1007/s11412-021-09357-3 PMID: 35002570

Hu, K. (2023, 02 2). ChatGPT sets record for fast-growing user base-analyst note. Reuters. Retrieved 07 30, 2024, from https://www.reuters.com/

Huang, L. (2023). Ethics of artificial intelligence in education: Student privacy and data protection. *Science Insights Education Frontiers*, 16(2), 2577–2587. DOI: 10.15354/sief.23.re202

Huang, R., & Lu, Z. (2019). Adaptive learning and intelligent tutoring systems: Review and perspectives. *Journal of Educational Technology Development and Exchange*, 12(1), 53–69. DOI: 10.18785/jetde.1201.05

Hunde, B. R., & Woldeyohannes, A. D. (2022). Future prospects of computer-aided design (CAD)–A review from the perspective of artificial intelligence (AI), extended reality, and 3D printing. *Results in Engineering*, 14, 100478. DOI: 10.1016/j.rineng.2022.100478

Hwang, G., Xie, H., & Gasevic, D. (2020). Vision, challenges, roles and research issues of Artificial Intelligence in Education . *Computers and Education: Artificial Intelligence 1 Article.*

Hwang, G. J., & Chang, C. Y. (2018). Innovative learning environments: Opportunities and challenges. *Journal of Educational Technology & Society*, 21(1), 1–9.

Hwang, G. J., Chu, H. C., & Yin, C. (2017). Objectives, methodologies and research issues of learning analytics. *Interactive Learning Environments*, 25(2), 143–146. DOI: 10.1080/10494820.2017.1287338

Hwang, G. J., Xie, H., Wah, B. W., & Gašević, D. (2020). Vision, challenges, roles and research issues of Artificial Intelligence in Education. *Computers and Education: Artificial Intelligence*, 1, 100001. DOI: 10.1016/j.caeai.2020.100001

Hwang, G., & Tu, Y. (2021). Roles and research trends of artificial intellignece in mathematics education: A bibliogmetric mapping and systematic review. *Mathematics*, 9(6), 584. DOI: 10.3390/math9060584

Hwang, S. (2022). Examining the effects of artificial intelligence on elementary students' mathematics achievement: A meta-analysis. *Sustainability (Basel)*, 14(20), 13185. DOI: 10.3390/su142013185

Ingrams, A., Kaufmann, W., & Jacobs, D. (2022). In AI we trust? Citizen perceptions of AI in government decision making. *Policy and Internet*, 14(2), 390–409. DOI: 10.1002/poi3.276

International Business Machines. (n.d.). *Deep Blue: IBM's computer checkmated a human chess champion in a computing tour de force.* IBM Heritage. https://www.ibm.com/history/deep-blue#:~:text=Deep%20Blue%20derived%20its%20chess,high%2Dspeed%20computations%20in%20parallel

International Design Center of the University of California. Irvine. (2019). The HCD [Human-Centered Design] Process. https://www.interaction-design.org/

International Society for Technology in Education. (2024). *StretchAI: An AI coach just for educators.* https://iste.org/ai#stretchai

Islam, M. K., Sarker, M. F. H., & Islam, M. S. (2022). Promoting student-centred blended learning in higher education: A model. *E-Learning and Digital Media*, 19(1), 36–54. DOI: 10.1177/20427530211027721

Januszewski, A., & Monlenda, M. (2007). *Educational Technology: A Definition with Commentary*. Routledge., DOI: 10.4324/9780203054000

Jermakowicz, E. (2023). The coming trnasformative impact of large language models and artificial intelligence on global business and education. *Journal of Global Awareness*, 4(2), 3. DOI: 10.24073/jga/4/02/03

Jessica-Mullins. (2023, March 10). Philosophy of Instructional Design. https://jessica-mullins.com/instructional-design-philosophy/

Jordan, M. I., & Mitchell, T. M. (2015, Jul 17). Machine learning: Trends, perspectives, and prospects. *Science*. https://www.science.org/doi/abs/10.1126/science.aaa8415

Jowallah, R. (2019). *Artificial intelligence in education* [Video]. YouTube. https://www.youtube.com/watch?v=-nsVW6c2OQU&list=PLk7RZ0ABlfPJHFtVgh9T6QI5I4sYgVH4x

Jowallah, R. (2024). *AI in higher education: Opportunities and challenges* [Video]. YouTube. https://youtu.be/rJYssMYJ52Y

Jowallah, R. (2024a). *Teachers are essential in the age of AI* [Video]. YouTube. https://youtu.be/R48kRHmCyak

Judijanto, L., Atsani, M. R., & Chadijah, S. (2024). Trends In The Development Of Artificial Intelligence-Based Technology In Education. *International Journal of Teaching and Learning*, 2(6), 1722–1723.

Kahn, B. (2020). *Ethical challenges in AI education*. Cambridge University Press.

Kaipa, R. (2021). Multiple choice questions and essay questions in curriculum. *Journal of Applied Research in Higher Education*, 13(1), 16–32. DOI: 10.1108/JARHE-01-2020-0011

Kajamaa, A., Kumpulainen, K., & Olkinuora, H. R. (2020). Teacher interventions in students' collaborative work in a technology-rich educational makerspace. *British Journal of Educational Technology*, 51(2), 371–386. DOI: 10.1111/bjet.12837

Kaldaras, L., Akaeze, H. O., & Reckase, M. D. (2024). Developing valid assessments in the era of generative artificial intelligence. *Frontiers in Education*, 9, 1399377. Advance online publication. DOI: 10.3389/feduc.2024.1399377

Kalla, D., Smith, N., Samaah, F., & Kuraku, S. (2023). Study and analysis of ChatGPT and its impact on different fields of study. *International Journal of Innovative Science and Research Technology*, 8(3).

Kammer, J., & Hays, L. (2023). *Digital Literacy Made Simple : Strategies for Building Skills Across the Curriculum*. International Society for Technology in Education.

Kapur, M. (2016). Examining productive failure, productive success, unproductive failure, and unproductive success in learning. *Educational Psychologist*, 51(2), 289–299. DOI: 10.1080/00461520.2016.1155457

Kaur, H. (2023, June 23). *Using AI in universal design for learning*. Edutopia. https://www.edutopia.org/article/using-ai-in-universal-design-for-learning/

Kenwright, B. (2024). Is it the end of undergraduate dissertations?: Exploring the advantages and challenges of Generative AI models in education. In Hai-Jew, S. (Ed.), *Generative AI in Teaching and Learning* (pp. 46–65). IGI Global., DOI: 10.4018/979-8-3693-0074-9.ch003

Kharbat, F. F., Alshawabkeh, A., & Woolsey, M. L. (2021). Identifying gaps in using artificial intelligence to support students with intellectual disabilities from education and health perspectives. *Aslib Journal of Information Management*, 73(1), 101–128. DOI: 10.1108/AJIM-02-2020-0054

Khosravi, H., & Cooper, A. (2019). Personalized adaptive learning: AI approaches in higher education. In *2019 IEEE International Conference on Artificial Intelligence in Education (AIED)* (pp. 59–68). IEEE. https://doi.org/DOI: 10.1109/AIED.2019.00015

Khosravi, H., Kitto, K., & Williams, J. (2019). RiPPLE: A Crowdsourced Adaptive Platform for Recommendation of Learning Activities. *Journal of Learning Analytics*, 6(3), 1–15. DOI: 10.18608/jla.2019.63.12

Kim, J. (2024). Leading teachers' perspective on teacher-AI collaboration in education. *Education and Information Technologies*, 29(7), 8693–8724. DOI: 10.1007/s10639-023-12109-5

Kim, J., Lee, H., & Cho, Y. H. (2022). Learning design to support student-AI collaboration: Perspectives of leading teachers for AI in education. *Education and Information Technologies*, 27(5), 6069–6104. DOI: 10.1007/s10639-021-10831-6

Kim, S., Jang, Y., Choi, S., Kim, W., Jung, H., Kim, S., & Kim, H. (2021). Analyzing teacher competency with TPACK for K-12 AI education. *Kunstliche Intelligenz*, 35(2), 139–151. DOI: 10.1007/s13218-021-00731-9

Kizilcec, R. F., & Lee, H. (2020). Algorithmic fairness in education. arXiv preprint arXiv:2007.05443.

Kleizen, B., Van Dooren, W., Verhoest, K., & Tan, E. (2023). Do citizens trust trustworthy artificial intelligence? Experimental evidence on the limits of ethical AI measures in government. *Government Information Quarterly*, 40(4), 101834. DOI: 10.1016/j.giq.2023.101834

Knewton. (2021). The Knewton platform: Adaptive learning technology. https://www.knewton.com/platform/

Knight, P. T. (2002). Summative assessment in higher education: Practices in disarray. *Studies in Higher Education*, 27(3), 275–286. DOI: 10.1080/03075070220000662

Kolb, B., & Whishaw, I. (2014). *An introduction to the brain and behaviour*. Worth Publishers.

Kop, R., Fournier, H., & Durand, G. (2017). A critical perspective on learning analytics and educational data mining. *Handbook of Learning Analytics, 319.*

Kose, U., & Deperlioglu, O. (2020). Intelligent tutoring systems and AI for personalized learning in higher education. *AI and Learning Review*, 11(3), 149–164. DOI: 10.1007/s40593-019-00185-6

Kose, U., Deperlioglu, O., & Erguvan, E. (2020). Innovative approaches to AI-based adaptive learning systems: Review and future perspectives. *AI and Education Journal*, 15(3), 101–123. DOI: 10.1007/s40593-019-00184-7

Kulkarni, C. E., Bernstein, M. S., & Klemmer, S. R. (2015). PeerStudio: Rapid Peer Feedback Emphasizes Revision and Improves Performance. *Proceedings of the Second (2015) ACM Conference on Learning @ Scale*, 75–84. DOI: 10.1145/2724660.2724670

Kumar, P., & Singh, A. (2023). Limitations and biases in AI-based assessment: A critical review. *Computers and Education: Artificial Intelligence*, 3, 100074. DOI: 10.1016/j.caeai.2023.100074

Laak, K. J., & Aru, J. (2024). AI and personalized learning: Bridging the gap with modern educational goals. *arXiv preprint arXiv:2404.02798.*

Lameras, P., & Arnab, S. (2021). Power to the teachers: An exploratory review on artificial intelligence in education. *Information (Basel)*, 13(1), 14. DOI: 10.3390/info13010014

Lee, A. V. Y. (2023). Supporting students' generation of feedback in large-scale online course with artificial intelligence-enabled evaluation. *Studies in Educational Evaluation*, 77, 101250. DOI: 10.1016/j.stueduc.2023.101250

Lee, I., Zhang, H., Moore, K., Zhou, X., Perret, B., Cheng, Y., & Pu, G. (2022, February). AI book club: An innovative professional development model for AI education. In *Proceedings of the 53rd ACM Technical Symposium on Computer Science Education-Volume 1* (pp. 202-208). DOI: 10.1145/3478431.3499318

Lee, J., & Kim, H. (2023). Implementing AI-based assessment in computer science courses: A case study. *Journal of Educational Computing Research*, 61(2), 458–481. DOI: 10.1177/07356331221142957

Lee, M., Zhao, T., & Fernandez, A. (2021). Authenticity Perception in AI Influencers: A Cross-Generational Analysis. *International Journal of Human-Computer Interaction*, 37(4), 351–366. DOI: 10.1080/10447318.2021.1898524

Lee, Y.-J., & Davis, R. O. (2024). Korean in-service teachers' perceptions of implementing artificial intelligence (AI) education for teaching in schools and their AI teacher training programs. *International Journal of Information and Education Technology (IJIET)*, 14(2), 214–219. Advance online publication. DOI: 10.18178/ijiet.2024.14.2.2042

Legris, P., Ingham, J., & Collerette, P. (2003). Why do people use information technology?A critical review of the Technology Acceptance Model. *Information & Management*, 40(3), 191–204. DOI: 10.1016/S0378-7206(01)00143-4

Lewis, M., & McNamara, K. (2021). A certified school librarian is a professional learning powerhouse. *The Learning Professional*, 42(4), 52.

Lim, C. P., & Chai, C. S. (2008). Rethinking classroom-oriented instructional development models to mediate instructional planning in technology-enhanced learning environments. *Teaching and Teacher Education*, 24(8), 2002–2013. DOI: 10.1016/j.tate.2008.05.004

Limna, P., Jakwatanatham, S., Siripipattanakul, S., Kaewpuang, P., & Sriboonruang, P. (2022). A review of artificial intelligence (AI) in education during the digital era. *Advance Knowledge for Executives*, 1(1), 1–9.

Ling Jen, S., & Abdul Rahim Hj Salam, A. R. (2024). A systematic review on the use of artificial intelligence in writing. *International Journal of Academic Research in Progressive Education and Development*, 13(1). https://www.researchgate.net/publication/378514867_A_Systematic_Review_on_The_Use_of_Artificial_Intelligence_in_Writing

Liu, Y., & Baucham, M. (2023). AI Technology: Key to successful assessment. In *Handbook of Research on Redesigning Teaching, Learning, and Assessment in the Digital Era* (pp. 304-325). IGI Global.

Liu, Q., & Wang, L. (2020). Intelligent systems in education: An overview. *Educational Technology Research and Development*, 68(3), 1345–1363.

Liu, X., & Zhong, B. (2024). What to consider before incorporating generative AI into schools? *AI & Society: Journal of Knowledge. AI & Society*, 1-3. Advance online publication. DOI: 10.1007/s00146-024-01872-9

Liu, Y., & Xu, F. (2020). Artificial intelligence for education and learning. *AI Open*, 1, 111–119. DOI: 10.1016/j.aiopen.2020.07.002

Liu, Y., & Xu, Y. (2020). The role of artificial intelligence in education: A review. *Journal of Educational Technology & Society*, 23(1), 1–12.

Lo, C. K., & Hew, K. F. (2023). *A review of integrating AI-based chatbots into flipped learning: New possibilities and challenges. Frontiers in Education*. doi:10.3389/feduc.2023.1175715

Lodge, J., Yang, S. J., Furze, L., & Dawson, P. (2023). It's not like a calculator, so what is the relationship between learners and generative artificial intelligence? *Learning: Research and Practice*, 9(2), 117–124. DOI: 10.1080/23735082.2023.2261106

Long, D., & Magerko, B. (2020). What is AI literacy? Competencies and design considerations. In *Proceedings of the 2020 CHI Conference on Human Factors in Computing Systems* (pp. 1-16). https://doi.org/DOI: 10.1145/3313831.3376727

Lorenzo, N., & Gallon, R. (2019). Smart pedagogy for smart learning. In Daniela, L. (Ed.), *Didactics of smart pedagogy* (pp. 41–69). Springer., DOI: 10.1007/978-3-030-01551-0_3

Luan, H., Geczy, P., Lai, H., Gobert, J., Yang, S. J., Ogata, H., Baltes, J., Guerra, R., Li, P., & Tsai, C. C. (2020). Challenges and future directions of big data and artificial intelligence in education. *Frontiers in Psychology*, 11, 580820. DOI: 10.3389/fpsyg.2020.580820 PMID: 33192896

Luckin, R., Holmes, W., Griffiths, M., & Forcier, L. B. (2016). Intelligence unleashed: An argument for AI in education. Pearson Education. https://www.pearson.com/content/dam/one-dot-com/one-dot-com/global/Files/about-pearson/innovation/Intelligence-Unleashed-Publication.pdf

Luckin, R. (2017). *Machine learning and human intelligence: The future of education for the 21st century*. UCL Institute of Education Press.

Luckin, R., & Cukurova, M. (2019). Designing educational technologies in the age of AI: A learning sciences-driven approach. *British Journal of Educational Technology*, 50(6), 2824–2838. DOI: 10.1111/bjet.12861

Luckin, R., & Holmes, W. (2019). AI in education: Opportunities, challenges, and ethical considerations. *AI & Society*, 34(3), 537–552. DOI: 10.1007/s00146-019-00849-1

Luckin, R., Holmes, W., & Forcier, L. B. (2016). *Intelligence unleashed: An argument for AI in education*. Pearson.

Luckin, R., Holmes, W., & Griffiths, M. (2019). The impact of AI on education: Current developments and future perspectives. *AI in Education Review*, 13(4), 101–119.

Luckin, R., Holmes, W., Griffiths, M., & Corcier, L. B. (2016). *Intelligence Unleashed: An Argument for AI in Education*. Pearson.

Luo, J. (2024). A critical review of GenAI policies in higher education assessment: A call to reconsider the "originality" of students' work. *Assessment & Evaluation in Higher Education*, 49(5), 651–664. DOI: 10.1080/02602938.2024.2309963

Mager, R. F., & Pipe, P. (1970). *Analyzing performance problems or you can't fix what you can't describe*. Fearon Publishers.

Mansaray, M., & Mutisya, P. (2017). Applied statistical models of assessment and evaluation of instructional efficiency. *International Journal of Academic Research in Business & Social Sciences*, 7(5), 233–257. DOI: 10.6007/IJARBSS/v7-i5/2928

Many, H., Shvetsova, M., & Forestier, G. (2024). Transformation numérique: comment enseigner (avec) l'IA générative dans l'enseignement supérieur ? https://doi.org/DOI: 10.1145/3457607

Marbun, T. O. (2023). The implementation of artificial intelligence, Chatgpt, and critical thinking method for academic endeavors at theological higher education. *Journal Didaskalia*, 6(2), 84–100. DOI: 10.33856/didaskalia.v6i2.309

Marchese, D. (2022, Dec. 21). An A. I. pioneer on what we should really fear. *NewYork Times Magazine* para. 7, note 4. https://www.nytimes.com/interactive/2022/12/26/magazine/yejin-choi-interview.html

Martin, A., & Lazendic, G. (2017). Computer-adaptive testing: Implications for students' achievement, motivation, engagement, and subjective test experience. *Journal of Educational Psychology*, •••, 1–57.

Marzano, R. J. (2001). *Classroom instruction that works: Research-based strategies for increasing student achievement*. ASCD.

Marzano, R. J. (2011). *Formative assessment & standards-based grading*. Solution Tree Press.

Masoud, B., & Kamran, K. (2024). *Transformative Influence of LLM and AI Tools in Student Social Media Engagement: Analyzing Personalization, Communication Efficiency, and Collaborative Learning*. Working Paper. http://arxiv.org/abs/2407.15012

Mazur, J. (2013). *Learning and behaviour*. Prentice Hall.

McCormack, M. (2023, 4 17). Educause QuickPoll Results: Adopting and Adapting to Generative AI in Higher Ed Tech. Educause Research Notes.

McDonald, G. (2013). Does size matter? The impact of student–staff ratios. *Journal of Higher Education Policy and Management*, 35(6), 652–667. DOI: 10.1080/1360080X.2013.844668

McGowan, M. J., & O'Reilly, T. (2021). Ethical challenges in using artificial intelligence in education. *Computers & Education*, 166, 104159.

Memarian, B., & Doleck, T. (2024). A review of assessment for learning with artificial intelligence. *Computers in Human Behavior: Artificial Humans*, 2, 1–12.

Merrill, D. M. (2007). The proper study of instructional design. In Reiser, R. A., & Dempsey, J. V. (Eds.), *Trends and Issues in Instructional Design and Technology* (2nd ed., pp. 336–341). Pearson Prentice Hall.

Mersand, S. (2021). The state of makerspace research: A review of the literature. *TechTrends*, 65(2), 174–186. DOI: 10.1007/s11528-020-00566-5

Miao, F., & Holmes, W. (2023). *Guidance for generative AI in education and research.* UNESCO. https://doi.org/https://doi.org/10.54675/EWZM9535

Miao, F., & Shiohira, K. (2024a). *AI competency framework for students* (UNESCO, Ed.). UNESCO. https://doi.org/https://doi.org/10.54675/JKJB9835

Miao, F., & Shiohira, K. (2024b). *AI competency framework for Teachers* (UNESCO, Ed.). UNESCO. https://doi.org/https://doi.org/10.54675/ZJTE2084

Miao, F., Holmes, W., Huang, R., & Zhang, H. (2021). *AI and education: A guidance for policymakers.* Unesco Publishing.

Miller, T., & Davis, R. (2023). The impact of AI-based assessment on educators: Efficiency, workload, and pedagogical implications. *British Journal of Educational Technology*, 54(3), 835–853. DOI: 10.1111/bjet.13242

Ministry of Education People Republic of China. (2019, 08 29). *UNESCO publishes Beijing Consensus on Artificial Intelligence and Education.* Retrieved from Ministry of Education People Republic of China: http://en.moe.gov.cn/news/press_releases/201909/t20190902_396913.html

Mishra, P., & Koehler, M. J. (2006). Technological pedagogical content knowledge: A framework for teacher knowledge. *Teachers College Record*, 108(6), 1017–1054. DOI: 10.1111/j.1467-9620.2006.00684.x

Mishra, P., Warr, M., & Islam, R. (2023). TPACK in the age of ChatGPT and Generative AI. *Journal of Digital Learning in Teacher Education*, 39(4), 235–251. DOI: 10.1080/21532974.2023.2247480

Mislevy, R., Almond, R., & Lukas, J. (2004). A Brief Introduction to Evidence-Centered Design CSE Report 632. Maryland: National Center for Research on Evaluation,Standards, and Student Testing (CRESST).

Mohammadi, Z., Kho ℵ rami, F., & Zarrabi, M. (2021). Instructional designers' perceptions of artificial intelligence: A thematic analysis. [doi: 10.1007/s11557-021-01823-5]. *TechTrends*, 65(6), 1222–1232.

Mohammadi, Z., Tavakol, M., & Arshadi, N. (2021). Artificial intelligence and instructional design: A review of literature. Computers & Education [DOI: 10.1016/j.caeai.2021.100014]. *Artificial Intelligence*, 2(2), 100014.

Molina, E., Cobo, C., Pineda, J., & Rovner, H. (2024). *AI revolution in education: what you need to know* (Digital Innovations in Education, Issue 1). W. Bank. https://documents1.worldbank.org/curated/en/099734306182493324/pdf/IDU152823b13109c514ebd19c241a289470b6902.pdf

Mollick, E. (2024). *Co-intelligence: Living and working with AI*. Penguin Publishing Group. https://books.google.nl/books?id=J2HgEAAAQBAJ

Moore, M. G., & Kearsley, G. (2012). *Distance education: A systems view of online learning* (3rd ed.). Wadsworth Cengage Learning.

Morjaria, L., Burns, L., Bracken, K., Levinson, A. J., Ngo, Q. N., Lee, M., & Sibbald, M. (2024). Examining the efficacy of ChatGPT in marking short-answer assessments in an undergraduate medical program. *International Medical Education*, 3(1), 32–43. DOI: 10.3390/ime3010004

Motawa, I., & Almarshad, A. (2013). A knowledge-based BIM system for building maintenance. *Automation in Construction*, 29, 173–182. DOI: 10.1016/j.autcon.2012.09.008

Mouti, S., & Rihawi, S. (2023). Special needs classroom assessment using a sign language communicator (CASC) based on artificial intelligence (AI) techniques. *International Journal of e-Collaboration*, 19(1), 1–15. DOI: 10.4018/IJeC.313960

Mulryan-Kyne, C. (2010). Teaching large classes at college and university level: Challenges and opportunities. *Teaching in Higher Education*, 15(2), 175–185. DOI: 10.1080/13562511003620001

Mwela, W. (2019). *Africa Open Science Capacity building and skills development Framework. In Academy of Science of South Africa (ASSAf). Mapping the current landscape of Open Science? Open Data initiatives in AFrica Draft Report.* in Press.

Mwelwa, J., Boulton, G., Wafula, J. M., & Loucoubar, C. (2020). Developing open science in Africa: Barriers, solutions and opportunities. *Data Science Journal*, 19(31), 1–17. DOI: 10.5334/dsj-2020-031

Naidoo, R. (2024, 08 8). *Artificial Intelligence is disrupting higher education*. Retrieved from Innovation Web: https://www.itweb.co.za/article/artificial-intelligence-is-disrupting-higher-education/Pero37Z3eoOMQb6m

Narciss, S. (2013). Designing and evaluating tutoring feedback strategies for digital learning environments on the basis of the Interactive Tutoring Feedback Model. *Digital Education Review*, (23), 7–26. DOI: 10.1344/der.2013.23.7-26

Narciss, S. (2017). Conditions and Effects of Feedback Viewed Through the Lens of the Interactive Tutoring Feedback Model. In Carless, D., Bridges, S. M., Chan, C. K. Y., & Glofcheski, R. (Eds.), *Scaling up Assessment for Learning in Higher Education* (Vol. 5, pp. 173–189). Springer Singapore., DOI: 10.1007/978-981-10-3045-1_12

Nassoura, A. (2022). Applied Artificial Intelligence Applications In Higher Education Institutions: A Systematic Review. *Webology*, 19(3), 1168–1183.

National Academies of Sciences, Engineering, and Medicine. (2018). *How people learn II: Learners, contexts, and cultures (2nd ed.)*. The National Academies Press.

National Council for the Social Studies (NCSS). (2013). *The college, career, and civic life (C3) framework for social studies state standards: Guidance for enhancing the rigor of K-12 civics, economics, geography, and history.*

National Governors Association Center for Best Practices & Council of Chief State School Officers. (2010a). *Common core state standards for English language arts & literacy in history: Social studies, science, and technical Subjects*. Author.

National Governors Association Center for Best Practices & Council of Chief State School Officers. (2010b). *Common core state standards for mathematics*. Author.

Nayyar, A., Kumar, R., Sachan, R., & Kumar, A. (2023). *AI-assisted special education for students with exceptional needs*. IGI Global Publishers.

Nazaretsky, T., Ariely, M., Cukurova, M., & Alexandron, G. (2022). Teachers' trust in AI-powered educational technology and a professional development program to improve it. *British Journal of Educational Technology*, 53(4), 914–931. DOI: 10.1111/bjet.13232

Nesbit, J. C., Adesope, O. O., Liu, Q., & Ma, W. (2014). How effective are intelligent tutoring systems in computer science education? In *2014 IEEE 14th international conference on advanced learning technologies* (pp. 99-103). IEEE. DOI: 10.1109/ICALT.2014.38

Neumann, M., Niessen, A., & Meijer, R. (2021). Implementing evidence-based assessment and selection in organizations: A review and an agenda for future research. *Organizational Psychology Review*, 11(3), 205–239. DOI: 10.1177/2041386620983419

News, S. D. (2023, August 31). *Education in today's time: Emerging trends and fields*. SD News. https://sdnews.com/education-in-todays-time-emerging-trends-and-fields/

Newton, S., Alemdar, M., Rutstein, D., Edwards, D., Helms, M., Hernandez, D., & Usselman, M. (2021). Utilising evidence based design to develop assessments: A high school introductory computer science course. *Frontiers in Education*, 6, 1–19. DOI: 10.3389/feduc.2021.695376

Next Generation Science Standards (NGSS) Lead States. (2013). *Next generation science standards: For states, by states*. National Academies Press.

Ng, D. T. K., Leung, J. K. L., Su, J., Ng, R. C. W., & Chu, S. K. W. (2023). Teachers' AI digital competencies and twenty-first century skills in the post-pandemic world. *Educational Technology Research and Development*, 71(1), 137–161. DOI: 10.1007/s11423-023-10203-6 PMID: 36844361

Ng, D. T. K., Wu, W., Leung, J. K. L., Chiu, T. K. F., & Chu, S. K. W. (2024). Design and validation of the AI literacy questionnaire: The affective, behavioural, cognitive and ethical approach. *British Journal of Educational Technology*, 55(3), 1082–1104. https://doi.org/https://doi.org/10.1111/bjet.13411. DOI: 10.1111/bjet.13411

Ng, D. T., Luo, W., Chan, H. M., & Chu, S. K. (2022). Using digital story writing as a pedagogy to develop AI literacy among primary students. *Computers and Education: Artificial Intelligence*, 3, 100054. DOI: 10.1016/j.caeai.2022.100054

Ng, K. (2020). The moderating role of trust and the theory of reasoned action. *Journal of Knowledge Management*, 24(6), 1221–1240. DOI: 10.1108/JKM-01-2020-0071

Ng, S. H. S., Chan, H., Wong, J. H. K., & Privitera, A. J. (2024). A scoping review of the use of generative AI in assessment in higher education. https://doi.org/DOI: 10.35542/osf.io/u5yge

Nguyen, N. (2023, 5 16). Opportunities and challenges for AI in higher education. https://feedbackfruits.com/blog/opportunities-and-challenges-of-ai-in-higher-education

Nguyen, A., Ngo, H. N., Hong, Y., Dang, B., & Nguyen, B.-P. T. (2023). Ethical principles for artificial intelligence in education. *Education and Information Technologies*, 28(4), 4221–4241. DOI: 10.1007/s10639-022-11316-w PMID: 36254344

Nguyen, H., & Kim, S. (2023). The Role of AI Influencers in Shaping Brand Perceptions Among Different Generations. *Journal of Consumer Behaviour*, 22(1), 15–30. DOI: 10.1002/cb.20984

Nguyen, L. A. T., & Habók, A. (2024). Tools for assessing teacher digital literacy: A review. *Journal of Computers in Education*, 11(1), 305–346. DOI: 10.1007/s40692-022-00257-5

Nguyen, T., & Patel, A. (2023). Designing and developing an AI-based assessment system: Technical considerations and best practices. *Journal of Computer Assisted Learning*, 39(2), 342–360. DOI: 10.1111/jcal.12687

Ng, W. (2022). AI literacy in K-12: A systematic literature review. Journal of Educational Technology & Society.

Nikolopoulou, K. (2024). Generative Artificial Intelligence in Higher Education: Exploring ways of harnessing pedagogical Practices with the assistance of ChatGPT. *International Journal of Changes in Education*, 1(2), 103–111. DOI: 10.47852/bonviewIJCE42022489

Niu, S. J., Luo, J., Niemi, H., Li, X., & Lu, Y. (2022). Teachers' and students' views of using an AI-aided educational platform for supporting teaching and learning at Chinese schools. *Education Sciences*, 12(12), 858. DOI: 10.3390/educsci12120858

NLQF. (2022). *Level 6 descriptors for Dutch bachelor's degree*. Dutch Qualification Framework [Het Nederlands kwalificatieraamwerk]. https://www.nlqf.nl/images/downloads/NLQF_niveaus/Niveau_6_NLQF_en_EQF.pdf

Noble, S. U. (2018). Algorithms of oppression: How search engines reinforce racism. New York university press. Luan, H., Geczy, P., Lai, H., Gobert, J., Yang, S. J., Ogata, H., ... & Tsai, C. C. (2020). Challenges and future directions of big data and artificial intelligence in education. *Frontiers in Psychology*, 11, 580820.

Nouraldeen, R. M. (2023). The impact of technology readiness and use perceptions on students' adoption of artificial intelligence: The moderating role of gender. *Development and Learning in Organizations*, 37(3), 7–10. DOI: 10.1108/DLO-07-2022-0133

Nourian, P., Azadi, S., & Oval, R. (2023). Generative design in architecture: From mathematical optimization to grammatical customization. In *Computational Design and Digital Manufacturing* (pp. 1–43). Springer International Publishing., DOI: 10.1007/978-3-031-21167-6_1

Nouri, J., & Eklund, J. (2020). The impact of artificial intelligence on education: A systematic literature review. *Education and Information Technologies*, 25(3), 2059–2084.

Nyhan, M., & Marshall, K. (2024). *Harnessing Emerging Technologies for Scalable, Global, Ethical & Equitable Education for Sustainability*. National University of Ireland.

O'neil, C. (2017). *Weapons of math destruction: How big data increases inequality and threatens democracy*. Crown.

OECD. (2017). *Starting strong V: Transitions from early childhood education and care to primary education*. OECD Publishing., DOI: 10.1787/9789264276253-

OECD. (2023). Opportunities, guidelines and guardrails for effective and equitable use of AI in education. In *OECD digital education Outlook: Towards an effective digital education system*. OECD Publishing.

Okolo, C., Aruleba, K., & Obaido, G. (2023). Responsible AI in Africa—Challenges and Opportunities. In Eke, D. (Ed.), *K. akunuma, & S. Akintoye, Responsible AI in Africa* (pp. 35–64). Palgrave McMillan. DOI: 10.1007/978-3-031-08215-3_3

Okoye, F. (2023). Shifting from the old frame of reference to (w)holistic teacher-student relationships in higher education institutions: A case of the University of the Free State. *South African Journal of Higher Education*, 37(5), 187–202. DOI: 10.20853/37-5-5406

Okudan, O., Budayan, C., & Dikmen, I. (2021). A knowledge-based risk management tool for construction projects using case-based reasoning. *Expert Systems with Applications*, 173, 114776. DOI: 10.1016/j.eswa.2021.114776

Onaolapo, S., & Oyewole, O. (2018). Performance expectancy, effort expectancy, and facilitating conditions as factors influencing smart phones use for mobile learning by postgraduate students of the university of Ibadan, Nigeria. *Interdisciplinary Journal of e-Skills and Lifelong Learning 14*, 95-115.

Open, A. I. (2024). *ChatGPT* (August 28 version). [Large language model]. https://chat.openai.com/chat

Open, A. I. T. (2023). ChatGpt: Optimizing language models for dialogue. OpenAI. 2022. *URL*https://openai.com/blog/chatgpt

Opesemowo, O., & Adekomaya, V. (2024). Harnessing Artificial Intelligence for Advancing Sustainable Development Goals in South Africa's Higher Education System: A Qualitative Study. *International Journal of Learning. Teaching and Educational Research*, 23(3), 68–86. DOI: 10.26803/ijlter.23.3.4

Ordonez, C., & Gacía, E. (2021). Ethical considerations of artificial intelligence in education. *International Journal of Educational Technology in Higher Education*, 18(1), 4. PMID: 34778518

Ottenbreit-Leftwich, A., Glazewski, K., Jeon, M., Jantaraweragul, K., Hmelo-Silver, C. E., Scribner, A., Lee, S., Mott, B., & Lester, J. (2023). Lessons learned for AI education with elementary students and teachers. *International Journal of Artificial Intelligence in Education*, 33(2), 267–289. DOI: 10.1007/s40593-022-00304-3

Ouyang, F., & Jiao, P. (2021). Artificial intelligence in education: The three paradigms. *Computers and Education: Artificial Intelligence, 2*, 100020. https://doi.org/https://doi.org/10.1016/j.caeai.2021.100020

Ouyang, L. e. (2020). Training language models to follow instructions with human feedback. Retrieved 07 31, 2024, from https://doi.org/

Ouyang, F., & Jiao, P. (2021). Artificial intelligence in education: The three paradigms. *Computers and Education: Artificial Intelligence*, 2, 100020. Advance online publication. DOI: 10.1016/j.caeai.2021.100020

Owoc, M. L., Sawicka, A., & Weichbroth, P. (2021). Artificial Intelligence Technologies in Education: Benefits, Challenges and Strategies of Implementation. In Owoc, M. L., & Pondel, M. (Eds.), *Artificial Intelligence for Knowledge Management. AI4KM 2019. IFIP Advances in Information and Communication Technology* (Vol. 599). Springer., DOI: 10.1007/978-3-030-85001-2_4

Owoc, M., Sawicka, A., & Weichbroth, P. (2021). *Artificial Intelligence Technologies in Education: Benefits, challenges and strategies of Implementation*. Gdansk University of Technology.

Pane, J. F., Griffin, B. A., McCaffrey, D. F., & Karam, R. (2014). Effectiveness of Cognitive Tutor Algebra I at scale. *Educational Evaluation and Policy Analysis*, 36(2), 127–144. https://www.jstor.org/stable/43773458. DOI: 10.3102/0162373713507480

Papert, S., & Harel, I. (1991). Situating constructionism. In Harel, I., & Papert, S. (Eds.), *Constructionism* (pp. 1–11). Ablex Publishing.

Paul, R., & Elder, L. (2006). *Critical thinking: Tools for taking charge of your learning and your life*. Pearson/Prentice Hall. https://books.google.nl/books?id=ZqJZAAAAYAAJ

Pedró, F. (2016). *Digital education: The future of education in a digital world*. OECD.

Pellegrino, J. W., & Hilton, M. L. (Eds.). (2012). *Education for life and work: Developing transferable knowledge and skills in the 21st century*. National Academies Press., DOI: 10.17226/13398

Perkins, M. (2023). Academic integrity considerations of AI Large Language Models in the post-pandemic era: ChatGPT and beyond. *Journal of University Teaching & Learning Practice*, 20(2). Advance online publication. DOI: 10.53761/1.20.02.07

Perrotta, R. (2023, Feb. 17). *Peabody EDI Office responds to MSU shooting with email written using ChatGPT.* https://vanderbilthustler.com/2023/02/17/peabody-edi-office-responds-to-msu-shooting-with-email-written-using-chatgpt/

Perrotta, C., & Selwyn, N. (2020). AI in education: A critical review of the literature. *Computers & Education*.

Pfeiffer, J., Kamath, A., Rücklé, A., Cho, K., & Gurevych, I. (2021). AdapterFusion: Non-Destructive Task Composition for Transfer Learning. *Proceedings of the 16th Conference of the European Chapter of the Association for Computational Linguistics: Main* Volume, 487–503. DOI: 10.18653/v1/2021.eacl-main.39

Piaget, J. (1976). *The child and reality: Problems of genetic psychology* (Rosin, A., Trans.). Basic Books.

Picciano, A. G. (2017). The role of artificial intelligence in education. *Journal of Online Learning Research*, 3(2), 119–134.

Pinkwart, N. (2016). Another 25 years of AIED? Challenges and opportunities for intelligent educational technologies of the future. *International Journal of Artificial Intelligence in Education*, 26(2), 771–783. DOI: 10.1007/s40593-016-0099-7

Pinochet, L. H. C., Moreira, M. Â. L., Fávero, L. P., Santos, M., & Pardim, V. I. (2023). Collaborative work alternatives with ChatGPT based on evaluation criteria for its use in higher education: Application of the PROMETHEE-SAPEVO-M1 method. *Procedia Computer Science*, 221, 177–184. DOI: 10.1016/j.procs.2023.07.025

Pinto, M., Garcia-Marco, J., Caballero, D., Manso, R., Uribe, A., & Gomez, C. (2024). Assessing information, media and data literacy in academic libraries: Approaches and challenges in the research literature on the topic. *Journal of Academic Librarianship*, 50(5), 102920. Advance online publication. DOI: 10.1016/j.acalib.2024.102920

Popenici, S. A., & Kerr, S. (2017). Exploring the impact of artificial intelligence on teaching and learning in higher education. *Research and Practice in Technology Enhanced Learning*, 12(1), 1–13. DOI: 10.1186/s41039-017-0062-8 PMID: 30595727

Popham, W. J. (2001). Teaching to the Test? *Educational Leadership*, 58(6), 16–21.

Prabawasari, V. W., Madenda, S., Suhendra, A., & Tahrir, R. (•••). Knowledge-Based Systems in the Information System of Indonesian Colonial Architecture. *Universitas*, 4, 1–4.

Press, G. (2018, Feb 7). *The brute force of IBM Deep Blue And Google DeepMind.* https://www.forbes.com/sites/gilpress/2018/02/07/the-brute-force-of-deep-blue-and-deep-learning/

Priest, M. (2024, March 7). *AI trainer: A job of the future.* Accessed September 10, 2024, https://boost.ai/blog/ai-trainer-a-job-of-the-future/

Puntambekar, S. G. Erkens, & Hmelo-Silver, C. (2011). *Analyzing interactions in CSCL.* Boston: Springer US.

QaQish. R., & Hanna, R. (1997). A World-wide Questionnaire Survey on the Use of Computers in Architectural Education. In *Challenges of the Future (15th eCAADe Conference Proceedings).*

Quy, V. K., Thanh, B. T., Chehri, A., Linh, D. M., & Tuan, D. A. (2023). AI and Digital Transformation in Higher Education: Vision and Approach of a Specific University in Vietnam. *Sustainability (Basel)*, 15(14), 11093. DOI: 10.3390/su151411093

Radianti, J., Majchrzak, T. A., Fromm, J., & Wohlgenannt, I. (2020). A systematic review of immersive virtual reality applications for higher education: Design elements, lessons learned, and research agenda. *Computers & Education*, 147, 103778. DOI: 10.1016/j.compedu.2019.103778

Rahim, S., & Shute, V. (2023). Stealth assessment: a theoretically grounded and psychometrically sound method to assess, support,and investigate learning in technology-rich environments. *Education Tech Research Dev*, 1-25.

Rahiman, H. U., & Kodikal, R. (2024). Revolutionizing education: Artificial intelligence empowered learning in higher education. *Cogent Education*, 11(1), 1–24. DOI: 10.1080/2331186X.2023.2293431

Rajagopal, K., Vrieling-Teunter, E., Hsiao, Y. P., Van Seggelen-Damen, I., & Verjans, S. (2021). Guiding thesis circles in higher education: towards a typology. *Professional Development in Education, 50*(2), 315-332. https://doi.org/DOI: 10.1080/19415257.2021.1973072

Rajan, T. (2022). The unusual case of BYJU's: Creating one of the world's most valued educational technology companies from India. *Indian Journal of Marketing*, 52(4), 8–23. https://www.researchgate.net/publication/359935437_The_Unusual_Case_of_BYJU's_Creating_One_of_the_World's_Most_Valued_Educational_Technology_Companies_from_India. DOI: 10.17010/ijom/2022/v52/i4/163181

Ra, S., Shrestha, U., Khatiwada, S., Seung, W. Y., & Kwon, K. (2019). The rise of technology and impact on skills. *International Journal of Training Research*, 17(sup1), 26–40. DOI: 10.1080/14480220.2019.1629727

Reich, J., & Ito, M. (2017). From good intentions to real outcomes: Equity by design in learning technologies. Digital Media and Learning Research Hub. https://clalliance.org/wp-content/uploads/2017/11/GIROreport_1031.pdf

Reiss, M. J. (2021). The Use of Al in Education: Practicalities and Ethical Considerations. *London Review of Education*, 19(1), n1. DOI: 10.14324/LRE.19.1.05

Reunanen, T., & Nieminen, N. (2024). Artificial intelligence as a catalyst: A case study on adaptive learning in programming education. In: V. Salminen (Eds.), *Human Factors, Business Management and Society. AHFE (2024) International Conference. AHFE Open Access, 135*. AHFE International, USA. http://doi.org/ DOI: 10.54941/ahfe1004957

Reynaud, D., & Northcote, M. (2015). The World Wars through tabletop wargaming: An innovative approach to university history teaching. *Arts and Humanities in Higher Education*, 14(4), 349–367. DOI: 10.1177/1474022214556899

Rizkalla, N., Tannady, H., & Bernando, R. (2023). Analysis of the influence of performance expectancy, effort expectancy, social influence,and attitude toward behavior on intention to adopt live.on. *Multidiscip. Rev.*, Published online.

Rjaibi, N., & Rabai, L. B. A. (2018). How Stakeholders Perceived Security Risks? A New Predictive Functional Level Model and its Application to E-Learning. *ICST Transactions on Security and Safety*, 5(15), 155738. DOI: 10.4108/eai.15-10-2018.155738

Roberts, L. N., Solomon, F. N., & Cummings, R. (2024). Navigating the AI Landscape: Student and Teacher Perceptions of AI in Assessments in High School and College Settings. In *AI-Enhanced Teaching Methods* (pp. 268-285). IGI Global.

Romero, C., Ventura, S., & García, E. (2020). Data mining techniques applied to education: A review of the literature. *Expert Systems with Applications*, 33(1), 135–146. DOI: 10.1016/j.eswa.2006.04.005

Romme, G., & Nijhuis, J. (2002). *Collaborative learning in thesis rings*https://www.researchgate.net/profile/Georges-Romme/publication/259145056_Collaborative_Learning_in_Thesis_Rings/links/00b4952a06e173cb9c000000/Collaborative-Learning-in-Thesis-Rings.pdf

Rosell, A., Rodríguez-Gómez, G., Gutiérrez-Cóbreces, G., & Barberà, E. (2023). Artificial intelligence in instructional design: A systematic review of research and applications. [DOI: 10.1007/s10639-022-11001-z]. *Education and Information Technologies*, 28(2), 1421–1450.

Rosell, D., Suarez, A., & Congosto, M. (2023). A review of artificial intelligence in technology-enhanced learning. [doi: 10.1109/TLT.2022.3229403]. *IEEE Transactions on Learning Technologies*, 16(2), 182–198.

Roshanaei, M. (2024). Towards best practices for mitigating artificial intelligence implicit bias in shaping diversity, inclusion and equity in higher education. *Education and Information Technologies*, 29(14), 1–26. DOI: 10.1007/s10639-024-12605-2

Royer, C. (2024). Outsourcing humanity? ChatGPT, critical thinking, and the crisis in higher education. *Studies in Philosophy and Education: An International Journal*, 1-19. DOI: 10.1007/s11217-024-09946-3

Rudolph, J., Tan, S., & Tan, S. (2023). ChatGPT: Bullshit spewer or the end of traditional assessments in higher education? *Journal of applied learning and teaching, 6*(1), 342-363.

Ruiz-Rojas, L. I., Acosta-Vargas, P., De-Moreta-Llovet, J., & Gonzalez-Rodriguez, M. (2023). Empowering education with generative artificial intelligence tools: Approach with an instructional design matrix. *Sustainability (Basel)*, 15(15), 11524. DOI: 10.3390/su151511524

Ryan, C. (2023, August 14). *Leveraging AI in instructional design*. Medium. https://medium.com/@crystal.ryanc/leveraging-ai-in-instructional-design-165fe152b2ee

Sabouni, A. R., & Al-Mourad, O. M. (1997). Quantitative knowledge based approach for preliminary design of tall buildings. *Artificial Intelligence in Engineering*, 11(2), 143–154. DOI: 10.1016/S0954-1810(96)00023-4

Safsouf, Y. 2021. Contributed to the development of decision models for improving learner success in an online learning environment, TEL - Thèses en ligne. France.

Salajan, F. D., Barnes, T. L., & Becker, A. (2024). Comparative regionalism cases of artificial intelligence governance in education: The Caribbean Community and the European Union. *The Round Table*, 113(1), 71–85. DOI: 10.1080/00358533.2024.2307793

Salas-Pilco, S. Z., Xiao, K., & Hu, X. (2022). Artificial intelligence and learning analytics in teacher education: A systematic review. *Education Sciences*, 12(8), 569. DOI: 10.3390/educsci12080569

Salas-Pilco, S., & Yang, Y. (2022). Artificial Intelligence application in Latin America higher education: A systematic review. *International Journal of Educational Technology in Higher Education*, 19(21), 1–20.

Samek, W., Montavon, G., Vedaldi, A., Hansen, L. K., & Müller, K. R. (Eds.). (2021). *Explainable AI: Interpreting, explaining and visualizing deep learning*. Springer Nature., DOI: 10.1007/978-3-030-98131-8

Sandoval, W. (2014). Conjecture mapping: An approach to systematic educational design research. *Journal of the Learning Sciences*, 23(1), 18–36. DOI: 10.1080/10508406.2013.778204

Schiavi, B., Havard, V., Beddiar, K., & Baudry, D. (2022). BIM data flow architecture with AR/VR technologies: Use cases in architecture, engineering and construction. *Automation in Construction*, 134, 104054. DOI: 10.1016/j.autcon.2021.104054

Schiff, D., Biddle, J., Borenstein, J., & Laas, K. (2020). What's next for AI ethics, policy, and governance? A global overview. In Proceedings of the AAAI/ ACM Conference on AI, Ethics, and Society (pp. 153-158). https://doi.org/DOI: 10.1145/3375627.3375804

Schiff, D. (2022). Education for AI, not AI for education: The role of education and ethics in national AI policy strategies. *International Journal of Artificial Intelligence in Education*, 32(3), 527–563. DOI: 10.1007/s40593-021-00270-2

Schmitt, G. (Ed.). (2010). *Future Cities:ECAADE 2010: Proceedings of the 28th Conference on Education in Computer Aided Architectural Design in Europe, September 15-18, 2010, Zurich, Switzerland, ETH Zurich*. vdf Hochschulverlag AG.

Schneider, K. (2024). What is learning? *Psychology (Irvine, Calif.)*, 15(5), 779–799. DOI: 10.4236/psych.2024.155047 PMID: 38278804

Selbst, A. D., Boyd, D., Friedler, S. A., Venkatasubramanian, S., & Vertesi, J. (2019). Fairness and Abstraction in Sociotechnical Systems. *Proceedings of the Conference on Fairness, Accountability, and Transparency*, 59–68. DOI: 10.1145/3287560.3287598

Seldon, A., & Abidoye, O. (2018). *The fourth education revolution*. Legend Press Ltd.

Selwyn, N. (2019). Should robots replace teachers?: AI and the future of education. John Wiley & Sons. https://www.wiley.com/en-us/Should+Robots+Replace+Teachers%3F%3A+AI+and+the+Future+of+Education-p-9781509528639

Selwyn, N. (2021). *Education and technology: Key issues and debates*. Bloomsbury Publishing.

Selwyn, N. (2023). Constructive Criticism? Working with (Rather than Against) the AIED Back-Lash. *International Journal of Artificial Intelligence in Education*. Advance online publication. DOI: 10.1007/s40593-023-00344-3

Sennott, S. C., Akagi, L., Lee, M., & Rhodes, A. (2019). AAC and artificial intelligence (AI). *Topics in Language Disorders*, 39(4), 389–403. DOI: 10.1097/TLD.0000000000000197 PMID: 34012187

Settles, B., & Meeder, B. (2016). A trainable spaced repetition model for language learning. In *Proceedings of the 54th Annual Meeting of the Association for Computational Linguistics* (Volume 1: Long Papers) (pp. 1848-1858). https://doi.org/ DOI: 10.18653/v1/P16-1174

Sey, A., & Mudongo, O. (2023). *Case Studies on AI Skills Capacity-building and AI in Workforce Development in Africa*. Research in ICT.

Shah, P. (2023). AI and the Future of Education: Teaching in the Age of artificial intelligence. *Welcome to TeachOnline*. https://teachonline.ca/tools-trends/must-read-books-on-online-learning/ai-and-future-education-teaching-age-artificial-intelligence

Shane, J. (2019). *You look like a thing and I love you*. Voracious.

Shaw, P., Cole, B., & Russell, J. (2013). 19: Determining our own tempos: Exploring slow pedagogy, curriculum, assessment, and professional development. *To Improve the Academy*, 32(20210331). Advance online publication. DOI: 10.3998/tia.17063888.0032.023

Shen, J., Xu, L., Majumdar, R., & Shu, L. (2021). Generative AI: A Survey of the State-of-the-Art and Future Trends. arXiv preprint arXiv:2112.05488.

Shen, L., Chen, I., Grey, A., & Su, A. (2021). Teaching and learning with artificial intelligence. In *Impact of AI technologies on teaching, learning, and research in higher education* (pp. 73–98). IGI Global. DOI: 10.4018/978-1-7998-4763-2.ch005

Shen, L., & Su, A. (2020). The changing roles of teachers with AI. In *Revolutionizing education in the age of AI and machine learning* (pp. 1–25). IGI Global. DOI: 10.4018/978-1-5225-7793-5.ch001

Shermis, M. D., & Burstein, J. (Eds.). (2013). *Handbook of automated essay evaluation: Current applications and new directions*. Routledge., DOI: 10.4324/9780203122761

Shermis, M. D., & Hamner, B. (2014). Contrasting State-of-the-Art Automated Scoring of Essays. In *Handbook of Automated Essay Evaluation*. Routledge., DOI: 10.4324/9780203122761.ch19

Shibata, T., & Uto, M. (2022). Analytic Automated Essay Scoring based on Deep Neural Networks: Integrating Multidimensional Item Response Theory. *Proceedings of the 29th International Conference on Computational Linguistics* (pp. 2917–2926). London: International Committee on Computational lingustics October 12–17.

Shnayder, V., & Parkes, D. C. (2016). Practical peer prediction for peer assessment. *Proceedings of the fourth AAAI conference on human computation and crowdcourcing* (pp. 199-209). Texas: e fourth AAAI conference.

Shoufan, A. (2023). Exploring students' perceptions of ChatGPT: Thematic analysis and follow-up survey. *IEEE Access : Practical Innovations, Open Solutions*, 11, 38805–38818. DOI: 10.1109/ACCESS.2023.3268224

Shute, V., Lu, X., & Rahimi, S. (2021). Stealth assessment. In J. Spector, *The Routledge Encyclopedia of Education* (pp. 1-9). London: Taylor & Francis group.

Shute, V. J., Sun, C., & Asbell-Clarke, J. (2017). Demystifying computational thinking. *Educational Research Review*, 22, 142–158. DOI: 10.1016/j.edurev.2017.09.003

Shute, V., Leighton, J., Jang, E., & Chu, M.-W. (2016). Advances in the science of assessment. *Educational Assessment*, 21(1), 34–59. DOI: 10.1080/10627197.2015.1127752

Shute, V., & Rahimi, S. (2017). Review of computer-based assessment for learning in elementary and secondary education. *Journal of Computer Assisted Learning*, 33(1), 1–19. DOI: 10.1111/jcal.12172

Shute, V., & Ventura, M. (2013). *Stealth Assessment: Measuring and Supporting Learning in Video Games*. The MIT Press., DOI: 10.7551/mitpress/9589.001.0001

Siemens, G. (2005). Connectivism: A learning theory for the digital age. *International Journal of Instructional Technology and Distance Learning*, 2(1), 3–10.

Siemens, G. (2014). Learning analytics: The emerging educational and ethical issues. *International Review of Research in Open and Distance Learning*, 15(2), 190–203.

Siemens, G., & Baker, R. S. J. d. (2020). Learning analytics and AI: The path to personalized education. *AI in Education Journal*, 14(2), 98–112.

Siemens, G., Dawson, S., & Lynch, G. (2019). Analytics, AI, and the future of education. *Learning Analytics Review*, 17(1), 1–12.

Siemens, G., Gašević, D., & Dawson, S. (2019). *Preparing for the digital university: A review of the history and current state of distance, blended, and online learning*. Athabasca University.

Siemens, G., & Long, P. (2011). Penetrating the fog: Analytics in learning and education. *EDUCAUSE Review*, 46(5), 30.

Sillat, L. H., Tammets, K., & Laanpere, M. (2021). Digital Competence Assessment Methods in Higher Education: A Systematic Literature Review. *Education Sciences*, 11(8), 402. DOI: 10.3390/educsci11080402

Sims, R. (2006). Beyond instructional design: Making learning design a reality. *Journal of Learning Design*, 1(2), 1–9.

Singh, V., & Gu, N. (2012). Towards an integrated generative design framework. *Design Studies*, 33(2), 185–207. DOI: 10.1016/j.destud.2011.06.001

Skill, Q. (n.d.). *AI & ADDIE: Leveraging artificial intelligence in instructional design*. SkillQ. https://skillq.com/ai_addie/

Slade, S., & Prinsloo, P. (2013). Learning analytics: A collaborative approach to the ethical use of student data. *Higher Education*, 66(4), 407–423.

Smerdon, D. (2024). AI in essay-based assessment: Student adoption, usage, and performance. *Computers and Education: Artificial Intelligence*, 100288, 100288. Advance online publication. DOI: 10.1016/j.caeai.2024.100288

Smith, H. J., Zheng, Q., Li, Y., Jain, S., & Hodgins, J. K. (2023). A Method for Animating Children's Drawings of the Human Figure. *ACM Transactions on Graphics*, 42(3), 1–15. Advance online publication. DOI: 10.1145/3592788

Smith, J., & Johnson, M. (2023). Revolutionizing assessment practices with AI: A comprehensive study. *Computers & Education*, 183, 104467. DOI: 10.1016/j.compedu.2023.104467

Smith, L., & Johnson, R. (2022). The Impact of AI Influencers on Millennials and Gen Z: A Comparative Study. *Journal of Digital Marketing*, 15(3), 45–60. DOI: 10.1016/j.jdmark.2022.01.005

Smith, P. L., & Ragan, G. Z. (2007). *Instructional design* (3rd ed.). John Wiley & Sons.

Soliman, S., Taha, D., & El Sayad, Z. (2019). Architectural education in the digital age: Computer applications: Between academia and practice. *Alexandria Engineering Journal*, 58(2), 809–818. DOI: 10.1016/j.aej.2019.05.016

Soulen, R. R. (2021). Enabling collaboration through mentorship: Examining the role of the school librarian. *School Library Research, 24*.

Spector, J. M. (2016, March). Smart learning environments: Concepts and issues. In *Society for Information Technology & teacher education international conference* (pp. 2728-2737). Association for the Advancement of Computing in Education (AACE).

Starkey, L. (2012). *Teaching and learning in the digital age*. Routledge. DOI: 10.4324/9780203117422

Stassen, L., Doherty, K., & Poe, M. (2001). Course based review and assessment methods for understanding student learning. Massachusettes: University of Massachusetts Amherst.

Statistical Modelling. (2024, 08 6). *Statistical Modelling*. Retrieved from What is Statistical Modelling?: https://www.alooba.com/skills/concepts/statistics/statistical-modelling/

Stiggins, R. J. (2005). *Student-involved assessment for learning* (4th ed.). Prentice Hall.

Stiggins, R. J., Arter, J. A., & Chappuis, J. (2004). *Classroom assessment for student learning: Doing it right, using it well.* Assessment Training Institute.

Su, F., & Wood, M. (2023). Relational pedagogy in higher education: What might it look like in practice and how do we develop it? *The International Journal for Academic Development*, 28(2), 230–233. DOI: 10.1080/1360144X.2023.2164859

Suresh Babu, C. V., Anniyappa, C. S., & Sastha, B. D. (2024). Unraveling the Inner Workings of Massive Language Models: Architecture, Training, and Linguistic Capacities. In B. Gupta (Ed.), Challenges in Large Language Model Development and AI Ethics (pp. 239-279). IGI Global. DOI: 10.4018/979-8-3693-3860-5.ch008

Suresh Babu, C. V., & Adhithya, S. (2023). ChatGPT and Other Generative AI Tools in Education: Transformative Potential and Ethical Considerations. In Keengwe, J. (Ed.), *Creative AI Tools and Ethical Implications in Teaching and Learning* (pp. 135–152). IGI Global., DOI: 10.4018/979-8-3693-0205-7.ch007

Suresh Babu, C. V., & Auroshaa, A. (2024). Influence of Data Analysis Tools in Teaching and Learning Economics. In Scott, B., & Fox, M. E. (Eds.), *Cases on Economics Education and Tools for Educators* (pp. 229–248). IGI Global., DOI: 10.4018/978-1-6684-7583-6.ch010

Suresh Babu, C. V., & Padma, R. (2023). Technology Transformation Through Skilled Teachers in Teaching Accountancy. In González-Lezcano, R. (Ed.), *Advancing STEM Education and Innovation in a Time of Distance Learning* (pp. 211–233). IGI Global., DOI: 10.4018/978-1-6684-5053-6.ch011

Suresh Babu, C. V., & Rohan, B. (2023). Evaluation and Quality Assurance for Rapid E-Learning and Development of Digital Learning Resources. In Santally, M., Rajabalee, Y., & Rajputh, R. (Eds.), *Implementing Rapid E-Learning Through Interactive Materials Development* (pp. 139–170). IGI Global., DOI: 10.4018/978-1-6684-4940-0.ch008

Sutherland, D., Warwick, P., & Anderson, J. (2019). What factors influence student satisfaction with module quality? A comparative analysis in a UK business school context. *International Journal of Management Education*, 17(3), 100312. DOI: 10.1016/j.ijme.2019.100312

Sweller, J. (2021). Instructional Design. In Shackelford, T. K., & Weekes-Shackelford, V. A. (Eds.), *Encyclopedia of Evolutionary Psychological Science*. Springer., DOI: 10.1007/978-3-319-19650-3_2438

Swiecki, Z., Khosravi, H., Chen, G., Martinez-Maldonado, R., Lodge, J., Milligan, S., Selwyn, N., & Gasevic, D. (2022). Assessment in the age of artificial intelligence. *Computers and Education-Artificial Intelligence*, 3, 1–10. DOI: 10.1016/j.caeai.2022.100075

Tait, E., & Pierson, C. M. (2022). Artificial intelligence and robots in libraries: Opportunities in LIS curriculum for preparing the librarians of tomorrow. *Journal of the Australian Library and Information Association*, 71(3), 256–274. https://doi-org.cyrano.ucmo.edu/10.1080/24750158.2022.2081111. DOI: 10.1080/24750158.2022.2081111

Talebi, M. R. Nili Ahmadabadi, H. Fardanesh, & A. Delavar. (2023). Investigating the effectiveness of "Instructional Design Thinking" on the instructional design capability of educational technology students. *Nashrīyah-i 'Ilmī pizhūhishī-i fannāvarī-i āmūzish, 17*(4), 709–728. https://doi.org/DOI: 10.22061/tej.2023.9329.2831

The Association of African Universities (AAU). (2023, 10 10). Artificial Intelligence in African Universities . *AAU*. AAU.

Timms, M. J. (2016). Letting artificial intelligence in education out of the box: Educational cobots and smart classrooms. *International Journal of Artificial Intelligence in Education*, 26(2), 701–712. DOI: 10.1007/s40593-016-0095-y

Todd, M., Bannister, P., & Clegg, S. (2004). Independent inquiry and the undergraduate dissertation: perceptions and experiences of final-year social science students. *Assessment & Evaluation in Higher Education, 29*(3), 335-355. DOI: 10.1080/0260293042000188285

Tomas, C., & Jessop, T. (2019). Struggling and juggling: A comparison of student assessment loads across research and teaching-intensive universities. *Assessment & Evaluation in Higher Education*, 44(1), 1–10. DOI: 10.1080/02602938.2018.1463355

Touretzky, D., Gardner-McCune, C., Martin, F., & Seehorn, D. (2019, July). Envisioning AI for K-12: What should every child know about AI? In *Proceedings of the AAAI conference on artificial intelligence* (Vol. 33, No. 01, pp. 9795-9799). https://ojs.aaai.org/index.php/AAAI/article/view/5053

Trilling, B., & Fadel, C. (2009). *21st century skills: Learning for life in our times.* John Wiley & Sons.

Tronto, J. (2020). *Moral boundaries: A political argument for an ethic of care.* Taylor & Francis. https://books.google.nl/books?id=A2HwDwAAQBAJ

Tronto, J. C. (1998). An ethic of care. *Generations: Journal of the American Society on Aging, 22*(3), 15-20. https://www.jstor.org/stable/44875693

Tuomi, I. (2018). The impact of artificial intelligence on learning, teaching, and education. Publications Office of the European Union._https://publications.jrc.ec.europa.eu/repository/handle/JRC113226

Turing, A. M. (1950). Computing machinery and intelligence. *Mind*, 59(236), 433–460. DOI: 10.1093/mind/LIX.236.433

Türker, O., & Kahraman, A. D. (2024). Artificial Intelligence Software in the Context of Educational Process. *The Turkish Online Journal of Educational Technology*, 23(1), 16–23.

Tuzunkan, D., Alper, M., & Ozkul, S. (2020). The impact of artificial intelligence on education: A systematic review. *Computers & Education*, 148, 103788. DOI: 10.1016/j.compedu.2020.103788

U.S. Department of Education. Office of Educational Technology [OET]. (2023). Artificial Intelligence and Future of Teaching and Learning: Insights and Recommendations, Washington, DC. https://tech.ed.gov

U.S. Department of Education. Office of Educational Technology [OET]. (2024). Designing for education with artificial intelligence: An essential guide for developers. Washington, D.C. https://tech.ed.gov

UNESCO. (2019). *BEIJING CONSENSUS on artifcial intelligence and education. BEIJING CONSENSUS on artifcial intelligence and education*. UNESCO.

UNESCO. (2021). *AI and education: Guidance for policy-makers*. UNESCO. https://unesdoc.unesco.org/ark:/48223/pf0000376709

UNESCO. (2021). *AI and education: Guidance for policy-makers*. United Nations Educational, Scientific and Cultural Organization.

UNESCO. (2022). *Recommendation on the Ethics of Artificial Intelligence* (UNESCO, Ed.). UNESCO.

UNESCO. (2023). ChatGPT and Artificial Intelligence in higher education: Quick start. In: United Nations Educational, Scientific and Cultural Organization (UNESCO).

UNESCO. (n.d.). Artificial intelligence. UNESCO. https://www.unesco.org/en/artificial-intelligence

United Nations Scientific and Cultural Organisation (UNESCO). (2019). *Artificial Intelliegence for sustainable development: A synthesis report*. UNESCO.

United Nations Scientific and Cultural Organisation. (2020). *Artificial Intelligence needs assessment and survey in Africa*. UNESCO.

University at Austin Center for teaching and Learning (2023). *Five things to know about ChatGPT.*https://ctl.utexas.edu/teaching-technology/5-things-know-about-chatgpt

University of South Florida Sarasota-Manatee. (2024). *Emerging technologies in education*. University of South Florida Sarasota-Manatee. https://www.sarasotamanatee.usf.edu/magazine/2020/emerging-technologies-in-education.aspx

van den Berg, S. (2023). *The acceptance of assessment AIs in formal higher education; An explolatory study.* A master degree thesis submitted to the Faculty of Behavioural Management and Social Sciences: University of Twente.

van den Berg, C., Verster, B., & Collett, K. (2018). Flipped out in the blended classroom, the good, the bad and the ugly: When academics become students. *South African Journal of Higher Education*, 32(6), 440–459. DOI: 10.20853/32-6-2984

Van Laar, E., Van Deursen, A. J., Van Dijk, J. A., & De Haan, J. (2017). The relation between 21st-century skills and digital skills: A systematic literature review. *Computers in Human Behavior*, 72, 577–588. DOI: 10.1016/j.chb.2017.03.010

Van Merriënboer, J. G. (1997). Training complex cognitive skills: A four-component instructional design model for technical training. *Educational Psychologist*, 32(3), 157–172.

Vartiainen, H., Tedre, M., & Valtonen, T. (2020). Learning machine learning with very young children: Who is teaching whom? *International Journal of Child-Computer Interaction*, 25, 1–11. DOI: 10.1016/j.ijcci.2020.100182

Venkatesh, V., Thong, J., & Xu, X. (2016). Unified Theory of Acceptance and Use of Technology A Synthesis and the Road Ahead. *Journal of the Association for Information Systems*, 17(5), 328–376. DOI: 10.17705/1jais.00428

Verster, B., van den Berg, C., & Collett, K. (2024). *Relational reading~writing~thinking~becoming in higher education: Possibilities for scholarly reading and writing in times of turbulence*. Critical Studies in Teaching and Learning. DOI: 10.14426/cristal.v11i2.2007

Vesselinov, R., & Grego, J. (2012). Duolingo effectiveness study. *City University of New York, USA*, 28, 1–25.

Von Ahn, L. (2013). Duolingo: *Learn a language for free while helping to translate the web*. In *Proceedings of the 2013 International Conference on Intelligent User Interfaces* (pp. 1–2). Association for Computing Machinery. https://doi.org/DOI: 10.1145/2449396.2449398

Vygotsky, L. S. (1978). *Mind in society: The development of higher psychological processes* (Cole, M., John-Steiner, V., Scribner, S., & Souberman, E., Eds.). Harvard University Press.

Wahbeh, W. (2017, October). Building skins, parametric design tools and BIM platforms. In *Conference Proceedings of the 12th Conference of Advanced Building Skins*, 1104-1111.

Walton Family Foundation. (2024). AI chatbots in schools: Findings from a poll of K-12 teachers, students, parents, and college undergraduates. https://8ce82b94a8c4fdc3ea6d-b1d233e3bc3cb10858bea65ff05e18f2.ssl.cf2.rackcdn.com/bf/24/cd3646584af89e7c668c7705a006/deck-impact-analysis-national-schools-tech-tracker-may-2024-1.pdf

Wang, F., & Wang, Q. (2018). Artificial intelligence in education: The future of learning. *International Journal of Information and Education Technology (IJIET)*, 8(4), 253–257.

Wang, H., & Liu, X. (2022). Artificial intelligence in education: A critical review of the literature. [doi: 10.1007/s40563-022-00356-x]. *International Journal of Artificial Intelligence in Education*, 33(2), 393–430.

Wang, H., Tlili, A., Huang, R., Cai, Z., Li, M., Cheng, Z., Yang, D., Li, M., Zhu, X., & Fei, C. (2023). Examining the applications of intelligent tutoring systems in real educational contexts: A systematic literature review from the social experiment perspective. *Education and Information Technologies*, 28(7), 9113–9148. Advance online publication. DOI: 10.1007/s10639-022-11555-x PMID: 36643383

Wang, L., & Zhang, Y. (2023). Ethical considerations in AI-based assessment: Ensuring fairness, transparency, and data privacy. *Journal of Educational Technology & Society*, 26(2), 187–203.

Wang, T., & Liu, X. (2022). Artificial intelligence in instructional design: A critical review of the literature and a proposed research framework. [DOI: 10.1007/s11423-021-09924-9]. *Educational Technology Research and Development*, 70(3), 825–844.

Wang, T., Lund, B. D., Marengo, A., Pagano, A., Mannuru, N. R., Teel, Z. A., & Pange, J. (2023). Exploring the potential impact of artificial intelligence (AI) on international students in higher education: Generative AI, chatbots, analytics, and international student success. *Applied Sciences (Basel, Switzerland)*, 13(11), 6716. DOI: 10.3390/app13116716

Wang, V. (Ed.). (2023). *Handbook of research on andragogical leadership and technology in a modern world* (1st ed.). IGI Global Information Science Reference. DOI: 10.4018/978-1-6684-7832-5

Wang, W., Wang, G., Ding, X., & Zhang, B. (Eds.). (2021). *Artificial Intelligence in Education and Teaching Assessment*. Springer., DOI: 10.1007/978-981-16-6502-8

Watson, W. R., & Watson, S. L. (2018). The role of artificial intelligence in higher education: Current trends and future directions. *Journal of Educational Technology & Society*, 21(1), 50–62.

Weiser, B. (2023, May 27). Here's what happens when your lawyer uses chatGPT. *The New York Times*.https://www.nytimes.com/2023/05/27/nyregion/avianca-airline-lawsuit-chatgpt.html

Weng, X., & Chiu, T. K. (2023). Instructional design and learning outcomes of intelligent computer assisted language learning: Systematic review in the field. *Computers and Education: Artificial Intelligence*, 4, 100117. DOI: 10.1016/j.caeai.2022.100117

West, D. M. (2018). *AI and the future of education: The potential impact of artificial intelligence on education and society*. Brookings Institution.

WifiTalents. (2024, 08 6). *Home education and learning statistics*. Retrieved from WifiTalents: https://wifitalents.com/statistic/ai-in-higher-education/#:~:text=68%25%20of%20universities%20plan%20to,million%20annually%20from%202020%2D2024

Wiggins, G. (2005). *Understanding by design*. Association for Supervision and Curriculum Development.

Wiley. (2023). ChatGPT and accounting education. Retrieved 7 31, 2924, from https://www.wiley.com/

Williamson, B., Bayne, S., & Shay, S. (2020). The datafication of teaching in Higher Education: Critical issues and perspectives. *Teaching in Higher Education*, 25(4), 351–365. DOI: 10.1080/13562517.2020.1748811

Williamson, B., Eynon, R., & Potter, J. (2020). Pandemic politics, pedagogies and practices: Digital technologies and distance education during the coronavirus emergency. *Learning, Media and Technology*, 45(2), 107–114. DOI: 10.1080/17439884.2020.1761641

Willians, M., Rana, N., & Dwivedi, Y. (2015). Unified theory of acceptance and use of technology. *Journal of Enterprise Information Management*, 28(3), 443–488. DOI: 10.1108/JEIM-09-2014-0088

Winkler, R., & Söllner, M. (2018). Unleashing the potential of chatbots in education: A state-of-the-art analysis. In *Academy of Management Annual Meeting (AOM)* (pp. 1-40). DOI: 10.5465/AMBPP.2018.15903abstract

Woolf, B. P. (2020). *Building intelligent interactive tutors: Student-centered strategies for revolutionizing e-learning*. Morgan Kaufmann.

Woolf, B. P. (2020). How artificial intelligence is transforming education: Implications for teaching and learning. *Educational Technology Research and Development*, 68(2), 255–277. DOI: 10.1007/s11423-019-09745-8

Woolf, B. P., & McLaren, B. M. (2020). Intelligent learning environments: Bridging the gap between AI research and education. *Journal of Educational Technology & Society*, 23(2), 3–16.

Wu, J. S., Chien, T. H., Chien, L. R., & Yang, C. Y. (2021). Using artificial intelligence to predict class loyalty and plagiarism in students in an online blended programming course during the COVID-19 pandemic. *Electronics (Basel)*, 10(18), 2203. DOI: 10.3390/electronics10182203

Wulandari, F., Astuti, M. T., & Marhamah, M. (2024). Enhancing Writing Literacy Teachers' through AI Development. *Jurnal Onoma: Pendidikan, Bahasa dan Sastra, 10*(1), 246 - 256. http://repository.uir.ac.id/id/eprint/23289

Wulandari, F., & Hadi, S. (2021). Development of computerized adaptive testing to measure students' logical thinking skills in science learning. *Psychology and Education*, 58(2), 4465–4474.

Xia, Q., Weng, X., Ouyang, F., Lin, T. J., & Chiu, T. K. F. (2024). A scoping review on how generative artificial intelligence transforms assessment in higher education. *International Journal of Educational Technology in Higher Education*, 21(1), 40. DOI: 10.1186/s41239-024-00468-z

Xu, X., Wang, X., Zhang, Y., & Zheng, R. (2024). Applying ChatGPT to tackle the side effects of personal learning environments from learner and learning perspective: An interview of experts in higher education. *PLoS One*, 19(1), e0295646. DOI: 10.1371/journal.pone.0295646 PMID: 38170691

Yadav, A., & Bhattacharya, A. (2021). Ethical challenges in the implementation of AI in education: Perspectives from educators. *International Journal of Information and Education Technology (IJIET)*, 11(5), 201–209.

Yang, G. R., & Wang, X. J. (2020). Artificial neural networks for neuroscientists: A primer. *Neuron*, 107(6), 1048–1070. DOI: 10.1016/j.neuron.2020.09.005 PMID: 32970997

Yang, L., & Xin, T. (2022). Changing Educational Assessments in the Post-COVID-19 Era: From Assessment of Learning (AoL) to Assessment as Learning (AaL). *Educational Measurement: Issues and Practice*, 41(1), 54–60. DOI: 10.1111/emip.12492

Yao, N., & Wang, Q. (2024). Factors influencing pre-service special education teachers' intention toward AI in education: Digital literacy, teacher self-efficacy, perceived ease of use, and perceived usefulness. *Heliyon*, 10(14), e34894. DOI: 10.1016/j.heliyon.2024.e34894 PMID: 39149079

Yau, M. Y., Lai, E. K., & Chun, H. W. (1994, March). FPDX: A knowledge-based system for architectural floor plan design. In *Proceedings of International Conference on Expert Systems for Development*, 309-314. IEEE. DOI: DOI: 10.1109/ICESD.1994.302261

Yegnanarayana, B. (1994). Artificial neural networks for pattern recognition. *Sadhana*, 19(2), 189–238. DOI: 10.1007/BF02811896

Yi, K., Turner, R., & Turner, S. (2019). Investigating technology integration practices and competencies of school librarians: A case study in Kentucky, USA. *School Libraries Worldwide*, 25(1), 35–56.

Yilmaz, H., Maxutov, S., Baitekov, A., & Balta, N. (2023). Student attitudes towards Chat GPT: A technology acceptance model survey. *International Educational Review, 1*(1), 57 - 83. https://int-er.com/article/student-attitudes-towards-chat-gpt-a-technology-acceptance-model-survey-13483

Yorio, K. (2023). The ChatGPT revolution: School librarians explore new AI technology. Will it dramatically change education? *School Library Journal*, 69(2), 10.

You-Jin, J., Yong-Jin, K., & Ok-Chol, R. (2023). *Review of feedback in Automated Essay Scoring*. Faculty of Mathematics.

Yuldashev, S., Akramov, M., Tursunova, F., Abdullaeva, K., Shakhmurodova, D., & Ubaydullayev, A. (2024). A development of AI connected system with adaptive assessments method for evaluation methods in education field. In 2024 4th International Conference on Advance Computing and Innovative Technologies in Engineering (ICACITE) (pp. 826-830). Greater Noida, India. https://doi.org/DOI: 10.1109/ICACITE60783.2024.10616960

Zapata-Cardona, L., & Martínez-Castro, C. (2023). Statistical modeling in teacher education. *Mathematical Thinking and Learning*, 25(1), 64–78. DOI: 10.1080/10986065.2021.1922859

Zawacki-Richter, O., Latchem, C., & Anderson, T. (2019). Systematic review of research on artificial intelligence in higher education: Where are we now and where do we go? *International Journal of Educational Technology in Higher Education*, 16(1), 1–20. DOI: 10.1186/s41239-019-0171-0

Zhai, X. (2022). ChatGPT: Artificial intelligence for education. *Supporting Instructional Decision Making: The Potential of An Automatically Scored Three-Dimensional Assessment System*

Zhai, Y.. (2021). Trends in AI applications in education: A systematic review. *Educational Technology Research and Development*.

Zhang, K., & Aslan, A. B. (2021). AI technologies for education: Recent research & future directions. *Computers and Education: Artificial Intelligence*, 2, 100025. Advance online publication. DOI: 10.1016/j.caeai.2021.100025

Zhang, Y., Ong, C. C., Zheng, J., Lie, S. T., & Guo, Z. (2022). Generative design of decorative architectural parts. *The Visual Computer*, 38(4), 1209–1225. DOI: 10.1007/s00371-021-02142-1

Zheng, L., & Yang, Z. (2020). Ethical implications of artificial intelligence in education. *AI & Society*, 35(4), 889–895.

Zhou, J., Chen, F., Berry, A., Reed, M. S., & Savage, S. (2020). A survey on ethical principles of AI and implementations. *2020 IEEE Symposium Seris on Computational Intelligence (SSCI)* (pp. 3010-3017). Australia: 2020 IEEE Symposium Seris on Computational Intelligence (SSCI). DOI: 10.1109/SSCI47803.2020.9308437

Zhou, Y., & Chen, J. (2020). The role of artificial intelligence in education: Opportunities and challenges. *Computers in Human Behavior*, 112, 106466.

Zhu, M., & Zhai, L. (2018). Adaptive learning in education: The role of intelligent systems. *International Journal of Emerging Technologies in Learning*, 13(4), 4–15. DOI: 10.3991/ijet.v13i11.9582

Zhu, X., & Evans, C. (2022). Enhancing the development and understanding of assessment literacy in higher education. *European Journal of Higher Education*, 14(1), 80–100. DOI: 10.1080/21568235.2022.2118149

About the Contributors

Scott Gregory is an Assistant Professor in the Department of Teacher Education at Fort Hays State University located in Hays, Kansas. Scott currently teaches foundations of education, classroom management, and secondary school field experience. Scott earned his Ed.D. from the University of Nebraska in 2023 and specializes in the areas of philosophy of education, social foundations of education, and artificial intelligence in education.

***

Natalie Bolton, PhD- Associate Professor and Director of Quality Assurance for the University of Missouri-St. Louis College of Education. She earned her Ph.D. in educational leadership from the University of Louisville. She has an M.A. in secondary education with emphasis in social studies education, and a B.A. in secondary education from the University of Kentucky. Dr. Bolton's work experiences include middle school teacher; middle school assistant principal, Kentucky Department of Education Social Studies Consultant, and University of Louisville Co-Director of the Nystrand Center of Excellence in Education; Director of the Office of Civic Education and Engagement; and assistant professor. Currently, Dr. Bolton conducts research on the science of learning, assessment literacy, standards-based grading and reporting, program evaluation, and social studies/civic education. She is also the PI of a $4 million six-year grant awarded in 2022 by the McDonnell Foundation to embed translational research in St. Louis charter school with post-doctoral fellows. She is also the project lead for UMSL and the Deans for Impact Learning by Scientific Design Network (a network of educator-preparation programs that want to ensure novice teachers understand basic principles of learning science and can employ these principles when they teach). She teaches courses related to instruction, learning and assessment, education research, quantitative statistics, program evaluation, and serves as a research methodologist on doctoral committees. Additionally, she is an assessment literacy and program evaluation consultant independently and with the Assessment Training Institute founded by Rick Stiggins, PhD. She works with schools and education organizations in the U.S. and internationally on designing and critiquing cognitive and affective assessments, developing and refining standards-based grading and reporting systems, conducting program evaluations, and supporting professional learning related to the science of learning and assessment literacy. Natalie demonstrates an unwavering commitment to students becoming successful learners by embedding formative assessment into her teaching practices. She was recognized in 2023 as UMSL's Co-Investigator of the Year and in 2012 for UMSL's most prestigious teaching award, The Gerald and Deanne Gitner Excellence in Teaching Award.

Jinal Boricha is an Architect and Urban Planner pursuing a Ph.D. in the Department of Architecture and Planning, Birla Institute of Technology, Mesra, Ranchi, India. She has done research in the field of Urban and Regional Planning. She has attended a few conferences on national and International levels and has a few in the pipeline for upcoming publications.

Ilham Boutob received her PhD degree in "Language, Culture and Communication" from Mohammed First University. Her dissertation was on "Cross-Cultural Discourses: A study of Some Orientalist and Occidentalist Texts". Currently, she is an associate professor at Ecole Normale Superieure (ENS), Moulay Ismail University, Meknes. She is a member in the research laboratory SCALEC; she is also an active member in the Research team on "Space & Culture", and a member in the "Culture & Art Studies Unit" of Oujda. She has participated in many study days, seminars, and international conferences in different Moroccan cities and abroad, and published many articles about "post-colonialism, Otherness, self & Other, Orientalism and Occidentalism, pedagogy .."

Rene Burress is a department chair of the Educational Technology and Library Science department and associate professor at the University of Central Missouri (UCM), where she has worked for 11 years. She is a former kindergarten teacher and elementary school librarian. Dr. Burress is an expert in school librarianship. She researches and presents on topics such as how school librarians impact student learning, educational technology use in education and libraries, curriculum and assessment for both libraries and higher education, and advocacy for libraries and education.

Chakabwata William holds a PhD in Curriculum and Instruction obtained from University of South Africa on 27 September 2023.He also holds a master degree in Curriculum and arts education which he earned from University of Zimbabwe. He has taught at Midlands State University in Namibia and also at Namibia University of Science and Technology(NUST). He may be contacted at williechaka@gmail.com

Elizabeth A. Gross is Associate Professor of Library Science and Technology at Sam Houston State University and holds a PhD in Learning Design & Technology. Post-Doctoral work in engineering education uncovered the differences between graduate returner and direct pathway engineering students, and led to five journal articles and over a dozen proceedings papers and presentations. Her research interests include information needs of master's and early career school librarians, perceptions of school librarianship, social justice in the school library, and generative artificial intelligence as a tool for librarians and library users.

Ya-Ping (Amy) Hsiao is a researcher at the Tilburg Center of Learning Sciences and the Teaching & Learning Center at Tilburg University. She holds a PhD in Educational Science and Technology from the Open University of the Netherlands. Her research interests include program-level assessment design, alternative assessments (such as authentic, performance-based, and portfolio assessments), grading, feedback literacy, and integrating AI into assessment design.

Sabrine Jmad received her Phd Degree in E-Learning and Pedagogical Engineering. Currently, she is an associate professor at the Faculty of Letters and Human Sciences, Mohammed I University, Oujda. She is an active member in the research laboratory CEDUC (Communication, Education, Digital Usage and Creativity) at Mohammed First University, OUJDA.

Rohan Jowallah has worked in education for over twenty years. He has taught at various levels: elementary school, middle school, high school, and university. He currently works as an associate instructional designer at the University of Central Florida (UCF). Before joining UCF's Instructional Design Team, Rohan was employed as an Academic Program Planner by The University of The West Indies Open Campus. Rohan has presented at several international conferences and has had several peer-reviewed publications. He continues to develop work for publication. He has also been a reviewer of several international journals. Rohan also teaches online as an adjunct lecturer for two universities. Rohan's current research interests are teaching and learning in higher education, with particular emphasis on online learning and teaching, blended learning and inclusive practices in higher education.

Grace Kaletski Maisel G. joined the Instructional Design team in May 2023. She holds a Master of Science in Information Studies and a Graduate Certificate in Information Architecture from Florida State University, a Master of Arts in Women's Studies from the University of Alabama, and a Bachelor of Arts in English and Political Science from Birmingham-Southern College. She comes to UCF with a background as an academic librarian and worked in libraries for 16 years, specializing in teaching information literacy and research skills at the university level. Her research interests include digital literacy in online learning.

Aditi Nag is an Architect and Urban Planner currently working as an Assistant Professor in School of Architecture and Design at Manipal University Jaipur with a Ph.D. from the Department of Architecture and Planning, Birla Institute of Technology, Mesra, Ranchi, India. She has done urban and rural planning research and has a few publications in her record. She is the 1st to have been awarded the DST Inspire Fellowship in the field of Architecture and planning by the Ministry of Science & Technology, Govt. of India for her Ph.D. work.

Kamakshi Rajagopal is a senior researcher and independent advisor in educational design and technology, with an interdisciplinary background in social sciences, artificial intelligence and linguistics. She completed her doctoral research at the Open Universiteit (NL) in 2013, on personal learning networks and their value for continuous professional development. Dr. Rajagopal has extensive experience in multilateral, multinational, (nationally-funded and European) research and innovation projects. Her research focuses on the complex nature of learning environments, as natural and designed spaces. She is specifically interested in developing instruments for teachers to design and work in this complexity. She works as a program manager for the European Association of Distance Teaching Universities (EADTU).

Leesha Roberts is an accomplished Assistant Professor at the Center of Education Programmes at The University of Trinidad and Tobago, with over two decades of experience in education and computing. Her expertise in Educational Technology/Instructional Design and TVET subjects is evident in her leadership role as Discipline Leader for the University's undergraduate and postgraduate programs. Leesha's research focuses on the integration of ICT in Caribbean Education. She not only supervises postgraduate students but also guides them to excel in their own research, demonstrating her commitment to academic support and mentorship. Her career journey began in the public service at the Ministry of Education, where she led projects to implement technology-based solutions in schools throughout Trinidad and Tobago. Her contributions extend beyond the classroom, as she has trained staff and lectured extensively at both the ministry level and at major local higher education institutions. With a PhD in education focused on ICT integration and instructional design, Leesha is dedicated to equipping students with the necessary skills for integrating technologies into teaching, learning, and research in those areas. Her work has significant implications for the future of education in Trinidad and Tobago and the Caribbean, contributing to the advancement of research in ICT integration at the educational level.

Amrita Sarkar is a graduate engineer in Information Technology with a post-graduate degree in Remote Sensing. She has completed her Ph.D. in Computer Science and Engineering from Birla Institute of Technology, Mesra. She has two years of experience at BIT, Mesra, as an SRF. After completing her Ph.D., she has almost six years of teaching experience. She is an Assistant Professor at the Department of Computer Science, BIT, Mesra, Off Campus Lalpur, Ranchi. She has several research publications in reputed journals. Her areas of interest include Artificial Intelligence, Machine Learning, Soft Computing, Data Mining, and Algorithms.

Sinem Sözen Özdoğan completed her secondary education in Uşak Abdulkadir Kılavuz Anatolian Teacher Training High School. In 2006, she started her undergraduate study in Elementary Mathematics Education Program at Middle East Technical University, Ankara. By means of Erasmus Exchange program, she also studied in Inholland Hogeschool, Rotterdam for one semester during undergraduate education and experienced the teaching practice in public elementary schools in Rotterdam, Netherlands. She completed her Master's Degree at METU Elementary Science and Mathematics Education Department with a focus on incorporation of the history of mathematics in elementary mathematics education. Meanwhile, she has been working as a research assistant at TED University Faculty of Education Elementary Education Department till her graduate studies ended. She got her Ph.D. degree from METU Elementary Education Department with a focus on domain-specific teaching and learning pathways through educational design research perspective on proportional reasoning.

C.V. Suresh Babu is a pioneer in content development. A true entrepreneur, he founded Anniyappa Publications, a company that is highly active in publishing books related to Computer Science and Management. Dr. C.V. Suresh Babu has also ventured into SB Institute, a center for knowledge transfer. He holds a Ph.D. in Engineering Education from the National Institute of Technical Teachers Training & Research in Chennai, along with seven master's degrees in various disciplines such as Engineering, Computer Applications, Management, Commerce, Economics, Psychology, Law, and Education. Additionally, he has UGC-NET/SET qualifications in the fields of Computer Science, Management, Commerce, and Education. Currently, Dr. C.V. Suresh Babu is a Professor in the Department of Information Technology at the School of Computing Science, Hindustan Institute of Technology and Science (Hindustan University) in Padur, Chennai, Tamil Nadu, India. For more information, you can visit his personal blog at https://sites.google.com/view/cvsureshbabu/.

Gamze Türkmen has been working as a researcher at Manisa Celal Bayar University for over four years. She completed her PhD in 2020 in the Department of Computer Education and Instructional Technology at Middle East Technical University. She also holds an MSc from the Cognitive Science department, earned in 2013. Her research focuses primarily on metacognition-centered instructional design and children's learning experiences in science centers. Additionally, she conducts studies on teacher trust in artificial intelligence and debugging processes in programming education.

Yashwant Waykar is a dedicated educator and researcher at Dr. Babasaheb Ambedkar Marathwada University, specializing in Software Engineering, Machine Learning, Artificial Intelligence, and Learning Management Systems (LMS). With over 14 years of experience and a Ph.D., Dr. Waykar has authored 40+ publications in prestigious journals indexed in SCOPUS, UGC CARE, and Web of Science. Their research has earned accolades and includes several book chapters and four patents (3 granted, 1 filed) in LMS and AI. Dr. Waykar's teaching in AI, Web Development, and Software Testing is highly regarded, fostering a dynamic learning environment. They have completed three research projects funded by UGC and Dr. B.A.M.U. and have mentored 3 M.Phil and 2 Ph.D. students, guiding them in Machine Learning and LMS research.

Holly Weimar is a Library Science Professor and Chair of the Department of Library Science and Technology. In addition, she has been the Field Experience Coordinator for the Library Science program for more than a decade. Her research interests include school librarian's use of generative artificial intelligence (GenAI) in the school library, advocacy, information literacy, and school librarian knowledge and skills. She holds an Ed.D. in Curriculum and Instruction with an emphasis on Teacher Education from University of Houston, a M.L.S. from Sam Houston State University, and a B.S. in Elementary Education with a minor in Mathematics from Stephen F. Austin State University. She is a current member of American Library Association, American Association of School Librarians, International Society for Technology in Education, Texas Computer Education Association, Texas Library Association, Texas Association of School Librarians, and Textbook & Academic Authors Association.

Charlotte Eliza Wolff, University of Iceland, School of Education is an Associate Professor with an interdisciplinary background in Applied Linguistics,

Anthropology, and Educational Psychology. As an educator, she prepares teachers to meet the professional challenges of language teaching in ever-changing contexts. She collaborates with an international network of researchers, educators, and practicing classroom teachers to research teacher cognition, alternative assessment, and evaluate the impact of innovative teaching interventions, such as AI-enhanced learning.

Sucheta S. Yambal has been an Assistant Professor in the Department of Management Science of Dr. Babasaheb Ambedkar Marathwada University in Chhatrapati Sambhaji Nagar, Maharashtra. Her total teaching experience is 19 years, and she has about 16 years of research experience. She has taken on several significant duties as a member of the Board of Directors, organized multiple workshops, and given guest lectures at numerous universities. Dr. Yambal has supervised four M.Phil. and four Ph.D. research students at Dr. Babasaheb Ambedkar Marathwada University to date. She has also reviewed Ph.D. theses for Tilak Maharastra Vidyapeeth, Pune. More than thirty national and international research papers have been published by her at prestigious institutes' international conferences, such as IIT Delhi and IIM Raipur. Her research has also been published in prestigious journals, such as SCOPUS and UGC- Care Listed. In November 2019, Dr. Yambal scored highly in the e-business course on the Nptel platform during an exam administered by IIT Kharagpur. She is deemed a "Women of Substance" 2018 Award which was organized at MGM, Chhtrapati Sambhaji Nagar. She had a stellar academic record from elementary school to the Dr. Babasaheb Ambedkar Marathwada University Ph.D. admission exam, where she received the best possible mark. Her areas of interest include employment, AI/ML, automation in industries, database management systems and data mining, modern and inclusive education, and employability.

Index

A

B

C

D

E

F

G

H

I

K

L

M

P

R

S

T

www.ingramcontent.com/pod-product-compliance
Lightning Source LLC
LaVergne TN
LVHW080348011026
849161LV00009B/2233
* 9 7 9 8 3 6 9 3 6 5 2 7 4 *